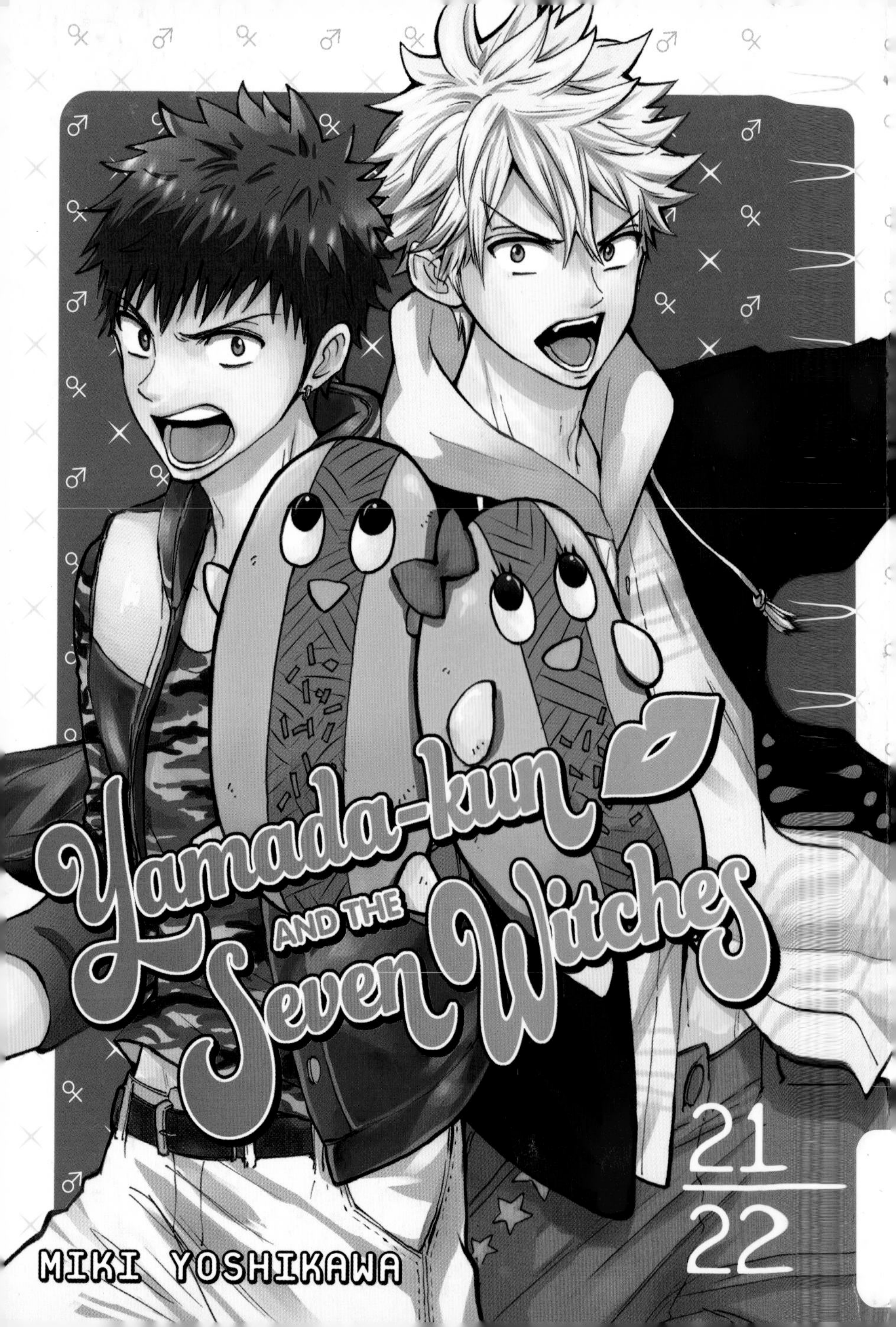
Yamada-kun
AND THE
Seven Witches
21
22
MIKI YOSHIKAWA

Yamada-kun and the Seven Witches

21

MIKI YOSHIKAWA

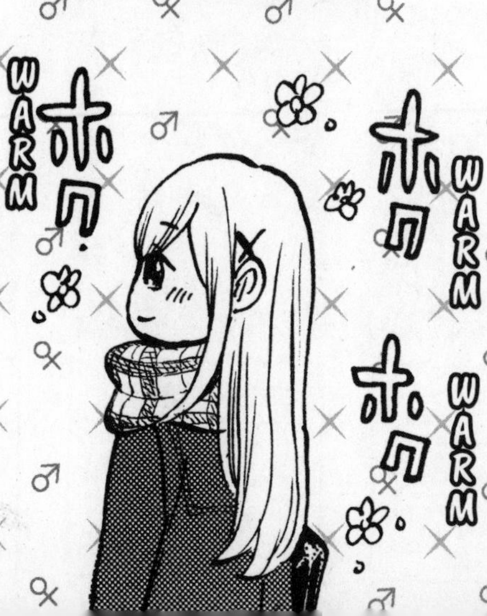
WARM
WARM
WARM

Urara Shiraishi

A second-year at Suzaku High School and president of the Supernatural Studies Club. She used to be known as the "Switch Witch," and she is Yamada's girlfriend. In anticipation of having her memory erased, she has prepared a journal in which she has recorded everything there is to know about Yamada.

Ryu Yamada

A second-year at Suzaku High School. He copied the "Seventh Witch's ability" from Nancy, but has been forgotten by the students at his school because Igarashi–who also stole Nancy's ability and was similarly forgotten–used the witch power.

Nene Odagiri

A second-year at Suzaku High School who used to be the "Charm Witch." Before her memory got erased, she directly expressed her feelings to Yamada. She's a member of the new Student Council.

Shinichi Tamaki

A second-year at Suzaku High School. He's known as the "Capture Guy" and steals the power of the witch whom he kisses. He claimed victory in the recall election and is now the president of the Student Council.

Toranosuke Miyamura

A second-year at Suzaku High School and former president of the Student Council. After the recall was established, he decided not to run in the next election, and instead has decided to support Tamaki along with Yamada and Noa.

Miyabi Itou

A second-year at Suzaku High School. She's a member of the Supernatural Studies Club and a huge fan of the occult. She's normally highly excitable.

Midori Arisugawa

A first-year at Suzaku High School. She appears to be mild-mannered, but she also displays a calculating side. Like Kurosaki, she has also continued on as a member of the new Student Council.

Jin Kurosaki

A first-year at Suzaku High School who reveres Miyamura. He has continued on as a member of the new Student Council following Tamaki's election.

Ushio Igarashi

A second-year at Suzaku High School and Yamada's old friend. He has the same ability as Tamaki, and he has used the ability he stole from Nancy to erase everyone's memories.

Noa Takigawa

A first-year at Suzaku High School and formerly a witch with the power to see into the past. She's smitten with Yamada, and through pure coincidence landed the role of Yamada's spotter (a.k.a wife).

Kentaro Tsubaki

A second-year at Suzaku High School. He's a member of the Supernatural Studies Club and a cheerful guy who used to live abroad. He has a habit of frying up tempura when he gets lonely.

Leona Miyamura

A third-year at Suzaku High School and Miyamura's older sister. She used to be in the Supernatural Studies Club with Yamazaki and had been pursuing the mystery of the witches.

Haruma Yamazaki

A third-year at Suzaku High School and the former president of the Student Council from two generations ago. After giving up his presidency, he has been studying hard to pass the entrance exam for Tono U.

Kotori Moegi

A second-year at Suzaku High School and a witch who can read minds after kissing someone with her doll. She's a gentle and kind-hearted girl.

CONTENTS

CHAPTER 173: You're a stalker, aren't you?!

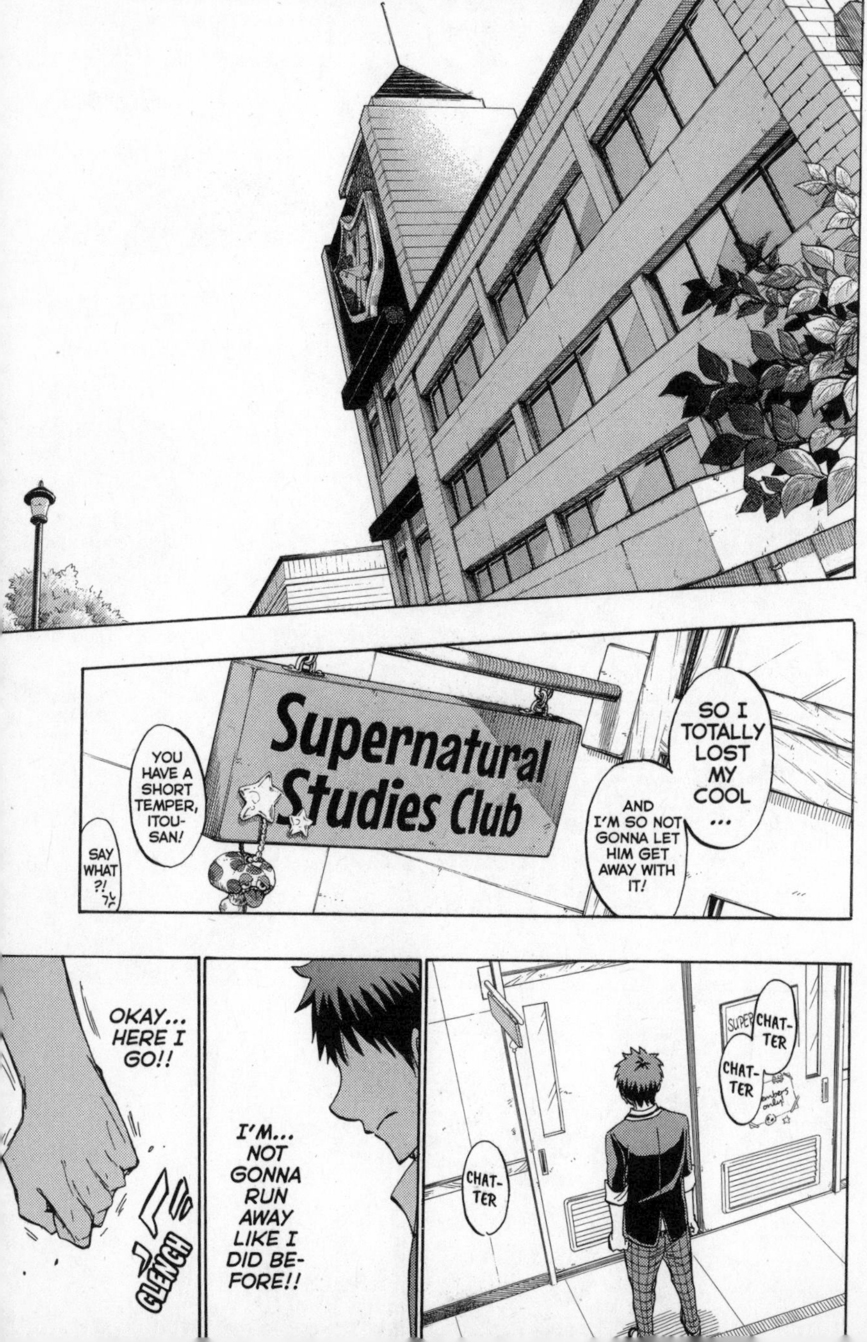

Supernatural Studies Club
SO I TOTALLY LOST MY COOL ...
AND I'M SO NOT GONNA LET HIM GET AWAY WITH IT!
YOU HAVE A SHORT TEMPER, ITOU-SAN!
SAY WHAT?!
CHAT-TER
CHAT-TER
CHAT-TER
I'M... NOT GONNA RUN AWAY LIKE I DID BE-FORE!!
OKAY... HERE I GO!!
CLENCH

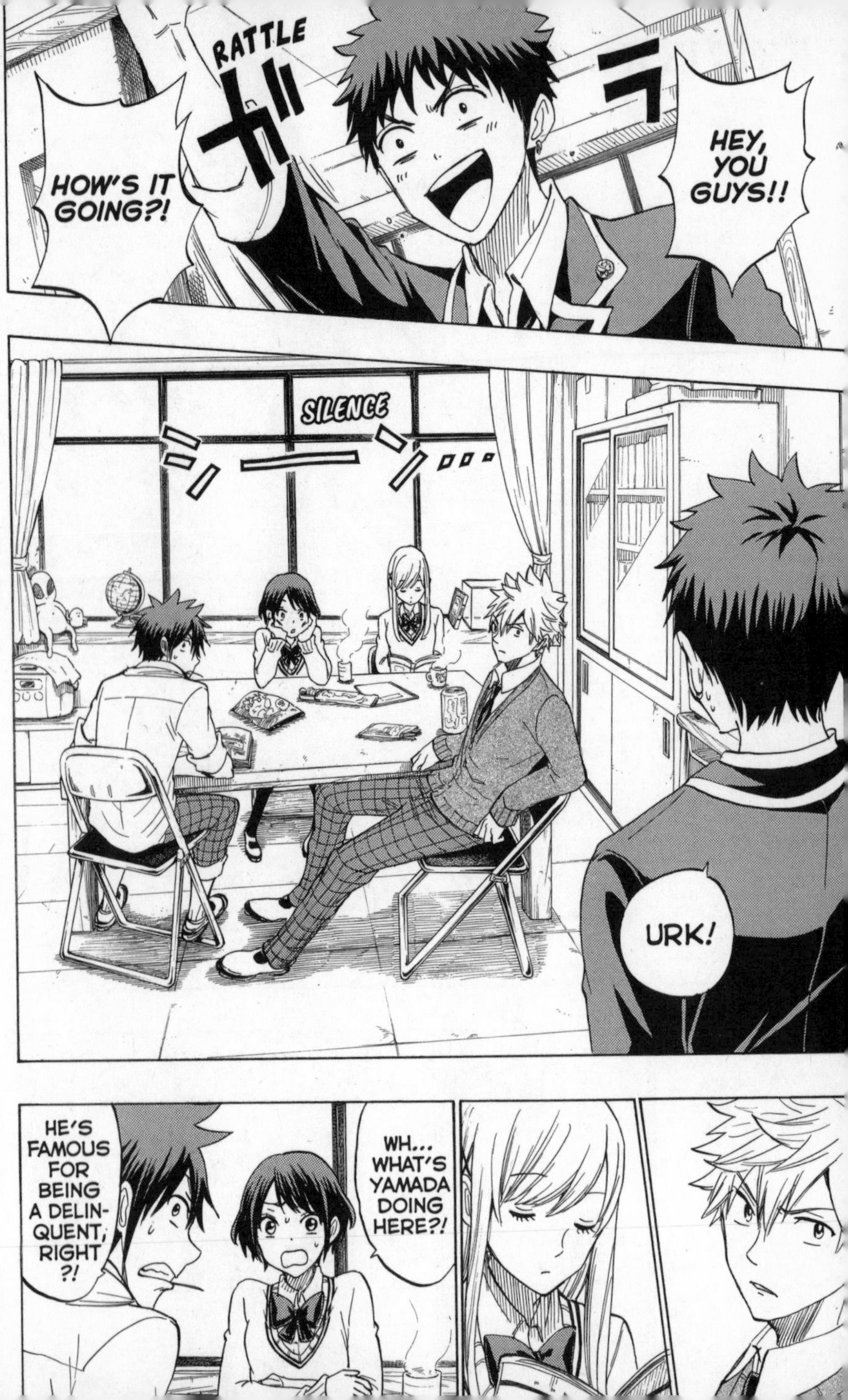
HEY, YOU GUYS!!
RATTLE
HOW'S IT GOING?!
URK!
SILENCE
WH... WHAT'S YAMADA DOING HERE?!
HE'S FAMOUS FOR BEING A DELINQUENT, RIGHT?!

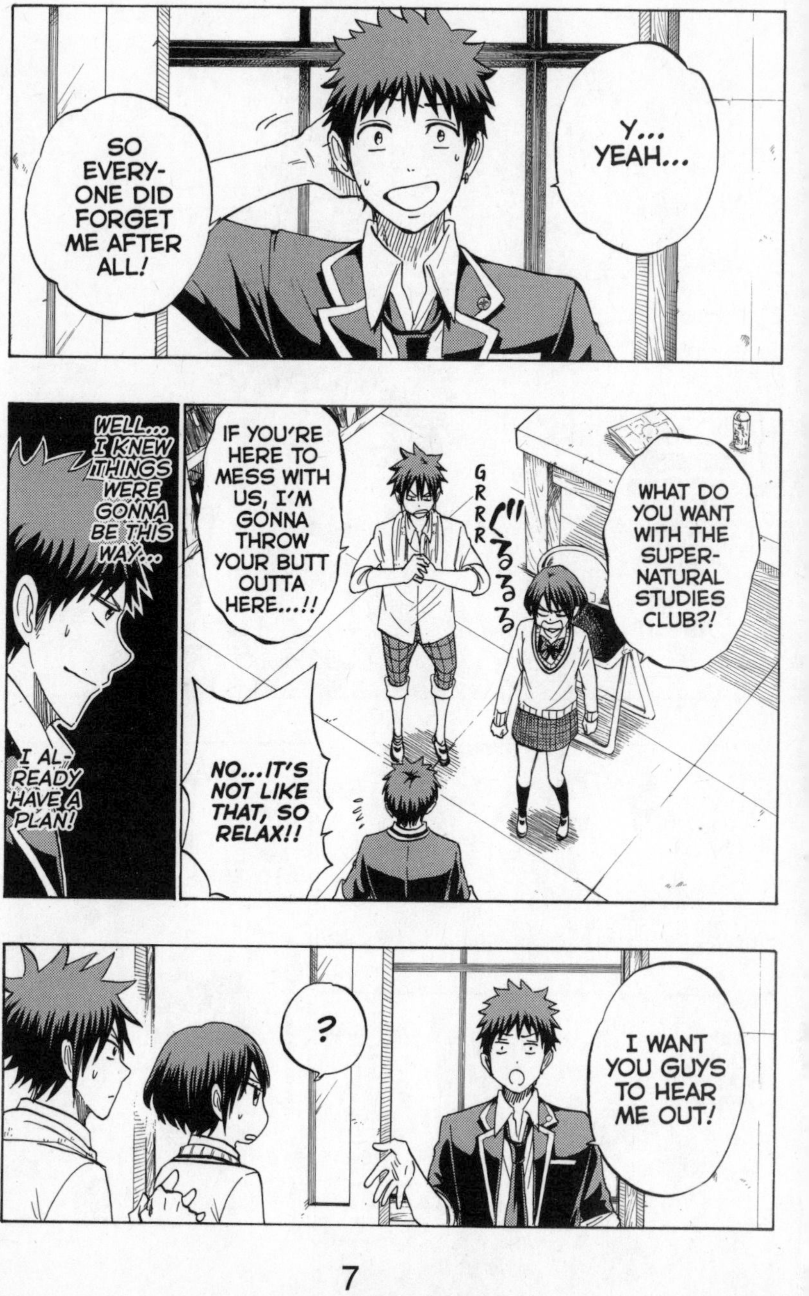
Y... YEAH...
SO EVERY-ONE DID FORGET ME AFTER ALL!
WHAT DO YOU WANT WITH THE SUPER-NATURAL STUDIES CLUB?!
GRRR
ぐるるるる
IF YOU'RE HERE TO MESS WITH US, I'M GONNA THROW YOUR BUTT OUTTA HERE...!!
NO...IT'S NOT LIKE THAT, SO RELAX!!
WELL... I KNEW THINGS WERE GONNA BE THIS WAY...
I AL-READY HAVE A PLAN!
I WANT YOU GUYS TO HEAR ME OUT!
?

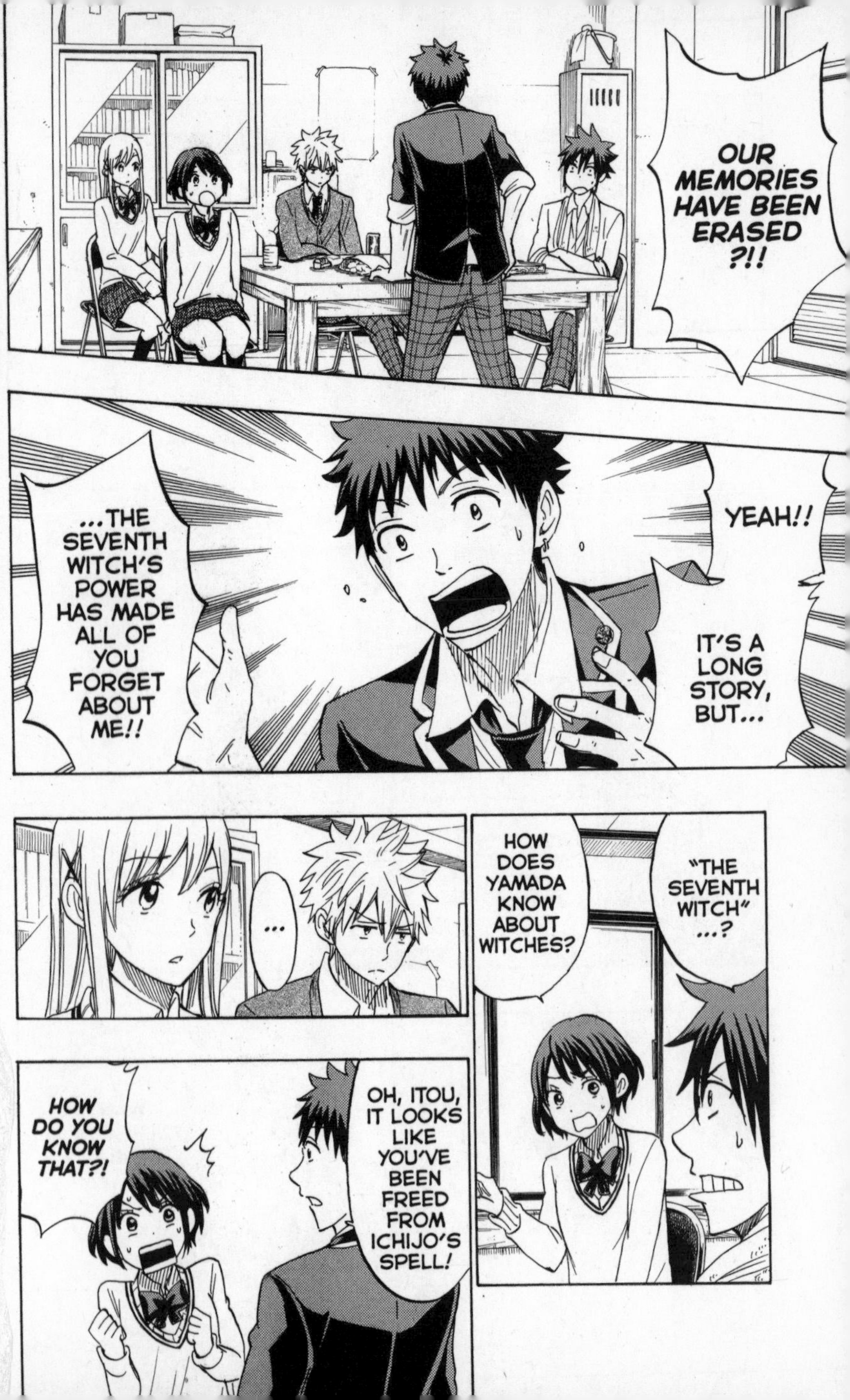
OUR MEMORIES HAVE BEEN ERASED ?!!
YEAH!!
IT'S A LONG STORY, BUT...
...THE SEVENTH WITCH'S POWER HAS MADE ALL OF YOU FORGET ABOUT ME!!
"THE SEVENTH WITCH" ...?
HOW DOES YAMADA KNOW ABOUT WITCHES?
...
OH, ITOU, IT LOOKS LIKE YOU'VE BEEN FREED FROM ICHIJO'S SPELL!
HOW DO YOU KNOW THAT?!

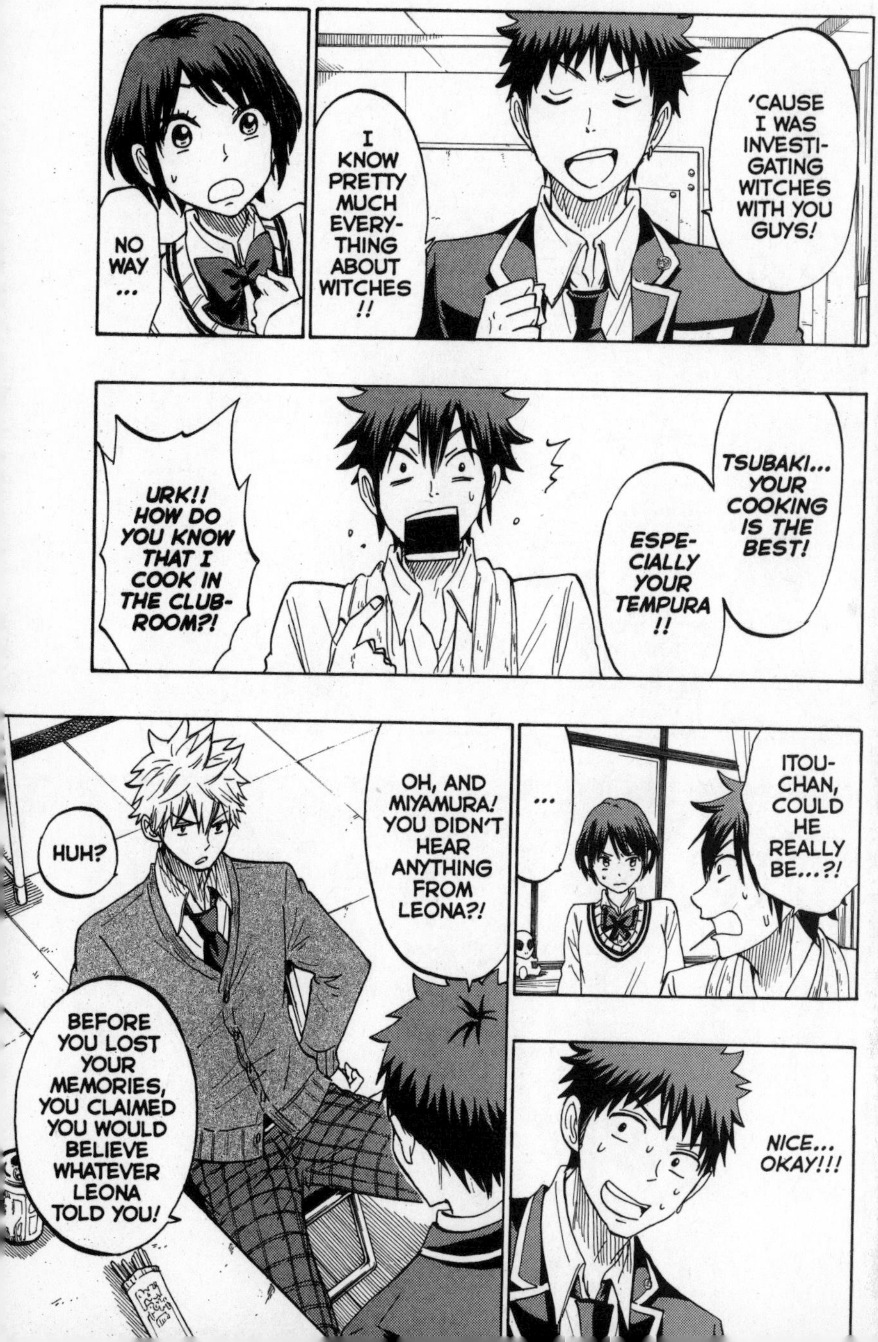
'CAUSE I WAS INVESTI-GATING WITCHES WITH YOU GUYS!
I KNOW PRETTY MUCH EVERY-THING ABOUT WITCHES!!
NO WAY...
TSUBAKI... YOUR COOKING IS THE BEST!
ESPE-CIALLY YOUR TEMPURA!!
URK!! HOW DO YOU KNOW THAT I COOK IN THE CLUB-ROOM?!
ITOU-CHAN, COULD HE REALLY BE...?!
...
NICE... OKAY!!!
OH, AND MIYAMURA! YOU DIDN'T HEAR ANYTHING FROM LEONA?!
HUH?
BEFORE YOU LOST YOUR MEMORIES, YOU CLAIMED YOU WOULD BELIEVE WHATEVER LEONA TOLD YOU!

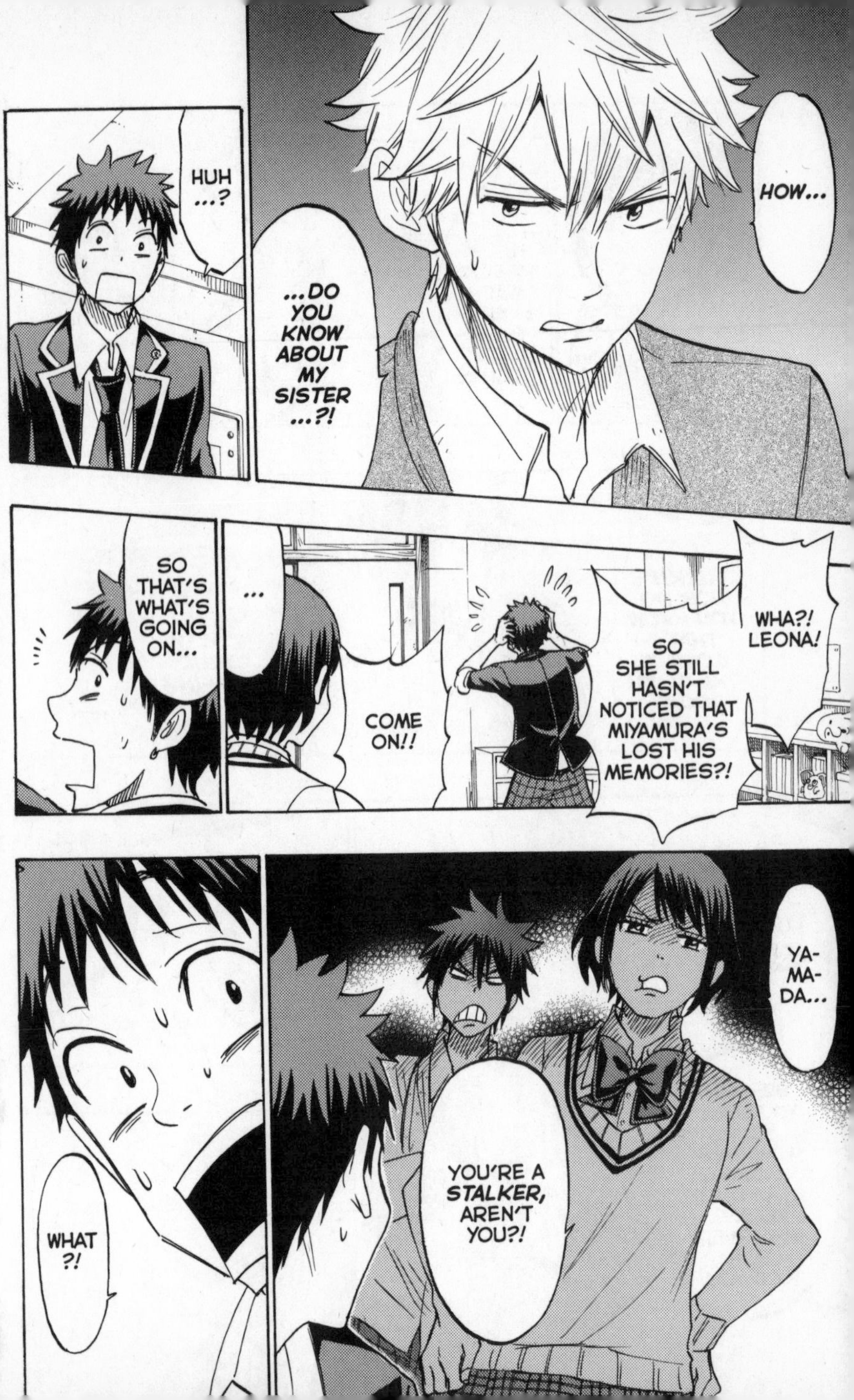
HOW...
...DO YOU KNOW ABOUT MY SISTER...?!
HUH...?
WHA?! LEONA!
SO SHE STILL HASN'T NOTICED THAT MIYAMURA'S LOST HIS MEMORIES?!
COME ON!!
...
SO THAT'S WHAT'S GOING ON...
YA-MA-DA...
YOU'RE A STALKER, AREN'T YOU?!
WHAT?!

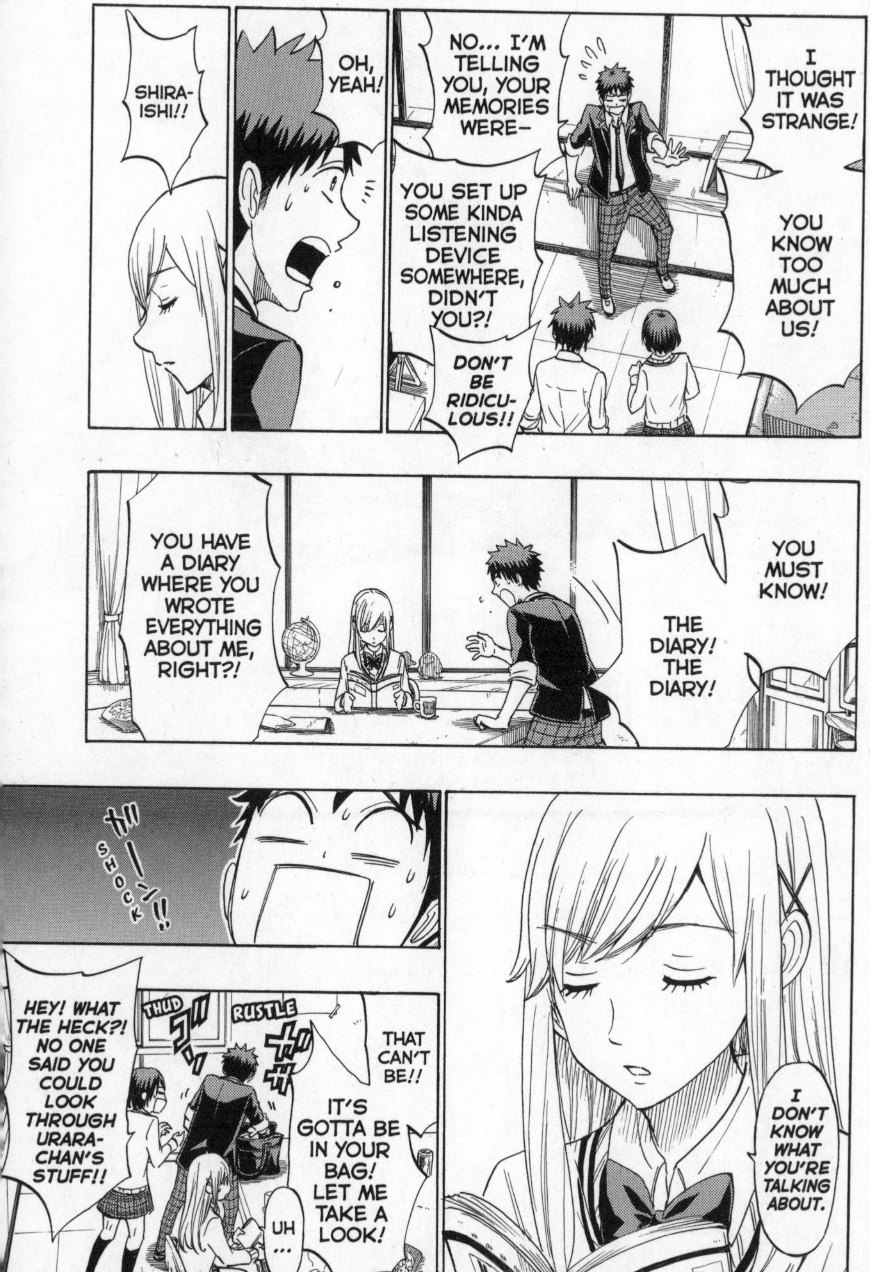
I THOUGHT IT WAS STRANGE!
YOU KNOW TOO MUCH ABOUT US!
NO... I'M TELLING YOU, YOUR MEMORIES WERE–
YOU SET UP SOME KINDA LISTENING DEVICE SOMEWHERE, DIDN'T YOU?!
DON'T BE RIDICULOUS!!
OH, YEAH!
SHIRAISHI!!
YOU MUST KNOW!
THE DIARY! THE DIARY!
YOU HAVE A DIARY WHERE YOU WROTE EVERYTHING ABOUT ME, RIGHT?!
I DON'T KNOW WHAT YOU'RE TALKING ABOUT.
Modern Japanese
SHOCK
THAT CAN'T BE!!
IT'S GOTTA BE IN YOUR BAG! LET ME TAKE A LOOK!
RUSTLE
THUD
HEY! WHAT THE HECK?! NO ONE SAID YOU COULD LOOK THROUGH URARA-CHAN'S STUFF!!
UH ...

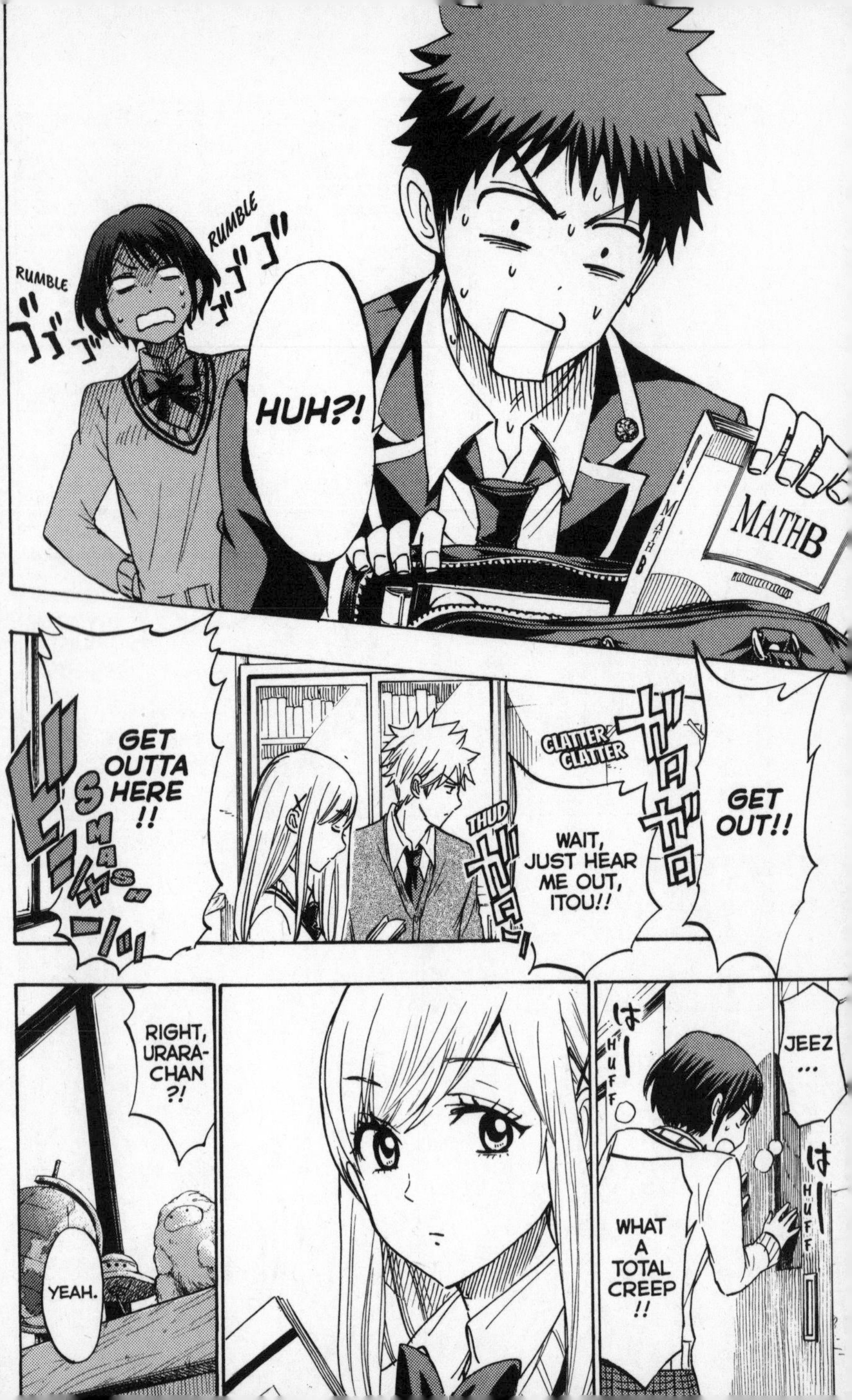
MATH B
HUH?!
RUMBLE
RUMBLE
GET OUT!!
CLATTER CLATTER
WAIT, JUST HEAR ME OUT, ITOU!!
THUD
GET OUTTA HERE!!
SMASH
JEEZ...
はー
HUFF
はー
HUFF
WHAT A TOTAL CREEP!!
RIGHT, URARA-CHAN?!
YEAH.

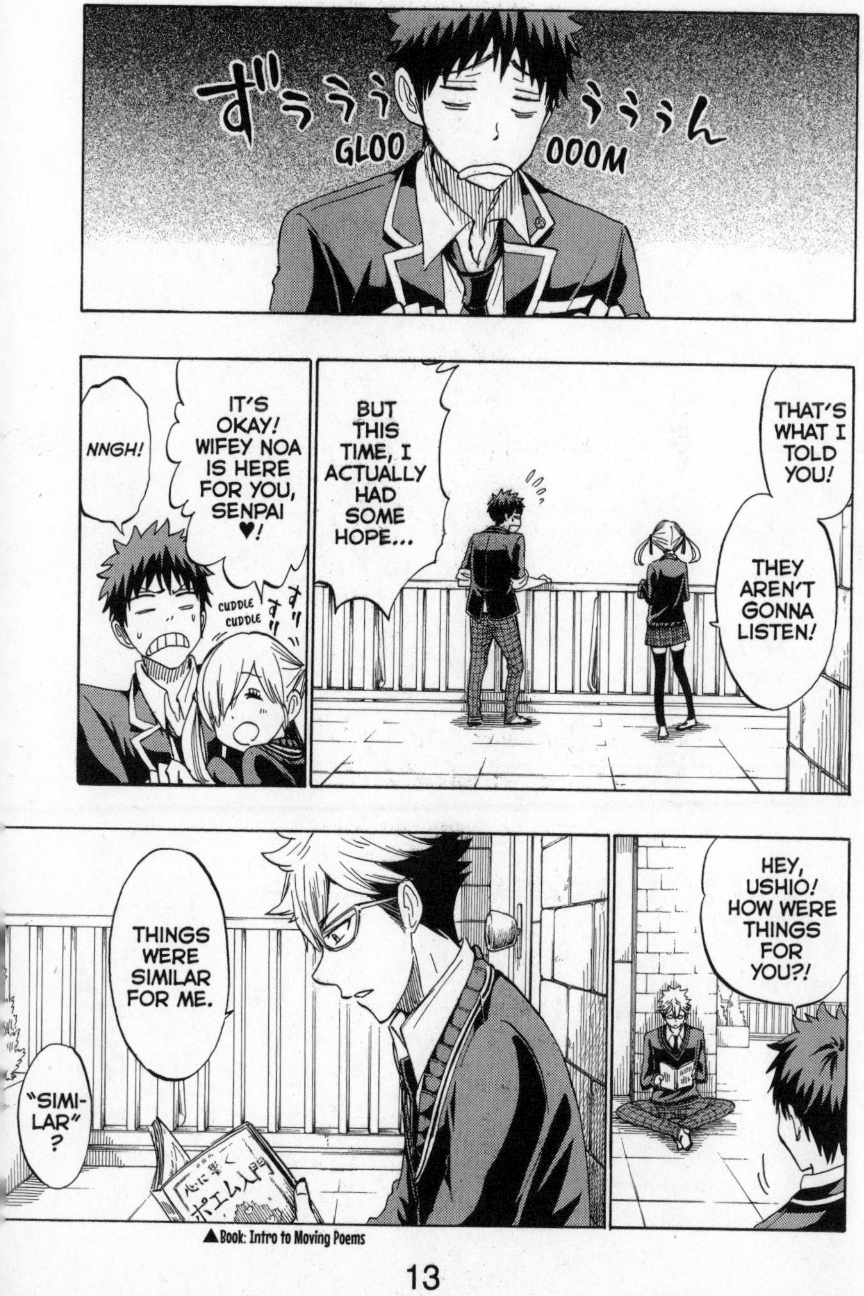
ずううう
GLOO
OOOM
うううん
THAT'S WHAT I TOLD YOU!
THEY AREN'T GONNA LISTEN!
BUT THIS TIME, I ACTUALLY HAD SOME HOPE...
IT'S OKAY! WIFEY NOA IS HERE FOR YOU, SENPAI ♥!
CUDDLE CUDDLE
NNGH!
HEY, USHIO! HOW WERE THINGS FOR YOU?!
THINGS WERE SIMILAR FOR ME.
"SIMI-LAR"?
心に響く ポエム入門

▲Book: Intro to Moving Poems

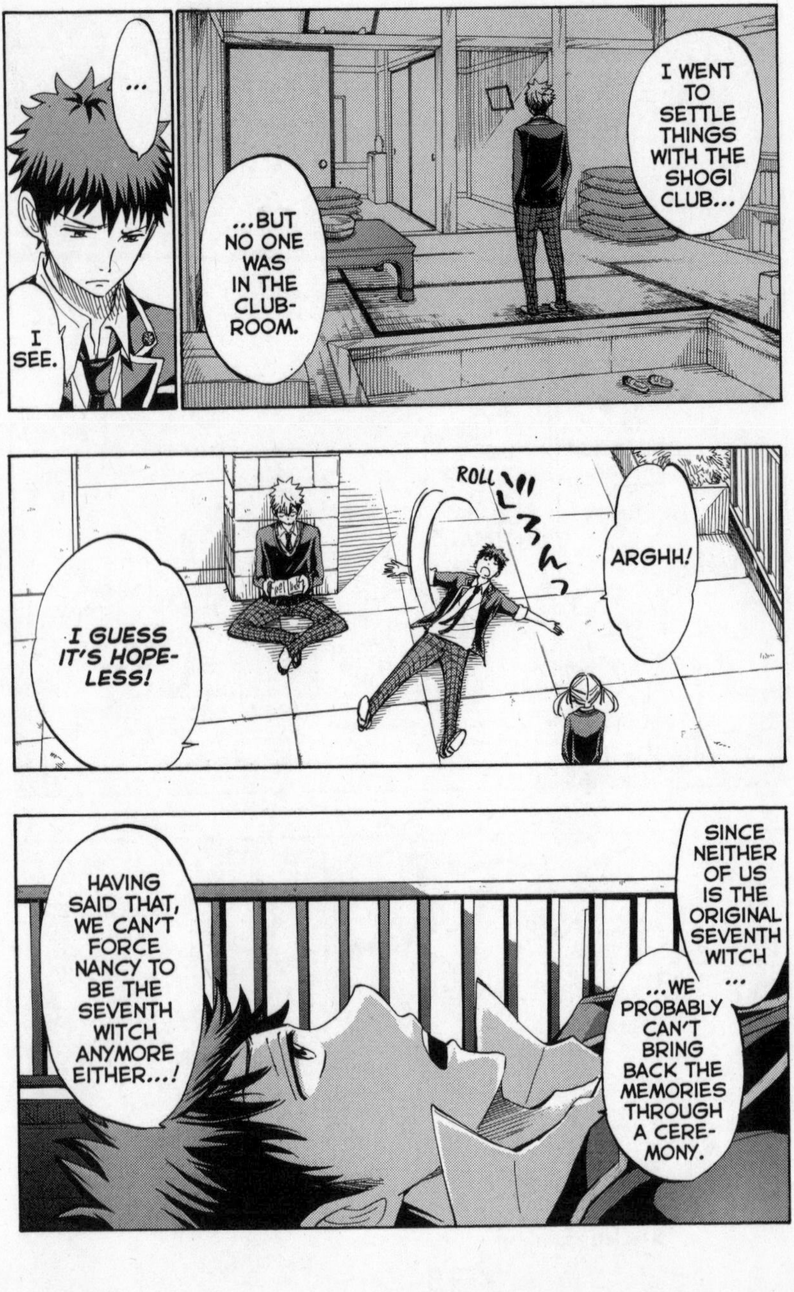
I WENT TO SETTLE THINGS WITH THE SHOGI CLUB...
...BUT NO ONE WAS IN THE CLUB-ROOM.
...
I SEE.
ARGHH!
ROLL
ごろんっ
I GUESS IT'S HOPE-LESS!
SINCE NEITHER OF US IS THE ORIGINAL SEVENTH WITCH...
...WE PROBABLY CAN'T BRING BACK THE MEMORIES THROUGH A CERE-MONY.
HAVING SAID THAT, WE CAN'T FORCE NANCY TO BE THE SEVENTH WITCH ANYMORE EITHER...!

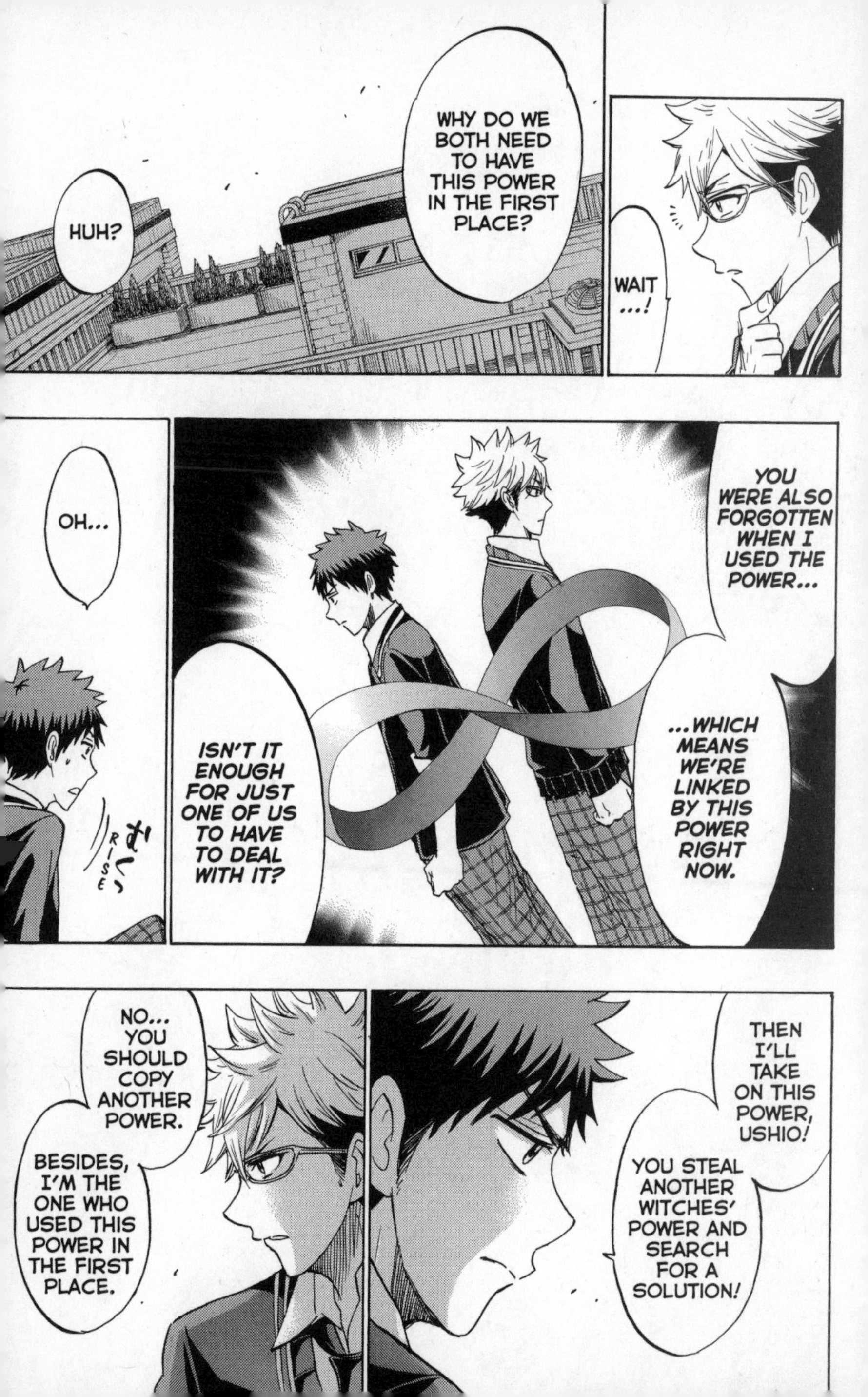
WAIT ...!
WHY DO WE BOTH NEED TO HAVE THIS POWER IN THE FIRST PLACE?
HUH?
YOU WERE ALSO FORGOTTEN WHEN I USED THE POWER...
...WHICH MEANS WE'RE LINKED BY THIS POWER RIGHT NOW.
ISN'T IT ENOUGH FOR JUST ONE OF US TO HAVE TO DEAL WITH IT?
OH...
RISE
THEN I'LL TAKE ON THIS POWER, USHIO!
YOU STEAL ANOTHER WITCHES' POWER AND SEARCH FOR A SOLUTION!
NO... YOU SHOULD COPY ANOTHER POWER.
BESIDES, I'M THE ONE WHO USED THIS POWER IN THE FIRST PLACE.

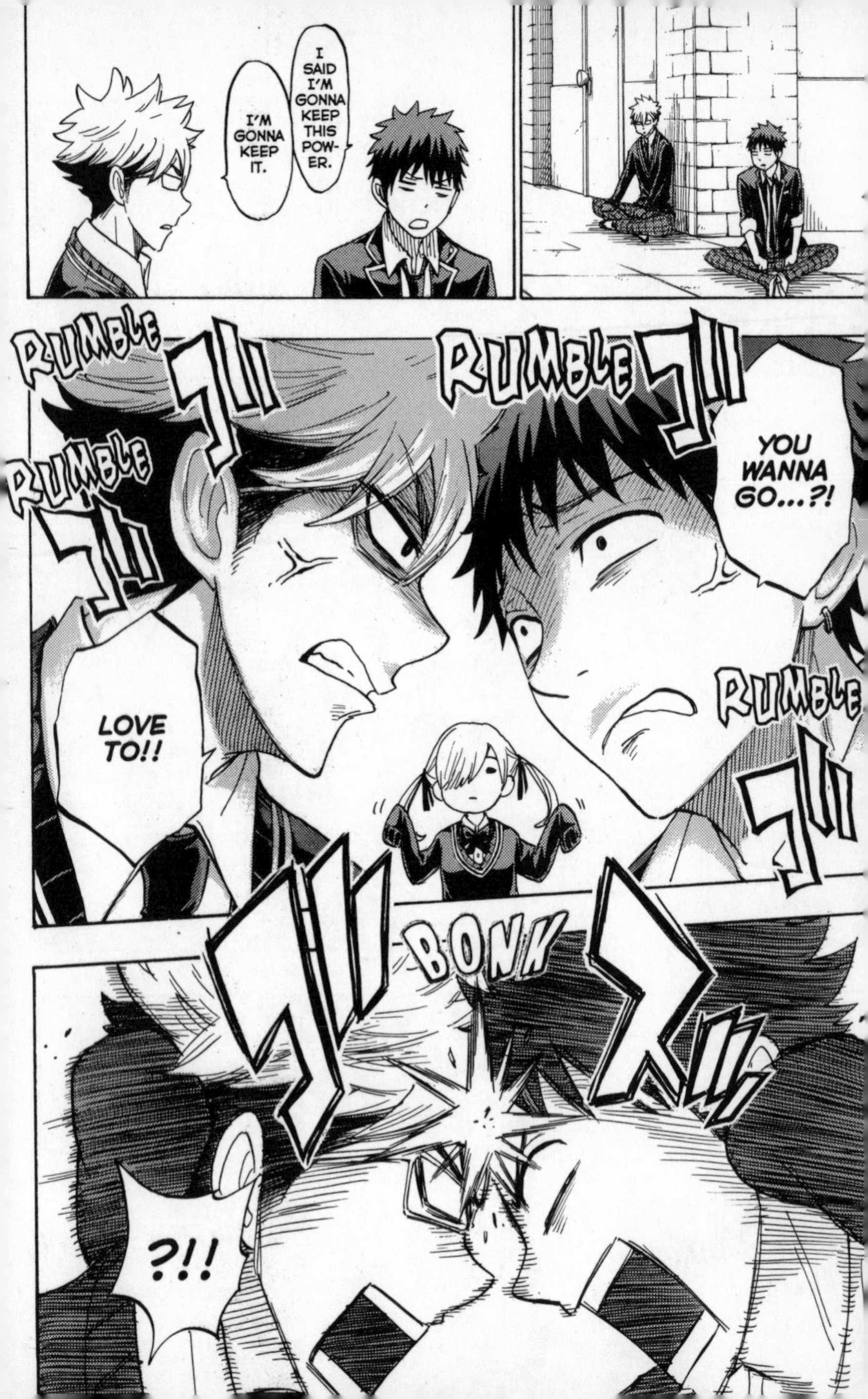

I SAID I'M GONNA KEEP THIS POW-ER.
I'M GONNA KEEP IT.
RUMBLE
RUMBLE
YOU WANNA GO...?!
RUMBLE
RUMBLE
LOVE TO!!
BONK
?!!

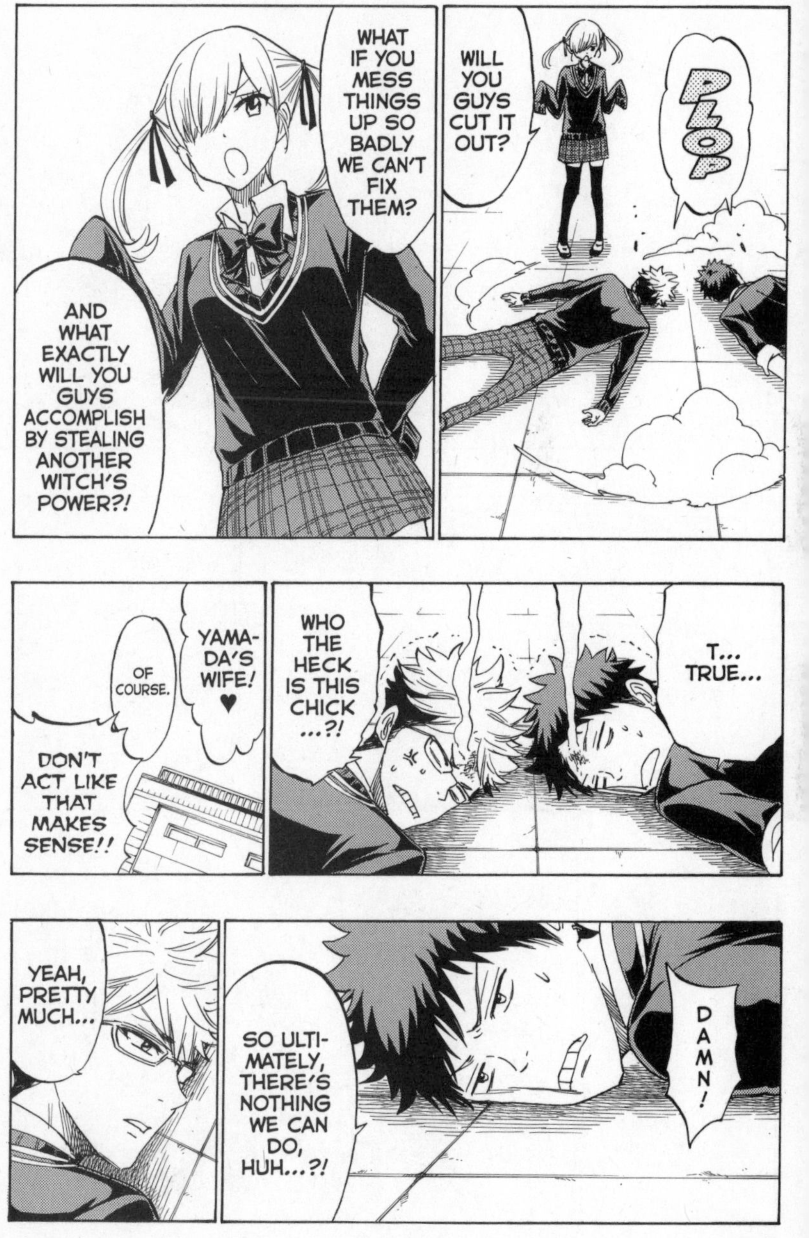
PLOP
WILL YOU GUYS CUT IT OUT?
WHAT IF YOU MESS THINGS UP SO BADLY WE CAN'T FIX THEM?
AND WHAT EXACTLY WILL YOU GUYS ACCOMPLISH BY STEALING ANOTHER WITCH'S POWER?!
T... TRUE...
WHO THE HECK IS THIS CHICK ...?!
YAMA-DA'S WIFE! ♥
OF COURSE.
DON'T ACT LIKE THAT MAKES SENSE!!
DAMN!
SO ULTI-MATELY, THERE'S NOTHING WE CAN DO, HUH...?!
YEAH, PRETTY MUCH...

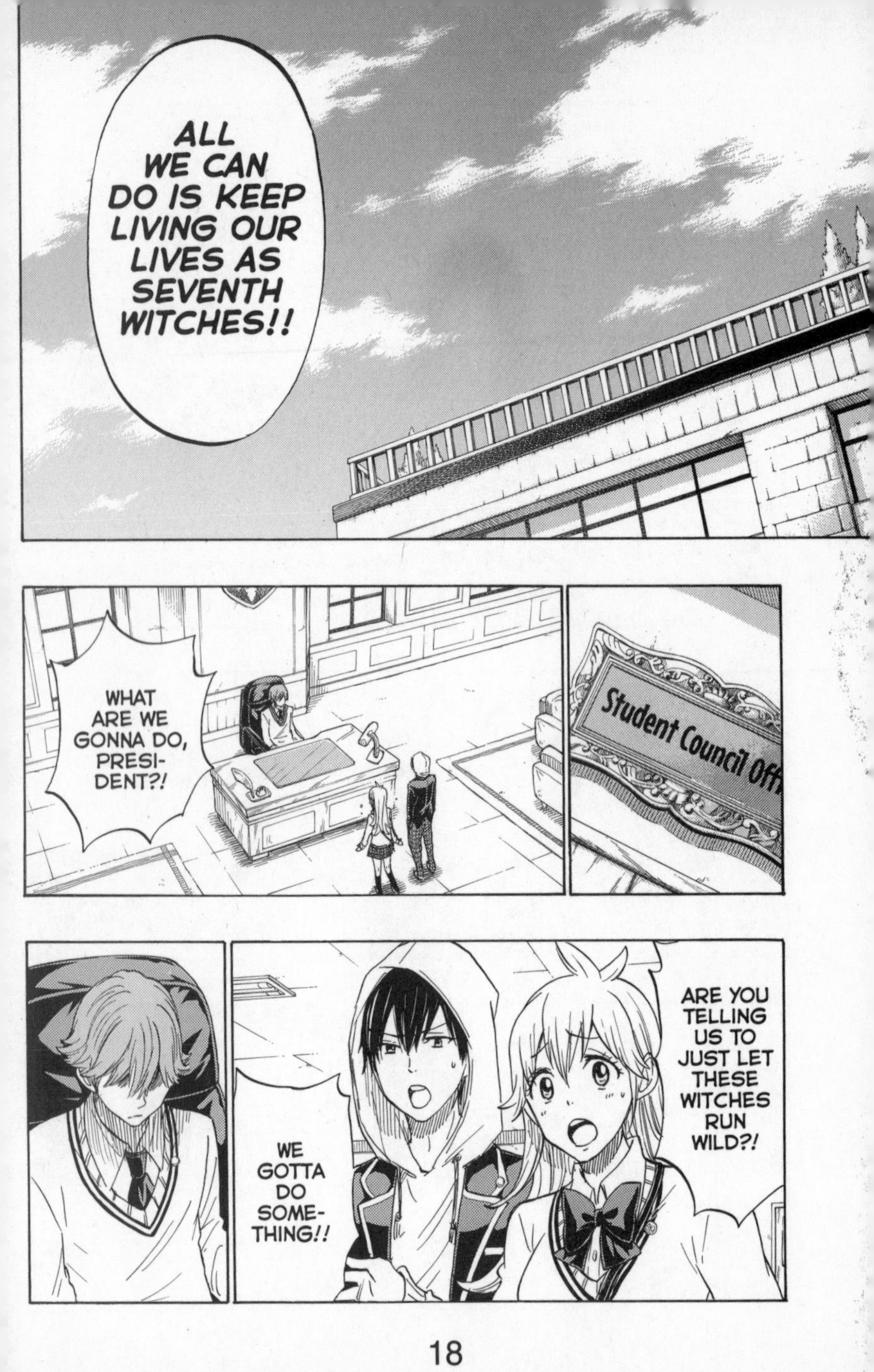
ALL WE CAN DO IS KEEP LIVING OUR LIVES AS SEVENTH WITCHES!!
Student Council
WHAT ARE WE GONNA DO, PRESI-DENT?!
ARE YOU TELLING US TO JUST LET THESE WITCHES RUN WILD?!
WE GOTTA DO SOME-THING!!

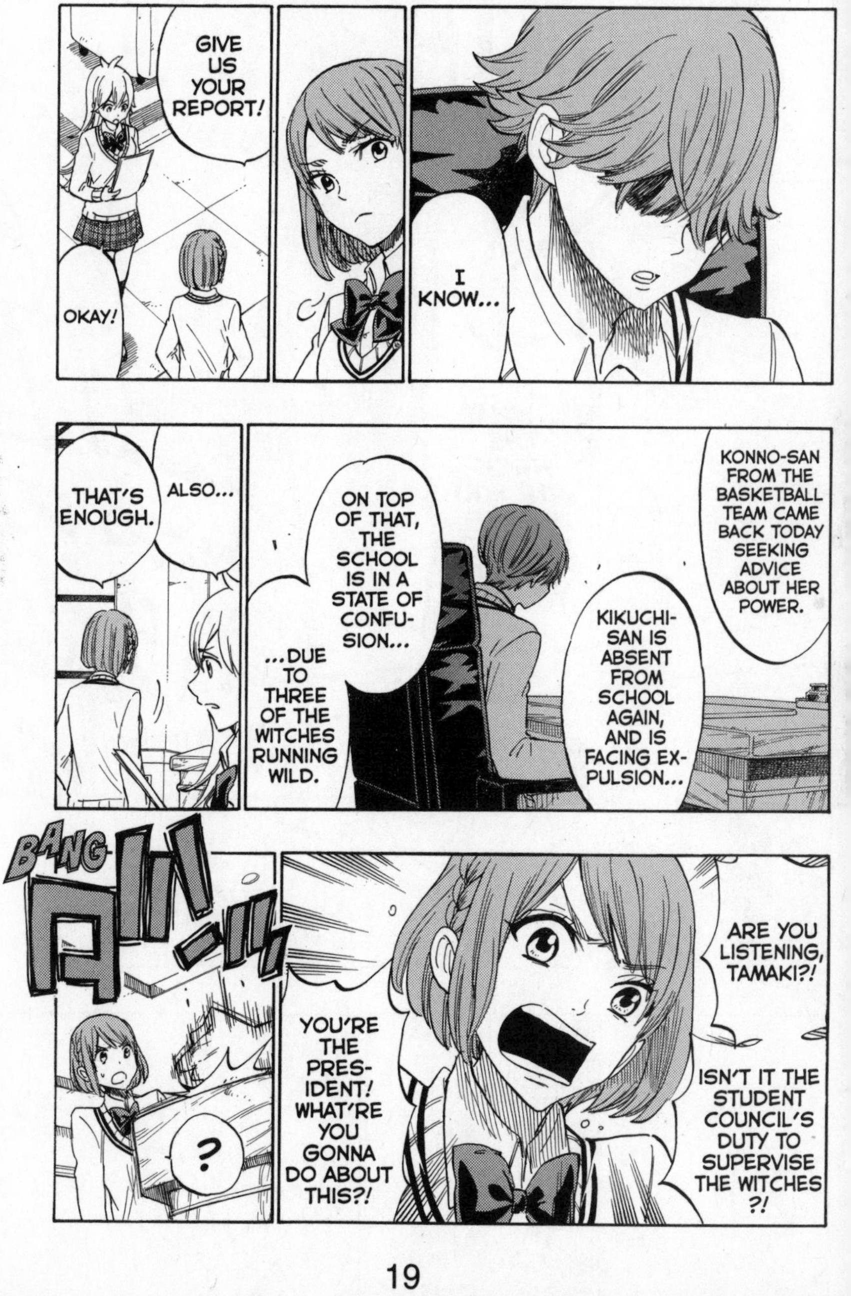
I KNOW...
GIVE US YOUR REPORT!
OKAY!
KONNO-SAN FROM THE BASKETBALL TEAM CAME BACK TODAY SEEKING ADVICE ABOUT HER POWER.
KIKUCHI-SAN IS ABSENT FROM SCHOOL AGAIN, AND IS FACING EXPULSION...
ON TOP OF THAT, THE SCHOOL IS IN A STATE OF CONFUSION...
...DUE TO THREE OF THE WITCHES RUNNING WILD.
ALSO...
THAT'S ENOUGH.
ARE YOU LISTENING, TAMAKI?!
ISN'T IT THE STUDENT COUNCIL'S DUTY TO SUPERVISE THE WITCHES?!
YOU'RE THE PRESIDENT! WHAT'RE YOU GONNA DO ABOUT THIS?!
BANG
?

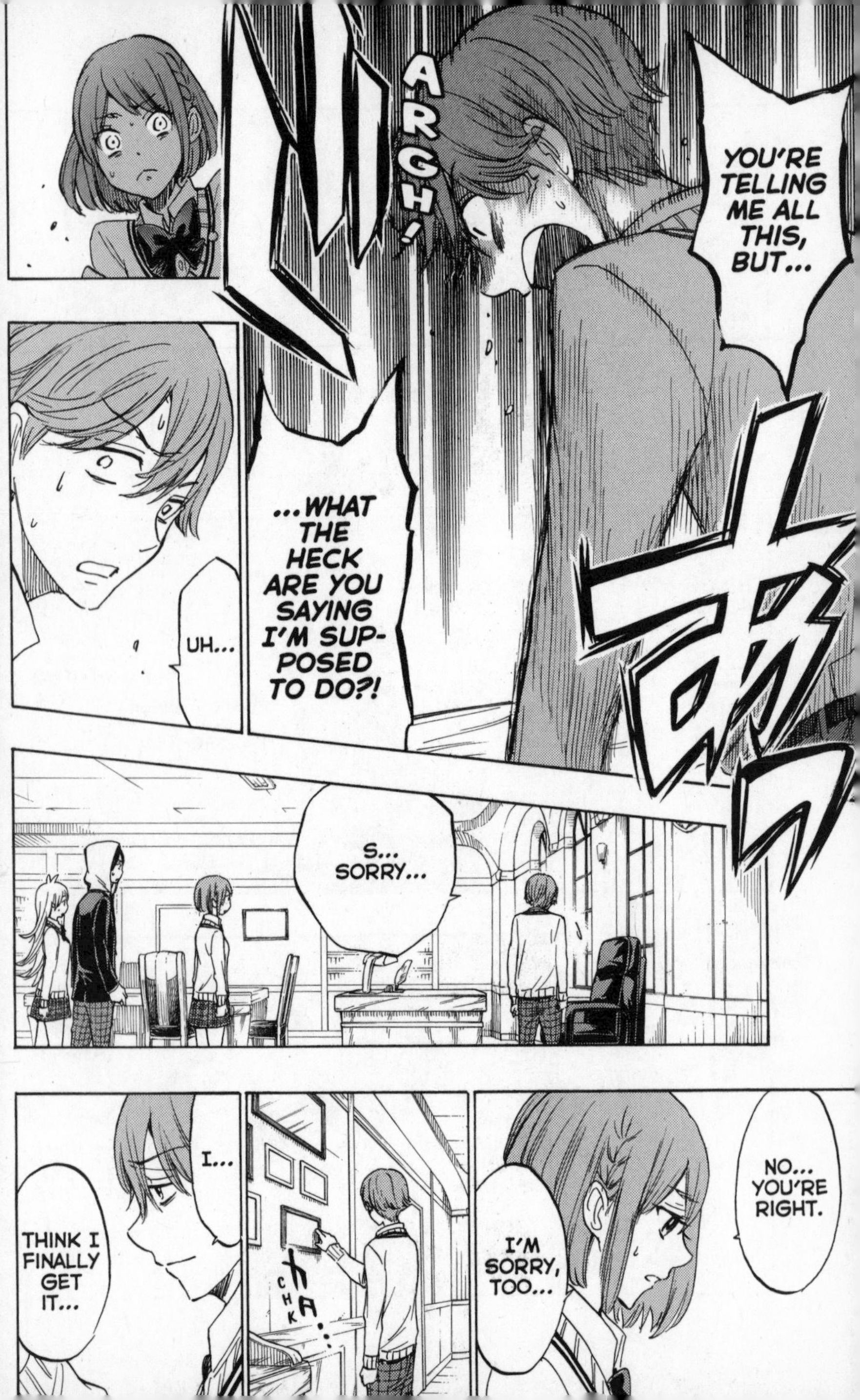
YOU'RE TELLING ME ALL THIS, BUT...
ARGH!
...WHAT THE HECK ARE YOU SAYING I'M SUPPOSED TO DO?!
UH...
S... SORRY...
NO... YOU'RE RIGHT.
I'M SORRY, TOO...
CHK
I...
THINK I FINALLY GET IT...

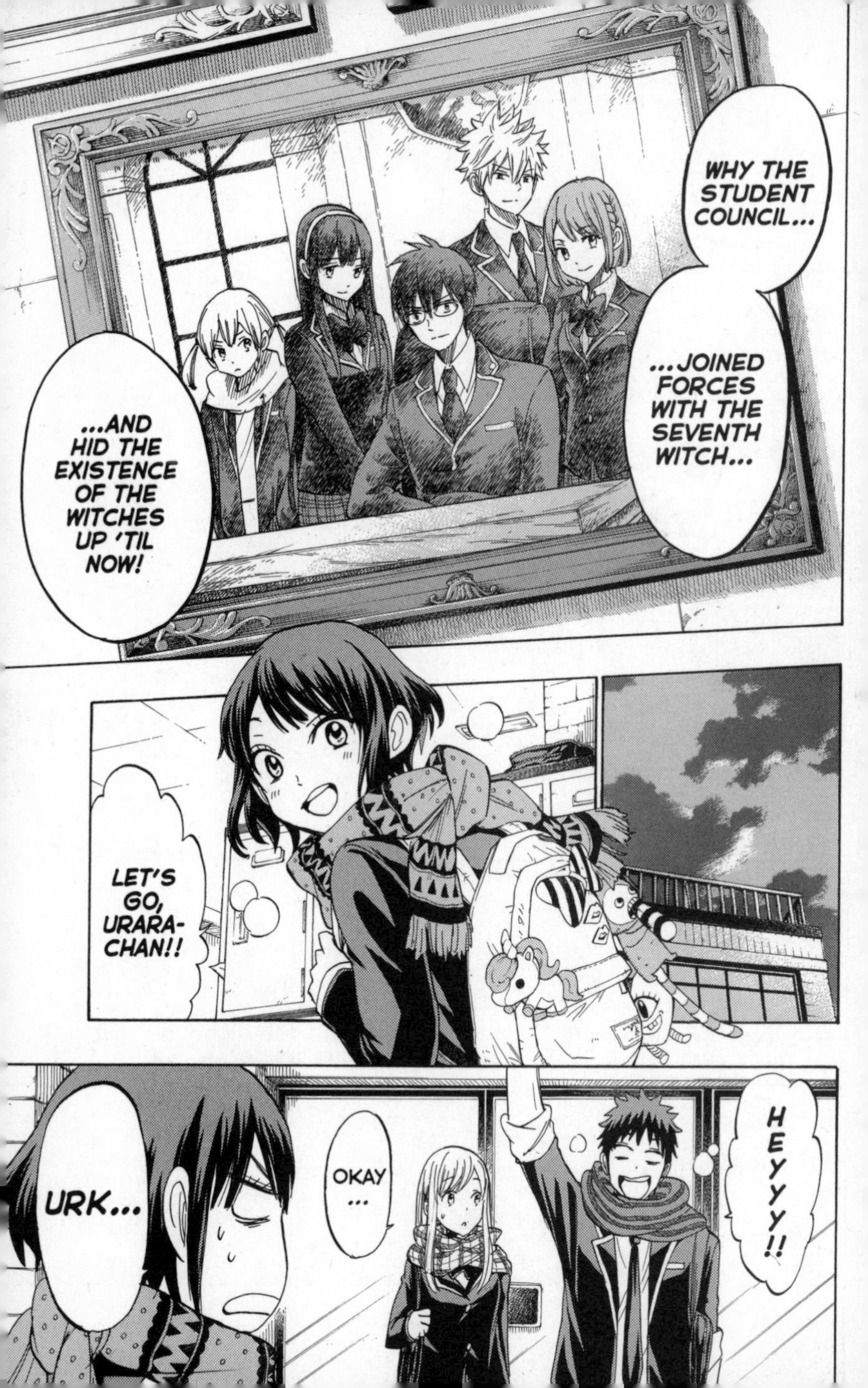
WHY THE STUDENT COUNCIL...
...JOINED FORCES WITH THE SEVENTH WITCH...
...AND HID THE EXISTENCE OF THE WITCHES UP 'TIL NOW!
LET'S GO, URARA-CHAN!!
HEYYY!!
OKAY ...
URK...

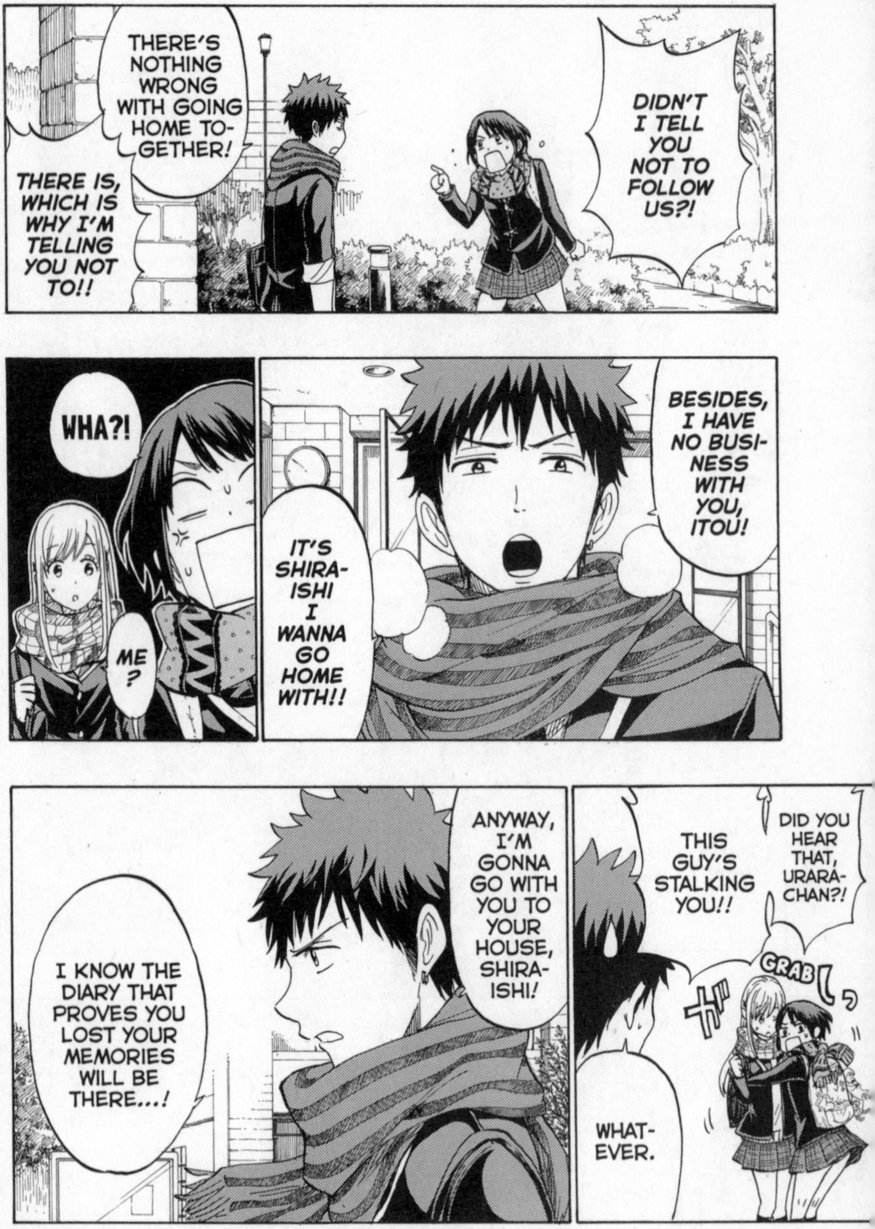
DIDN'T I TELL YOU NOT TO FOLLOW US?!
THERE'S NOTHING WRONG WITH GOING HOME TO-GETHER!
THERE IS, WHICH IS WHY I'M TELLING YOU NOT TO!!
BESIDES, I HAVE NO BUSI-NESS WITH YOU, ITOU!
IT'S SHIRA-ISHI I WANNA GO HOME WITH!!
WHA?!
ME?
DID YOU HEAR THAT, URARA-CHAN?!
THIS GUY'S STALKING YOU!!
GRAB
WHAT-EVER.
ANYWAY, I'M GONNA GO WITH YOU TO YOUR HOUSE, SHIRA-ISHI!
I KNOW THE DIARY THAT PROVES YOU LOST YOUR MEMORIES WILL BE THERE...!

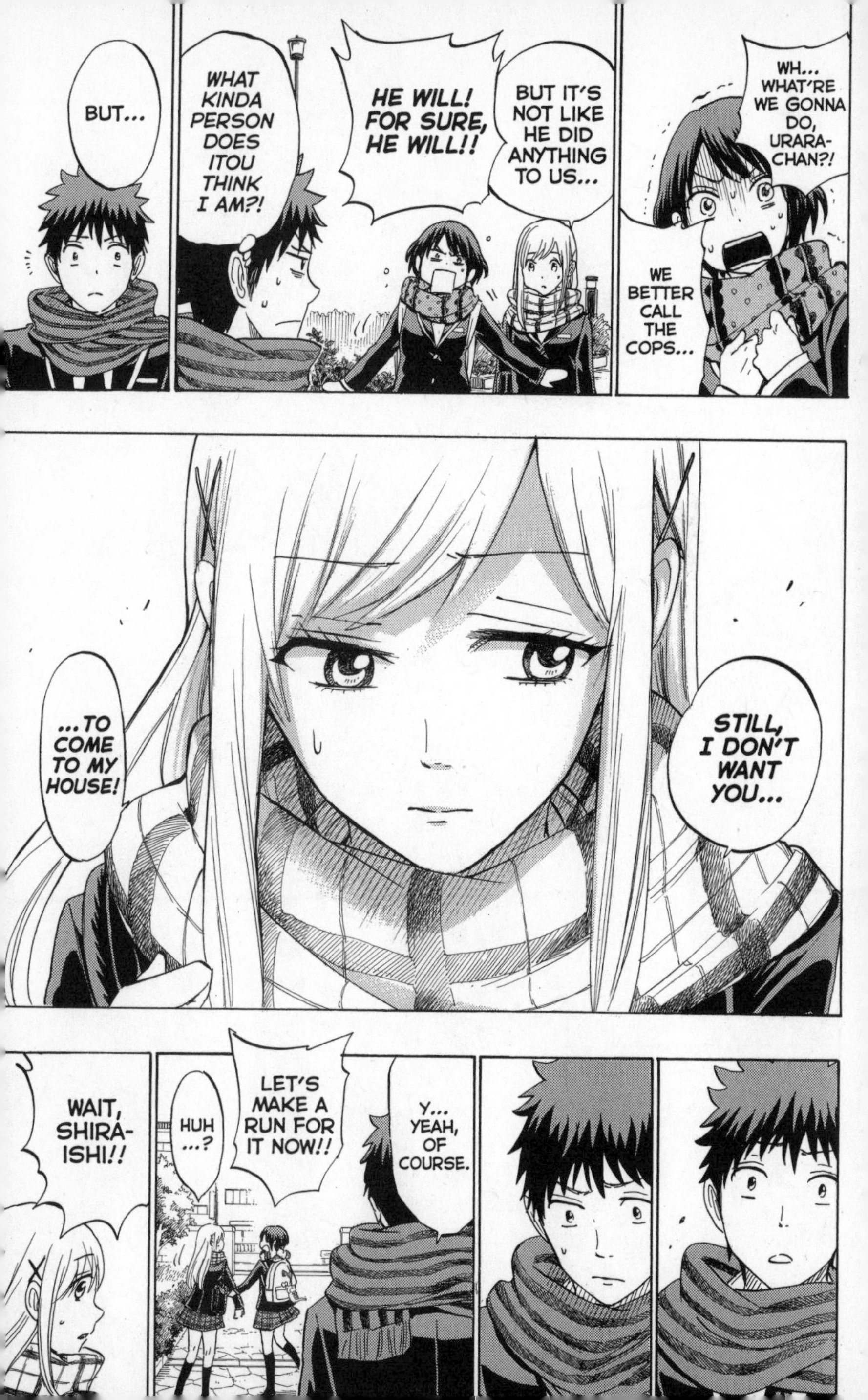
WH... WHAT'RE WE GONNA DO, URARA-CHAN?!
WE BETTER CALL THE COPS...
BUT IT'S NOT LIKE HE DID ANYTHING TO US...
HE WILL! FOR SURE, HE WILL!!
WHAT KINDA PERSON DOES ITOU THINK I AM?!
BUT...
STILL, I DON'T WANT YOU...
...TO COME TO MY HOUSE!
Y... YEAH, OF COURSE.
LET'S MAKE A RUN FOR IT NOW!!
HUH ...?
WAIT, SHIRAISHI!!

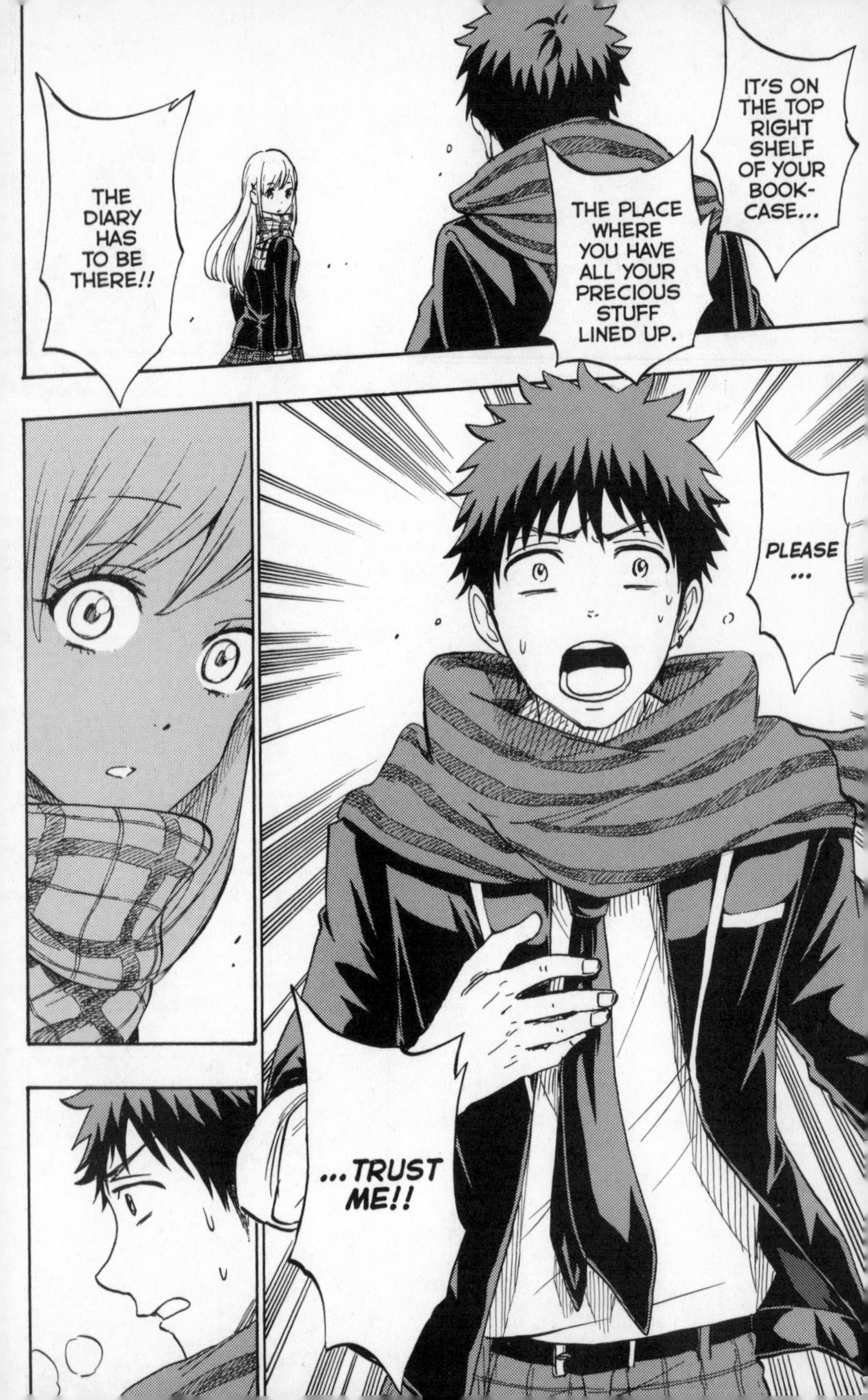
IT'S ON THE TOP RIGHT SHELF OF YOUR BOOK-CASE...
THE PLACE WHERE YOU HAVE ALL YOUR PRECIOUS STUFF LINED UP.
THE DIARY HAS TO BE THERE!!
PLEASE ...
...TRUST ME!!

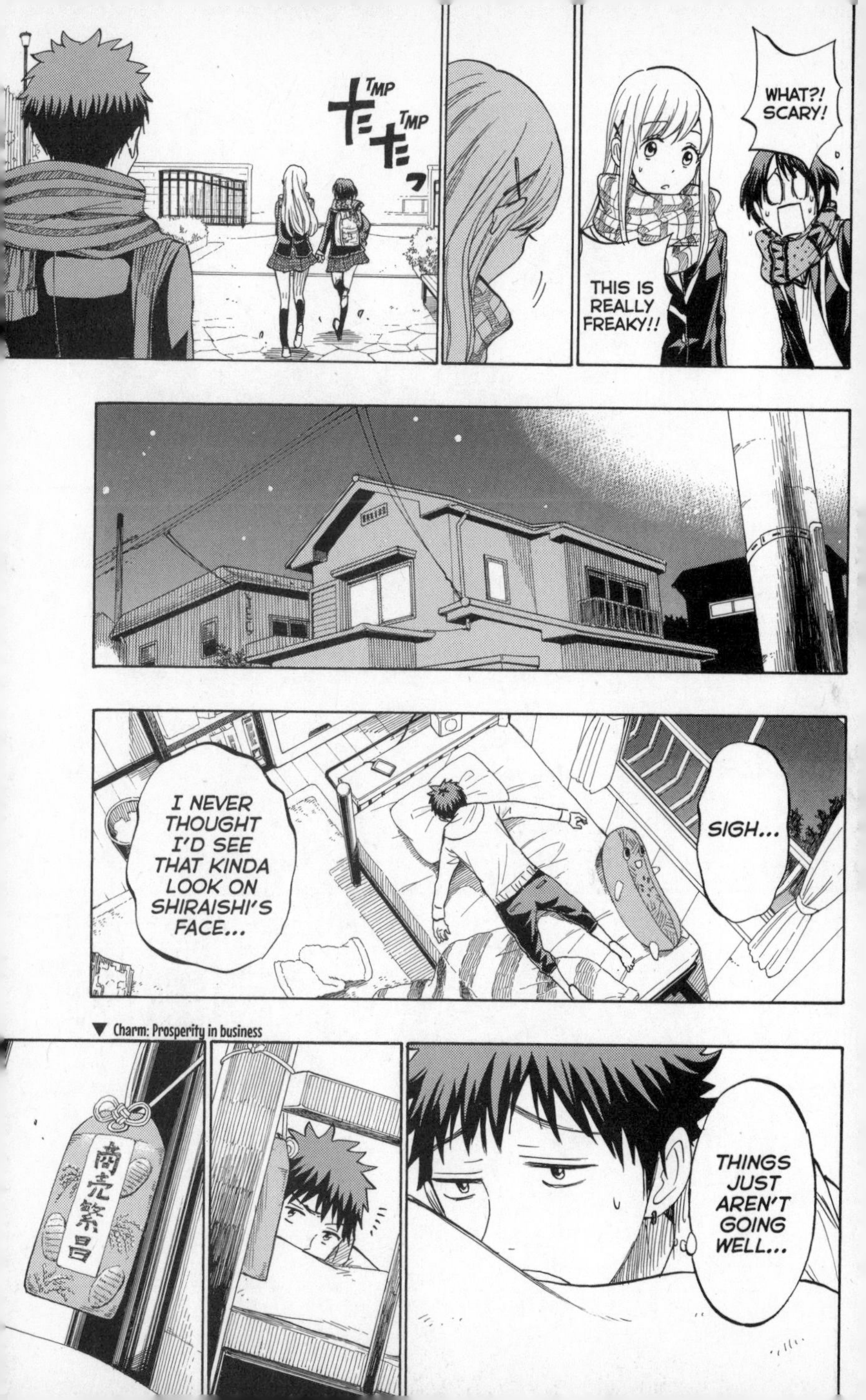
WHAT?! SCARY!
THIS IS REALLY FREAKY!!
TMP TMP
SIGH...
I NEVER THOUGHT I'D SEE THAT KINDA LOOK ON SHIRAISHI'S FACE...
Charm: Prosperity in business
THINGS JUST AREN'T GOING WELL...
商売繁昌

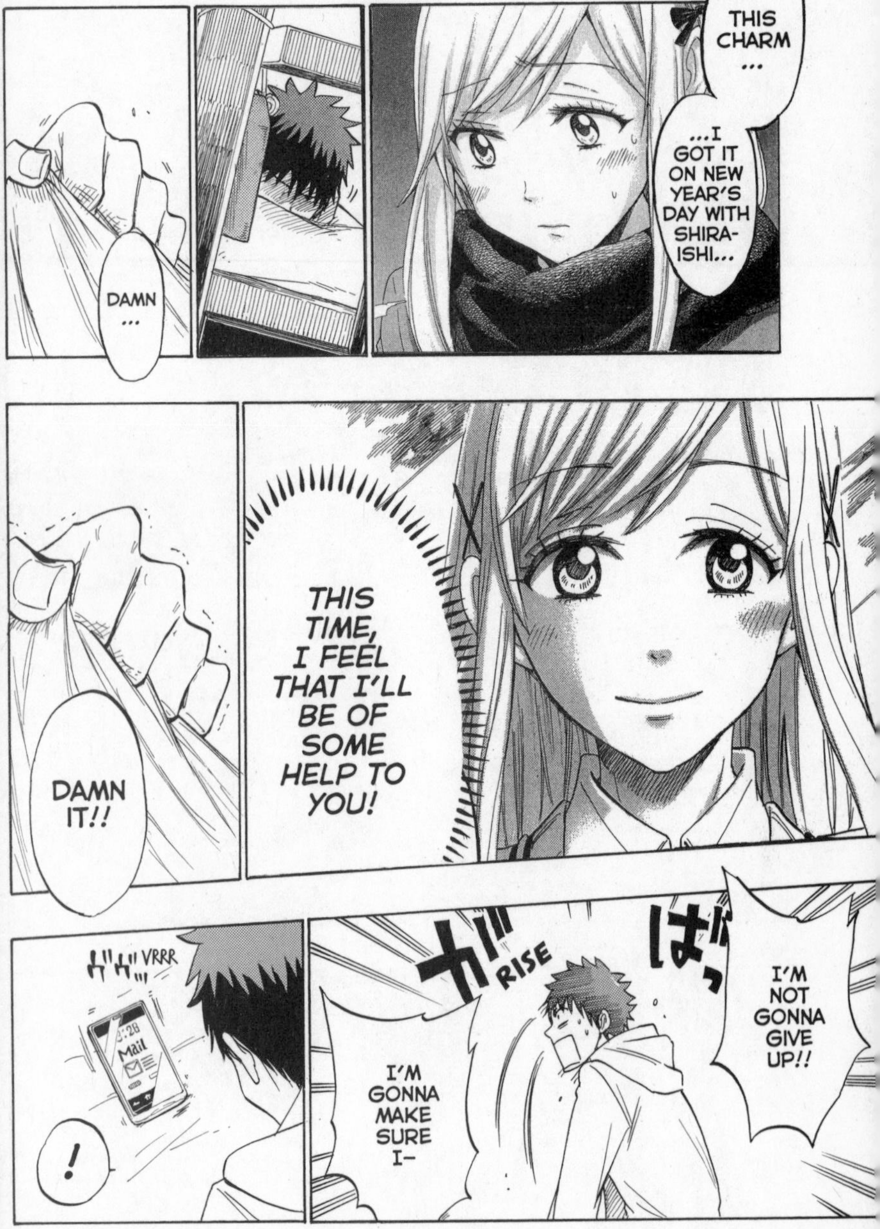
THIS CHARM ...
...I GOT IT ON NEW YEAR'S DAY WITH SHIRAISHI...
DAMN ...
THIS TIME, I FEEL THAT I'LL BE OF SOME HELP TO YOU!
DAMN IT!!
I'M NOT GONNA GIVE UP!!
RISE
I'M GONNA MAKE SURE I-
VRRR
Mail
!

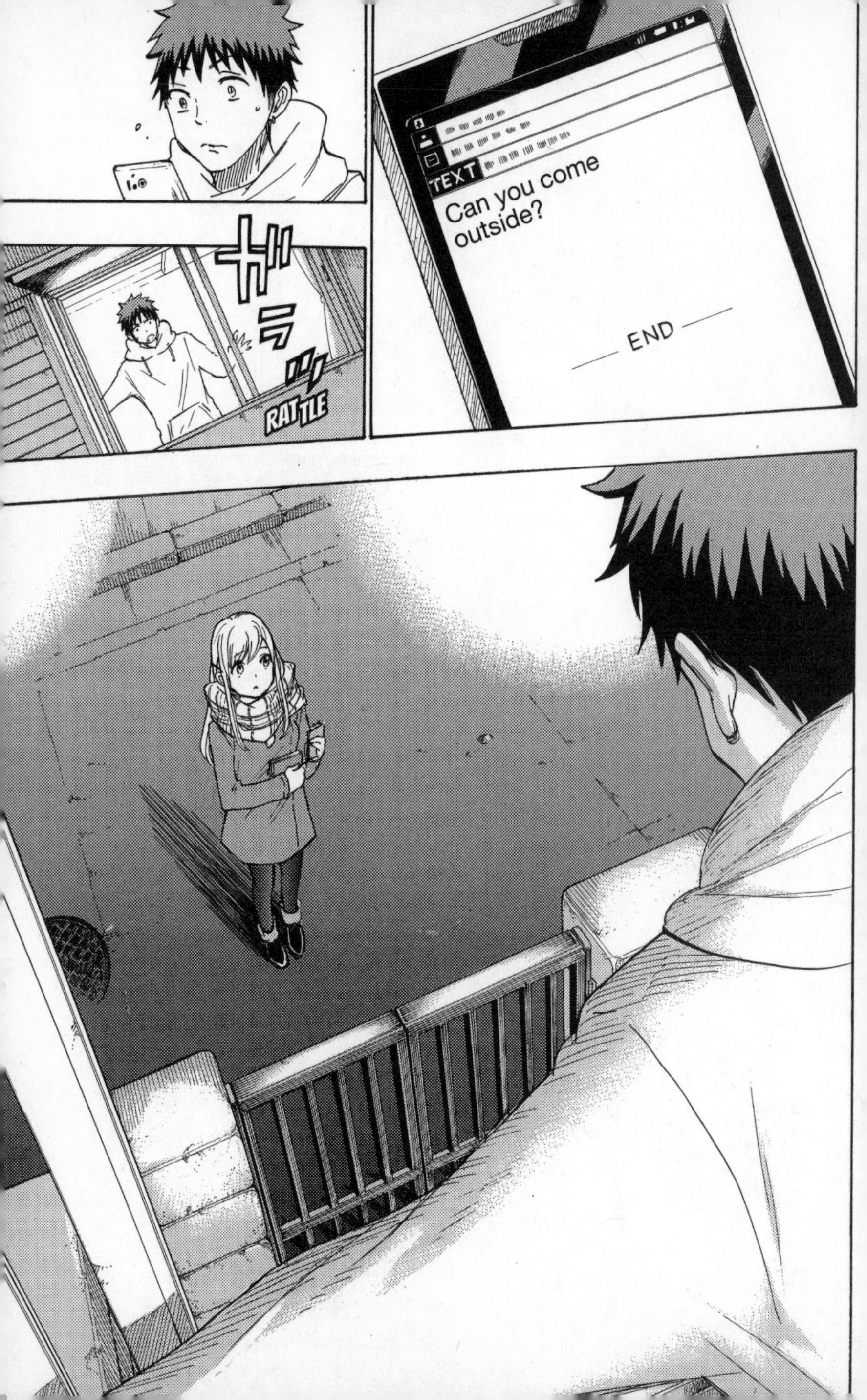
TEXT
Can you come outside?
END
ガラッ
RATTLE

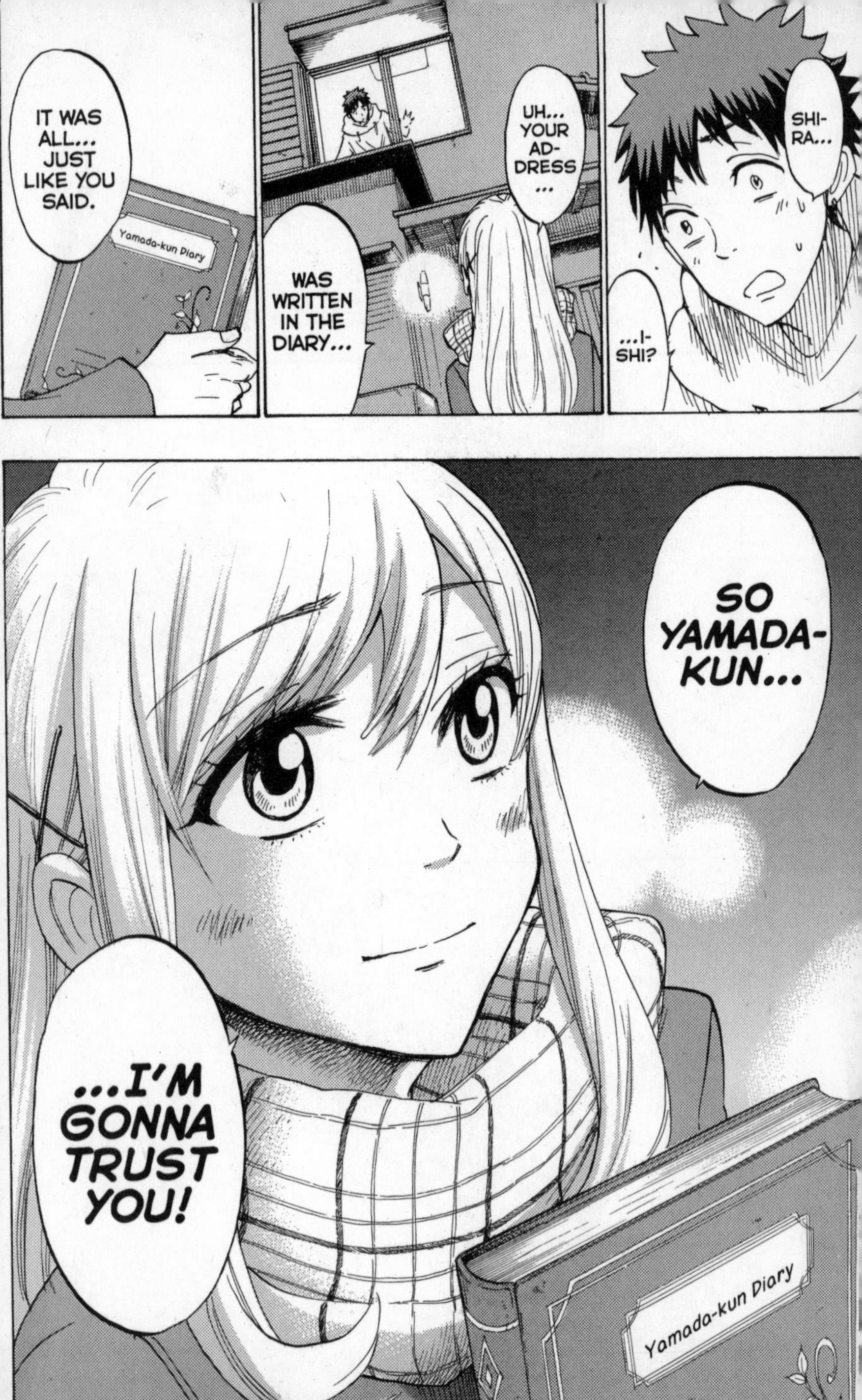
SHI-RA...
...I-SHI?
UH... YOUR AD-DRESS...
WAS WRITTEN IN THE DIARY...
IT WAS ALL... JUST LIKE YOU SAID.
Yamada-kun Diary
SO YAMADA-KUN...
...I'M GONNA TRUST YOU!
Yamada-kun Diary

CHAPTER 174: You're scared!

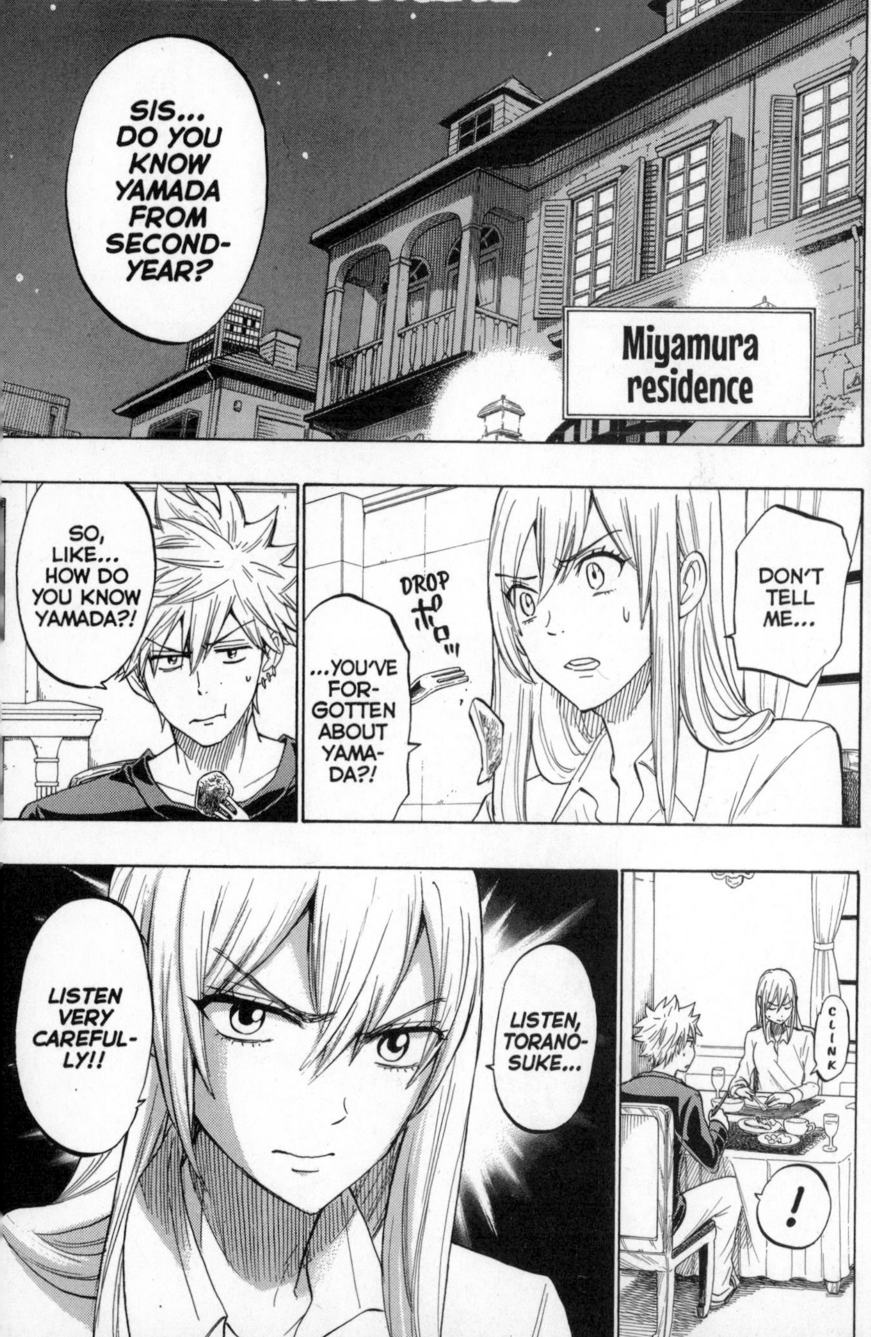
SIS... DO YOU KNOW YAMADA FROM SECOND-YEAR?
Miyamura residence
DON'T TELL ME...
DROP
...YOU'VE FOR-GOTTEN ABOUT YAMA-DA?!
SO, LIKE... HOW DO YOU KNOW YAMADA?!
CLINK
!
LISTEN, TORANO-SUKE...
LISTEN VERY CAREFUL-LY!!

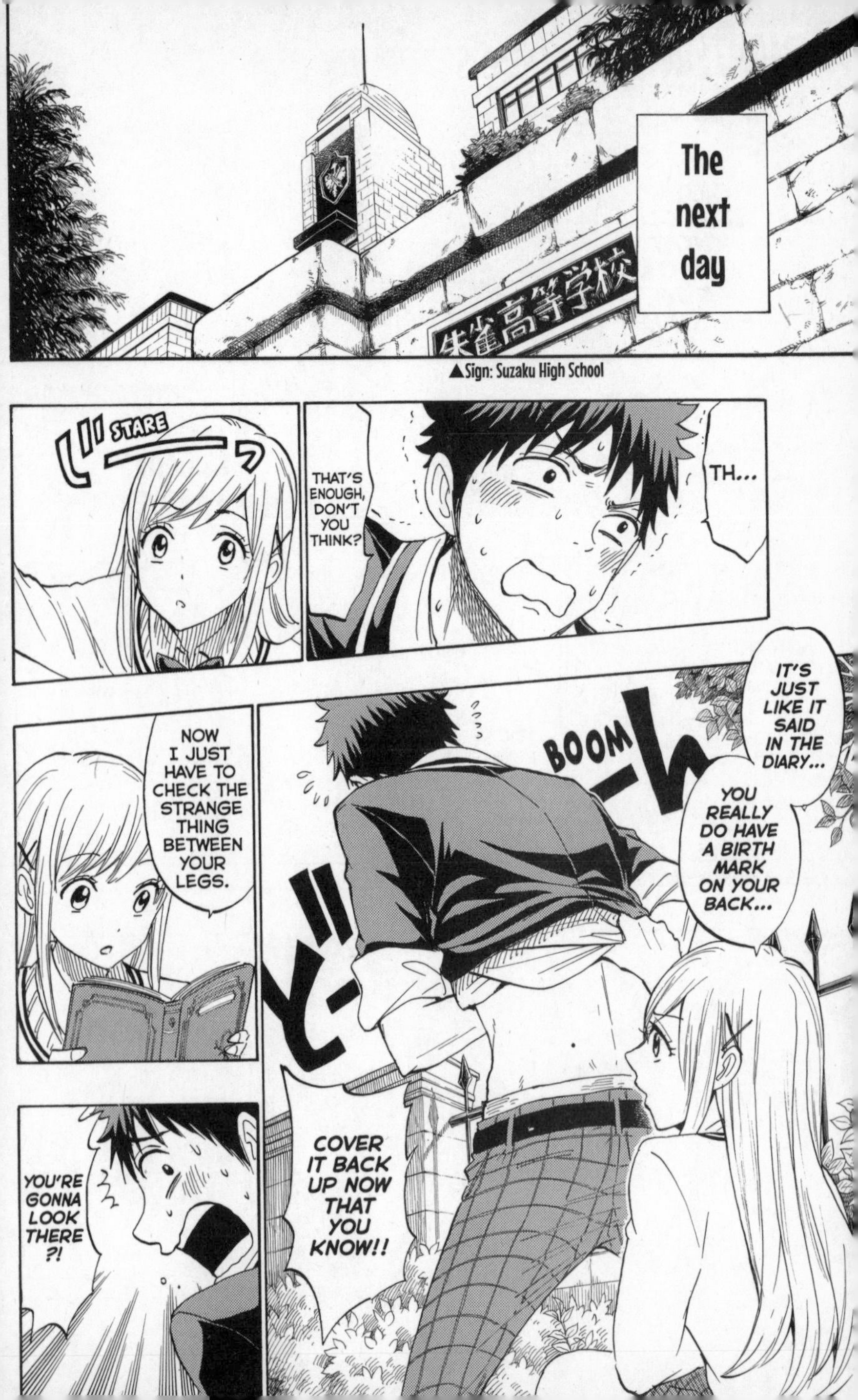
The next day
朱雀高等学校
TH...
THAT'S ENOUGH, DON'T YOU THINK?
STARE
IT'S JUST LIKE IT SAID IN THE DIARY...
YOU REALLY DO HAVE A BIRTH MARK ON YOUR BACK...
BOOM
COVER IT BACK UP NOW THAT YOU KNOW!!
NOW I JUST HAVE TO CHECK THE STRANGE THING BETWEEN YOUR LEGS.
YOU'RE GONNA LOOK THERE?!

▲Sign: Suzaku High School

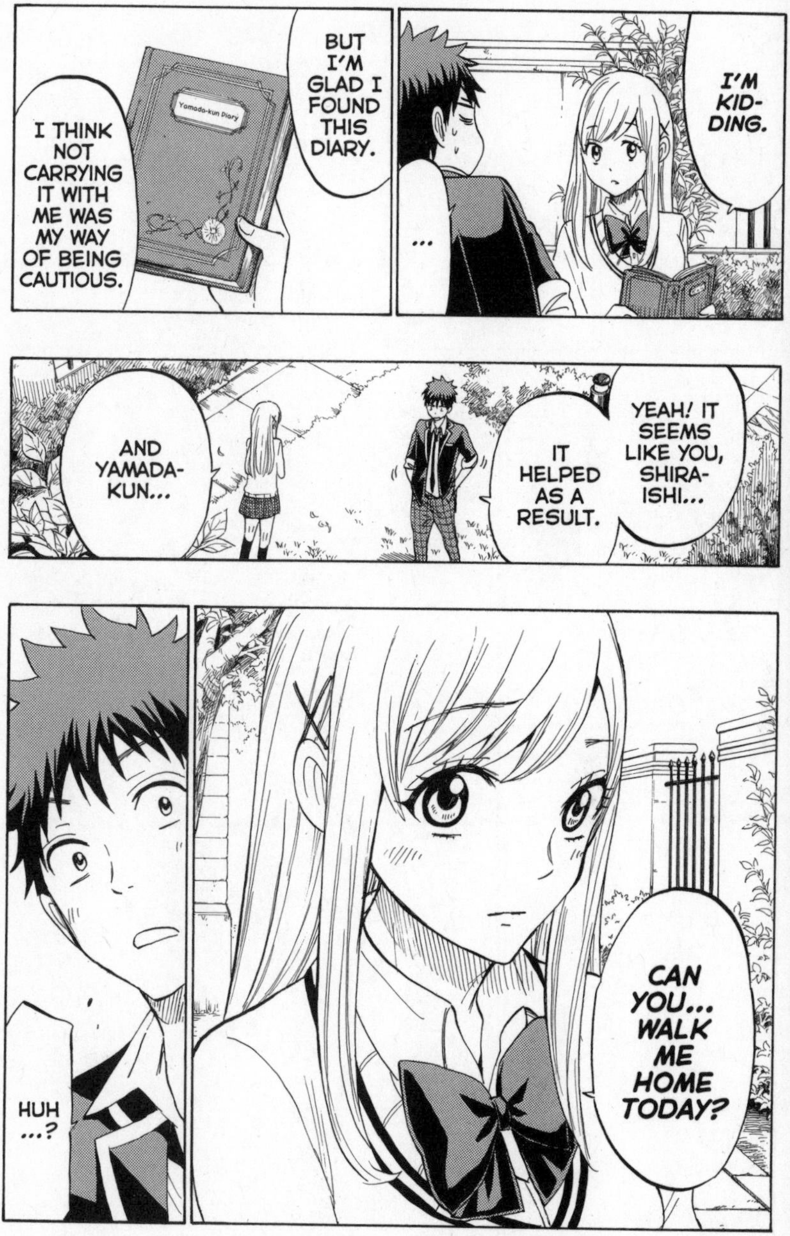
I'M KID-DING.
...
BUT I'M GLAD I FOUND THIS DIARY.
Yamada-kun Diary
I THINK NOT CARRYING IT WITH ME WAS MY WAY OF BEING CAUTIOUS.
YEAH! IT SEEMS LIKE YOU, SHIRA-ISHI...
IT HELPED AS A RESULT.
AND YAMADA-KUN...
CAN YOU... WALK ME HOME TODAY?
HUH ...?

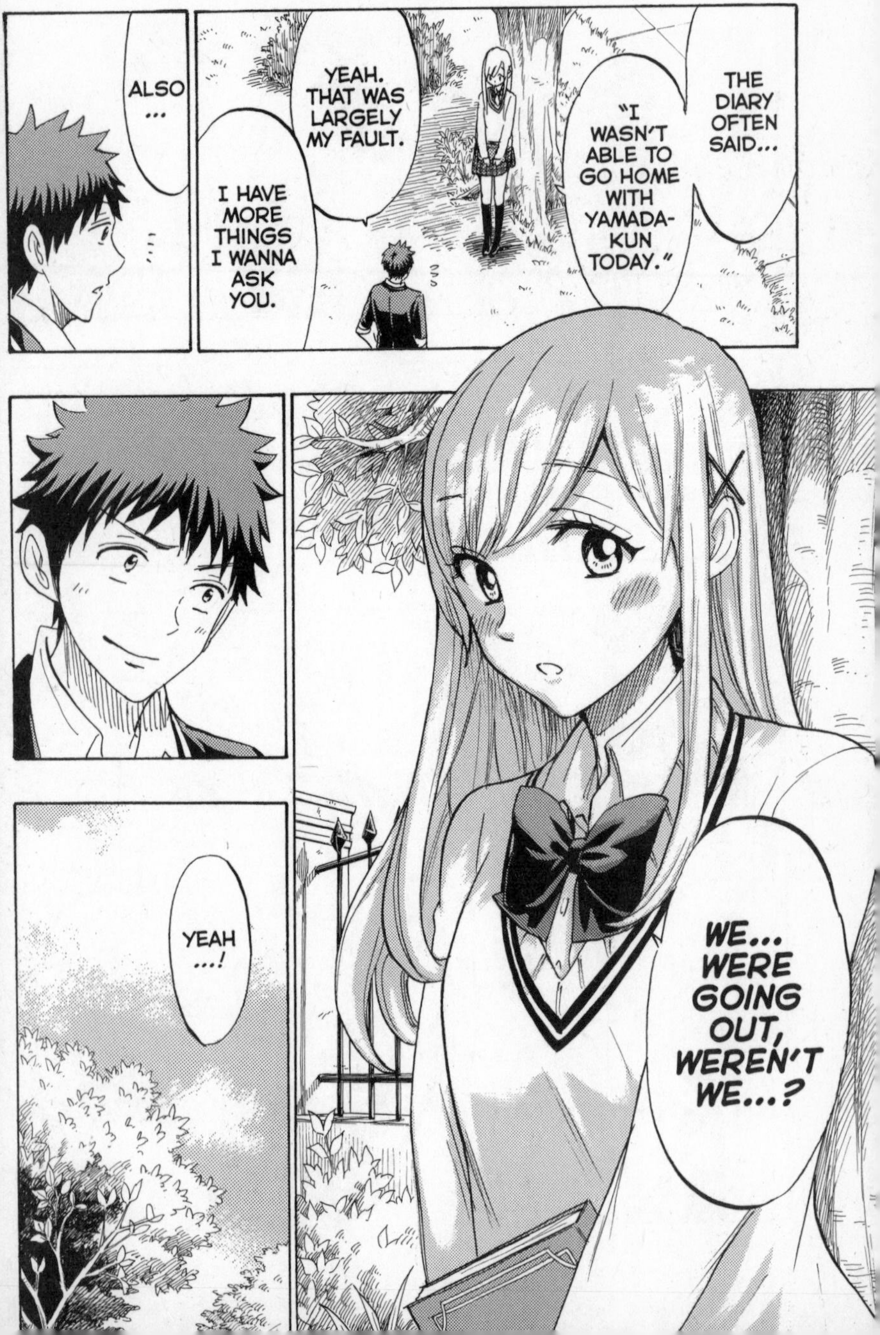
THE DIARY OFTEN SAID...
“I WASN'T ABLE TO GO HOME WITH YAMADA-KUN TODAY.”
YEAH. THAT WAS LARGELY MY FAULT.
I HAVE MORE THINGS I WANNA ASK YOU.
ALSO ...
WE... WERE GOING OUT, WEREN'T WE...?
YEAH ...!

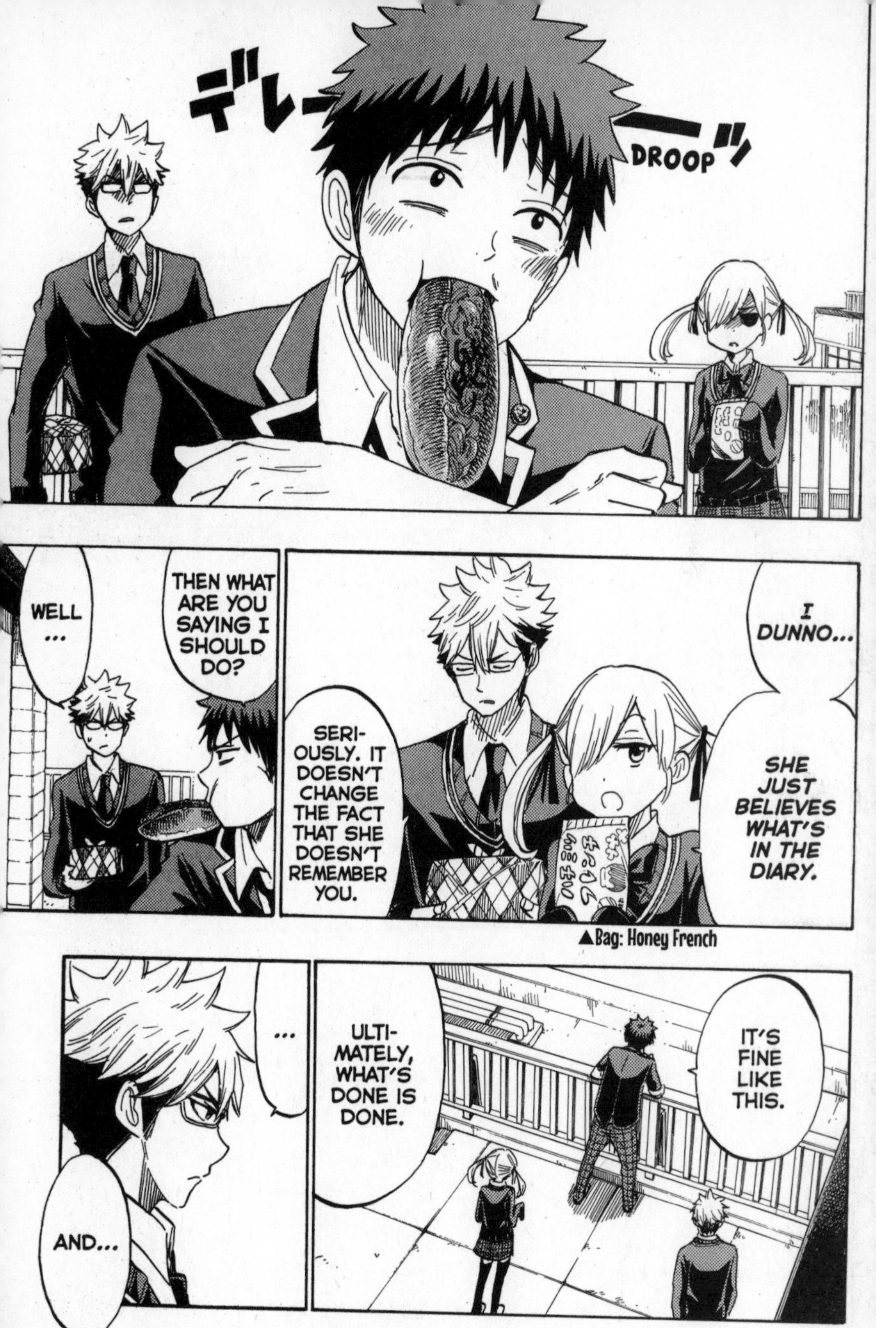
デレーーー
DROOP
I DUNNO...
SHE JUST BELIEVES WHAT'S IN THE DIARY.
SERI-OUSLY. IT DOESN'T CHANGE THE FACT THAT SHE DOESN'T REMEMBER YOU.
THEN WHAT ARE YOU SAYING I SHOULD DO?
WELL...
▲Bag: Honey French
IT'S FINE LIKE THIS.
ULTI-MATELY, WHAT'S DONE IS DONE.
...
AND...

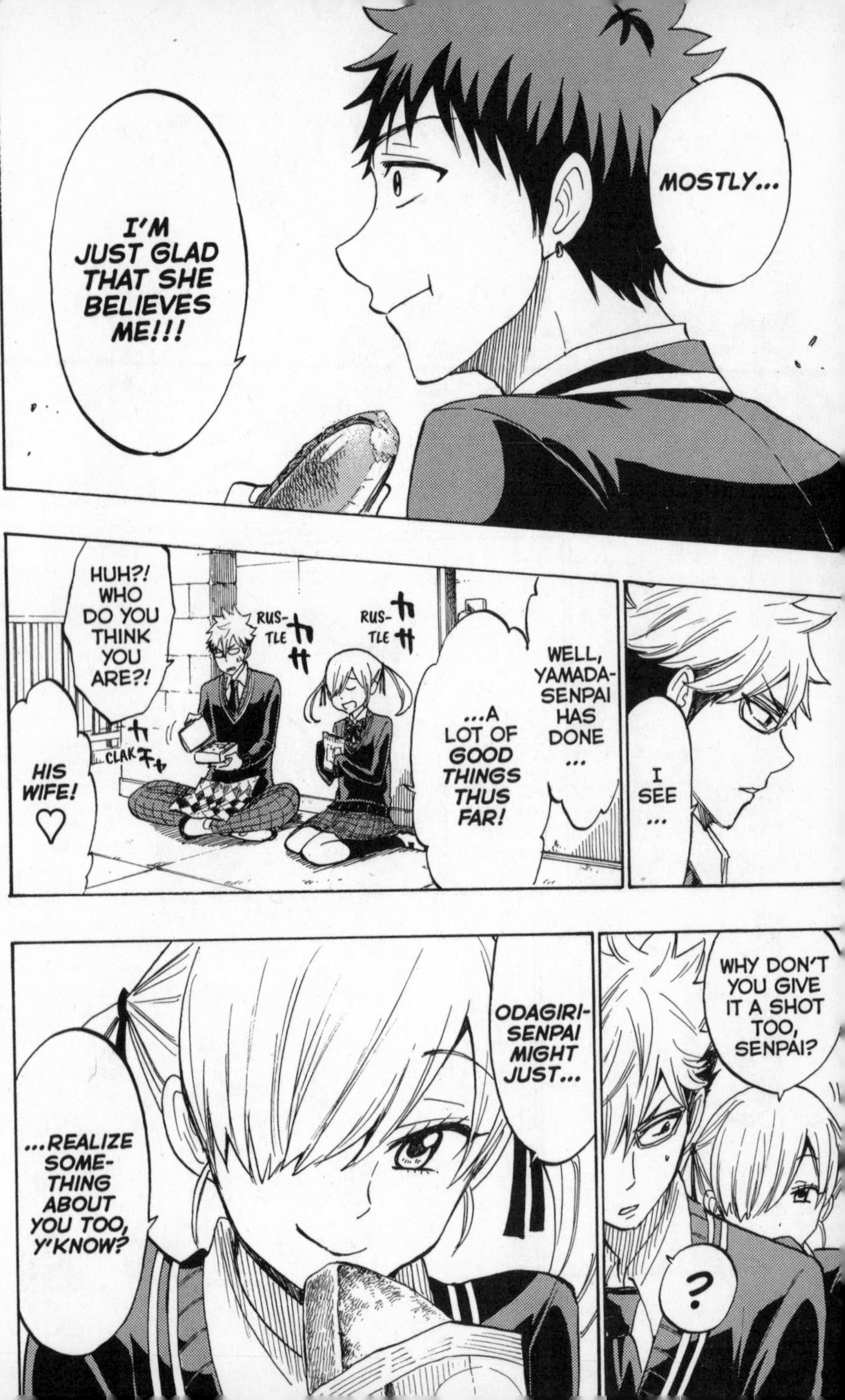
MOSTLY...
I'M JUST GLAD THAT SHE BELIEVES ME!!!
I SEE...
WELL, YAMADA-SENPAI HAS DONE...
...A LOT OF GOOD THINGS THUS FAR!
RUS-TLE
RUS-TLE
HUH?! WHO DO YOU THINK YOU ARE?!
CLAK
HIS WIFE! ♡
WHY DON'T YOU GIVE IT A SHOT TOO, SENPAI?
?
ODAGIRI-SENPAI MIGHT JUST...
...REALIZE SOMETHING ABOUT YOU TOO, Y'KNOW?

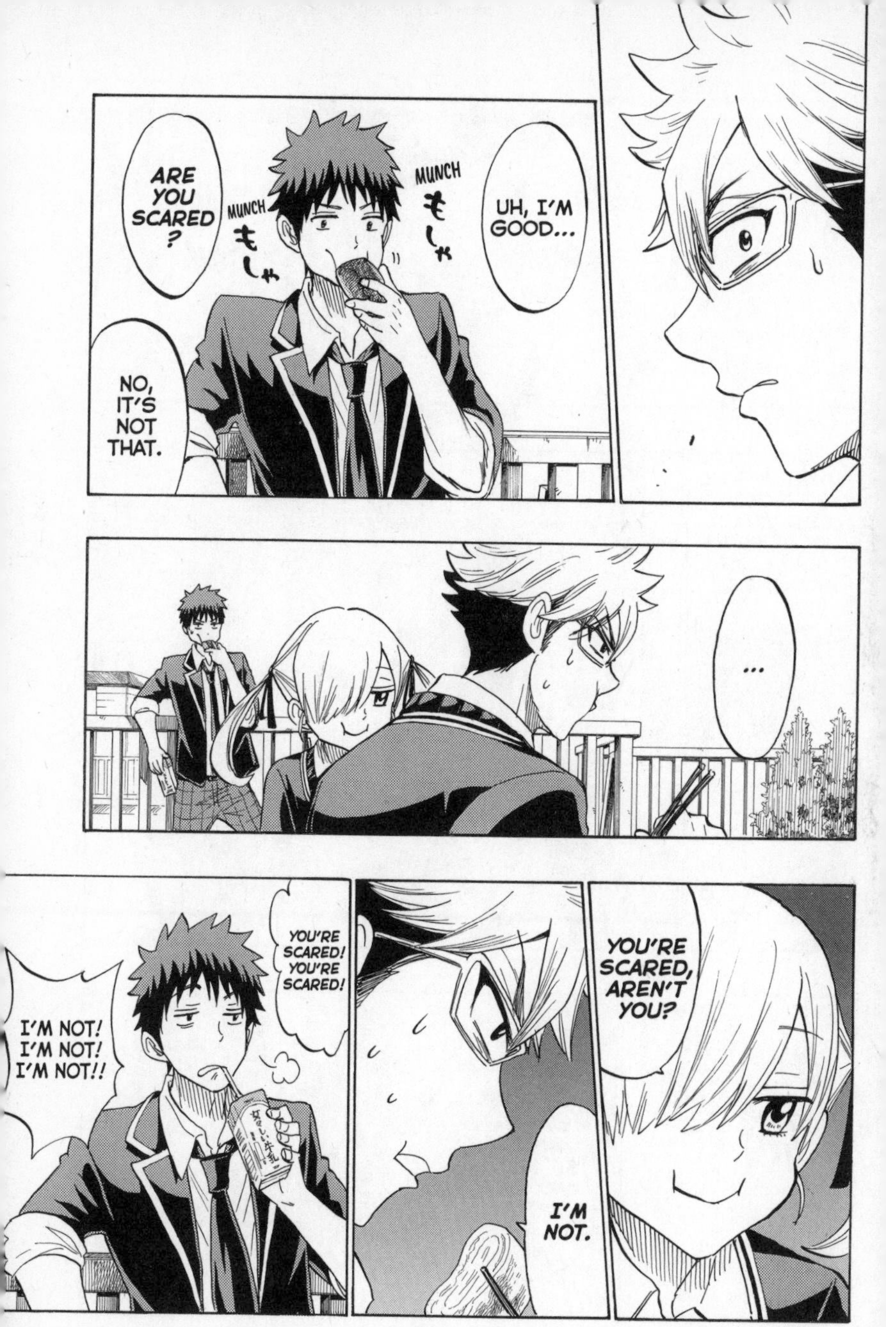
UH, I'M GOOD...
MUNCH
もしゃ
MUNCH
もしゃ
ARE YOU SCARED?
NO, IT'S NOT THAT.
...
YOU'RE SCARED, AREN'T YOU?
I'M NOT.
YOU'RE SCARED! YOU'RE SCARED!
I'M NOT! I'M NOT! I'M NOT!!

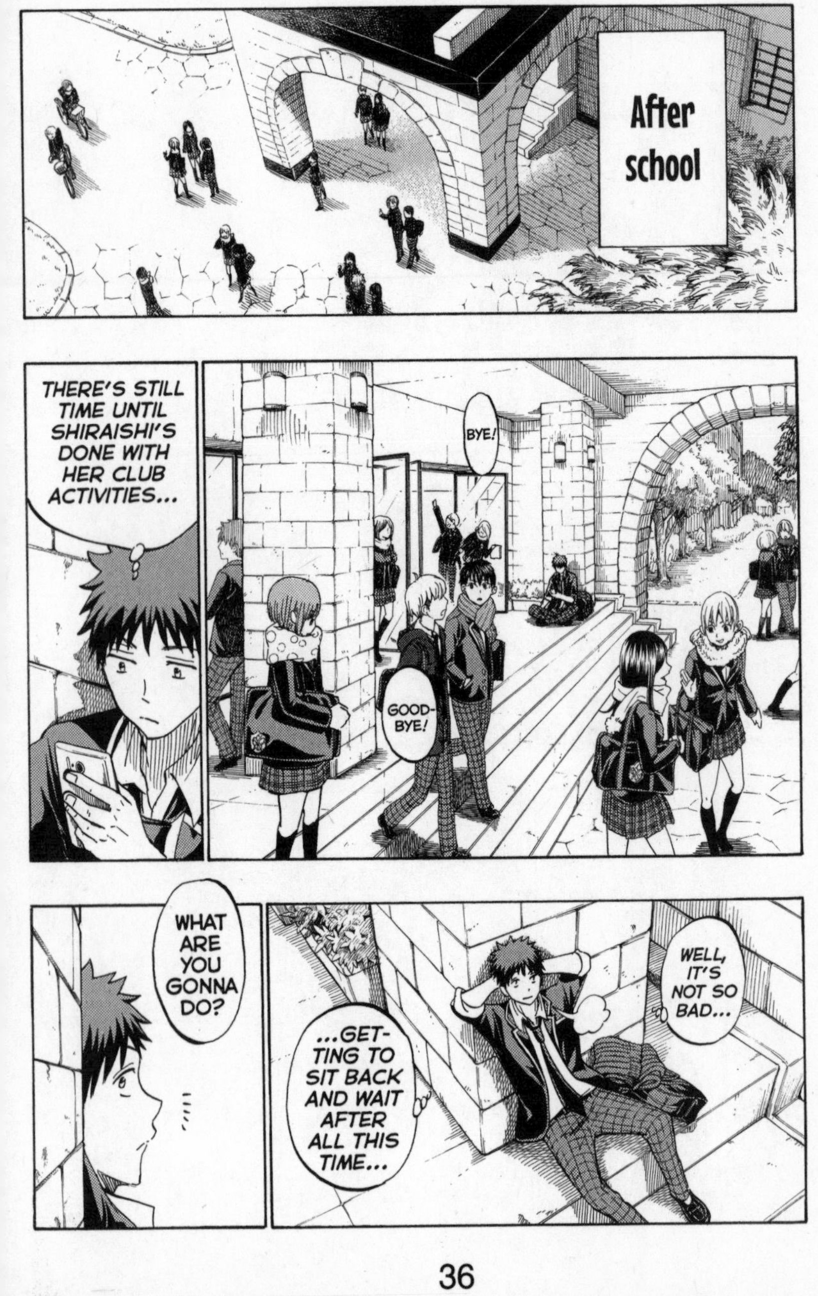
After school
BYE!
GOOD-BYE!
THERE'S STILL TIME UNTIL SHIRAISHI'S DONE WITH HER CLUB ACTIVITIES...
WELL, IT'S NOT SO BAD...
...GETTING TO SIT BACK AND WAIT AFTER ALL THIS TIME...
WHAT ARE YOU GONNA DO?
......

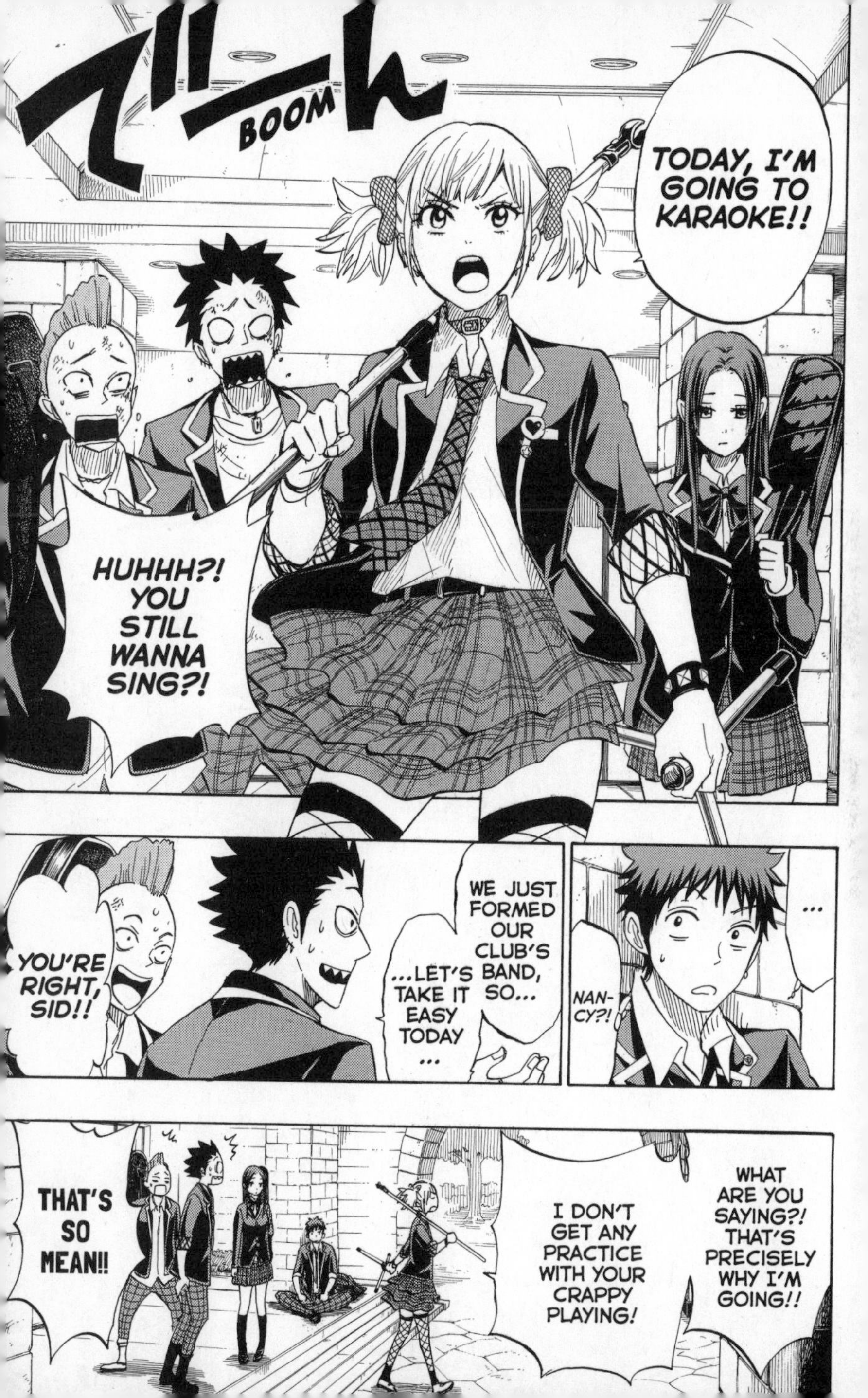
TODAY, I'M GOING TO KARAOKE!!
BOOM
HUHHH?! YOU STILL WANNA SING?!
...
NAN-CY?!
WE JUST FORMED OUR CLUB'S BAND, SO...
...LET'S TAKE IT EASY TODAY ...
YOU'RE RIGHT, SID!!
WHAT ARE YOU SAYING?! THAT'S PRECISELY WHY I'M GOING!!
I DON'T GET ANY PRACTICE WITH YOUR CRAPPY PLAYING!
THAT'S SO MEAN!!

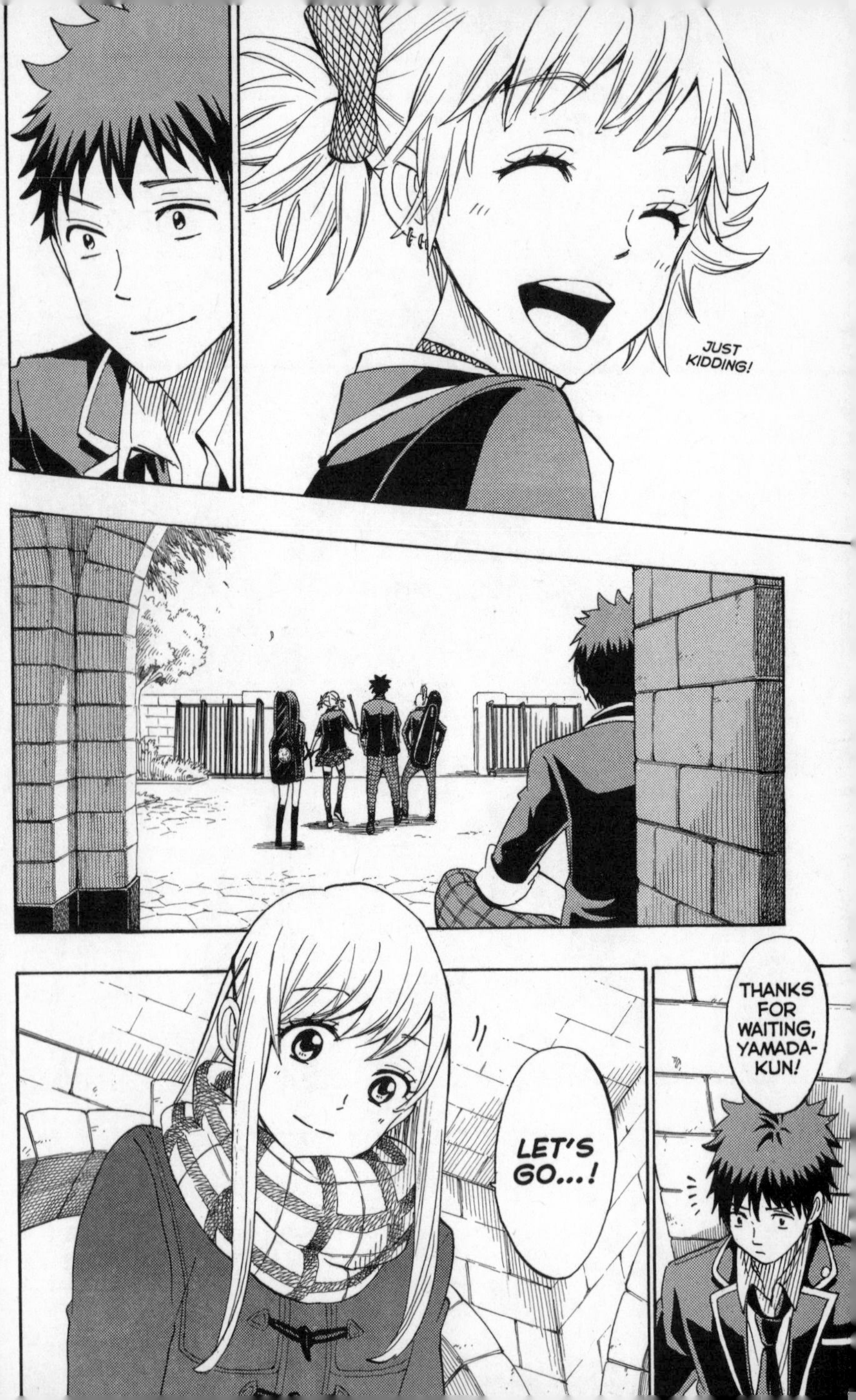
JUST KIDDING!
THANKS FOR WAITING, YAMADA-KUN!
LET'S GO...!

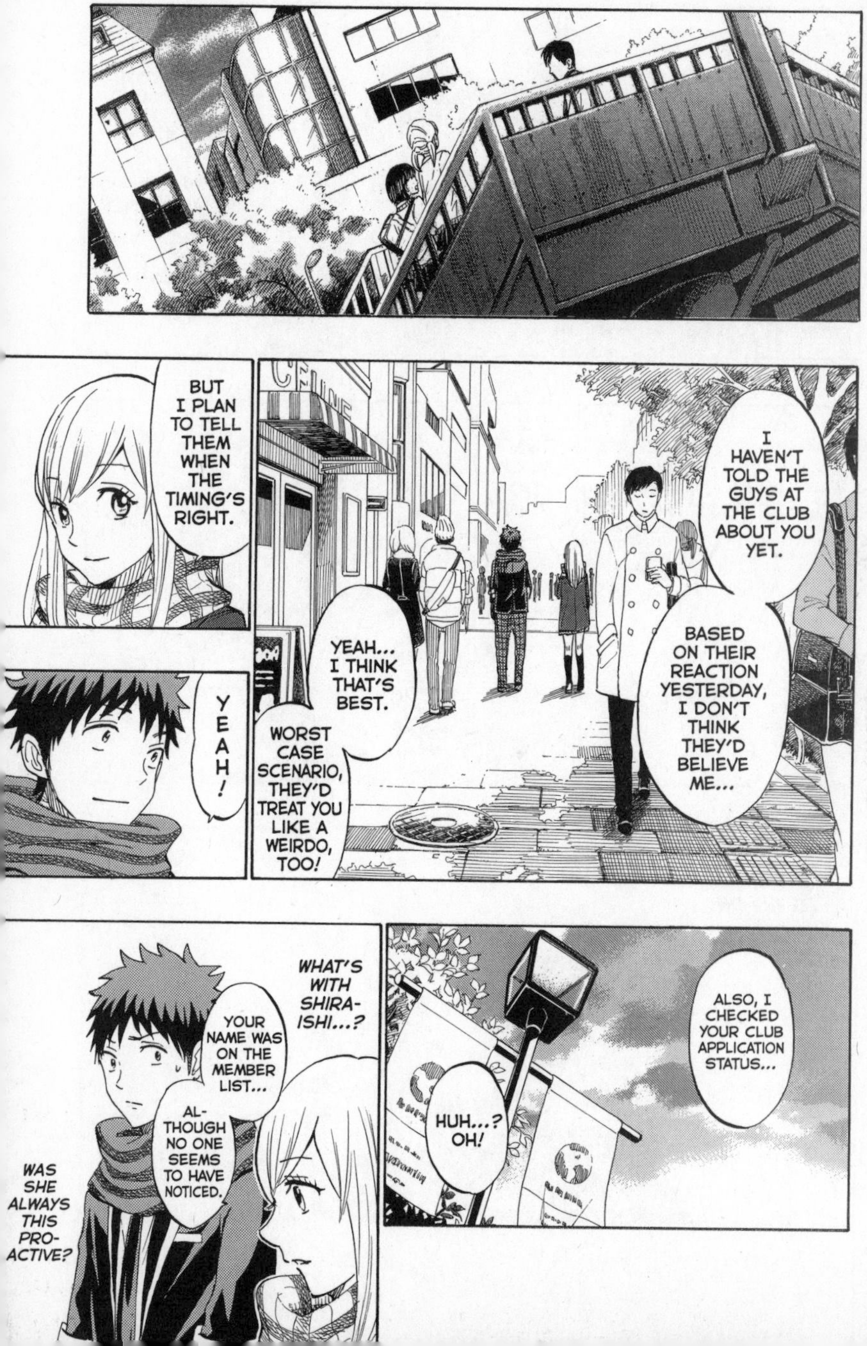
I HAVEN'T TOLD THE GUYS AT THE CLUB ABOUT YOU YET.
BASED ON THEIR REACTION YESTERDAY, I DON'T THINK THEY'D BELIEVE ME...
YEAH... I THINK THAT'S BEST.
WORST CASE SCENARIO, THEY'D TREAT YOU LIKE A WEIRDO, TOO!
BUT I PLAN TO TELL THEM WHEN THE TIMING'S RIGHT.
YEAH!
ALSO, I CHECKED YOUR CLUB APPLICATION STATUS...
HUH...? OH!
WHAT'S WITH SHIRAISHI...?
YOUR NAME WAS ON THE MEMBER LIST...
ALTHOUGH NO ONE SEEMS TO HAVE NOTICED.
WAS SHE ALWAYS THIS PROACTIVE?

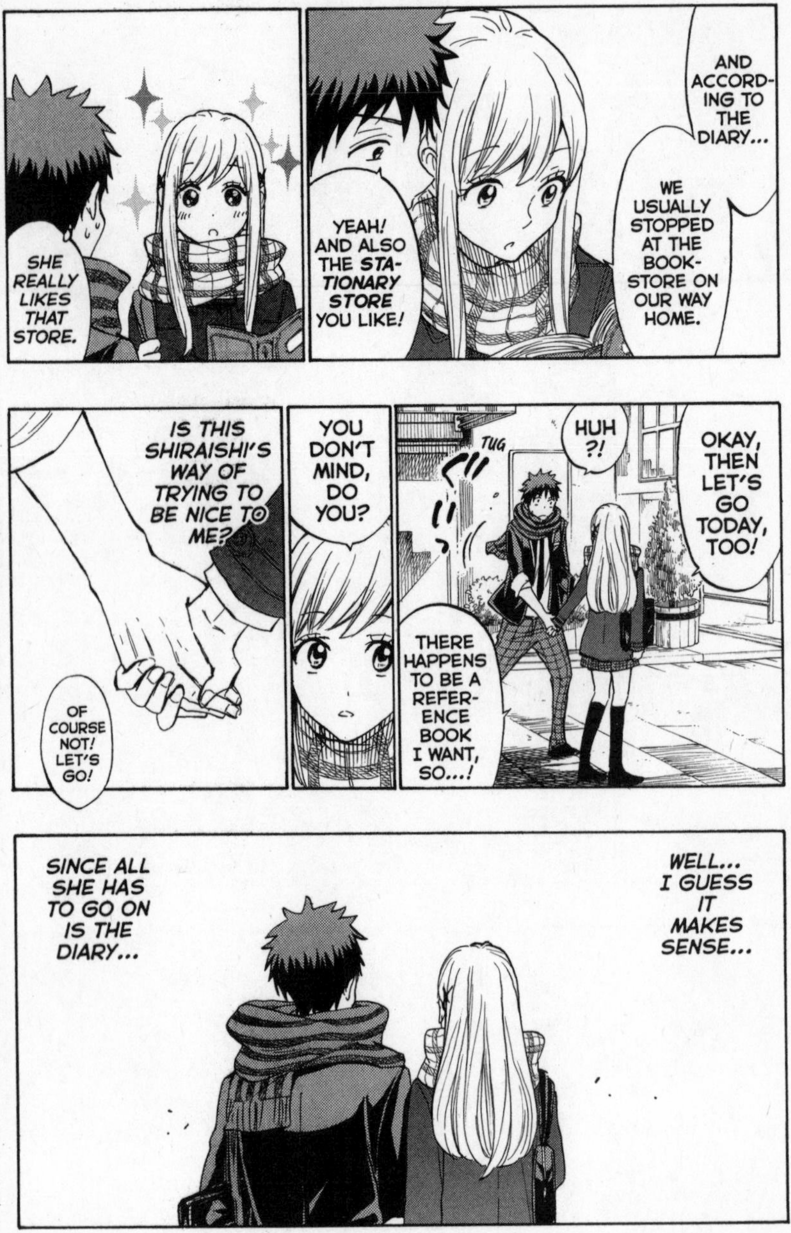
AND ACCORDING TO THE DIARY...
WE USUALLY STOPPED AT THE BOOKSTORE ON OUR WAY HOME.
YEAH! AND ALSO THE STATIONARY STORE YOU LIKE!
SHE REALLY LIKES THAT STORE.
OKAY, THEN LET'S GO TODAY, TOO!
HUH ?!
TUG
THERE HAPPENS TO BE A REFERENCE BOOK I WANT, SO...!
YOU DON'T MIND, DO YOU?
IS THIS SHIRAISHI'S WAY OF TRYING TO BE NICE TO ME?
OF COURSE NOT! LET'S GO!
WELL... I GUESS IT MAKES SENSE...
SINCE ALL SHE HAS TO GO ON IS THE DIARY...

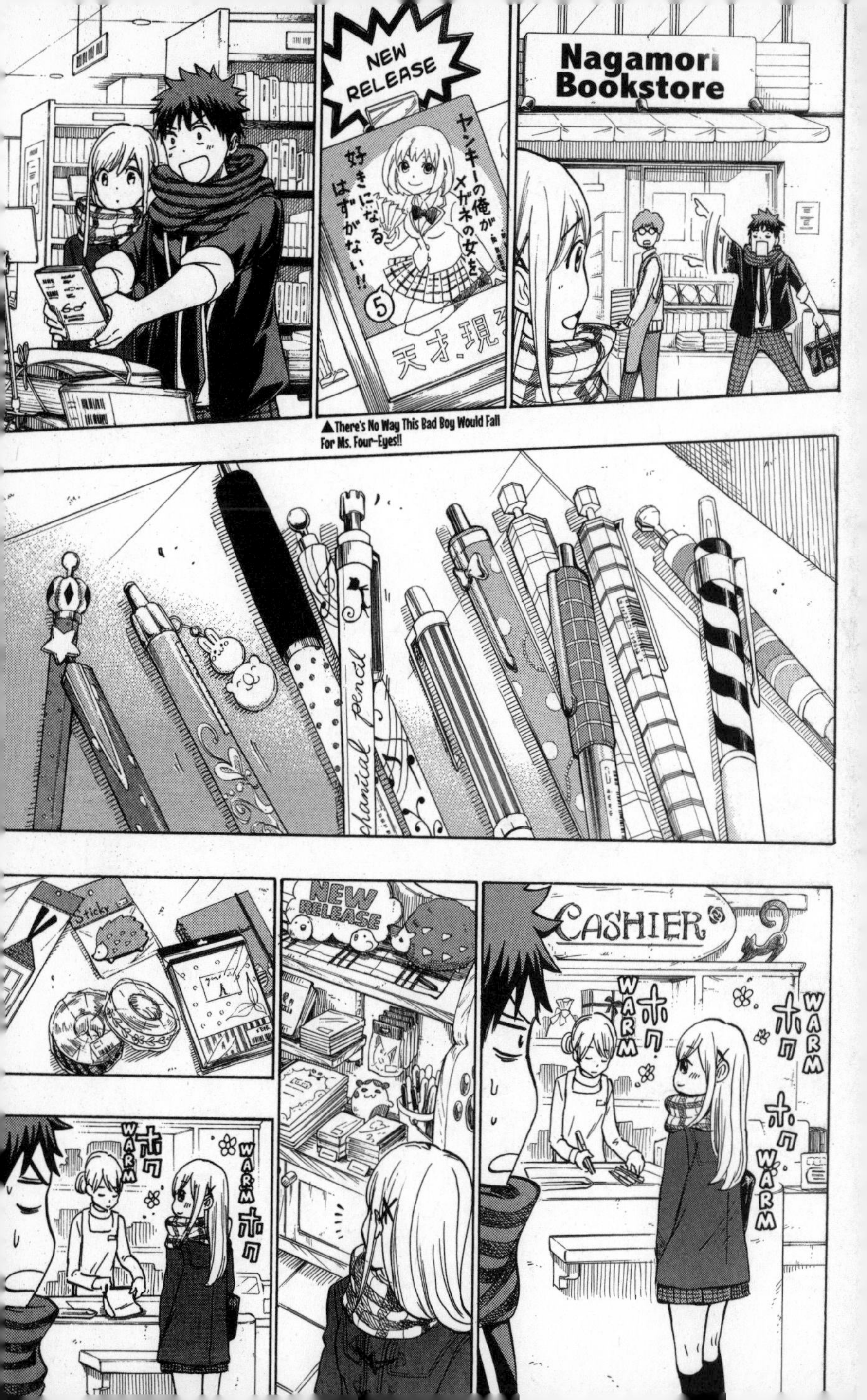
Nagamori Bookstore
NEW RELEASE
ヤンキーの俺がメガネの女を好きになるはずがない!!
5
▲There's No Way This Bad Boy Would Fall For Ms. Four-Eyes!!
pencil
CASHIER
WARM ホク
WARM ホク
WARM ホク
NEW RELEASE
Sticky
WARM ホク
WARM ホク

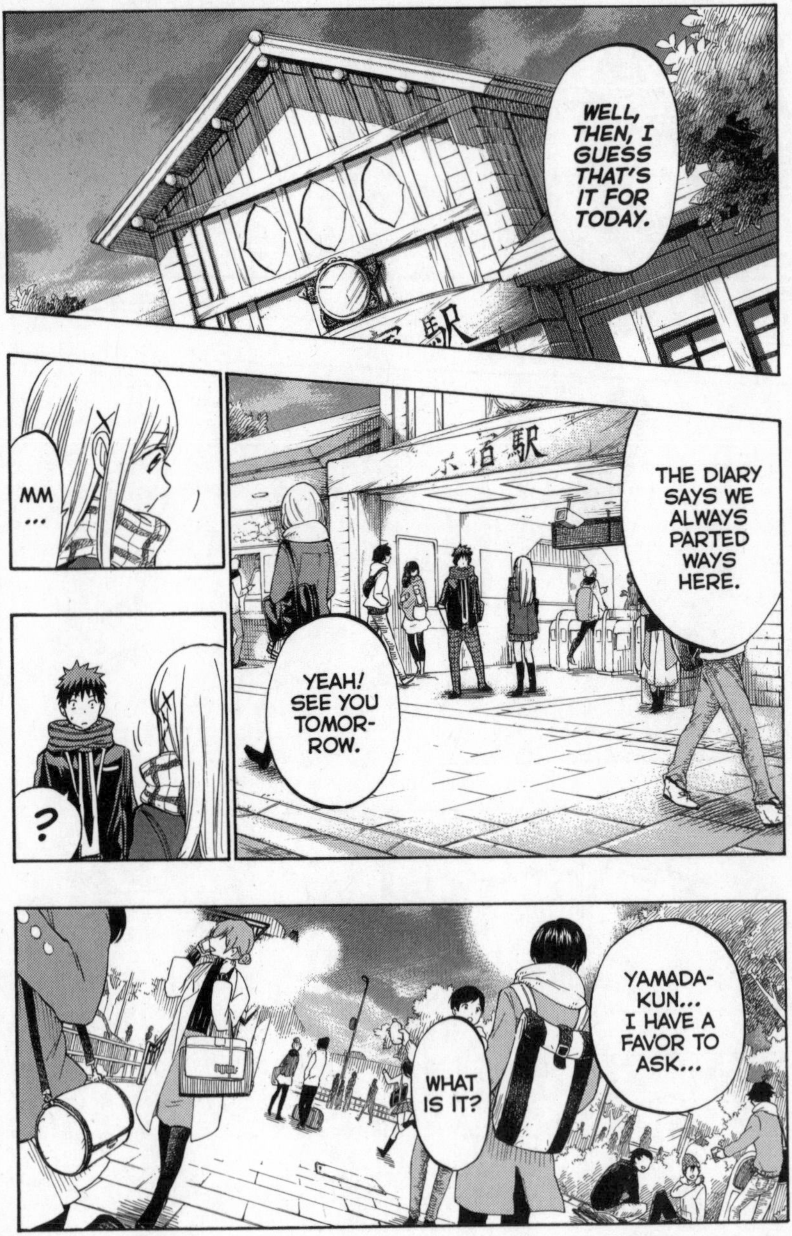
WELL, THEN, I GUESS THAT'S IT FOR TODAY.
THE DIARY SAYS WE ALWAYS PARTED WAYS HERE.
YEAH! SEE YOU TOMORROW.
MM ...
?
YAMADA-KUN... I HAVE A FAVOR TO ASK...
WHAT IS IT?

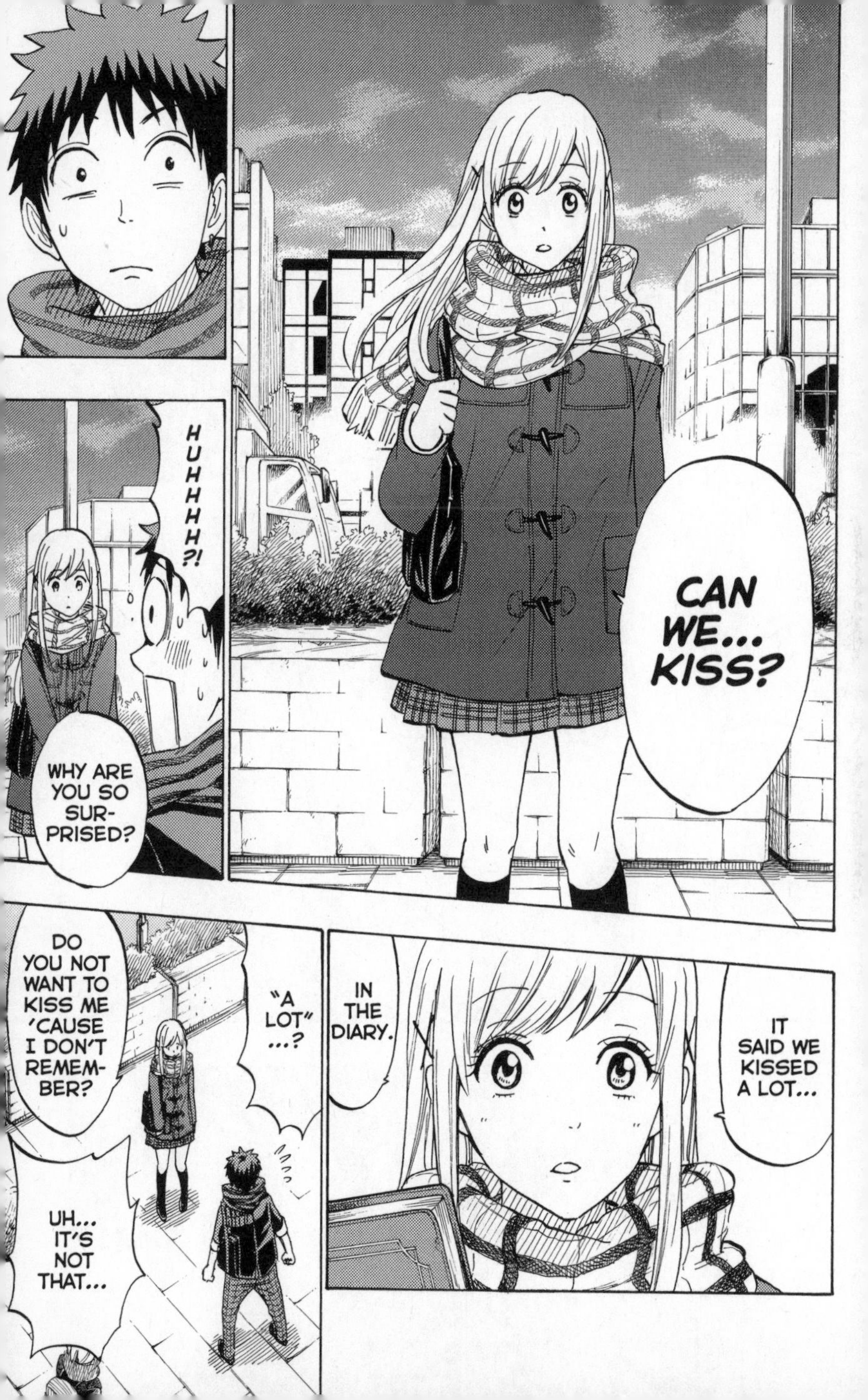
CAN WE... KISS?
HUHHHHH?!
WHY ARE YOU SO SURPRISED?
IT SAID WE KISSED A LOT...
IN THE DIARY.
"A LOT"...?
DO YOU NOT WANT TO KISS ME 'CAUSE I DON'T REMEMBER?
UH... IT'S NOT THAT...

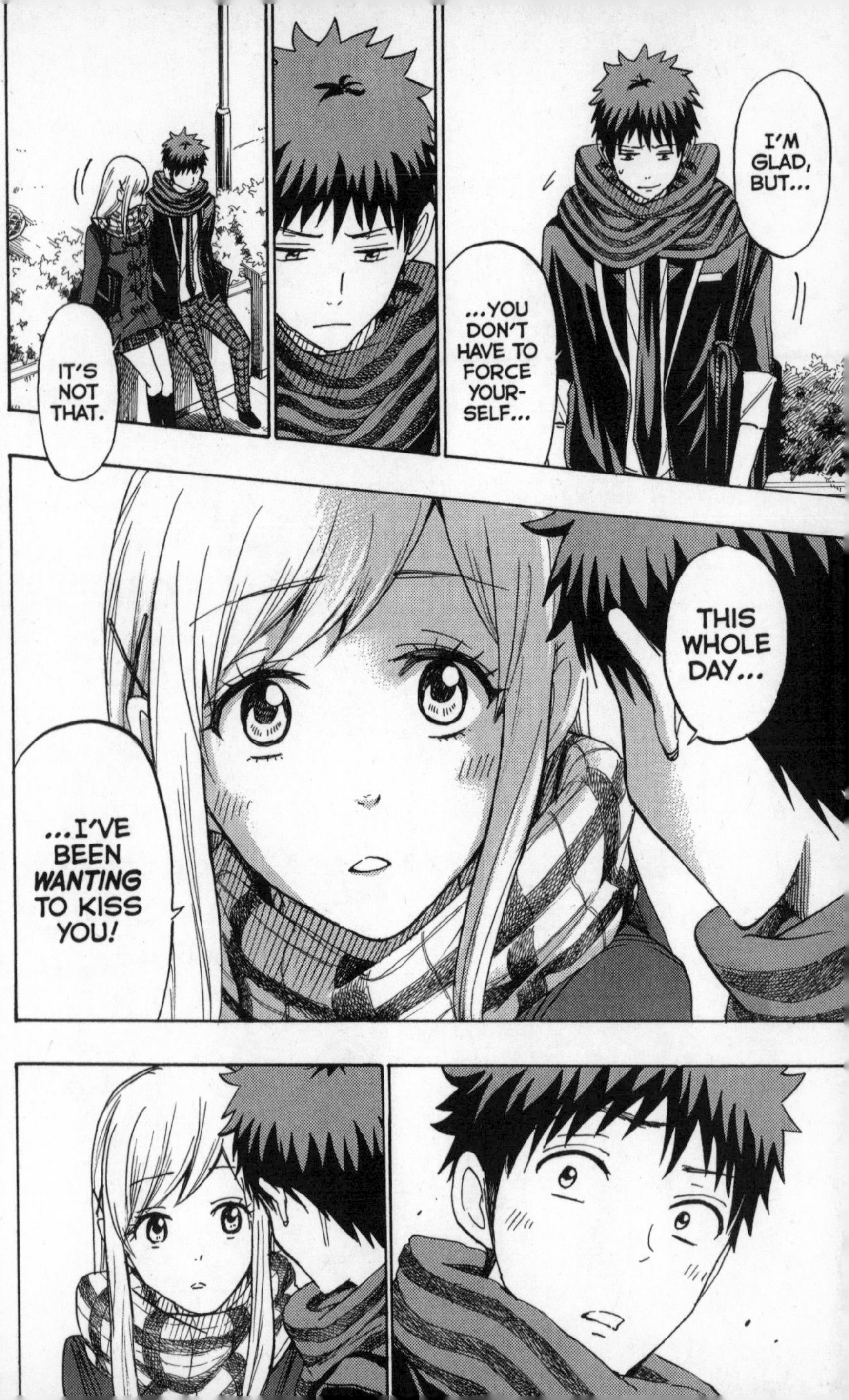
I'M GLAD, BUT...
...YOU DON'T HAVE TO FORCE YOUR-SELF...
IT'S NOT THAT.
THIS WHOLE DAY...
...I'VE BEEN *WANTING* TO KISS YOU!

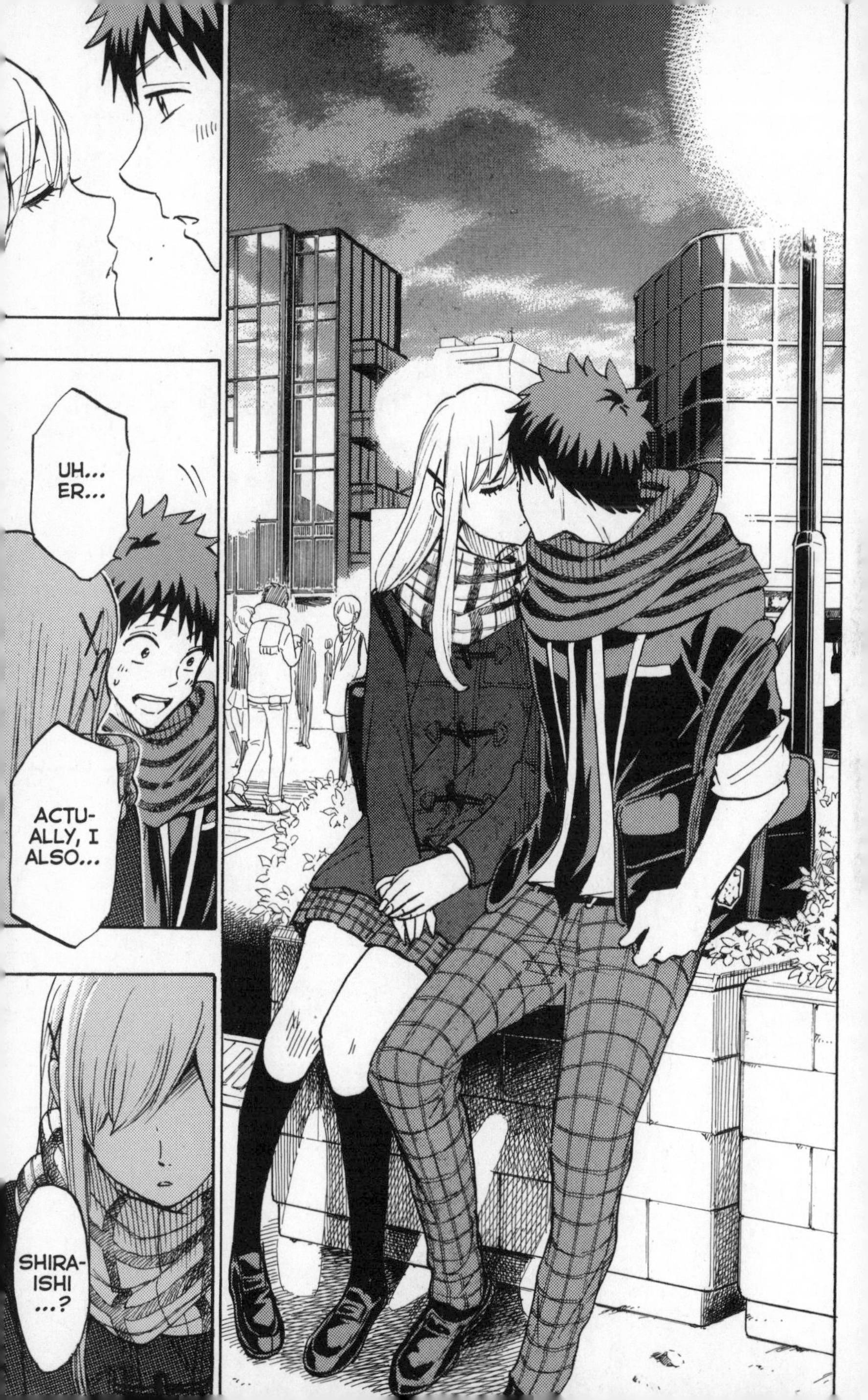
UH... ER...
ACTU-ALLY, I ALSO...
SHIRA-ISHI ...?

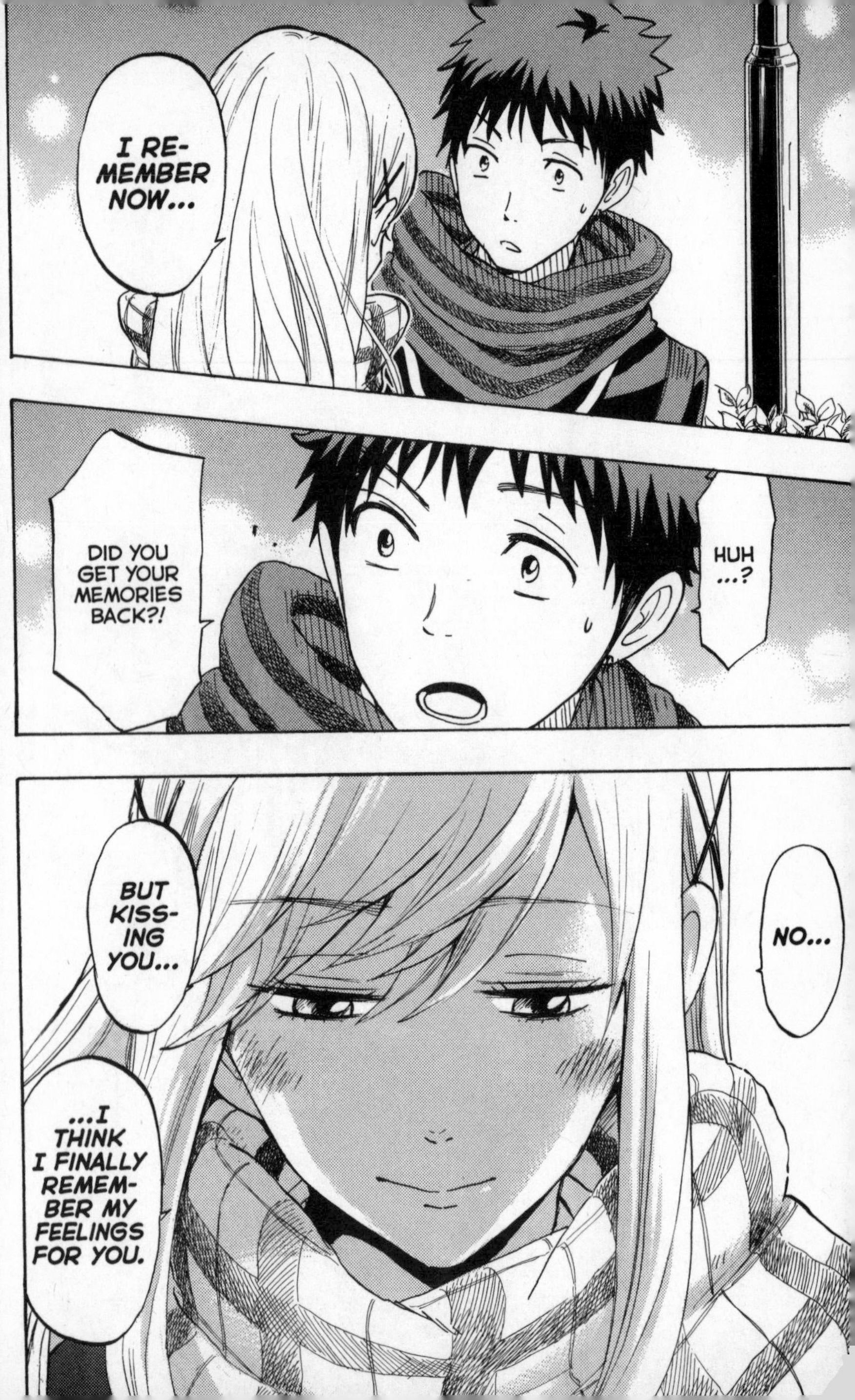
I RE-MEMBER NOW...
HUH ...?
DID YOU GET YOUR MEMORIES BACK?!
NO...
BUT KISS-ING YOU...
...I THINK I FINALLY REMEM-BER MY FEELINGS FOR YOU.

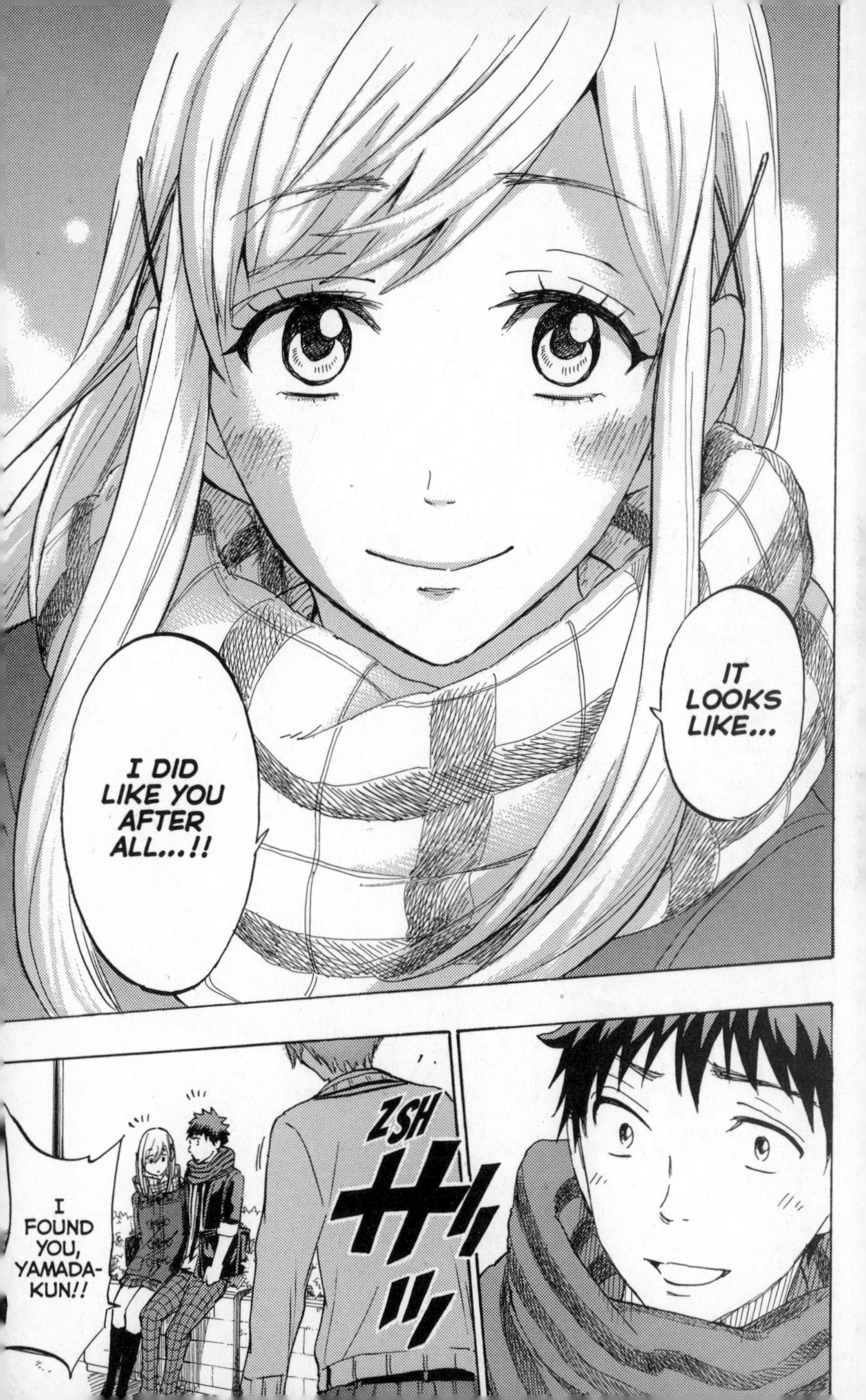
IT LOOKS LIKE...
I DID LIKE YOU AFTER ALL...!!
ZSH
I FOUND YOU, YAMADA-KUN!!

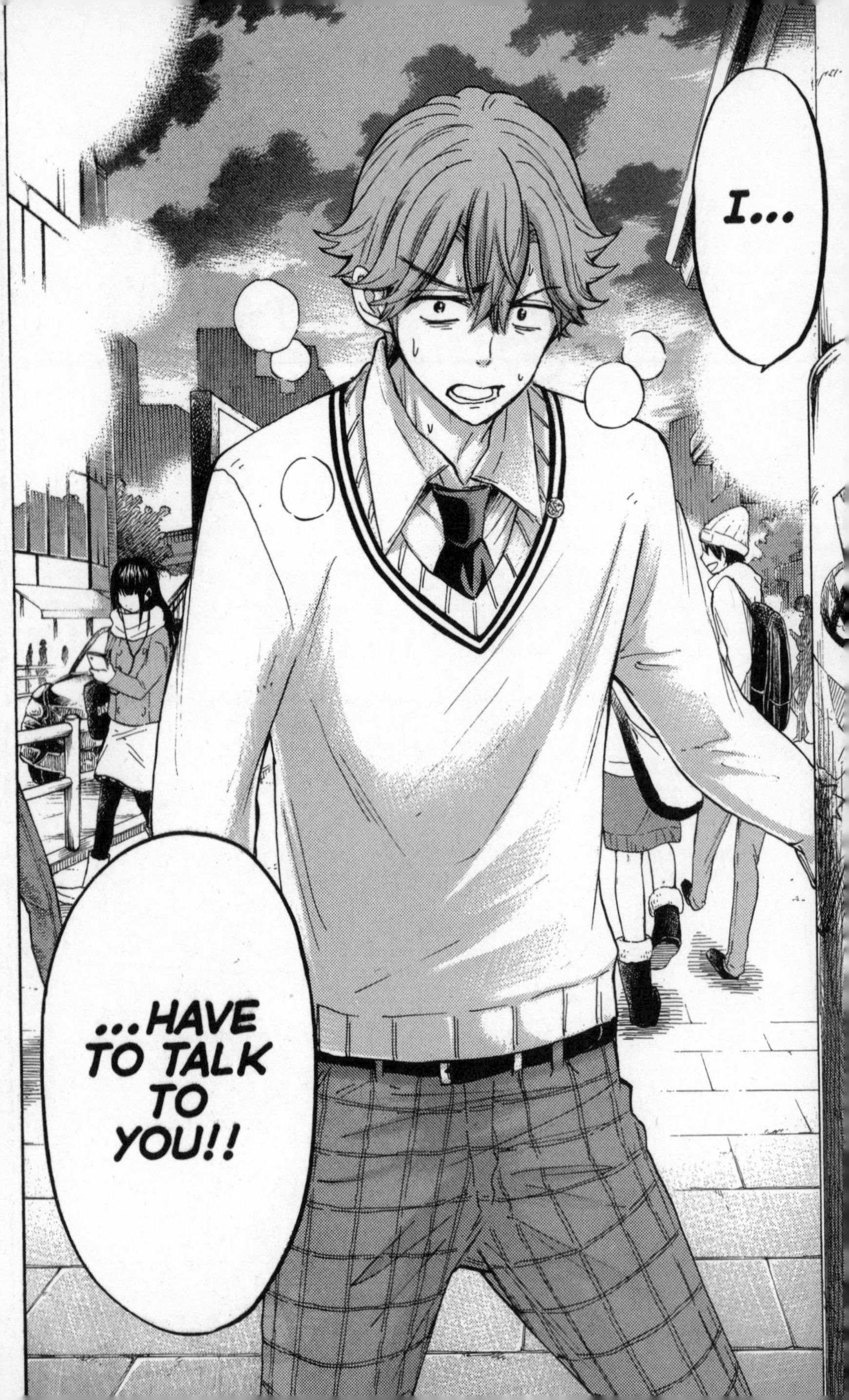
I...
...HAVE TO TALK TO YOU!!

CHAPTER 175: You're looking for a secret notebook?

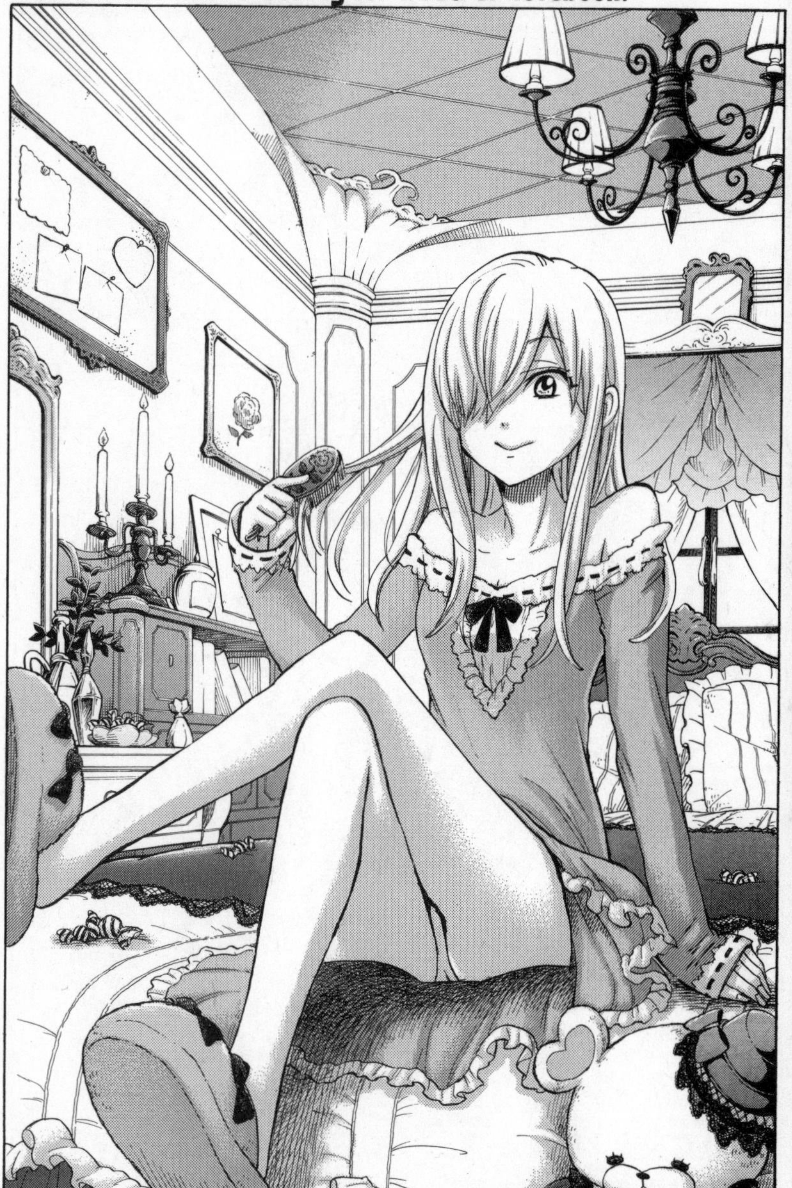

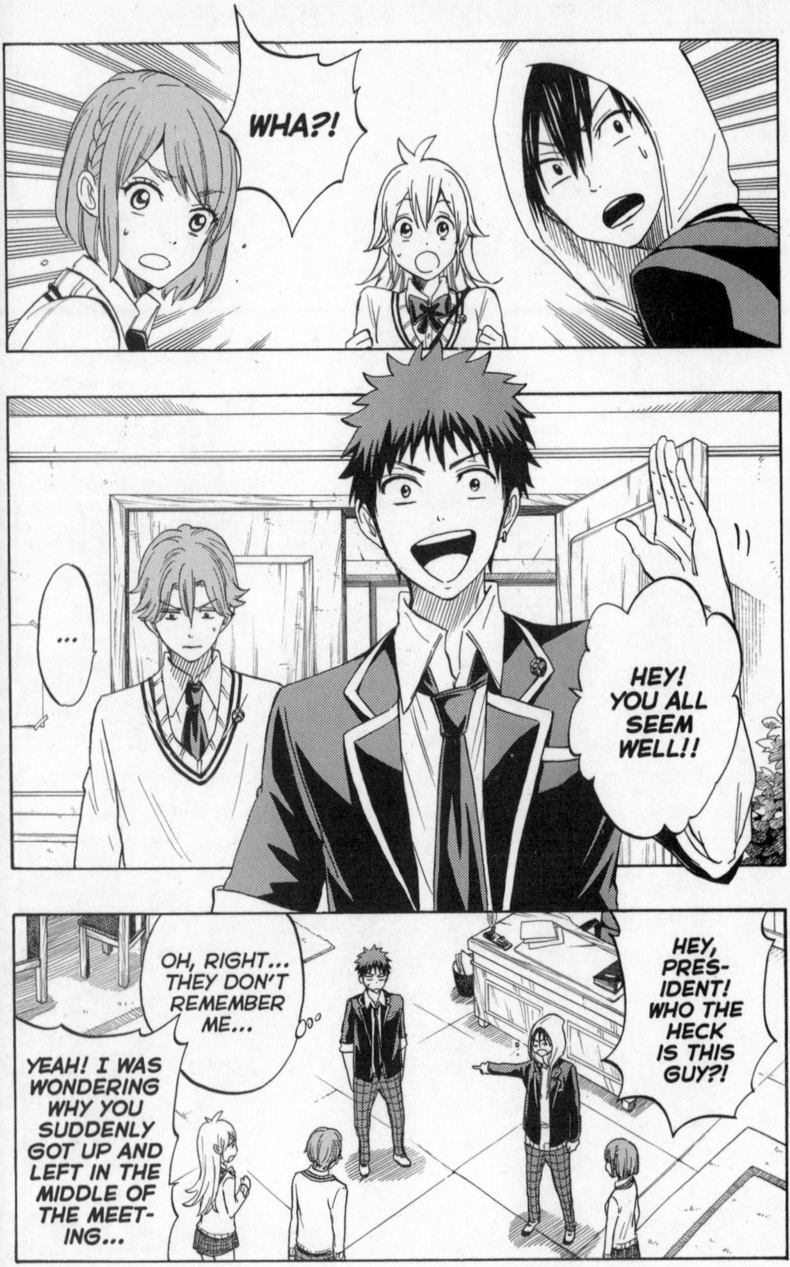
WHA?!
HEY! YOU ALL SEEM WELL!!
...
HEY, PRES-IDENT! WHO THE HECK IS THIS GUY?!
OH, RIGHT... THEY DON'T REMEMBER ME...
YEAH! I WAS WONDERING WHY YOU SUDDENLY GOT UP AND LEFT IN THE MIDDLE OF THE MEET-ING...

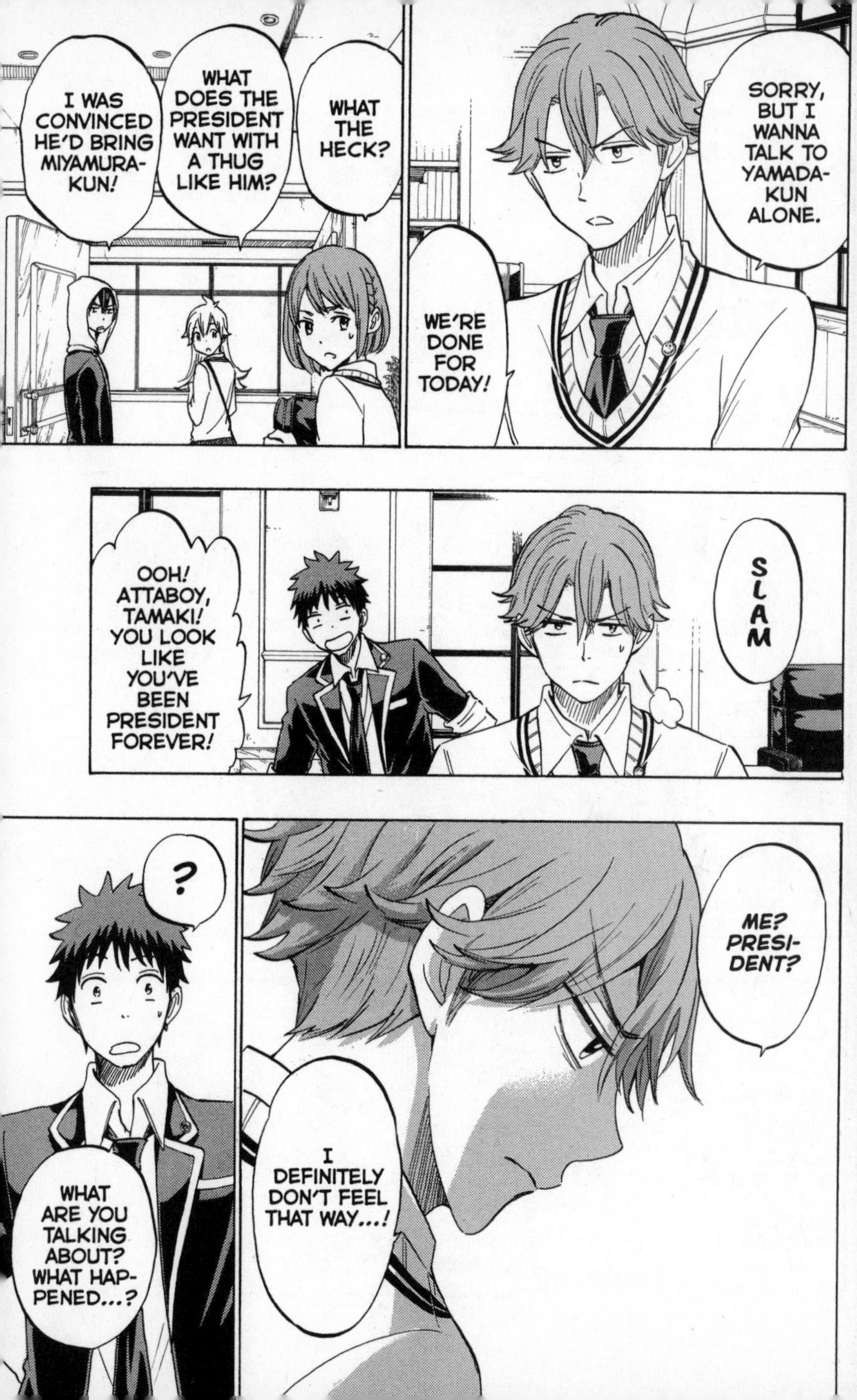
SORRY, BUT I WANNA TALK TO YAMADA-KUN ALONE.
WE'RE DONE FOR TODAY!
WHAT THE HECK?
WHAT DOES THE PRESIDENT WANT WITH A THUG LIKE HIM?
I WAS CONVINCED HE'D BRING MIYAMURA-KUN!
SLAM
OOH! ATTABOY, TAMAKI! YOU LOOK LIKE YOU'VE BEEN PRESIDENT FOREVER!
ME? PRESI-DENT?
I DEFINITELY DON'T FEEL THAT WAY...!
?
WHAT ARE YOU TALKING ABOUT? WHAT HAPPENED...?

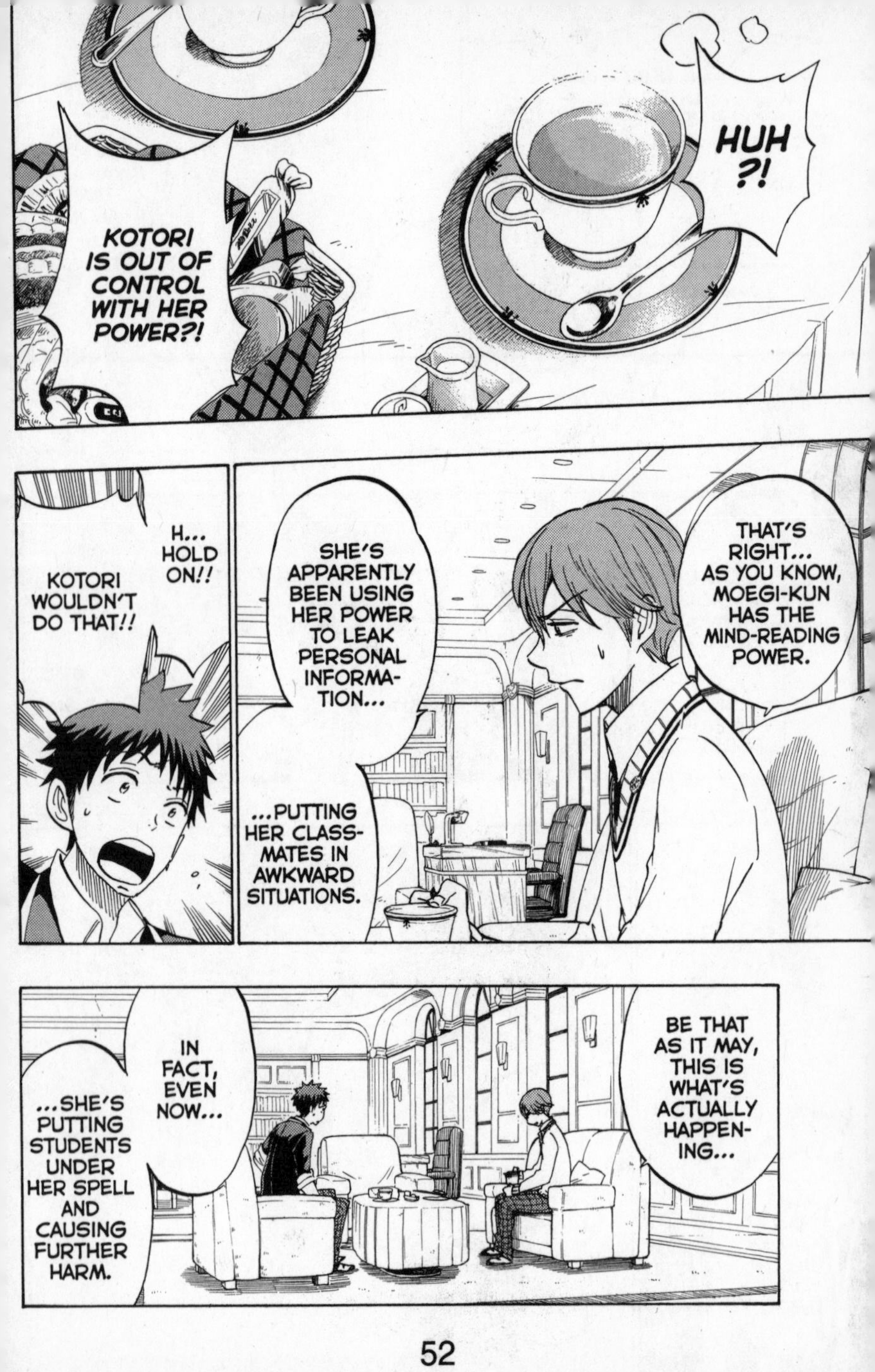
HUH ?!
KOTORI IS OUT OF CONTROL WITH HER POWER?!
THAT'S RIGHT... AS YOU KNOW, MOEGI-KUN HAS THE MIND-READING POWER.
SHE'S APPARENTLY BEEN USING HER POWER TO LEAK PERSONAL INFORMATION...
...PUTTING HER CLASSMATES IN AWKWARD SITUATIONS.
H... HOLD ON!!
KOTORI WOULDN'T DO THAT!!
BE THAT AS IT MAY, THIS IS WHAT'S ACTUALLY HAPPENING...
IN FACT, EVEN NOW...
...SHE'S PUTTING STUDENTS UNDER HER SPELL AND CAUSING FURTHER HARM.

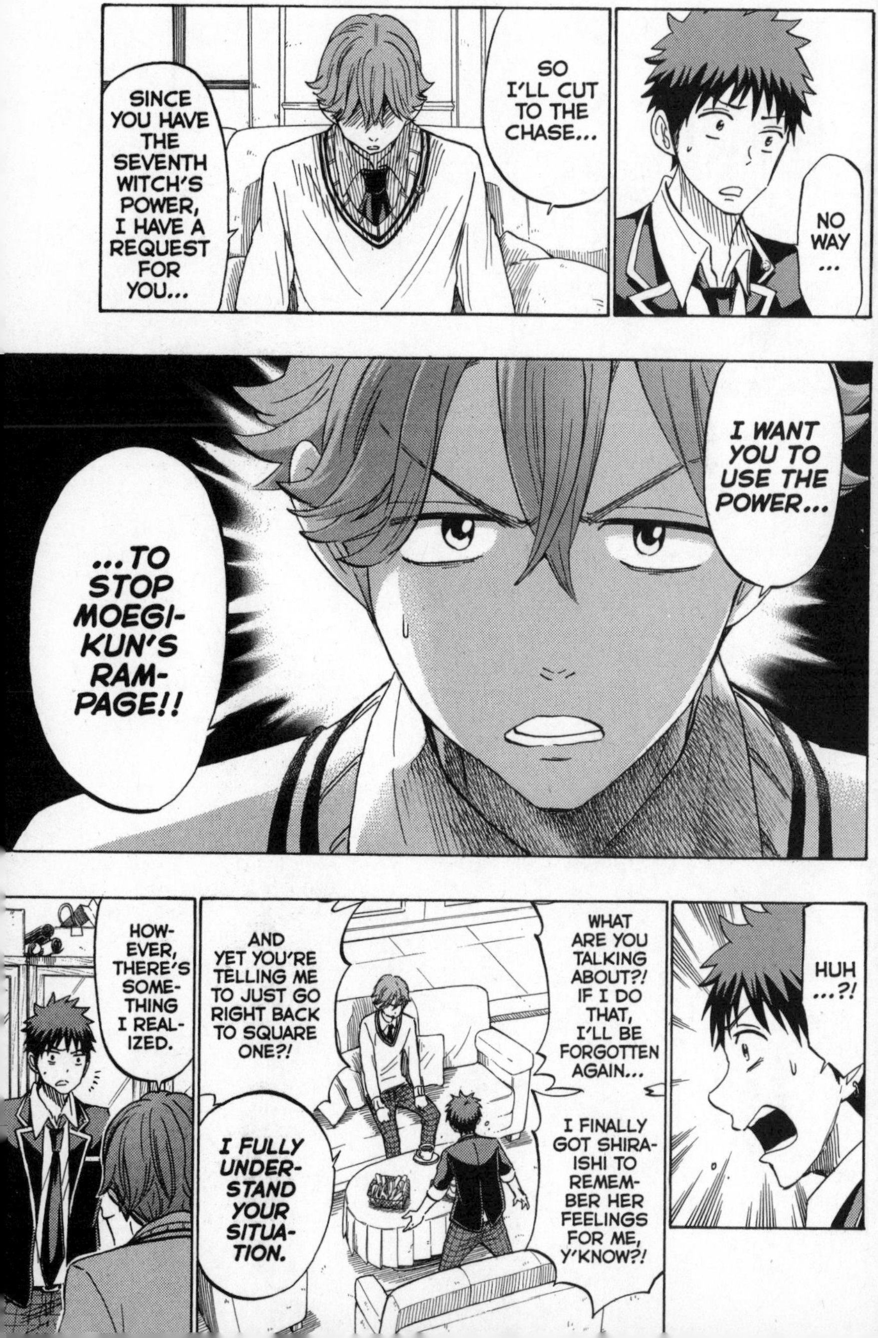
NO WAY ...
SO I'LL CUT TO THE CHASE...
SINCE YOU HAVE THE SEVENTH WITCH'S POWER, I HAVE A REQUEST FOR YOU...
I WANT YOU TO USE THE POWER...
...TO STOP MOEGI-KUN'S RAMPAGE!!
HUH ...?!
WHAT ARE YOU TALKING ABOUT?! IF I DO THAT, I'LL BE FORGOTTEN AGAIN...
I FINALLY GOT SHIRAISHI TO REMEMBER HER FEELINGS FOR ME, Y'KNOW?!
AND YET YOU'RE TELLING ME TO JUST GO RIGHT BACK TO SQUARE ONE?!
I FULLY UNDERSTAND YOUR SITUATION.
HOWEVER, THERE'S SOMETHING I REALIZED.

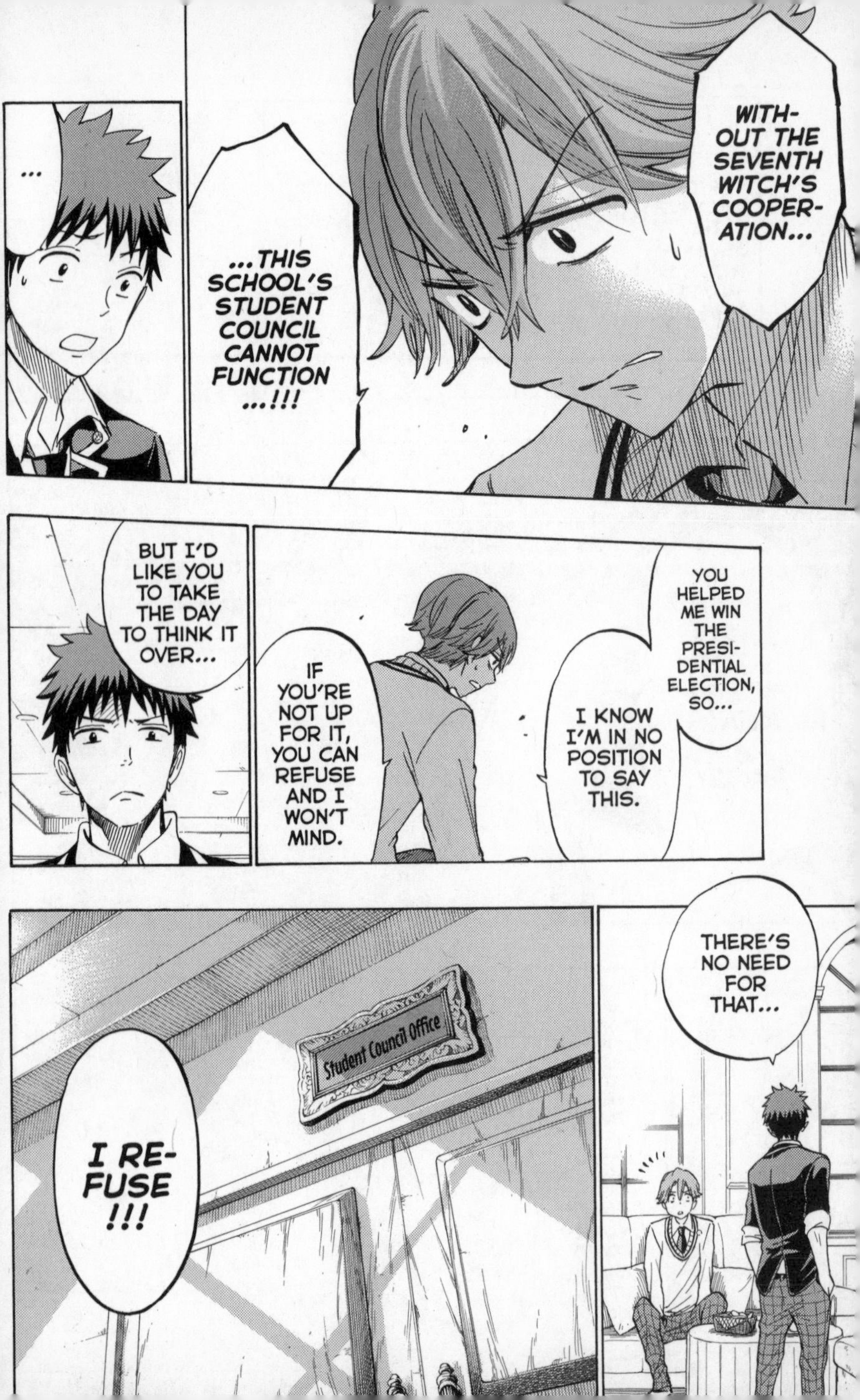
WITH-OUT THE SEVENTH WITCH'S COOPER-ATION...
...THIS SCHOOL'S STUDENT COUNCIL CANNOT FUNCTION ...!!!
...
YOU HELPED ME WIN THE PRESI-DENTIAL ELECTION, SO...
I KNOW I'M IN NO POSITION TO SAY THIS.
IF YOU'RE NOT UP FOR IT, YOU CAN REFUSE AND I WON'T MIND.
BUT I'D LIKE YOU TO TAKE THE DAY TO THINK IT OVER...
THERE'S NO NEED FOR THAT...
Student Council Office
I RE-FUSE !!!

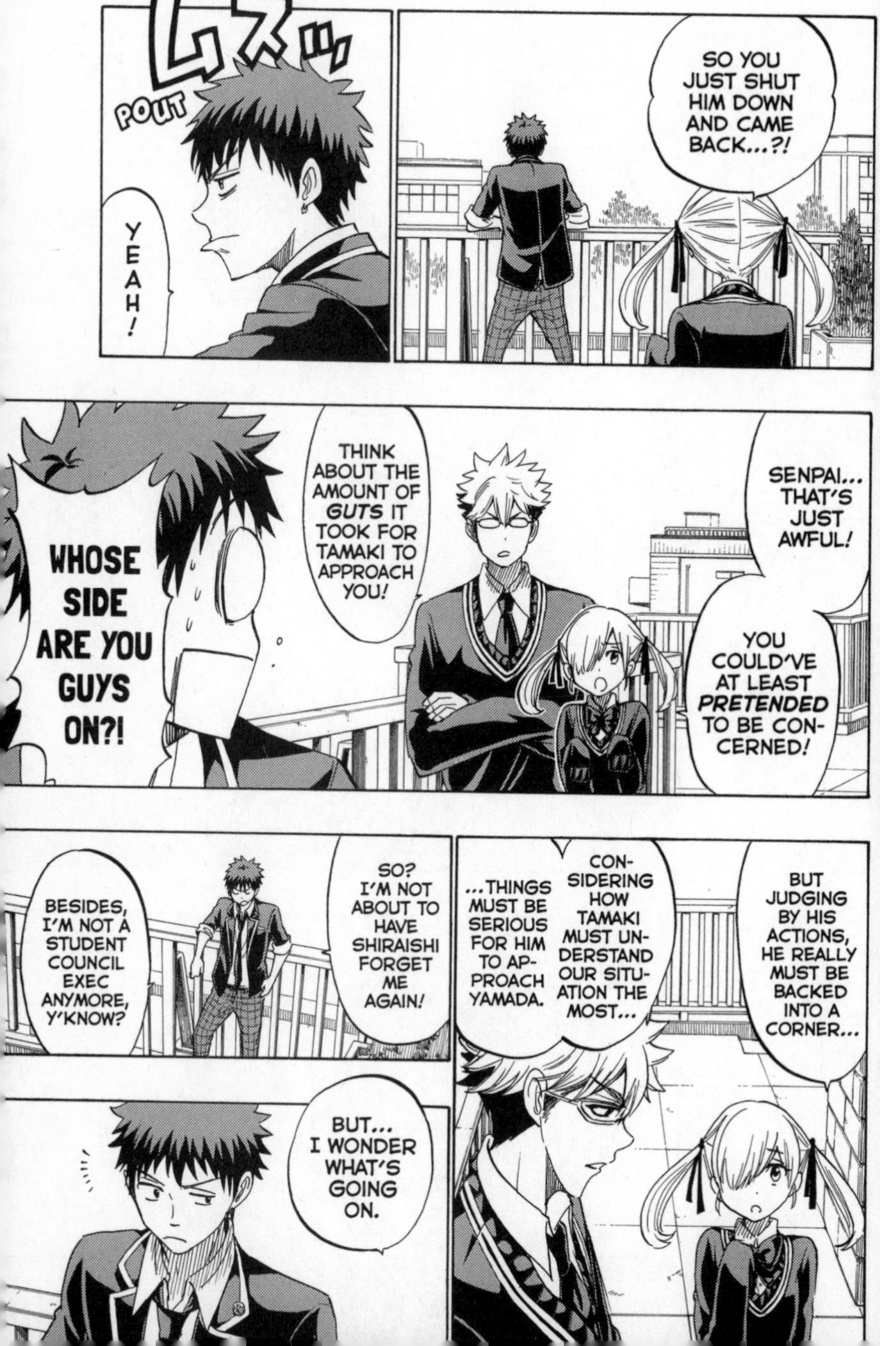
SO YOU JUST SHUT HIM DOWN AND CAME BACK...?!
ムスッ
POUT
YEAH!
SENPAI... THAT'S JUST AWFUL!
YOU COULD'VE AT LEAST *PRETENDED* TO BE CONCERNED!
THINK ABOUT THE AMOUNT OF *GUTS* IT TOOK FOR TAMAKI TO APPROACH YOU!
WHOSE SIDE ARE YOU GUYS ON?!
BUT JUDGING BY HIS ACTIONS, HE REALLY MUST BE BACKED INTO A CORNER...
CONSIDERING HOW TAMAKI MUST UNDERSTAND OUR SITUATION THE MOST...
...THINGS MUST BE SERIOUS FOR HIM TO APPROACH YAMADA.
SO? I'M NOT ABOUT TO HAVE SHIRAISHI FORGET ME AGAIN!
BESIDES, I'M NOT A STUDENT COUNCIL EXEC ANYMORE, Y'KNOW?
BUT... I WONDER WHAT'S GOING ON.

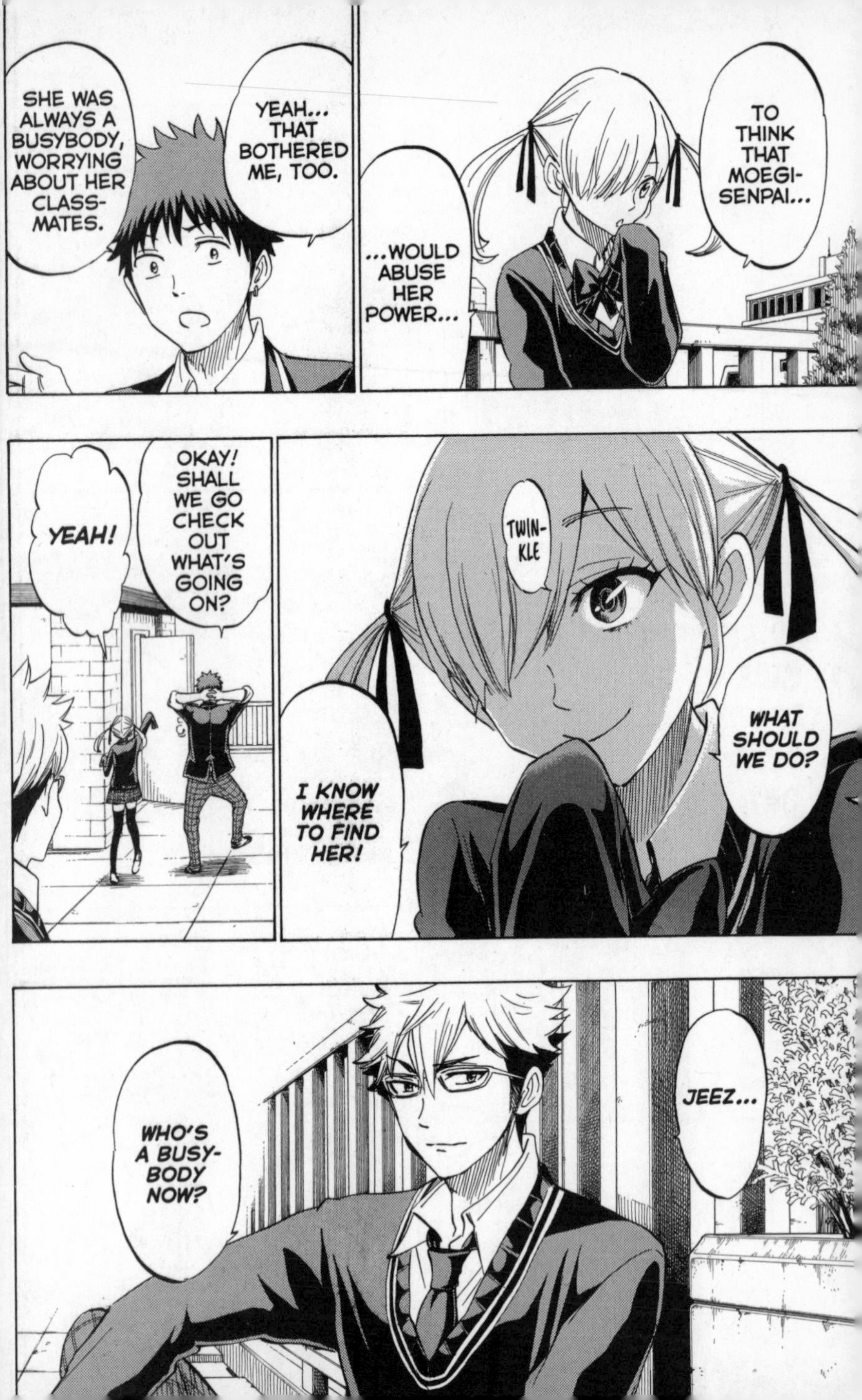
TO THINK THAT MOEGI-SENPAI...
...WOULD ABUSE HER POWER...
YEAH... THAT BOTHERED ME, TOO.
SHE WAS ALWAYS A BUSYBODY, WORRYING ABOUT HER CLASSMATES.
TWINKLE
WHAT SHOULD WE DO?
I KNOW WHERE TO FIND HER!
OKAY! SHALL WE GO CHECK OUT WHAT'S GOING ON?
YEAH!
JEEZ...
WHO'S A BUSYBODY NOW?

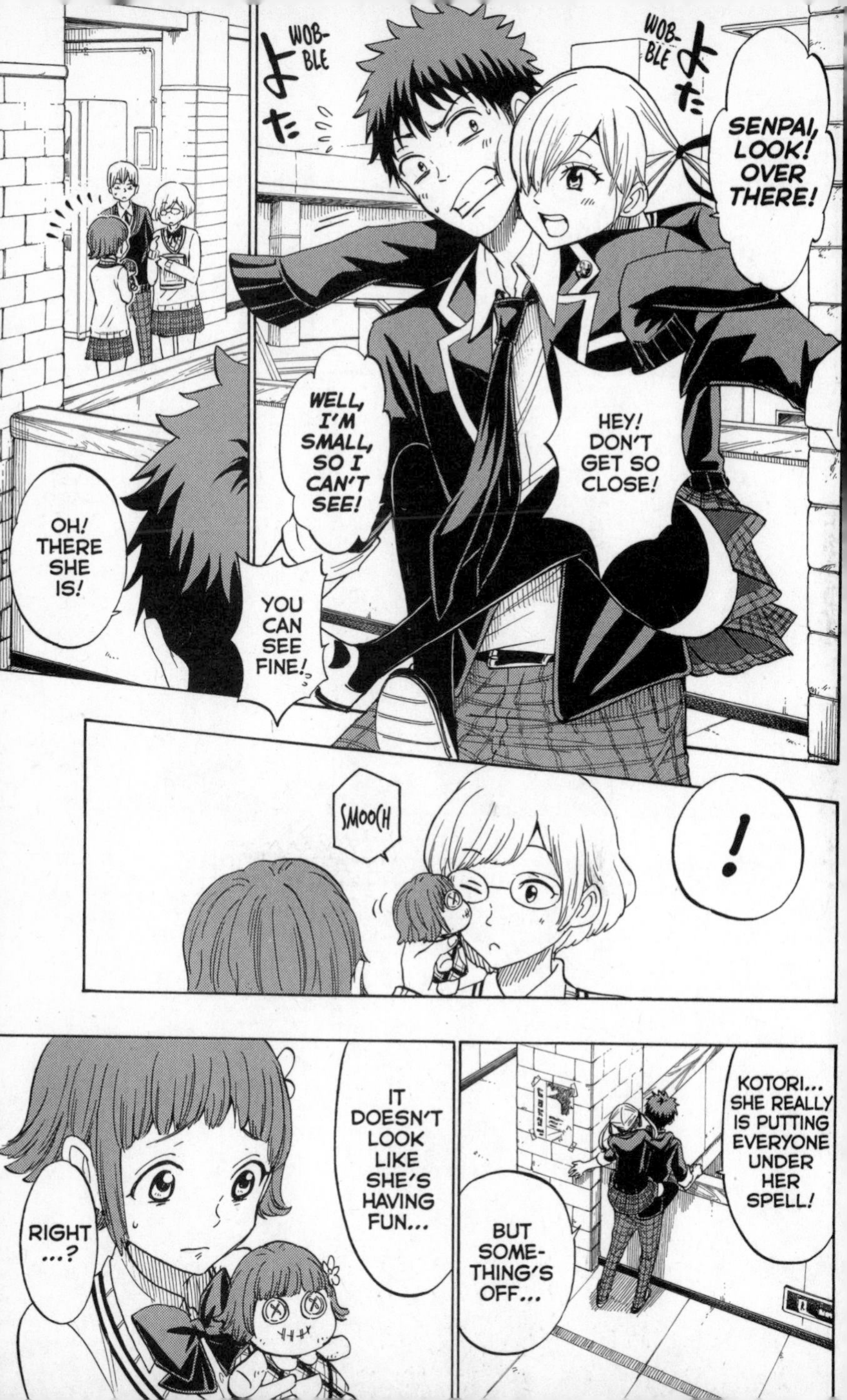
SENPAI, LOOK! OVER THERE!
よた WOB-BLE
よた WOB-BLE
HEY! DON'T GET SO CLOSE!
WELL, I'M SMALL, SO I CAN'T SEE!
YOU CAN SEE FINE!
OH! THERE SHE IS!
!
SMOOCH
KOTORI... SHE REALLY IS PUTTING EVERYONE UNDER HER SPELL!
BUT SOME-THING'S OFF...
IT DOESN'T LOOK LIKE SHE'S HAVING FUN...
RIGHT ...?

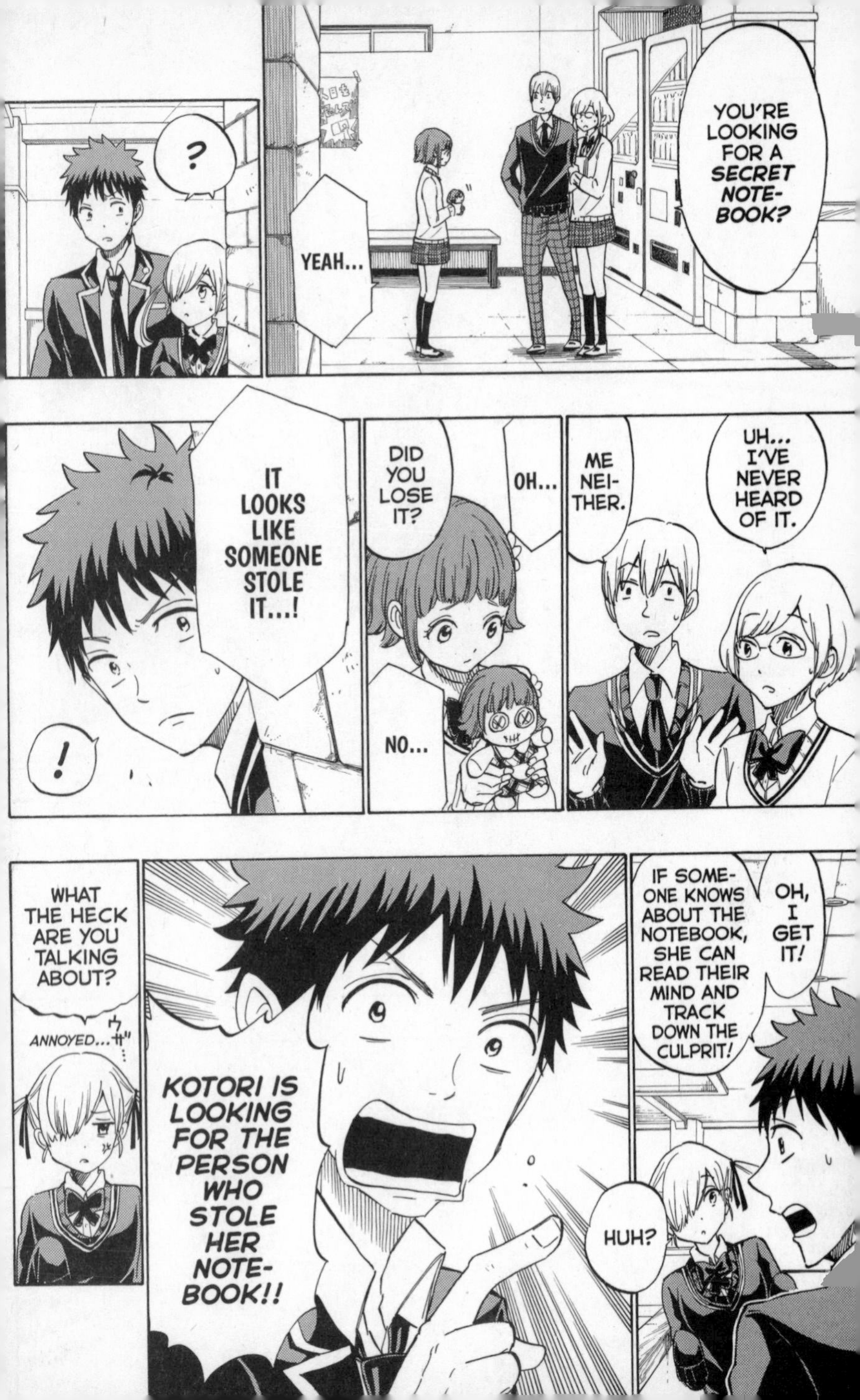
YOU'RE LOOKING FOR A SECRET NOTE-BOOK?
YEAH...
?
UH... I'VE NEVER HEARD OF IT.
ME NEI-THER.
OH...
DID YOU LOSE IT?
NO...
IT LOOKS LIKE SOMEONE STOLE IT...!
!
OH, I GET IT!
IF SOME-ONE KNOWS ABOUT THE NOTEBOOK, SHE CAN READ THEIR MIND AND TRACK DOWN THE CULPRIT!
HUH?
KOTORI IS LOOKING FOR THE PERSON WHO STOLE HER NOTE-BOOK!!
WHAT THE HECK ARE YOU TALKING ABOUT?
ANNOYED...
ウザ

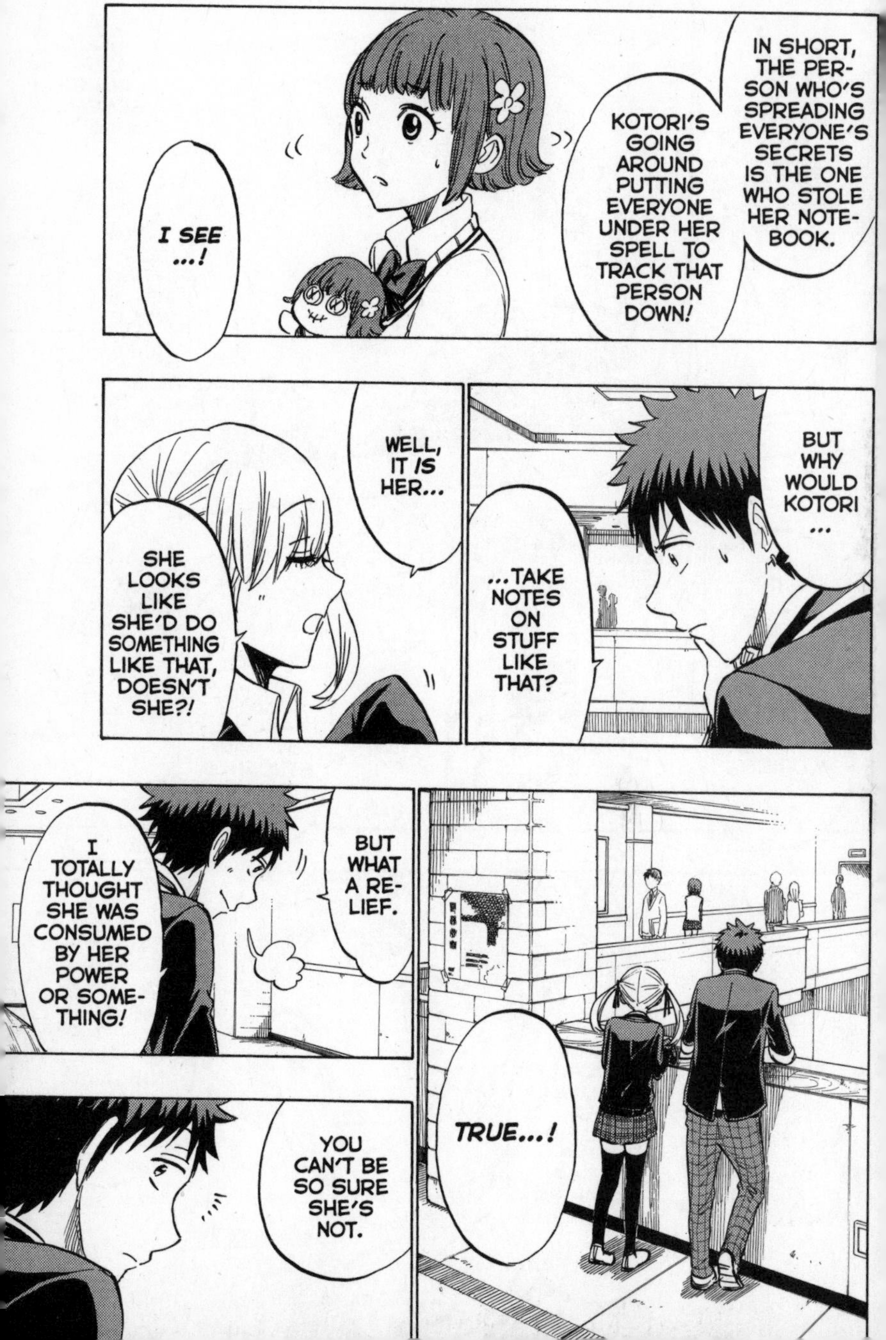
IN SHORT, THE PERSON WHO'S SPREADING EVERYONE'S SECRETS IS THE ONE WHO STOLE HER NOTEBOOK.
KOTORI'S GOING AROUND PUTTING EVERYONE UNDER HER SPELL TO TRACK THAT PERSON DOWN!
I SEE...!
BUT WHY WOULD KOTORI...
...TAKE NOTES ON STUFF LIKE THAT?
WELL, IT *IS* HER...
SHE LOOKS LIKE SHE'D DO SOMETHING LIKE THAT, DOESN'T SHE?!
TRUE...!
BUT WHAT A RELIEF.
I TOTALLY THOUGHT SHE WAS CONSUMED BY HER POWER OR SOMETHING!
YOU CAN'T BE SO SURE SHE'S NOT.

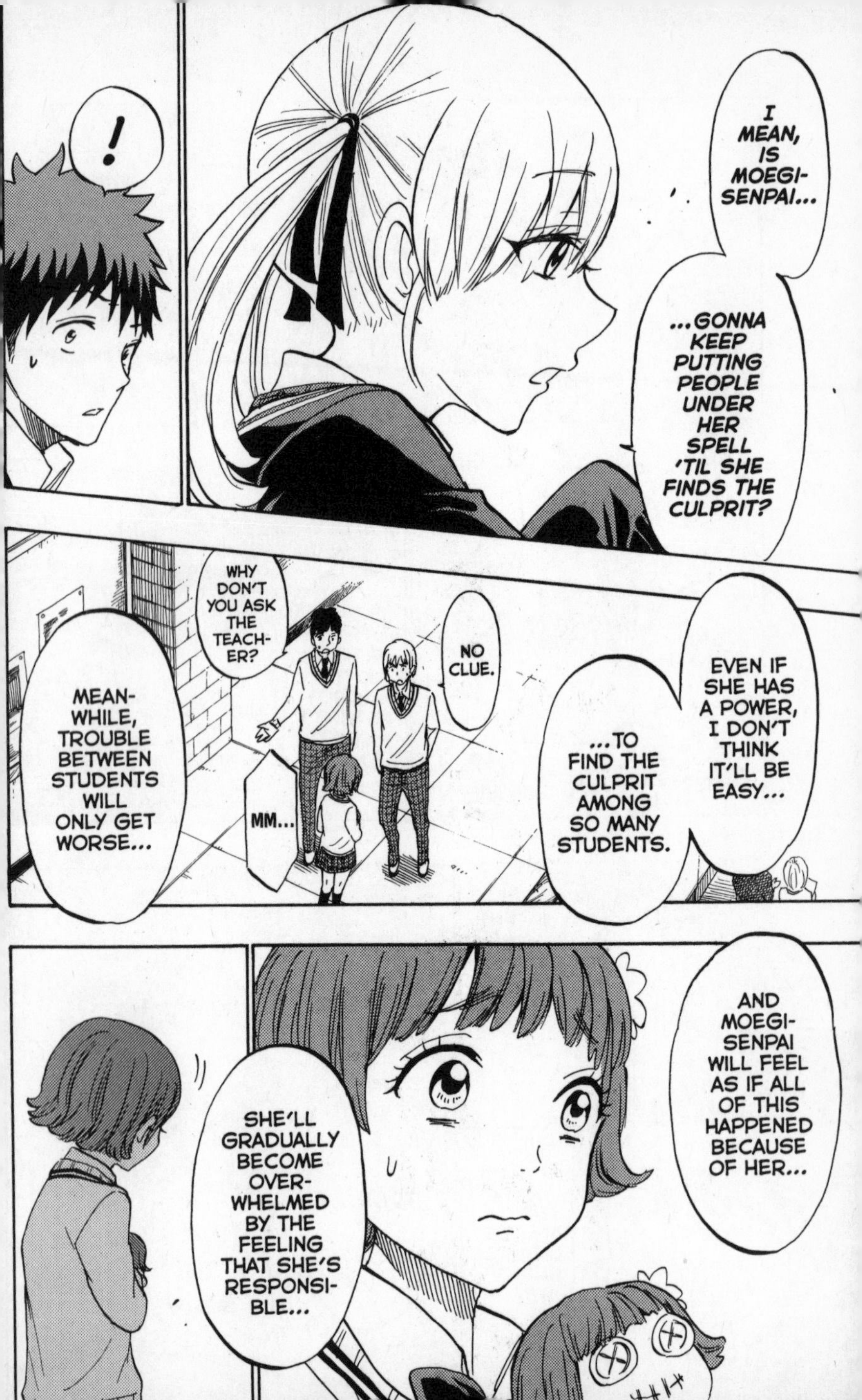
I MEAN, IS MOEGI-SENPAI...
...GONNA KEEP PUTTING PEOPLE UNDER HER SPELL 'TIL SHE FINDS THE CULPRIT?
!
EVEN IF SHE HAS A POWER, I DON'T THINK IT'LL BE EASY...
...TO FIND THE CULPRIT AMONG SO MANY STUDENTS.
NO CLUE.
WHY DON'T YOU ASK THE TEACHER?
MM...
MEAN-WHILE, TROUBLE BETWEEN STUDENTS WILL ONLY GET WORSE...
AND MOEGI-SENPAI WILL FEEL AS IF ALL OF THIS HAPPENED BECAUSE OF HER...
SHE'LL GRADUALLY BECOME OVER-WHELMED BY THE FEELING THAT SHE'S RESPONSI-BLE...

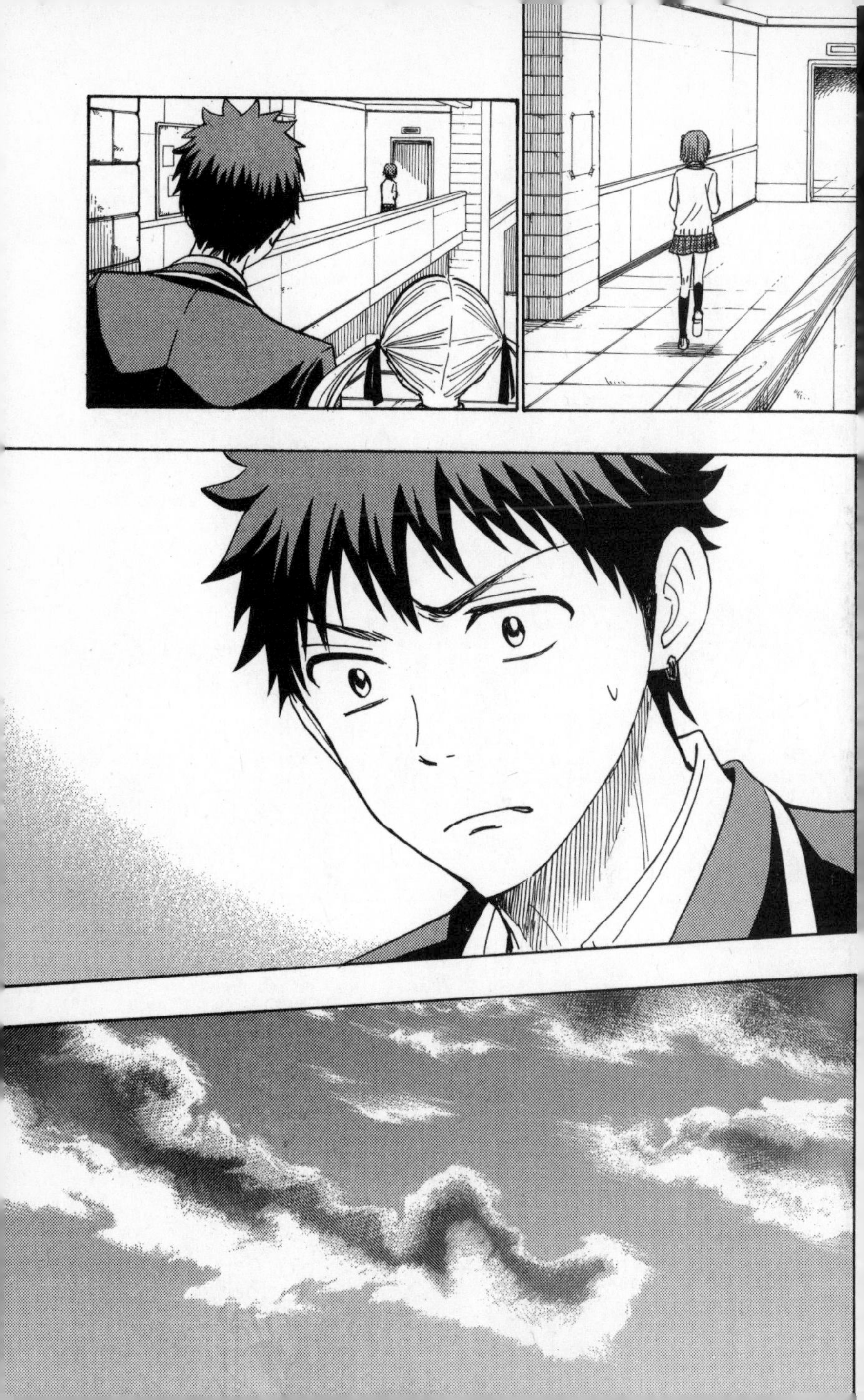

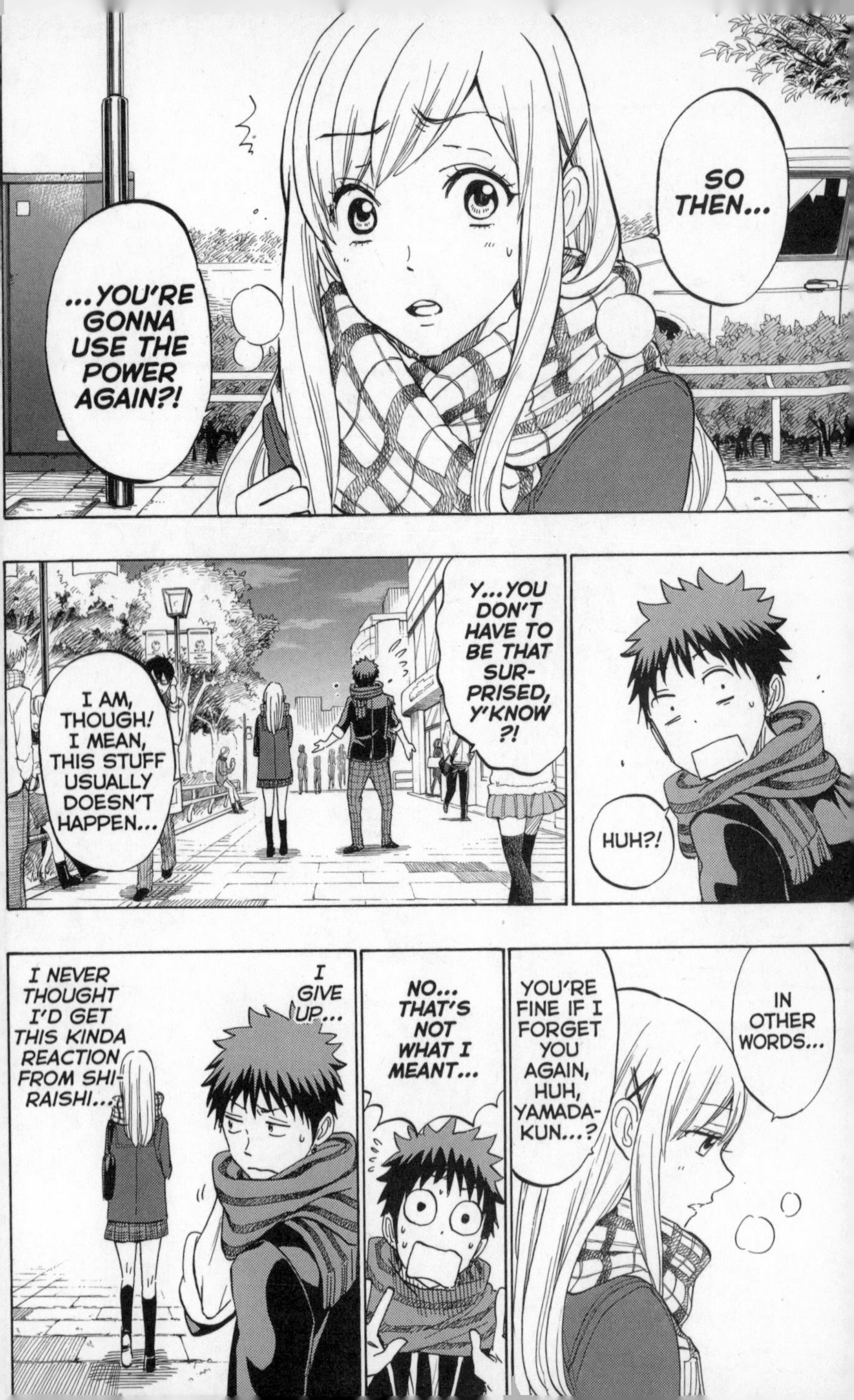
SO THEN...
...YOU'RE GONNA USE THE POWER AGAIN?!
HUH?!
Y...YOU DON'T HAVE TO BE THAT SUR-PRISED, Y'KNOW?!
I AM, THOUGH! I MEAN, THIS STUFF USUALLY DOESN'T HAPPEN...
IN OTHER WORDS...
YOU'RE FINE IF I FORGET YOU AGAIN, HUH, YAMADA-KUN...?
NO... THAT'S NOT WHAT I MEANT...
I GIVE UP...
I NEVER THOUGHT I'D GET THIS KINDA REACTION FROM SHI-RAISHI...

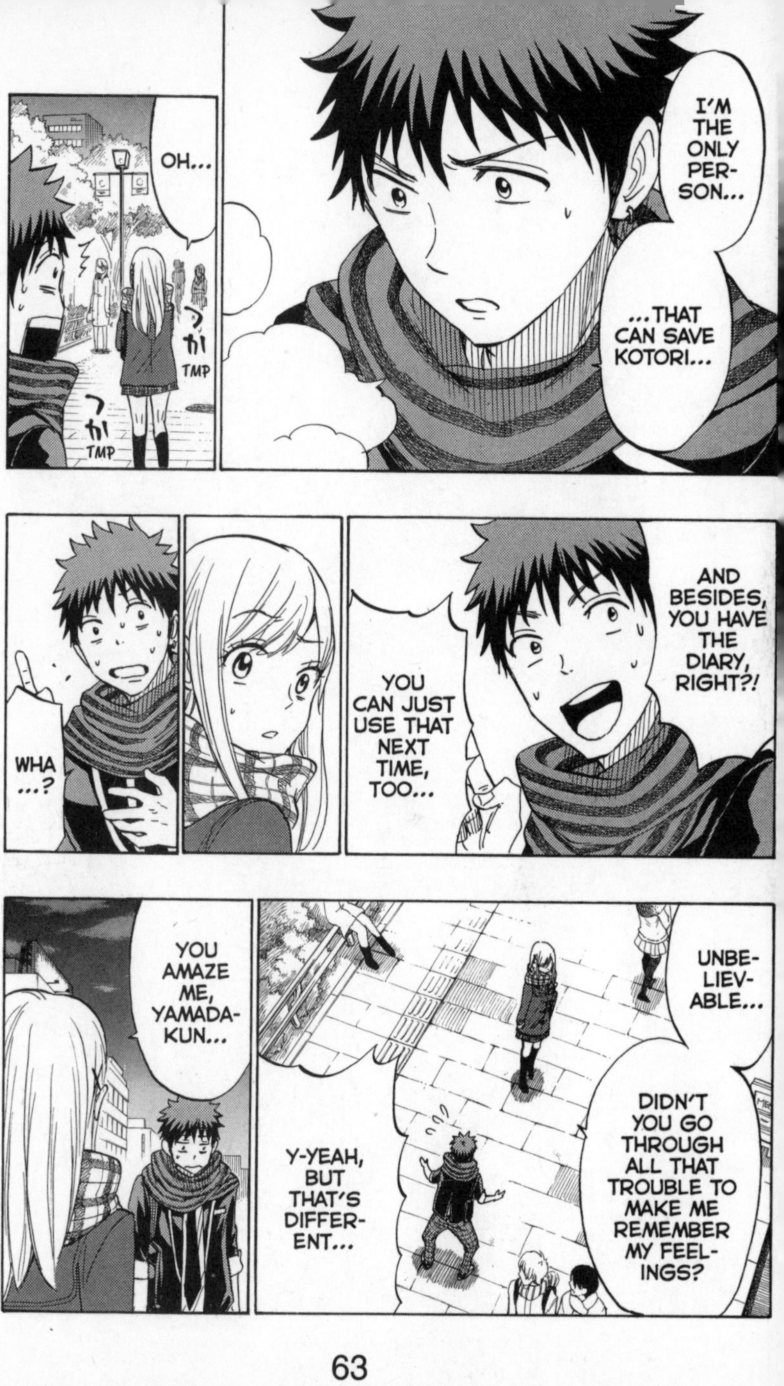
I'M THE ONLY PER-SON...
...THAT CAN SAVE KOTORI...
OH...
TMP
TMP
AND BESIDES, YOU HAVE THE DIARY, RIGHT?!
YOU CAN JUST USE THAT NEXT TIME, TOO...
WHA ...?
UNBE-LIEV-ABLE...
DIDN'T YOU GO THROUGH ALL THAT TROUBLE TO MAKE ME REMEMBER MY FEEL-INGS?
Y-YEAH, BUT THAT'S DIFFER-ENT...
YOU AMAZE ME, YAMADA-KUN...

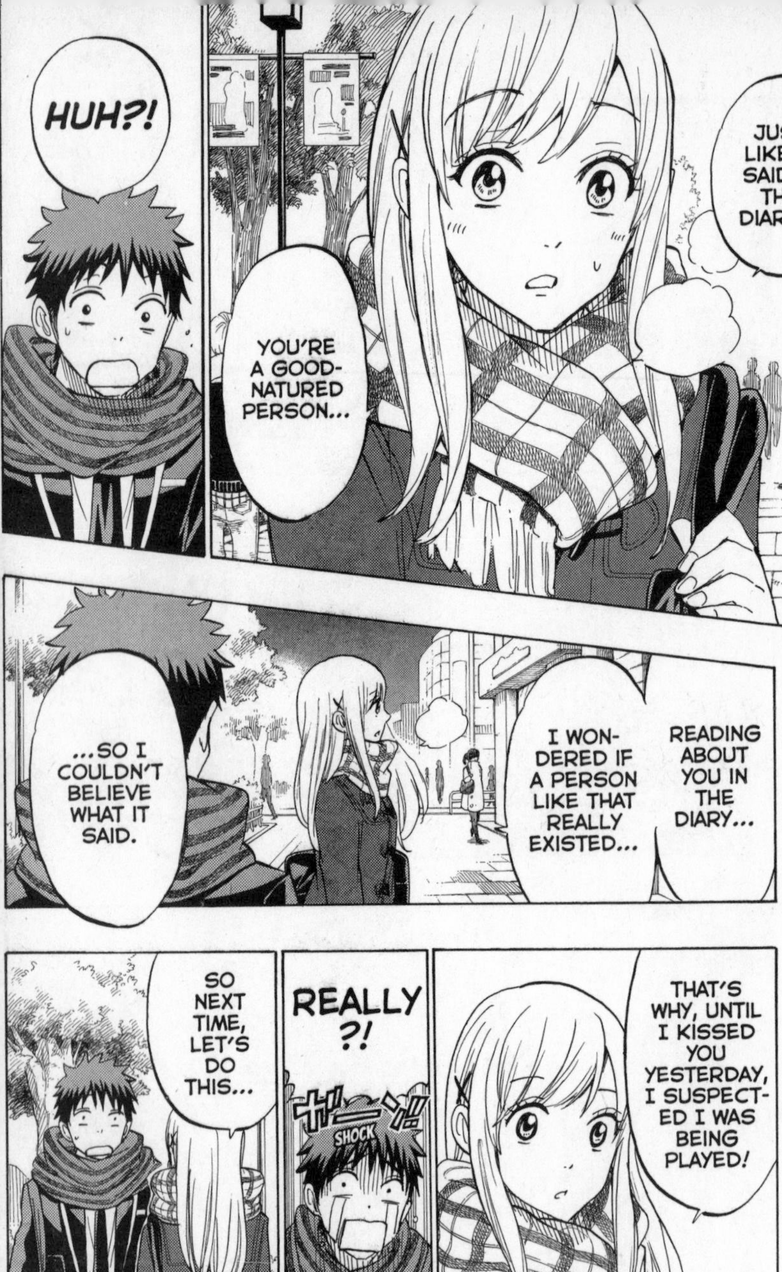
JUST LIKE IT SAID IN THE DIARY...
YOU'RE A GOOD-NATURED PERSON...
HUH?!
READING ABOUT YOU IN THE DIARY...
I WONDERED IF A PERSON LIKE THAT REALLY EXISTED...
...SO I COULDN'T BELIEVE WHAT IT SAID.
THAT'S WHY, UNTIL I KISSED YOU YESTERDAY, I SUSPECTED I WAS BEING PLAYED!
REALLY?!
SHOCK
SO NEXT TIME, LET'S DO THIS...

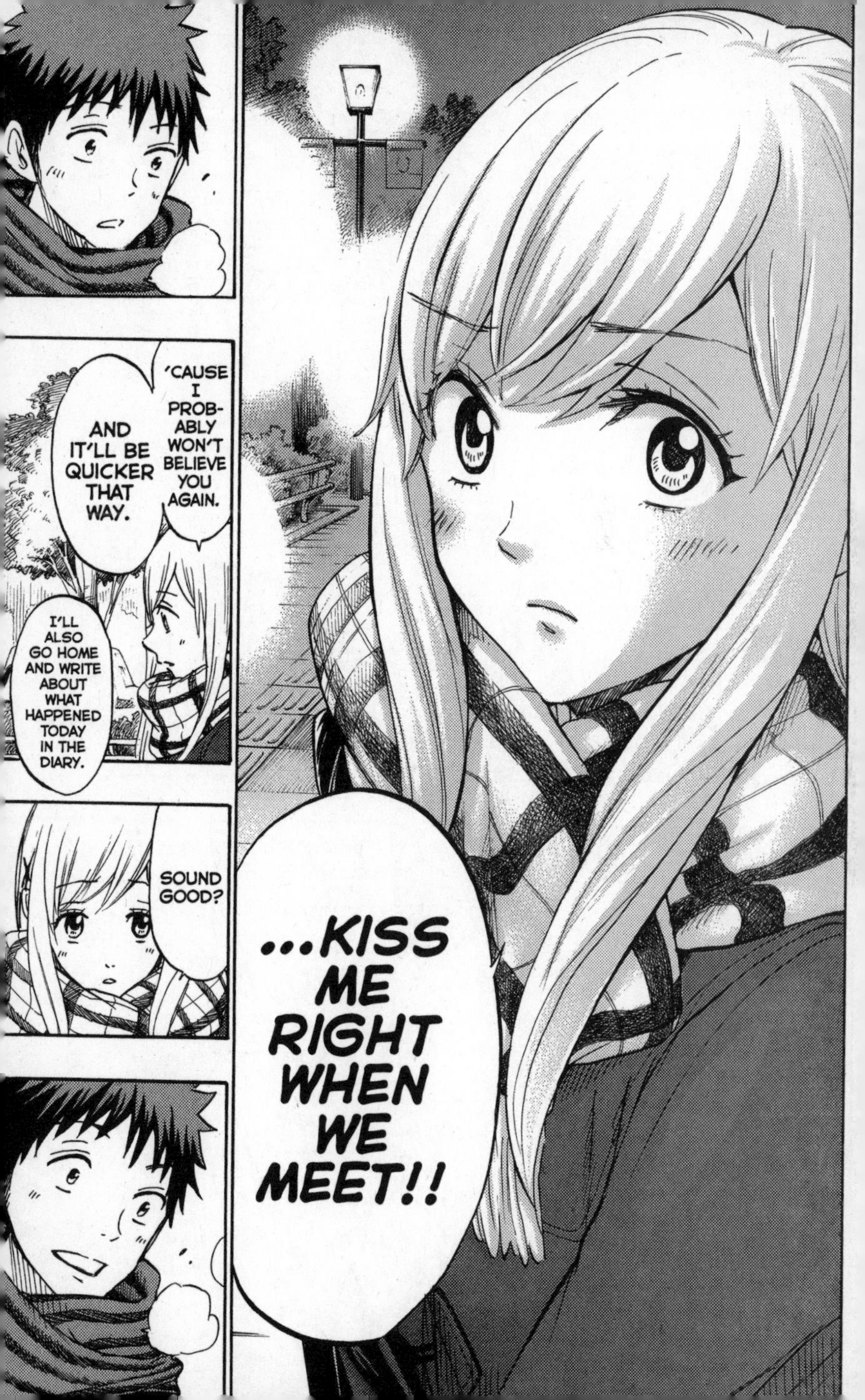
...KISS ME RIGHT WHEN WE MEET!!
'CAUSE I PROBABLY WON'T BELIEVE YOU AGAIN.
AND IT'LL BE QUICKER THAT WAY.
I'LL ALSO GO HOME AND WRITE ABOUT WHAT HAPPENED TODAY IN THE DIARY.
SOUND GOOD?

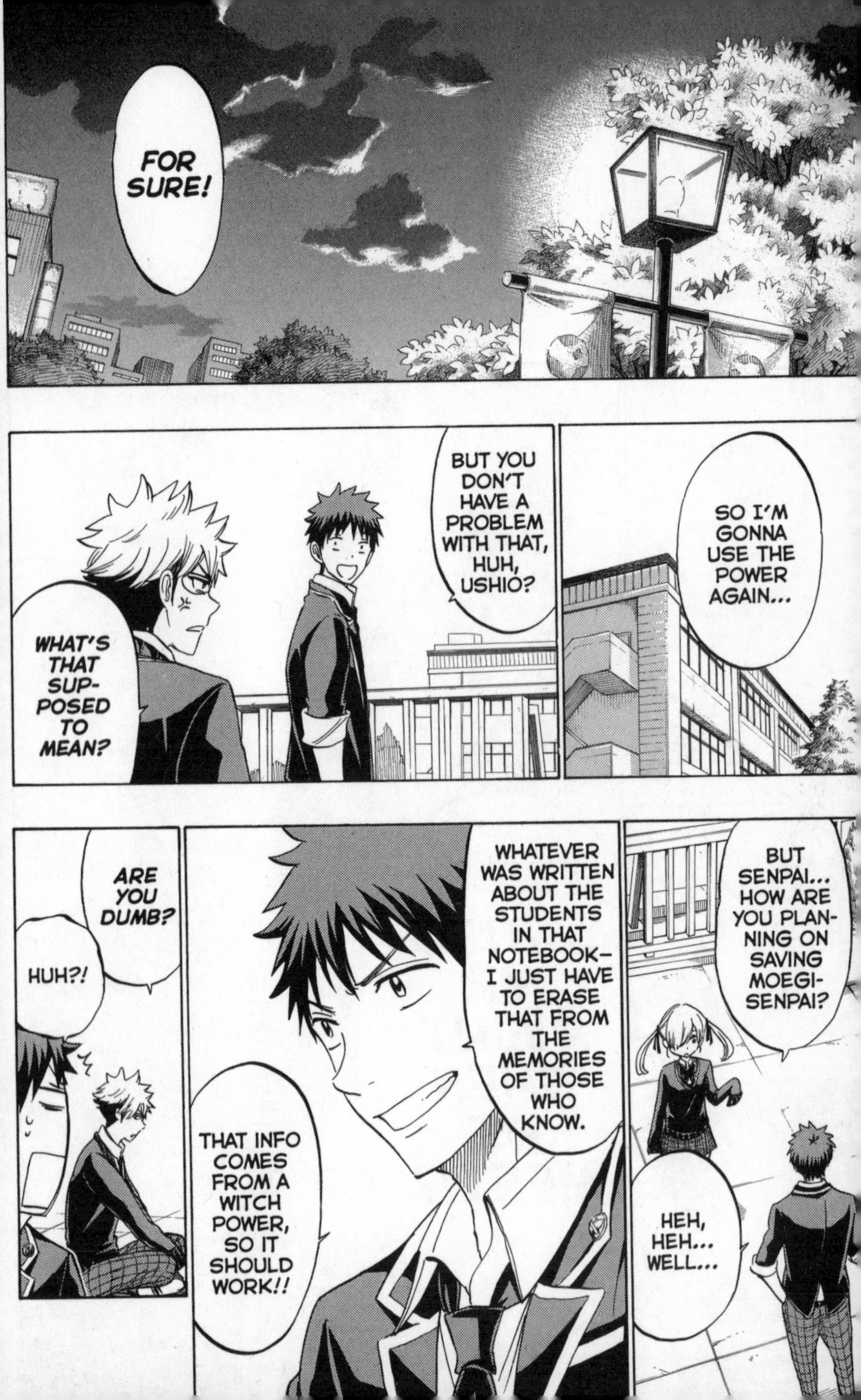
FOR SURE!
SO I'M GONNA USE THE POWER AGAIN...
BUT YOU DON'T HAVE A PROBLEM WITH THAT, HUH, USHIO?
WHAT'S THAT SUP-POSED TO MEAN?
BUT SENPAI... HOW ARE YOU PLAN-NING ON SAVING MOEGI-SENPAI?
HEH, HEH... WELL...
WHATEVER WAS WRITTEN ABOUT THE STUDENTS IN THAT NOTEBOOK– I JUST HAVE TO ERASE THAT FROM THE MEMORIES OF THOSE WHO KNOW.
THAT INFO COMES FROM A WITCH POWER, SO IT SHOULD WORK!!
ARE YOU DUMB?
HUH?!

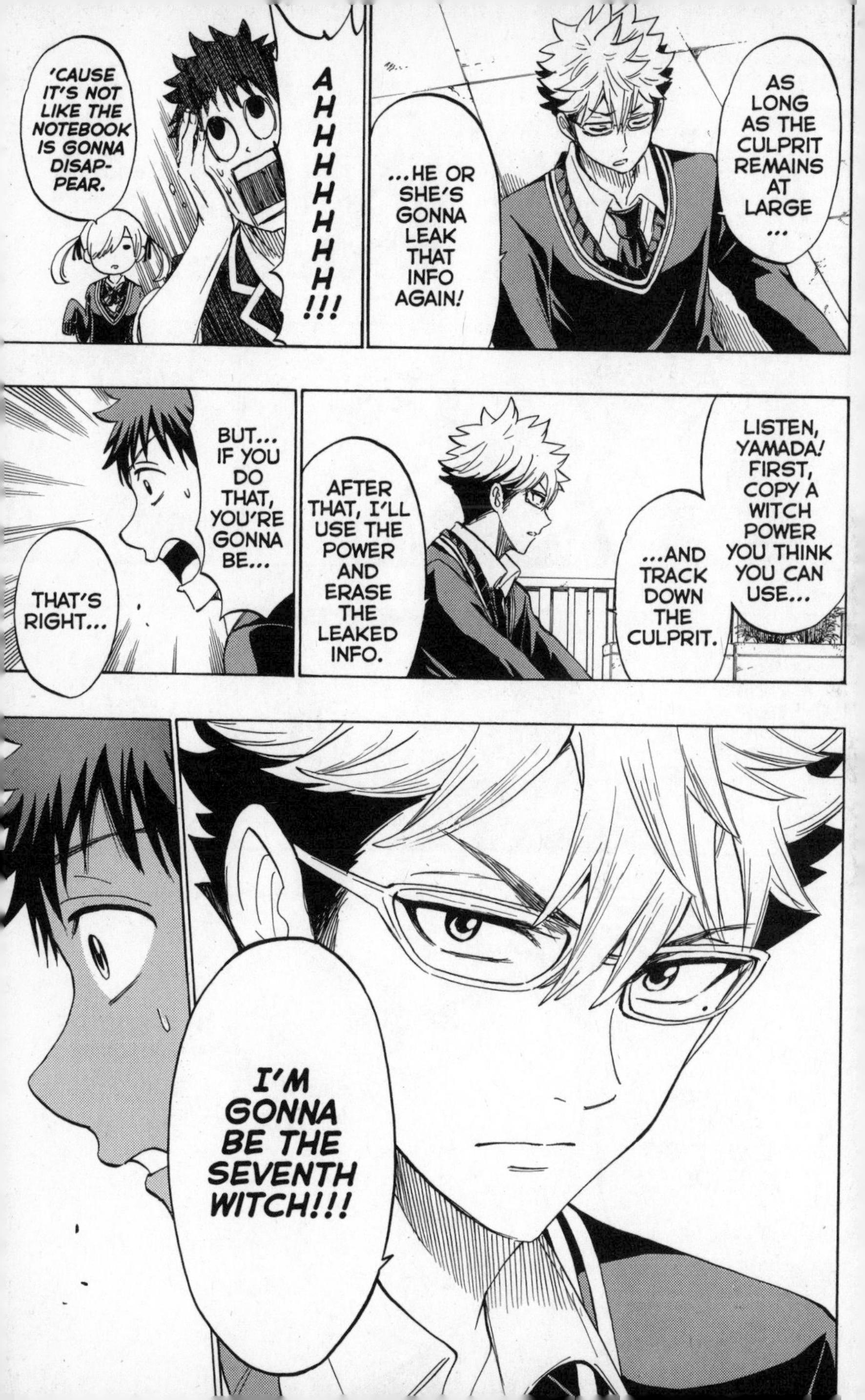
AS LONG AS THE CULPRIT REMAINS AT LARGE...
...HE OR SHE'S GONNA LEAK THAT INFO AGAIN!
AHHHHHH!!!
'CAUSE IT'S NOT LIKE THE NOTEBOOK IS GONNA DISAP-PEAR.
LISTEN, YAMADA! FIRST, COPY A WITCH POWER YOU THINK YOU CAN USE...
...AND TRACK DOWN THE CULPRIT.
AFTER THAT, I'LL USE THE POWER AND ERASE THE LEAKED INFO.
BUT... IF YOU DO THAT, YOU'RE GONNA BE...
THAT'S RIGHT...
I'M GONNA BE THE SEVENTH WITCH!!!

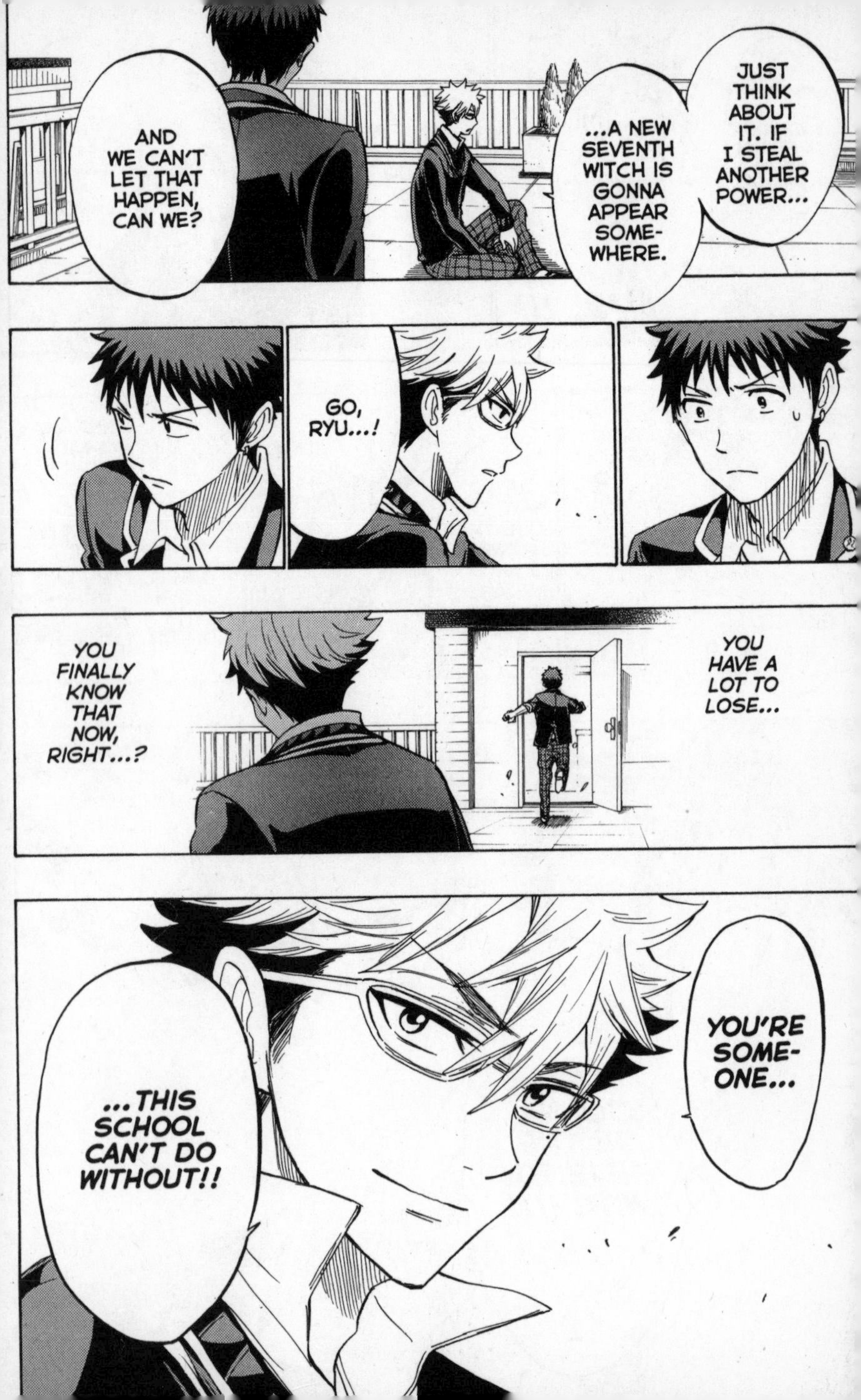
JUST THINK ABOUT IT. IF I STEAL ANOTHER POWER...
...A NEW SEVENTH WITCH IS GONNA APPEAR SOME-WHERE.
AND WE CAN'T LET THAT HAPPEN, CAN WE?
GO, RYU...!
YOU HAVE A LOT TO LOSE...
YOU FINALLY KNOW THAT NOW, RIGHT...?
YOU'RE SOME-ONE...
...THIS SCHOOL CAN'T DO WITHOUT!!

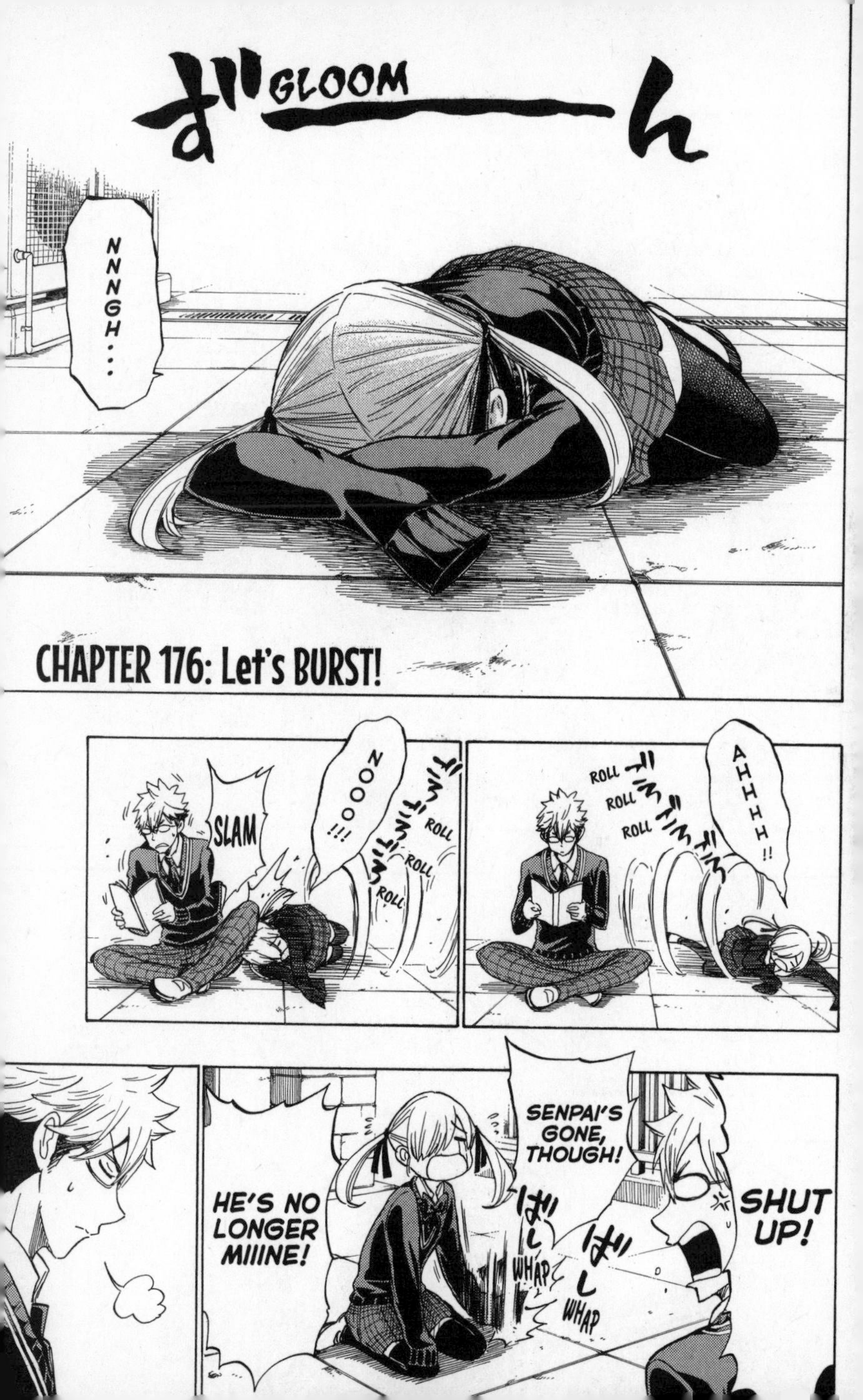
GLOOM
NNNGH...
CHAPTER 176: Let's BURST!
ROLL ROLL ROLL
AHHHH!!
NOOOO!!!
ROLL ROLL ROLL
SLAM
SENPAI'S GONE, THOUGH!
HE'S NO LONGER MIIINE!
ばし ばし
WHAP WHAP
SHUT UP!

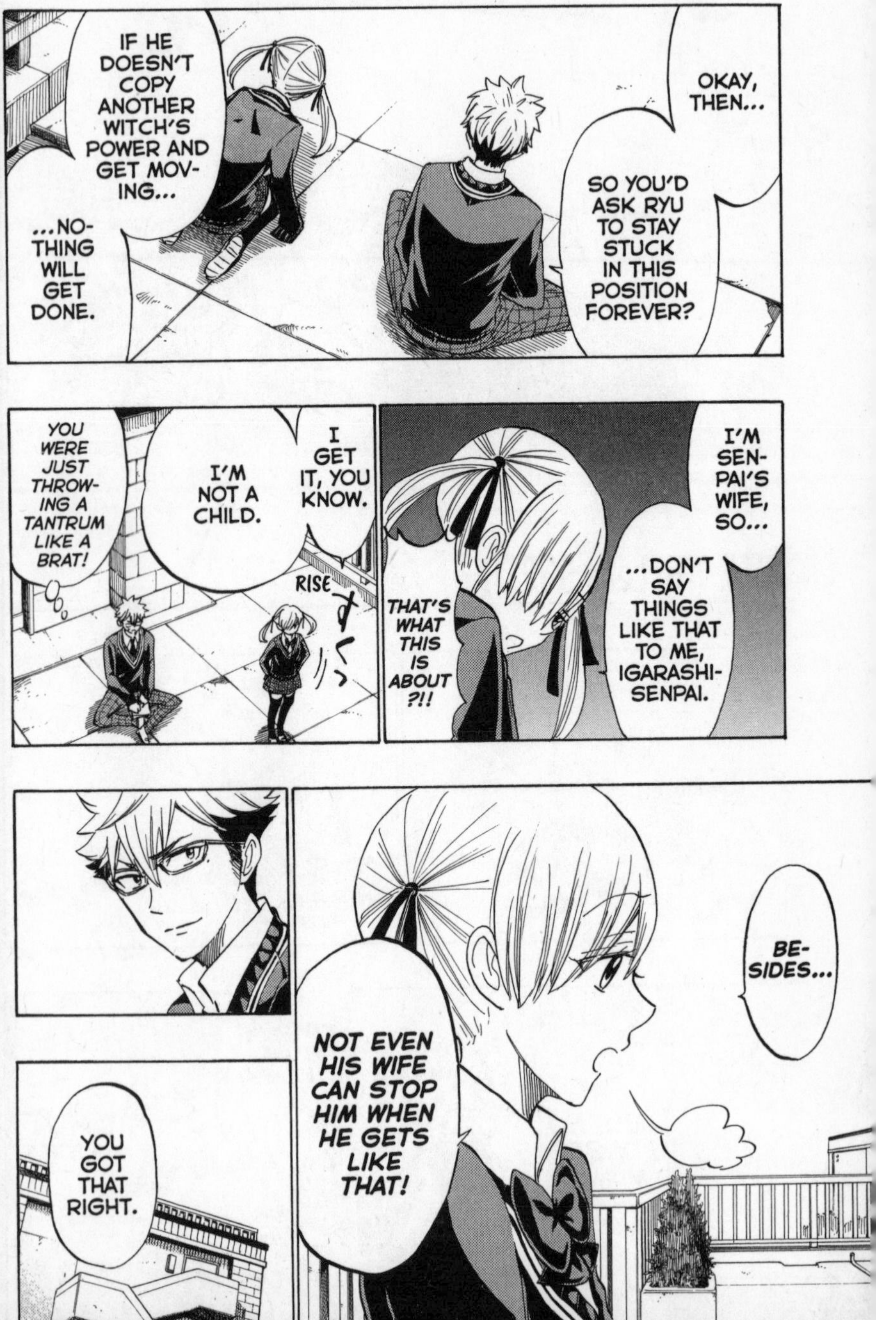
OKAY, THEN...
SO YOU'D ASK RYU TO STAY STUCK IN THIS POSITION FOREVER?
IF HE DOESN'T COPY ANOTHER WITCH'S POWER AND GET MOVING...
...NOTHING WILL GET DONE.
I'M SENPAI'S WIFE, SO...
...DON'T SAY THINGS LIKE THAT TO ME, IGARASHI-SENPAI.
THAT'S WHAT THIS IS ABOUT?!!
I GET IT, YOU KNOW.
I'M NOT A CHILD.
RISE
YOU WERE JUST THROWING A TANTRUM LIKE A BRAT!
BESIDES...
NOT EVEN HIS WIFE CAN STOP HIM WHEN HE GETS LIKE THAT!
YOU GOT THAT RIGHT.

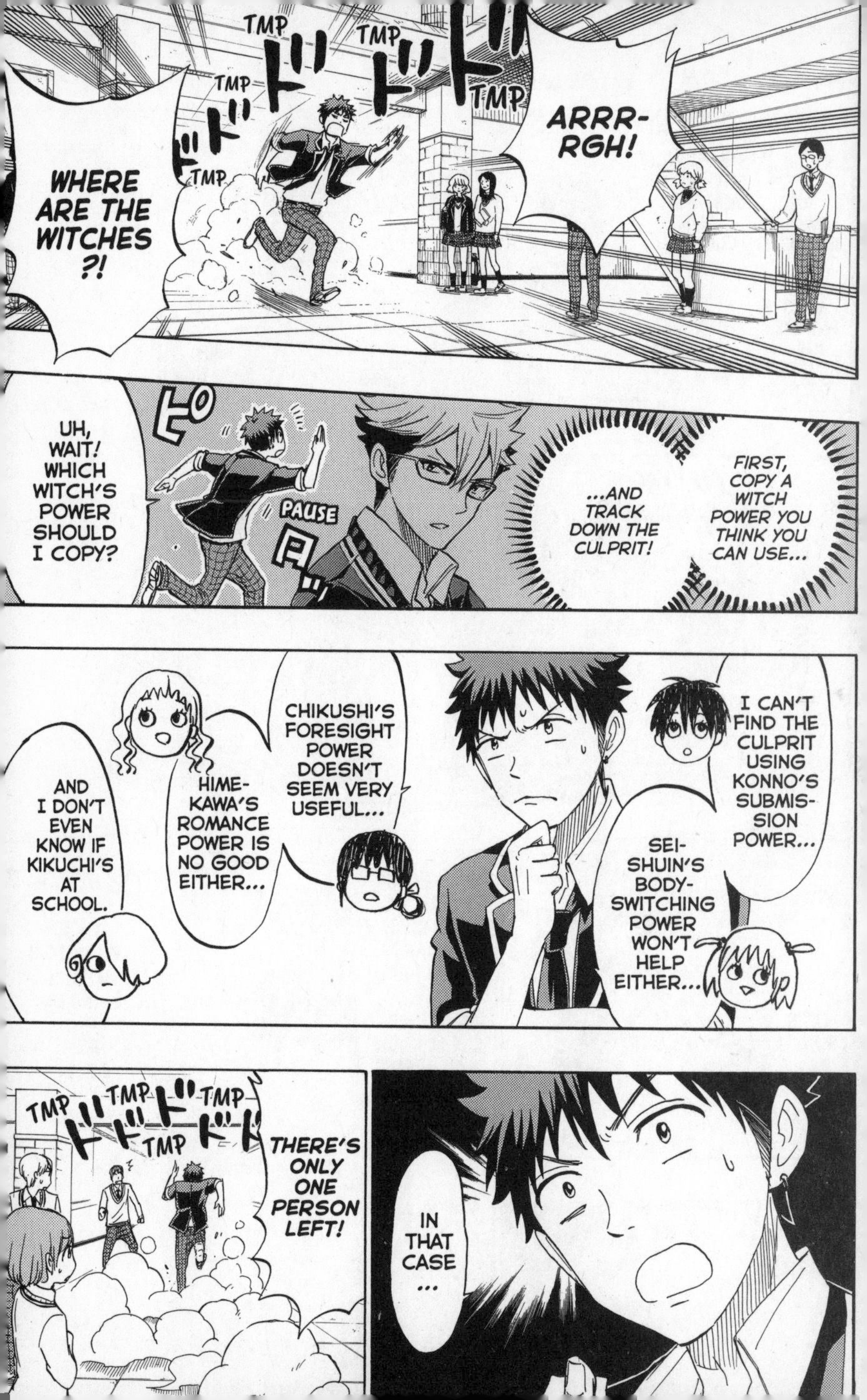
TMP TMP TMP TMP TMP
ARRR-RGH!
WHERE ARE THE WITCHES?!
FIRST, COPY A WITCH POWER YOU THINK YOU CAN USE...
...AND TRACK DOWN THE CULPRIT!
PAUSE
UH, WAIT! WHICH WITCH'S POWER SHOULD I COPY?
I CAN'T FIND THE CULPRIT USING KONNO'S SUBMISSION POWER...
SEISHUIN'S BODY-SWITCHING POWER WON'T HELP EITHER...
CHIKUSHI'S FORESIGHT POWER DOESN'T SEEM VERY USEFUL...
HIMEKAWA'S ROMANCE POWER IS NO GOOD EITHER...
AND I DON'T EVEN KNOW IF KIKUCHI'S AT SCHOOL.
IN THAT CASE...
TMP TMP TMP TMP
THERE'S ONLY ONE PERSON LEFT!

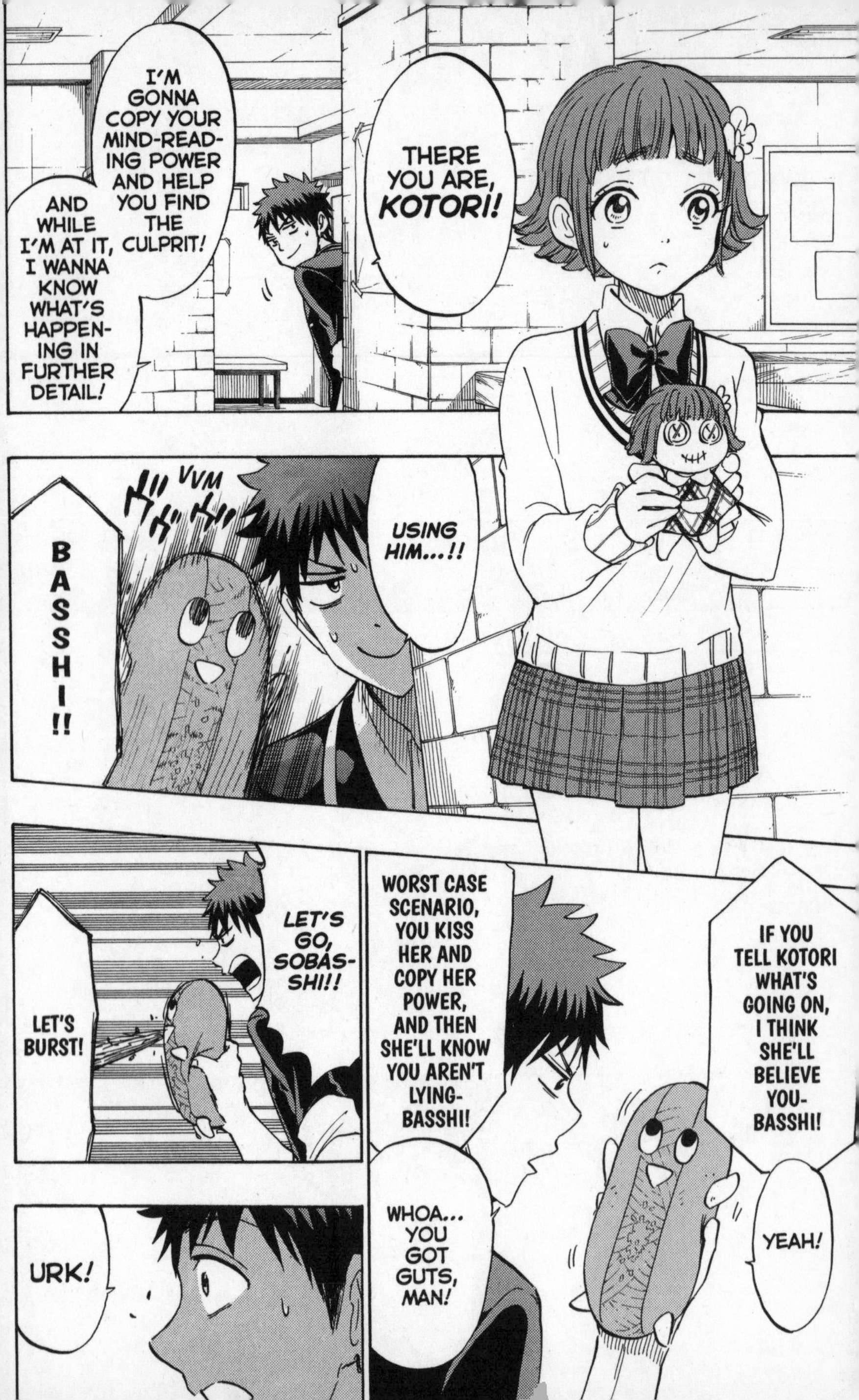
THERE YOU ARE, KOTORI!
I'M GONNA COPY YOUR MIND-READING POWER AND HELP YOU FIND THE CULPRIT!
AND WHILE I'M AT IT, I WANNA KNOW WHAT'S HAPPENING IN FURTHER DETAIL!
USING HIM...!!
VVM
BASSHI!!
IF YOU TELL KOTORI WHAT'S GOING ON, I THINK SHE'LL BELIEVE YOU-BASSHI!
WORST CASE SCENARIO, YOU KISS HER AND COPY HER POWER, AND THEN SHE'LL KNOW YOU AREN'T LYING-BASSHI!
YEAH!
WHOA... YOU GOT GUTS, MAN!
LET'S GO, SOBASSHI!!
LET'S BURST!
URK!

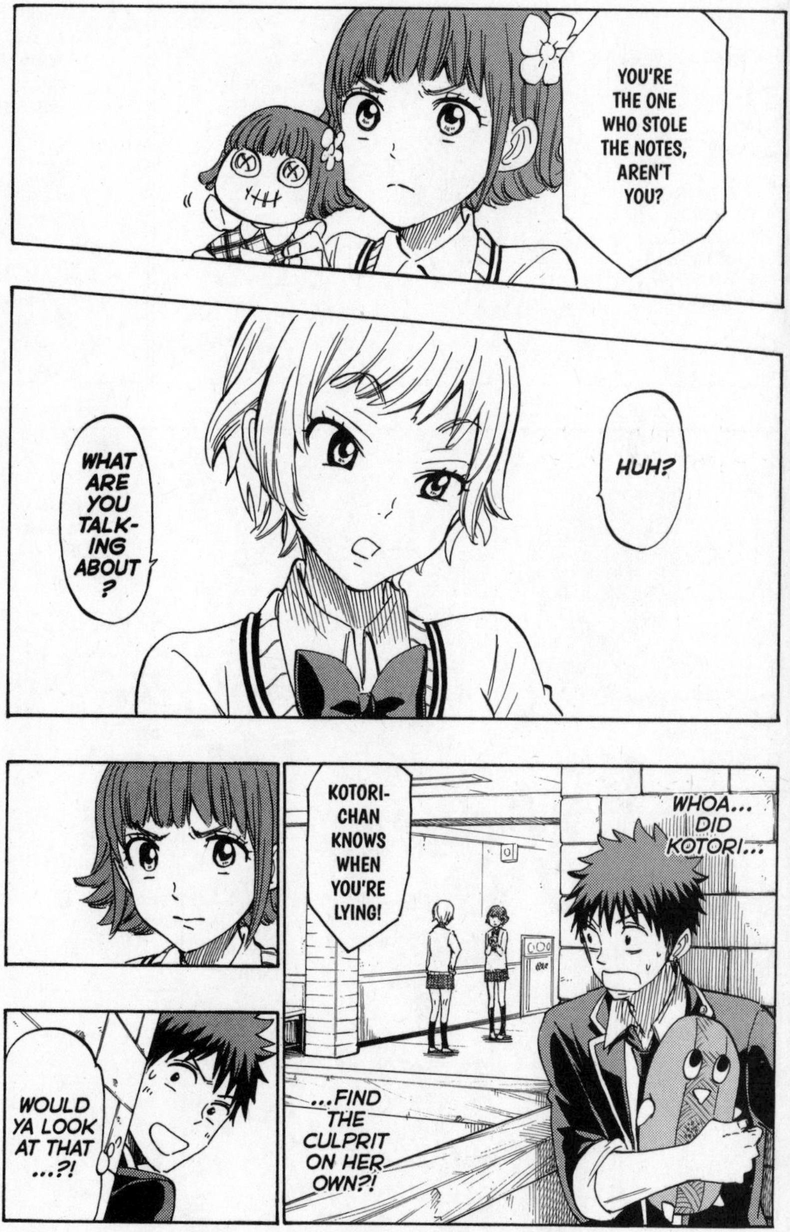
YOU'RE THE ONE WHO STOLE THE NOTES, AREN'T YOU?
HUH?
WHAT ARE YOU TALKING ABOUT?
WHOA... DID KOTORI...
KOTORI-CHAN KNOWS WHEN YOU'RE LYING!
...FIND THE CULPRIT ON HER OWN?!
WOULD YA LOOK AT THAT...?!

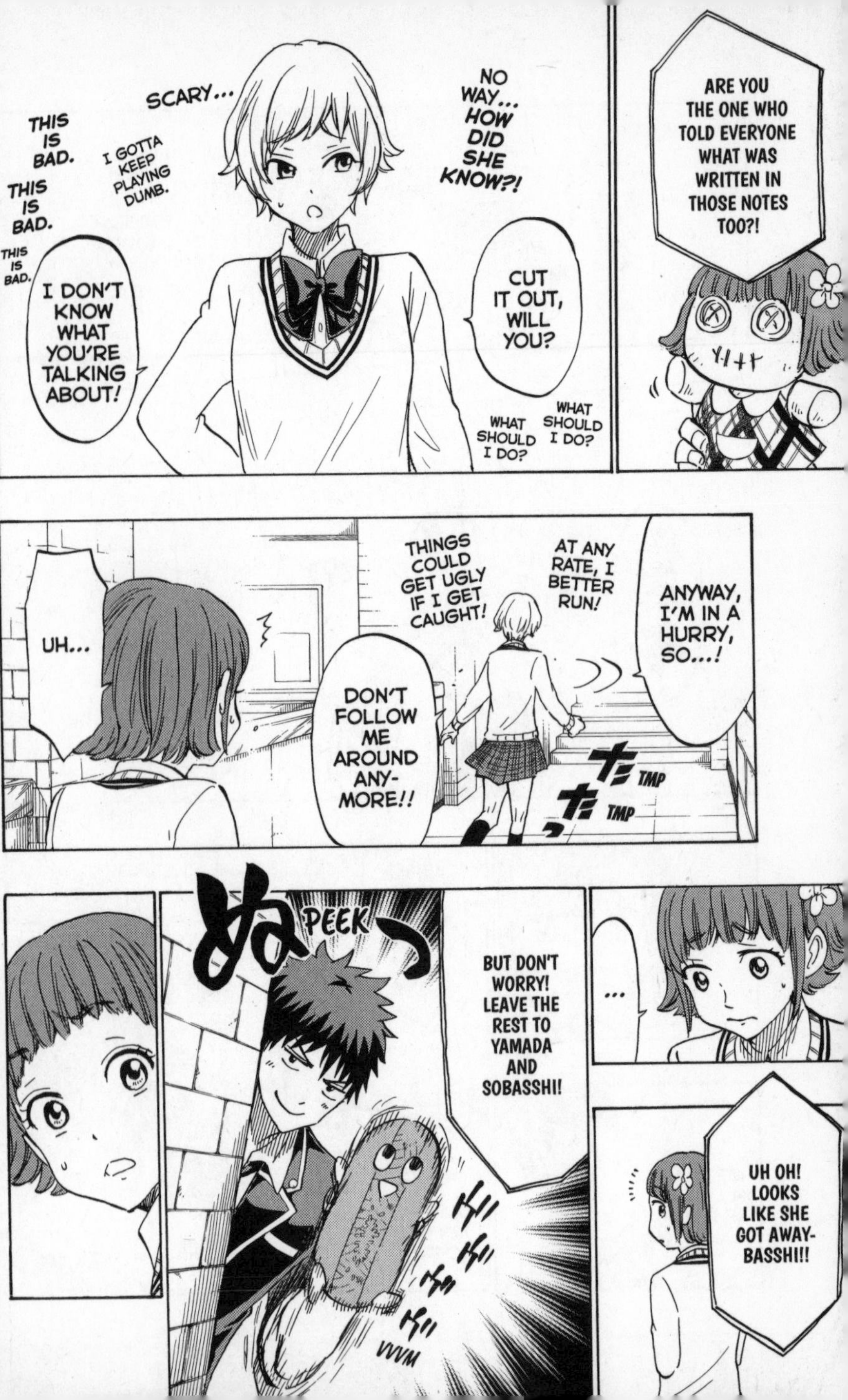
ARE YOU THE ONE WHO TOLD EVERYONE WHAT WAS WRITTEN IN THOSE NOTES TOO?!
NO WAY... HOW DID SHE KNOW?!
SCARY...
CUT IT OUT, WILL YOU?
I GOTTA KEEP PLAYING DUMB.
THIS IS BAD.
THIS IS BAD.
THIS IS BAD.
I DON'T KNOW WHAT YOU'RE TALKING ABOUT!
WHAT SHOULD I DO?
WHAT SHOULD I DO?
ANYWAY, I'M IN A HURRY, SO...!
AT ANY RATE, I BETTER RUN!
THINGS COULD GET UGLY IF I GET CAUGHT!
DON'T FOLLOW ME AROUND ANY-MORE!!
TMP
TMP
UH...
...
UH OH! LOOKS LIKE SHE GOT AWAY-BASSHI!!
BUT DON'T WORRY! LEAVE THE REST TO YAMADA AND SOBASSHI!
PEEK
VVVM

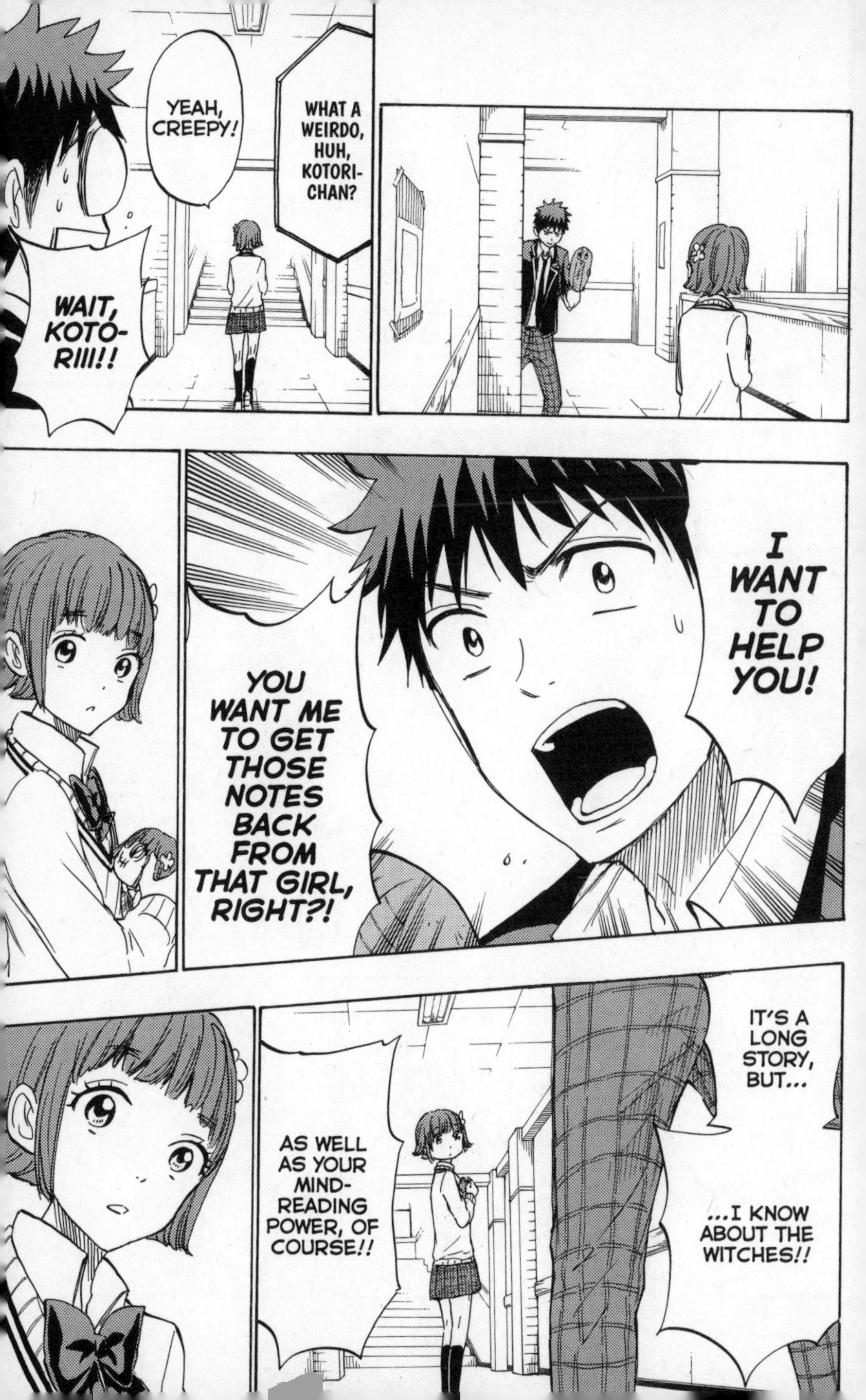
WHAT A WEIRDO, HUH, KOTORI-CHAN?
YEAH, CREEPY!
WAIT, KOTO-RIII!!
I WANT TO HELP YOU!
YOU WANT ME TO GET THOSE NOTES BACK FROM THAT GIRL, RIGHT?!
IT'S A LONG STORY, BUT...
...I KNOW ABOUT THE WITCHES!!
AS WELL AS YOUR MIND-READING POWER, OF COURSE!!

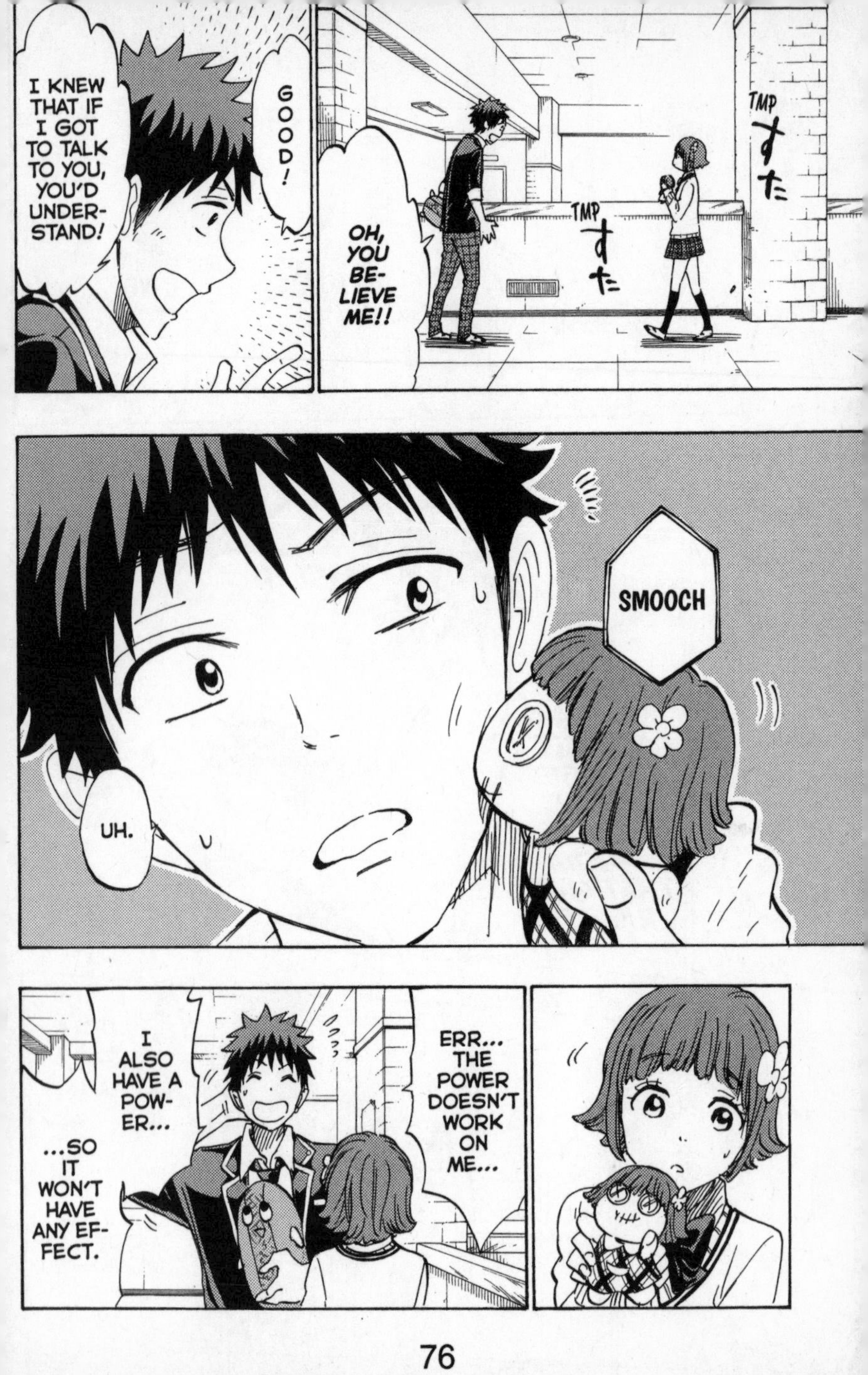

TMP すた
TMP すた
OH, YOU BELIEVE ME!!
GOOD!
I KNEW THAT IF I GOT TO TALK TO YOU, YOU'D UNDERSTAND!
SMOOCH
UH.
ERR... THE POWER DOESN'T WORK ON ME...
I ALSO HAVE A POWER...
...SO IT WON'T HAVE ANY EFFECT.

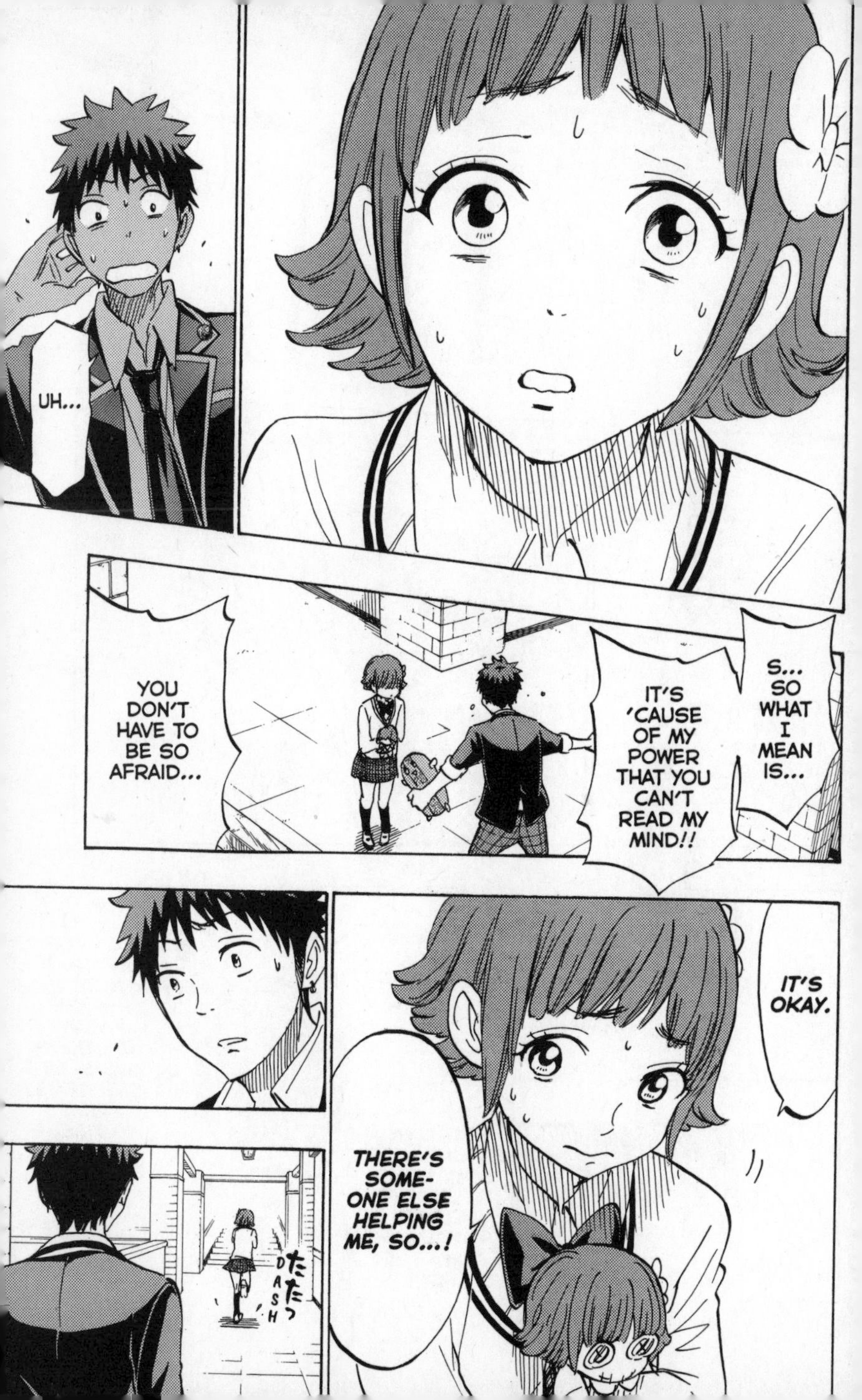
UH...
S... SO WHAT I MEAN IS...
IT'S 'CAUSE OF MY POWER THAT YOU CAN'T READ MY MIND!!
YOU DON'T HAVE TO BE SO AFRAID...
IT'S OKAY.
THERE'S SOME-ONE ELSE HELPING ME, SO...!
たたっ
DASH

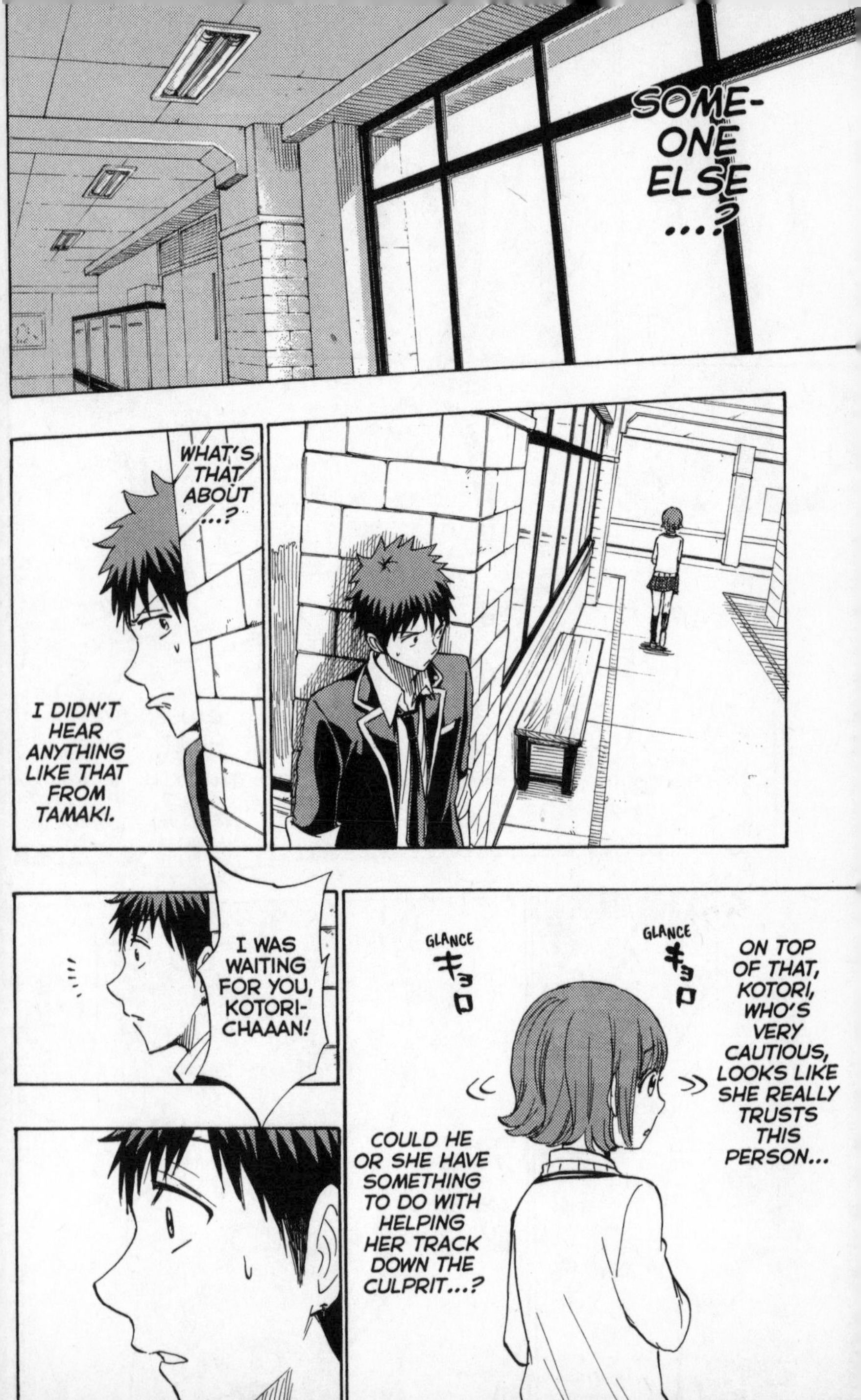
SOME-ONE ELSE ...?
WHAT'S THAT ABOUT ...?
I DIDN'T HEAR ANYTHING LIKE THAT FROM TAMAKI.
ON TOP OF THAT, KOTORI, WHO'S VERY CAUTIOUS, LOOKS LIKE SHE REALLY TRUSTS THIS PERSON...
GLANCE キョロ
GLANCE キョロ
COULD HE OR SHE HAVE SOMETHING TO DO WITH HELPING HER TRACK DOWN THE CULPRIT...?
I WAS WAITING FOR YOU, KOTORI-CHAAAN!

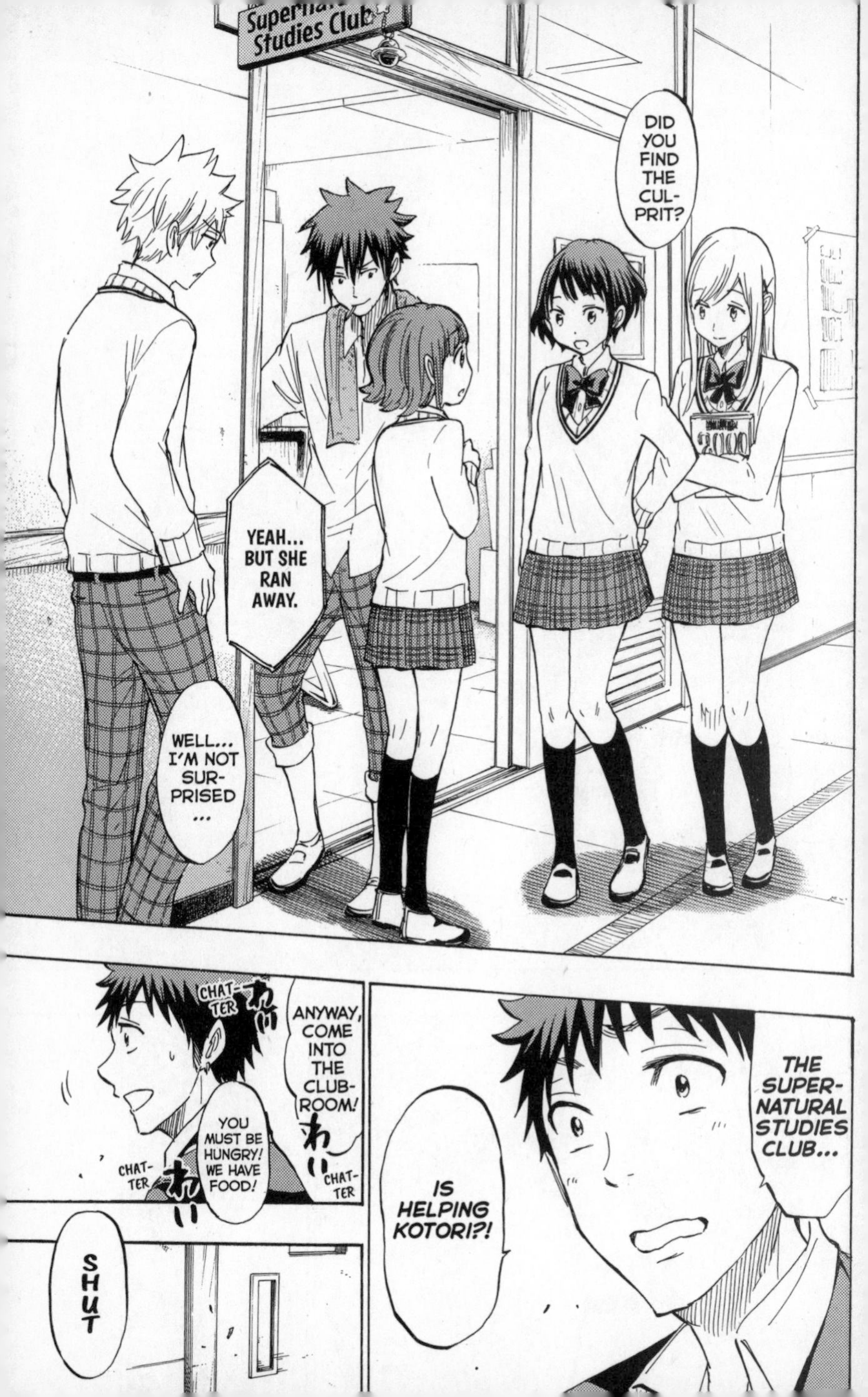
Studies Club
DID YOU FIND THE CULPRIT?
YEAH... BUT SHE RAN AWAY.
WELL... I'M NOT SURPRISED...
THE SUPERNATURAL STUDIES CLUB...
IS HELPING KOTORI?!
CHATTER
ANYWAY, COME INTO THE CLUBROOM!
YOU MUST BE HUNGRY! WE HAVE FOOD!
CHATTER
CHATTER
SHUT

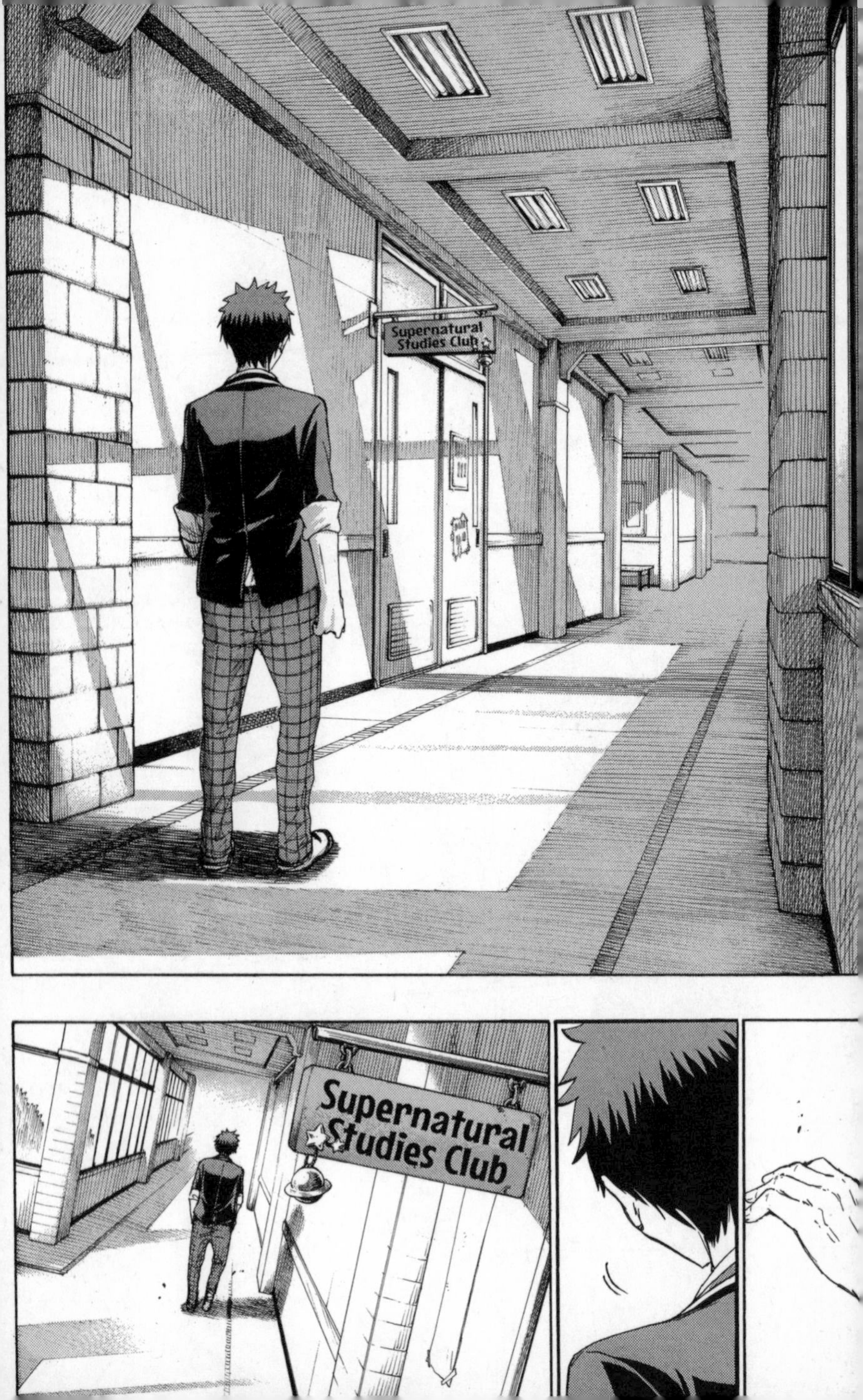
Supernatural Studies Club
Supernatural Studies Club

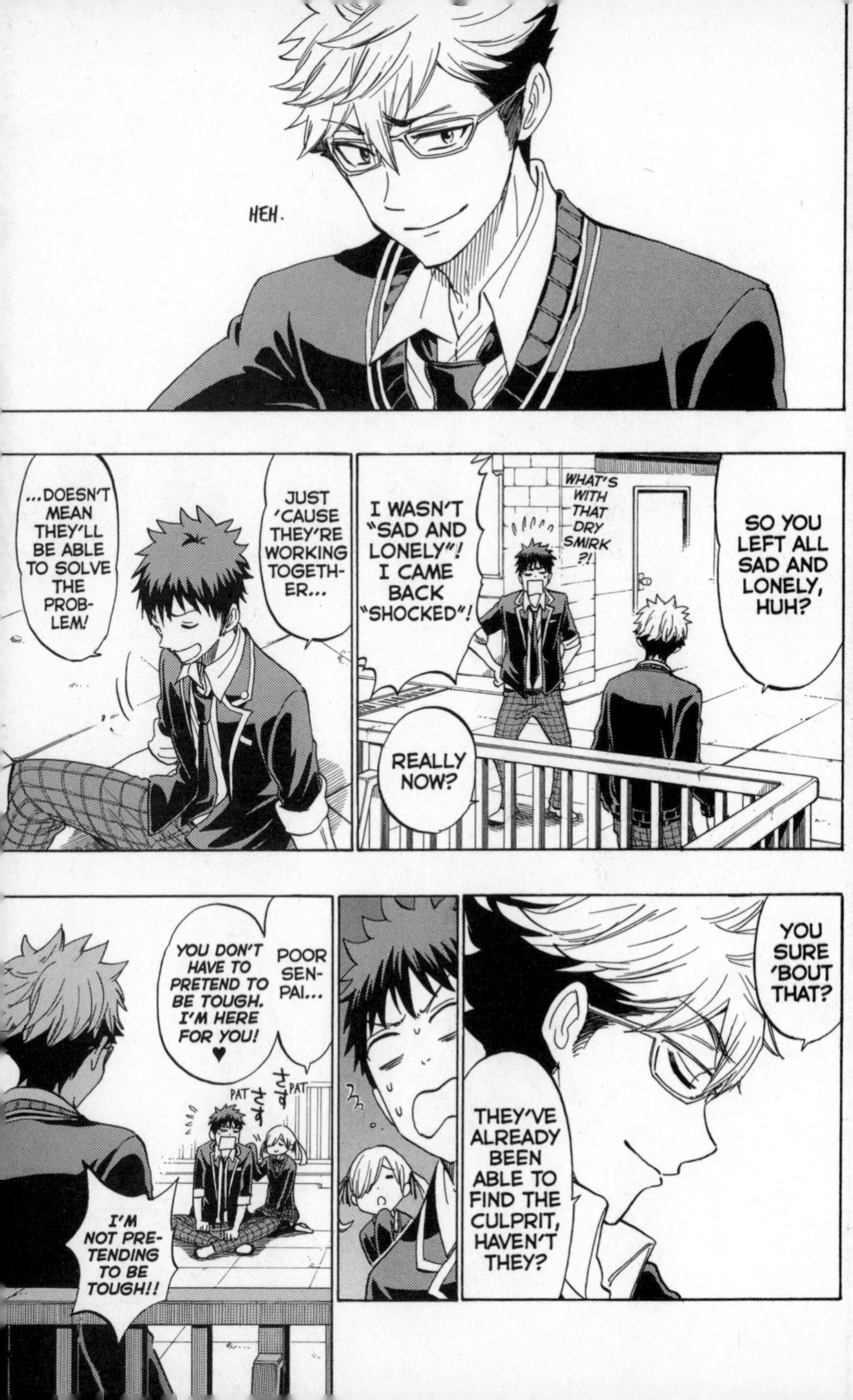
HEH.
SO YOU LEFT ALL SAD AND LONELY, HUH?
WHAT'S WITH THAT DRY SMIRK ?!
I WASN'T "SAD AND LONELY"! I CAME BACK "SHOCKED"!
REALLY NOW?
JUST 'CAUSE THEY'RE WORKING TOGETH-ER...
...DOESN'T MEAN THEY'LL BE ABLE TO SOLVE THE PROB-LEM!
YOU SURE 'BOUT THAT?
THEY'VE ALREADY BEEN ABLE TO FIND THE CULPRIT, HAVEN'T THEY?
POOR SEN-PAI...
YOU DON'T HAVE TO PRETEND TO BE TOUGH. I'M HERE FOR YOU! ♥
PAT さす
PAT さす
I'M NOT PRE-TENDING TO BE TOUGH!!

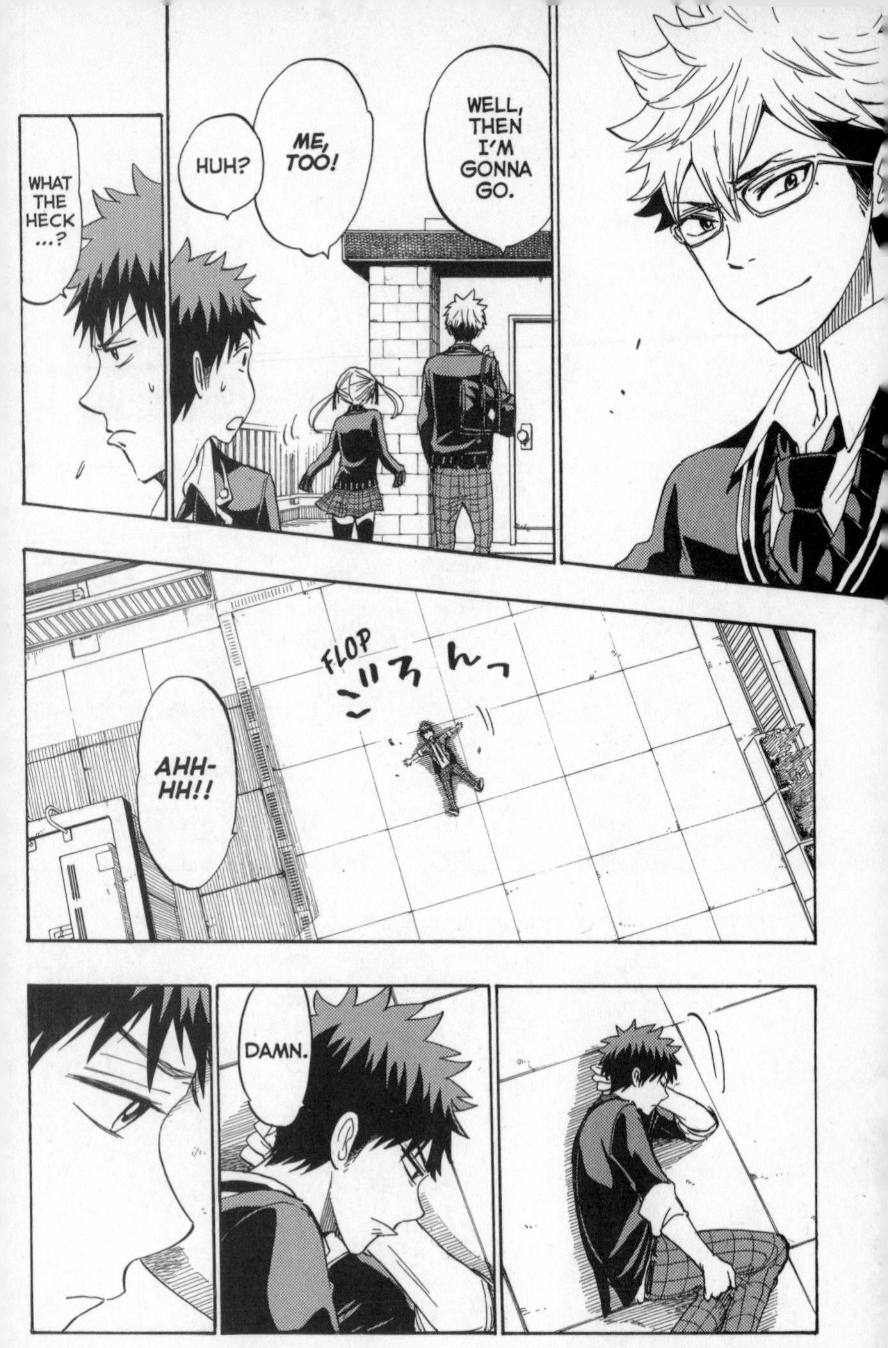
WELL, THEN I'M GONNA GO.
ME, TOO!
HUH?
WHAT THE HECK ...?
FLOP
ごろんっ
AHH-HH!!
DAMN.

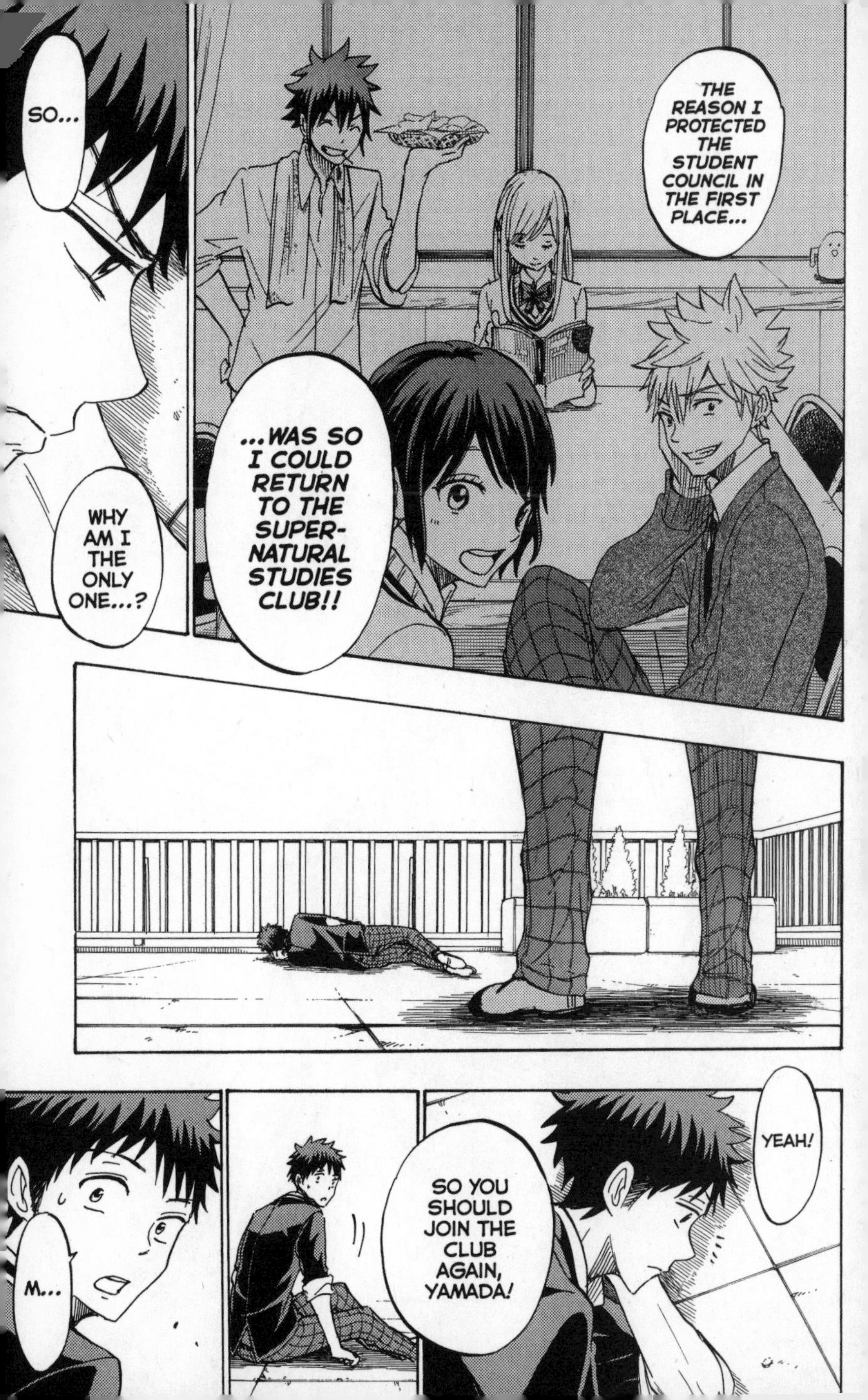
THE REASON I PROTECTED THE STUDENT COUNCIL IN THE FIRST PLACE...
...WAS SO I COULD RETURN TO THE SUPER-NATURAL STUDIES CLUB!!
SO...
WHY AM I THE ONLY ONE...?
YEAH!
SO YOU SHOULD JOIN THE CLUB AGAIN, YAMADA!
M...

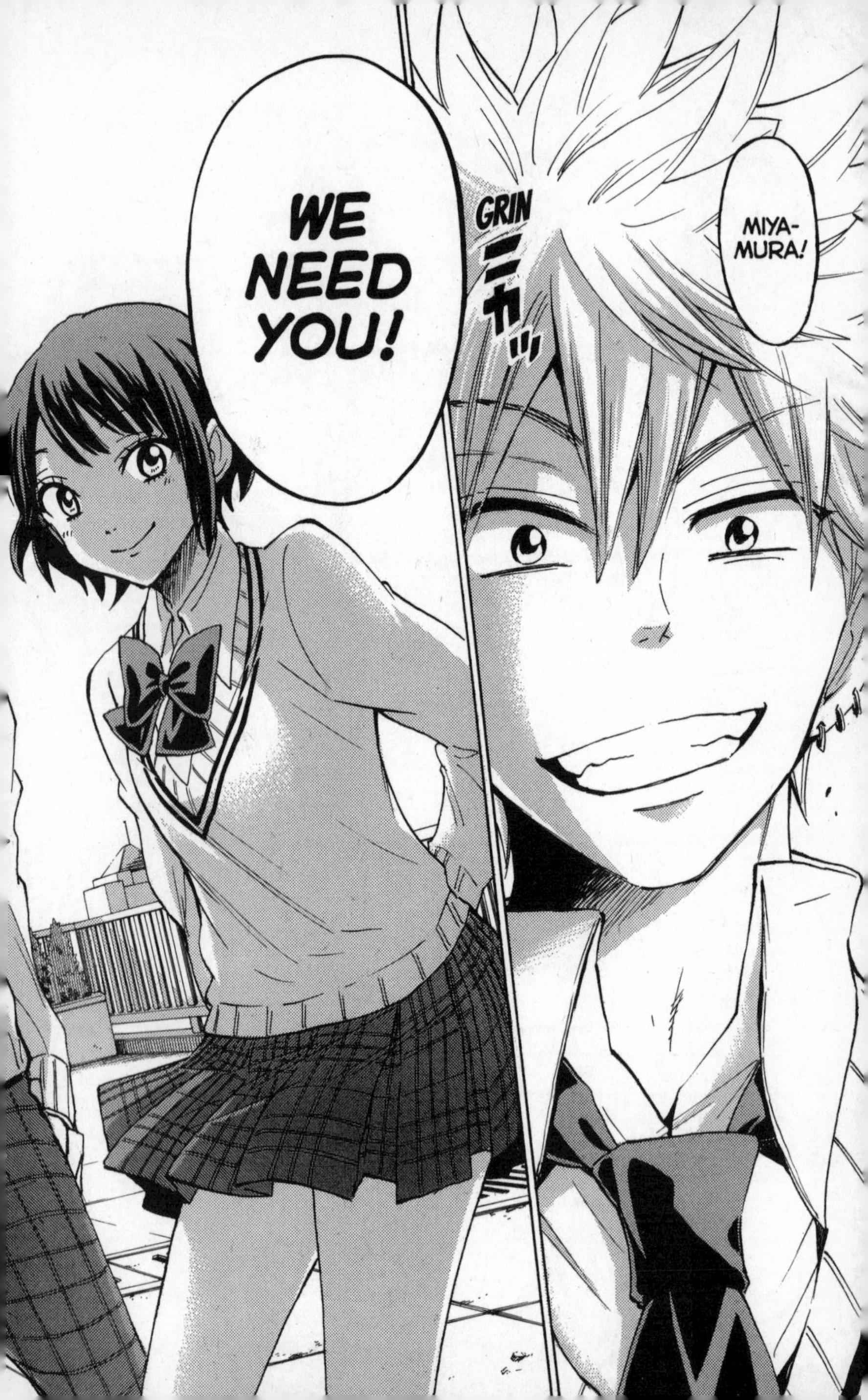
MIYA-
MURA!
GRIN
ニカッ
WE
NEED
YOU!

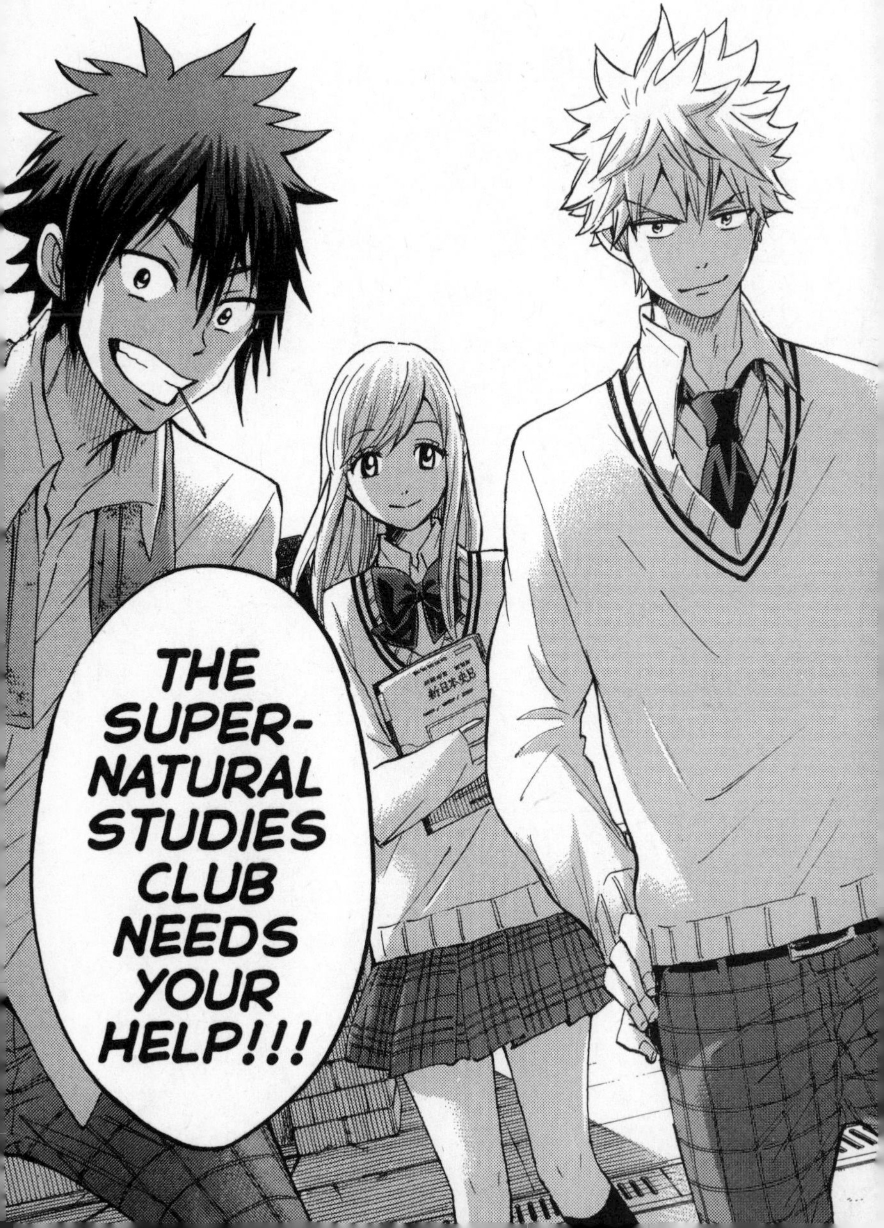
THE SUPER-NATURAL STUDIES CLUB NEEDS YOUR HELP!!!

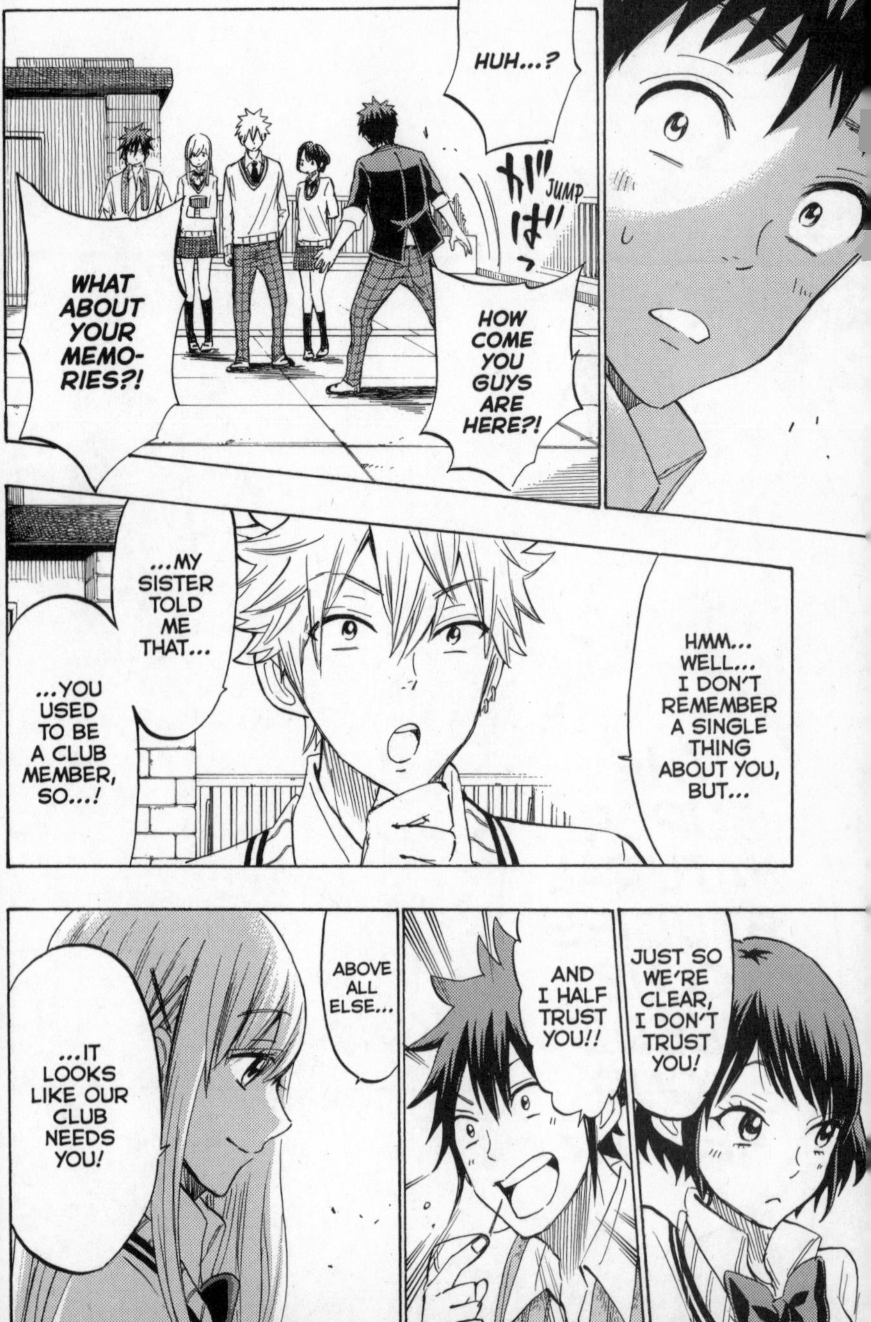
HUH...?
がばっ
JUMP
HOW COME YOU GUYS ARE HERE?!
WHAT ABOUT YOUR MEMO-RIES?!
HMM... WELL... I DON'T REMEMBER A SINGLE THING ABOUT YOU, BUT...
...MY SISTER TOLD ME THAT...
...YOU USED TO BE A CLUB MEMBER, SO...!
JUST SO WE'RE CLEAR, I DON'T TRUST YOU!
AND I HALF TRUST YOU!!
ABOVE ALL ELSE...
...IT LOOKS LIKE OUR CLUB NEEDS YOU!

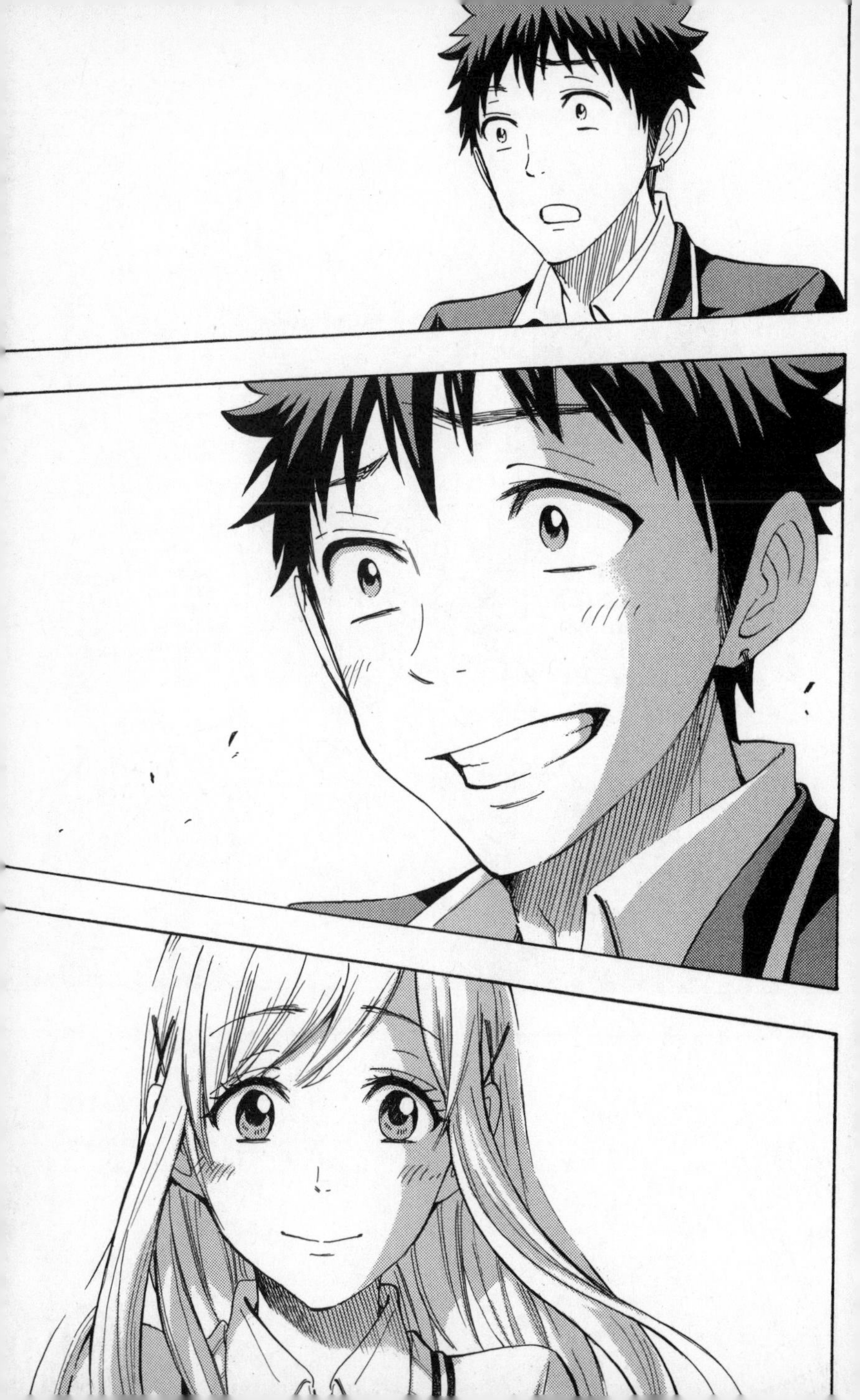

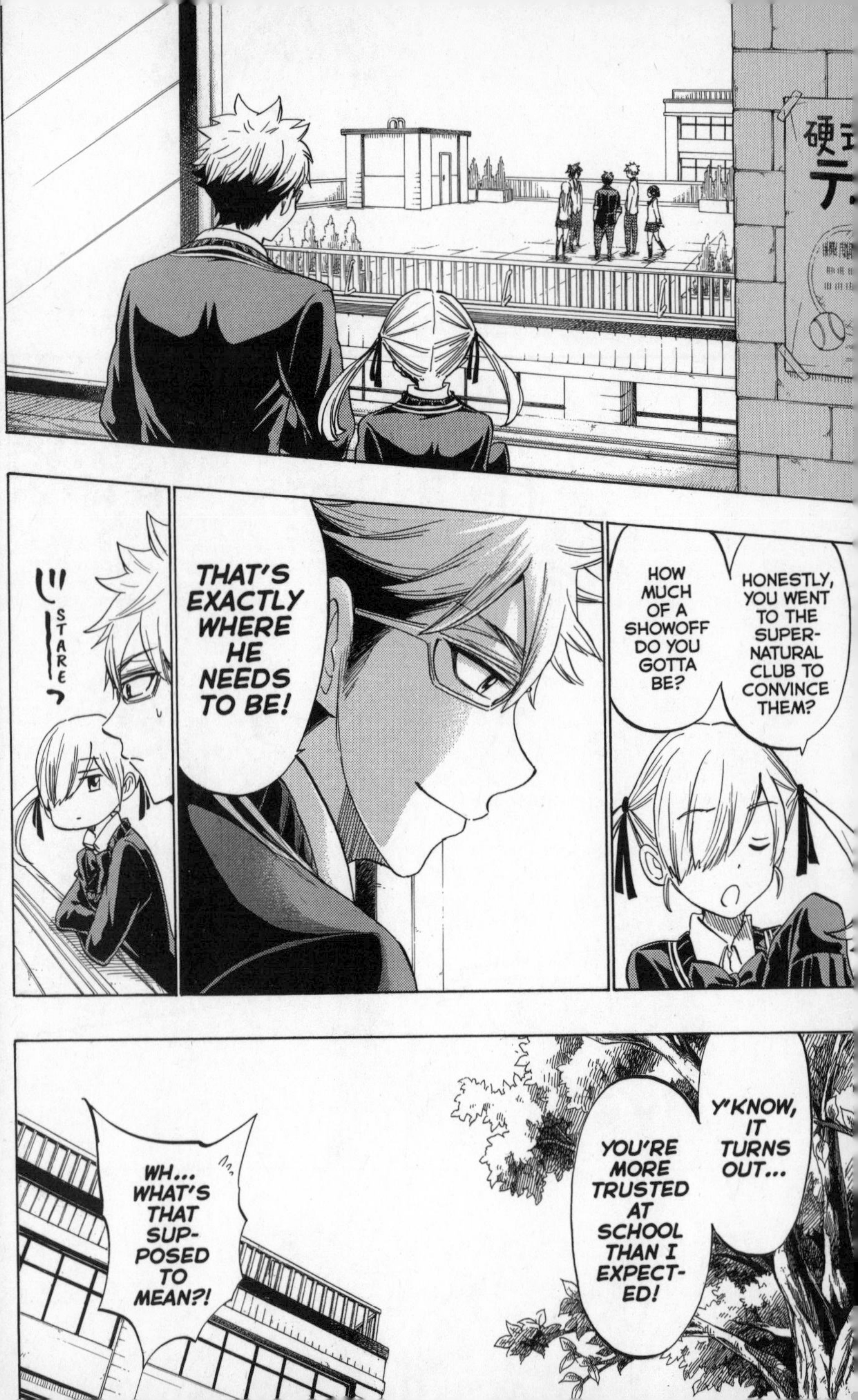
HONESTLY, YOU WENT TO THE SUPER-NATURAL CLUB TO CONVINCE THEM?
HOW MUCH OF A SHOWOFF DO YOU GOTTA BE?
THAT'S EXACTLY WHERE HE NEEDS TO BE!
じー STARE
Y'KNOW, IT TURNS OUT...
YOU'RE MORE TRUSTED AT SCHOOL THAN I EXPECTED!
WH... WHAT'S THAT SUPPOSED TO MEAN?!

CHAPTER 177: She's a high school girl, y'now?!

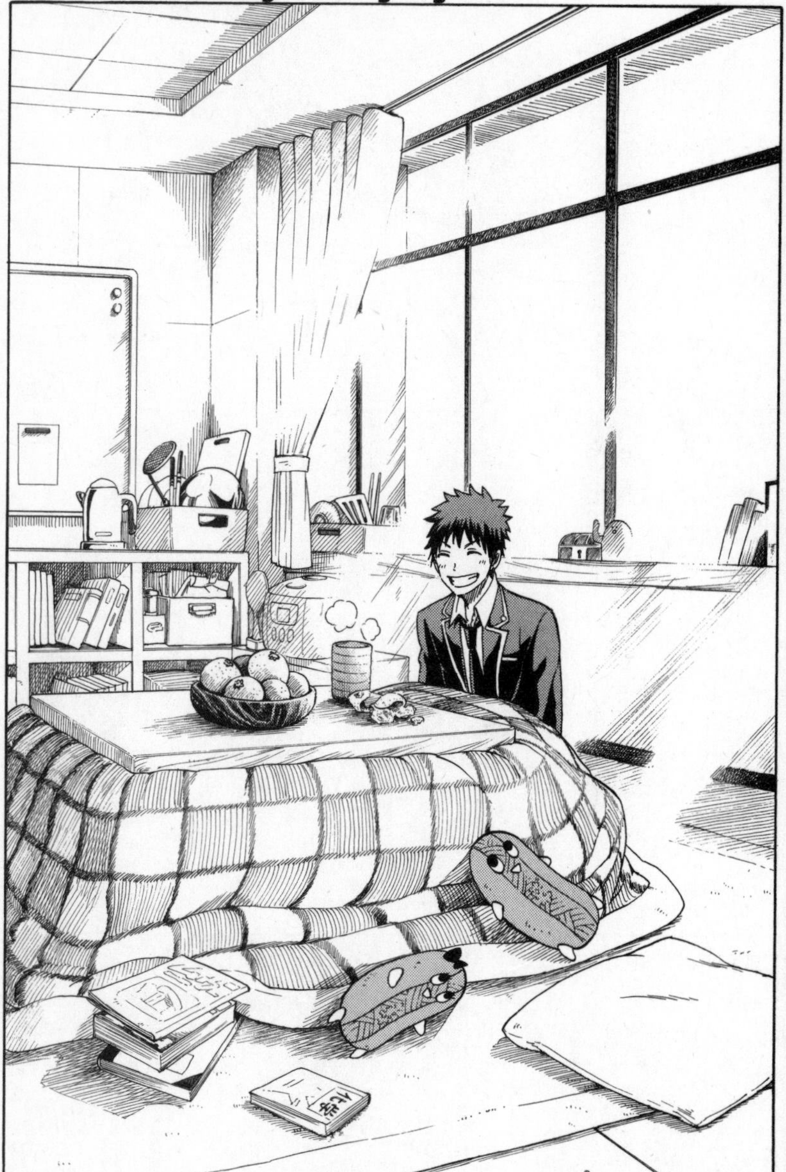

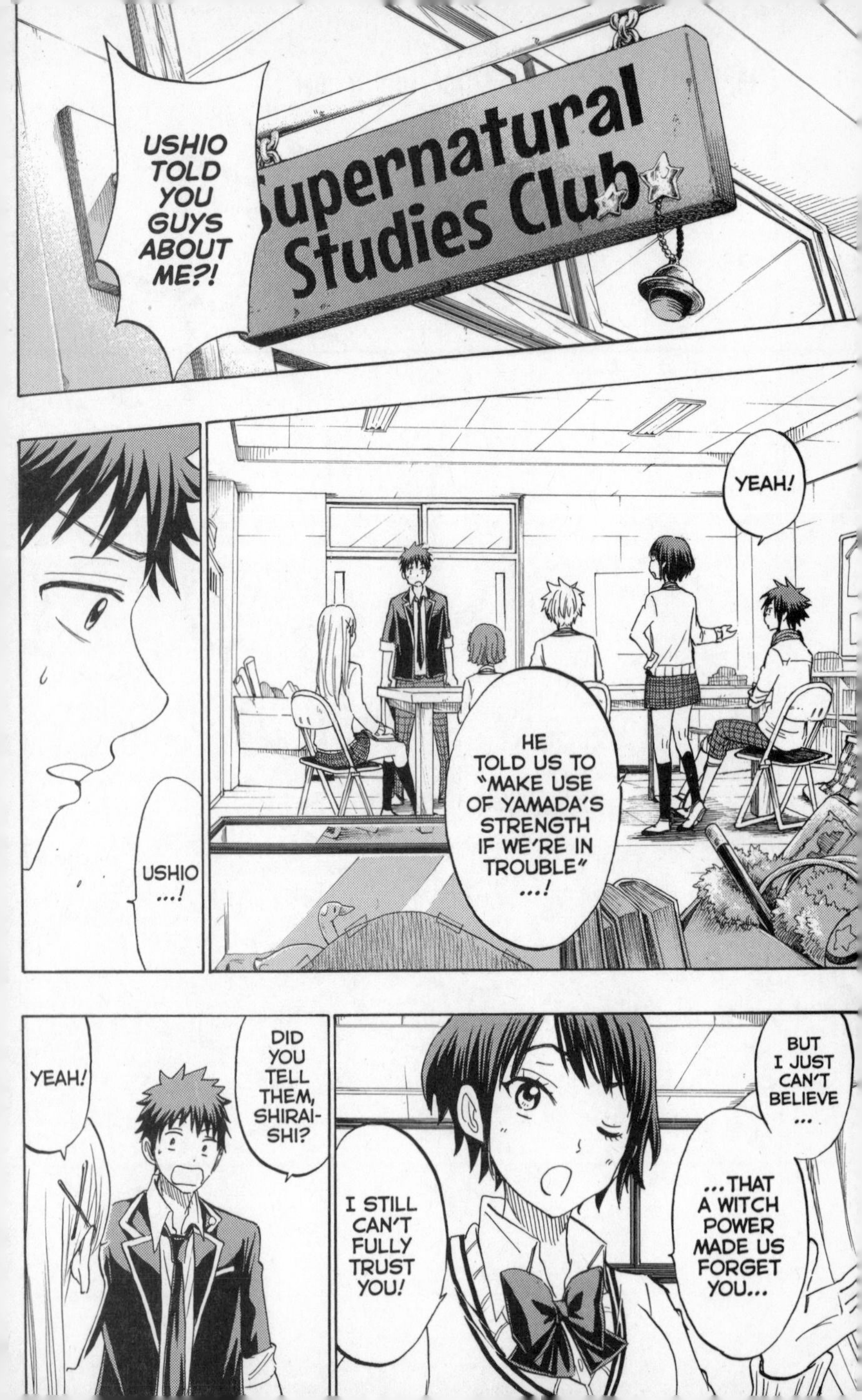
Supernatural Studies Club
USHIO TOLD YOU GUYS ABOUT ME?!
YEAH!
HE TOLD US TO "MAKE USE OF YAMADA'S STRENGTH IF WE'RE IN TROUBLE" ...!
USHIO ...!
BUT I JUST CAN'T BELIEVE ...
...THAT A WITCH POWER MADE US FORGET YOU...
I STILL CAN'T FULLY TRUST YOU!
DID YOU TELL THEM, SHIRAISHI?
YEAH!

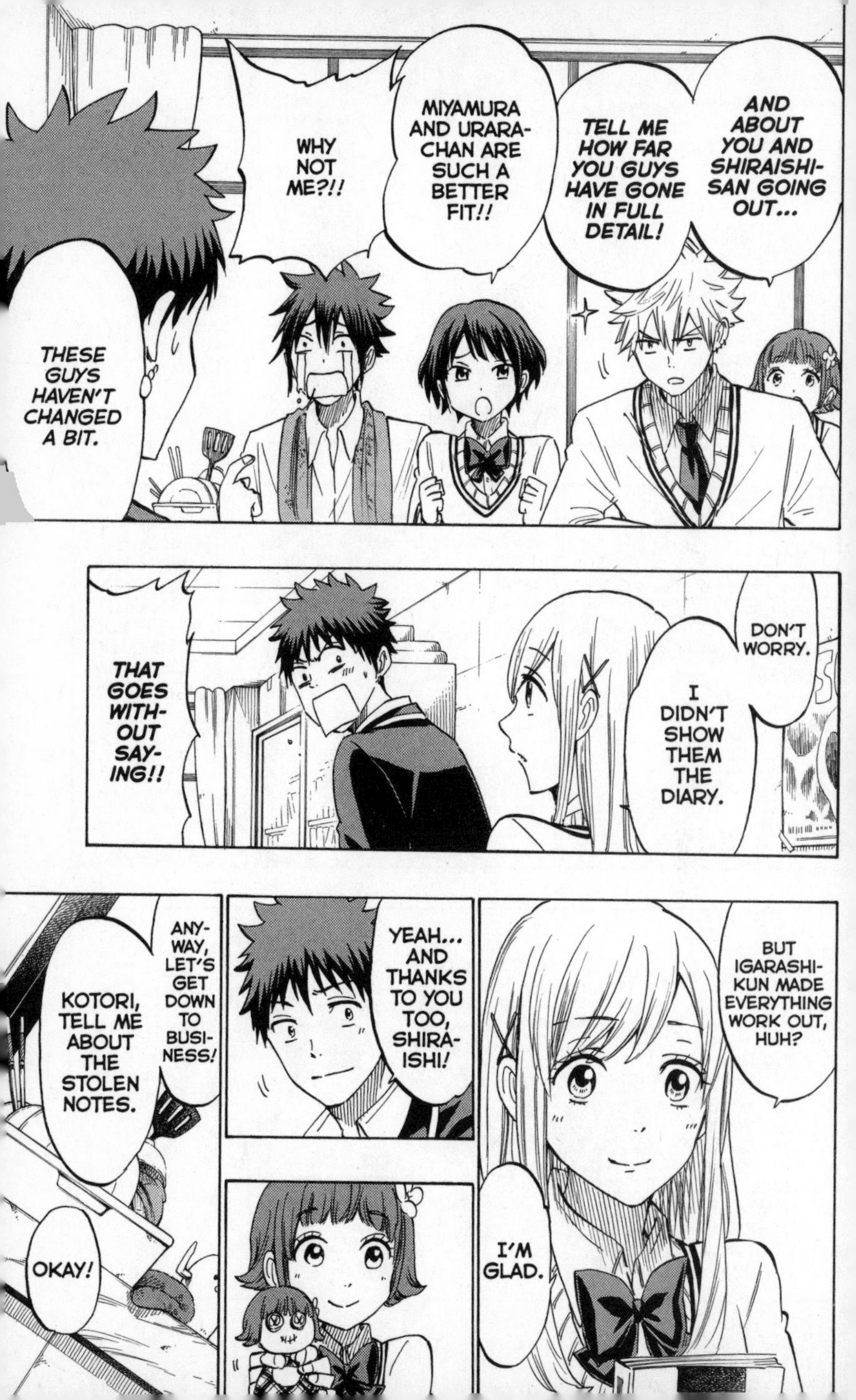
AND ABOUT YOU AND SHIRAISHI-SAN GOING OUT...
TELL ME HOW FAR YOU GUYS HAVE GONE IN FULL DETAIL!
MIYAMURA AND URARA-CHAN ARE SUCH A BETTER FIT!!
WHY NOT ME?!!
THESE GUYS HAVEN'T CHANGED A BIT.
DON'T WORRY.
I DIDN'T SHOW THEM THE DIARY.
THAT GOES WITH-OUT SAY-ING!!
BUT IGARASHI-KUN MADE EVERYTHING WORK OUT, HUH?
I'M GLAD.
YEAH... AND THANKS TO YOU TOO, SHIRA-ISHI!
ANY-WAY, LET'S GET DOWN TO BUSI-NESS!
KOTORI, TELL ME ABOUT THE STOLEN NOTES.
OKAY!

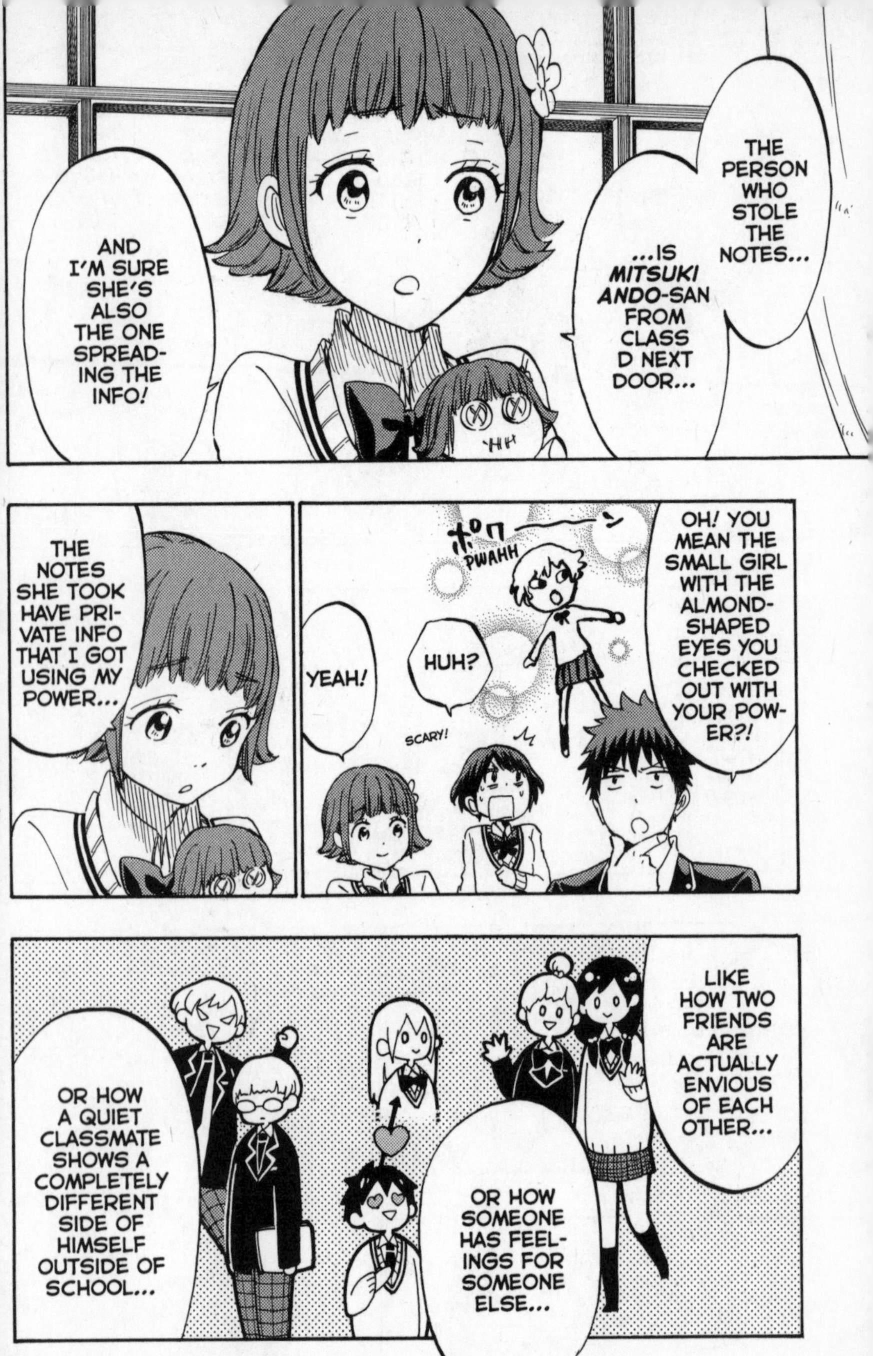
THE PERSON WHO STOLE THE NOTES...
...IS MITSUKI ANDO-SAN FROM CLASS D NEXT DOOR...
AND I'M SURE SHE'S ALSO THE ONE SPREADING THE INFO!
OH! YOU MEAN THE SMALL GIRL WITH THE ALMOND-SHAPED EYES YOU CHECKED OUT WITH YOUR POWER?!
ポワーン
PWAHH
HUH?
SCARY!
YEAH!
THE NOTES SHE TOOK HAVE PRIVATE INFO THAT I GOT USING MY POWER...
LIKE HOW TWO FRIENDS ARE ACTUALLY ENVIOUS OF EACH OTHER...
OR HOW SOMEONE HAS FEELINGS FOR SOMEONE ELSE...
OR HOW A QUIET CLASSMATE SHOWS A COMPLETELY DIFFERENT SIDE OF HIMSELF OUTSIDE OF SCHOOL...

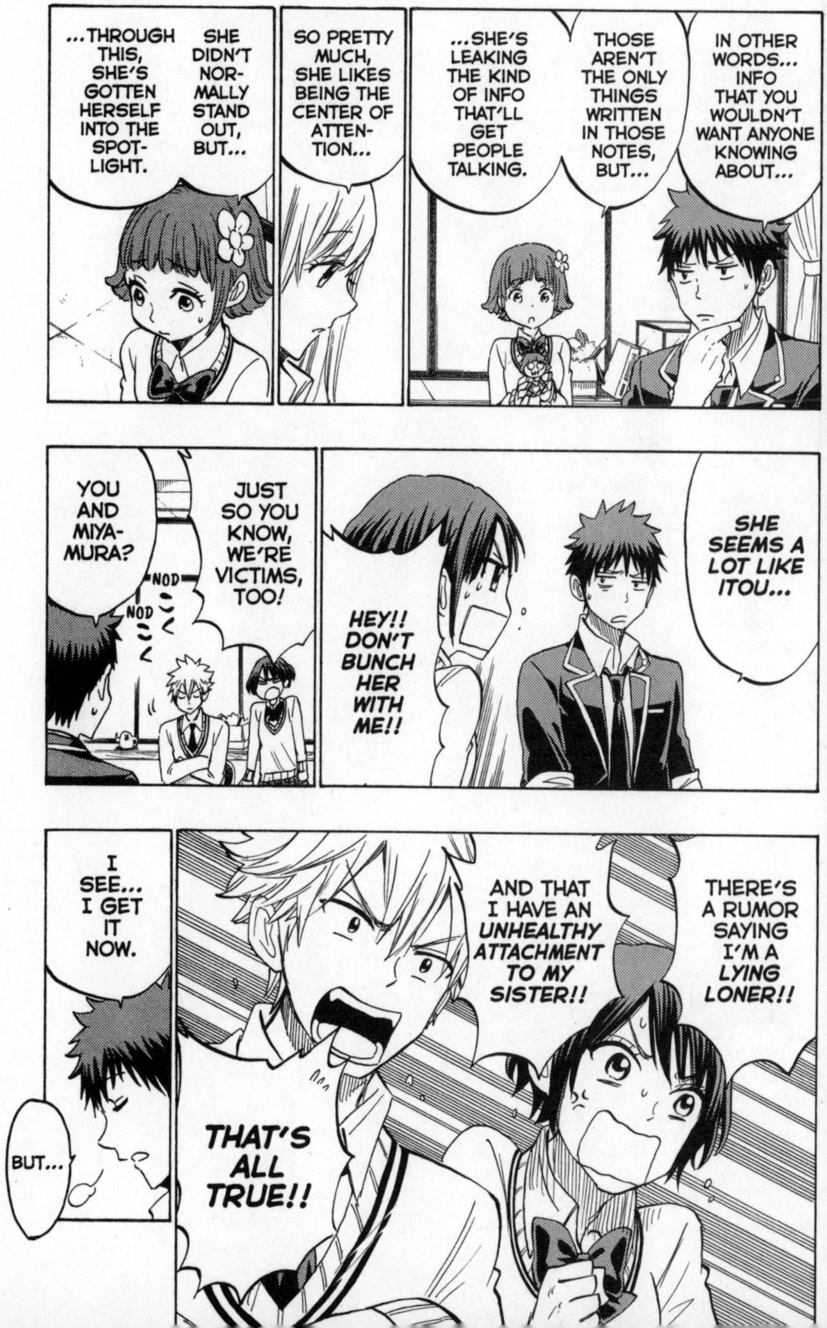
IN OTHER WORDS... INFO THAT YOU WOULDN'T WANT ANYONE KNOWING ABOUT...
THOSE AREN'T THE ONLY THINGS WRITTEN IN THOSE NOTES, BUT...
...SHE'S LEAKING THE KIND OF INFO THAT'LL GET PEOPLE TALKING.
SO PRETTY MUCH, SHE LIKES BEING THE CENTER OF ATTENTION...
SHE DIDN'T NORMALLY STAND OUT, BUT...
...THROUGH THIS, SHE'S GOTTEN HERSELF INTO THE SPOTLIGHT.
SHE SEEMS A LOT LIKE ITOU...
HEY!! DON'T BUNCH HER WITH ME!!
JUST SO YOU KNOW, WE'RE VICTIMS, TOO!
YOU AND MIYAMURA?
NOD こく
NOD こく
THERE'S A RUMOR SAYING I'M A LYING LONER!!
AND THAT I HAVE AN UNHEALTHY ATTACHMENT TO MY SISTER!!
THAT'S ALL TRUE!!
I SEE... I GET IT NOW.
BUT...

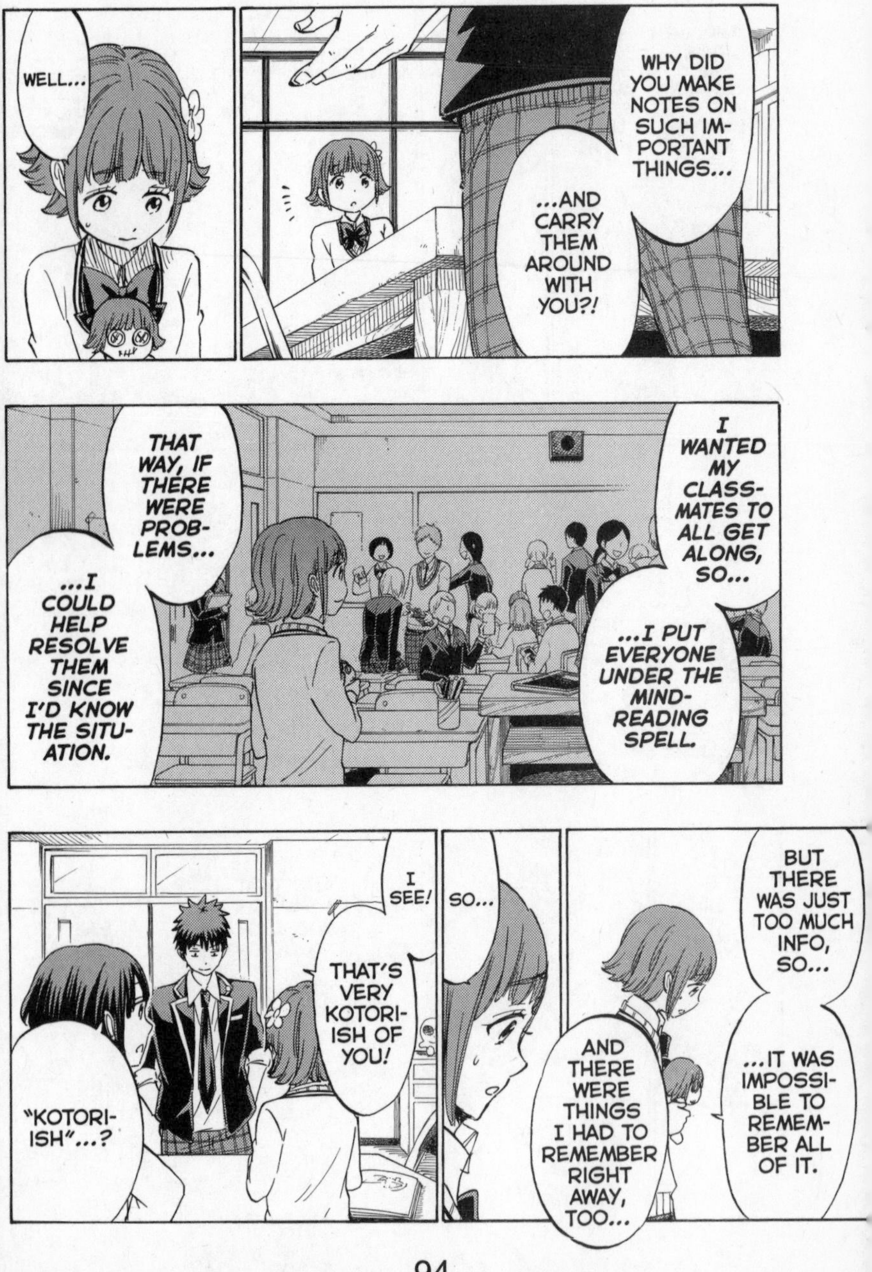
WHY DID YOU MAKE NOTES ON SUCH IMPORTANT THINGS...
...AND CARRY THEM AROUND WITH YOU?!
WELL...
I WANTED MY CLASSMATES TO ALL GET ALONG, SO...
...I PUT EVERYONE UNDER THE MIND-READING SPELL.
THAT WAY, IF THERE WERE PROBLEMS...
...I COULD HELP RESOLVE THEM SINCE I'D KNOW THE SITUATION.
BUT THERE WAS JUST TOO MUCH INFO, SO...
...IT WAS IMPOSSIBLE TO REMEMBER ALL OF IT.
AND THERE WERE THINGS I HAD TO REMEMBER RIGHT AWAY, TOO...
SO...
I SEE!
THAT'S VERY KOTORI-ISH OF YOU!
"KOTORI-ISH"...?

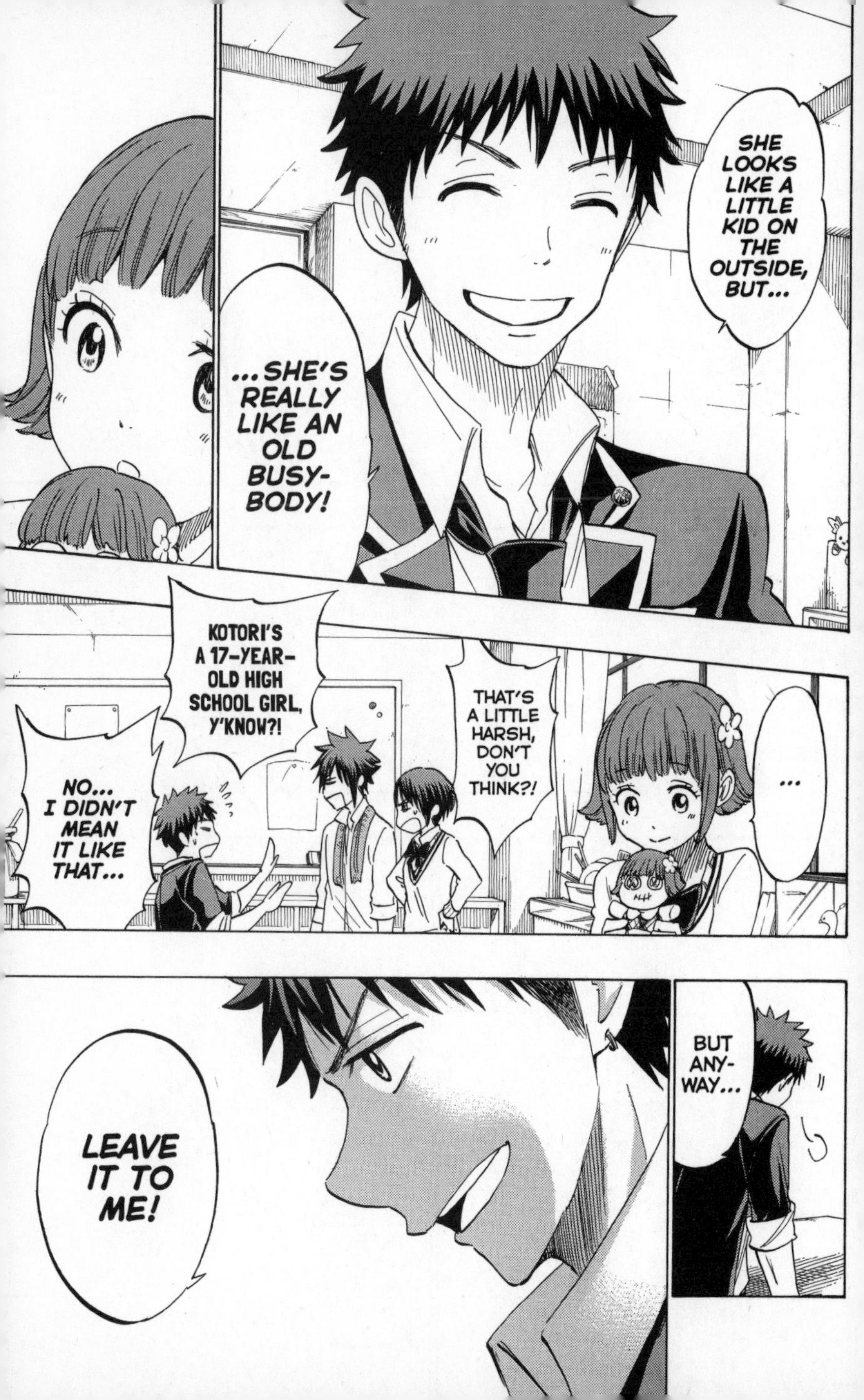
SHE LOOKS LIKE A LITTLE KID ON THE OUTSIDE, BUT...
...SHE'S REALLY LIKE AN OLD BUSY-BODY!
...
THAT'S A LITTLE HARSH, DON'T YOU THINK?!
KOTORI'S A 17-YEAR-OLD HIGH SCHOOL GIRL, Y'KNOW?!
NO... I DIDN'T MEAN IT LIKE THAT...
BUT ANY-WAY...
LEAVE IT TO ME!

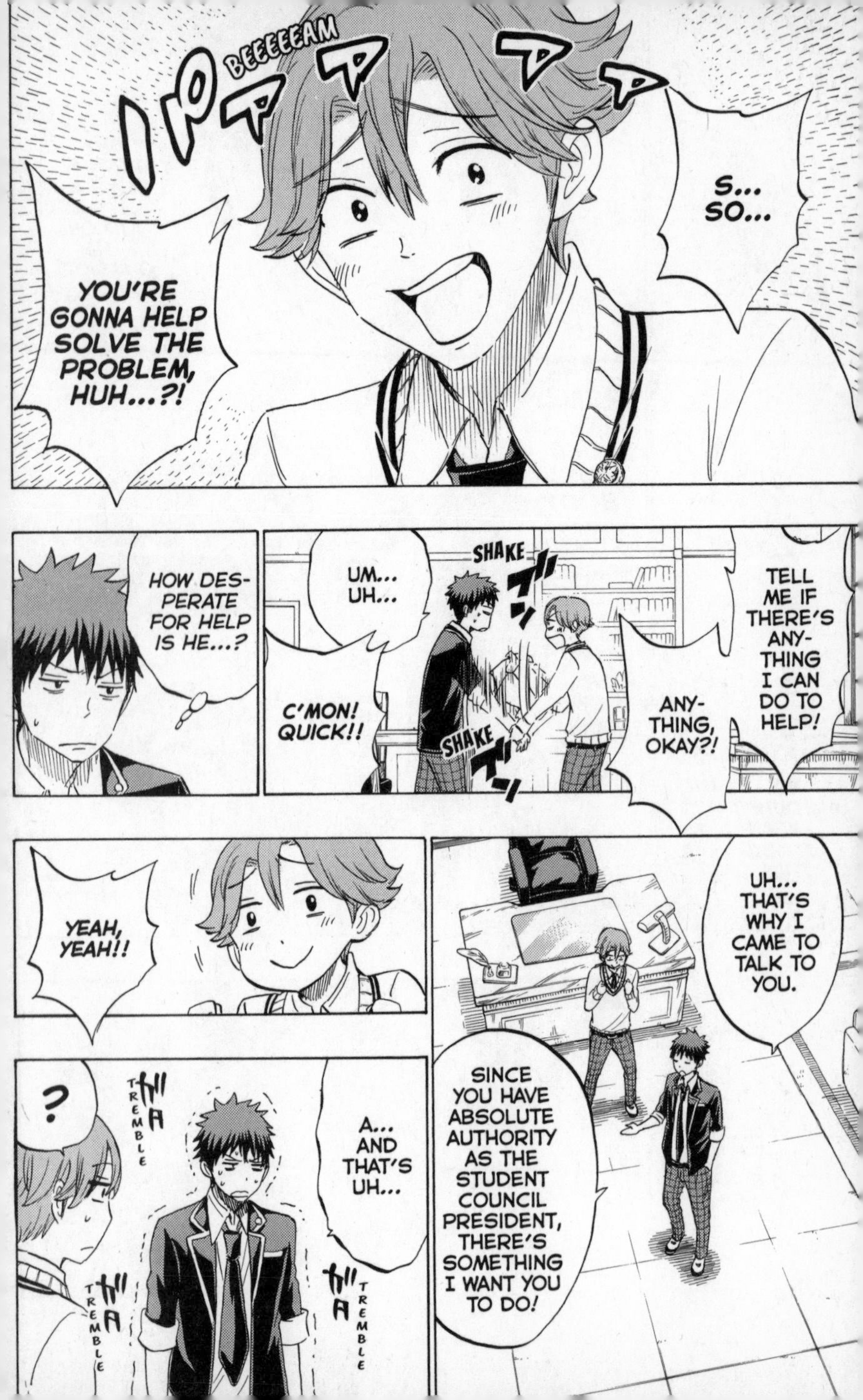
BEEEEEAM
S... SO...
YOU'RE GONNA HELP SOLVE THE PROBLEM, HUH...?!
TELL ME IF THERE'S ANY-THING I CAN DO TO HELP!
ANY-THING, OKAY?!
SHAKE
UM... UH...
C'MON! QUICK!!
SHAKE
HOW DES-PERATE FOR HELP IS HE...?
UH... THAT'S WHY I CAME TO TALK TO YOU.
SINCE YOU HAVE ABSOLUTE AUTHORITY AS THE STUDENT COUNCIL PRESIDENT, THERE'S SOMETHING I WANT YOU TO DO!
YEAH, YEAH!!
A... AND THAT'S UH...
TREMBLE
TREMBLE
TREMBLE
?

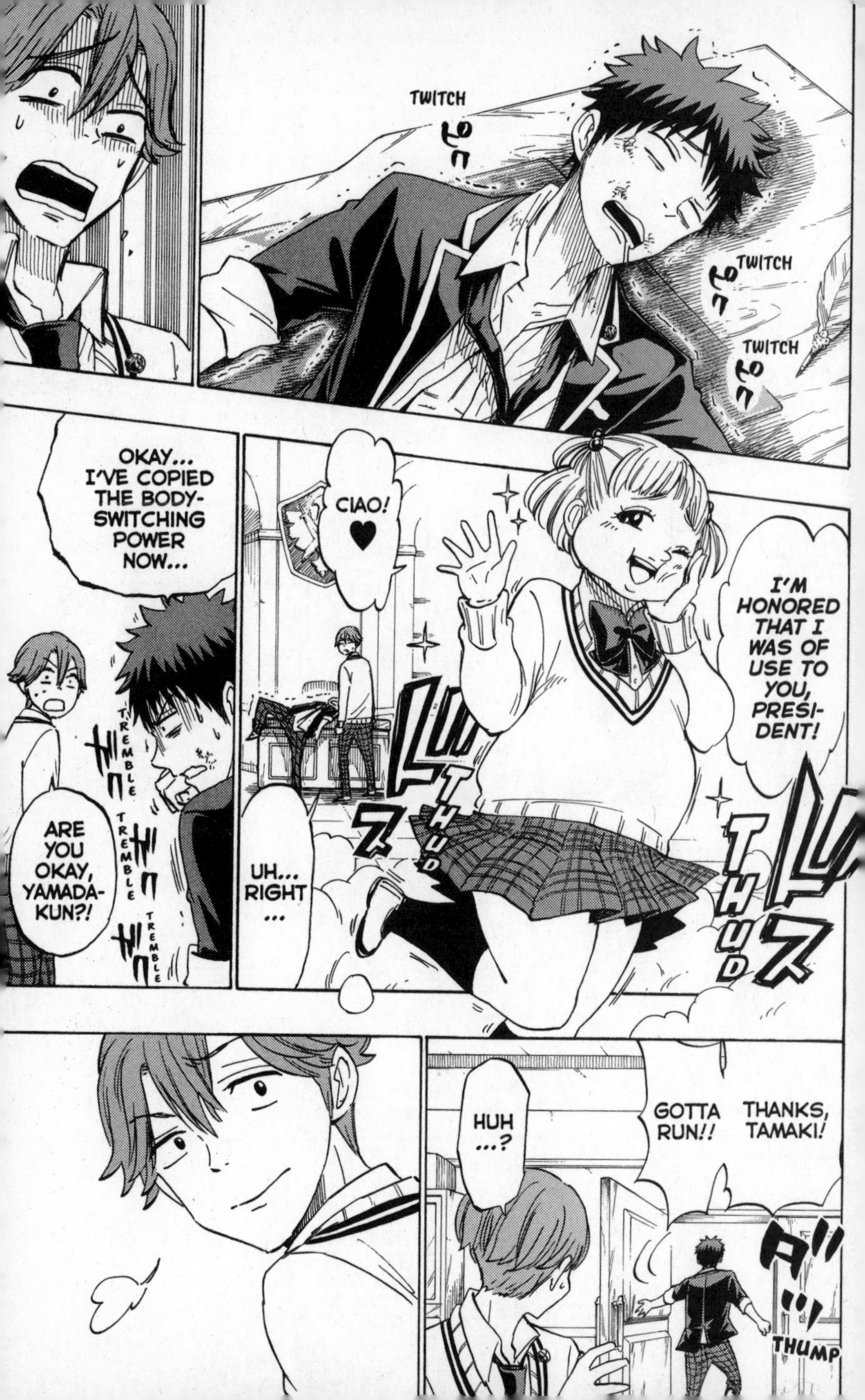
TWITCH
TWITCH
TWITCH
I'M HONORED THAT I WAS OF USE TO YOU, PRESIDENT!
THUD
CIAO! ♥
THUD
UH... RIGHT...
OKAY... I'VE COPIED THE BODY-SWITCHING POWER NOW...
TREMBLE
TREMBLE
TREMBLE
ARE YOU OKAY, YAMADA-KUN?!
THANKS, TAMAKI!
GOTTA RUN!!
THUMP
HUH...?

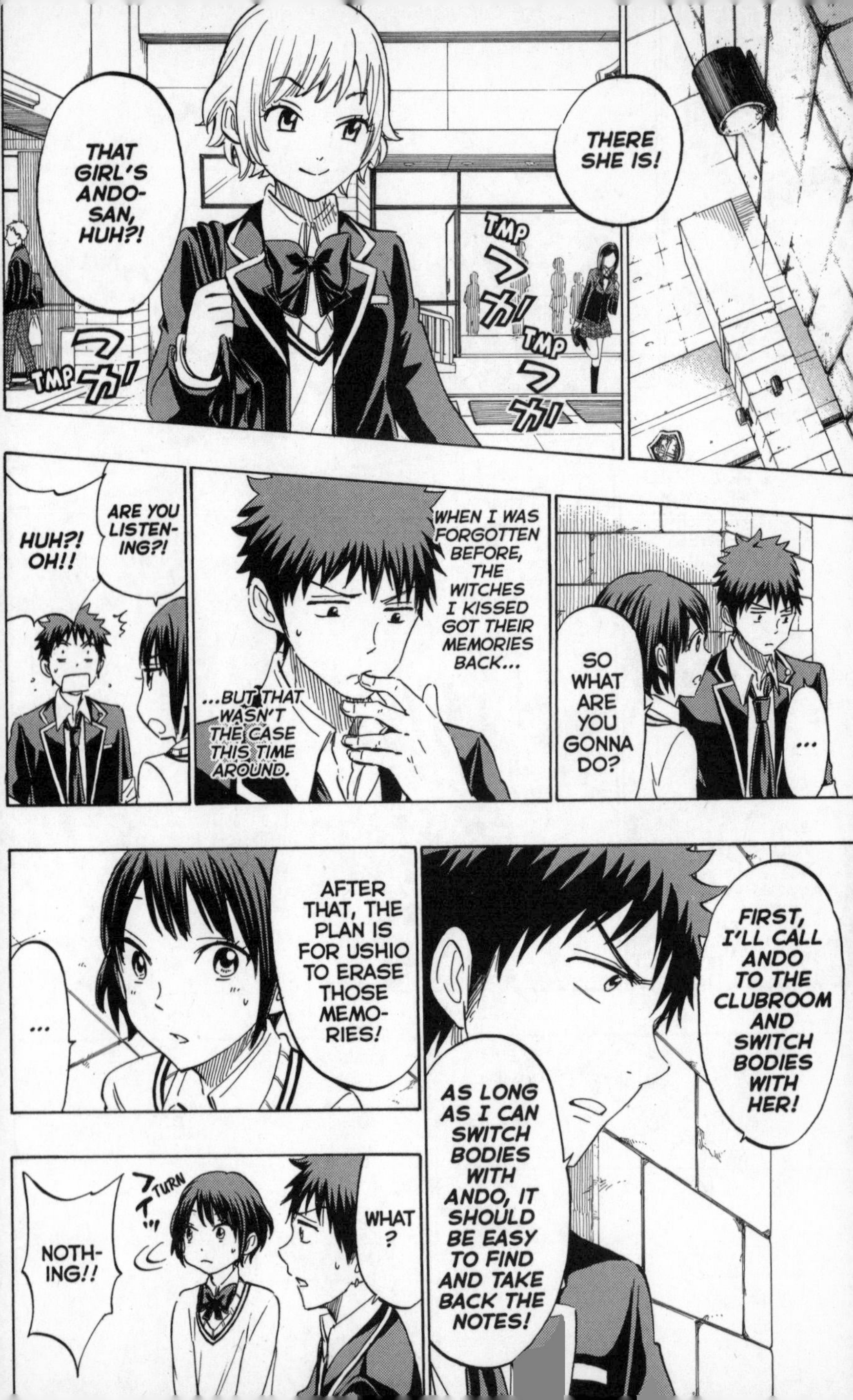
THERE SHE IS!
TMP
TMP
THAT GIRL'S ANDO-SAN, HUH?!
TMP
SO WHAT ARE YOU GONNA DO?
...
WHEN I WAS FORGOTTEN BEFORE, THE WITCHES I KISSED GOT THEIR MEMORIES BACK...
...BUT THAT WASN'T THE CASE THIS TIME AROUND.
ARE YOU LISTEN-ING?!
HUH?! OH!!
FIRST, I'LL CALL ANDO TO THE CLUBROOM AND SWITCH BODIES WITH HER!
AFTER THAT, THE PLAN IS FOR USHIO TO ERASE THOSE MEMO-RIES!
...
AS LONG AS I CAN SWITCH BODIES WITH ANDO, IT SHOULD BE EASY TO FIND AND TAKE BACK THE NOTES!
WHAT?
TURN
NOTH-ING!!

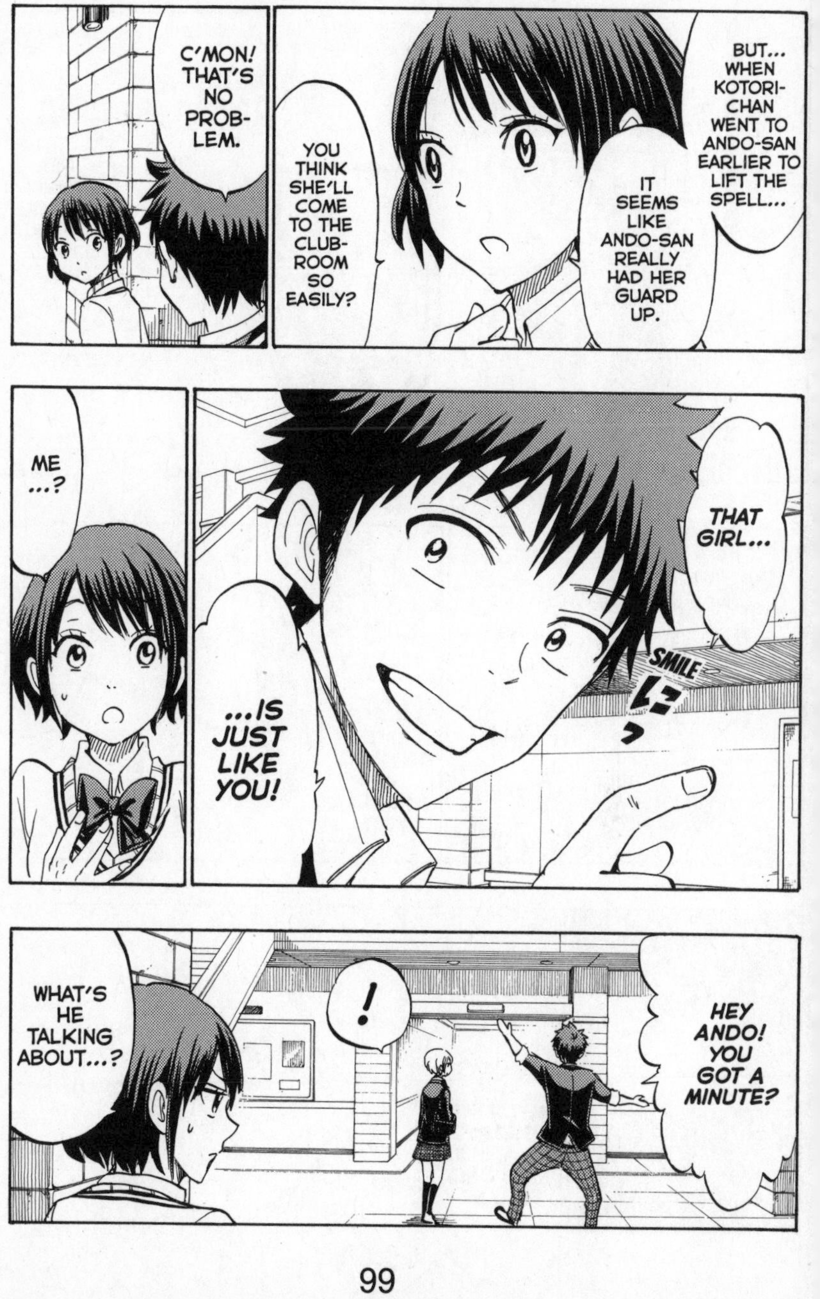
BUT... WHEN KOTORI-CHAN WENT TO ANDO-SAN EARLIER TO LIFT THE SPELL...
IT SEEMS LIKE ANDO-SAN REALLY HAD HER GUARD UP.
YOU THINK SHE'LL COME TO THE CLUB-ROOM SO EASILY?
C'MON! THAT'S NO PROB-LEM.
THAT GIRL...
SMILE
...IS JUST LIKE YOU!
ME ...?
HEY ANDO! YOU GOT A MINUTE?
!
WHAT'S HE TALKING ABOUT...?

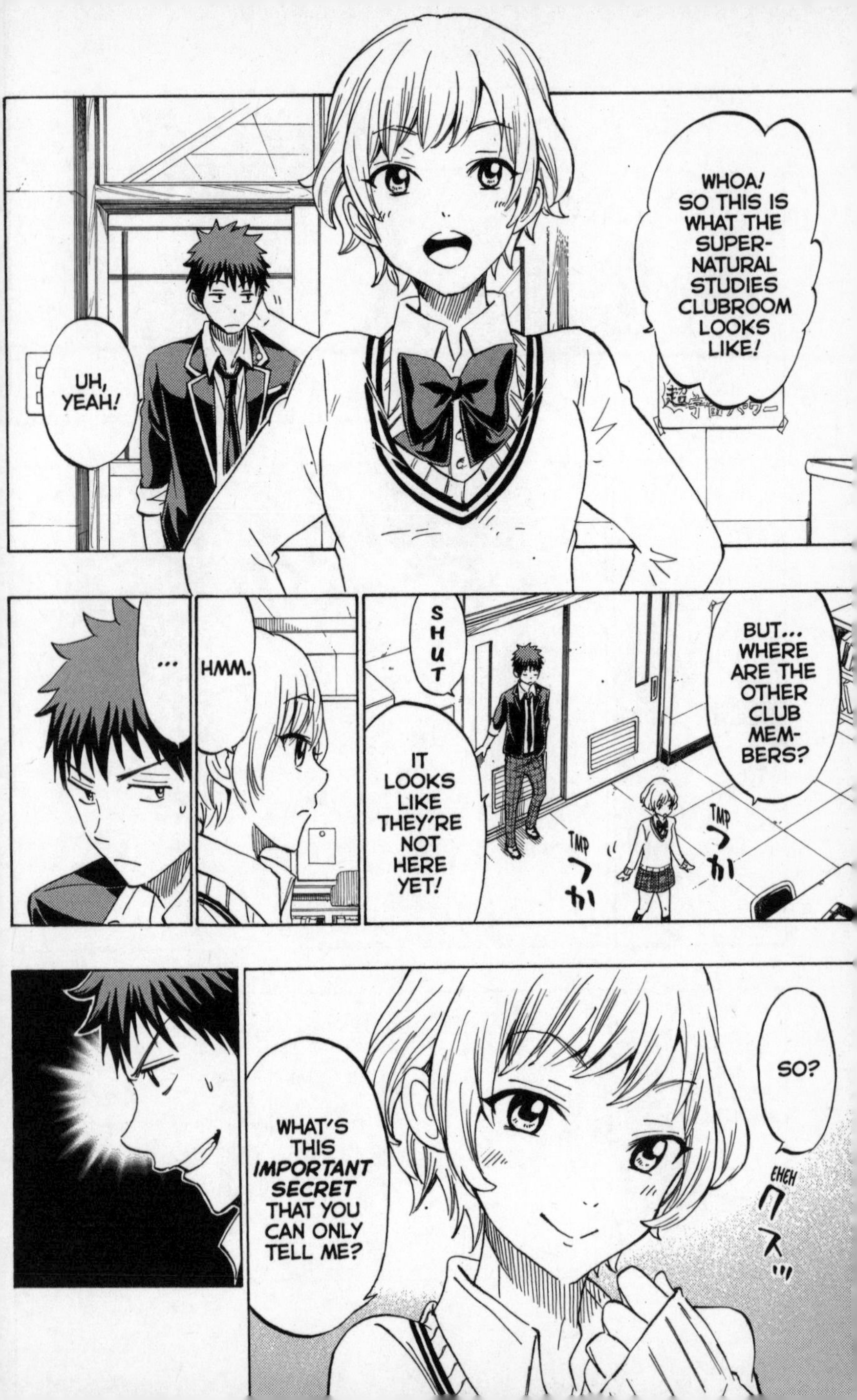
WHOA! SO THIS IS WHAT THE SUPER-NATURAL STUDIES CLUBROOM LOOKS LIKE!
UH, YEAH!
BUT... WHERE ARE THE OTHER CLUB MEM-BERS?
TMP つか
SHUT
IT LOOKS LIKE THEY'RE NOT HERE YET!
TMP つか
HMM.
...
SO?
EHEH クスッ
WHAT'S THIS *IMPORTANT SECRET* THAT YOU CAN ONLY TELL ME?

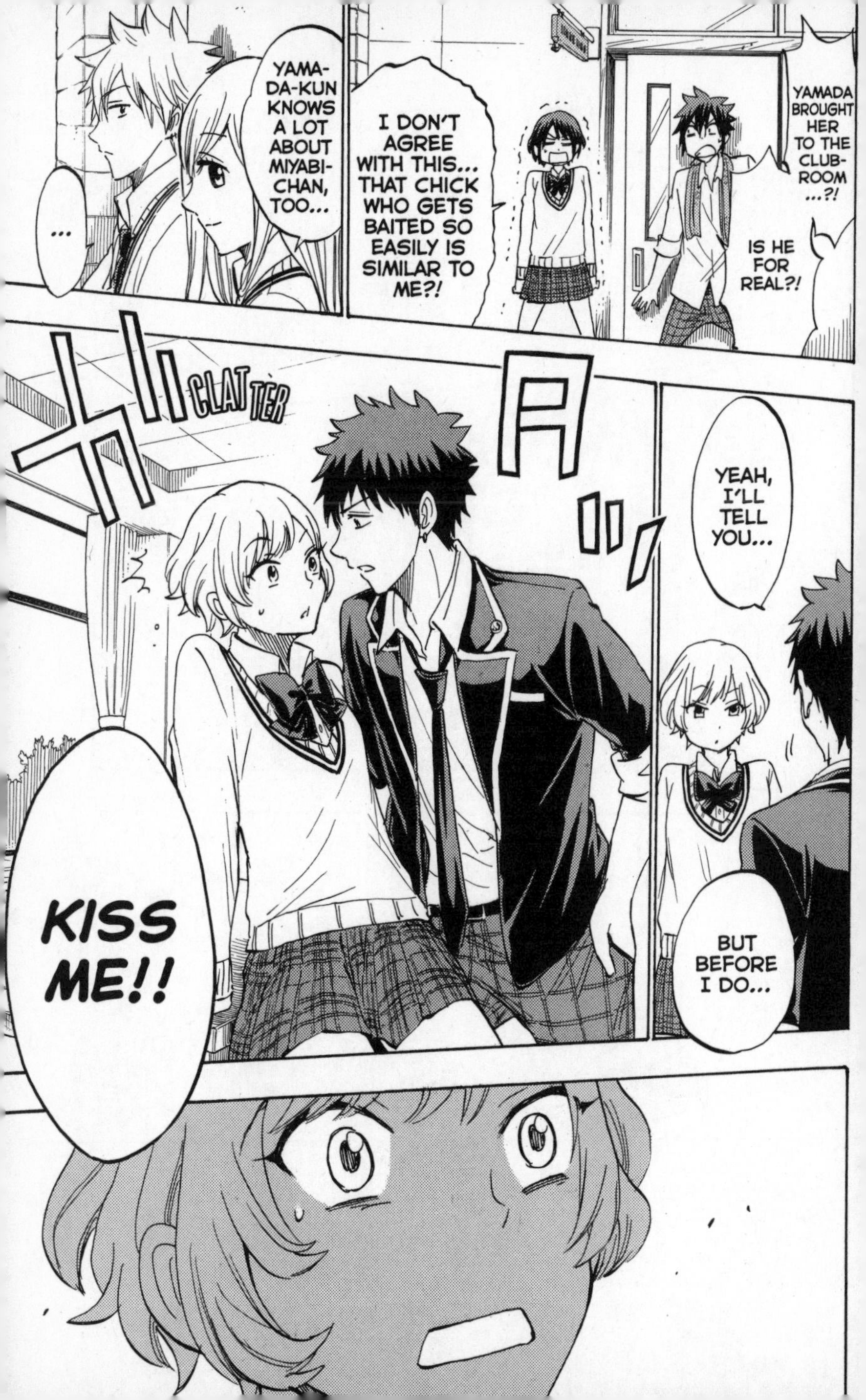
YAMADA BROUGHT HER TO THE CLUB-ROOM...?!
IS HE FOR REAL?!
I DON'T AGREE WITH THIS... THAT CHICK WHO GETS BAITED SO EASILY IS SIMILAR TO ME?!
YAMA-DA-KUN KNOWS A LOT ABOUT MIYABI-CHAN, TOO...
...
YEAH, I'LL TELL YOU...
BUT BEFORE I DO...
CLATTER
KISS ME!!

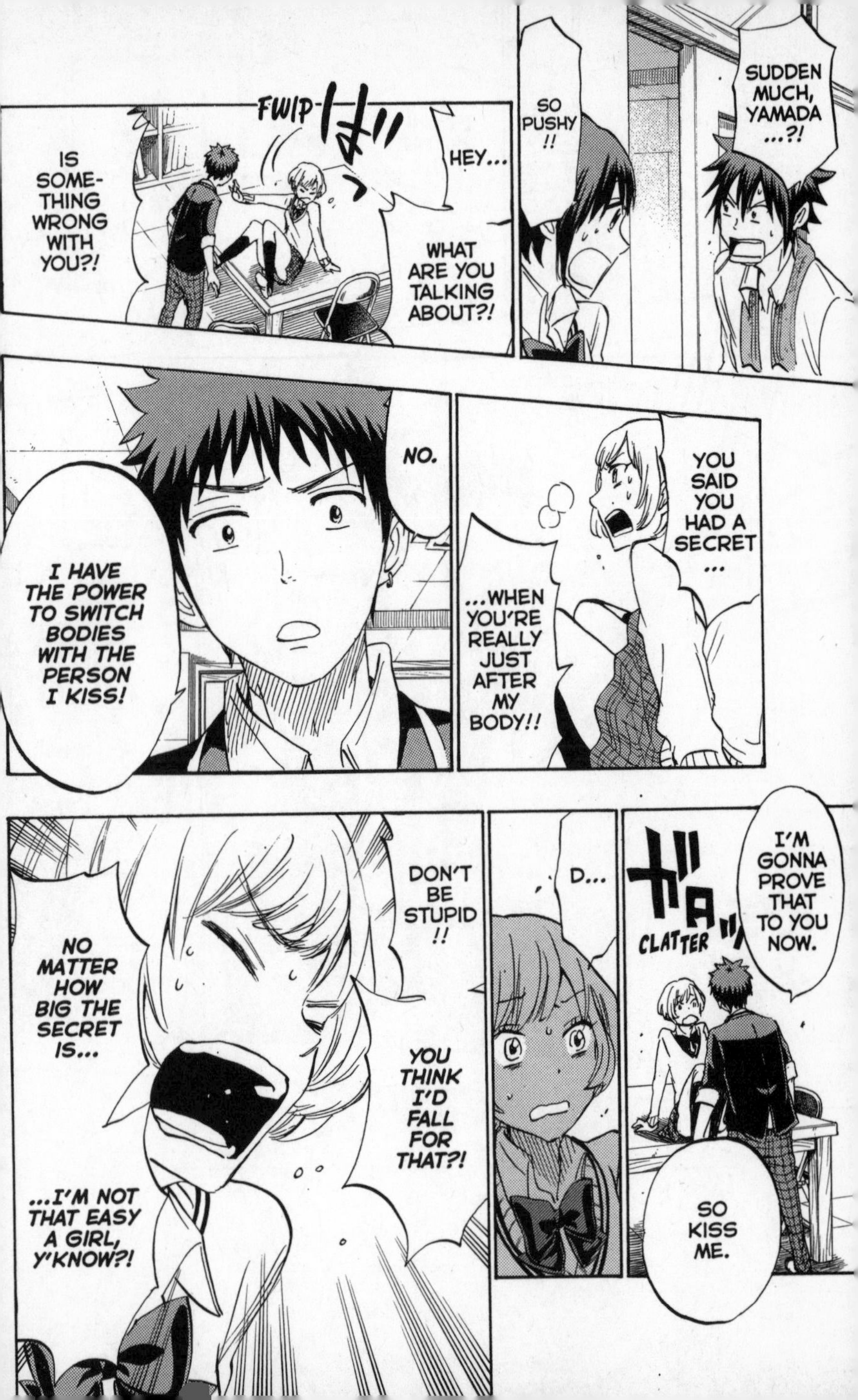
SUDDEN MUCH, YAMADA...?!
SO PUSHY!!
FWIP
HEY...
WHAT ARE YOU TALKING ABOUT?!
IS SOMETHING WRONG WITH YOU?!
YOU SAID YOU HAD A SECRET...
...WHEN YOU'RE REALLY JUST AFTER MY BODY!!
NO.
I HAVE THE POWER TO SWITCH BODIES WITH THE PERSON I KISS!
I'M GONNA PROVE THAT TO YOU NOW.
CLATTER
SO KISS ME.
D...
DON'T BE STUPID!!
NO MATTER HOW BIG THE SECRET IS...
YOU THINK I'D FALL FOR THAT?!
...I'M NOT THAT EASY A GIRL, Y'KNOW?!

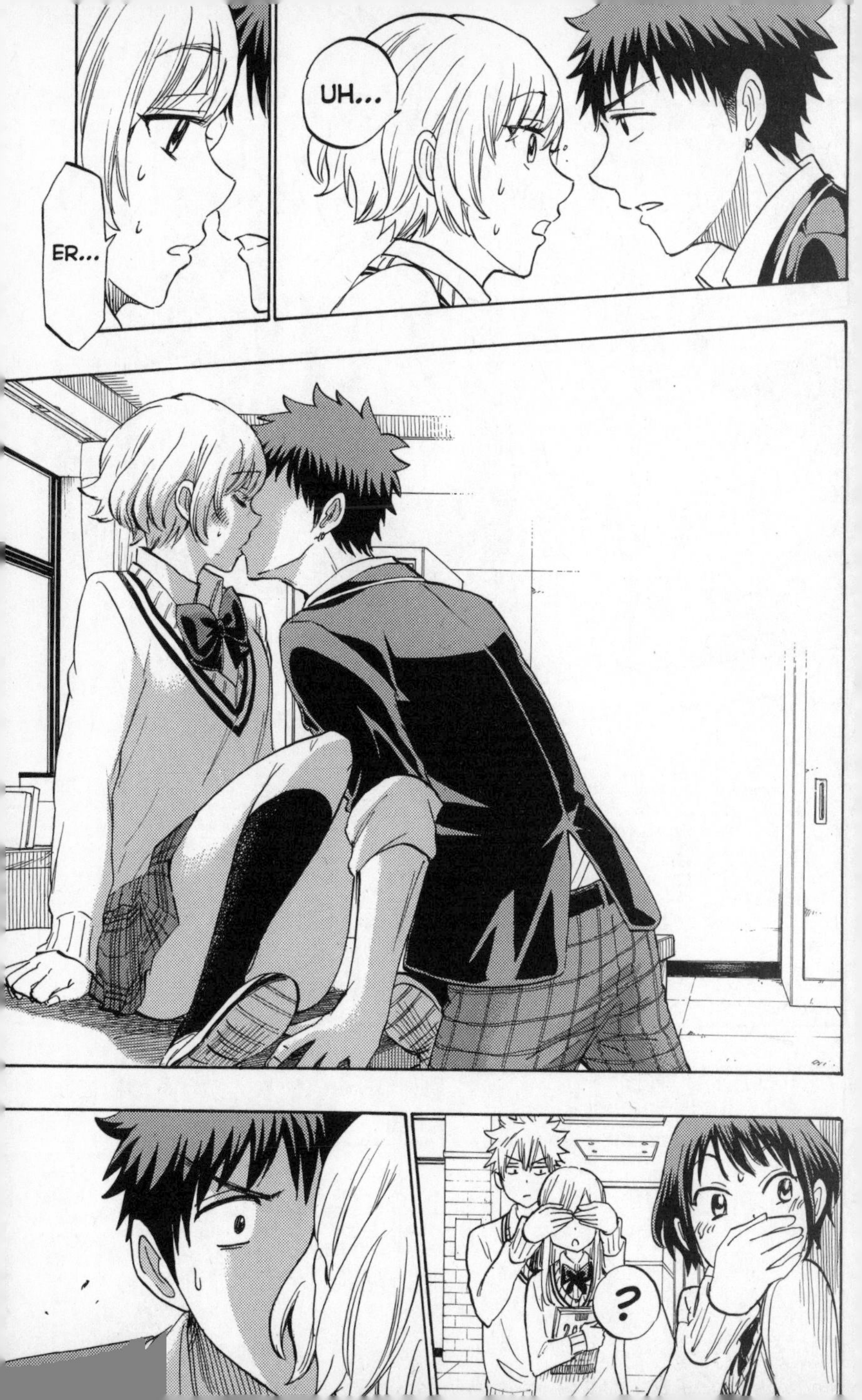
UH...
ER...
?

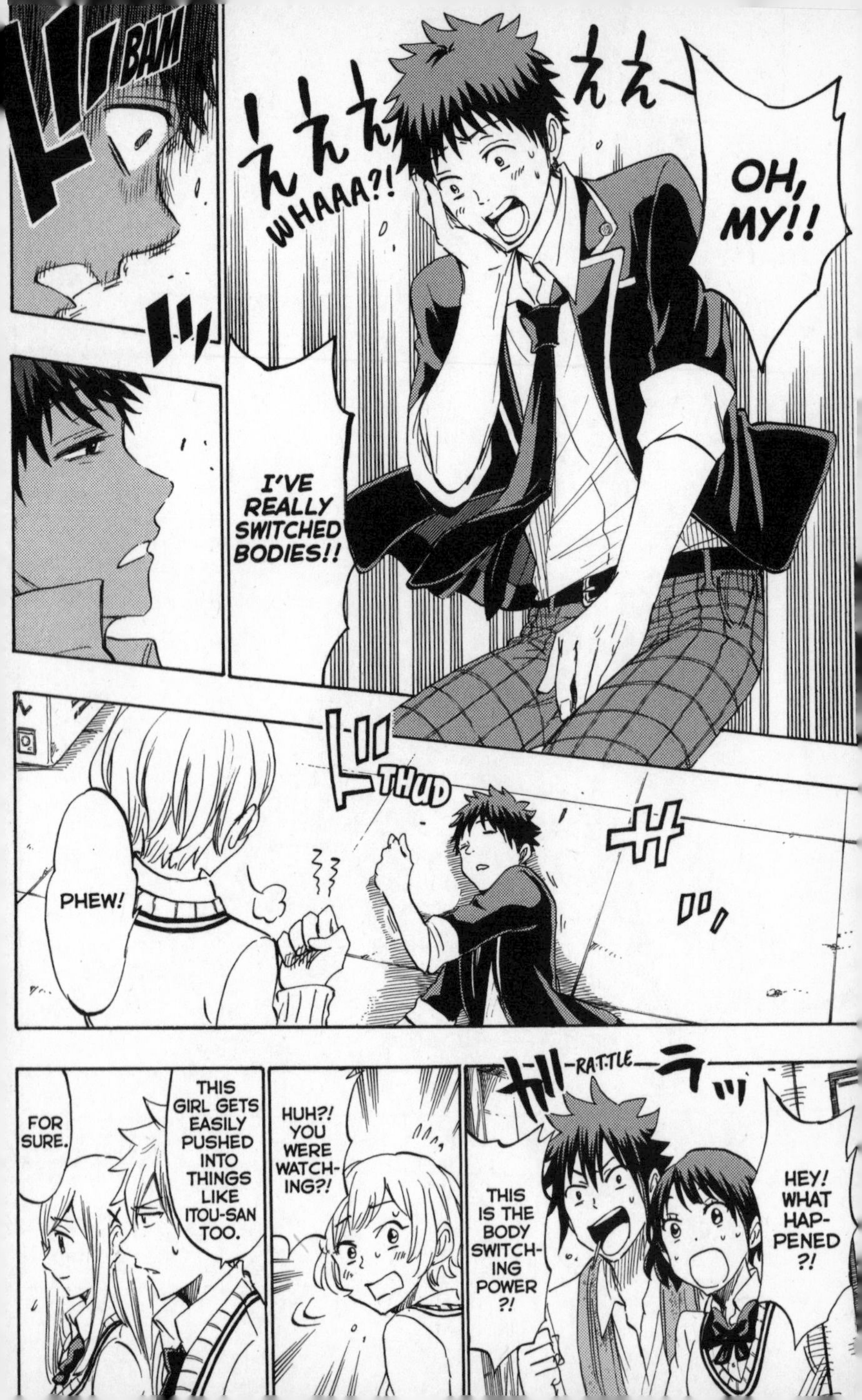
OH, MY!!
WHAAA?!
I'VE REALLY SWITCHED BODIES!!
BAM
THUD
PHEW!
RATTLE
HEY! WHAT HAP-PENED?!
THIS IS THE BODY SWITCH-ING POWER?!
HUH?! YOU WERE WATCH-ING?!
THIS GIRL GETS EASILY PUSHED INTO THINGS LIKE ITOU-SAN TOO.
FOR SURE.

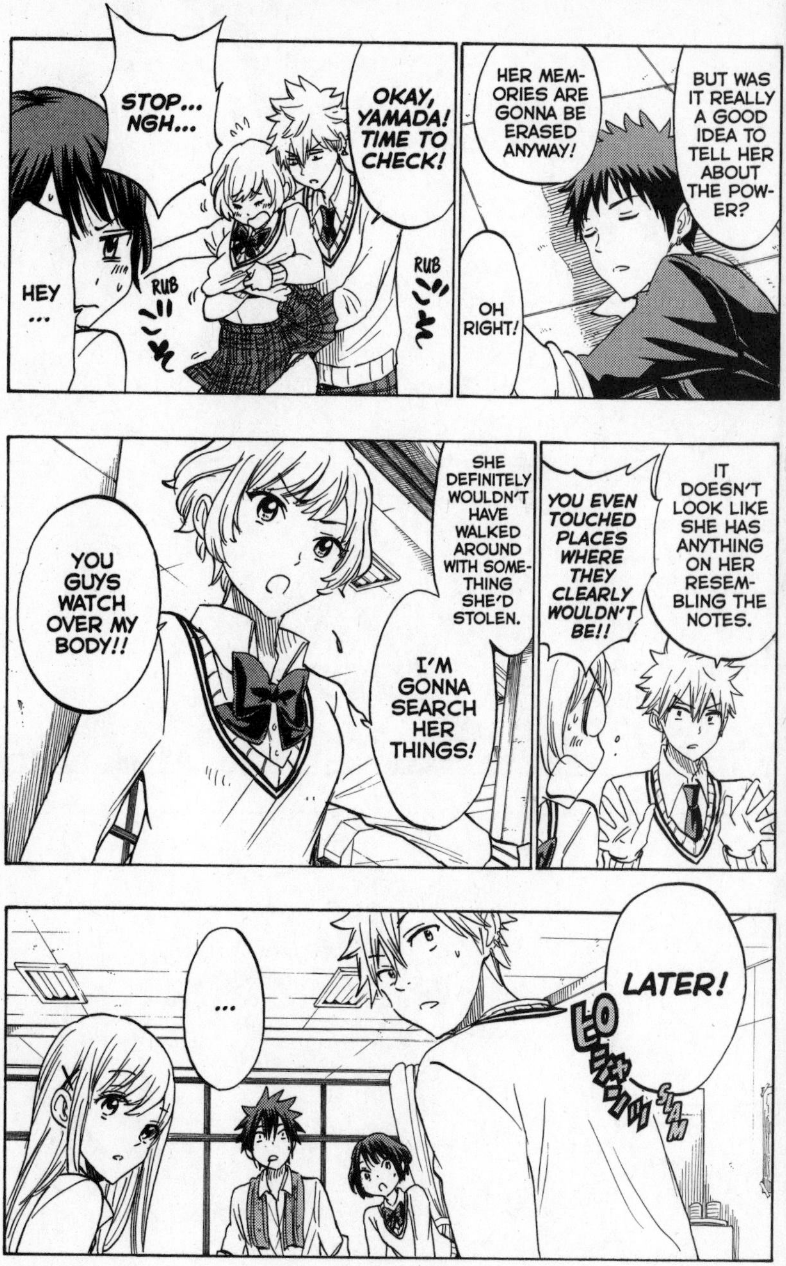
BUT WAS IT REALLY A GOOD IDEA TO TELL HER ABOUT THE POWER?
HER MEMORIES ARE GONNA BE ERASED ANYWAY!
OH RIGHT!
OKAY, YAMADA! TIME TO CHECK!
STOP... NGH...
RUB
RUB
HEY ...
IT DOESN'T LOOK LIKE SHE HAS ANYTHING ON HER RESEMBLING THE NOTES.
YOU EVEN TOUCHED PLACES WHERE THEY CLEARLY WOULDN'T BE!!
SHE DEFINITELY WOULDN'T HAVE WALKED AROUND WITH SOMETHING SHE'D STOLEN.
I'M GONNA SEARCH HER THINGS!
YOU GUYS WATCH OVER MY BODY!!
LATER!
SLAM
...

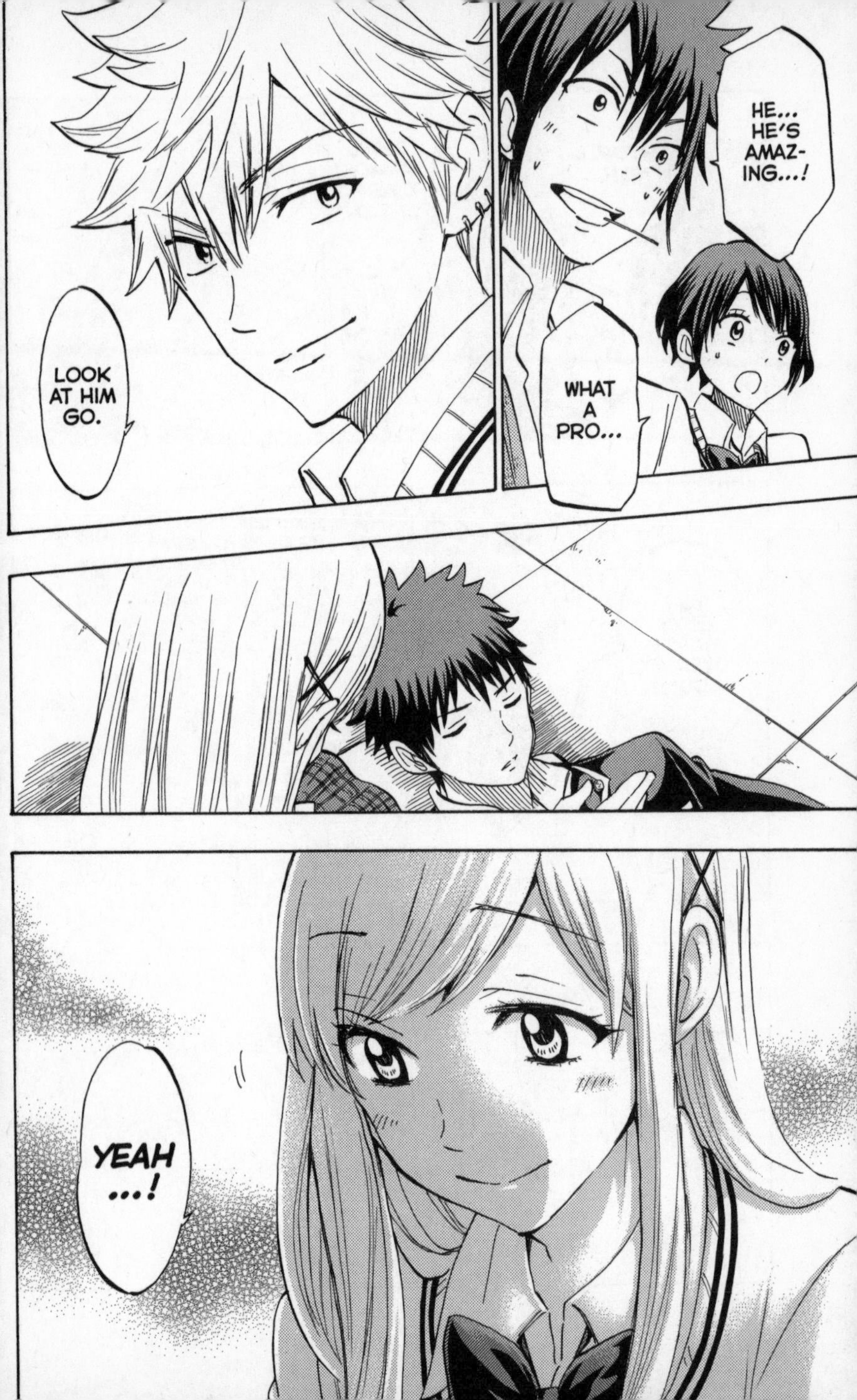
HE... HE'S AMAZ-ING...!
WHAT A PRO...
LOOK AT HIM GO.
YEAH ...!

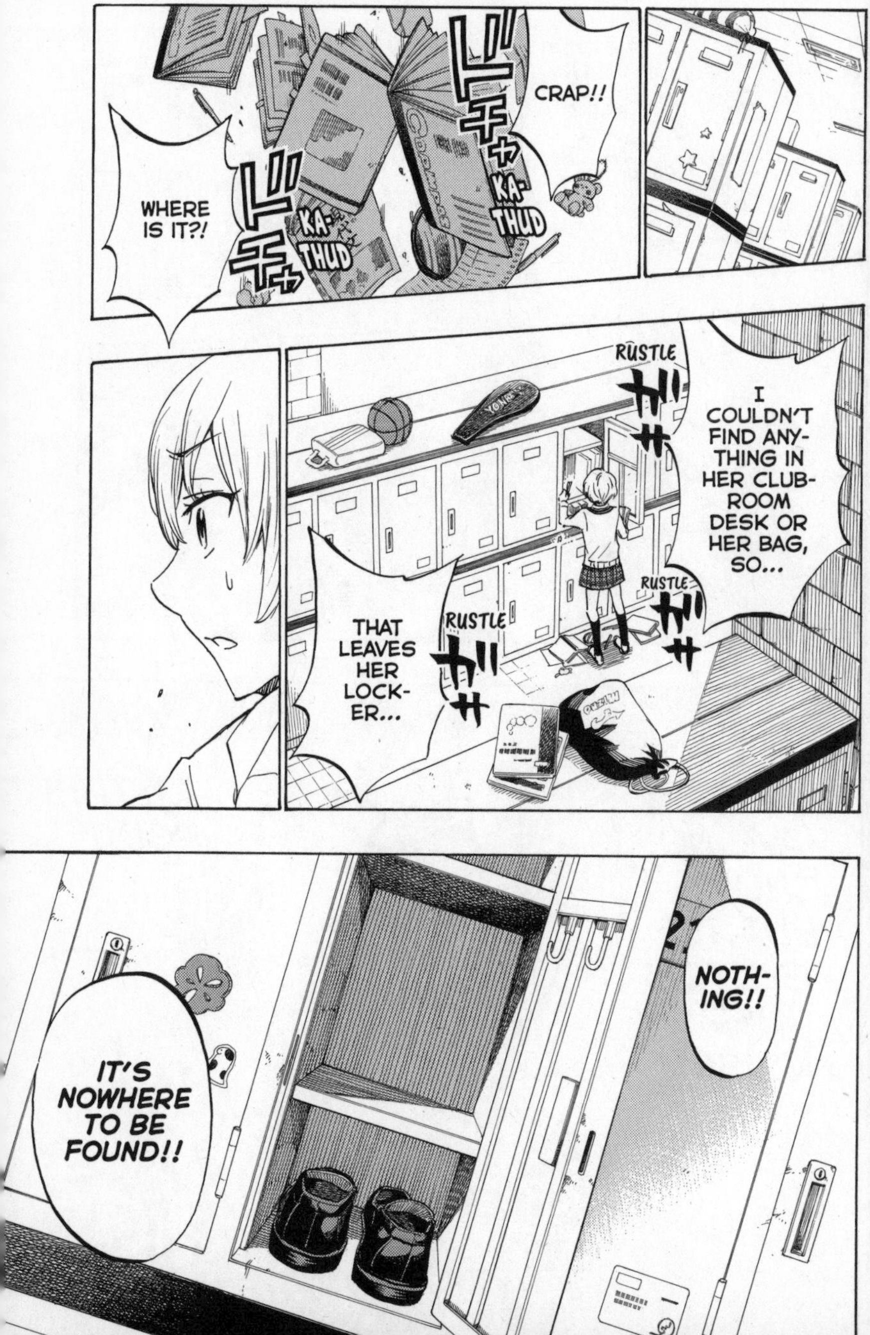
CRAP!!
KA-THUD
WHERE IS IT?!
KA-THUD
I COULDN'T FIND ANY-THING IN HER CLUB-ROOM DESK OR HER BAG, SO...
RUSTLE
RUSTLE
THAT LEAVES HER LOCK-ER...
RUSTLE
NOTH-ING!!
IT'S NOWHERE TO BE FOUND!!

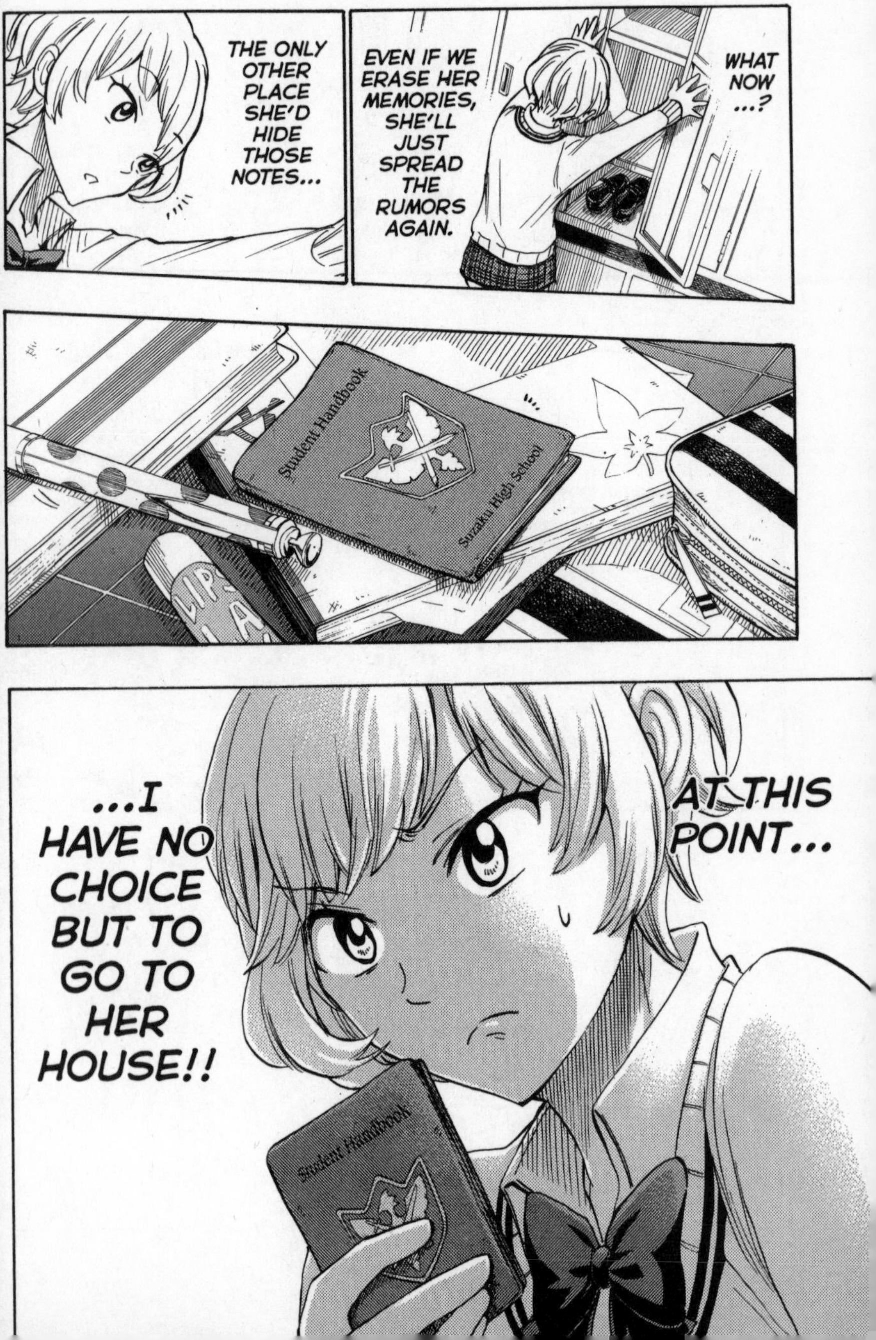
WHAT NOW ...?
EVEN IF WE ERASE HER MEMORIES, SHE'LL JUST SPREAD THE RUMORS AGAIN.
THE ONLY OTHER PLACE SHE'D HIDE THOSE NOTES...
Student Handbook
Suzaku High School
AT THIS POINT...
...I HAVE NO CHOICE BUT TO GO TO HER HOUSE!!
Student Handbook

CHAPTER 178: Right there.

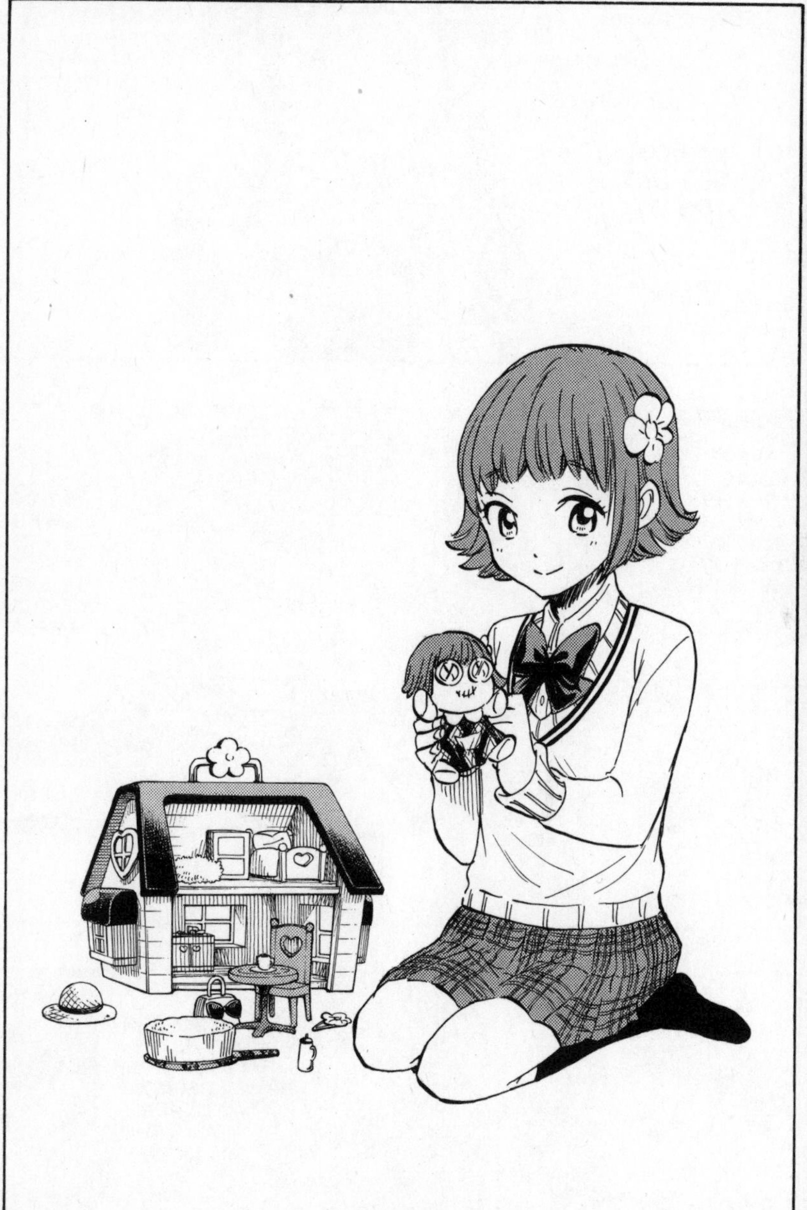

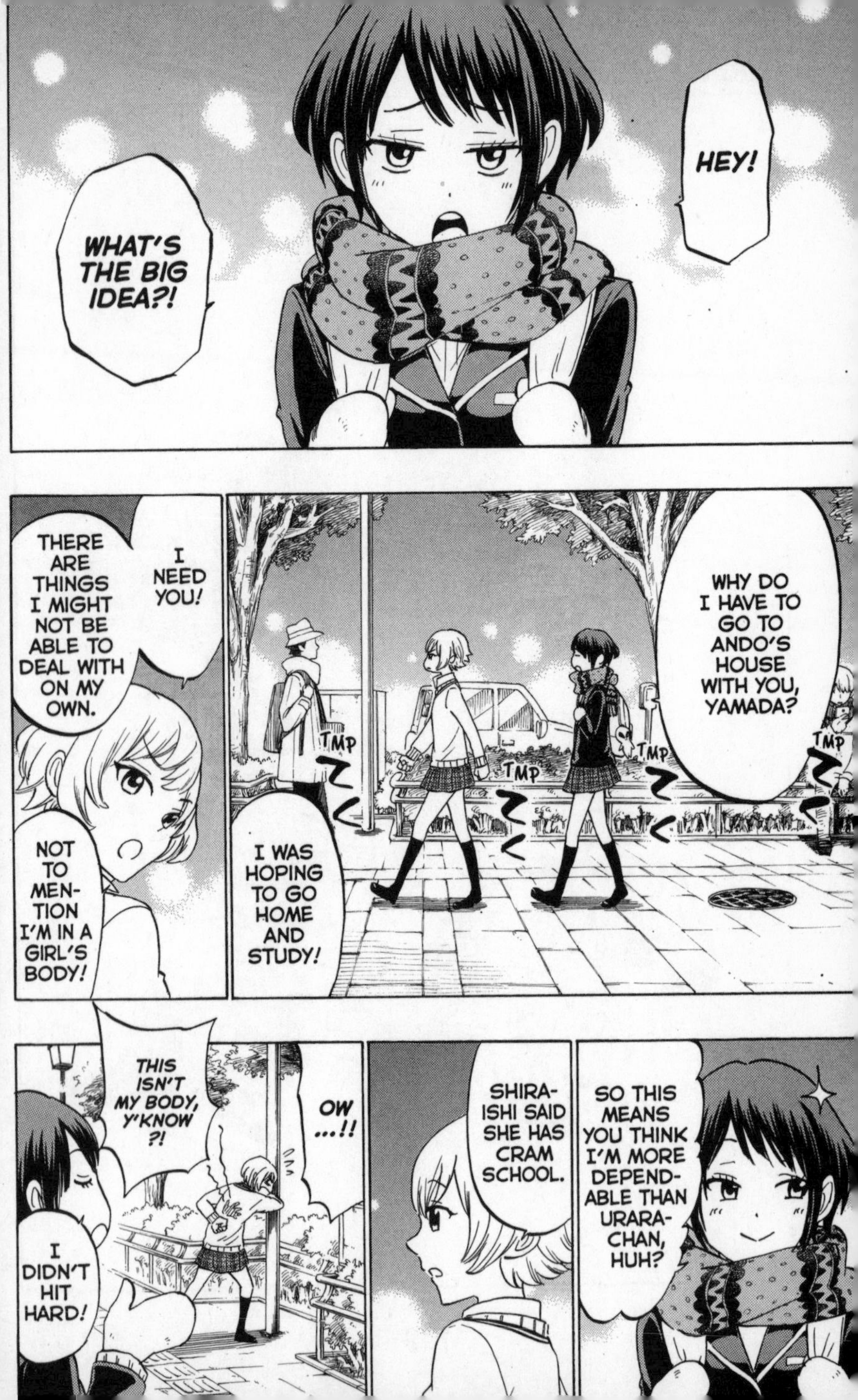
HEY!
WHAT'S THE BIG IDEA?!
WHY DO I HAVE TO GO TO ANDO'S HOUSE WITH YOU, YAMADA?
TMP
TMP
TMP
TMP
I WAS HOPING TO GO HOME AND STUDY!
I NEED YOU!
THERE ARE THINGS I MIGHT NOT BE ABLE TO DEAL WITH ON MY OWN.
NOT TO MENTION I'M IN A GIRL'S BODY!
SO THIS MEANS YOU THINK I'M MORE DEPENDABLE THAN URARA-CHAN, HUH?
SHIRAISHI SAID SHE HAS CRAM SCHOOL.
OW ...!!
THIS ISN'T MY BODY, Y'KNOW?!
I DIDN'T HIT HARD!

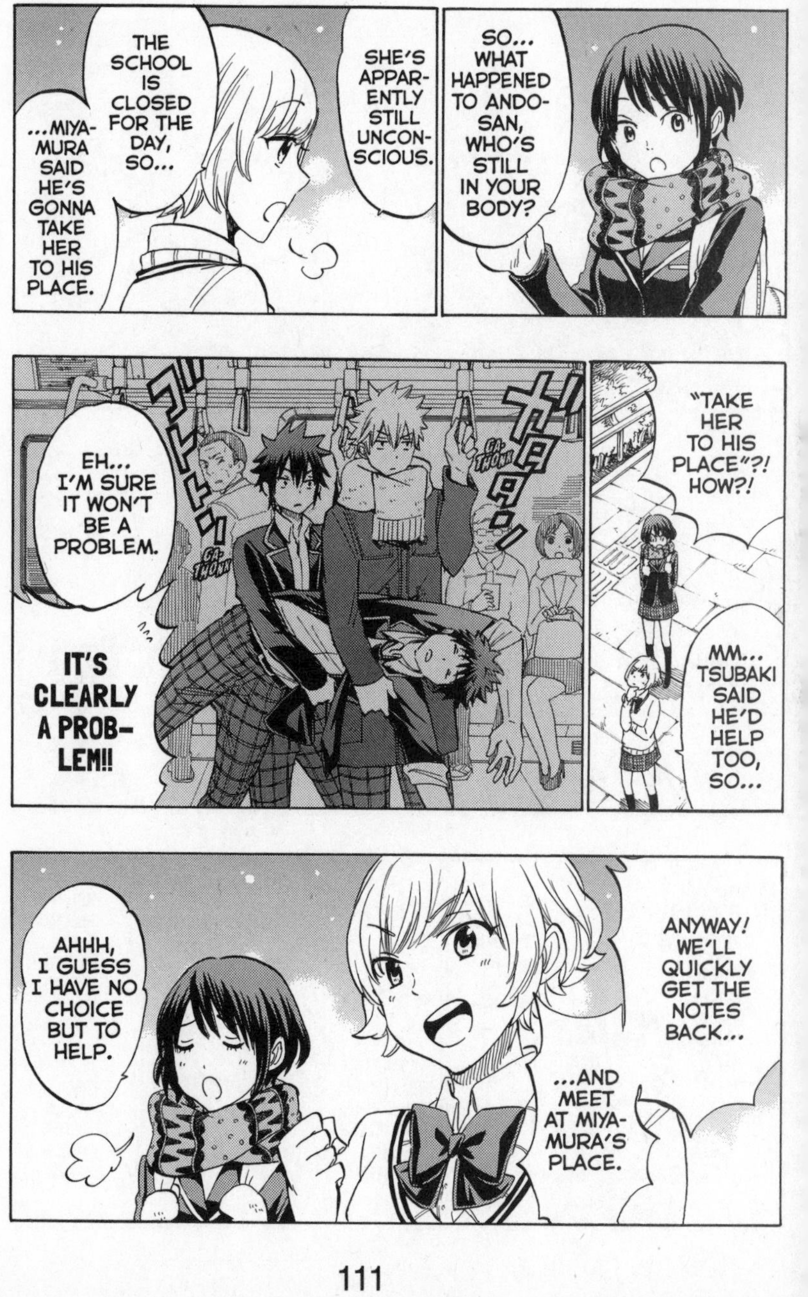
SO... WHAT HAPPENED TO ANDO-SAN, WHO'S STILL IN YOUR BODY?
SHE'S APPARENTLY STILL UNCONSCIOUS.
THE SCHOOL IS CLOSED FOR THE DAY, SO...
...MIYAMURA SAID HE'S GONNA TAKE HER TO HIS PLACE.
"TAKE HER TO HIS PLACE"?! HOW?!
MM... TSUBAKI SAID HE'D HELP TOO, SO...
GA-THONK
EH... I'M SURE IT WON'T BE A PROBLEM.
GA-THONK
IT'S CLEARLY A PROBLEM!!
ANYWAY! WE'LL QUICKLY GET THE NOTES BACK...
...AND MEET AT MIYAMURA'S PLACE.
AHHH, I GUESS I HAVE NO CHOICE BUT TO HELP.

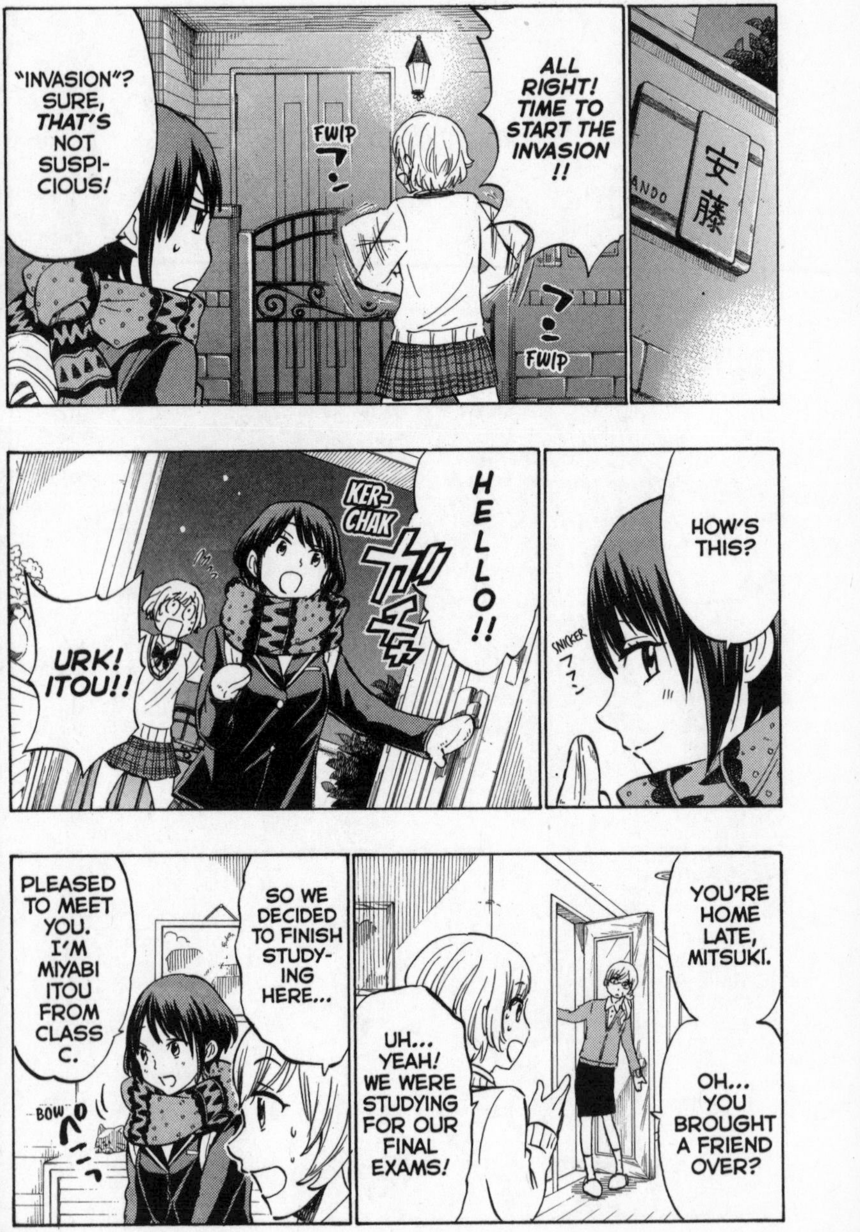
ANDO
安藤
ALL RIGHT! TIME TO START THE INVASION!!
FWIP
FWIP
"INVASION"? SURE, THAT'S NOT SUSPICIOUS!
HOW'S THIS?
SNICKER
HELLO!!
KER-CHAK
URK! ITOU!!
YOU'RE HOME LATE, MITSUKI.
OH... YOU BROUGHT A FRIEND OVER?
UH... YEAH! WE WERE STUDYING FOR OUR FINAL EXAMS!
SO WE DECIDED TO FINISH STUDYING HERE...
PLEASED TO MEET YOU. I'M MIYABI ITOU FROM CLASS C.
BOW

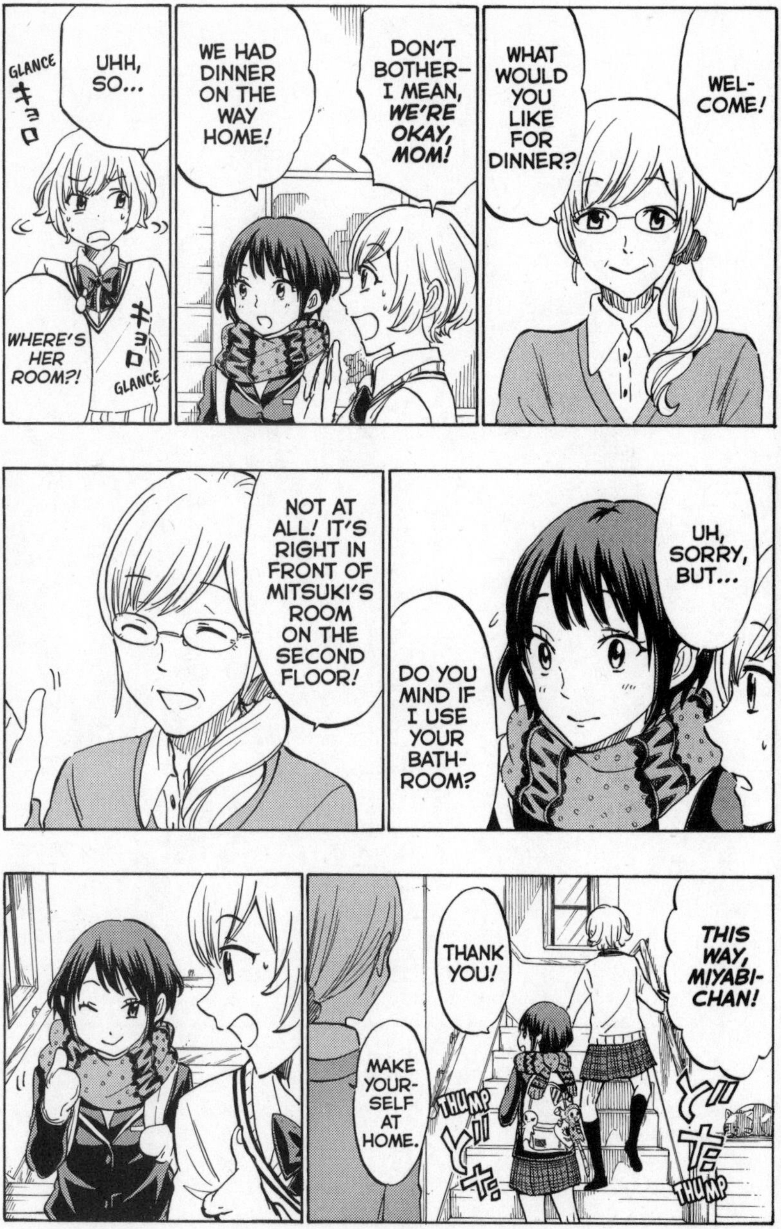
WEL-COME!
WHAT WOULD YOU LIKE FOR DINNER?
DON'T BOTHER— I MEAN, WE'RE OKAY, MOM!
WE HAD DINNER ON THE WAY HOME!
UHH, SO...
GLANCE キョロ
WHERE'S HER ROOM?!
キョロ GLANCE
UH, SORRY, BUT...
DO YOU MIND IF I USE YOUR BATH-ROOM?
NOT AT ALL! IT'S RIGHT IN FRONT OF MITSUKI'S ROOM ON THE SECOND FLOOR!
THIS WAY, MIYABI-CHAN!
ドッ THUMP
THANK YOU!
MAKE YOUR-SELF AT HOME.
THUMP ドッ

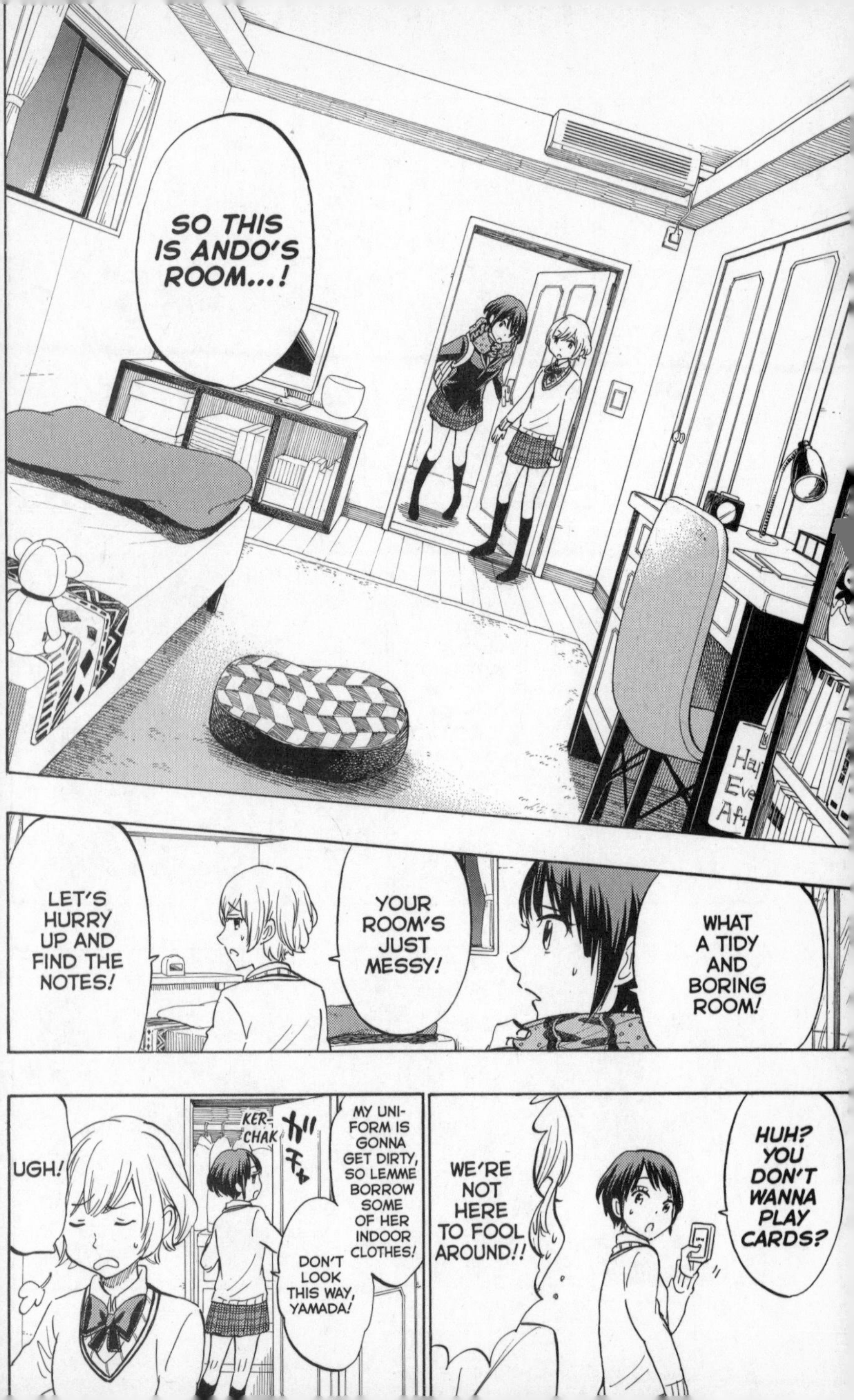
SO THIS IS ANDO'S ROOM...!
WHAT A TIDY AND BORING ROOM!
YOUR ROOM'S JUST MESSY!
LET'S HURRY UP AND FIND THE NOTES!
HUH? YOU DON'T WANNA PLAY CARDS?
WE'RE NOT HERE TO FOOL AROUND!!
MY UNI-FORM IS GONNA GET DIRTY, SO LEMME BORROW SOME OF HER INDOOR CLOTHES!
KER-CHAK
ガチャ
DON'T LOOK THIS WAY, YAMADA!
UGH!

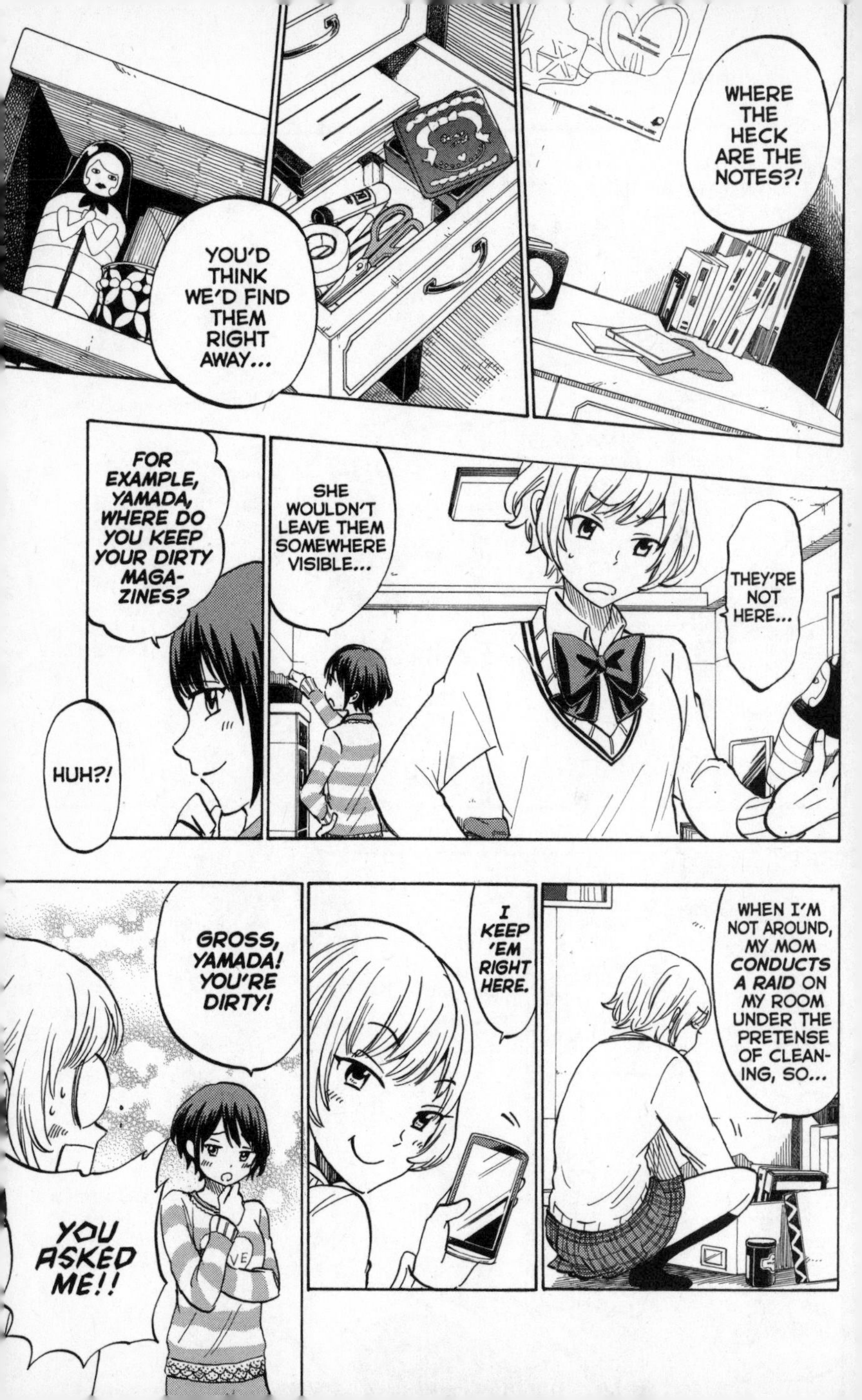
WHERE THE HECK ARE THE NOTES?!
YOU'D THINK WE'D FIND THEM RIGHT AWAY...
THEY'RE NOT HERE...
SHE WOULDN'T LEAVE THEM SOMEWHERE VISIBLE...
FOR EXAMPLE, YAMADA, WHERE DO YOU KEEP YOUR DIRTY MAGA-ZINES?
HUH?!
WHEN I'M NOT AROUND, MY MOM CONDUCTS A RAID ON MY ROOM UNDER THE PRETENSE OF CLEAN-ING, SO...
I KEEP 'EM RIGHT HERE.
GROSS, YAMADA! YOU'RE DIRTY!
YOU ASKED ME!!

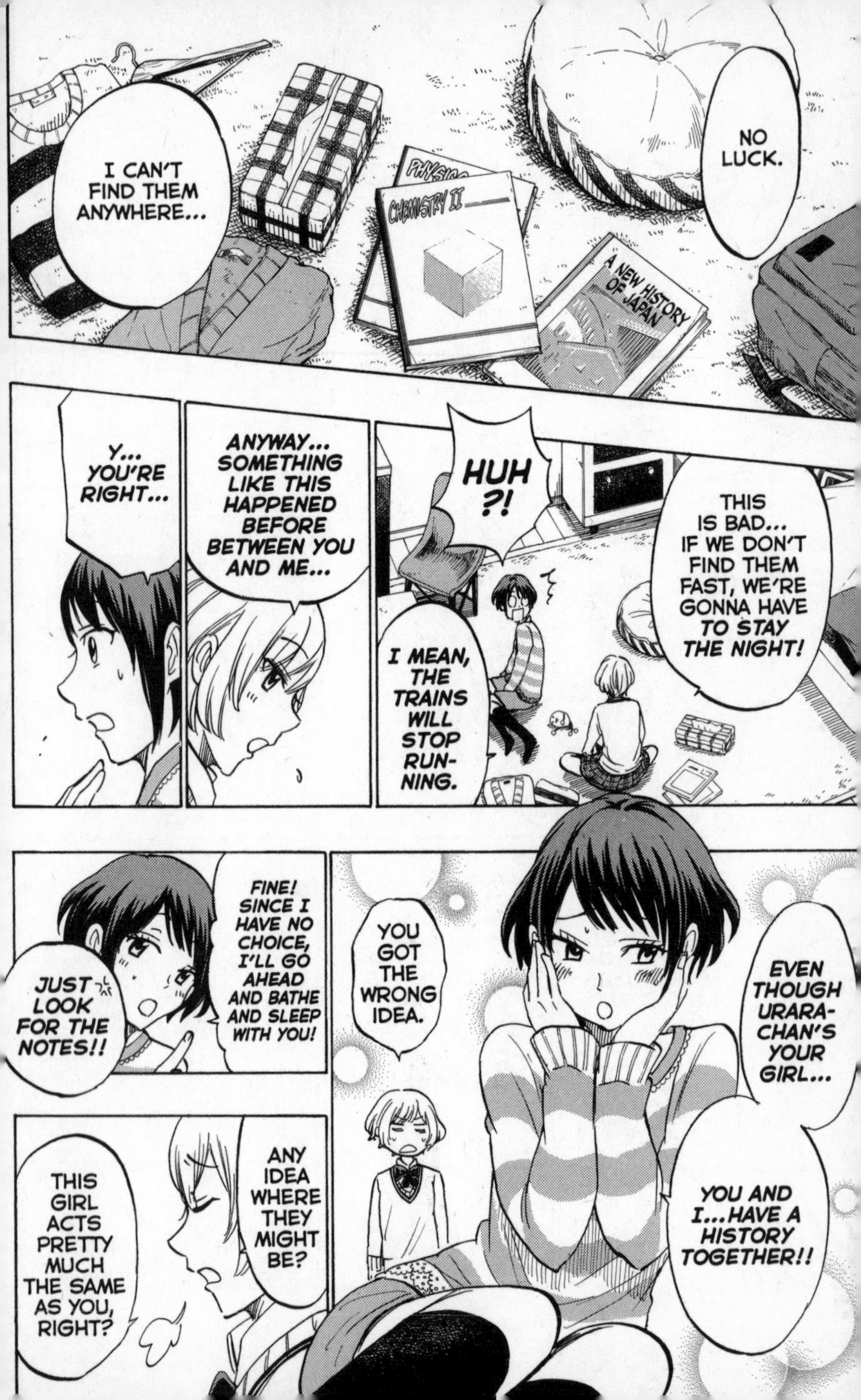
NO LUCK.
I CAN'T FIND THEM ANYWHERE...
CHEMISTRY II
A NEW HISTORY OF JAPAN
THIS IS BAD... IF WE DON'T FIND THEM FAST, WE'RE GONNA HAVE TO STAY THE NIGHT!
HUH ?!
I MEAN, THE TRAINS WILL STOP RUNNING.
ANYWAY... SOMETHING LIKE THIS HAPPENED BEFORE BETWEEN YOU AND ME...
Y... YOU'RE RIGHT...
EVEN THOUGH URARA-CHAN'S YOUR GIRL...
YOU AND I...HAVE A HISTORY TOGETHER!!
YOU GOT THE WRONG IDEA.
FINE! SINCE I HAVE NO CHOICE, I'LL GO AHEAD AND BATHE AND SLEEP WITH YOU!
JUST LOOK FOR THE NOTES!!
ANY IDEA WHERE THEY MIGHT BE?
THIS GIRL ACTS PRETTY MUCH THE SAME AS YOU, RIGHT?

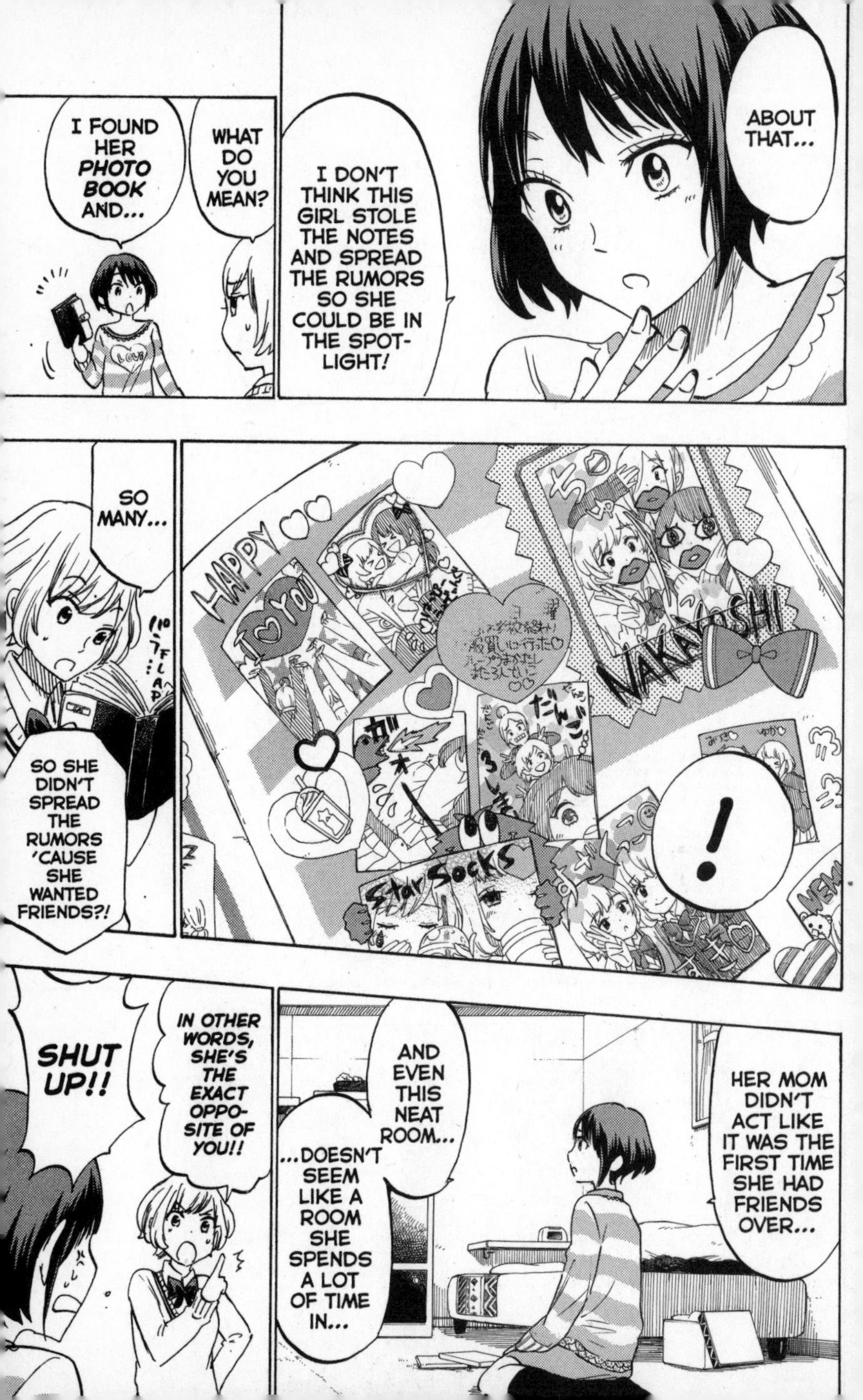
ABOUT THAT...
I DON'T THINK THIS GIRL STOLE THE NOTES AND SPREAD THE RUMORS SO SHE COULD BE IN THE SPOT-LIGHT!
WHAT DO YOU MEAN?
I FOUND HER PHOTO BOOK AND...
!
HAPPY
I ♥ YOU
NAKAYOSHI
Star Socks
SO MANY...
FLAP
SO SHE DIDN'T SPREAD THE RUMORS 'CAUSE SHE WANTED FRIENDS?!
HER MOM DIDN'T ACT LIKE IT WAS THE FIRST TIME SHE HAD FRIENDS OVER...
AND EVEN THIS NEAT ROOM...
...DOESN'T SEEM LIKE A ROOM SHE SPENDS A LOT OF TIME IN...
IN OTHER WORDS, SHE'S THE EXACT OPPOSITE OF YOU!!
SHUT UP!!

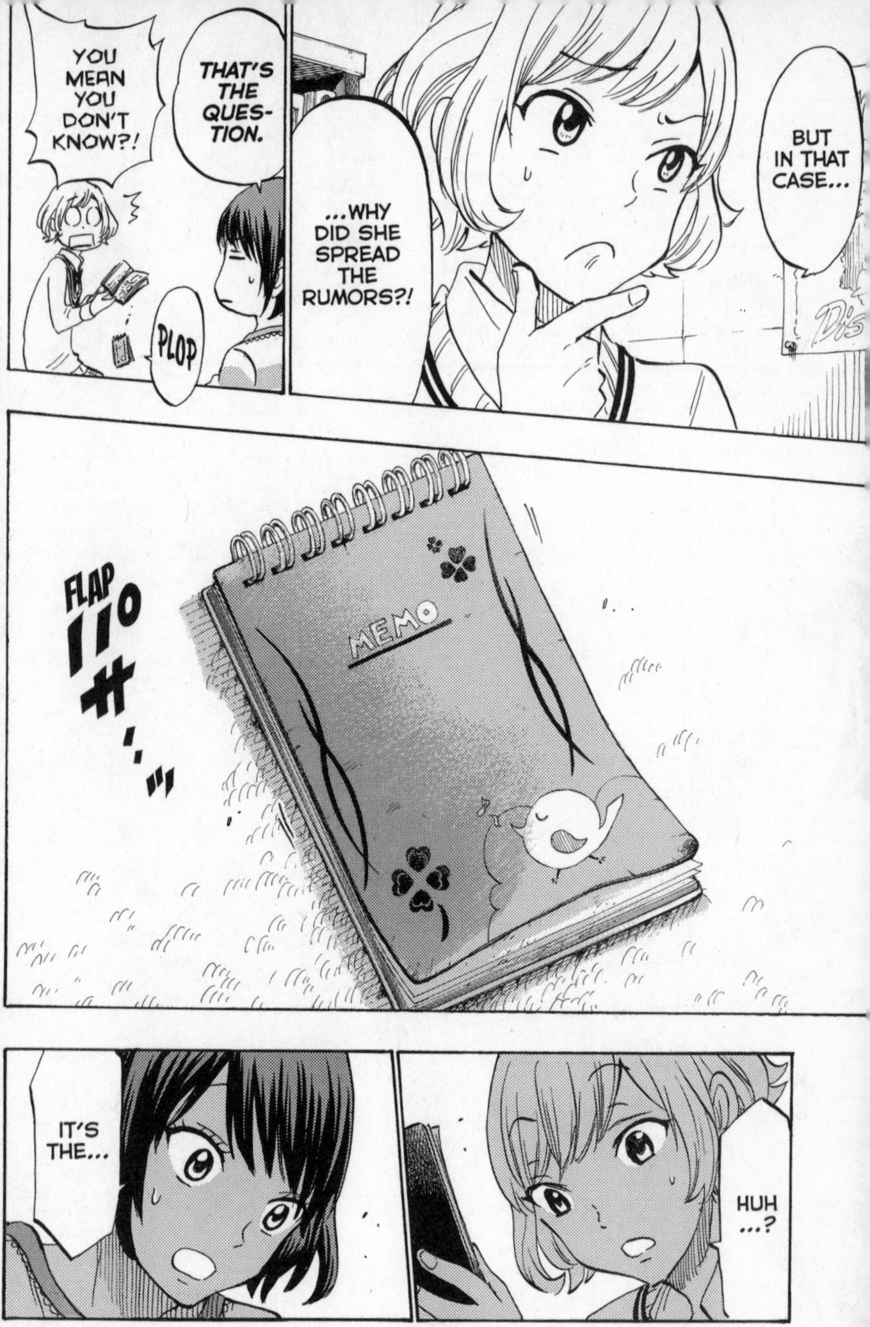
BUT IN THAT CASE...
...WHY DID SHE SPREAD THE RUMORS?!
THAT'S THE QUES-TION.
YOU MEAN YOU DON'T KNOW?!
PLOP
FLAP
HUH ...?
IT'S THE...

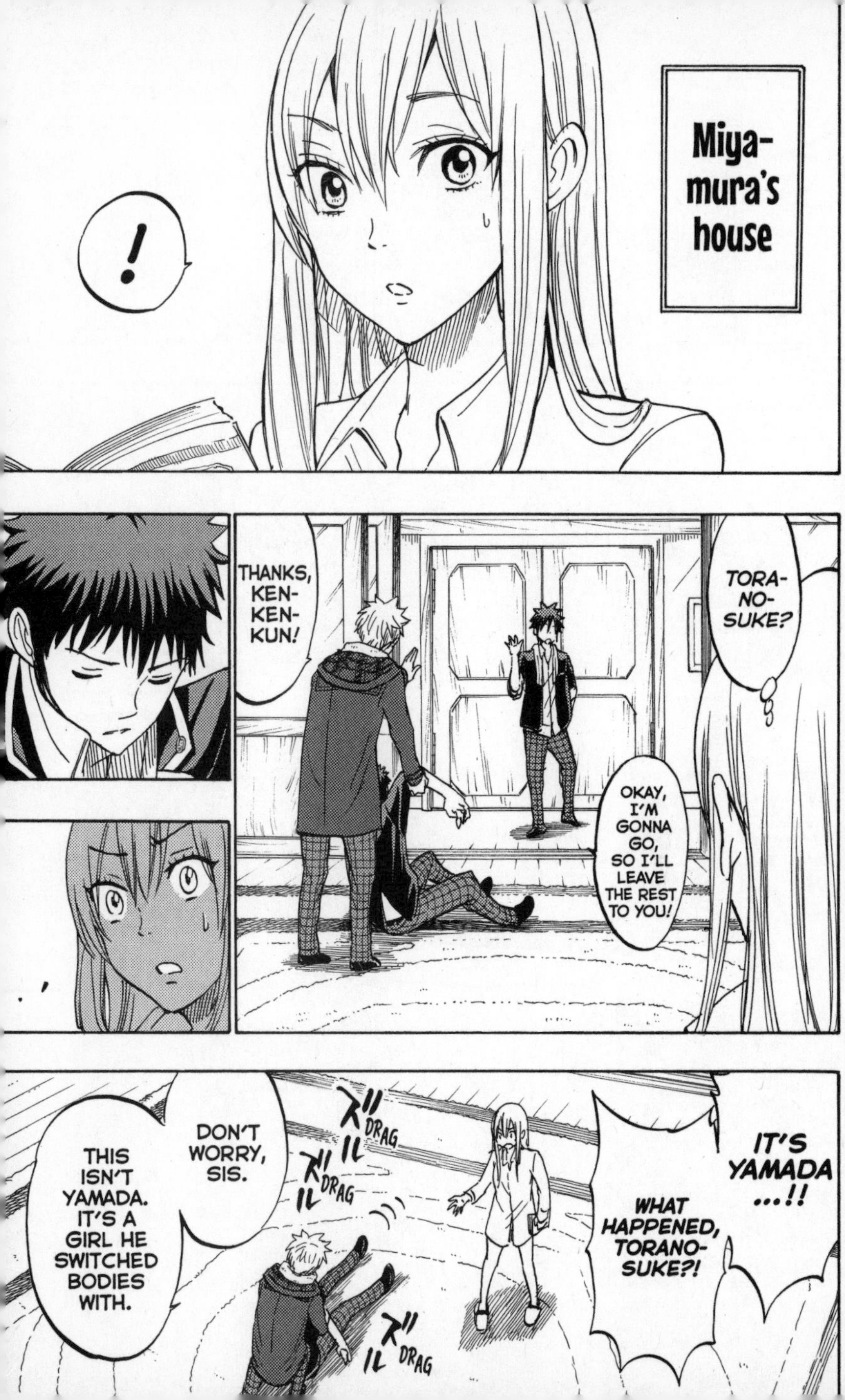
Miya-mura's house
!
TORA-NO-SUKE?
THANKS, KEN-KEN-KUN!
OKAY, I'M GONNA GO, SO I'LL LEAVE THE REST TO YOU!
IT'S YAMADA ...!!
WHAT HAPPENED, TORANO-SUKE?!
DRAG
DRAG
DON'T WORRY, SIS.
THIS ISN'T YAMADA. IT'S A GIRL HE SWITCHED BODIES WITH.
DRAG

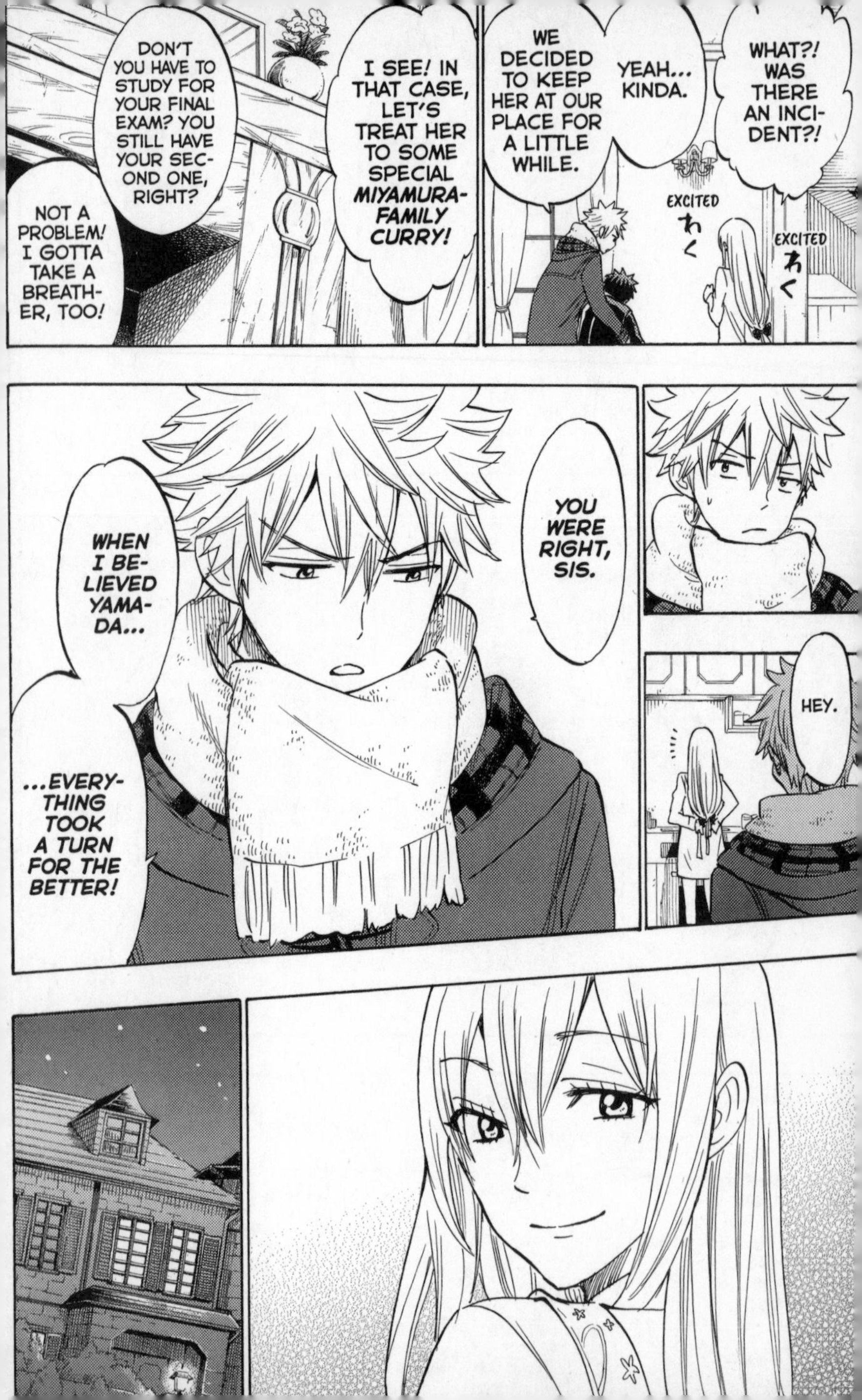
WHAT?! WAS THERE AN INCIDENT?!
EXCITED わく
EXCITED わく
YEAH... KINDA.
WE DECIDED TO KEEP HER AT OUR PLACE FOR A LITTLE WHILE.
I SEE! IN THAT CASE, LET'S TREAT HER TO SOME SPECIAL MIYAMURA-FAMILY CURRY!
DON'T YOU HAVE TO STUDY FOR YOUR FINAL EXAM? YOU STILL HAVE YOUR SECOND ONE, RIGHT?
NOT A PROBLEM! I GOTTA TAKE A BREATHER, TOO!
HEY.
YOU WERE RIGHT, SIS.
WHEN I BELIEVED YAMADA...
...EVERYTHING TOOK A TURN FOR THE BETTER!

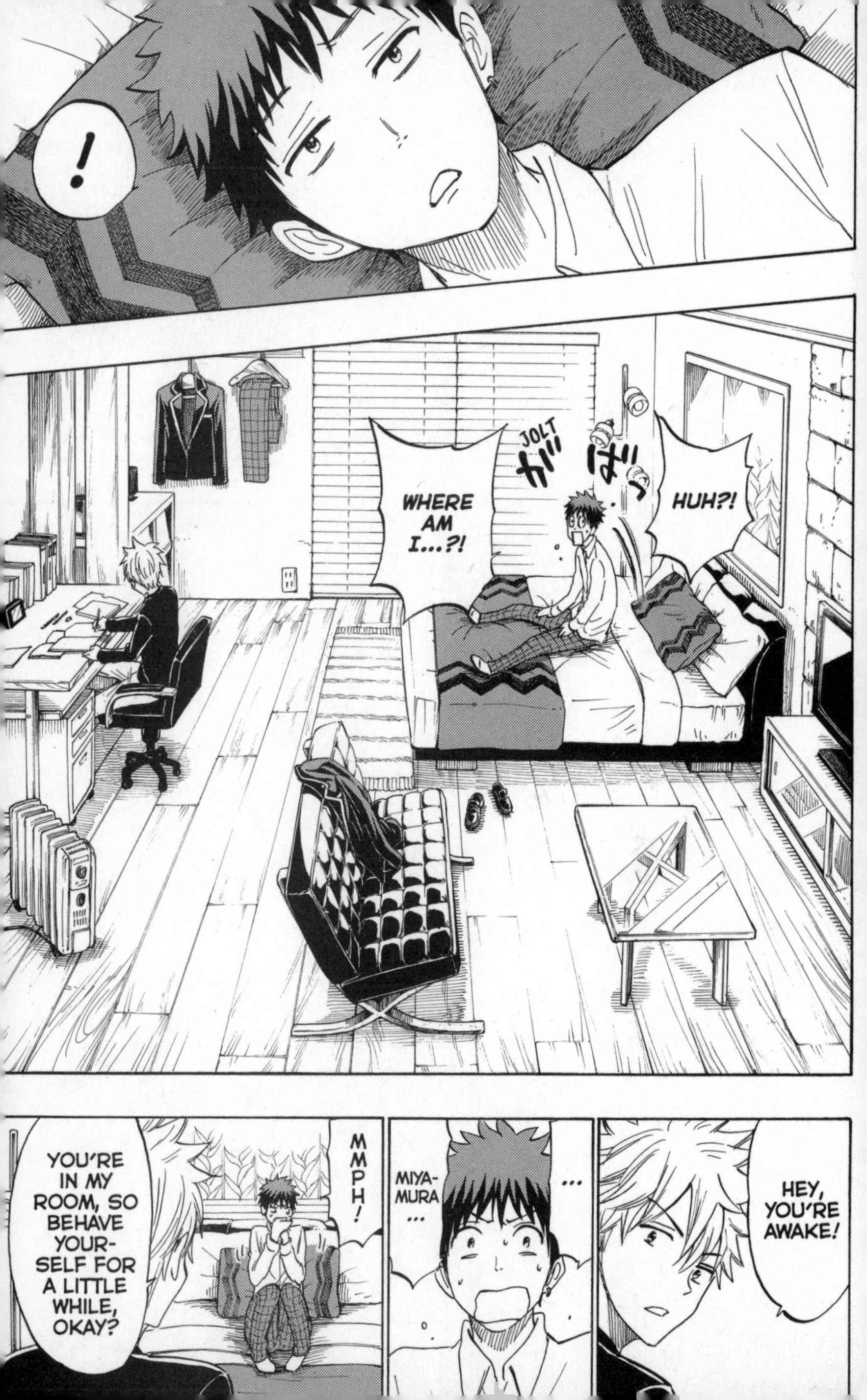
!
HUH?!
JOLT
がばっ
WHERE AM I...?!
HEY, YOU'RE AWAKE!
...
MIYA-MURA ...
MMPH!
YOU'RE IN MY ROOM, SO BEHAVE YOUR-SELF FOR A LITTLE WHILE, OKAY?

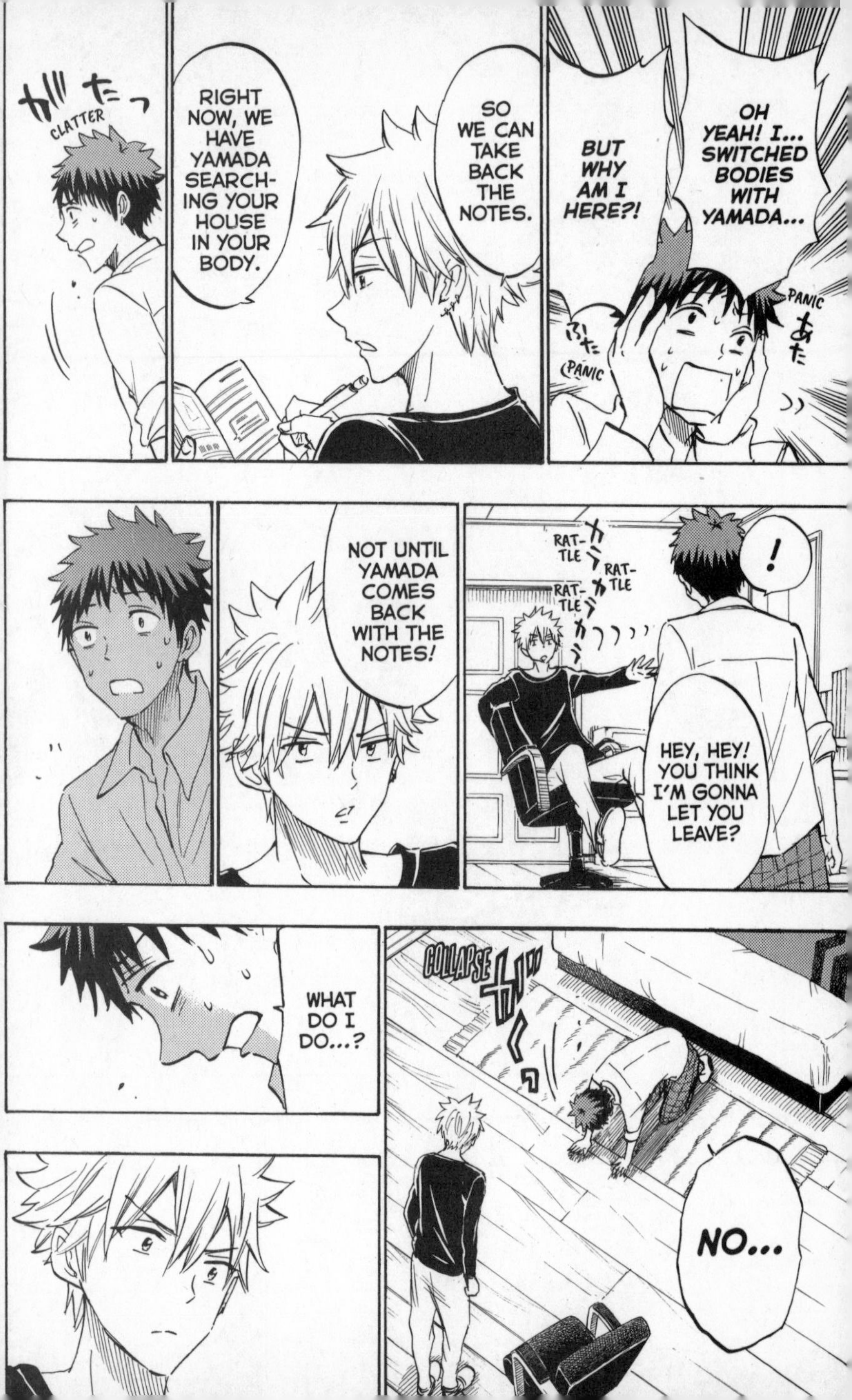
OH YEAH! I... SWITCHED BODIES WITH YAMADA...
BUT WHY AM I HERE?!
PANIC
PANIC
RIGHT NOW, WE HAVE YAMADA SEARCHING YOUR HOUSE IN YOUR BODY.
SO WE CAN TAKE BACK THE NOTES.
CLATTER
!
RATTLE RATTLE RATTLE
HEY, HEY! YOU THINK I'M GONNA LET YOU LEAVE?
NOT UNTIL YAMADA COMES BACK WITH THE NOTES!
COLLAPSE
NO...
WHAT DO I DO...?

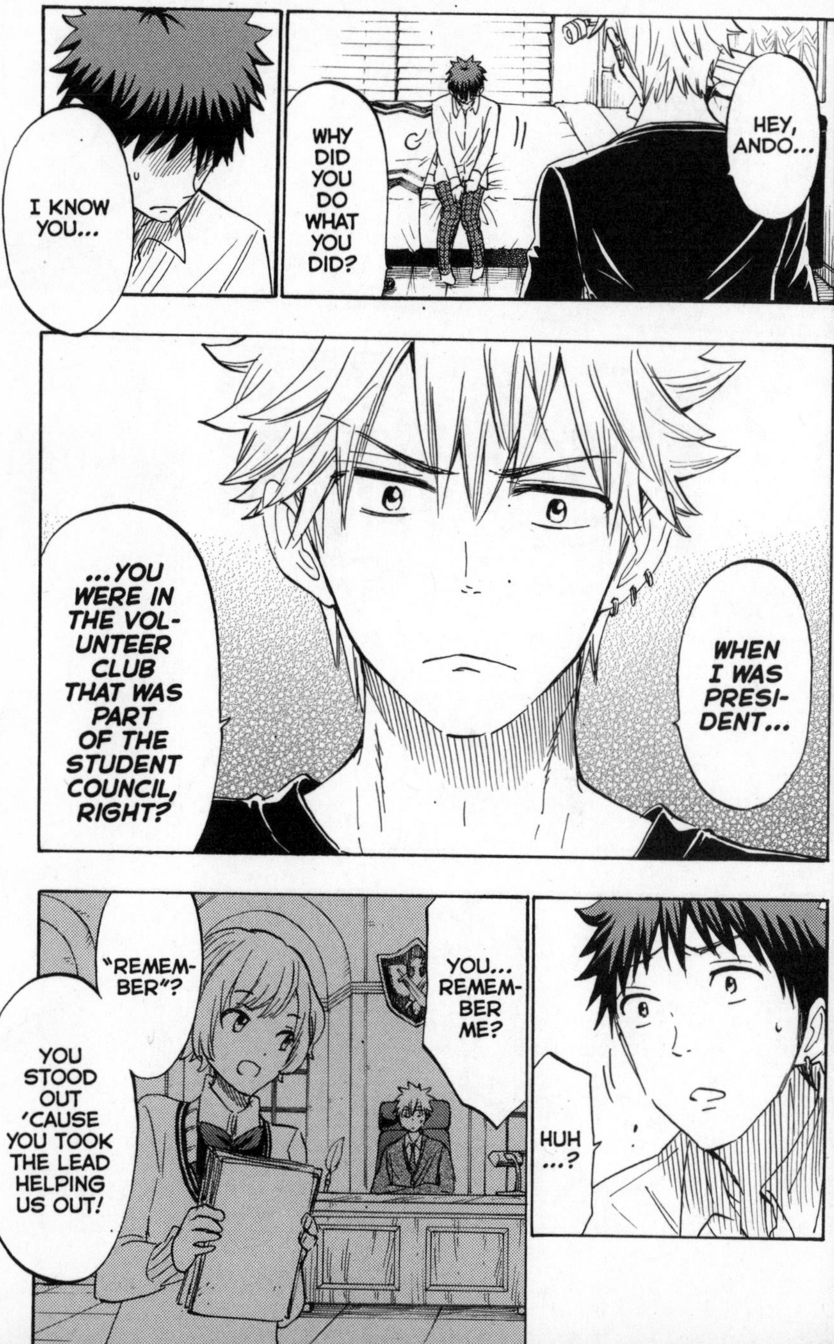
HEY, ANDO...
WHY DID YOU DO WHAT YOU DID?
I KNOW YOU...
WHEN I WAS PRESIDENT...
...YOU WERE IN THE VOL-UNTEER CLUB THAT WAS PART OF THE STUDENT COUNCIL, RIGHT?
HUH ...?
YOU... REMEM-BER ME?
"REMEM-BER"?
YOU STOOD OUT 'CAUSE YOU TOOK THE LEAD HELPING US OUT!

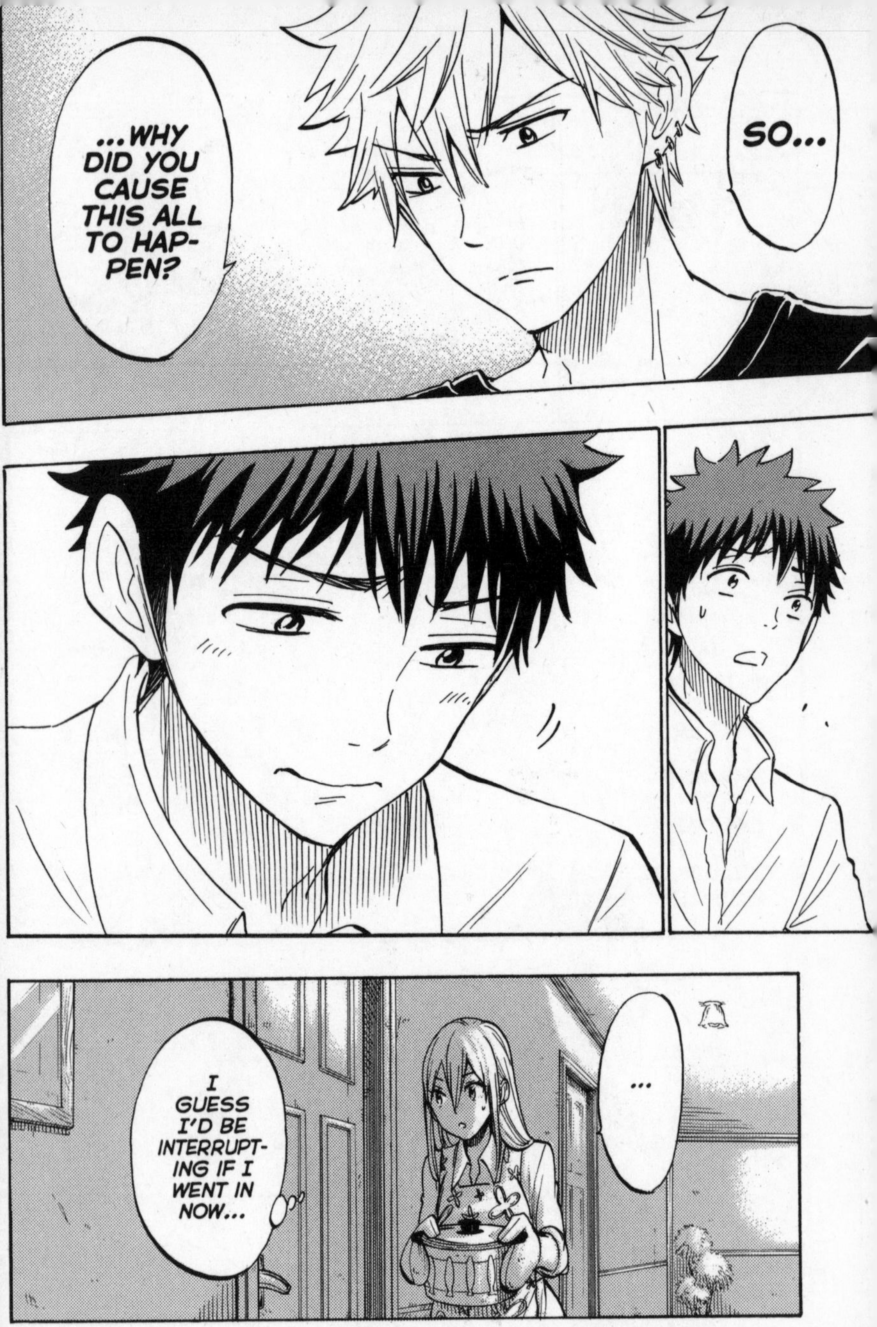
SO...
...WHY DID YOU CAUSE THIS ALL TO HAP-PEN?
...
I GUESS I'D BE INTERRUPT-ING IF I WENT IN NOW...

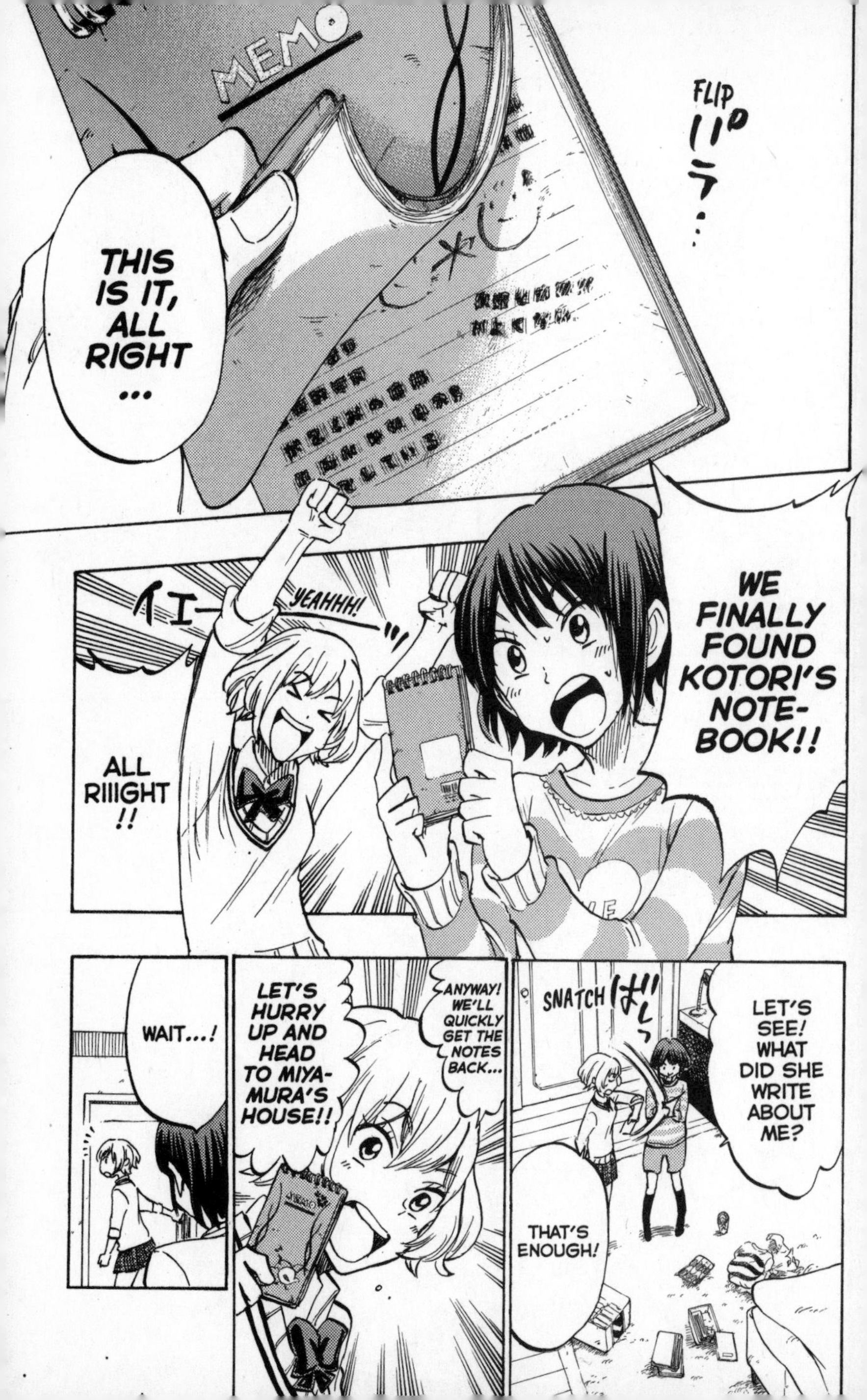
MEMO
FLIP
パラ…
THIS IS IT, ALL RIGHT...
WE FINALLY FOUND KOTORI'S NOTE-BOOK!!
イエー
YEAHHH!
ALL RIIIGHT!!
SNATCH
ばっ
LET'S SEE! WHAT DID SHE WRITE ABOUT ME?
THAT'S ENOUGH!
ANYWAY! WE'LL QUICKLY GET THE NOTES BACK...
LET'S HURRY UP AND HEAD TO MIYA-MURA'S HOUSE!!
WAIT...!

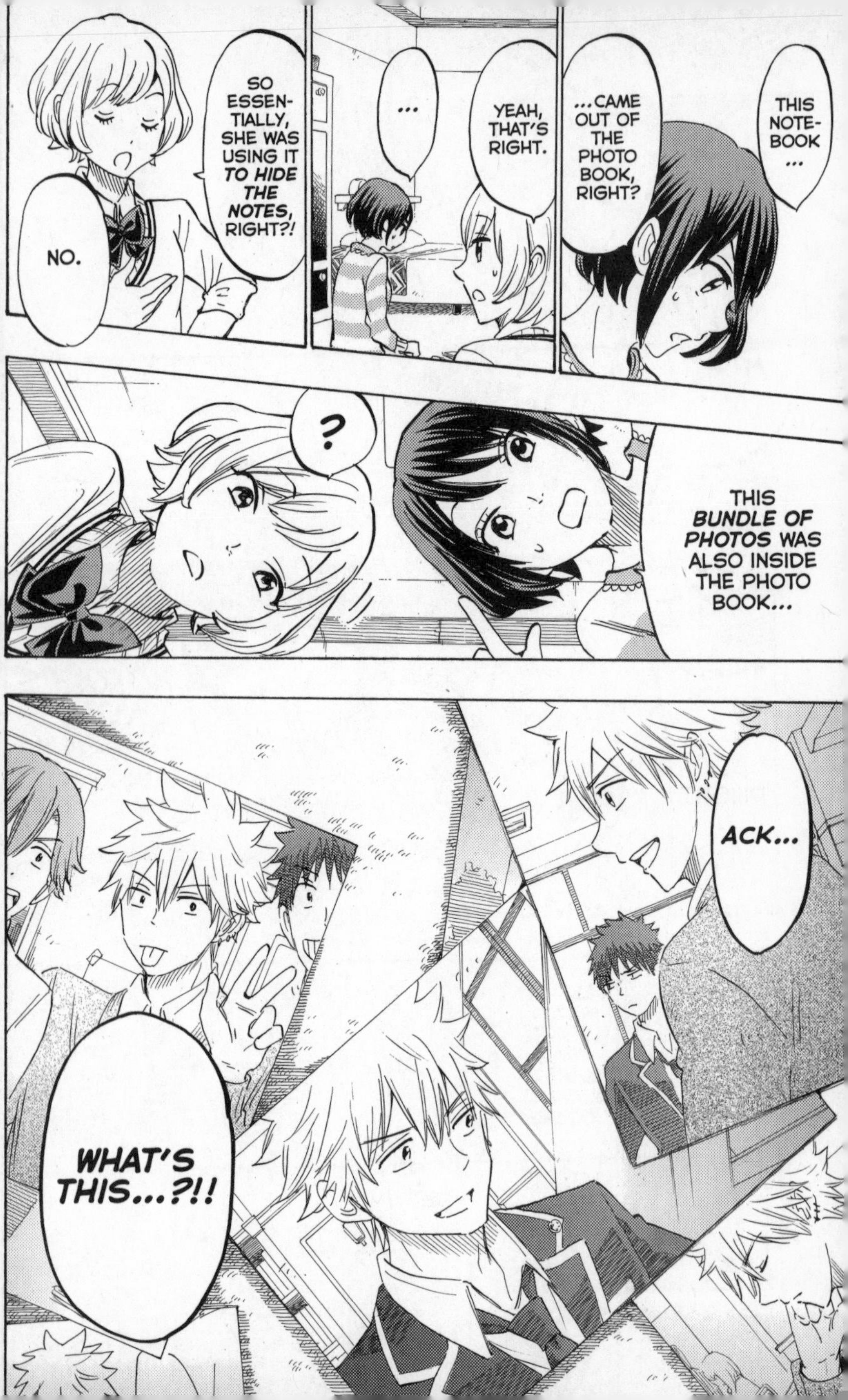
THIS NOTE-BOOK ...
...CAME OUT OF THE PHOTO BOOK, RIGHT?
YEAH, THAT'S RIGHT.
...
SO ESSENTIALLY, SHE WAS USING IT TO HIDE THE NOTES, RIGHT?!
NO.
THIS BUNDLE OF PHOTOS WAS ALSO INSIDE THE PHOTO BOOK...
?
ACK...
WHAT'S THIS...?!!

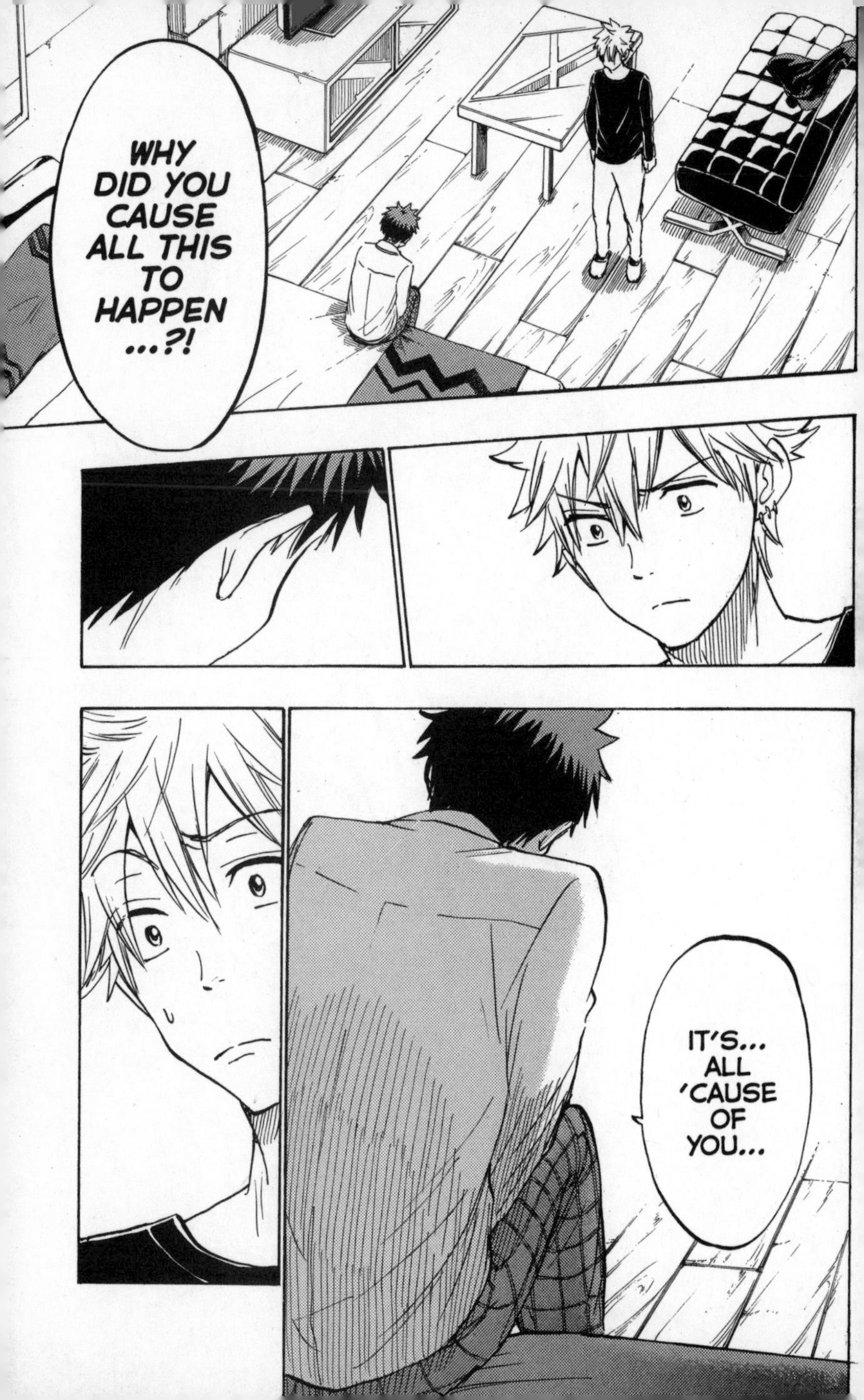
WHY DID YOU CAUSE ALL THIS TO HAPPEN ...?!
IT'S... ALL 'CAUSE OF YOU...

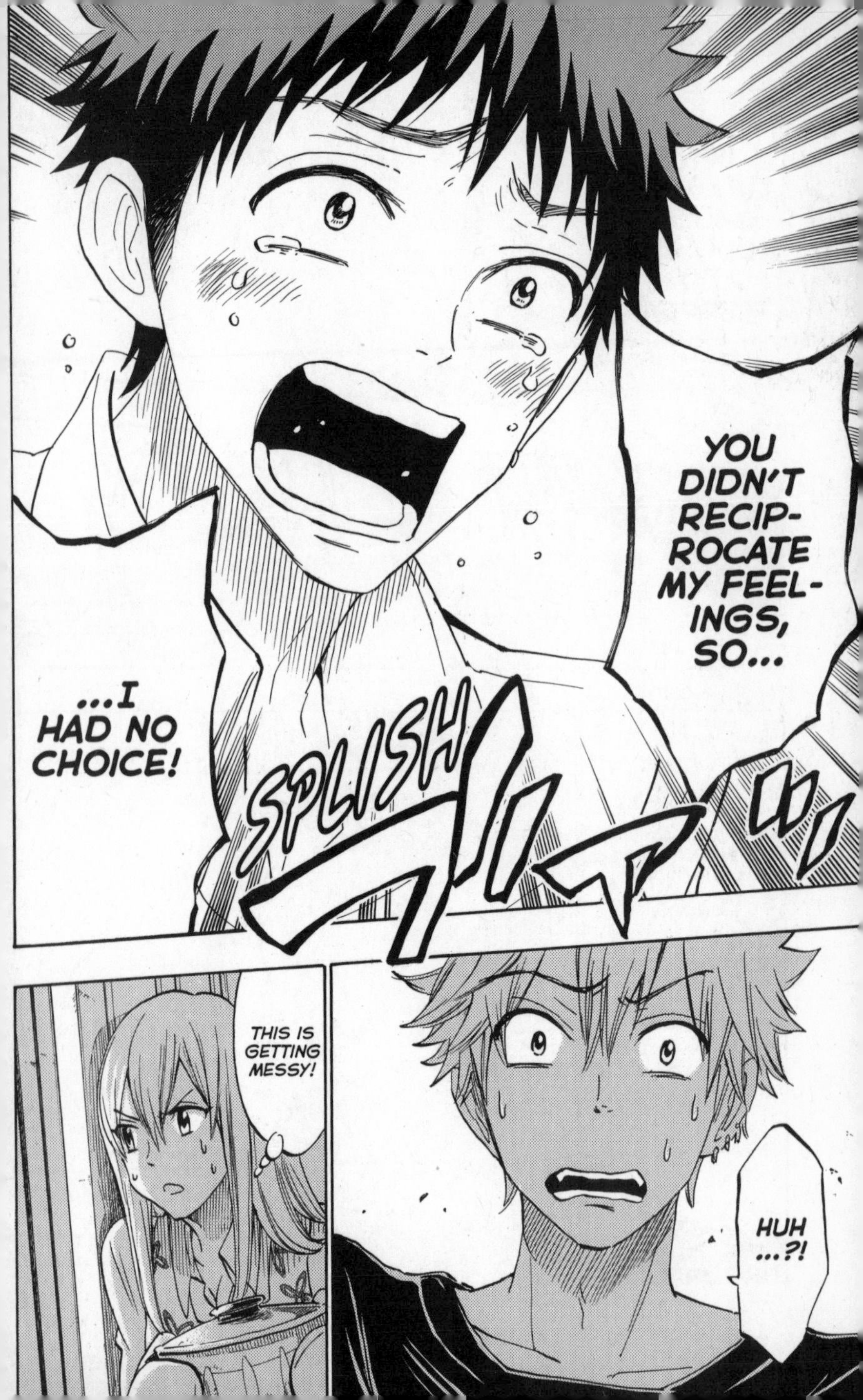
YOU DIDN'T RECIP- ROCATE MY FEEL- INGS, SO...
...I HAD NO CHOICE!
SPLISH
HUH ...?!
THIS IS GETTING MESSY!

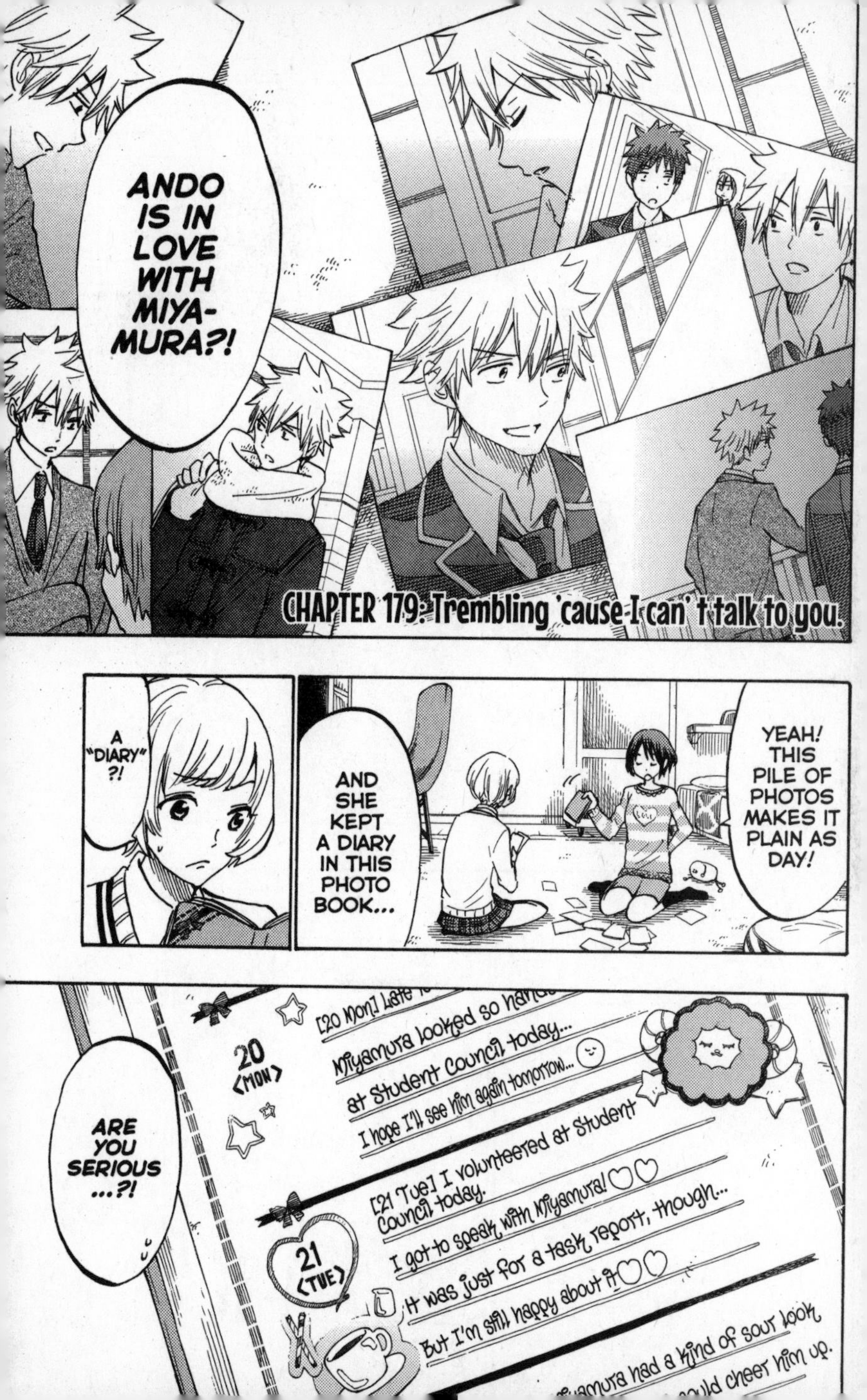
ANDO IS IN LOVE WITH MIYAMURA?!
CHAPTER 179: Trembling 'cause I can't talk to you.
YEAH! THIS PILE OF PHOTOS MAKES IT PLAIN AS DAY!
AND SHE KEPT A DIARY IN THIS PHOTO BOOK...
A "DIARY" ?!
20 (MON)
at Student Council today...
I hope I'll see him again tomorrow...
21 (TUE)
[21 Tue] I volunteered at Student Council today.
I got to speak with Miyamura!
It was just for a task report, though...
But I'm still happy about it!
ARE YOU SERIOUS...?!

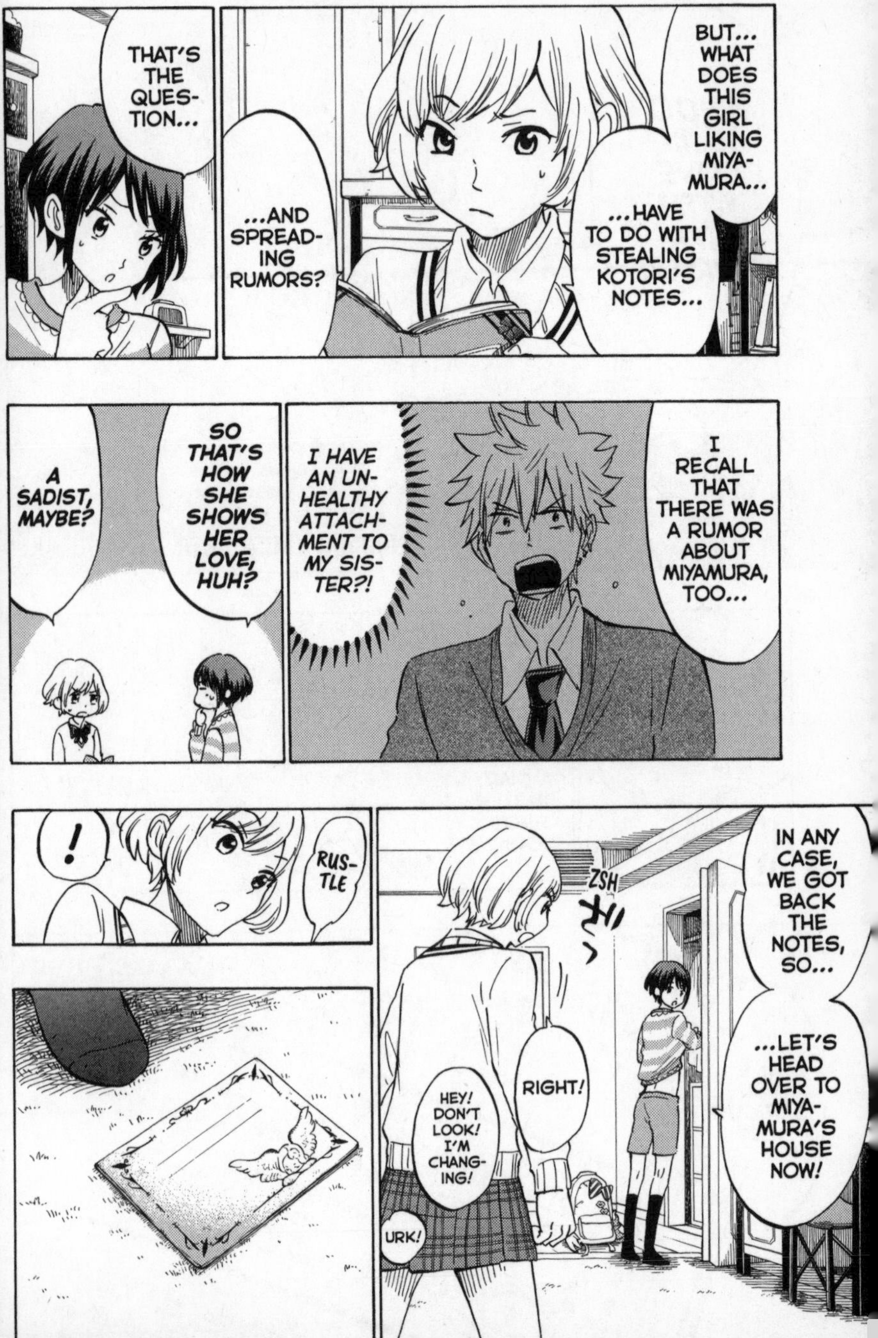
BUT... WHAT DOES THIS GIRL LIKING MIYAMURA...
...HAVE TO DO WITH STEALING KOTORI'S NOTES...
...AND SPREADING RUMORS?
THAT'S THE QUESTION...
I RECALL THAT THERE WAS A RUMOR ABOUT MIYAMURA, TOO...
I HAVE AN UNHEALTHY ATTACHMENT TO MY SISTER?!
SO THAT'S HOW SHE SHOWS HER LOVE, HUH?
A SADIST, MAYBE?
IN ANY CASE, WE GOT BACK THE NOTES, SO...
...LET'S HEAD OVER TO MIYAMURA'S HOUSE NOW!
ZSH
RIGHT!
HEY! DON'T LOOK! I'M CHANGING!
URK!
RUSTLE
!

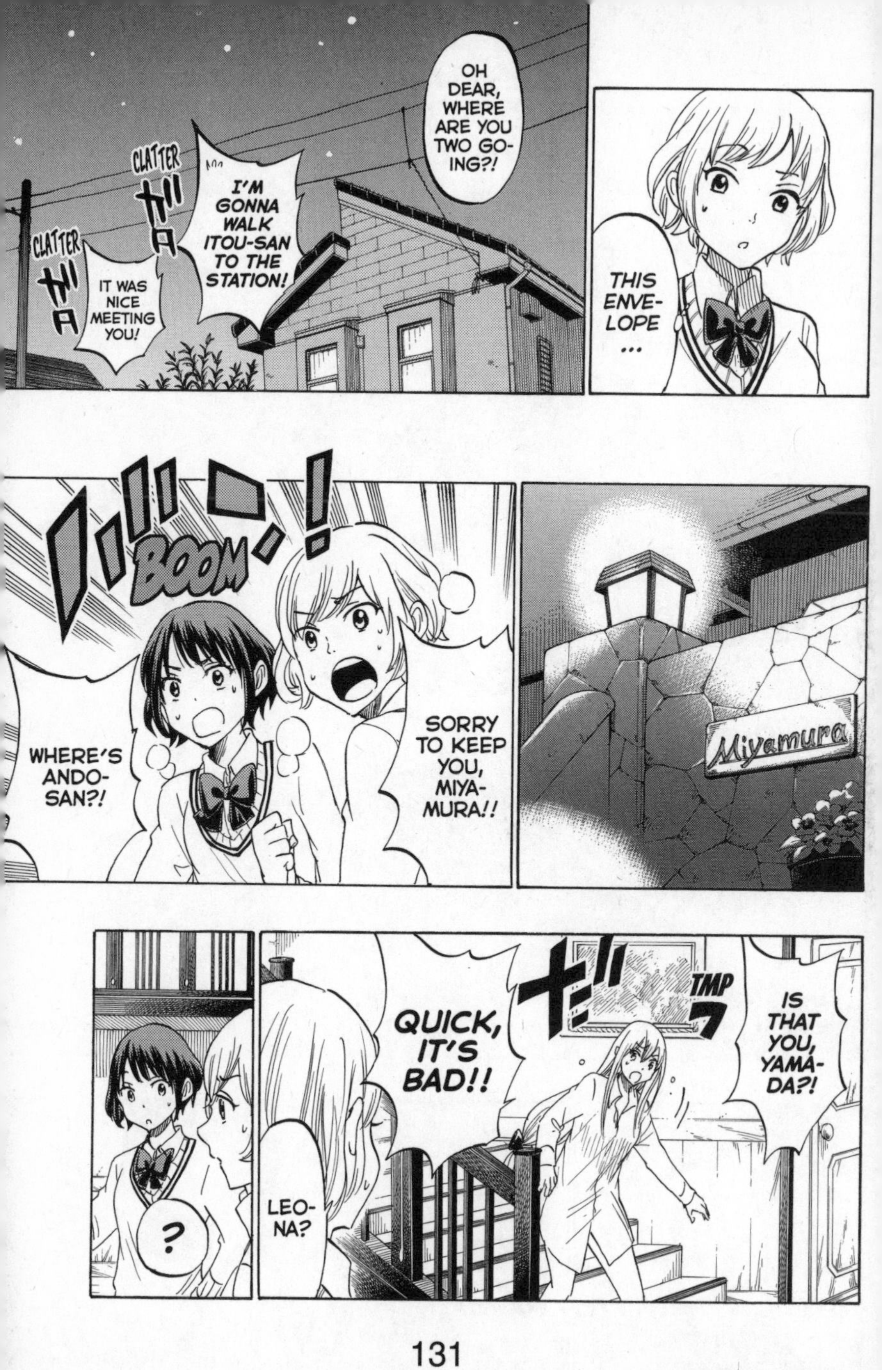
THIS ENVE- LOPE ...
OH DEAR, WHERE ARE YOU TWO GO- ING?!
I'M GONNA WALK ITOU-SAN TO THE STATION!
CLATTER
IT WAS NICE MEETING YOU!
CLATTER
Miyamura
BOOM
SORRY TO KEEP YOU, MIYA- MURA!!
WHERE'S ANDO- SAN?!
IS THAT YOU, YAMA- DA?!
TMP
QUICK, IT'S BAD!!
LEO- NA?
?

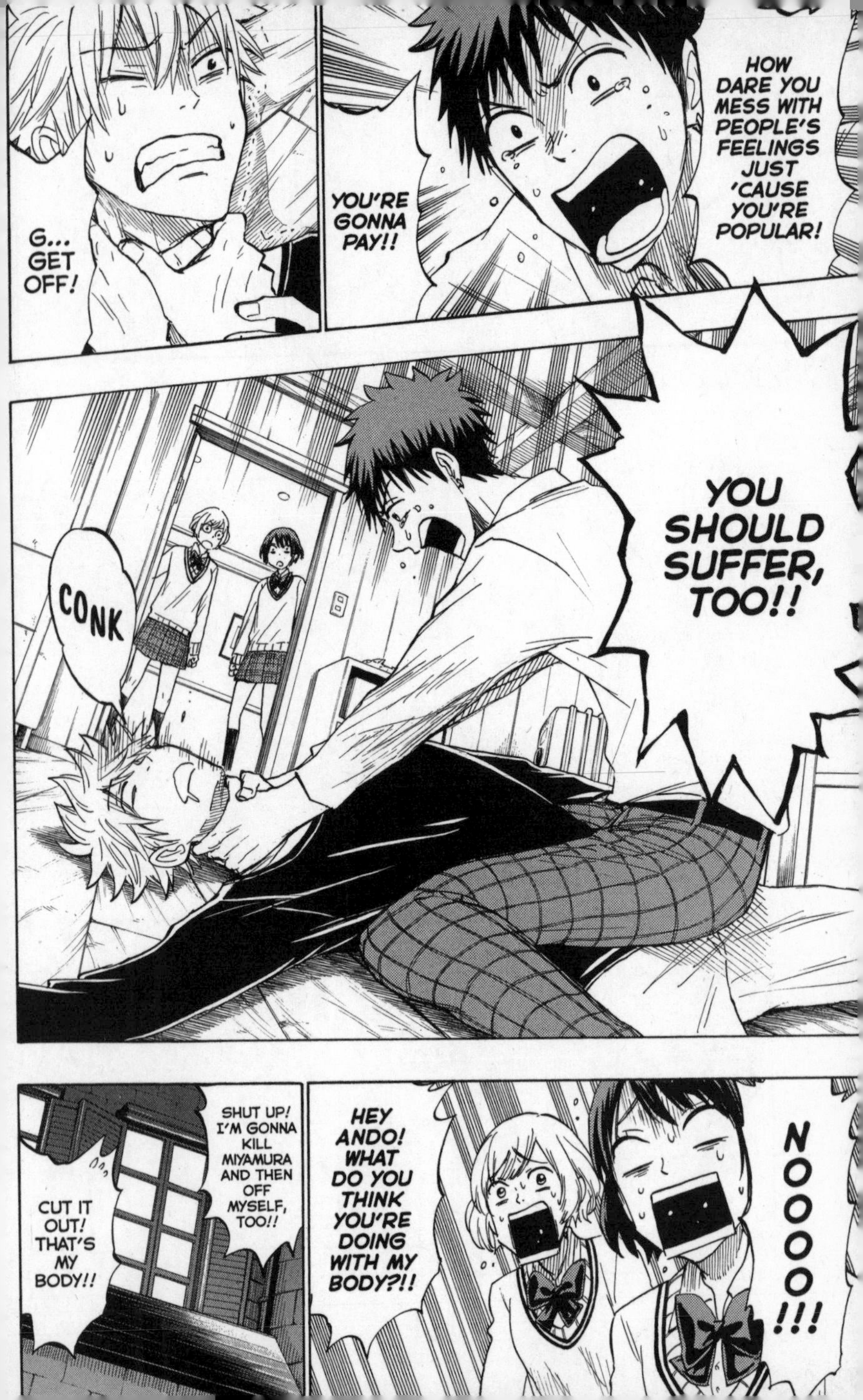
HOW DARE YOU MESS WITH PEOPLE'S FEELINGS JUST 'CAUSE YOU'RE POPULAR!
YOU'RE GONNA PAY!!
G... GET OFF!
YOU SHOULD SUFFER, TOO!!
CONK
NOOOOO!!!
HEY ANDO! WHAT DO YOU THINK YOU'RE DOING WITH MY BODY?!!
SHUT UP! I'M GONNA KILL MIYAMURA AND THEN OFF MYSELF, TOO!!
CUT IT OUT! THAT'S MY BODY!!

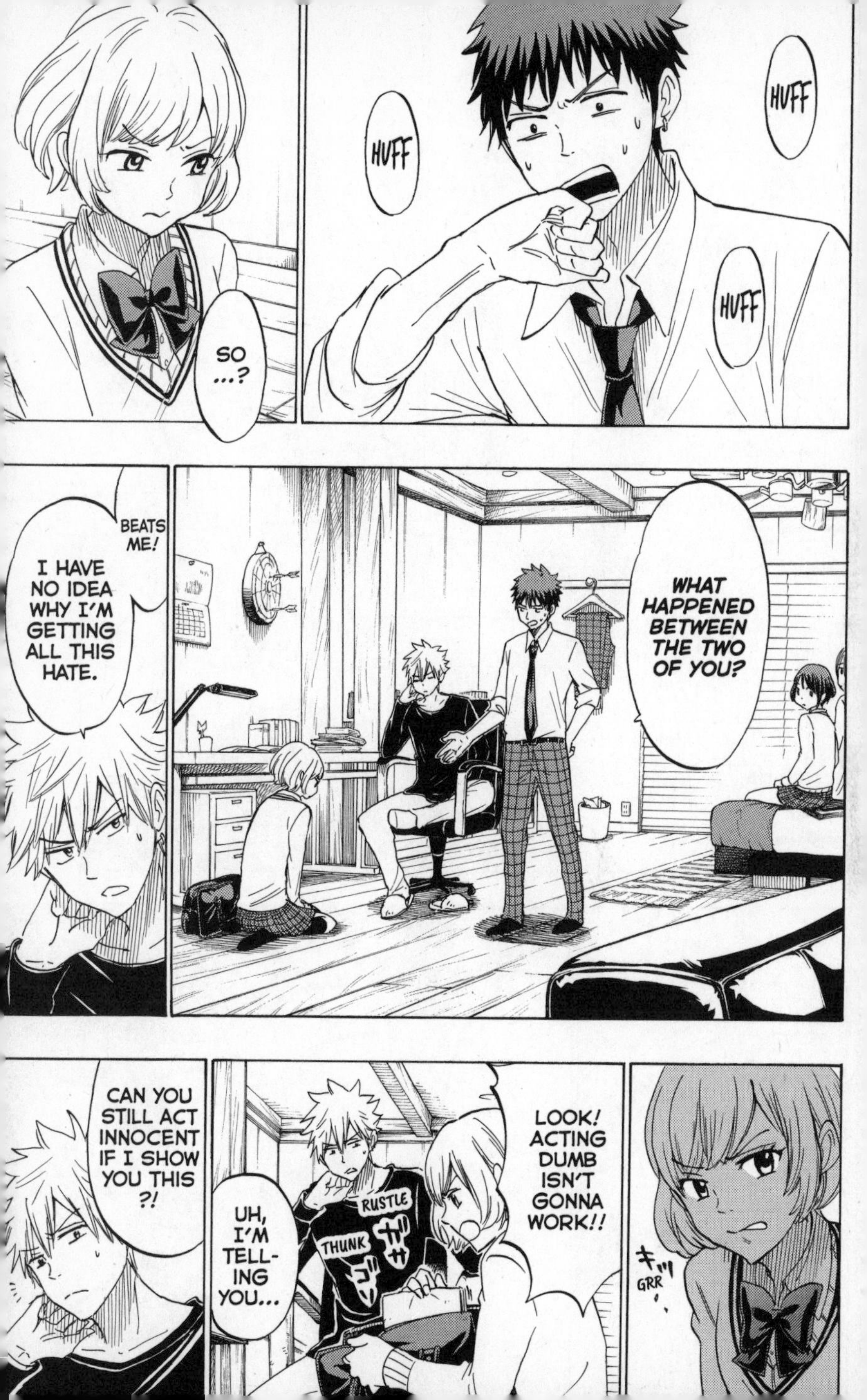
HUFF
HUFF
HUFF
SO ...?
WHAT HAPPENED BETWEEN THE TWO OF YOU?
BEATS ME!
I HAVE NO IDEA WHY I'M GETTING ALL THIS HATE.
キッ
GRR
LOOK! ACTING DUMB ISN'T GONNA WORK!!
RUSTLE
ガサ
THUNK
ゴソ
UH, I'M TELL-ING YOU...
CAN YOU STILL ACT INNOCENT IF I SHOW YOU THIS?!

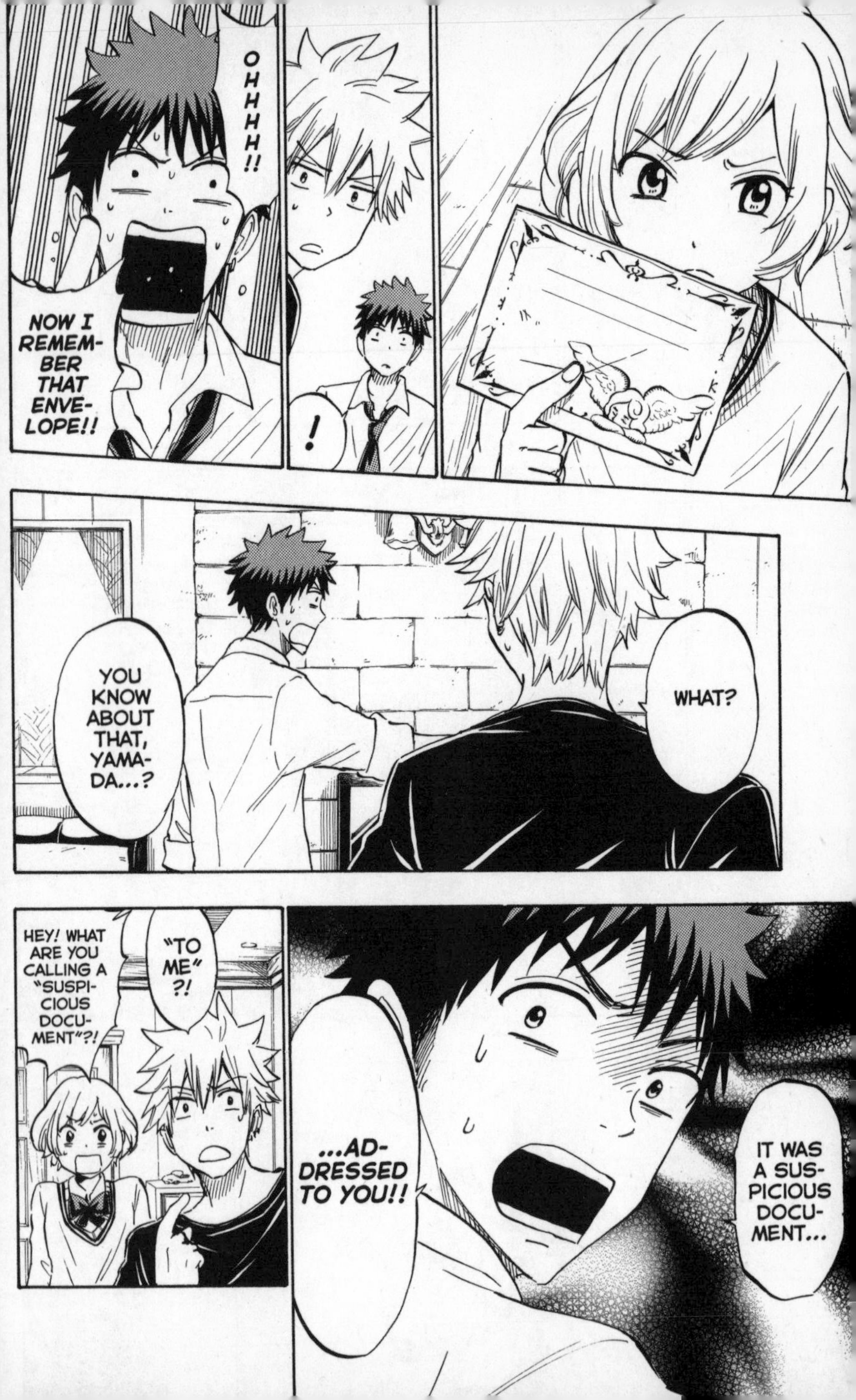
!
OHHHH!!
NOW I REMEM-BER THAT ENVE-LOPE!!
WHAT?
YOU KNOW ABOUT THAT, YAMA-DA...?
IT WAS A SUS-PICIOUS DOCU-MENT...
...AD-DRESSED TO YOU!!
“TO ME”?!
HEY! WHAT ARE YOU CALLING A “SUSPI-CIOUS DOCU-MENT”?!

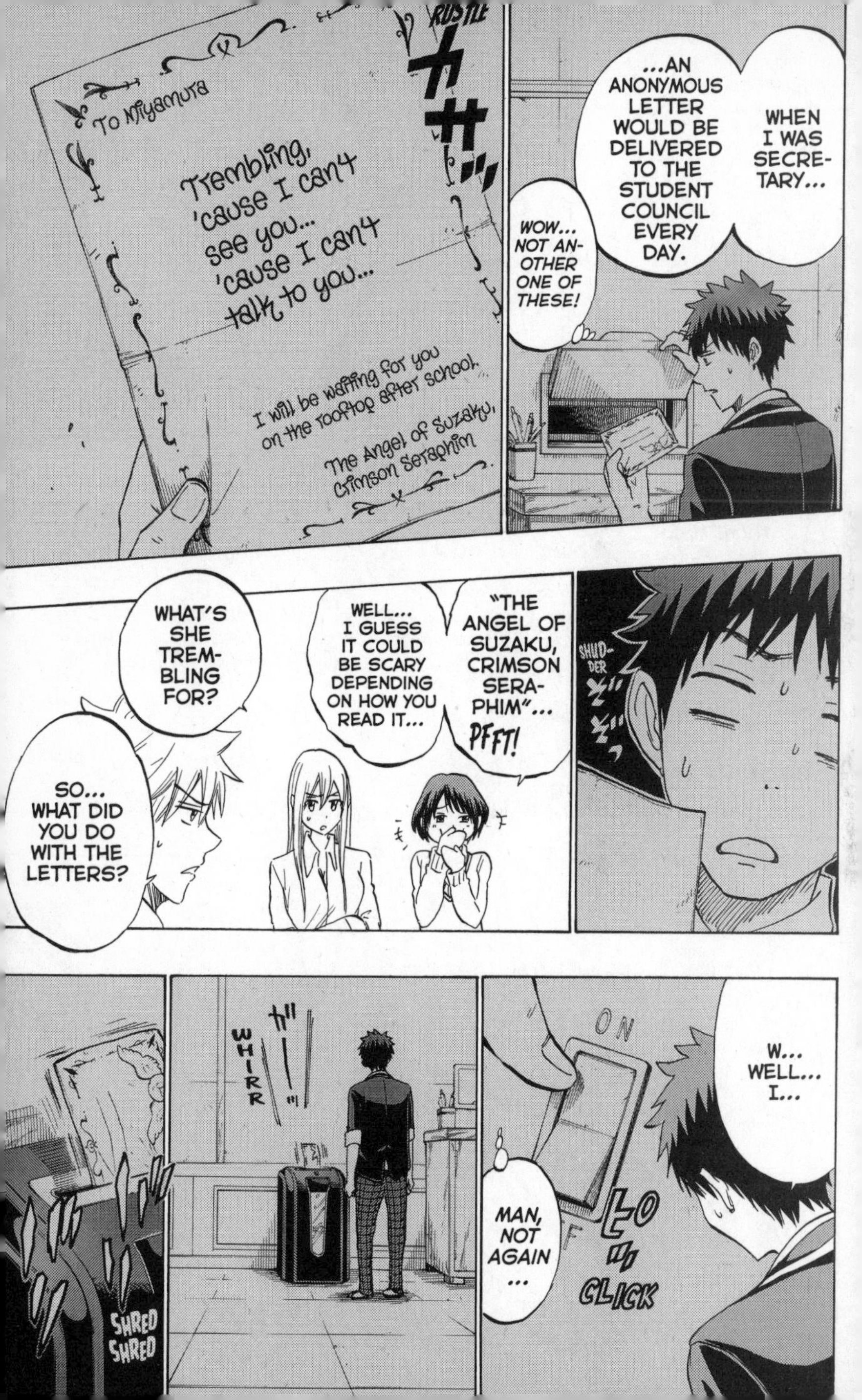
WHEN I WAS SECRE-TARY...
...AN ANONYMOUS LETTER WOULD BE DELIVERED TO THE STUDENT COUNCIL EVERY DAY.
WOW... NOT AN-OTHER ONE OF THESE!
RUSTLE
To Miyamura
Trembling, 'cause I can't see you... 'cause I can't talk to you...
I will be waiting for you on the rooftop after school.
The Angel of Suzaku, Crimson Seraphim
SHUD-DER
"THE ANGEL OF SUZAKU, CRIMSON SERA-PHIM"... PFFT!
WELL... I GUESS IT COULD BE SCARY DEPENDING ON HOW YOU READ IT...
WHAT'S SHE TREM-BLING FOR?
SO... WHAT DID YOU DO WITH THE LETTERS?
W... WELL... I...
ON
MAN, NOT AGAIN...
CLICK
WHIRR
SHRED SHRED

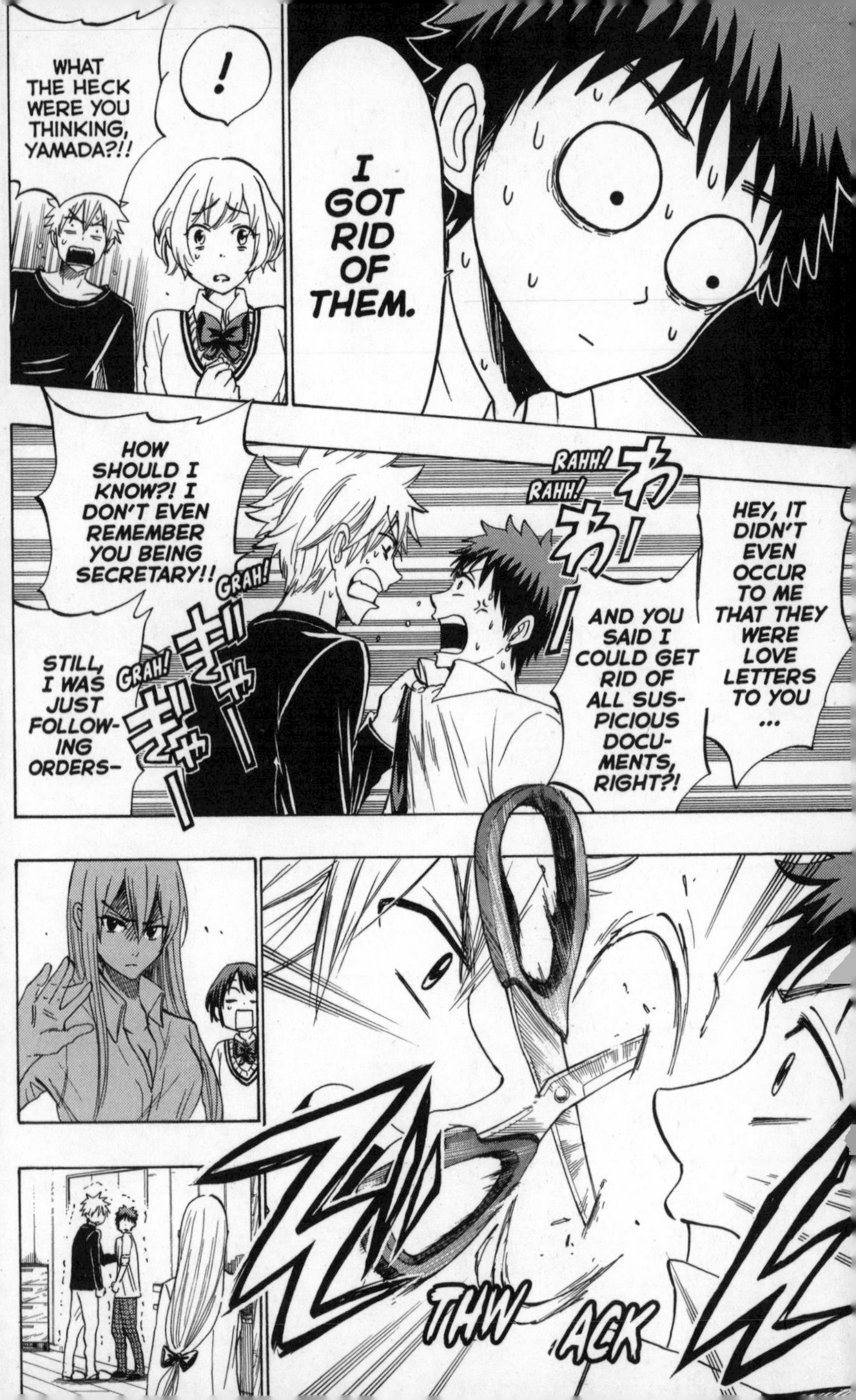
I GOT RID OF THEM.
!
WHAT THE HECK WERE YOU THINKING, YAMADA?!!
HEY, IT DIDN'T EVEN OCCUR TO ME THAT THEY WERE LOVE LETTERS TO YOU ...
RAHH! RAHH!
わーわー
AND YOU SAID I COULD GET RID OF ALL SUS-PICIOUS DOCU-MENTS, RIGHT?!
HOW SHOULD I KNOW?! I DON'T EVEN REMEMBER YOU BEING SECRETARY!!
GRAH! GRAH!
ぎゃーぎゃー
STILL, I WAS JUST FOLLOW-ING ORDERS–
THWACK

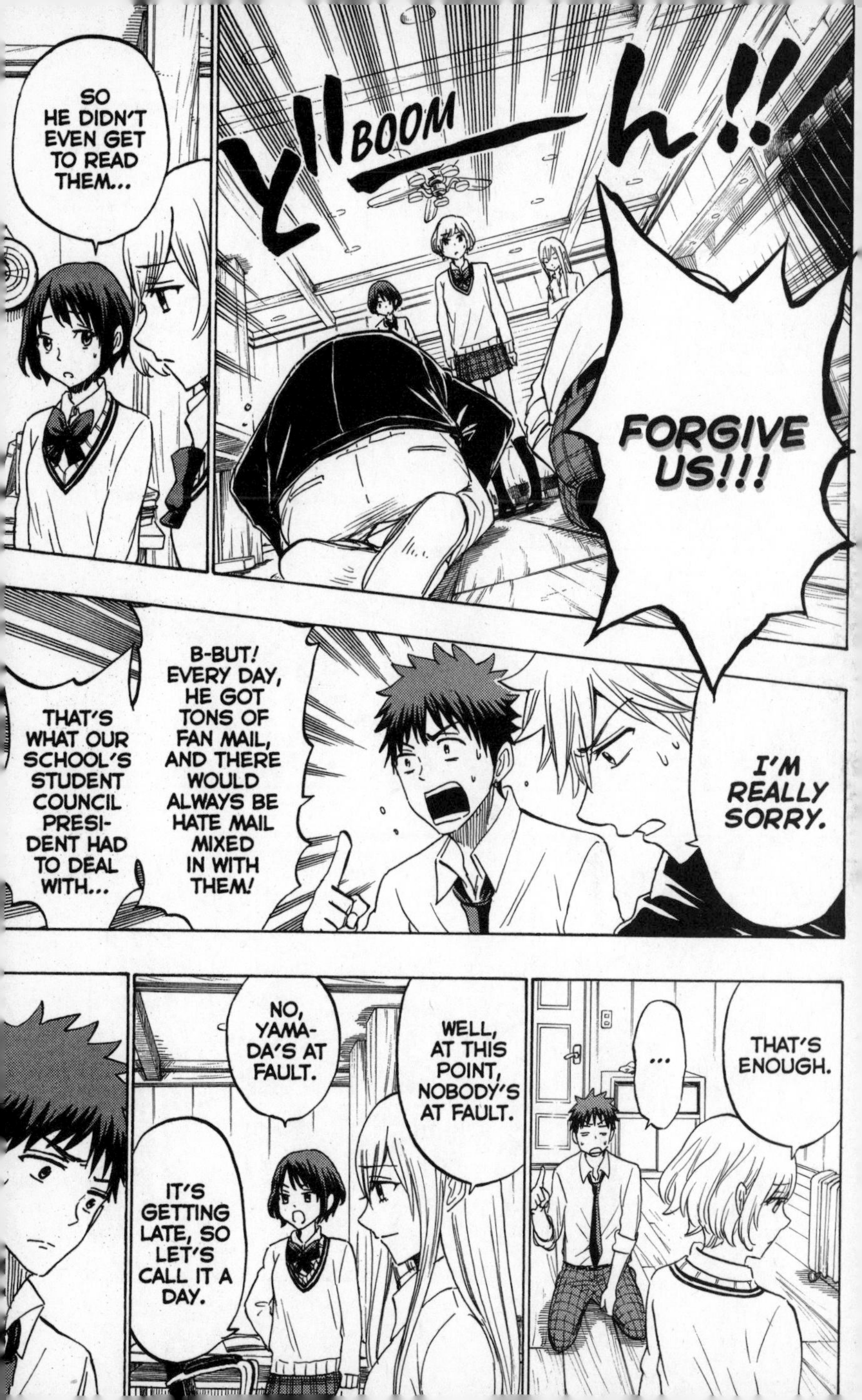
BOOM
FORGIVE US!!!
SO HE DIDN'T EVEN GET TO READ THEM...
I'M REALLY SORRY.
B-BUT! EVERY DAY, HE GOT TONS OF FAN MAIL, AND THERE WOULD ALWAYS BE HATE MAIL MIXED IN WITH THEM!
THAT'S WHAT OUR SCHOOL'S STUDENT COUNCIL PRESI-DENT HAD TO DEAL WITH...
THAT'S ENOUGH.
...
WELL, AT THIS POINT, NOBODY'S AT FAULT.
NO, YAMA-DA'S AT FAULT.
IT'S GETTING LATE, SO LET'S CALL IT A DAY.

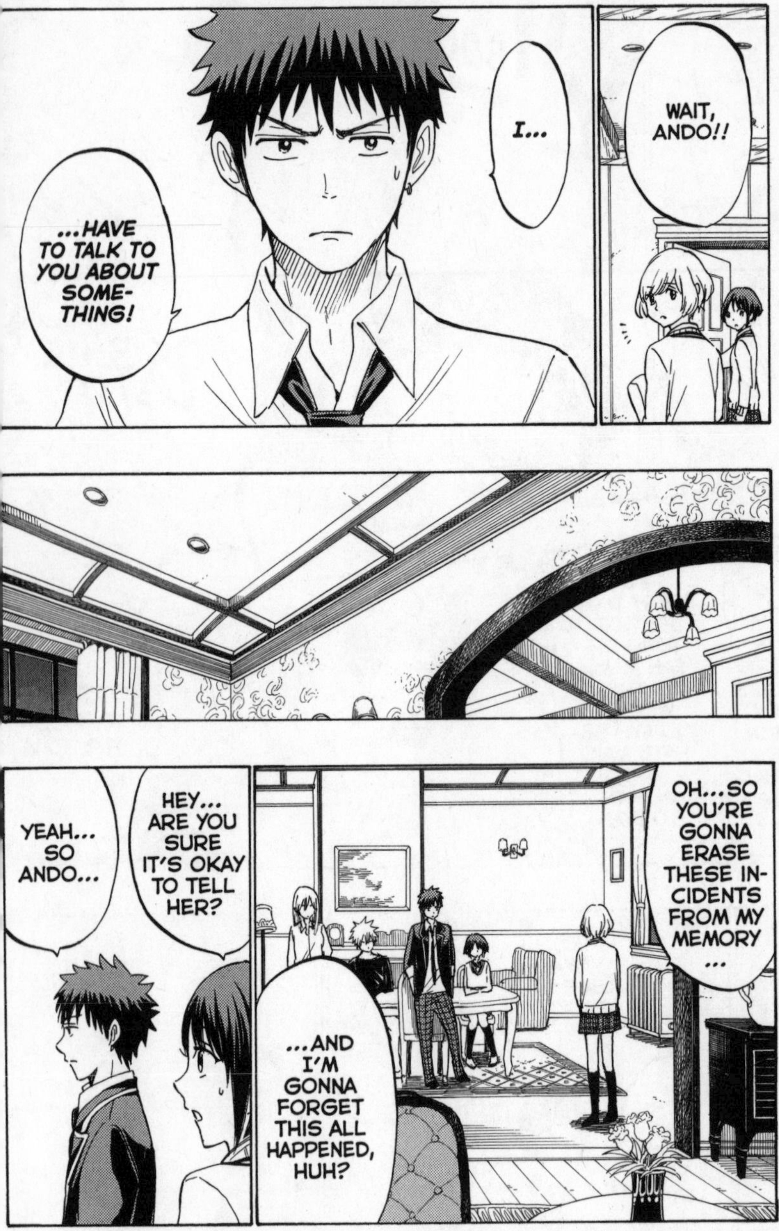
WAIT, ANDO!!
I...
...HAVE TO TALK TO YOU ABOUT SOME-THING!
OH...SO YOU'RE GONNA ERASE THESE IN-CIDENTS FROM MY MEMORY...
...AND I'M GONNA FORGET THIS ALL HAPPENED, HUH?
HEY... ARE YOU SURE IT'S OKAY TO TELL HER?
YEAH... SO ANDO...

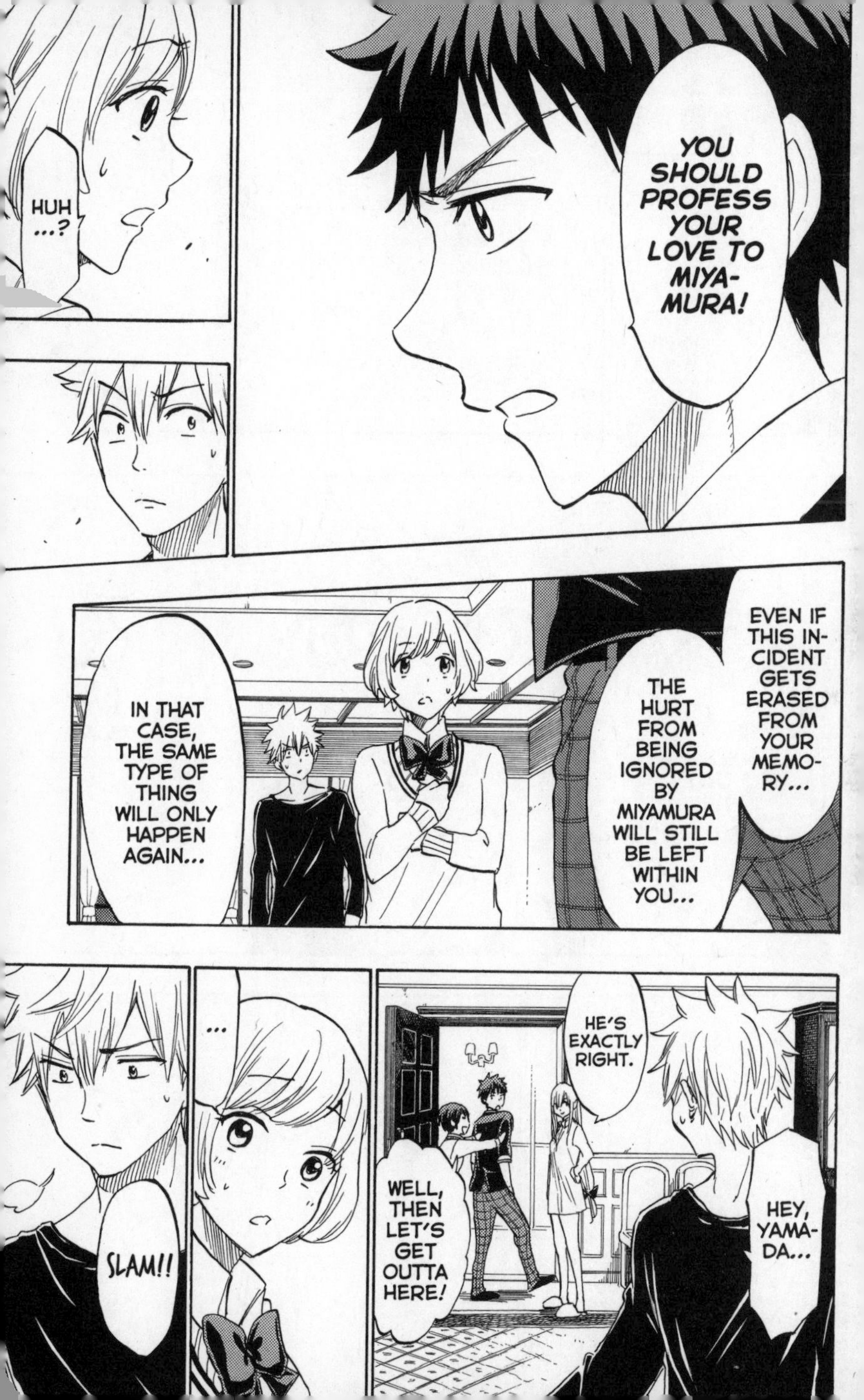
YOU SHOULD PROFESS YOUR LOVE TO MIYAMURA!
HUH ...?
EVEN IF THIS INCIDENT GETS ERASED FROM YOUR MEMORY...
THE HURT FROM BEING IGNORED BY MIYAMURA WILL STILL BE LEFT WITHIN YOU...
IN THAT CASE, THE SAME TYPE OF THING WILL ONLY HAPPEN AGAIN...
HE'S EXACTLY RIGHT.
HEY, YAMADA...
WELL, THEN LET'S GET OUTTA HERE!
...
SLAM!!

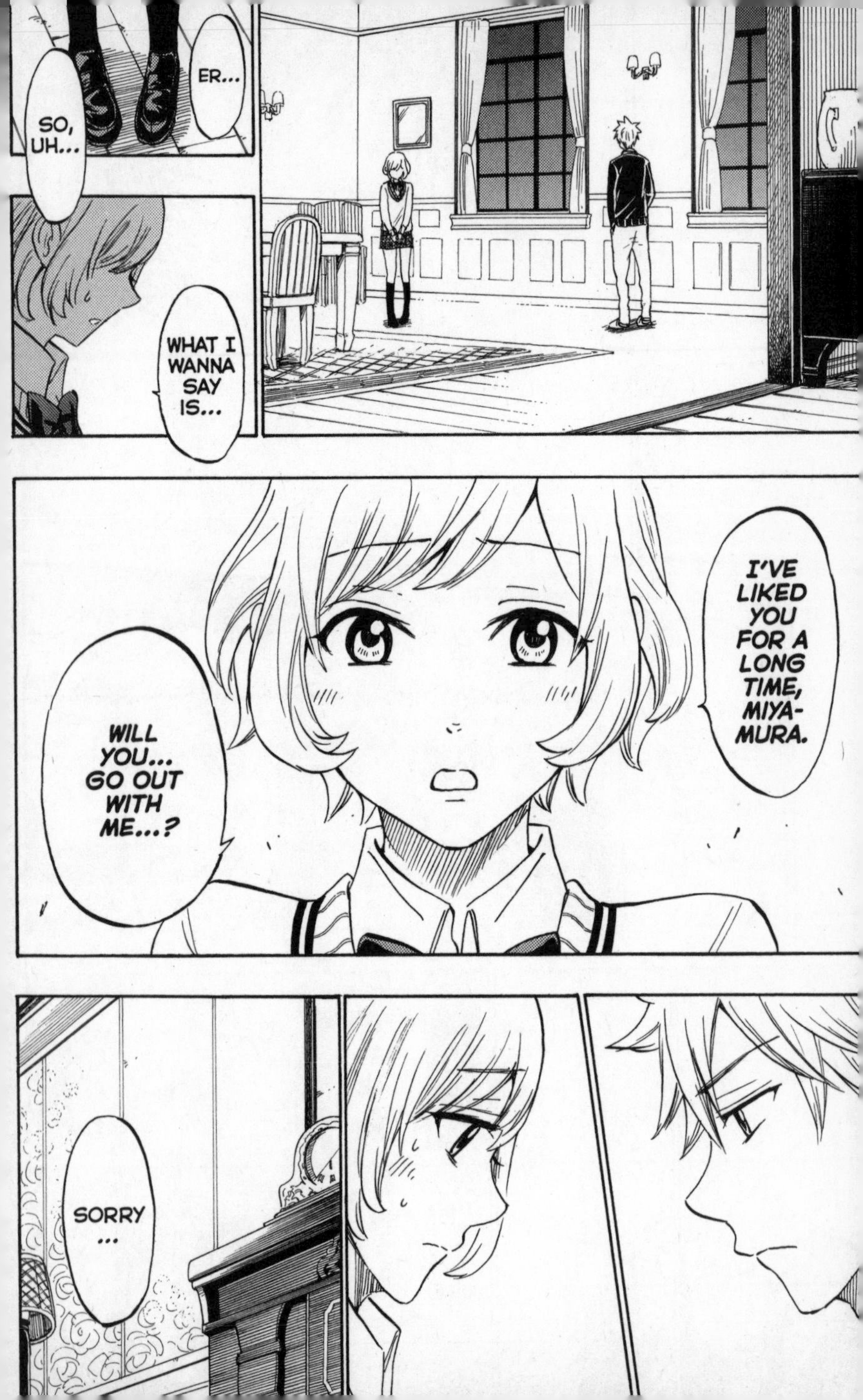
ER...
SO, UH...
WHAT I WANNA SAY IS...
I'VE LIKED YOU FOR A LONG TIME, MIYA-MURA.
WILL YOU... GO OUT WITH ME...?
SORRY...

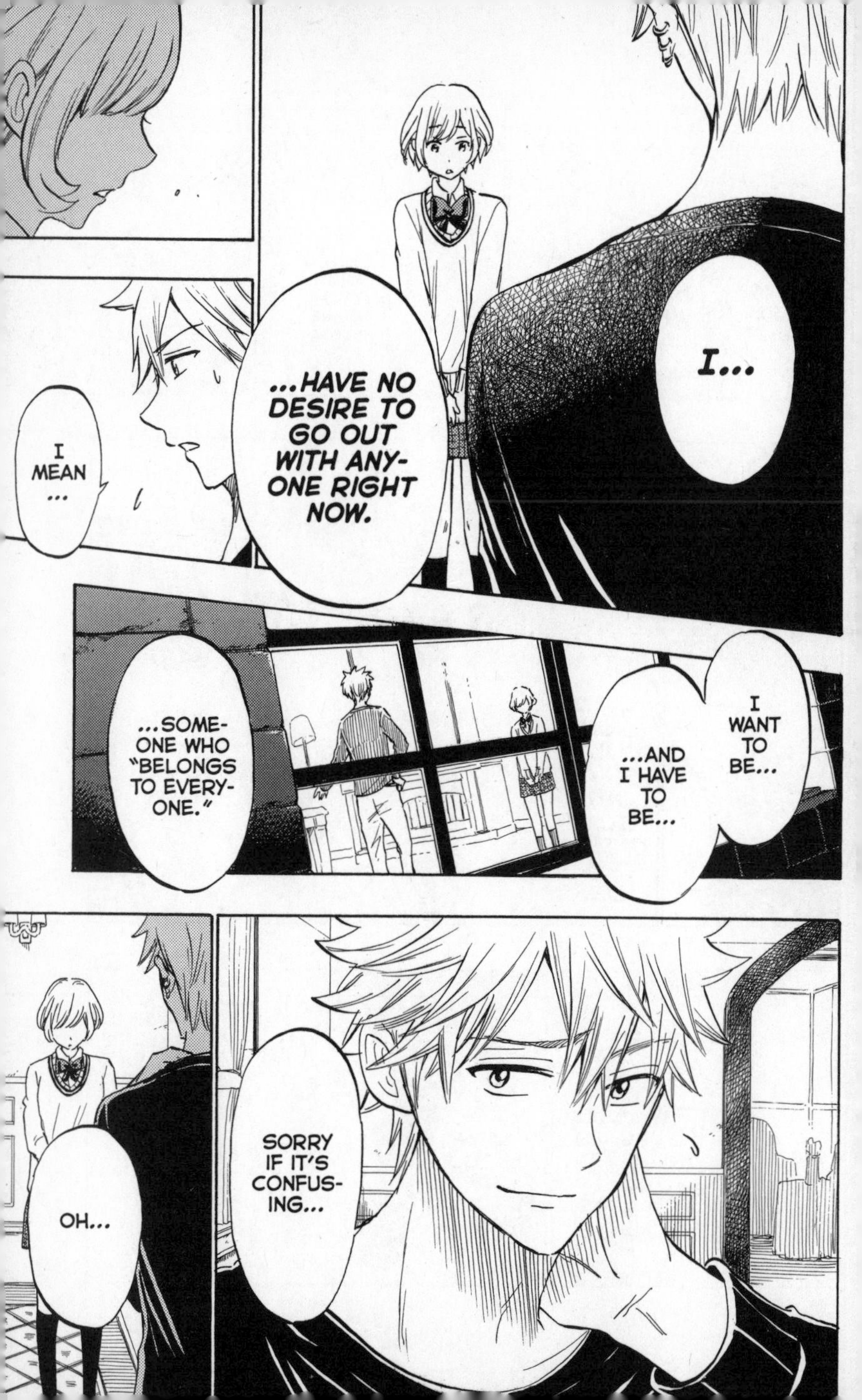
I...
...HAVE NO DESIRE TO GO OUT WITH ANY-ONE RIGHT NOW.
I MEAN ...
I WANT TO BE...
...AND I HAVE TO BE...
...SOME-ONE WHO "BELONGS TO EVERY-ONE."
SORRY IF IT'S CONFUS-ING...
OH...

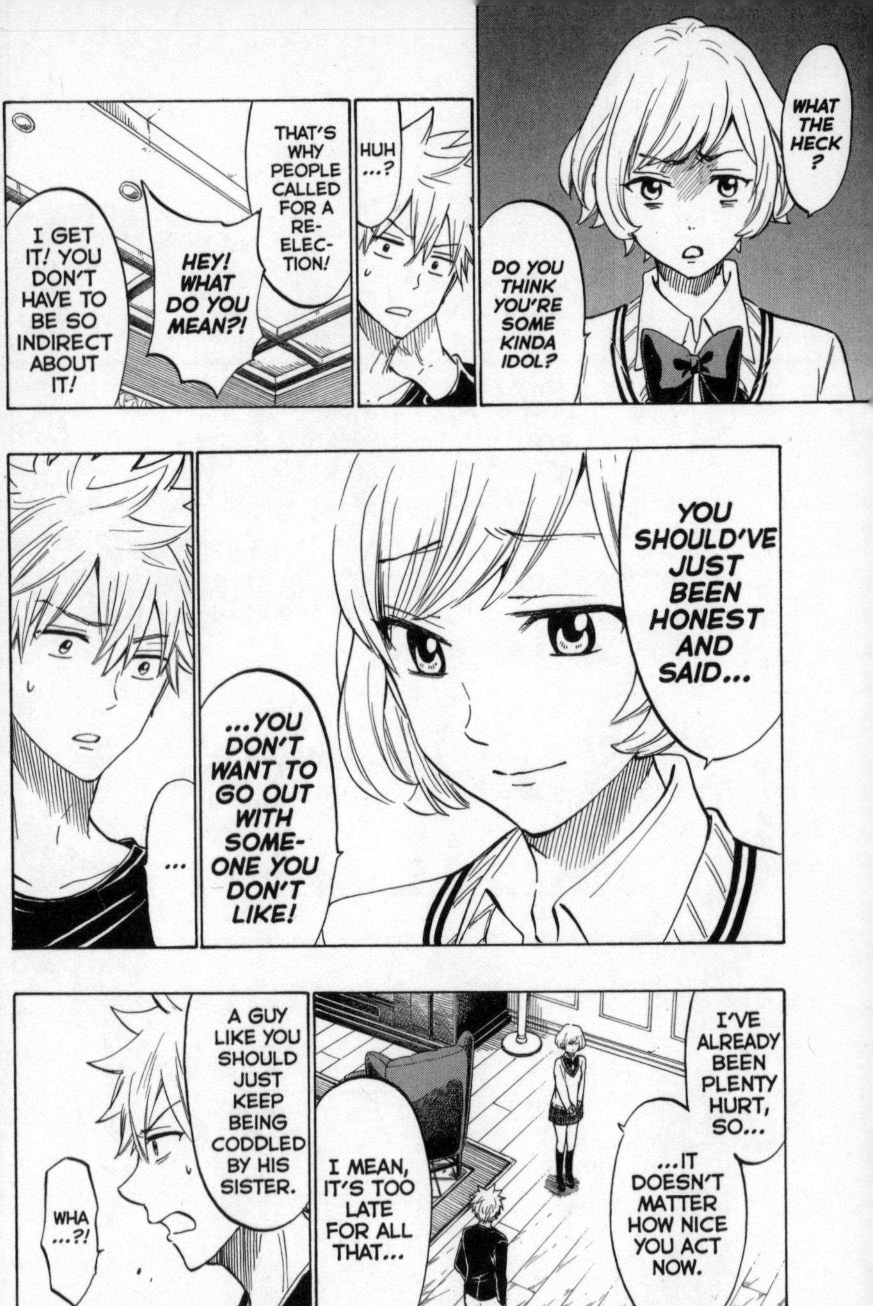
WHAT THE HECK?
DO YOU THINK YOU'RE SOME KINDA IDOL?
HUH ...?
THAT'S WHY PEOPLE CALLED FOR A RE-ELECTION!
HEY! WHAT DO YOU MEAN?!
I GET IT! YOU DON'T HAVE TO BE SO INDIRECT ABOUT IT!
YOU SHOULD'VE JUST BEEN HONEST AND SAID...
...YOU DON'T WANT TO GO OUT WITH SOME-ONE YOU DON'T LIKE!
...
I'VE ALREADY BEEN PLENTY HURT, SO...
...IT DOESN'T MATTER HOW NICE YOU ACT NOW.
I MEAN, IT'S TOO LATE FOR ALL THAT...
A GUY LIKE YOU SHOULD JUST KEEP BEING CODDLED BY HIS SISTER.
WHA ...?!

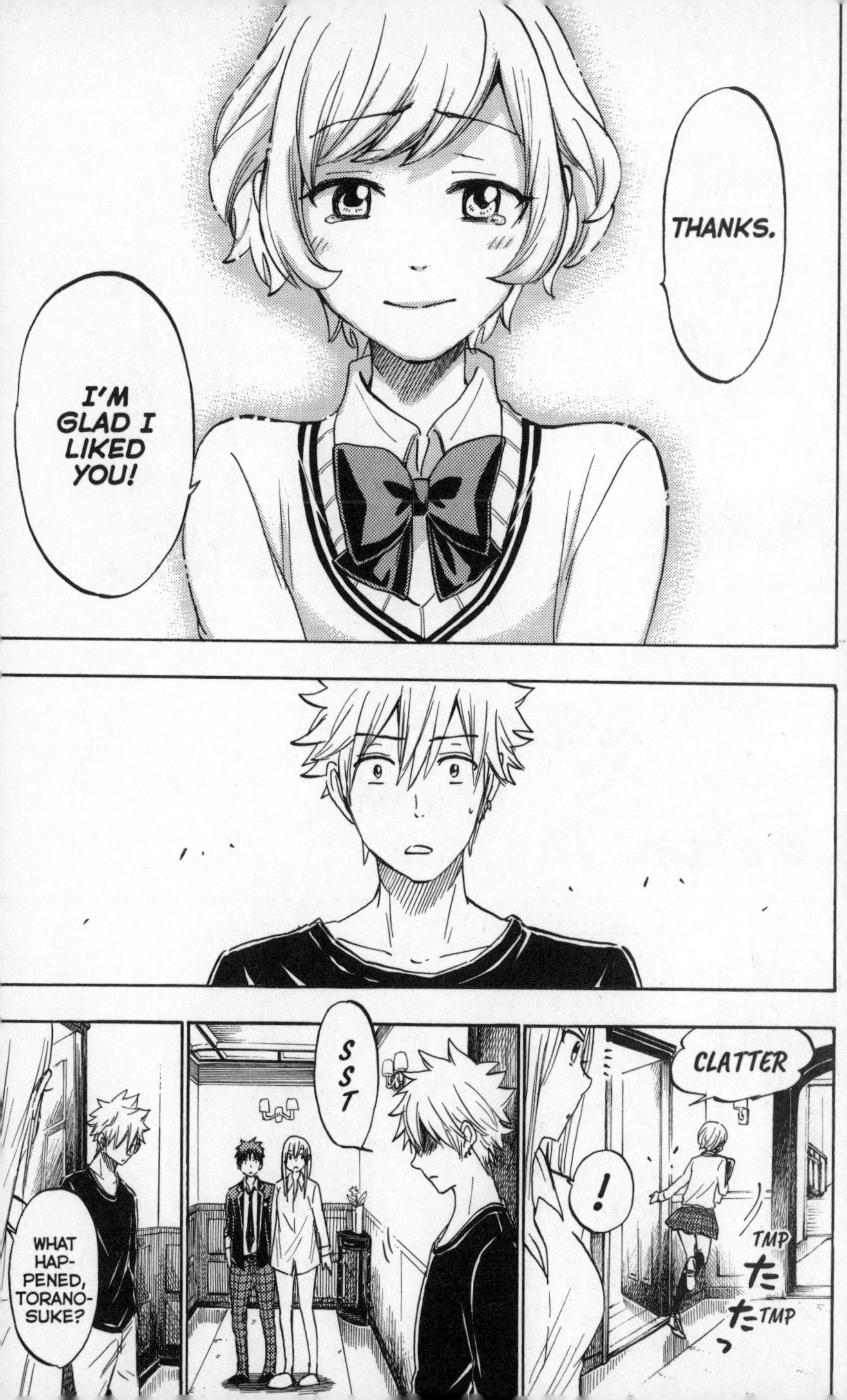
THANKS.
I'M GLAD I LIKED YOU!
CLATTER
!
TMP た
た TMP
SST
WHAT HAP-PENED, TORANO-SUKE?

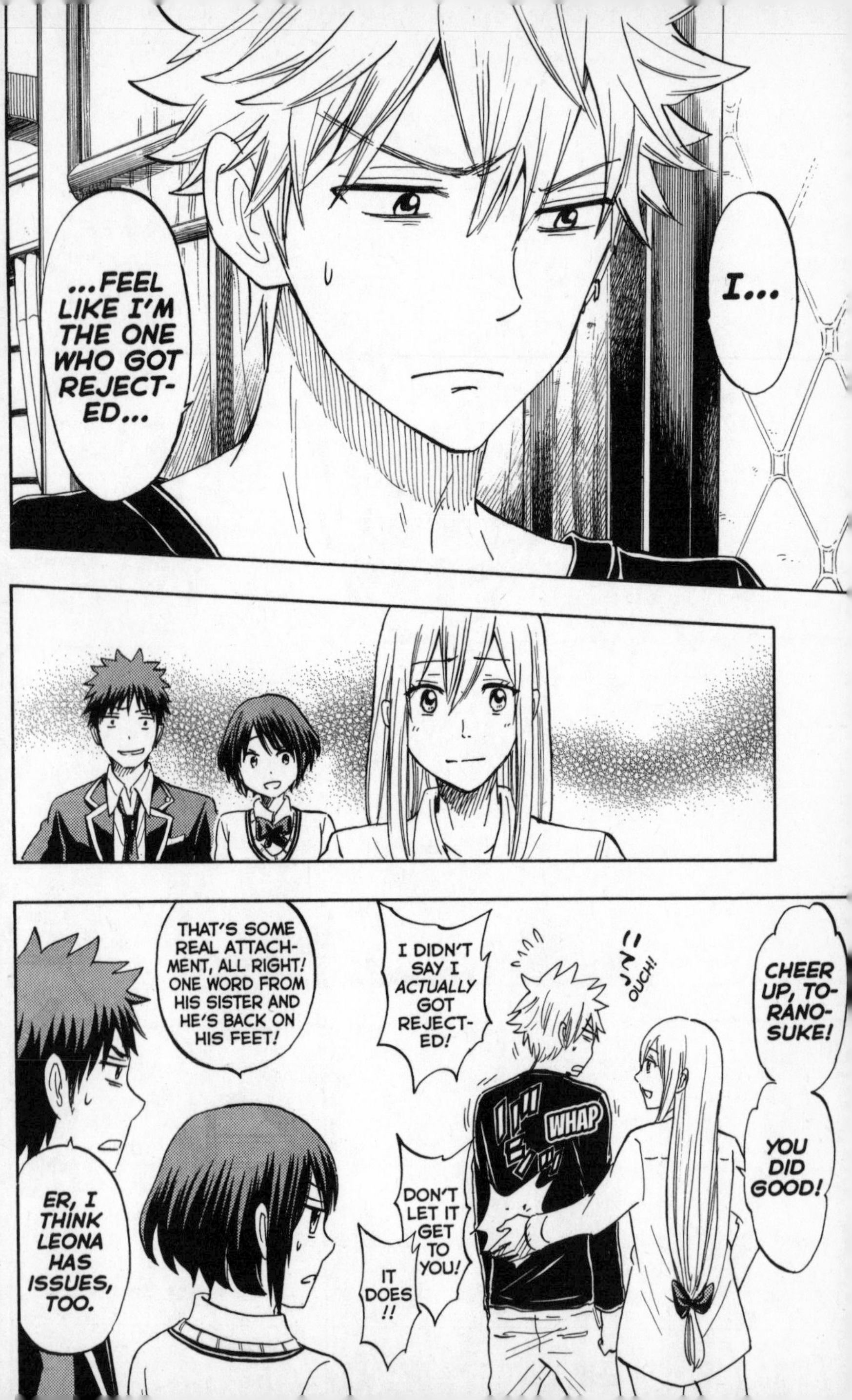
I...
...FEEL LIKE I'M THE ONE WHO GOT REJECT-ED...
CHEER UP, TO-RANO-SUKE!
YOU DID GOOD!
OUCH!
I DIDN'T SAY I ACTUALLY GOT REJECT-ED!
THAT'S SOME REAL ATTACH-MENT, ALL RIGHT! ONE WORD FROM HIS SISTER AND HE'S BACK ON HIS FEET!
WHAP
DON'T LET IT GET TO YOU!
IT DOES!!
ER, I THINK LEONA HAS ISSUES, TOO.

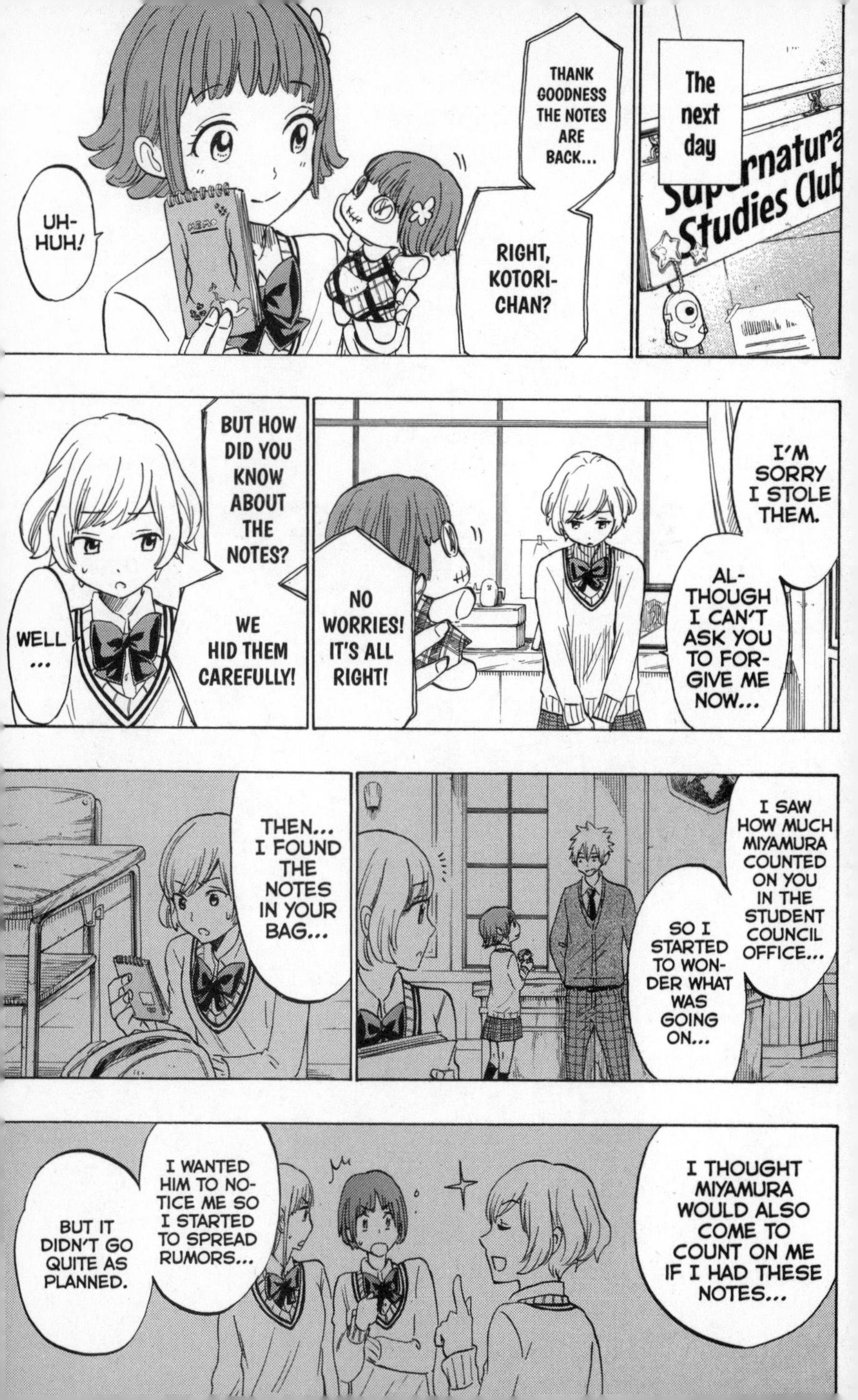
The next day
Supernatura
Studies Club
THANK GOODNESS THE NOTES ARE BACK...
RIGHT, KOTORI-CHAN?
UH-HUH!
I'M SORRY I STOLE THEM.
AL-THOUGH I CAN'T ASK YOU TO FOR-GIVE ME NOW...
NO WORRIES! IT'S ALL RIGHT!
BUT HOW DID YOU KNOW ABOUT THE NOTES?
WE HID THEM CAREFULLY!
WELL...
I SAW HOW MUCH MIYAMURA COUNTED ON YOU IN THE STUDENT COUNCIL OFFICE...
SO I STARTED TO WON-DER WHAT WAS GOING ON...
THEN... I FOUND THE NOTES IN YOUR BAG...
I THOUGHT MIYAMURA WOULD ALSO COME TO COUNT ON ME IF I HAD THESE NOTES...
I WANTED HIM TO NO-TICE ME SO I STARTED TO SPREAD RUMORS...
BUT IT DIDN'T GO QUITE AS PLANNED.

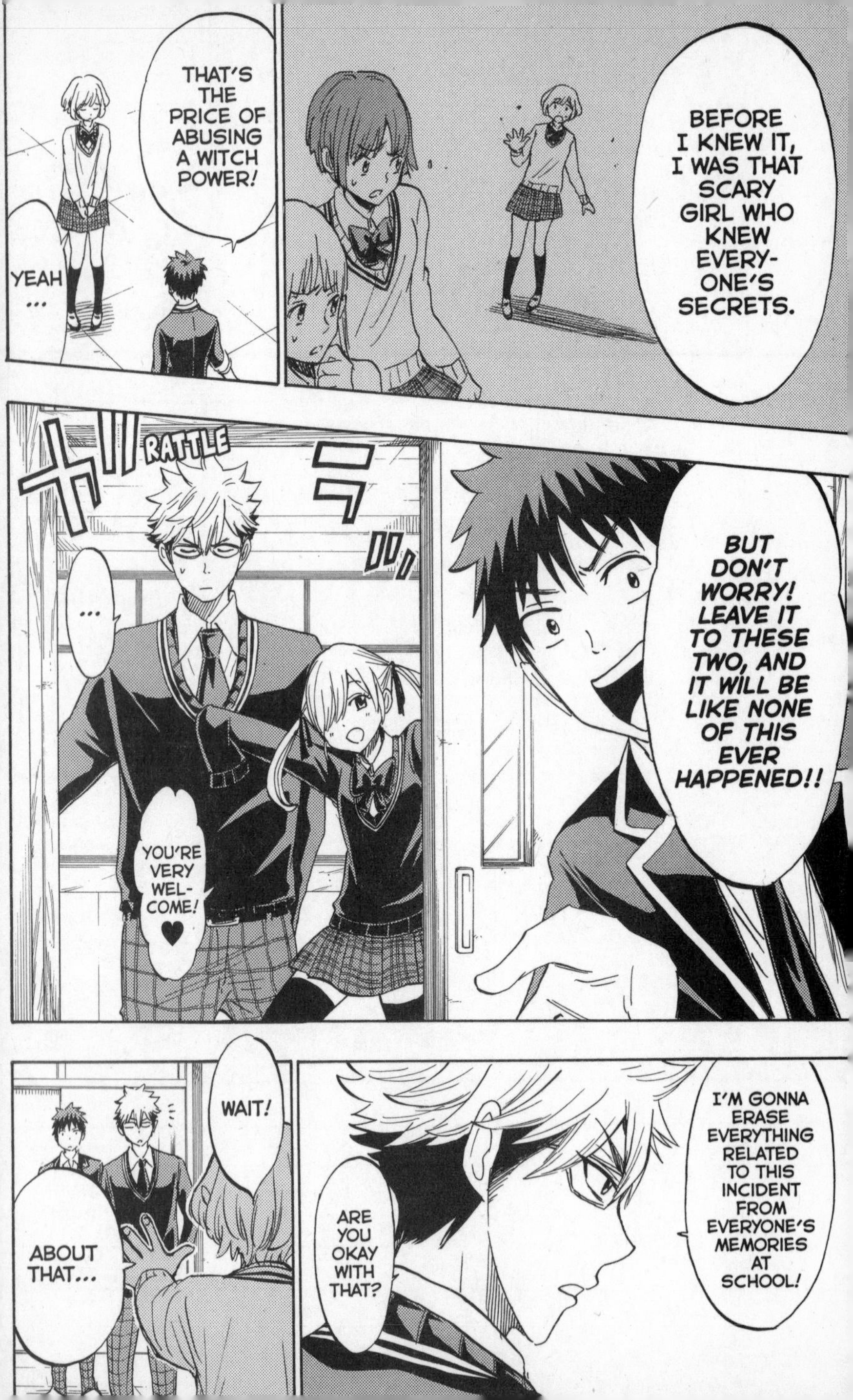
BEFORE I KNEW IT, I WAS THAT SCARY GIRL WHO KNEW EVERYONE'S SECRETS.
THAT'S THE PRICE OF ABUSING A WITCH POWER!
YEAH...
BUT DON'T WORRY! LEAVE IT TO THESE TWO, AND IT WILL BE LIKE NONE OF THIS EVER HAPPENED!!
RATTLE
...
YOU'RE VERY WELCOME! ♥
I'M GONNA ERASE EVERYTHING RELATED TO THIS INCIDENT FROM EVERYONE'S MEMORIES AT SCHOOL!
ARE YOU OKAY WITH THAT?
WAIT!
ABOUT THAT...

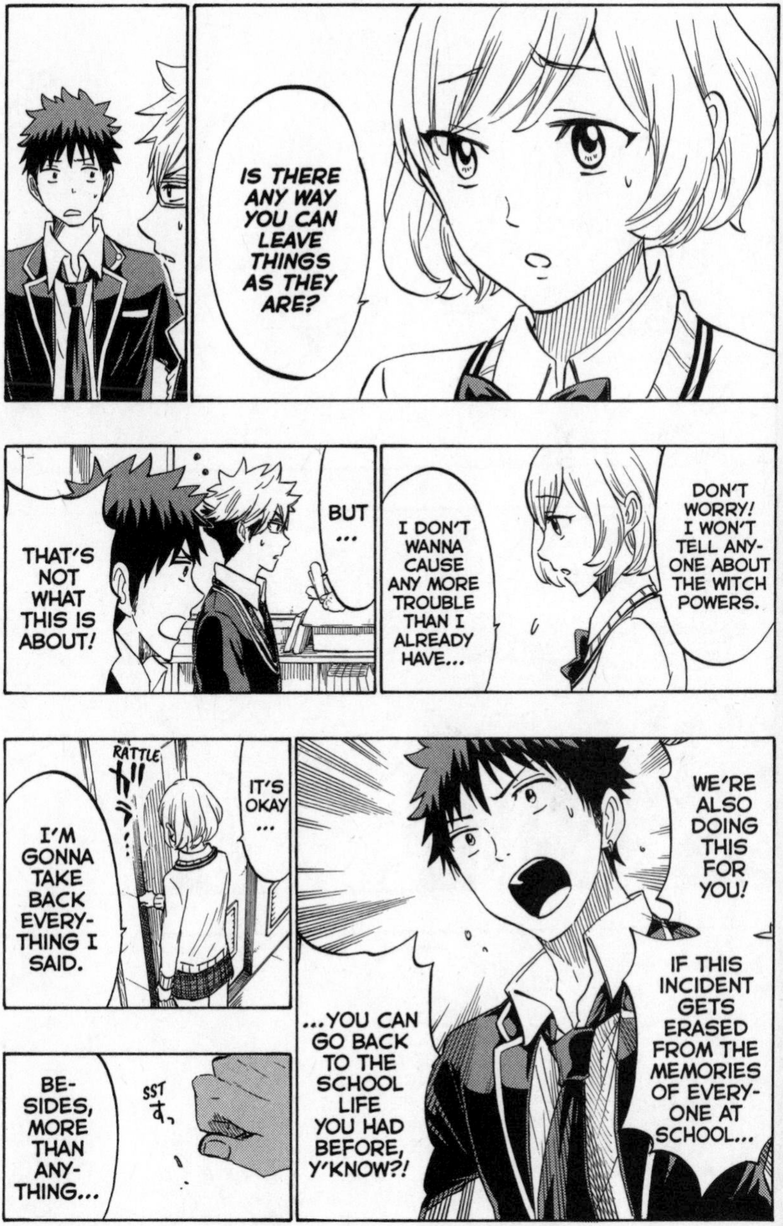
IS THERE ANY WAY YOU CAN LEAVE THINGS AS THEY ARE?
DON'T WORRY! I WON'T TELL ANYONE ABOUT THE WITCH POWERS.
I DON'T WANNA CAUSE ANY MORE TROUBLE THAN I ALREADY HAVE...
BUT...
THAT'S NOT WHAT THIS IS ABOUT!
WE'RE ALSO DOING THIS FOR YOU!
IF THIS INCIDENT GETS ERASED FROM THE MEMORIES OF EVERYONE AT SCHOOL...
...YOU CAN GO BACK TO THE SCHOOL LIFE YOU HAD BEFORE, Y'KNOW?!
IT'S OKAY...
RATTLE
ガラ
I'M GONNA TAKE BACK EVERYTHING I SAID.
SST
すっ
BESIDES, MORE THAN ANYTHING...

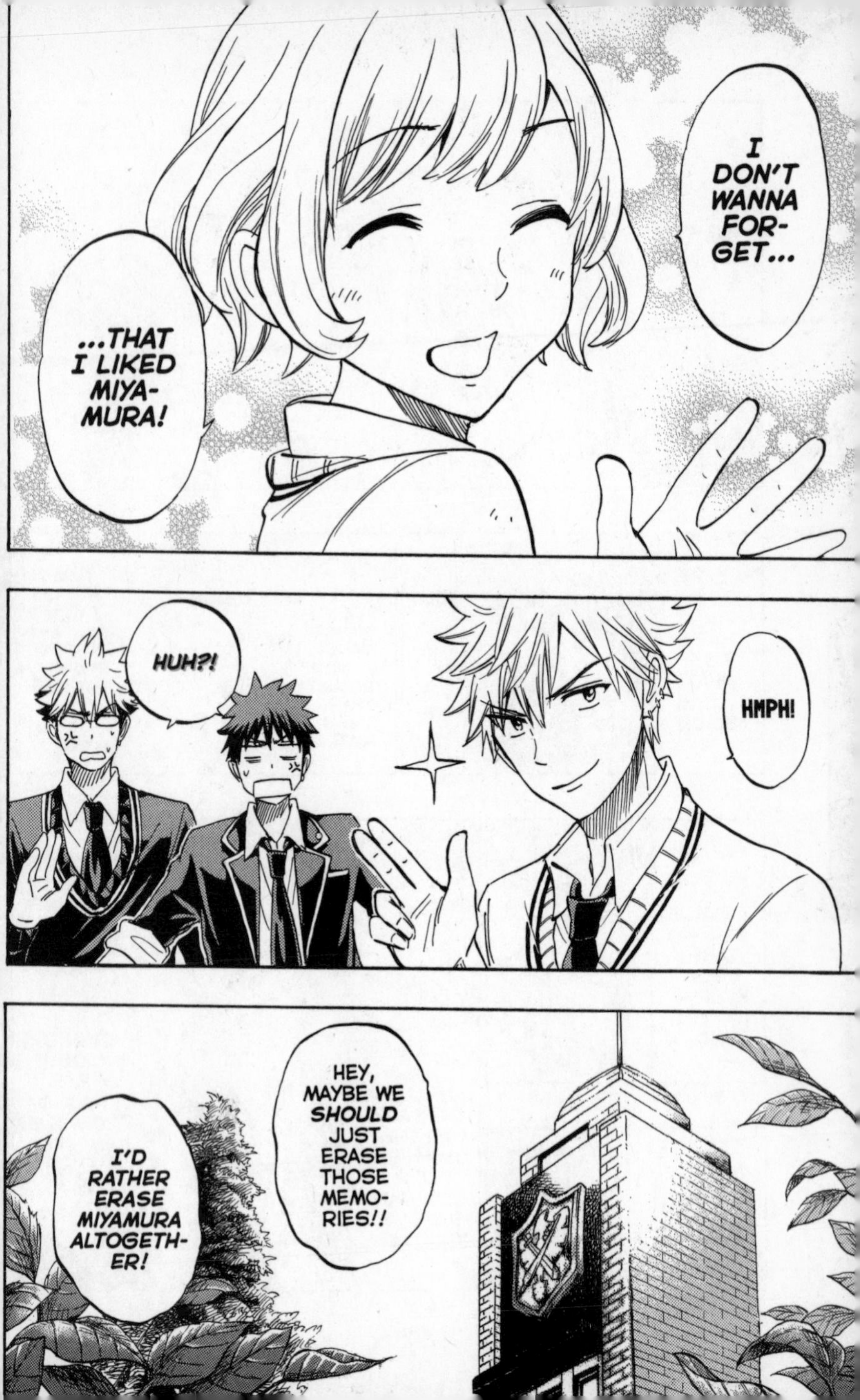
I DON'T WANNA FOR-GET...
...THAT I LIKED MIYA-MURA!
HMPH!
HUH?!
HEY, MAYBE WE SHOULD JUST ERASE THOSE MEMO-RIES!!
I'D RATHER ERASE MIYAMURA ALTOGETH-ER!

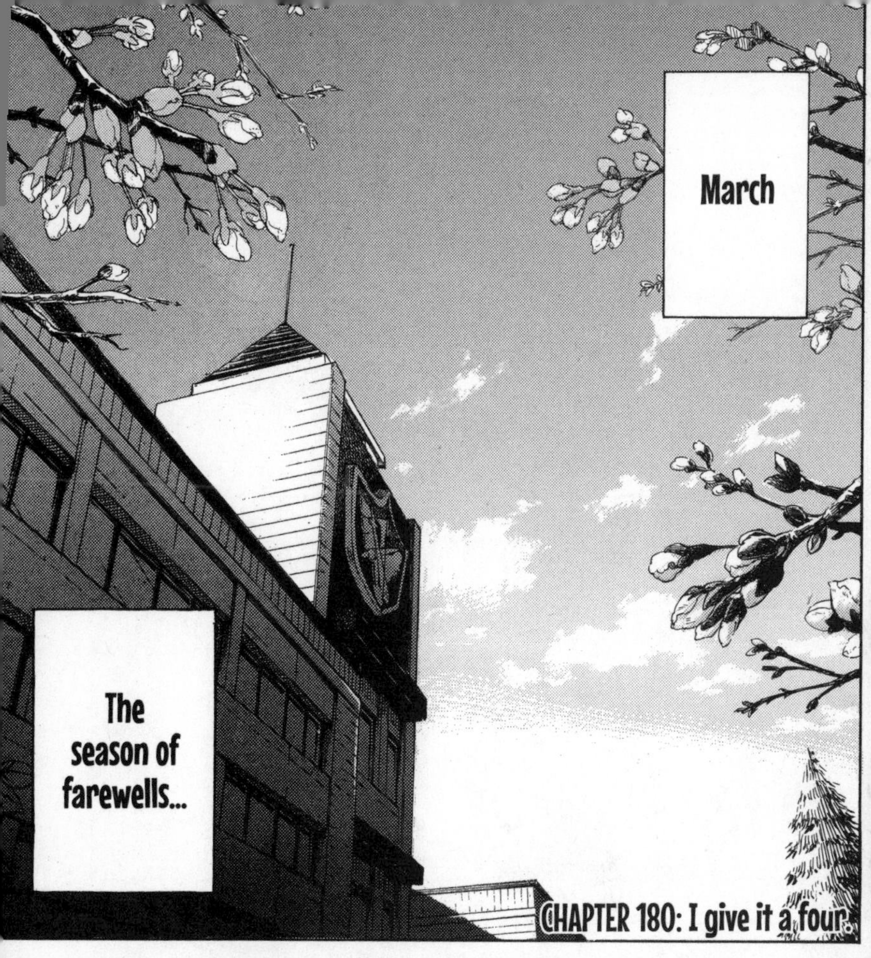
March
The season of farewells...
CHAPTER 180: I give it a four.

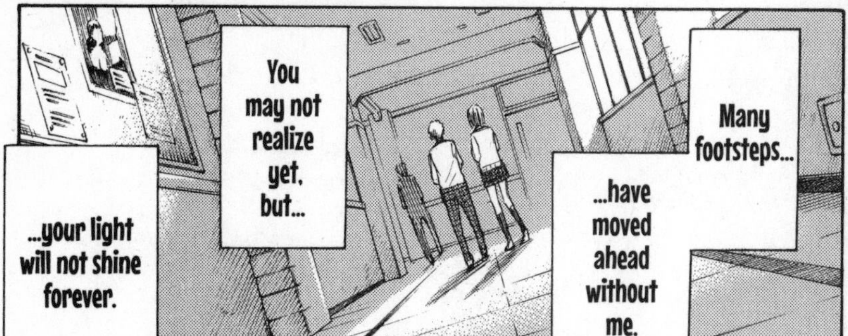
Many footsteps...
...have moved ahead without me.
You may not realize yet, but...
...your light will not shine forever.

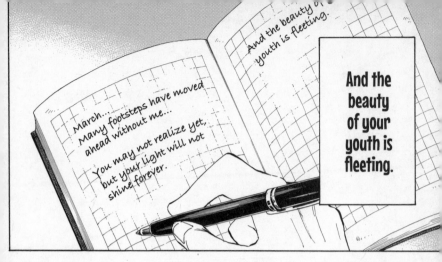

And the beauty of your youth is fleeting.

March...
Many footsteps have moved ahead without me...
You may not realize yet, but your light will not shine forever.

And the beauty of youth is fleeting.

SHUT

I GIVE IT A FOUR.

DON'T LOOK!!

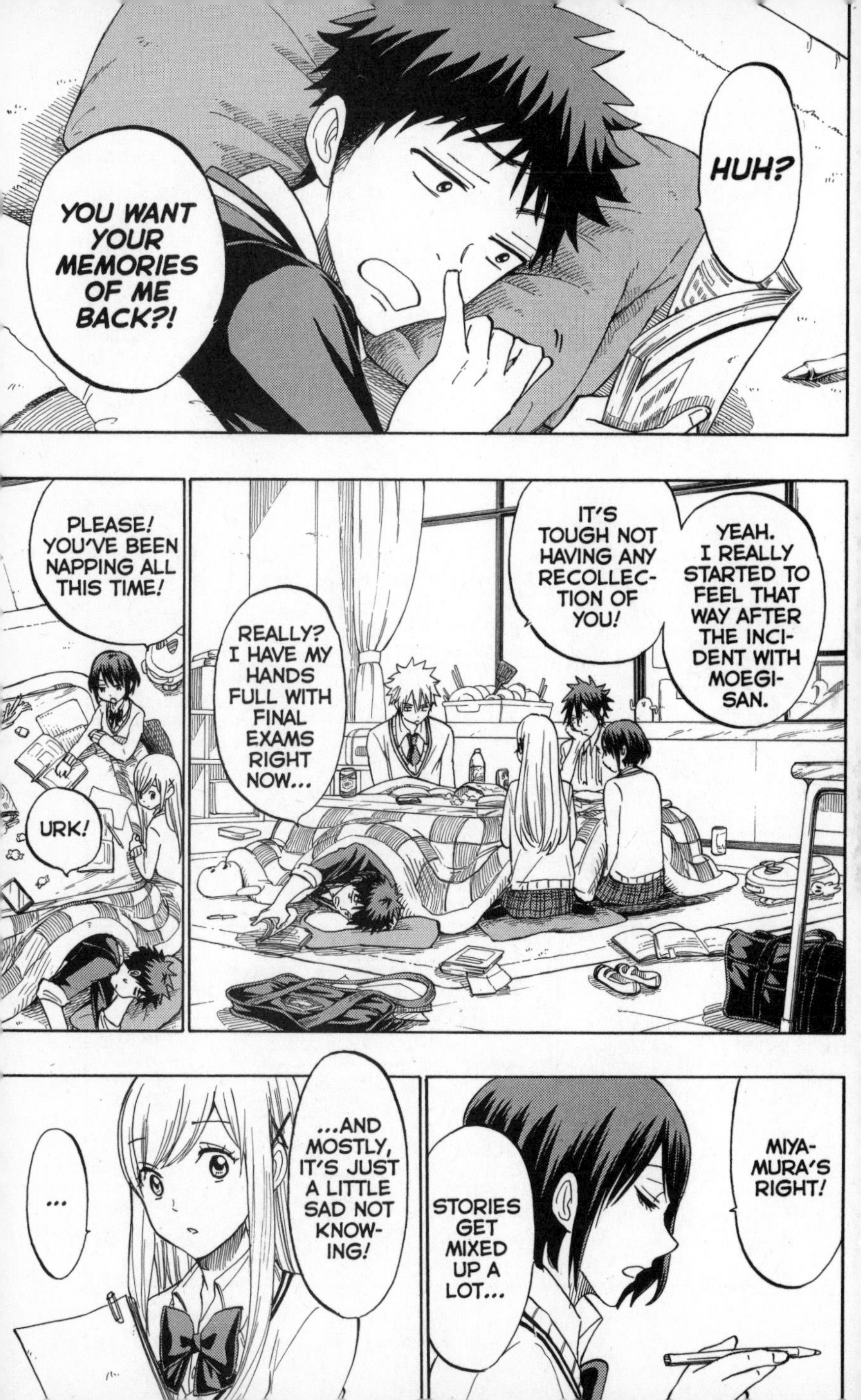
HUH?
YOU WANT YOUR MEMORIES OF ME BACK?!
YEAH. I REALLY STARTED TO FEEL THAT WAY AFTER THE INCIDENT WITH MOEGI-SAN.
IT'S TOUGH NOT HAVING ANY RECOLLECTION OF YOU!
REALLY? I HAVE MY HANDS FULL WITH FINAL EXAMS RIGHT NOW...
PLEASE! YOU'VE BEEN NAPPING ALL THIS TIME!
URK!
MIYAMURA'S RIGHT!
STORIES GET MIXED UP A LOT...
...AND MOSTLY, IT'S JUST A LITTLE SAD NOT KNOWING!
...

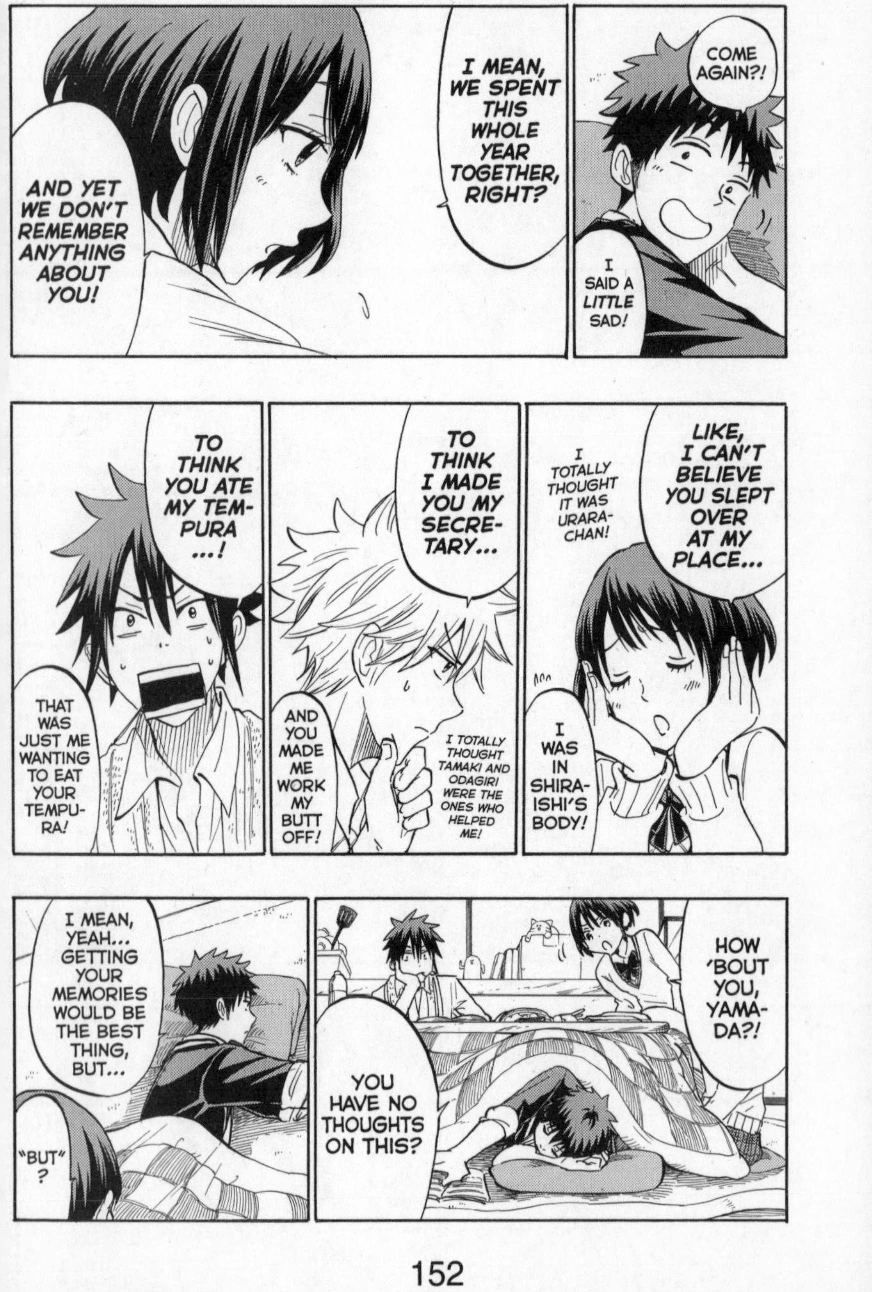
COME AGAIN?!
I SAID A LITTLE SAD!
I MEAN, WE SPENT THIS WHOLE YEAR TOGETHER, RIGHT?
AND YET WE DON'T REMEMBER ANYTHING ABOUT YOU!
LIKE, I CAN'T BELIEVE YOU SLEPT OVER AT MY PLACE...
I TOTALLY THOUGHT IT WAS URARA-CHAN!
I WAS IN SHIRAISHI'S BODY!
TO THINK I MADE YOU MY SECRETARY...
I TOTALLY THOUGHT TAMAKI AND ODAGIRI WERE THE ONES WHO HELPED ME!
AND YOU MADE ME WORK MY BUTT OFF!
TO THINK YOU ATE MY TEMPURA...!
THAT WAS JUST ME WANTING TO EAT YOUR TEMPURA!
HOW 'BOUT YOU, YAMADA?!
YOU HAVE NO THOUGHTS ON THIS?
I MEAN, YEAH... GETTING YOUR MEMORIES WOULD BE THE BEST THING, BUT...
"BUT"?

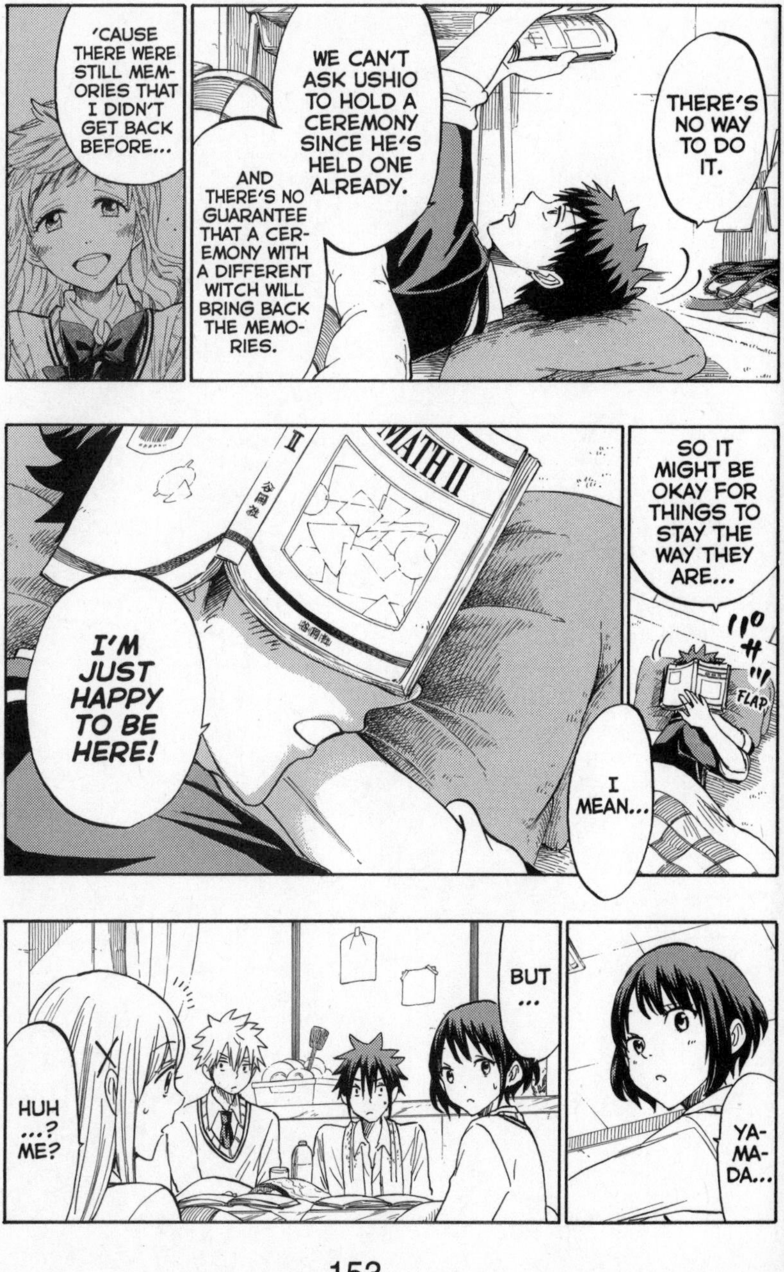
THERE'S NO WAY TO DO IT.
WE CAN'T ASK USHIO TO HOLD A CEREMONY SINCE HE'S HELD ONE ALREADY.
AND THERE'S NO GUARANTEE THAT A CEREMONY WITH A DIFFERENT WITCH WILL BRING BACK THE MEMORIES.
'CAUSE THERE WERE STILL MEMORIES THAT I DIDN'T GET BACK BEFORE...
SO IT MIGHT BE OKAY FOR THINGS TO STAY THE WAY THEY ARE...
FLAP
I MEAN...
MATH II
I'M JUST HAPPY TO BE HERE!
YAMADA...
BUT ...
HUH ...? ME?

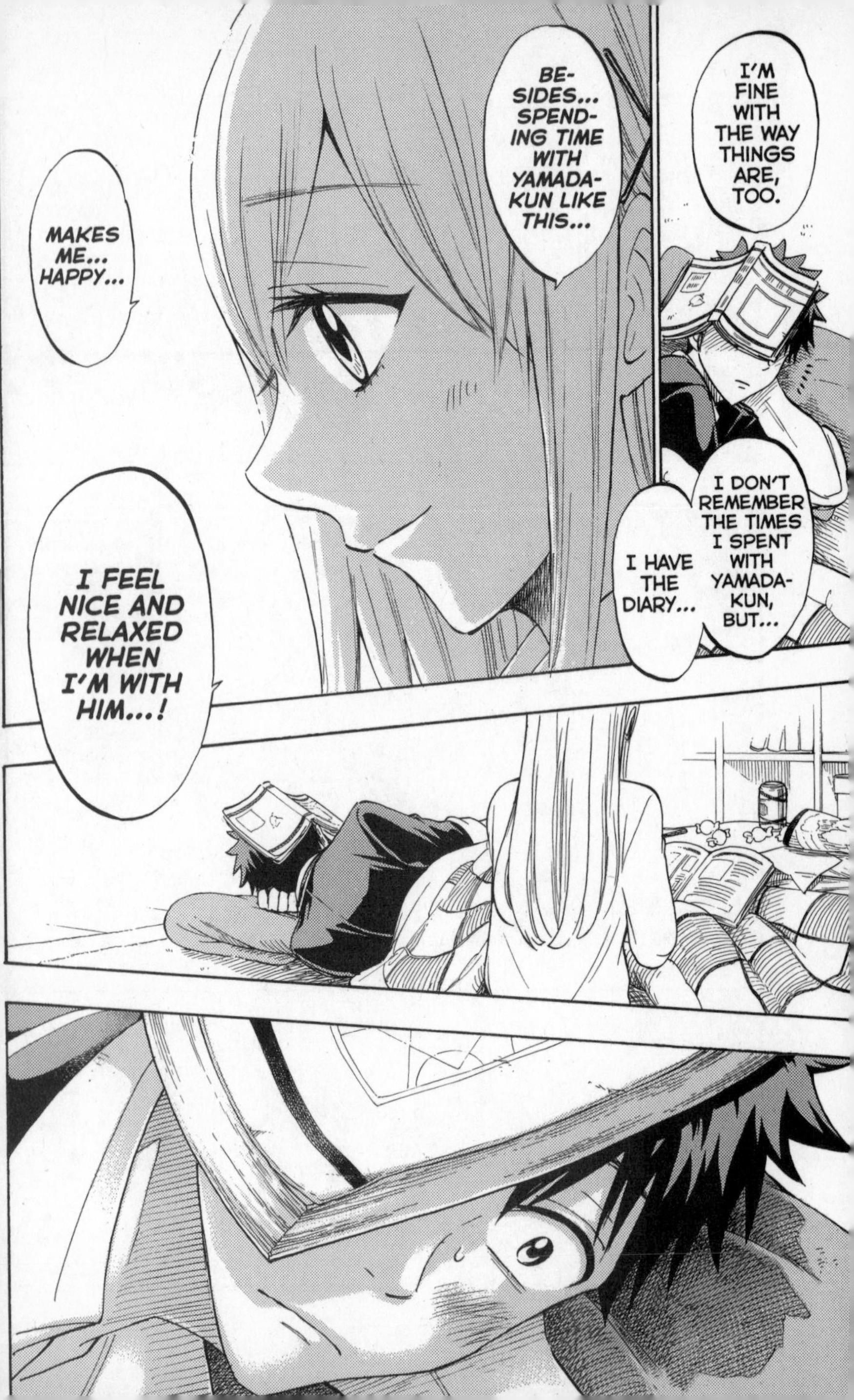

I'M FINE WITH THE WAY THINGS ARE, TOO.
I DON'T REMEMBER THE TIMES I SPENT WITH YAMADA-KUN, BUT...
I HAVE THE DIARY...
BESIDES... SPENDING TIME WITH YAMADA-KUN LIKE THIS...
MAKES ME... HAPPY...
I FEEL NICE AND RELAXED WHEN I'M WITH HIM...!

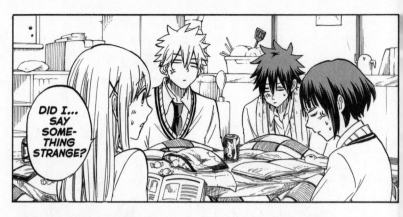

DID I... SAY SOME-THING STRANGE?
DAMN IT, YAMADA! I'M NOT NICE AND RELAXED! I'M FREAKIN' FRUSTRAT-ED!!
AARGH!!
URARA-CHAN CAN DO SO MUCH BETTER THAN YAMADA!!
CLAT-TER
OKAY, YAMADA! MAKE ME FEEL NICE AND RELAXED TOO!!
CLAT-TER
YEAH... BUT HOW'M I SUP-POSED TO— AUGH!
OH?
I GUESS YOU'RE BUSY NOW?
HUH ...?

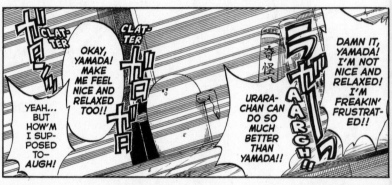

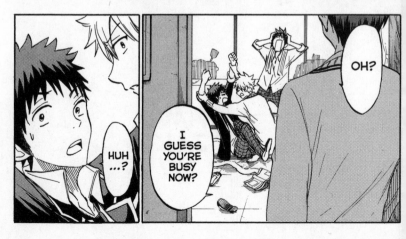

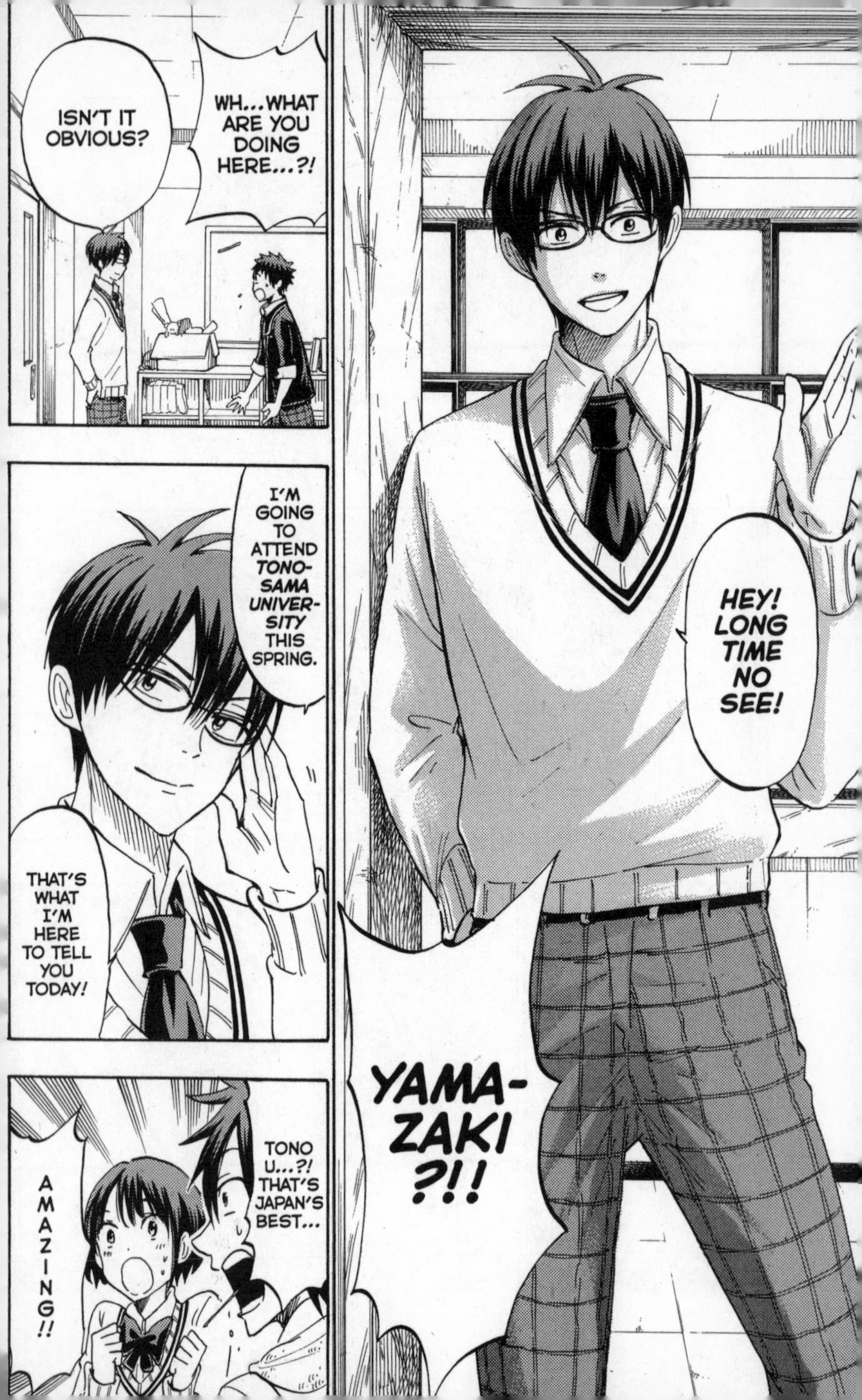
HEY! LONG TIME NO SEE!
YAMA-ZAKI ?!!
WH...WHAT ARE YOU DOING HERE...?!
ISN'T IT OBVIOUS?
I'M GOING TO ATTEND *TONO-SAMA UNIVERSITY* THIS SPRING.
THAT'S WHAT I'M HERE TO TELL YOU TODAY!
TONO U...?! THAT'S JAPAN'S BEST...
AMAZING!!

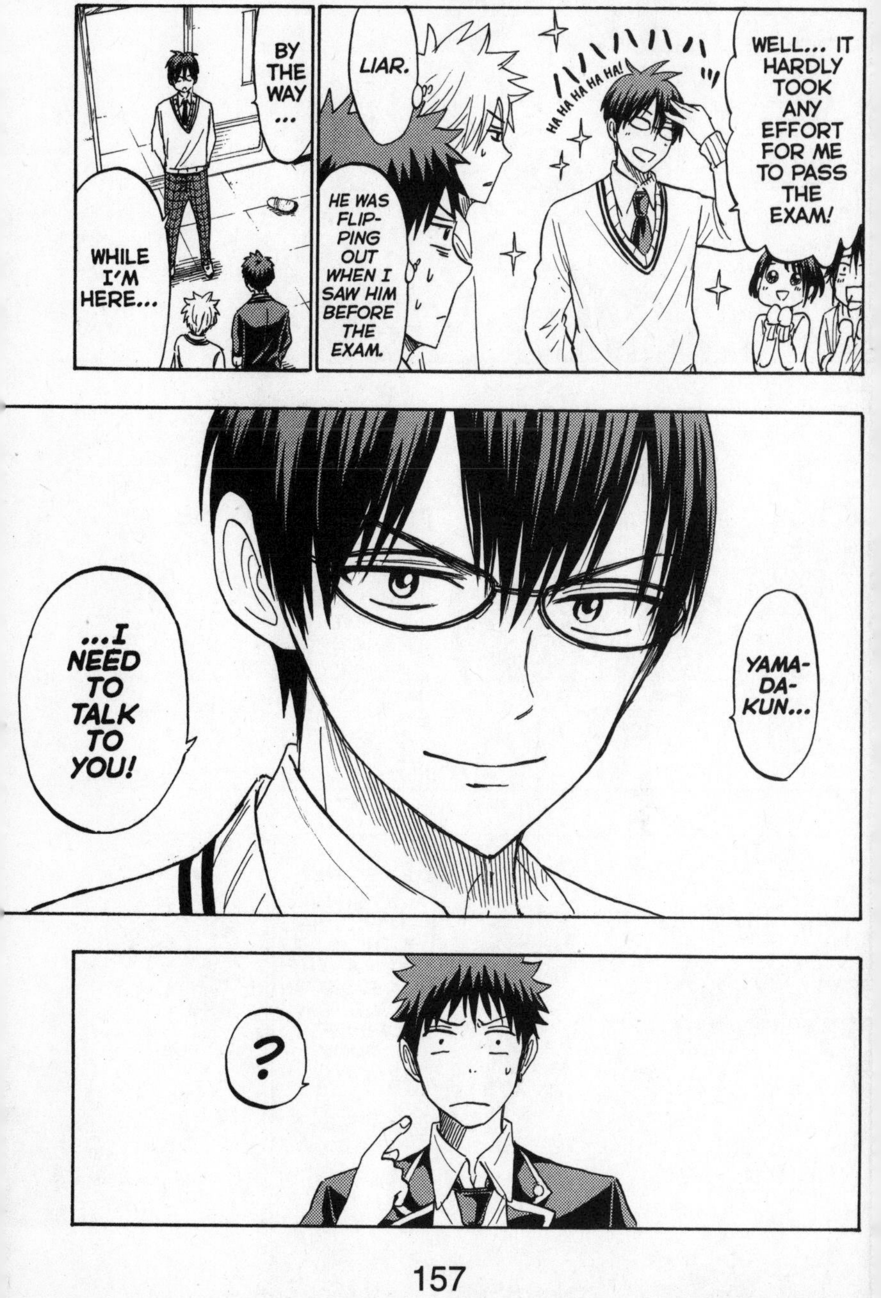
WELL... IT HARDLY TOOK ANY EFFORT FOR ME TO PASS THE EXAM!
HA HA HA HA HA!
LIAR.
HE WAS FLIP-PING OUT WHEN I SAW HIM BEFORE THE EXAM.
BY THE WAY ...
WHILE I'M HERE...
YAMA-DA-KUN...
...I NEED TO TALK TO YOU!
?

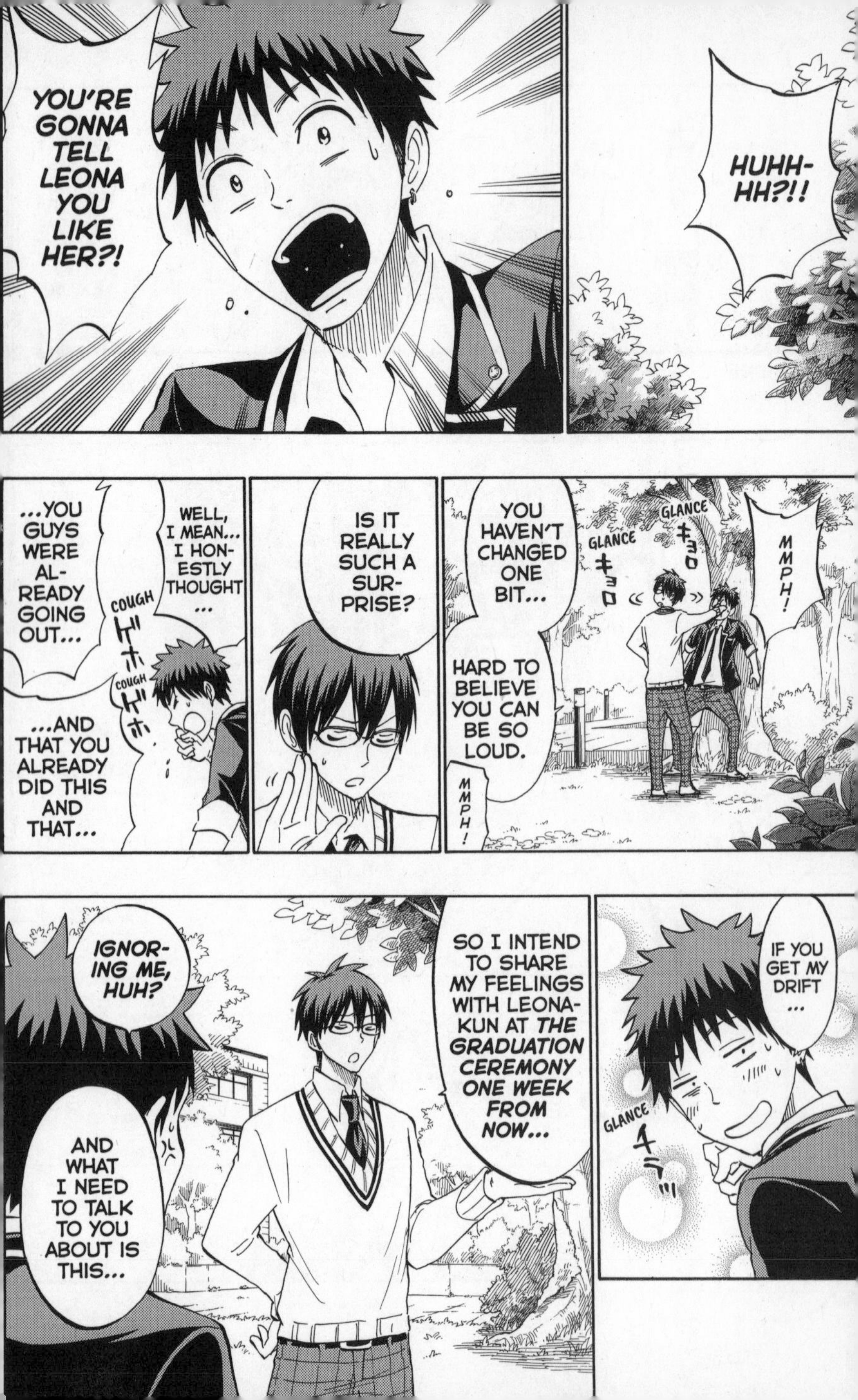
HUHHHH?!!
YOU'RE GONNA TELL LEONA YOU LIKE HER?!
MMPH!
GLANCE キョロ
GLANCE キョロ
YOU HAVEN'T CHANGED ONE BIT...
HARD TO BELIEVE YOU CAN BE SO LOUD.
MMPH!
IS IT REALLY SUCH A SURPRISE?
WELL, I MEAN... I HONESTLY THOUGHT...
...YOU GUYS WERE ALREADY GOING OUT...
COUGH ゲホ
COUGH ゲホ
...AND THAT YOU ALREADY DID THIS AND THAT...
IF YOU GET MY DRIFT...
GLANCE チラッ
SO I INTEND TO SHARE MY FEELINGS WITH LEONA-KUN AT THE GRADUATION CEREMONY ONE WEEK FROM NOW...
IGNORING ME, HUH?
AND WHAT I NEED TO TALK TO YOU ABOUT IS THIS...

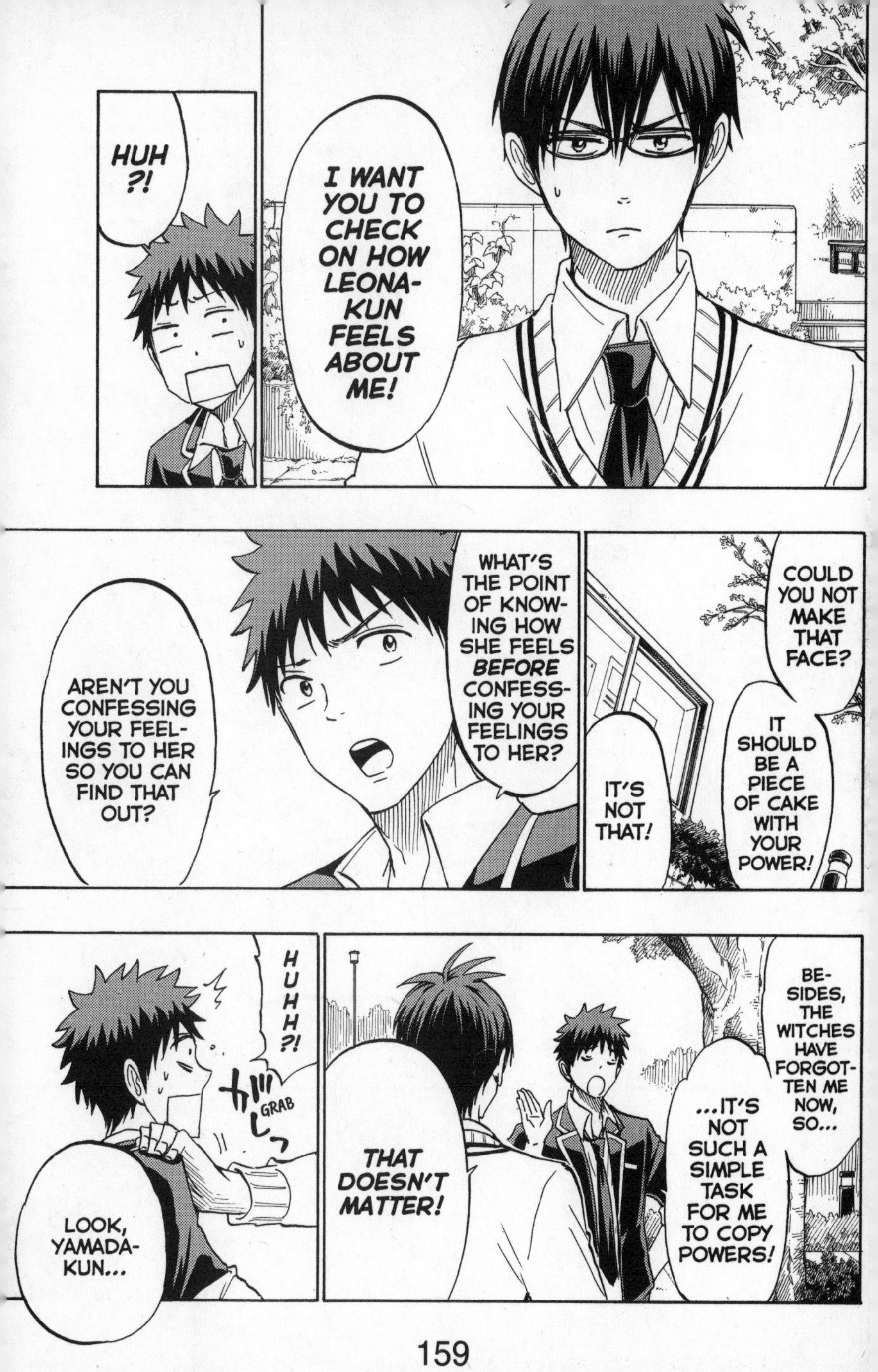
I WANT YOU TO CHECK ON HOW LEONA-KUN FEELS ABOUT ME!
HUH?!
COULD YOU NOT MAKE THAT FACE?
IT SHOULD BE A PIECE OF CAKE WITH YOUR POWER!
IT'S NOT THAT!
WHAT'S THE POINT OF KNOWING HOW SHE FEELS *BEFORE* CONFESSING YOUR FEELINGS TO HER?
AREN'T YOU CONFESSING YOUR FEELINGS TO HER SO YOU CAN FIND THAT OUT?
BESIDES, THE WITCHES HAVE FORGOTTEN ME NOW, SO...
...IT'S NOT SUCH A SIMPLE TASK FOR ME TO COPY POWERS!
THAT DOESN'T MATTER!
HUHH?!
GRAB
LOOK, YAMADA-KUN...

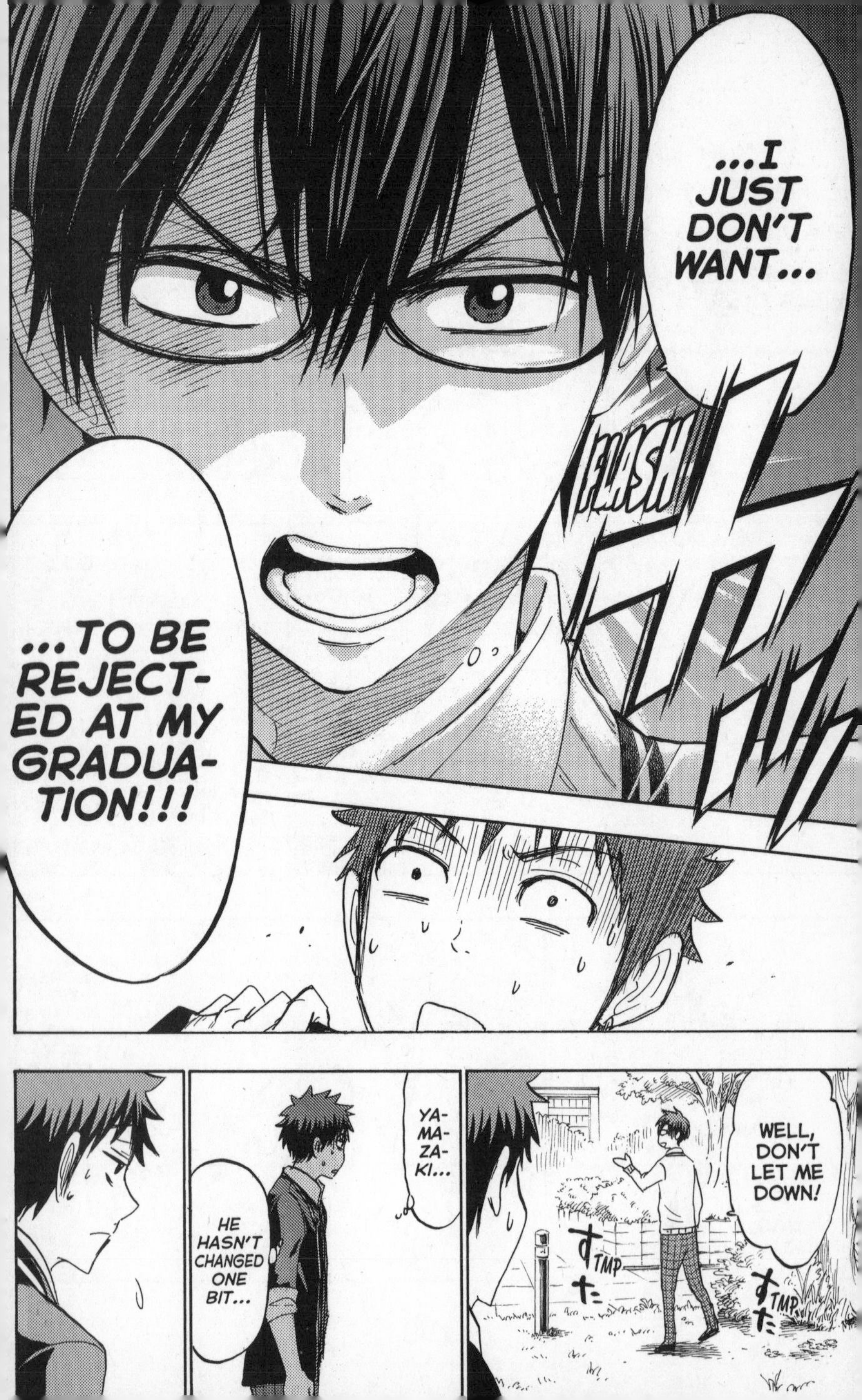
...I JUST DON'T WANT...
FLASH
...TO BE REJECT-ED AT MY GRADUA-TION!!!
WELL, DON'T LET ME DOWN!
TMP
TMP
YA-MA-ZA-KI...
HE HASN'T CHANGED ONE BIT...

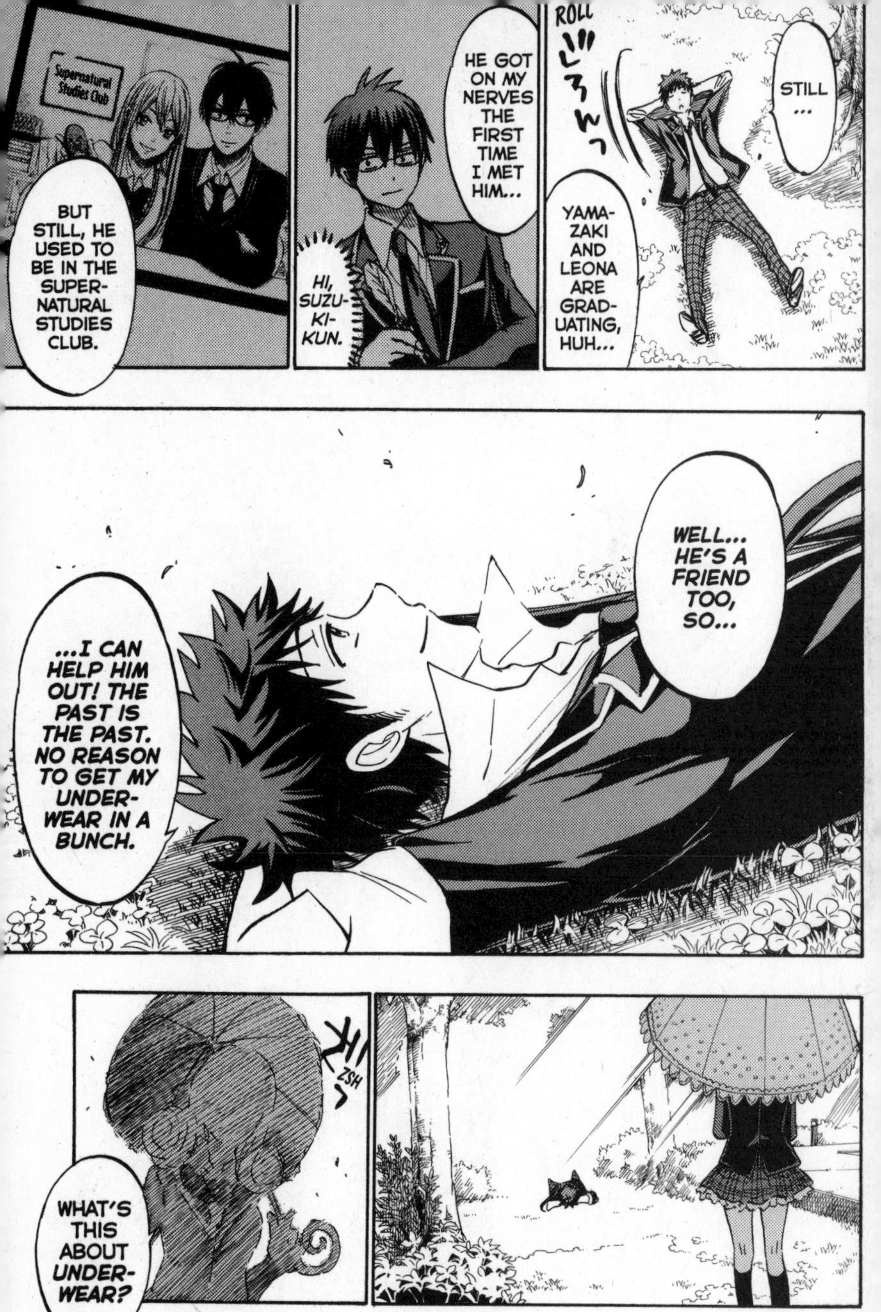
STILL...
ROLL
YAMAZAKI AND LEONA ARE GRADUATING, HUH...
HE GOT ON MY NERVES THE FIRST TIME I MET HIM...
HI, SUZUKI-KUN.
Supernatural Studies Club
BUT STILL, HE USED TO BE IN THE SUPERNATURAL STUDIES CLUB.
WELL... HE'S A FRIEND TOO, SO...
...I CAN HELP HIM OUT! THE PAST IS THE PAST. NO REASON TO GET MY UNDERWEAR IN A BUNCH.
ZSH
WHAT'S THIS ABOUT UNDERWEAR?

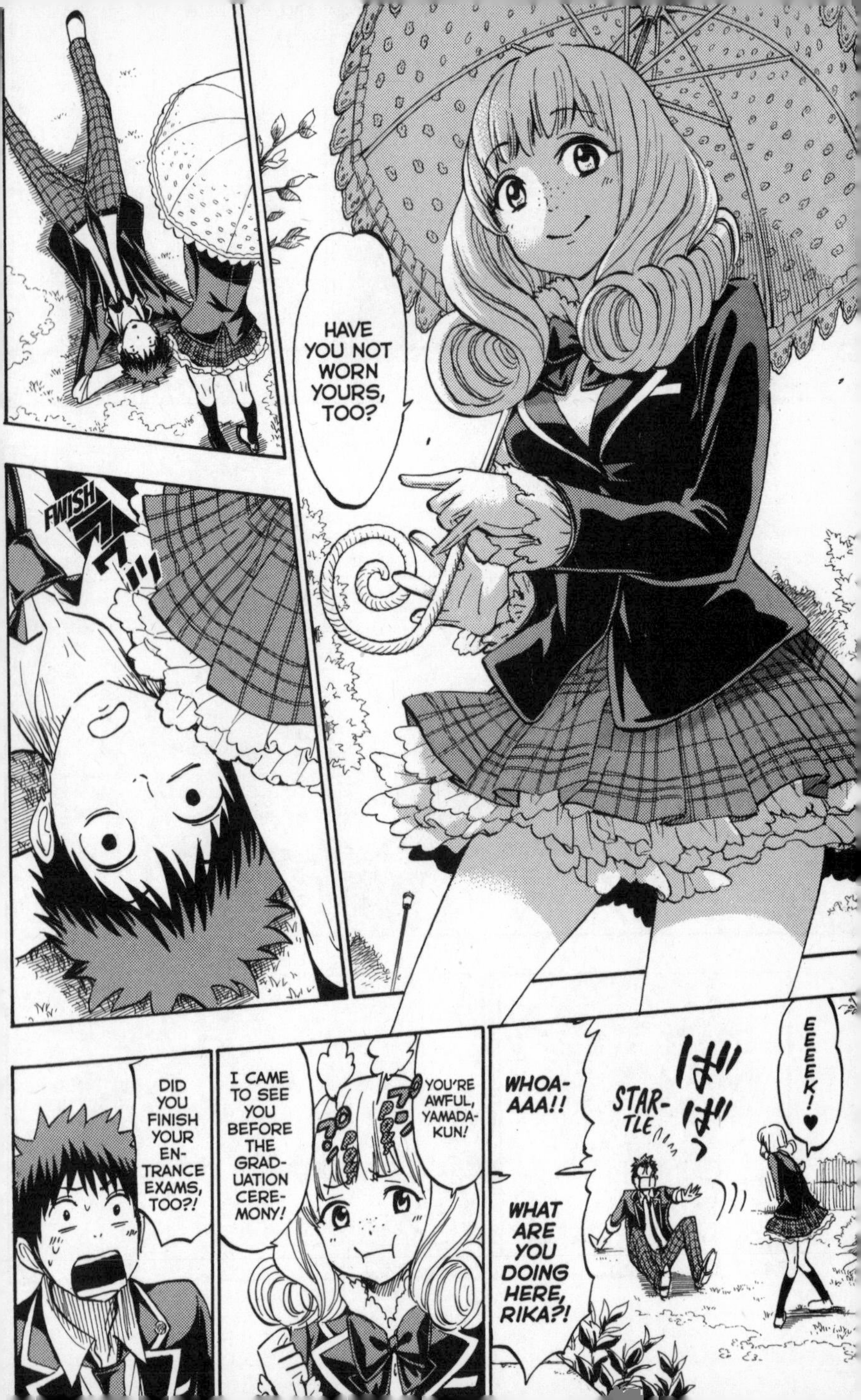
HAVE YOU NOT WORN YOURS, TOO?
FWISH
EEEEK! ♥
ばばっ
STAR-TLE
WHOA-AAA!!
WHAT ARE YOU DOING HERE, RIKA?!
YOU'RE AWFUL, YAMADA-KUN!
I CAME TO SEE YOU BEFORE THE GRAD-UATION CERE-MONY!
DID YOU FINISH YOUR EN-TRANCE EXAMS, TOO?!

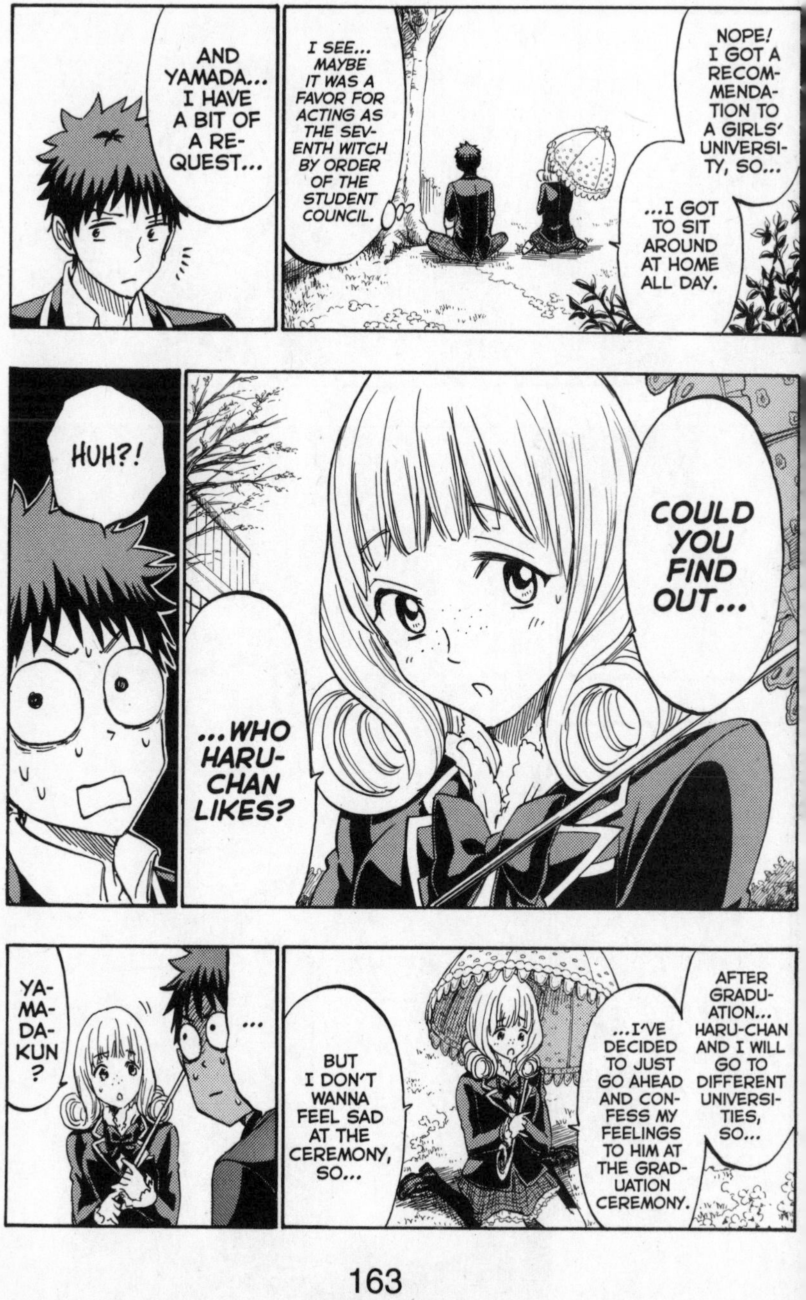
NOPE! I GOT A RECOMMENDATION TO A GIRLS' UNIVERSITY, SO...
...I GOT TO SIT AROUND AT HOME ALL DAY.
I SEE... MAYBE IT WAS A FAVOR FOR ACTING AS THE SEVENTH WITCH BY ORDER OF THE STUDENT COUNCIL.
AND YAMADA... I HAVE A BIT OF A REQUEST...
COULD YOU FIND OUT...
...WHO HARU-CHAN LIKES?
HUH?!
AFTER GRADUATION... HARU-CHAN AND I WILL GO TO DIFFERENT UNIVERSITIES, SO...
...I'VE DECIDED TO JUST GO AHEAD AND CONFESS MY FEELINGS TO HIM AT THE GRADUATION CEREMONY.
BUT I DON'T WANNA FEEL SAD AT THE CEREMONY, SO...
...
YAMADA-KUN?

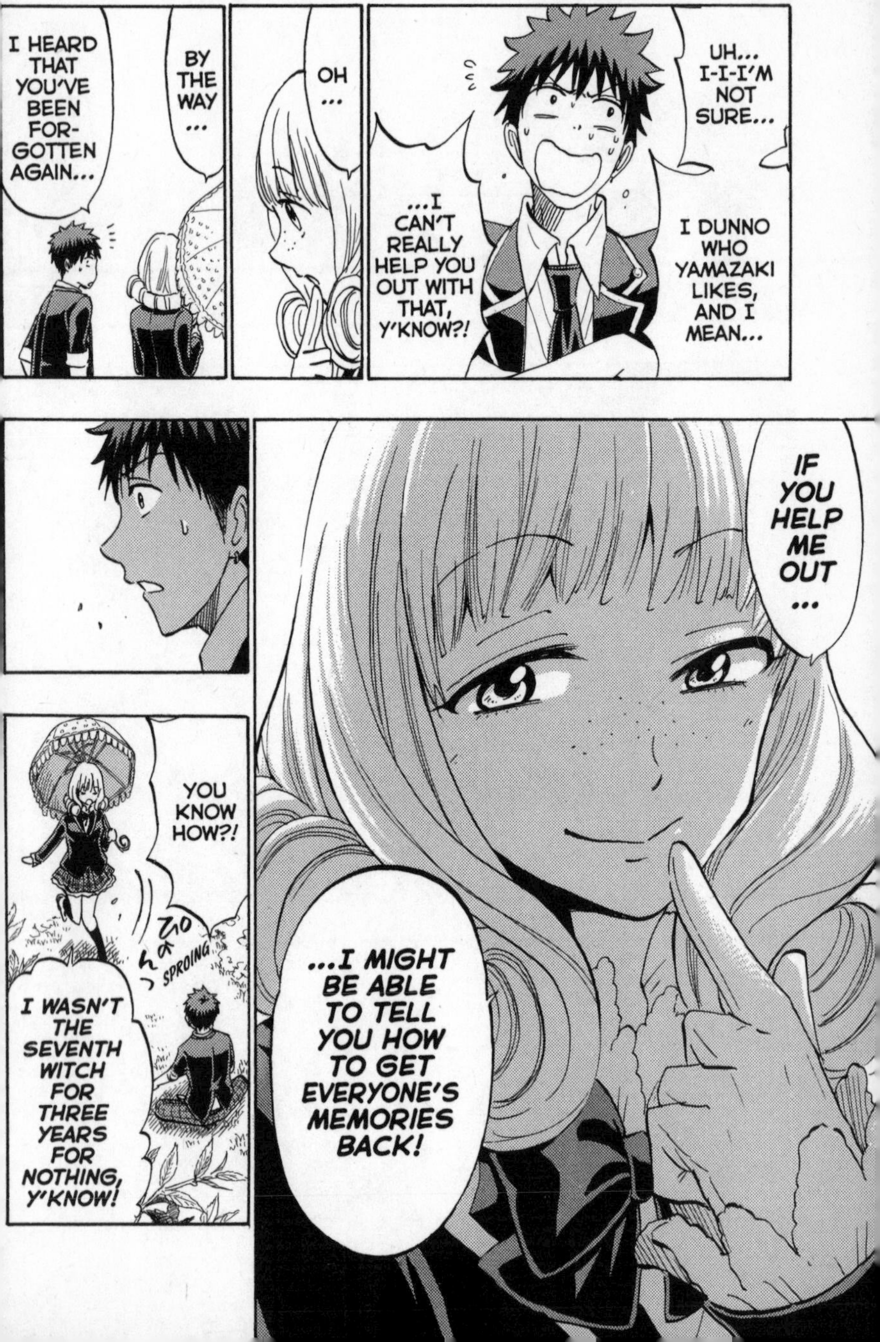
UH... I-I-I'M NOT SURE...
I DUNNO WHO YAMAZAKI LIKES, AND I MEAN...
...I CAN'T REALLY HELP YOU OUT WITH THAT, Y'KNOW?!
OH ...
BY THE WAY ...
I HEARD THAT YOU'VE BEEN FOR-GOTTEN AGAIN...
IF YOU HELP ME OUT ...
...I MIGHT BE ABLE TO TELL YOU HOW TO GET EVERYONE'S MEMORIES BACK!
YOU KNOW HOW?!
SPROING
I WASN'T THE SEVENTH WITCH FOR THREE YEARS FOR NOTHING, Y'KNOW!

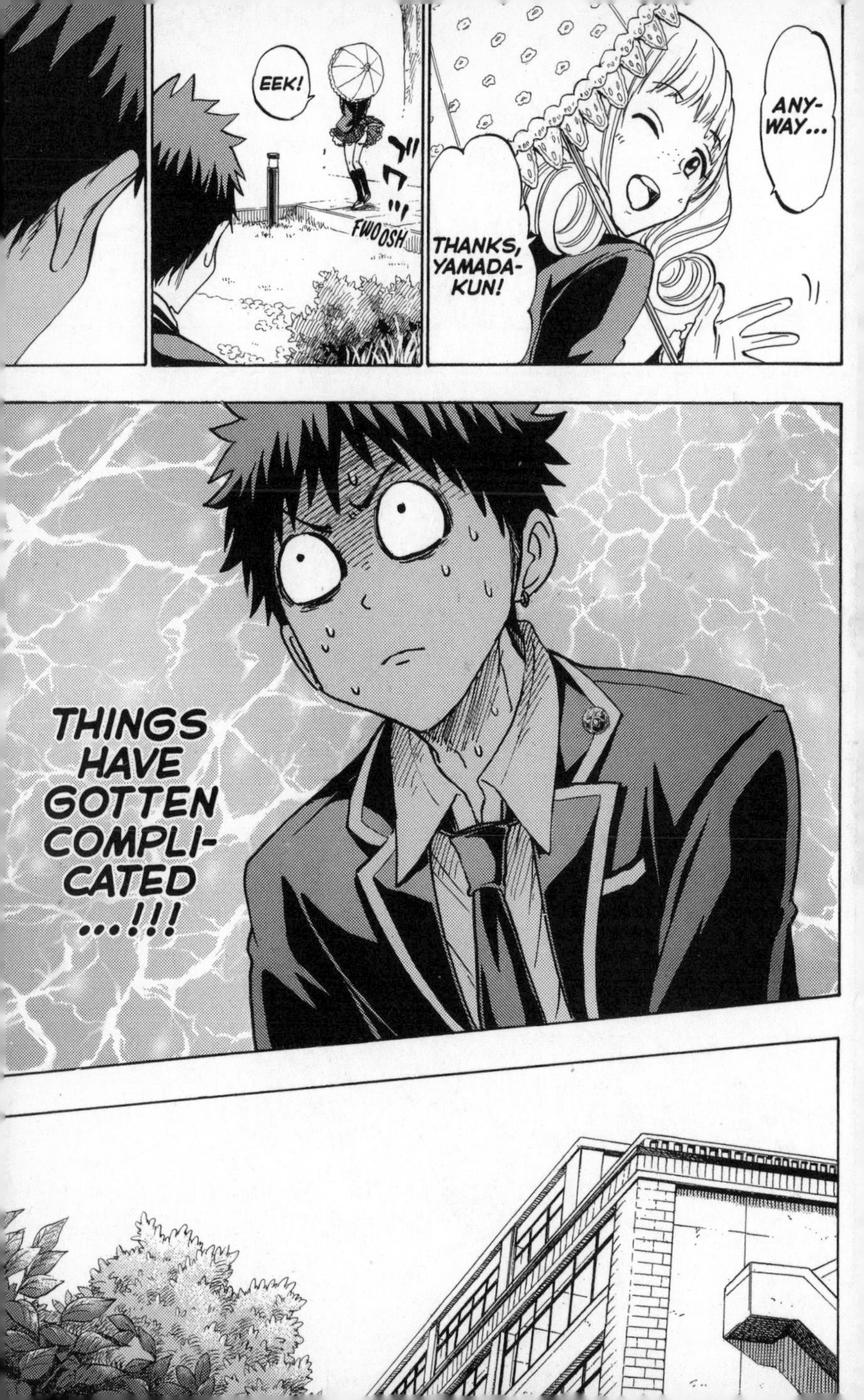
ANY-WAY...
THANKS, YAMADA-KUN!
EEK!
FWOOSH
THINGS HAVE GOTTEN COMPLI-CATED ...!!!

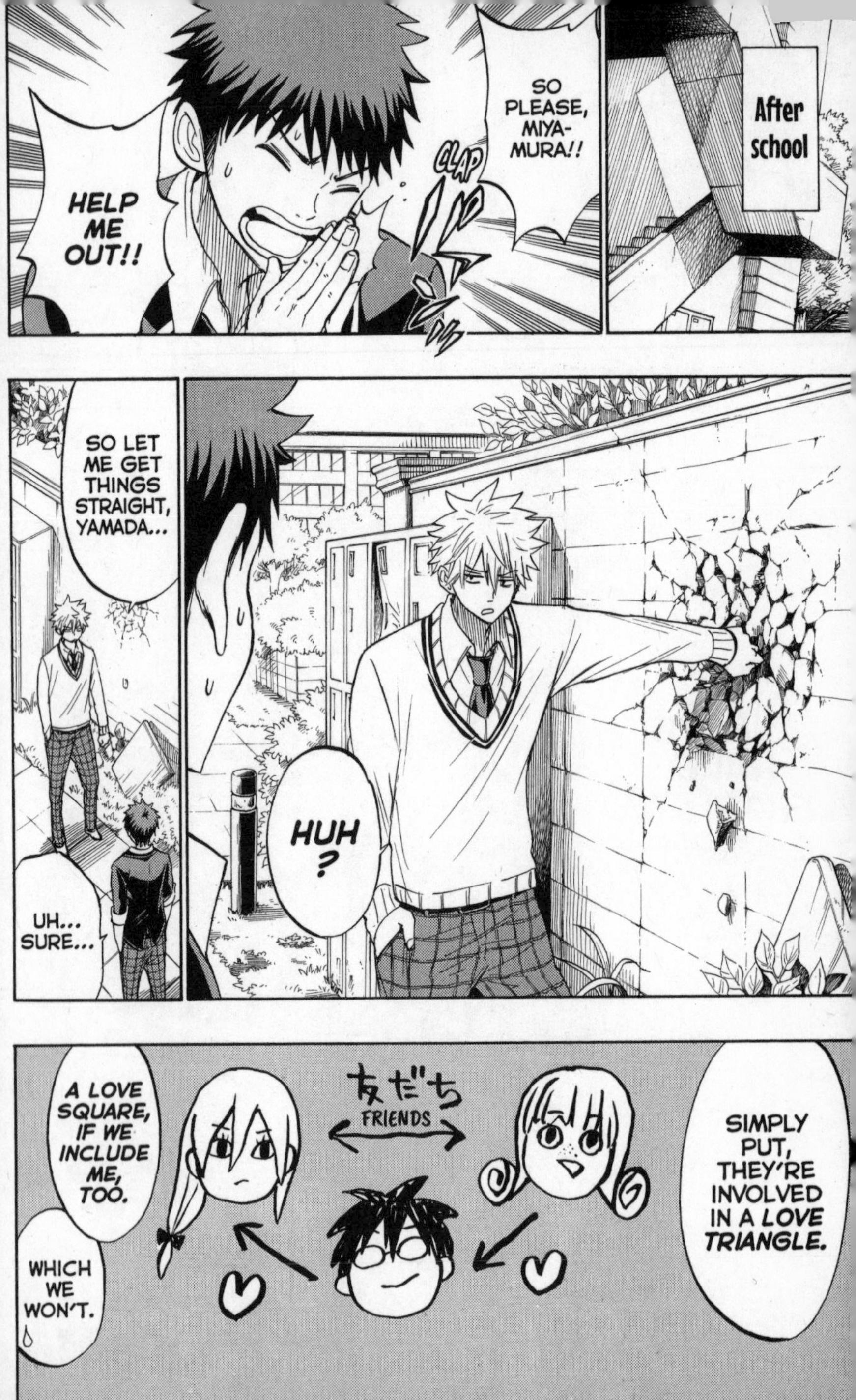
After school
SO PLEASE, MIYA-MURA!!
CLAP
HELP ME OUT!!
HUH?
SO LET ME GET THINGS STRAIGHT, YAMADA...
UH... SURE...
SIMPLY PUT, THEY'RE INVOLVED IN A LOVE TRIANGLE.
友だち
FRIENDS
A LOVE SQUARE, IF WE INCLUDE ME, TOO.
WHICH WE WON'T.

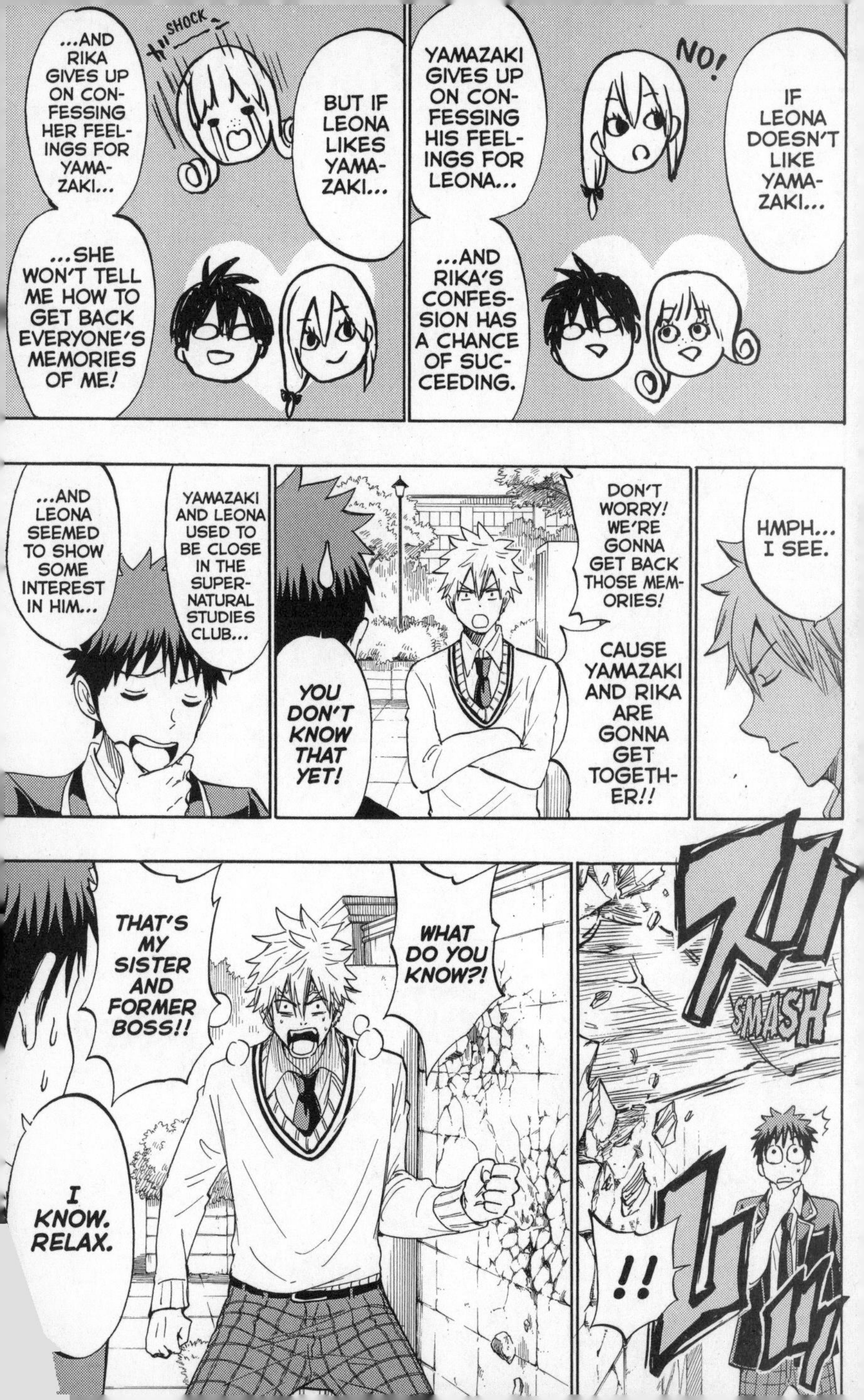
IF LEONA DOESN'T LIKE YAMAZAKI...
NO!
YAMAZAKI GIVES UP ON CONFESSING HIS FEELINGS FOR LEONA...
...AND RIKA'S CONFESSION HAS A CHANCE OF SUCCEEDING.
BUT IF LEONA LIKES YAMAZAKI...
SHOCK
...AND RIKA GIVES UP ON CONFESSING HER FEELINGS FOR YAMAZAKI...
...SHE WON'T TELL ME HOW TO GET BACK EVERYONE'S MEMORIES OF ME!
HMPH... I SEE.
DON'T WORRY! WE'RE GONNA GET BACK THOSE MEMORIES!
CAUSE YAMAZAKI AND RIKA ARE GONNA GET TOGETHER!!
YOU DON'T KNOW THAT YET!
YAMAZAKI AND LEONA USED TO BE CLOSE IN THE SUPERNATURAL STUDIES CLUB...
...AND LEONA SEEMED TO SHOW SOME INTEREST IN HIM...
SMASH
!!
WHAT DO YOU KNOW?!
THAT'S MY SISTER AND FORMER BOSS!!
I KNOW. RELAX.

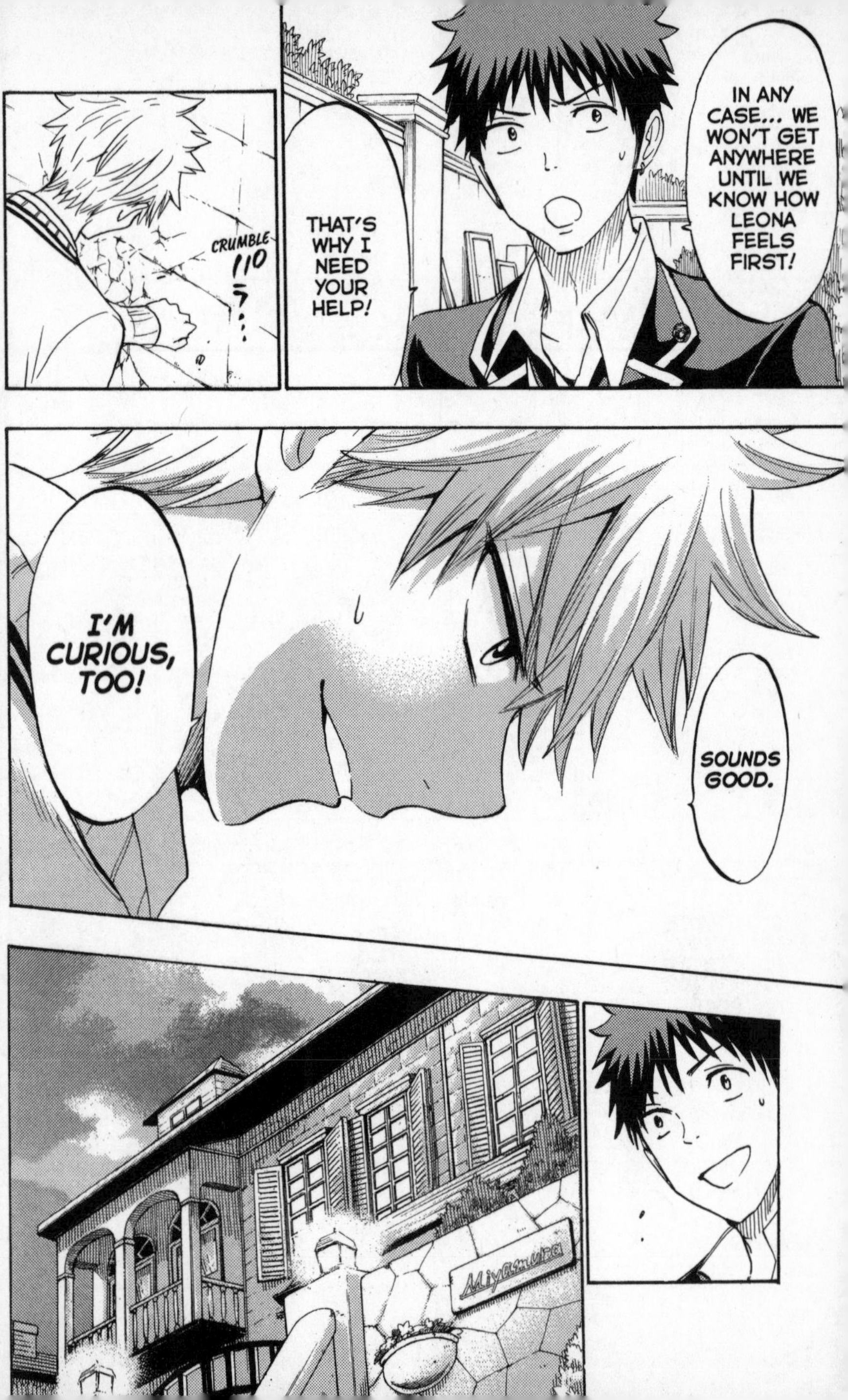
IN ANY CASE... WE WON'T GET ANYWHERE UNTIL WE KNOW HOW LEONA FEELS FIRST!
THAT'S WHY I NEED YOUR HELP!
CRUMBLE
SOUNDS GOOD.
I'M CURIOUS, TOO!
Miyamura

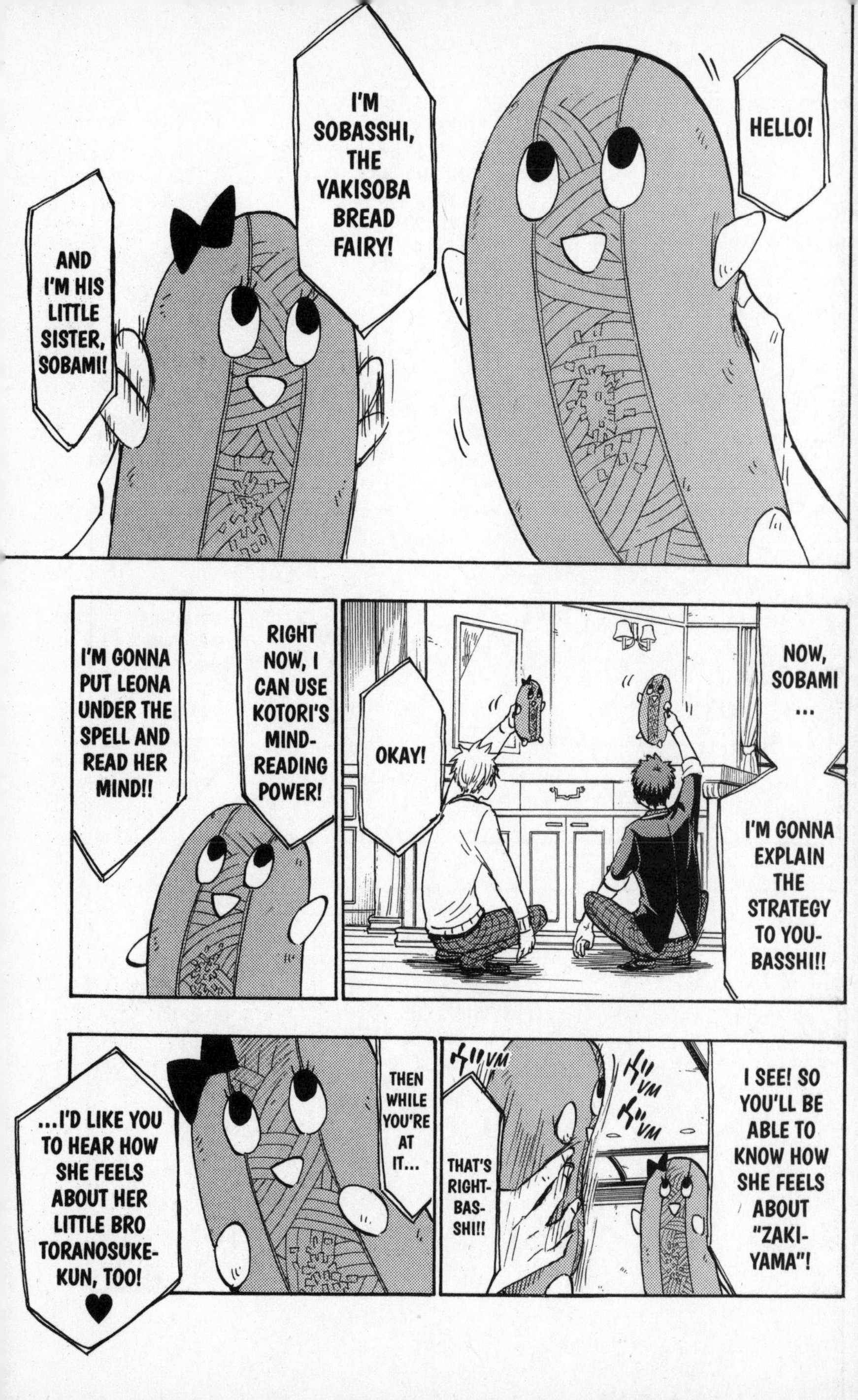
HELLO!
I'M SOBASSHI, THE YAKISOBA BREAD FAIRY!
AND I'M HIS LITTLE SISTER, SOBAMI!
NOW, SOBAMI ...
I'M GONNA EXPLAIN THE STRATEGY TO YOU-BASSHI!!
OKAY!
RIGHT NOW, I CAN USE KOTORI'S MIND-READING POWER!
I'M GONNA PUT LEONA UNDER THE SPELL AND READ HER MIND!!
I SEE! SO YOU'LL BE ABLE TO KNOW HOW SHE FEELS ABOUT "ZAKI-YAMA"!
VM
VM
VM
THAT'S RIGHT-BASSHI!!
THEN WHILE YOU'RE AT IT...
...I'D LIKE YOU TO HEAR HOW SHE FEELS ABOUT HER LITTLE BRO TORANOSUKE-KUN, TOO! ♥

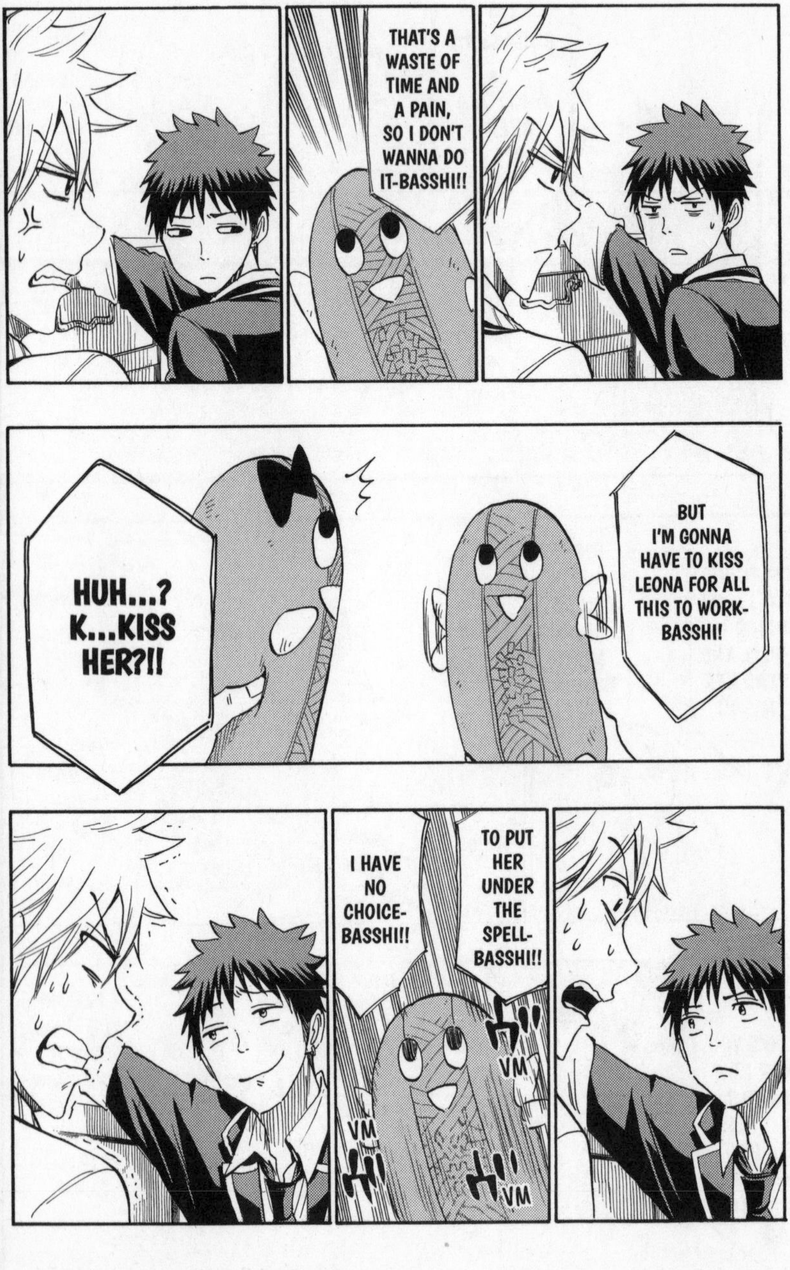
THAT'S A WASTE OF TIME AND A PAIN, SO I DON'T WANNA DO IT-BASSHI!!
BUT I'M GONNA HAVE TO KISS LEONA FOR ALL THIS TO WORK-BASSHI!
HUH...? K...KISS HER?!!
TO PUT HER UNDER THE SPELL-BASSHI!!
I HAVE NO CHOICE-BASSHI!!
VM
VM
VM

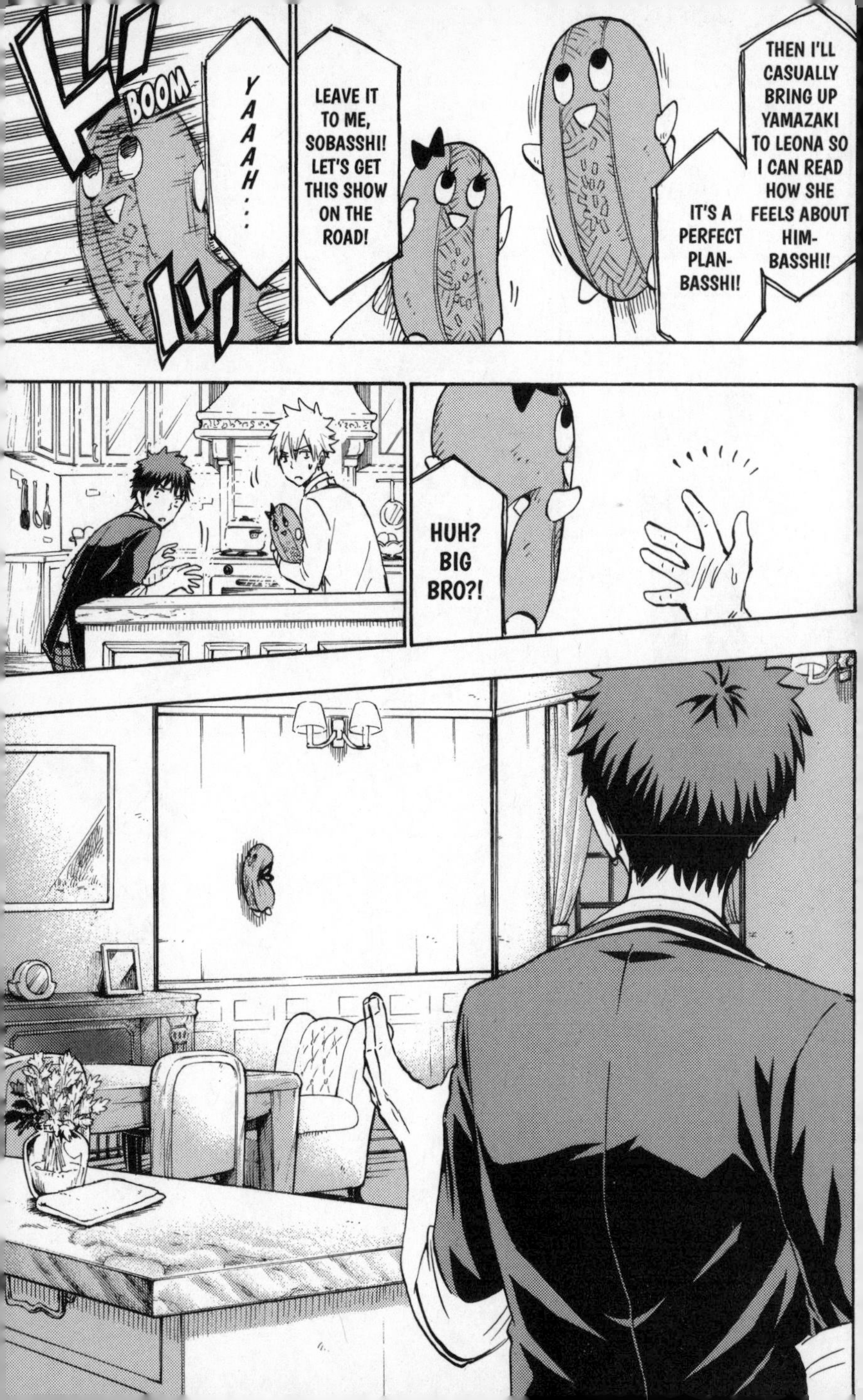
THEN I'LL CASUALLY BRING UP YAMAZAKI TO LEONA SO I CAN READ HOW SHE FEELS ABOUT HIM-BASSHI!
IT'S A PERFECT PLAN-BASSHI!
LEAVE IT TO ME, SOBASSHI! LET'S GET THIS SHOW ON THE ROAD!
YAAAH...
BOOM
HUH? BIG BRO?!

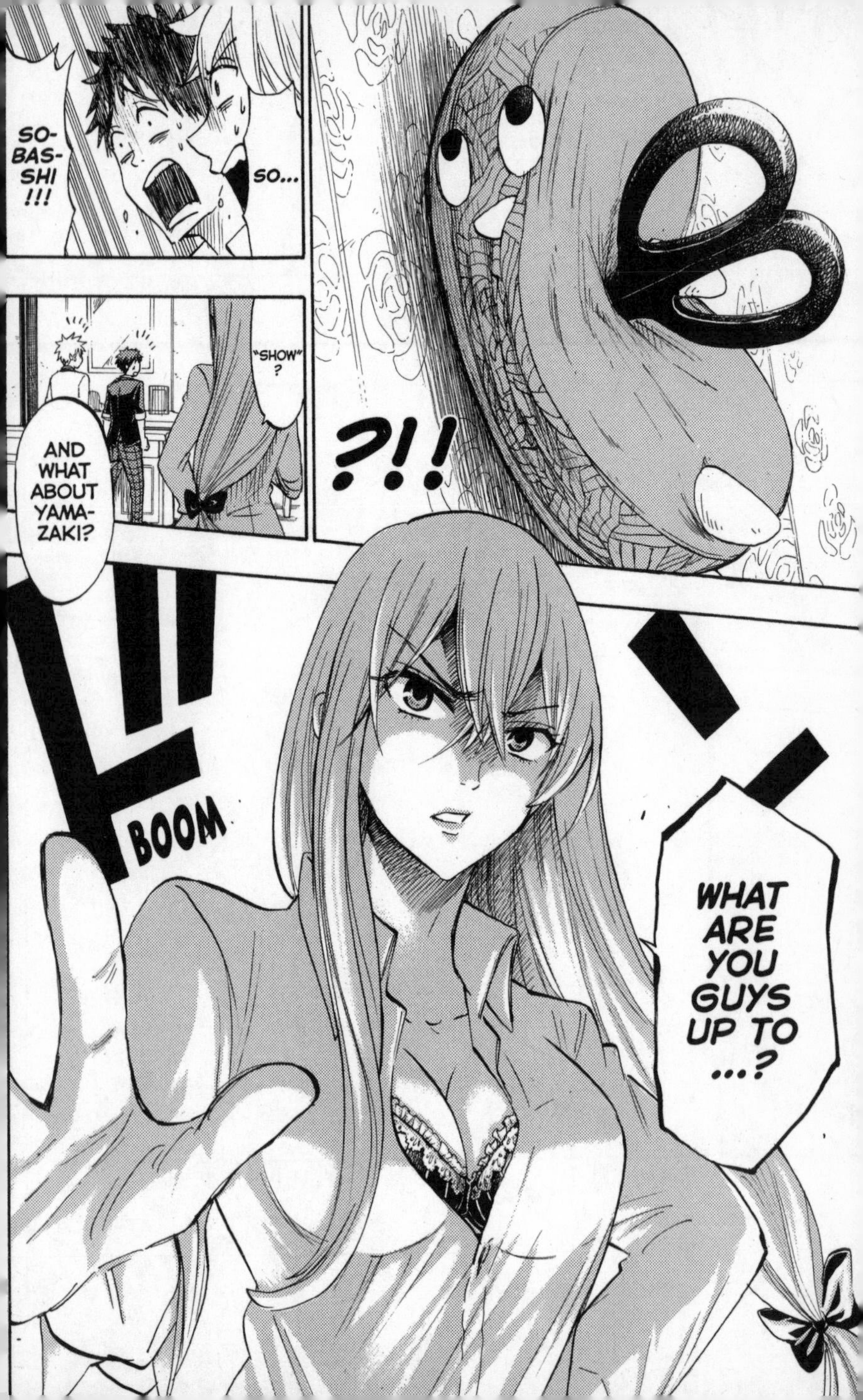

?!!
SO...
SO-BAS-SHI !!!
"SHOW" ?
AND WHAT ABOUT YAMA-ZAKI?
WHAT ARE YOU GUYS UP TO ...?
BOOM

CHAPTER 181: Although I always knew.

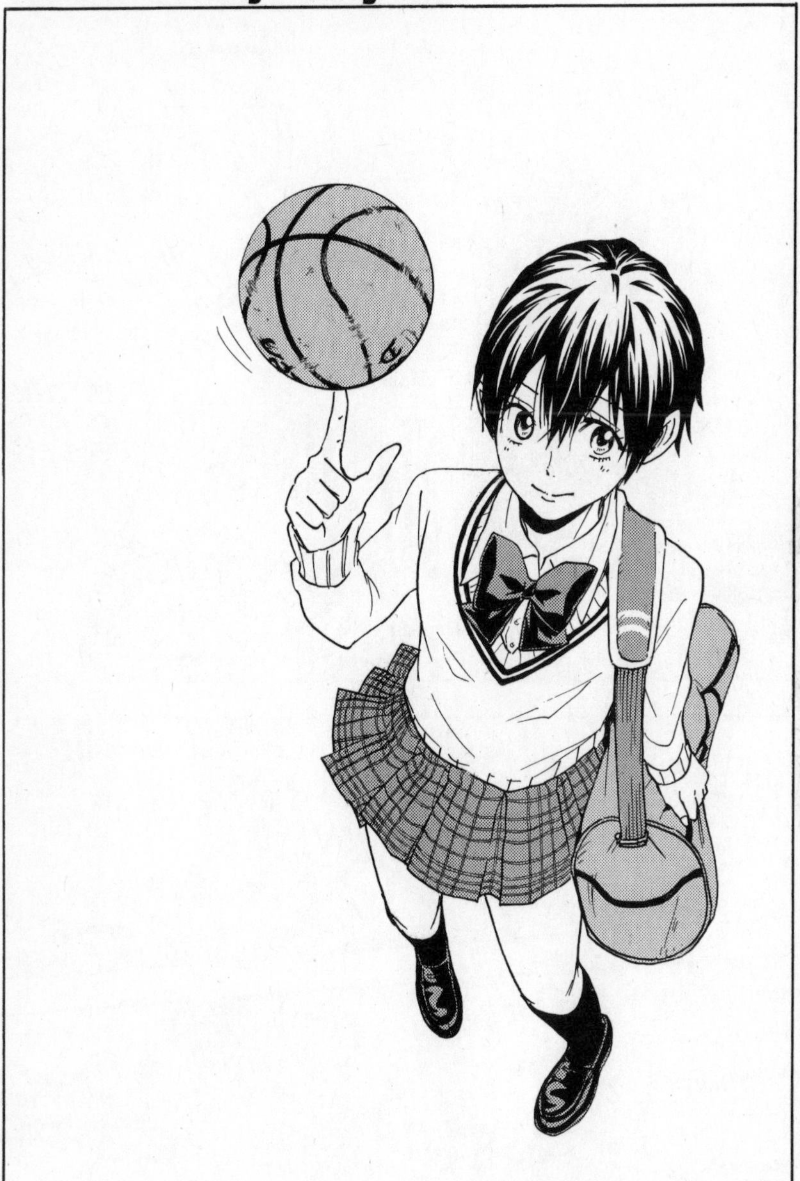

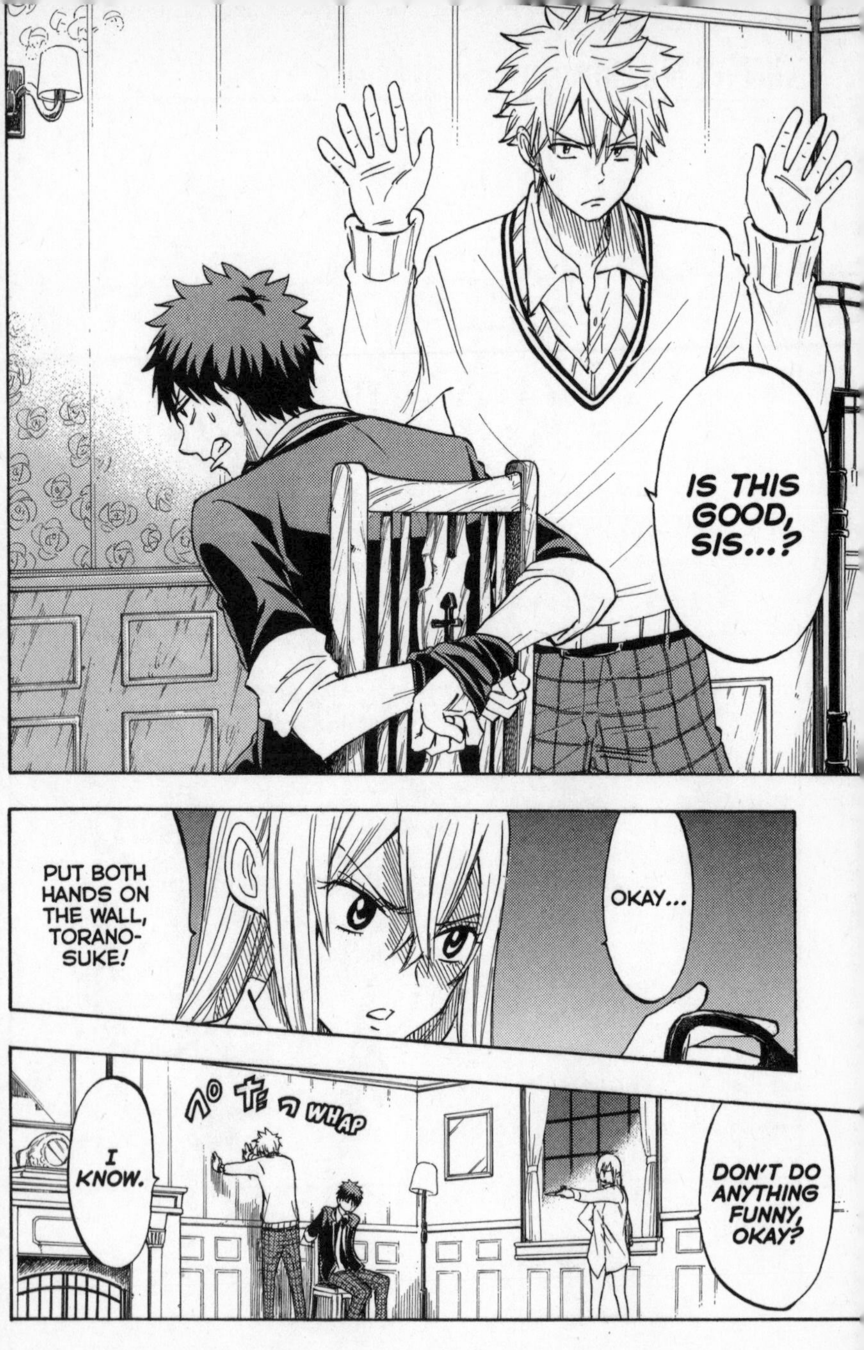
IS THIS GOOD, SIS...?
OKAY...
PUT BOTH HANDS ON THE WALL, TORANO-SUKE!
DON'T DO ANYTHING FUNNY, OKAY?
ぺたっ WHAP
I KNOW.

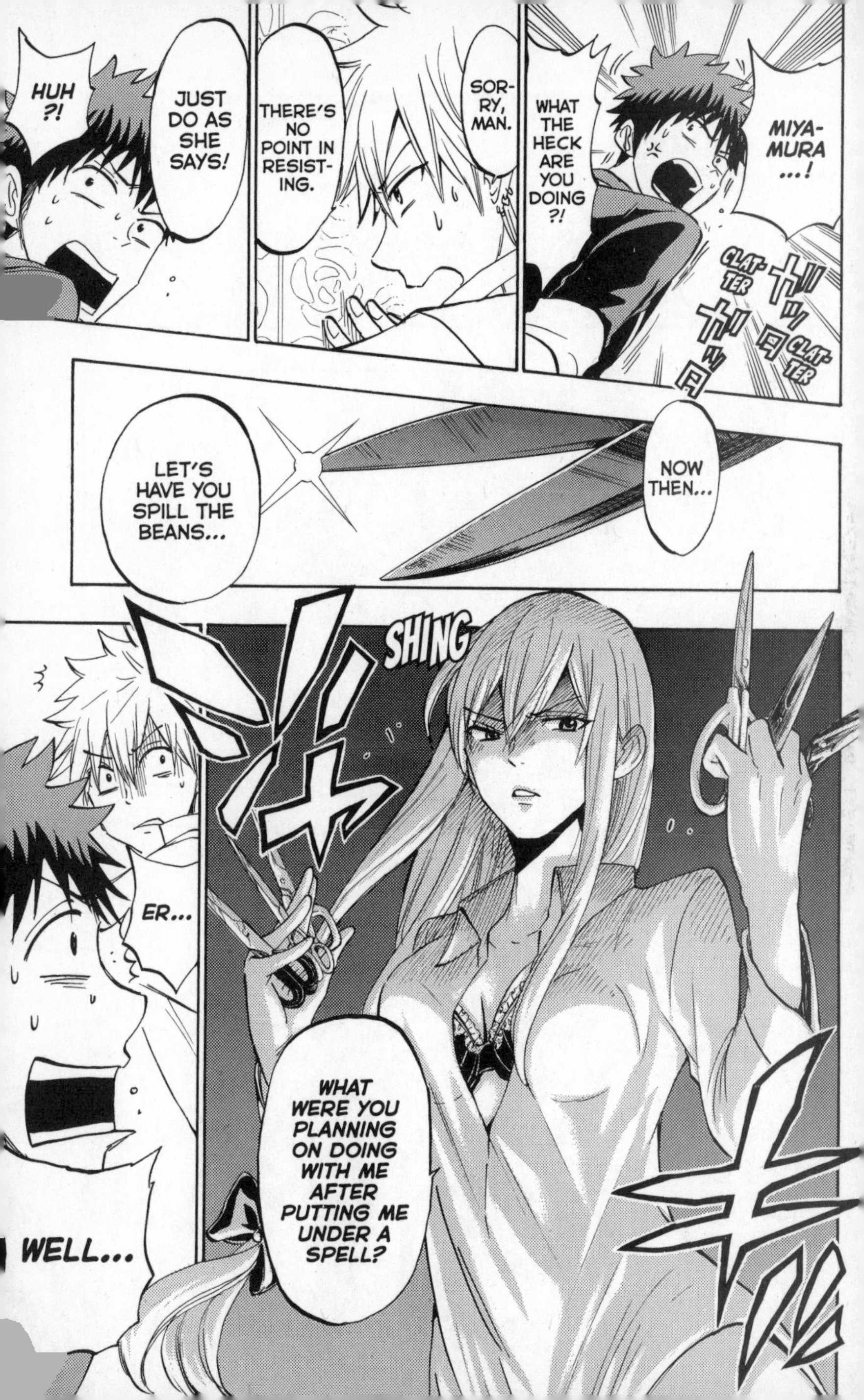
MIYA-MURA...!
WHAT THE HECK ARE YOU DOING?!
CLATTER
CLATTER
SORRY, MAN.
THERE'S NO POINT IN RESISTING.
JUST DO AS SHE SAYS!
HUH?!
NOW THEN...
LET'S HAVE YOU SPILL THE BEANS...
SHING
WHAT WERE YOU PLANNING ON DOING WITH ME AFTER PUTTING ME UNDER A SPELL?
ER...
WELL...

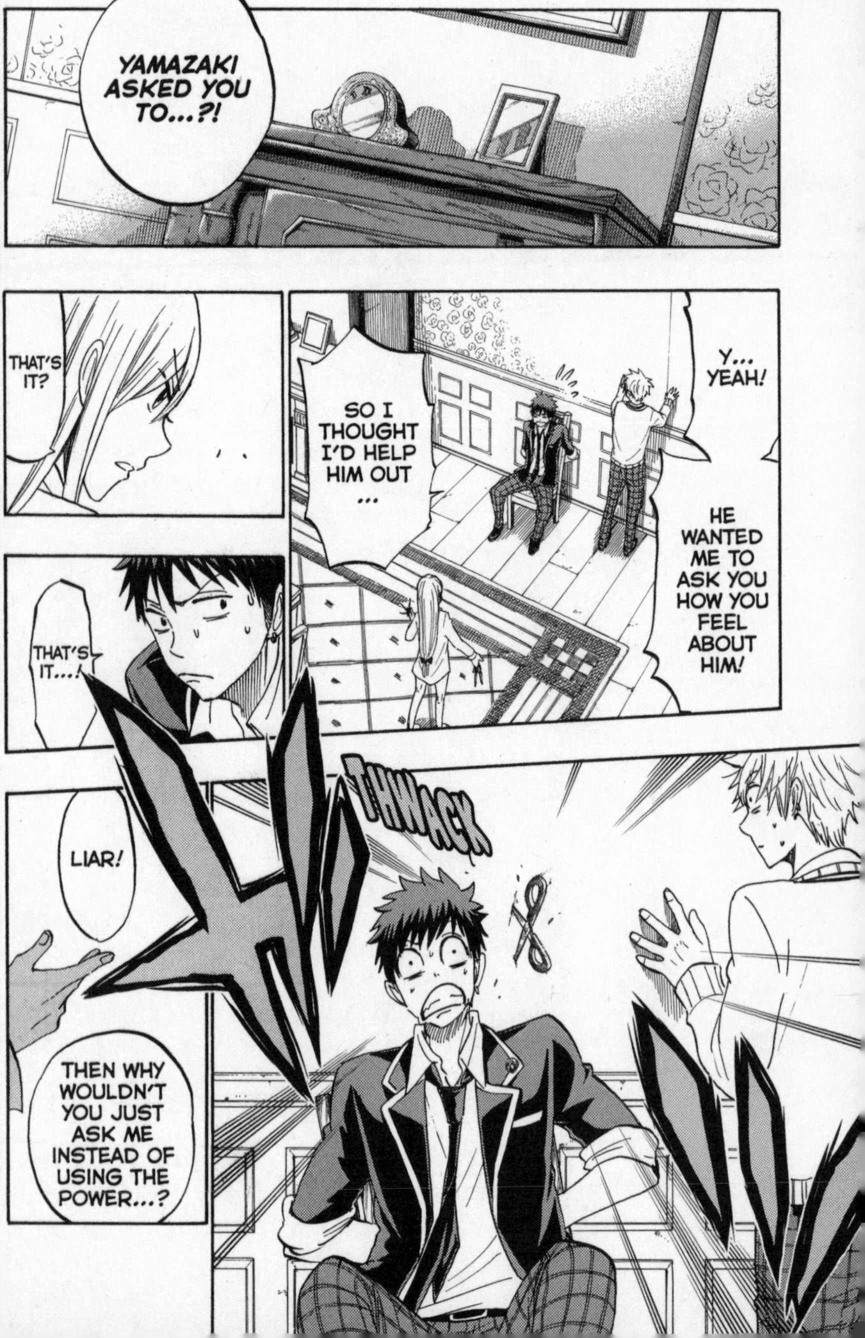
YAMAZAKI ASKED YOU TO...?!
Y... YEAH!
HE WANTED ME TO ASK YOU HOW YOU FEEL ABOUT HIM!
SO I THOUGHT I'D HELP HIM OUT ...
THAT'S IT?
THAT'S IT...!
THWACK
LIAR!
THEN WHY WOULDN'T YOU JUST ASK ME INSTEAD OF USING THE POWER...?

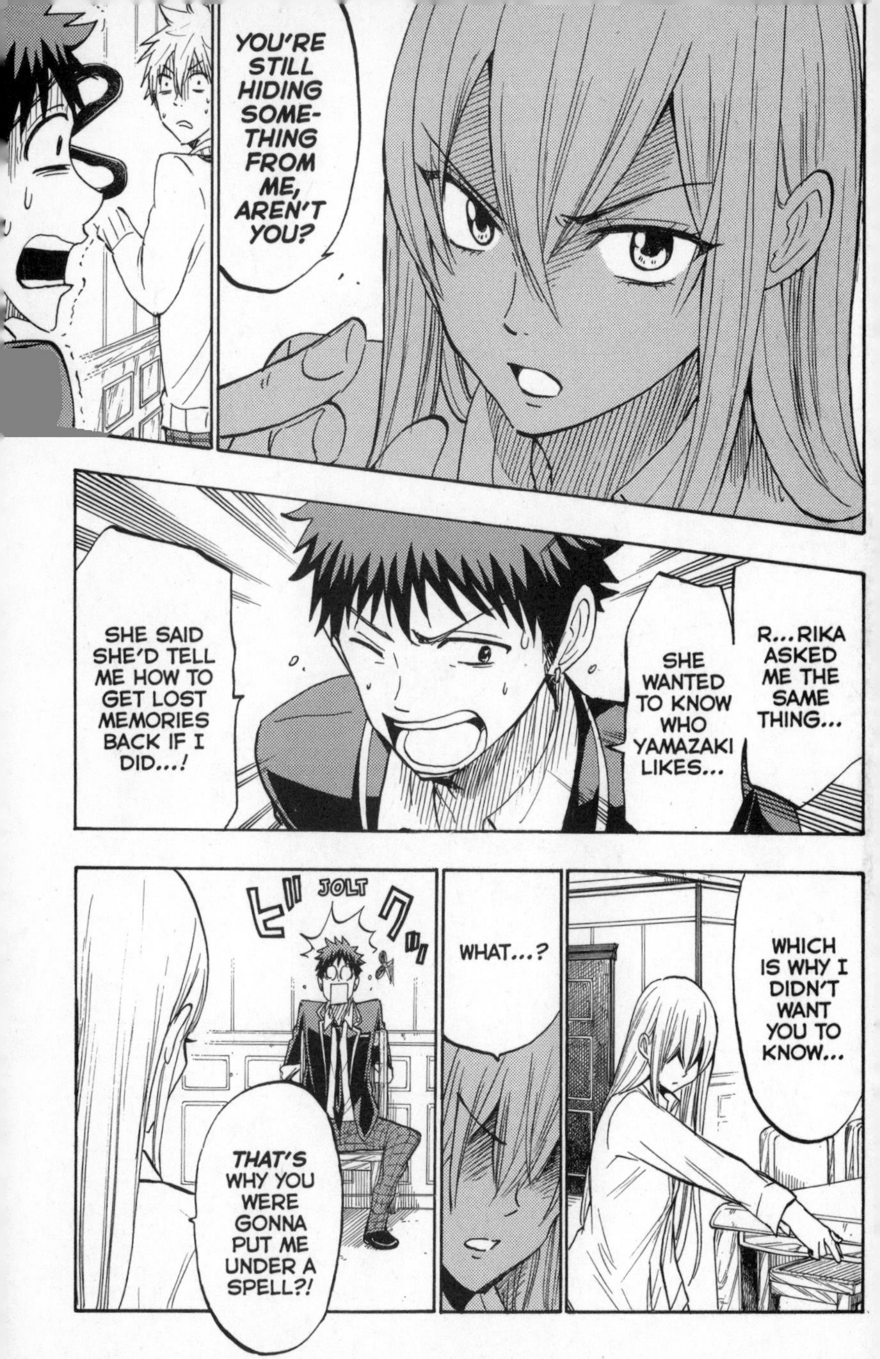
YOU'RE STILL HIDING SOME-THING FROM ME, AREN'T YOU?
R...RIKA ASKED ME THE SAME THING...
SHE WANTED TO KNOW WHO YAMAZAKI LIKES...
SHE SAID SHE'D TELL ME HOW TO GET LOST MEMORIES BACK IF I DID...!
WHICH IS WHY I DIDN'T WANT YOU TO KNOW...
WHAT...?
JOLT
THAT'S WHY YOU WERE GONNA PUT ME UNDER A SPELL?!

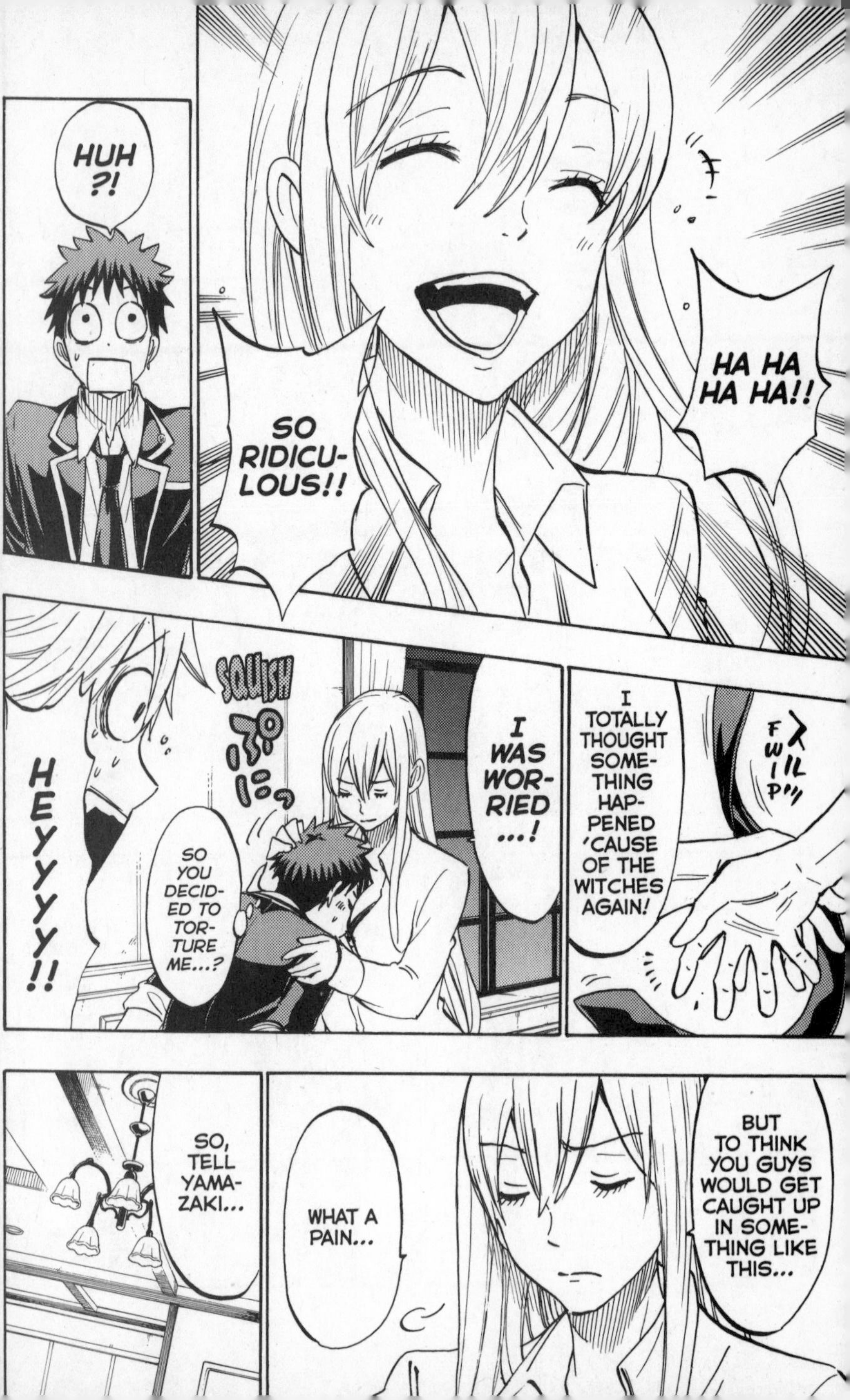

HA HA HA HA!!
SO RIDICULOUS!!
HUH ?!
FWIP
I TOTALLY THOUGHT SOMETHING HAPPENED 'CAUSE OF THE WITCHES AGAIN!
I WAS WORRIED...!
SQUISH
HEYYYYY!!
SO YOU DECIDED TO TORTURE ME...?
BUT TO THINK YOU GUYS WOULD GET CAUGHT UP IN SOMETHING LIKE THIS...
WHAT A PAIN...
SO, TELL YAMAZAKI...

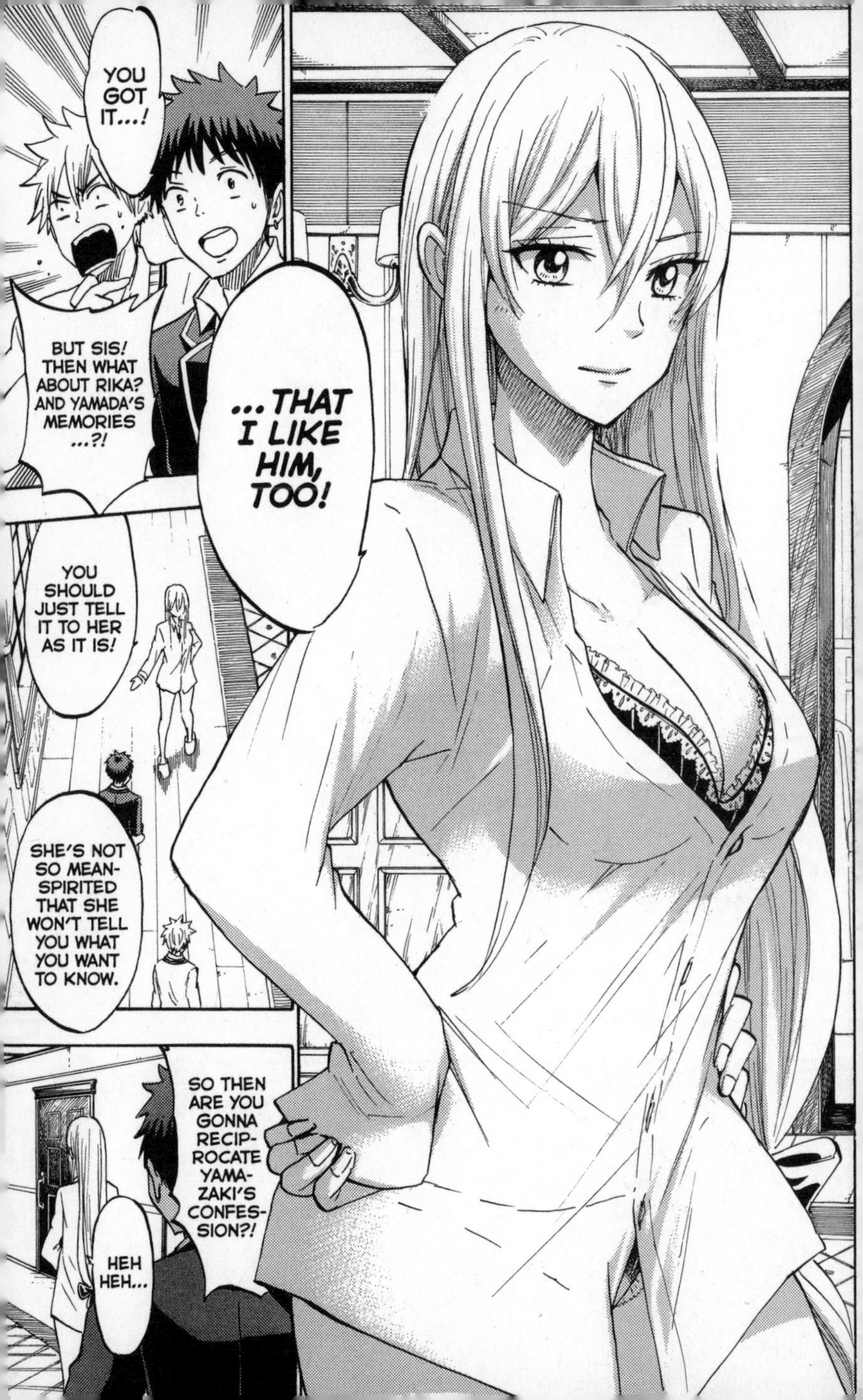

...THAT I LIKE HIM, TOO!
YOU GOT IT...!
BUT SIS! THEN WHAT ABOUT RIKA? AND YAMADA'S MEMORIES ...?!
YOU SHOULD JUST TELL IT TO HER AS IT IS!
SHE'S NOT SO MEAN-SPIRITED THAT SHE WON'T TELL YOU WHAT YOU WANT TO KNOW.
SO THEN ARE YOU GONNA RECIP-ROCATE YAMA-ZAKI'S CONFES-SION?!
HEH HEH...

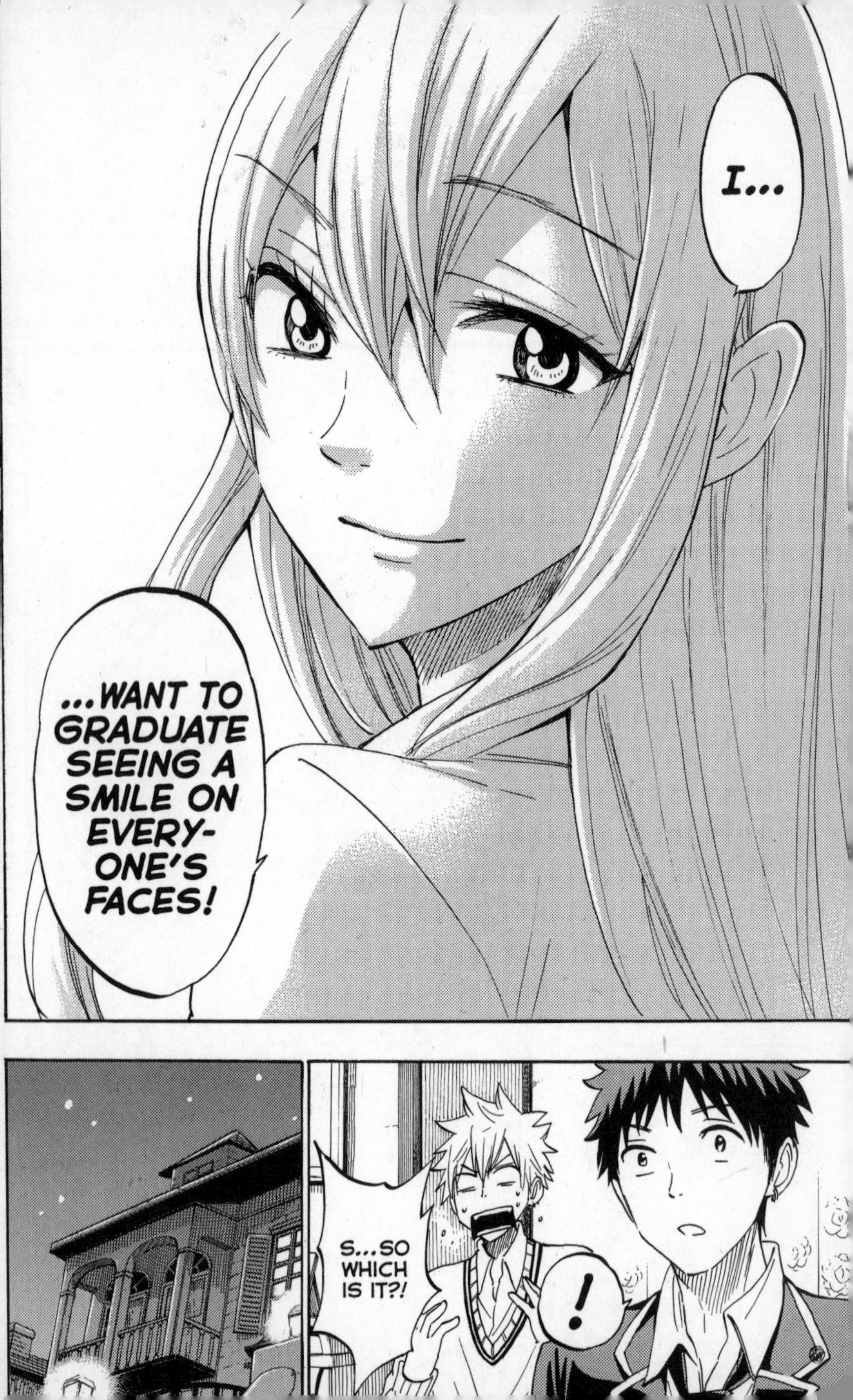
I...
...WANT TO GRADUATE SEEING A SMILE ON EVERY-ONE'S FACES!
S...SO WHICH IS IT?!
!

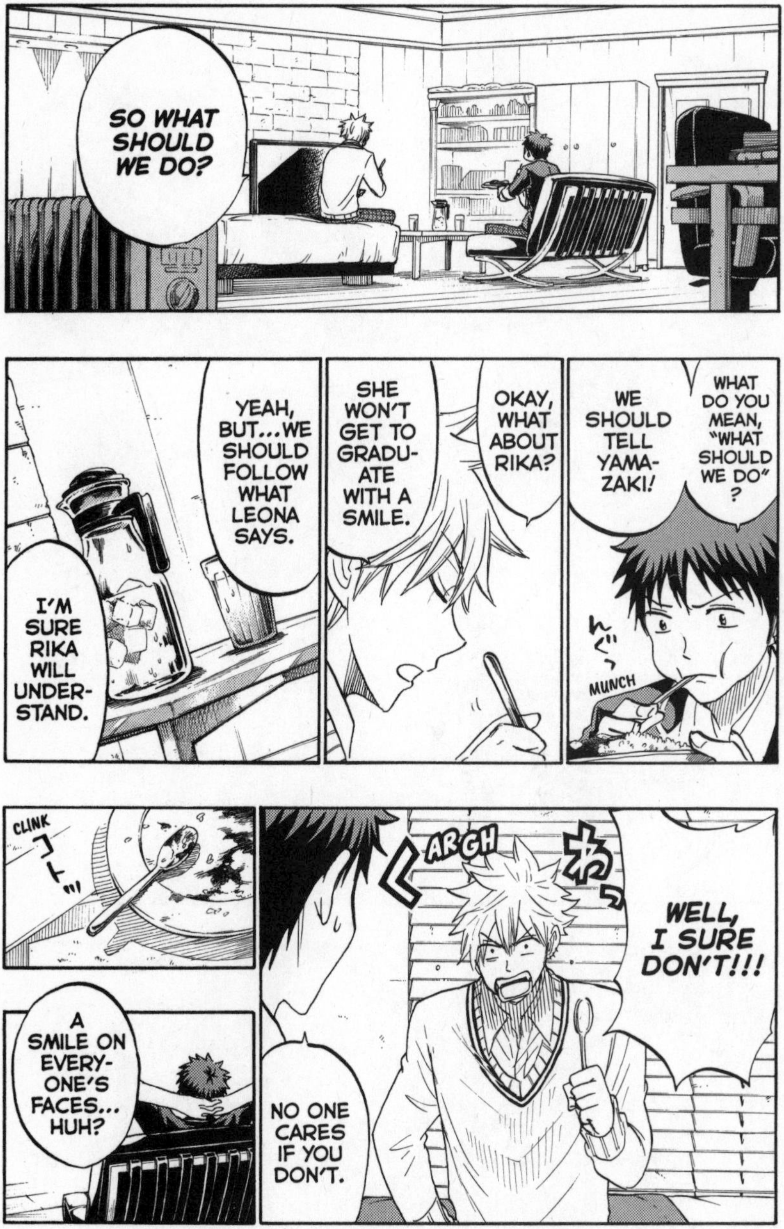
SO WHAT SHOULD WE DO?
WHAT DO YOU MEAN, "WHAT SHOULD WE DO"?
WE SHOULD TELL YAMA-ZAKI!
んぐっ
MUNCH
OKAY, WHAT ABOUT RIKA?
SHE WON'T GET TO GRADU-ATE WITH A SMILE.
YEAH, BUT...WE SHOULD FOLLOW WHAT LEONA SAYS.
I'M SURE RIKA WILL UNDER-STAND.
WELL, I SURE DON'T!!!
わっ
ARGH
NO ONE CARES IF YOU DON'T.
CLINK
コトッ
A SMILE ON EVERY-ONE'S FACES... HUH?

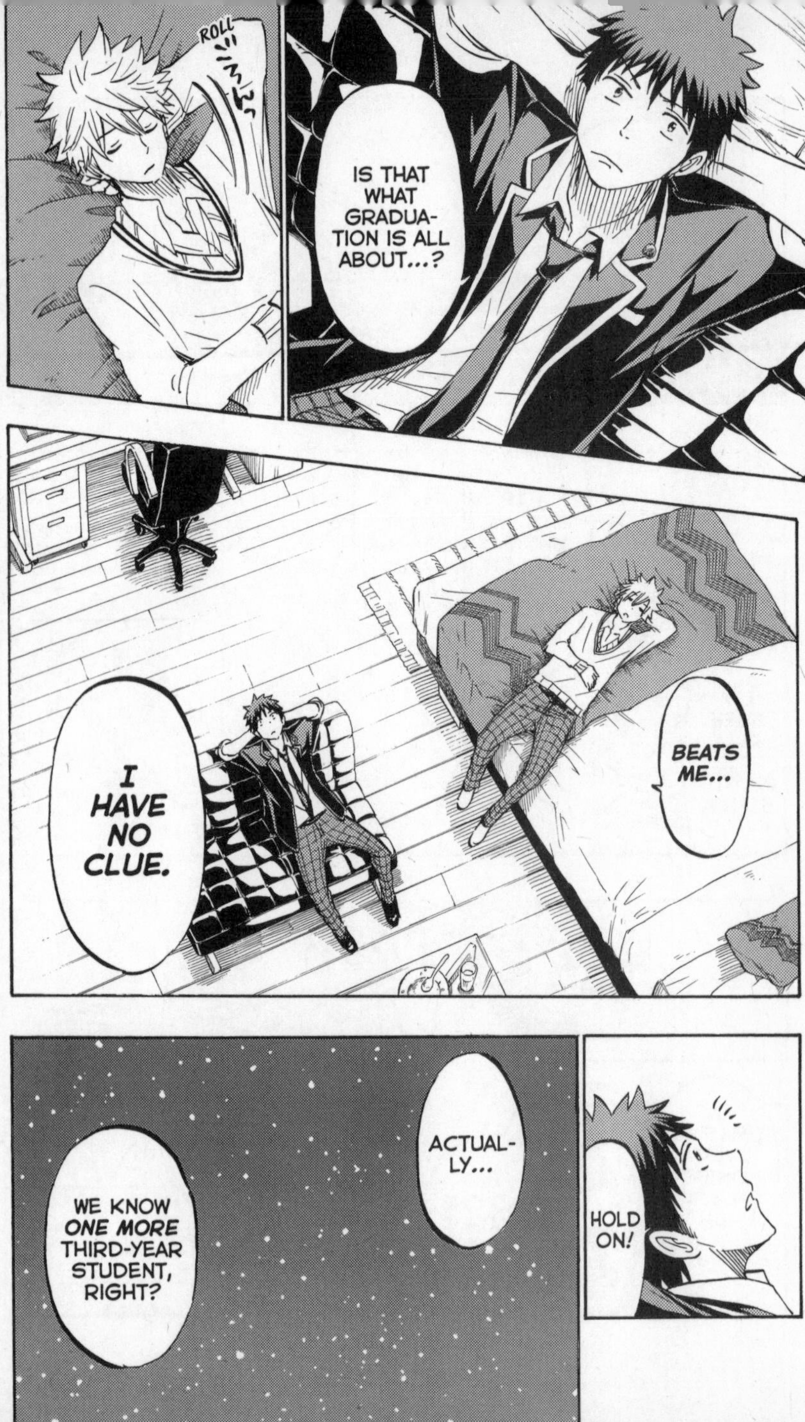
IS THAT WHAT GRADUATION IS ALL ABOUT...?
ROLL
BEATS ME...
I HAVE NO CLUE.
HOLD ON!
ACTUALLY...
WE KNOW ONE MORE THIRD-YEAR STUDENT, RIGHT?

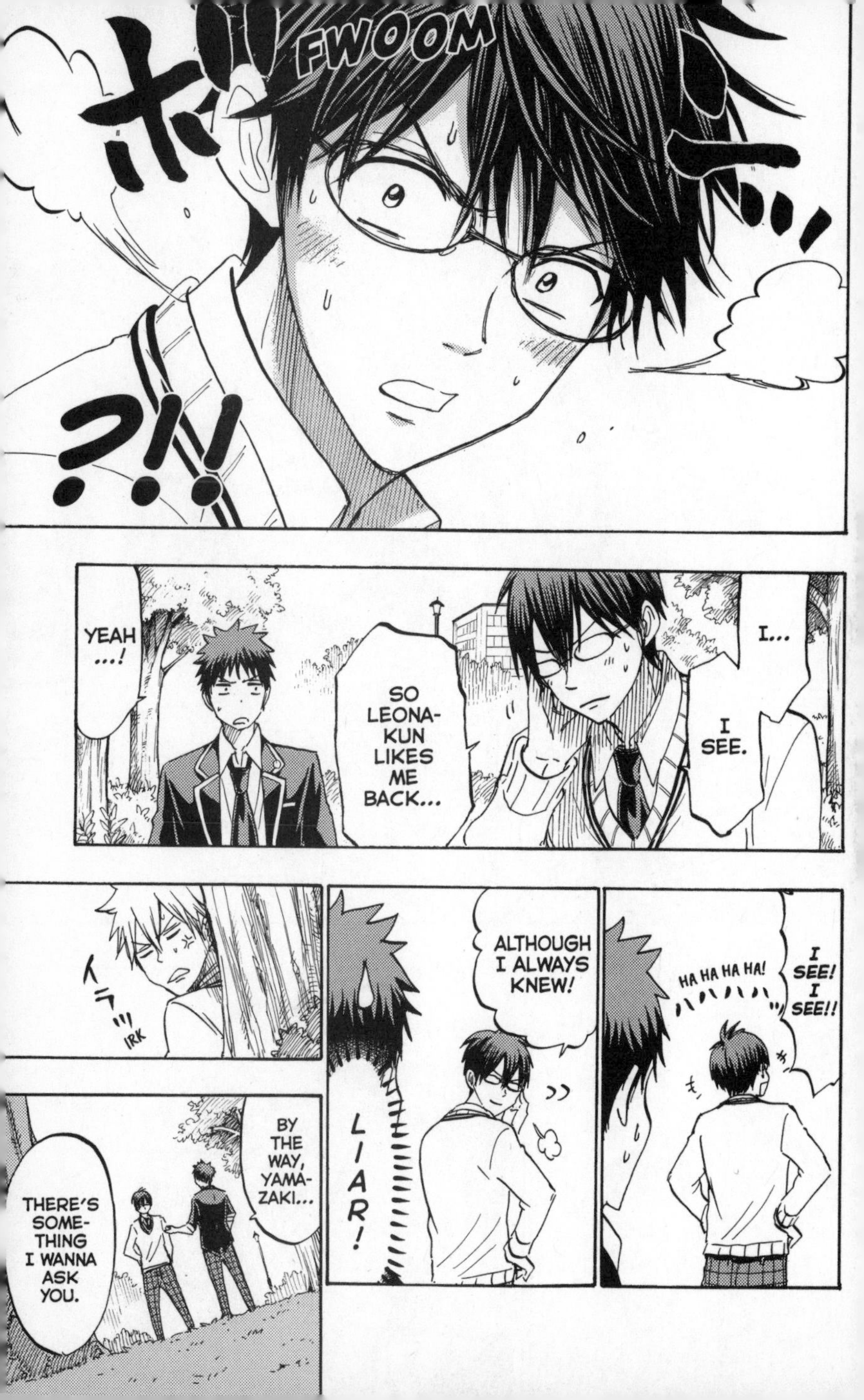
FWOOM
?!!
I...
I SEE.
SO LEONA-KUN LIKES ME BACK...
YEAH ...!
I SEE! I SEE!!
HA HA HA HA!
ALTHOUGH I ALWAYS KNEW!
LIAR!
IRK
BY THE WAY, YAMA-ZAKI...
THERE'S SOME-THING I WANNA ASK YOU.

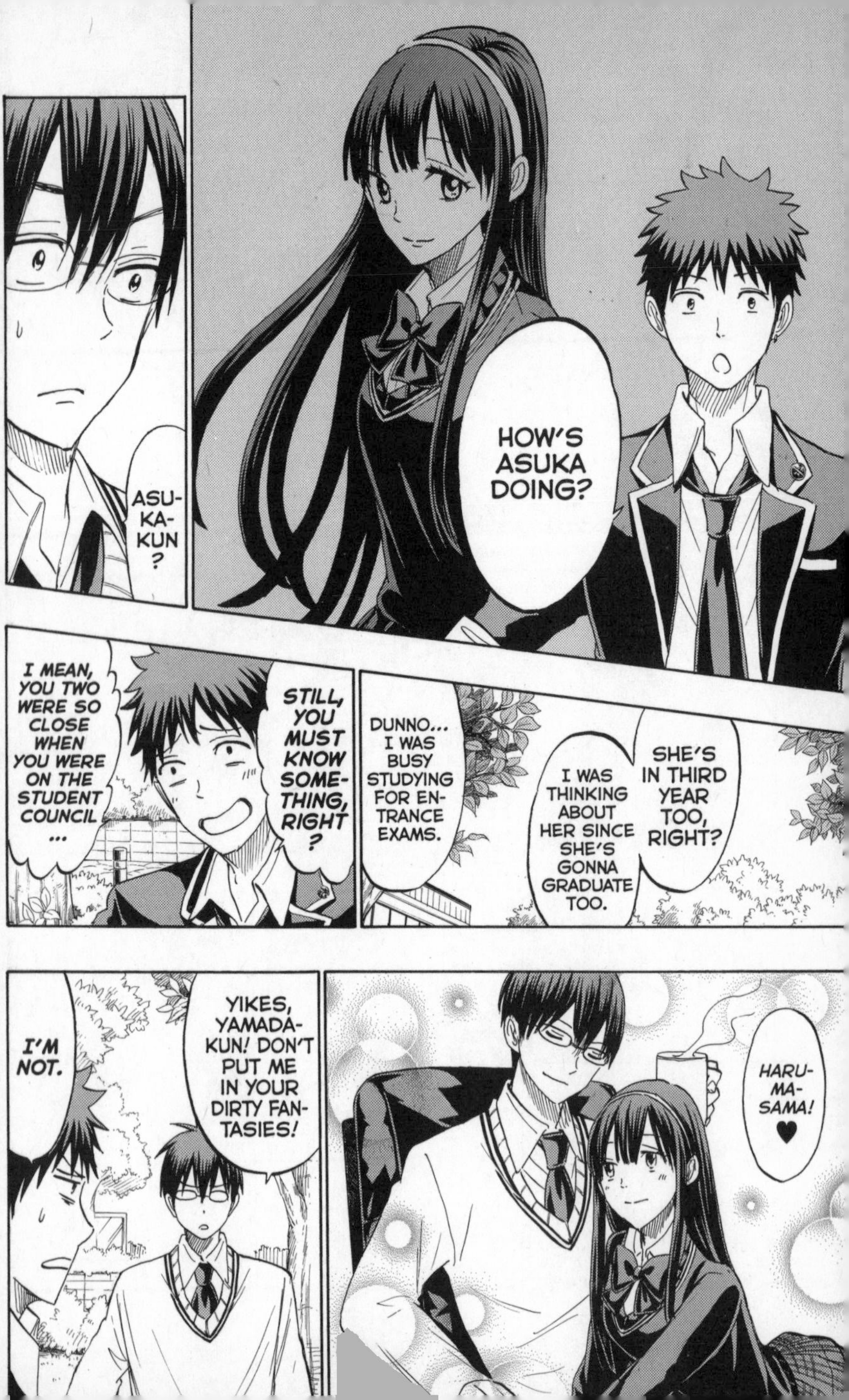
HOW'S ASUKA DOING?
ASUKA-KUN?
SHE'S IN THIRD YEAR TOO, RIGHT?
I WAS THINKING ABOUT HER SINCE SHE'S GONNA GRADUATE TOO.
DUNNO... I WAS BUSY STUDYING FOR ENTRANCE EXAMS.
STILL, YOU MUST KNOW SOMETHING, RIGHT?
I MEAN, YOU TWO WERE SO CLOSE WHEN YOU WERE ON THE STUDENT COUNCIL...
HARUMA-SAMA! ♥
YIKES, YAMADA-KUN! DON'T PUT ME IN YOUR DIRTY FANTASIES!
I'M NOT.

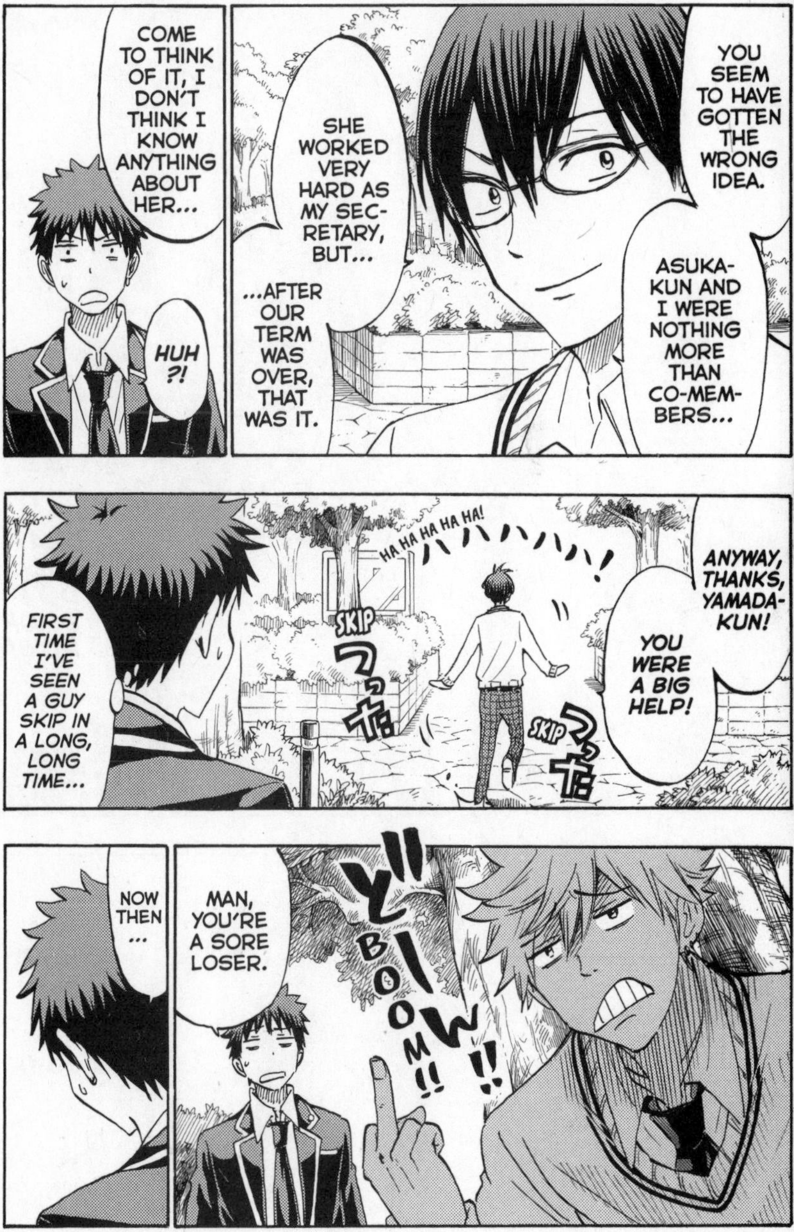
YOU SEEM TO HAVE GOTTEN THE WRONG IDEA.
ASUKA-KUN AND I WERE NOTHING MORE THAN CO-MEMBERS...
SHE WORKED VERY HARD AS MY SECRETARY, BUT...
...AFTER OUR TERM WAS OVER, THAT WAS IT.
COME TO THINK OF IT, I DON'T THINK I KNOW ANYTHING ABOUT HER...
HUH ?!
ANYWAY, THANKS, YAMADA-KUN!
YOU WERE A BIG HELP!
HA HA HA HA HA!
SKIP
SKIP
FIRST TIME I'VE SEEN A GUY SKIP IN A LONG, LONG TIME...
BOOM!!
MAN, YOU'RE A SORE LOSER.
NOW THEN ...

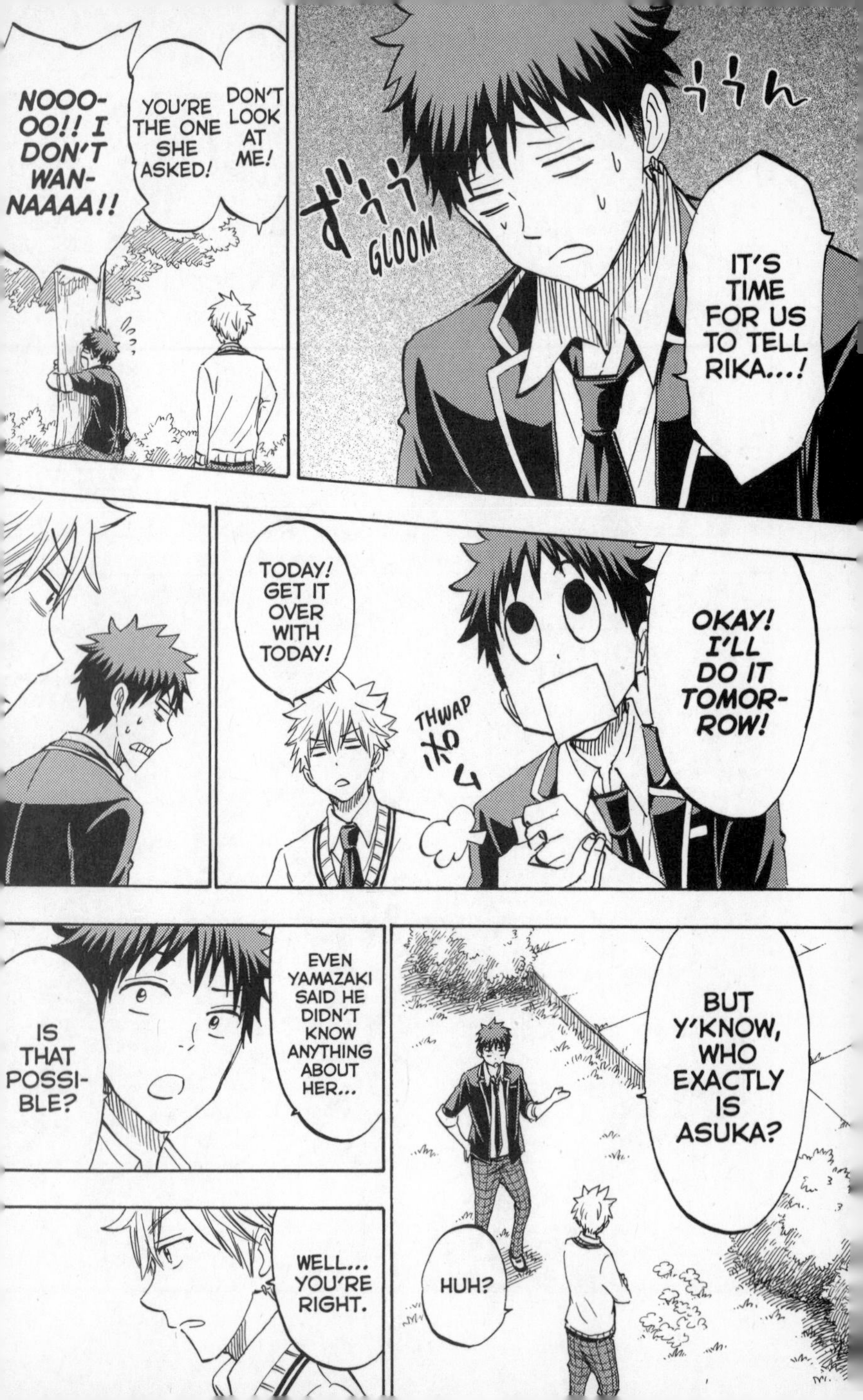
ううん
ずううう
GLOOM
IT'S TIME FOR US TO TELL RIKA...!
DON'T LOOK AT ME!
YOU'RE THE ONE SHE ASKED!
NOOOOO!! I DON'T WANNAAAA!!
OKAY! I'LL DO IT TOMORROW!
THWAP
ポム
TODAY! GET IT OVER WITH TODAY!
BUT Y'KNOW, WHO EXACTLY IS ASUKA?
HUH?
EVEN YAMAZAKI SAID HE DIDN'T KNOW ANYTHING ABOUT HER...
IS THAT POSSIBLE?
WELL... YOU'RE RIGHT.

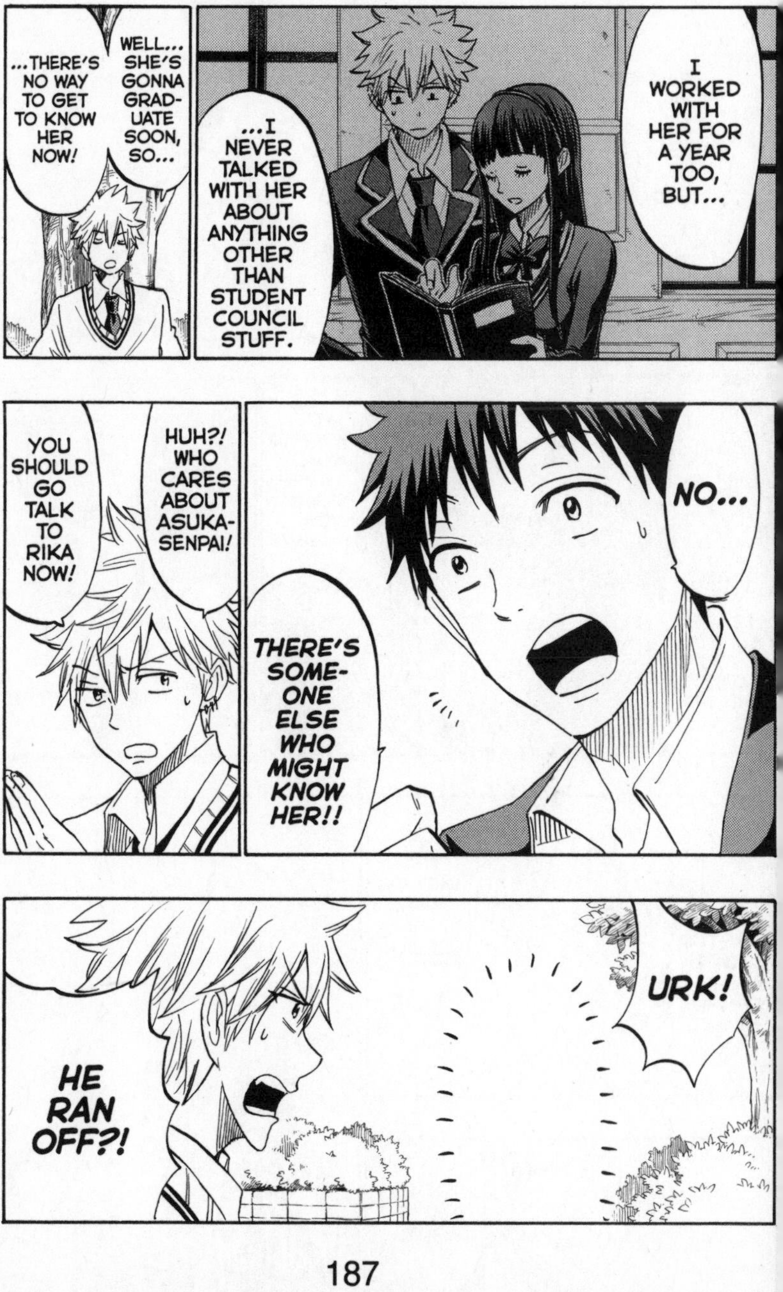
I WORKED WITH HER FOR A YEAR TOO, BUT...
...I NEVER TALKED WITH HER ABOUT ANYTHING OTHER THAN STUDENT COUNCIL STUFF.
WELL... SHE'S GONNA GRAD-UATE SOON, SO...
...THERE'S NO WAY TO GET TO KNOW HER NOW!
NO...
THERE'S SOME-ONE ELSE WHO MIGHT KNOW HER!!
HUH?! WHO CARES ABOUT ASUKA-SENPAI!
YOU SHOULD GO TALK TO RIKA NOW!
URK!
HE RAN OFF?!

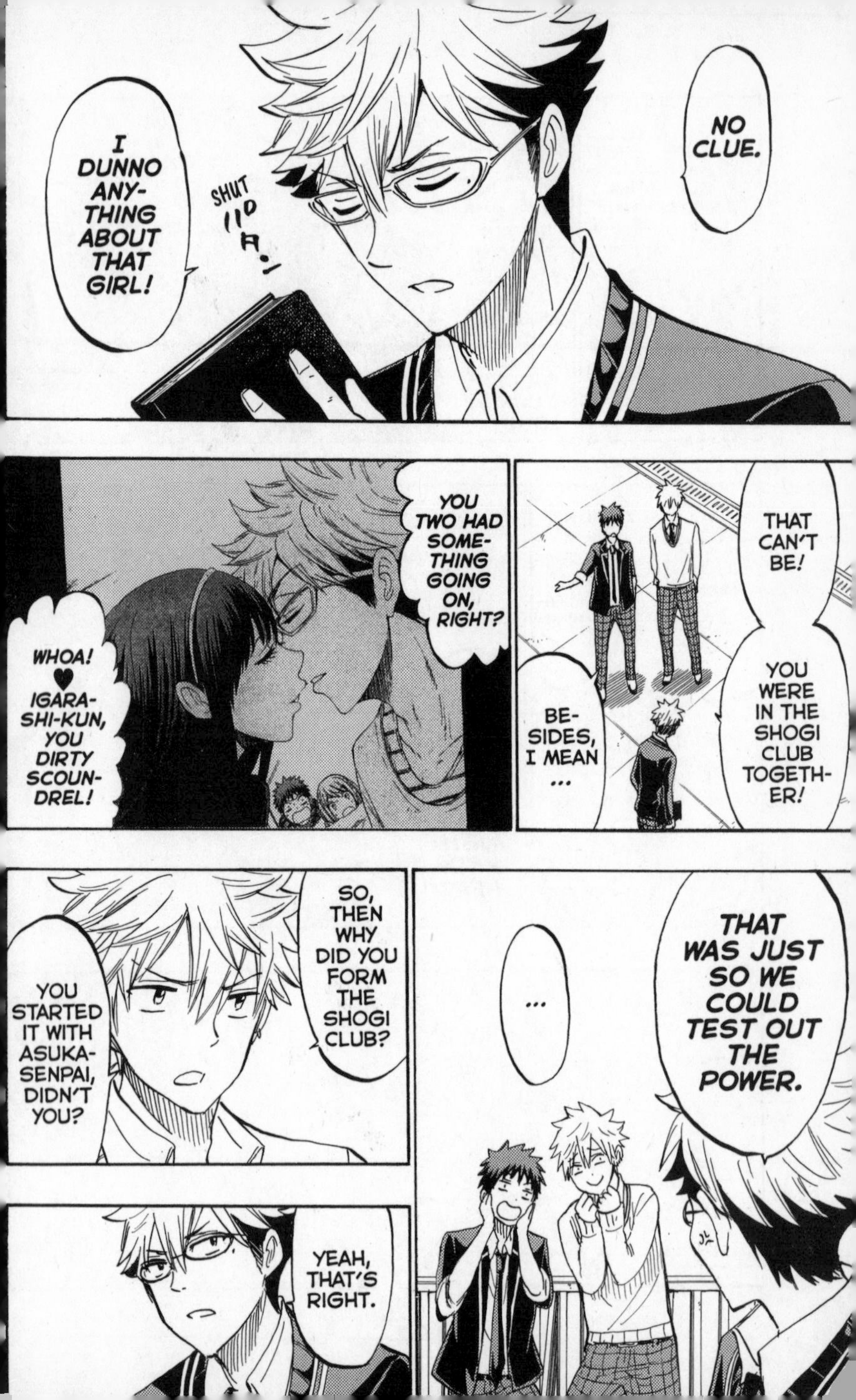
NO CLUE.
SHUT
I DUNNO ANYTHING ABOUT THAT GIRL!
THAT CAN'T BE!
YOU WERE IN THE SHOGI CLUB TOGETHER!
BESIDES, I MEAN ...
YOU TWO HAD SOMETHING GOING ON, RIGHT?
WHOA! ♥ IGARASHI-KUN, YOU DIRTY SCOUNDREL!
THAT WAS JUST SO WE COULD TEST OUT THE POWER.
...
SO, THEN WHY DID YOU FORM THE SHOGI CLUB?
YOU STARTED IT WITH ASUKA-SENPAI, DIDN'T YOU?
YEAH, THAT'S RIGHT.

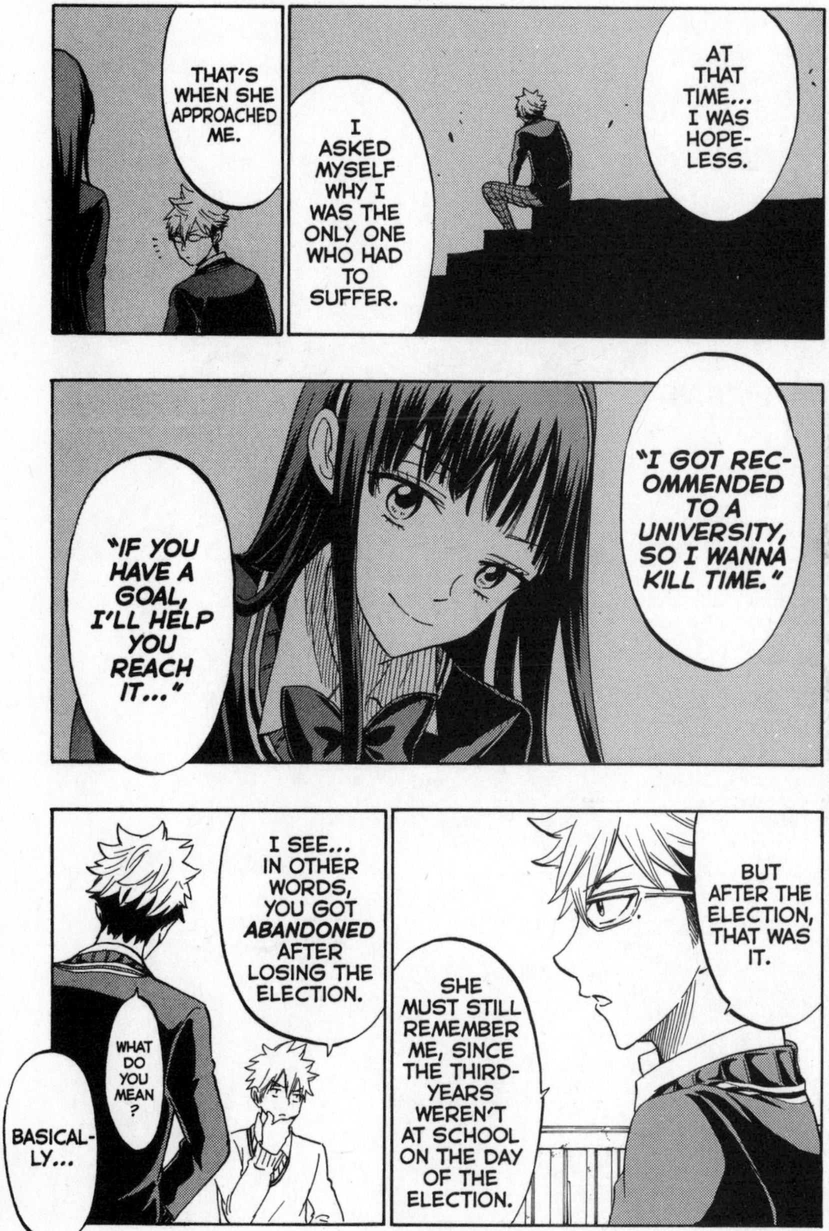
AT THAT TIME... I WAS HOPE-LESS.
I ASKED MYSELF WHY I WAS THE ONLY ONE WHO HAD TO SUFFER.
THAT'S WHEN SHE APPROACHED ME.
"I GOT REC-OMMENDED TO A UNIVERSITY, SO I WANNA KILL TIME."
"IF YOU HAVE A GOAL, I'LL HELP YOU REACH IT..."
BUT AFTER THE ELECTION, THAT WAS IT.
SHE MUST STILL REMEMBER ME, SINCE THE THIRD-YEARS WEREN'T AT SCHOOL ON THE DAY OF THE ELECTION.
I SEE... IN OTHER WORDS, YOU GOT *ABANDONED* AFTER LOSING THE ELECTION.
WHAT DO YOU MEAN?
BASICAL-LY...

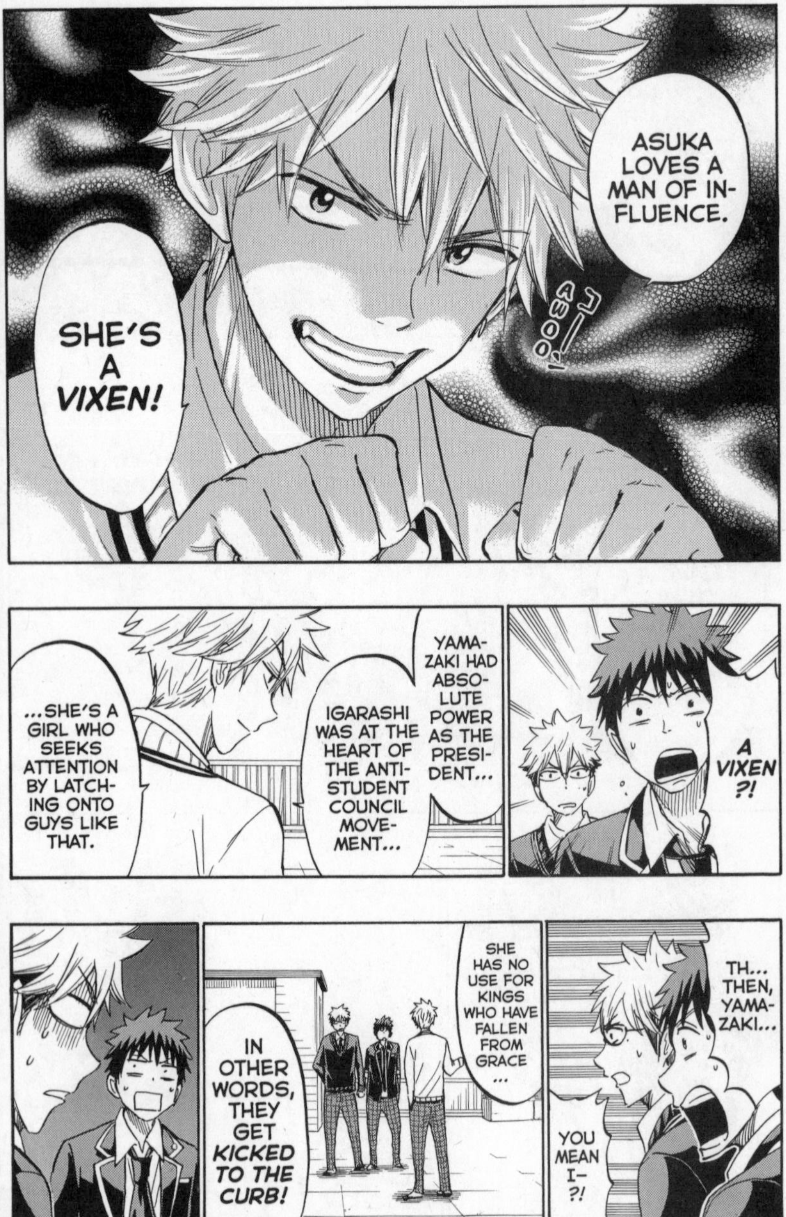
ASUKA LOVES A MAN OF IN-FLUENCE.
SHE'S A *VIXEN!*
A VIXEN ?!
YAMAZAKI HAD ABSOLUTE POWER AS THE PRESIDENT...
IGARASHI WAS AT THE HEART OF THE ANTI-STUDENT COUNCIL MOVEMENT...
...SHE'S A GIRL WHO SEEKS ATTENTION BY LATCHING ONTO GUYS LIKE THAT.
TH... THEN, YAMAZAKI...
YOU MEAN I—?!
SHE HAS NO USE FOR KINGS WHO HAVE FALLEN FROM GRACE...
IN OTHER WORDS, THEY GET *KICKED TO THE CURB!*

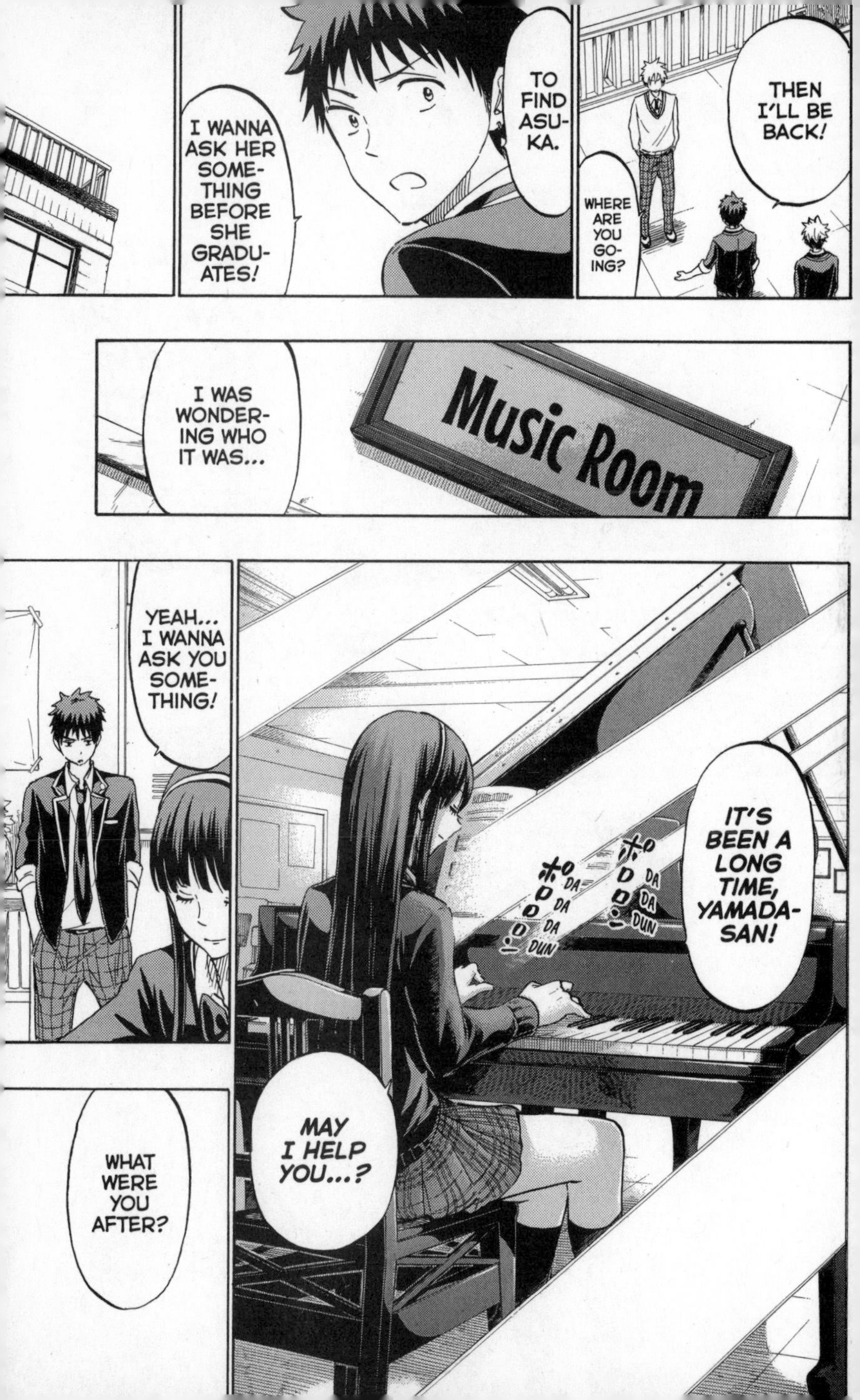
THEN I'LL BE BACK!
WHERE ARE YOU GOING?
TO FIND ASUKA.
I WANNA ASK HER SOMETHING BEFORE SHE GRADUATES!
Music Room
I WAS WONDERING WHO IT WAS...
IT'S BEEN A LONG TIME, YAMADA-SAN!
DA DA DUN
DA DA DA DUN
MAY I HELP YOU...?
YEAH... I WANNA ASK YOU SOMETHING!
WHAT WERE YOU AFTER?

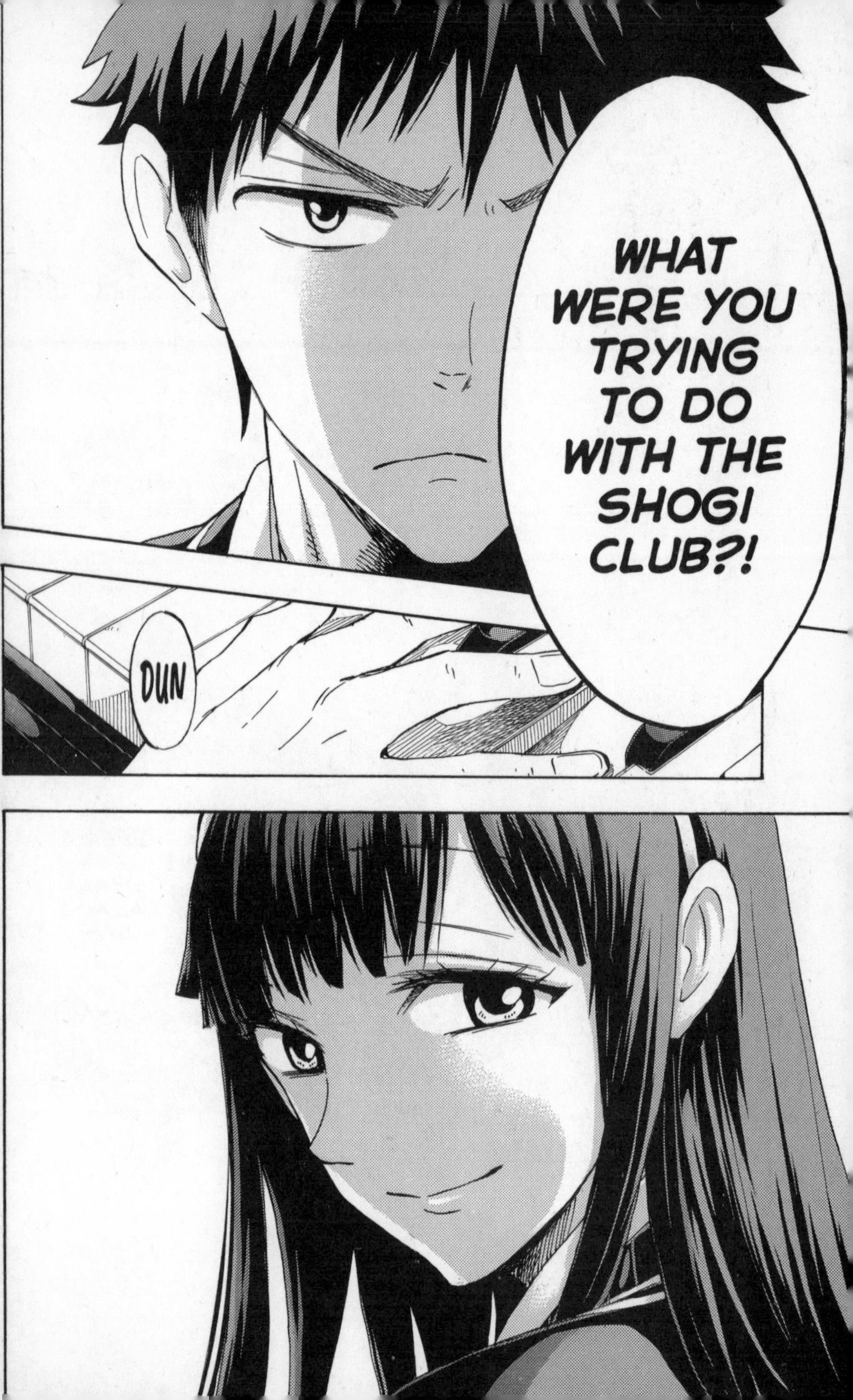
WHAT WERE YOU TRYING TO DO WITH THE SHOGI CLUB?!
DUN

朱雀高等学校
裏ホームページ
SUZAKU HIGH SCHOOL UNDERGROUND WEBSITE

Q&A Corner #14!! Let's go!!

Time to introduce today's guest!

Hey guys, this is Shinichi Tamaki from class 2-H *twinkle*.

What's up with him? Gross.

Well, since I will be the **star** of this Q&A Corner... I will do everything I can to answer your questions so that I may satisfy all of you, my fans...!

Sorry, you guys... This is what you're stuck with.

Hey, what's that supposed to mean?!

Anyway, I'm relieved that people sent questions for you.

If they didn't, our Q&A Corner would be in

jeopardy.

H...hey, cut it out with the pressure!

Q1. Do you like big boobs? Kanagawa Prefecture, H.N Makaron-san

Whoa, this question came from left field!

Earlier, you said that you'd be **"troubled with ones that are too big,"** right?

Hey! Don't pipe in before I get a chance to answer!

(What does he mean by "troubled"?)

Q2. You seem to be bad at sports, but how are your grades? What's your best subject?
Iwate Prefecture, H.N Hinemossu-san

What?! Who said I'm bad at sports?!

It's the truth.

No, it's not! I may not be good at ball sports or track-and-field, but I'm great at **dancing**, believe it or not! *twinkle*

Moving on!

Hey! I'm not finished! My best subject is Social Studies!!

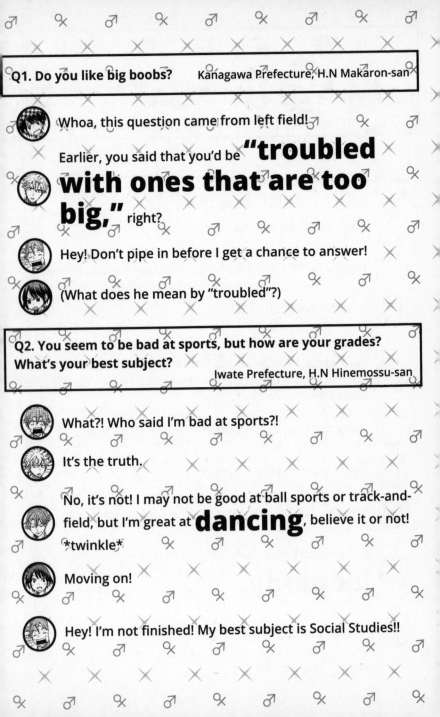

Q3. Tell us what's your favorite genre for light novels! I want to check it out!

Nagano Prefecture, H.N Fanta-san

 Heh heh! I was expecting this question! In my case, I check out new publications regardless of the genre, but I'll recommend a series that I shared with Yama-da-kun...

The **"There's No Way This Bad Boy Would Fall for Ms. Four-Eyes!!"** series!

It takes place at a school, but once you start, you won't be able to put it down. I actually recommend any work by the series author, Mikihiko Yoshikawa-sensei, and her debut work is–Uh, are you guys listening?

Oh, we dozed off.

Q4. Tell us about your family! Tokushima Prefecture, H.N Chiyo-san

 My family consists of four members: My dad, my mom, my little sister, and me.

 You have a little sister?! Is she cute?!

 I'm her older brother, how should I know?! Anyway, she has quite the attitude!

She's two years younger than me, but we've barely talk-ed since she entered junior high. Unlike me, she has a lot of friends, and these days, she just looks at me and says,

"Gross."

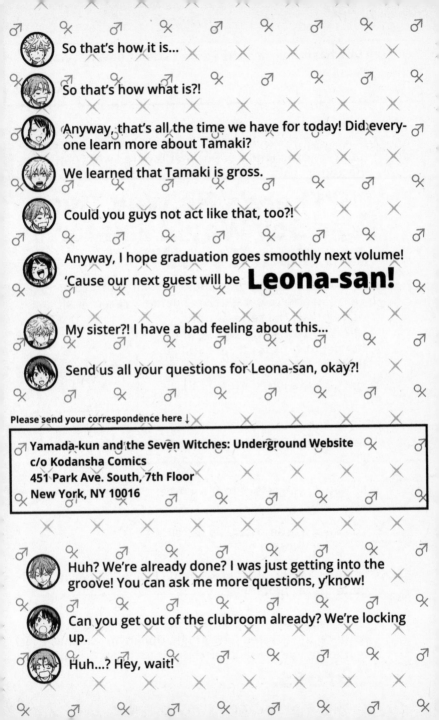

So that's how it is...

So that's how what is?!

Anyway, that's all the time we have for today! Did everyone learn more about Tamaki?

We learned that Tamaki is gross.

Could you guys not act like that, too?!

Anyway, I hope graduation goes smoothly next volume! 'Cause our next guest will be **Leona-san!**

My sister?! I have a bad feeling about this...

Send us all your questions for Leona-san, okay?!

Please send your correspondence here ↓

Yamada-kun and the Seven Witches: Underground Website
c/o Kodansha Comics
451 Park Ave. South, 7th Floor
New York, NY 10016

Huh? We're already done? I was just getting into the groove! You can ask me more questions, y'know!

Can you get out of the clubroom already? We're locking up.

Huh...? Hey, wait!

Suzaku Gallery

This is where we'll introduce illustrations that we've received from all of you!

Selected artists will receive **a signed shikishi from the series creator!** When you make a submission, please make sure to clearly write your address, name, and phone number! If you don't, we won't be able to send you a prize even if you're selected! Looking forward to all your submissions!

7人目の魔女
ナンシー

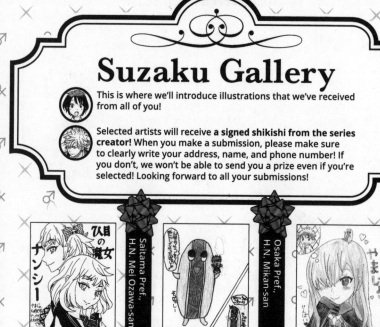

Saitama Pref.,
H.N. Mei Ozawa-san

I hear she's been working hard on her band since becoming a regular student!

山田くんと7人の魔女

Osaka Pref.,
H.N. Mikan-san

Sobasshi turns the tables! It seems that this was coming...

やまじょ

Okayama Pref.,
H.N. Yamanatsu-san

A lot of people like seeing Takigawa with her hair down. I also think it looks great.

Please send your art here ↓

Yamada-kun and the Seven Witches:
Suzaku Gallery
c/o Kodansha Comics
451 Park Ave. South, 7th Floor
New York, NY 10016

※ Please clearly write your address, name, and phone number. If your address, name, and phone number aren't included with your submission, we won't be able to send you a prize.

※ And if necessary, don't forget to include your handle name (pen name)!

Please send your letters with the understanding that your zip code, address, name and other personal information included in your correspondence may be given to the author of this work.

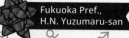

Fukuoka Pref.,
H.N. Yuzumaru-san

S
O
R
a

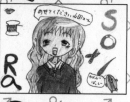

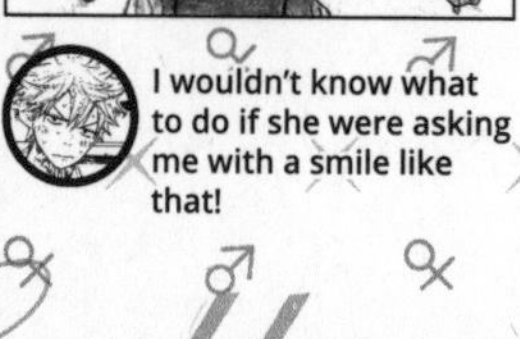

I wouldn't know what to do if she were asking me with a smile like that!

Suzaku Gallery

Translation Notes

Let's BURST!, page 72

As explained in a previous volume, Sobasshi is based on a Japanese mascot named Funassyi, who is a pear fairy representing the city of Funabashi, Chiba. One of Funassyi's catchphrases is *"Nashijiru bushaa!"* which loosely translates to "I'm bursting with pear juice!" and also denotes the character's hyperactive personality. As a parody, Sobasshi uses a similar phrase and says "Let's BURST!"

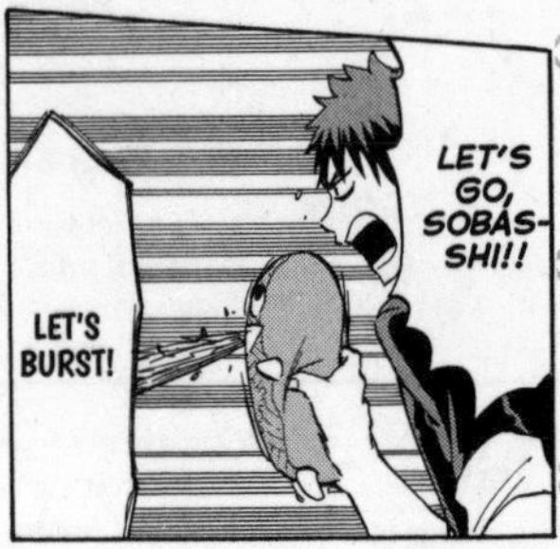
LET'S GO, SOBAS-SHI!!
LET'S BURST!

University recommendations, page 163

Avid manga readers may know that it's common for high school students to take entrance exams in order to advance to Japanese universities, but an alternative way to enter into a university is through recommendations. A recommendation is usually administered by the principal of the high school, and once granted, it gives the recipient an easier path towards the university for which they were recommended.

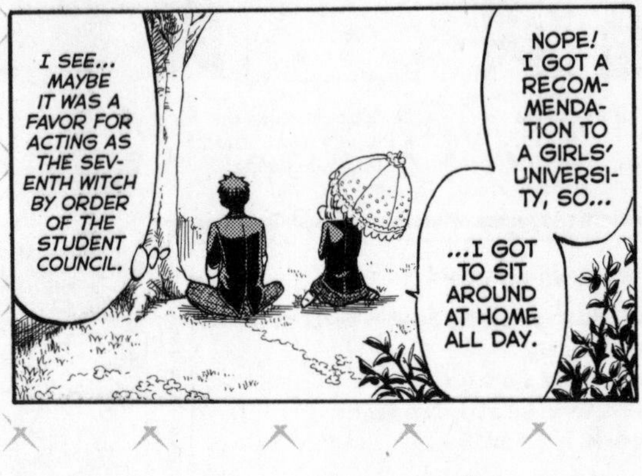
NOPE! I GOT A RECOM-MENDA-TION TO A GIRLS' UNIVERSI-TY, SO...
...I GOT TO SIT AROUND AT HOME ALL DAY.
I SEE... MAYBE IT WAS A FAVOR FOR ACTING AS THE SEV-ENTH WITCH BY ORDER OF THE STUDENT COUNCIL.

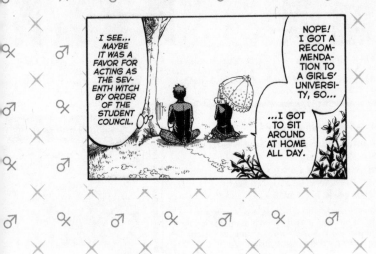

Yamada-kun
AND THE
Seven Witches

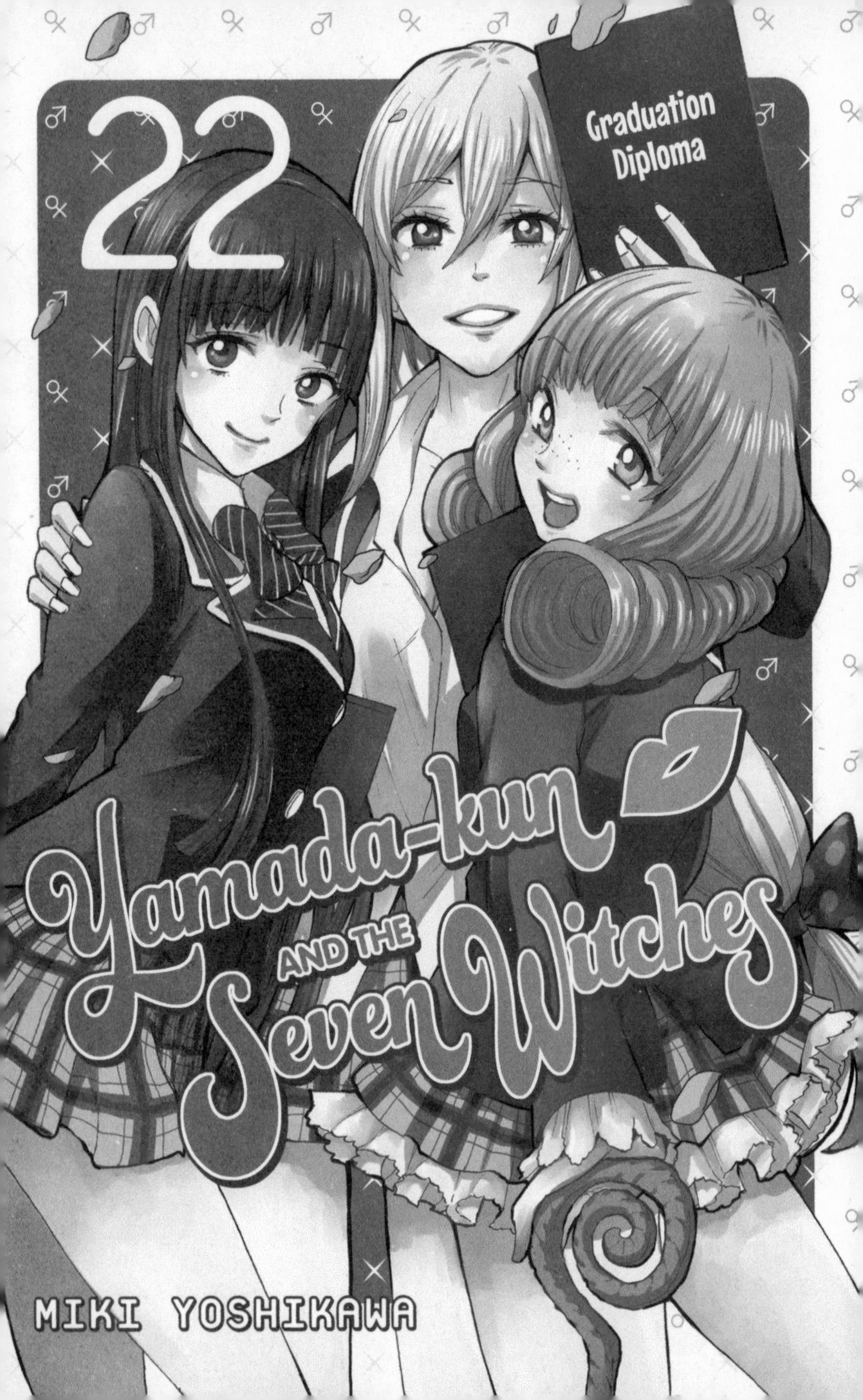
22
Graduation Diploma
Yamada-kun AND THE Seven Witches
MIKI YOSHIKAWA

Yamada-kun AND THE Seven Witches

22

MIKI YOSHIKAWA

Yamada-kun and the Seven Witches

Cast of Characters

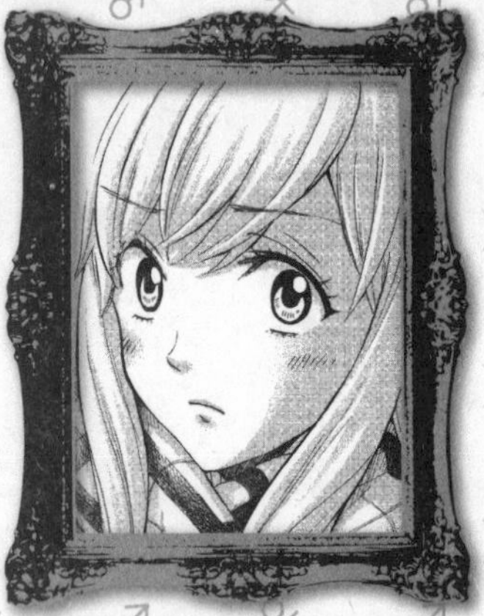

Urara Shiraishi

A second-year at Suzaku High School and president of the Supernatural Studies Club. She's Yamada's girlfriend despite having lost her memories of him… However, the existence of her diary has helped her remember her feelings for Yamada!

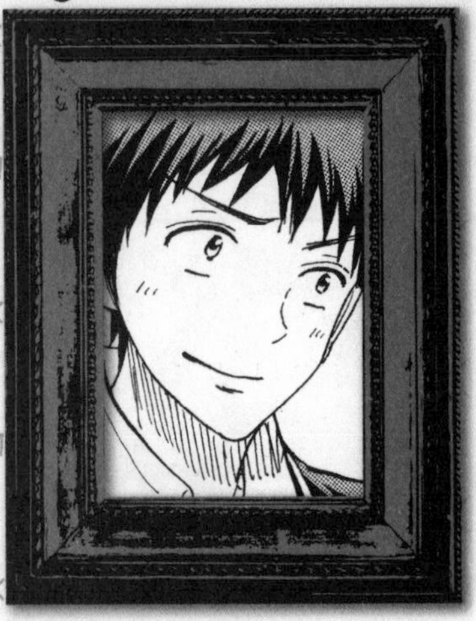

Ryu Yamada

A second-year at Suzaku High School. He's found himself in a tough spot and is helping others out in the middle of a love triangle with Yamazaki, who wants to profess his love to Leona, and Rika, who wants to confess to Yamazaki. He's also trying to confirm what Asuka's intentions are, but…!

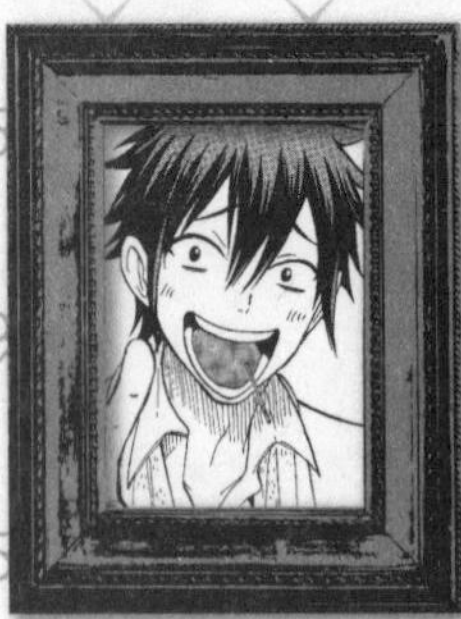

Kentaro Tsubaki

A second-year at Suzaku High School and the mood-maker of the Supernatural Studies Club. He used to live abroad, is good at cooking, and has a habit of frying up some tempura when he gets lonely.

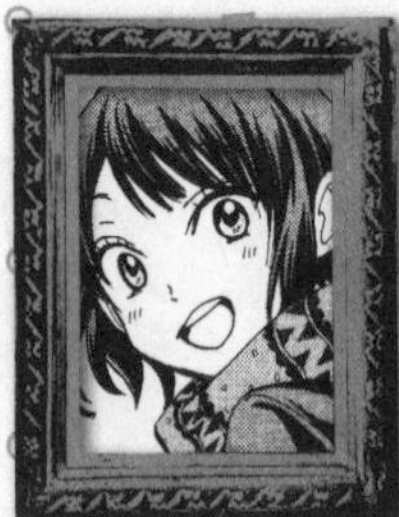

Miyabi Itou

A second-year at Suzaku High School and a member of the Supernatural Studies Club. A huge occult fan. Once she gets talking, she falls into her own world. She always seems to be full of energy.

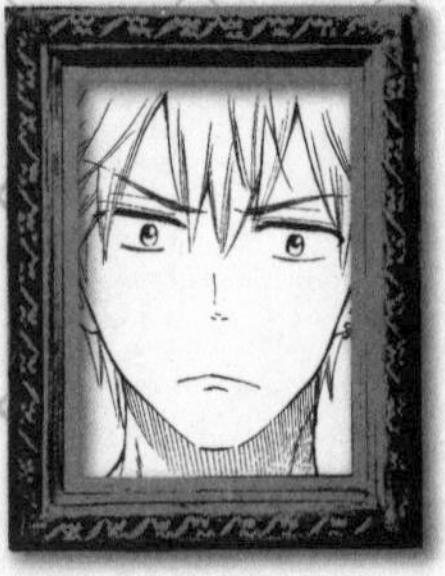

Toranosuke Miyamura

A second-year at Suzaku High School and former president of the Student Council. It seems that he currently spends his time hanging around the clubroom for the Supernatural Studies Club as a member. He has a slightly unhealthy attachment to his sister.

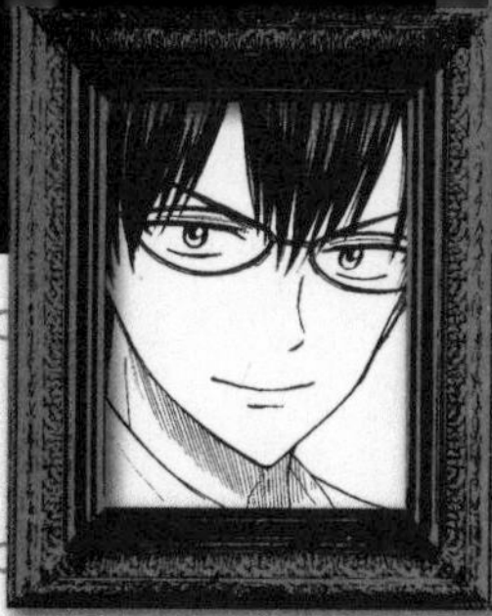

Haruma Yamazaki

A third-year at Suzaku High School and the former president of the Student Council from two years ago. He used to be in the Supernatural Studies Club with Leona and has always had feelings for her. He's going to use graduation as a chance to confess his love for Leona, but…!

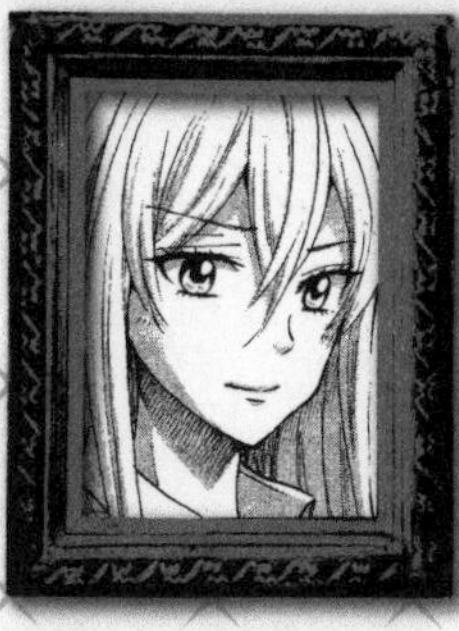

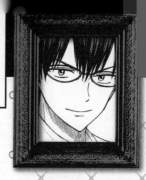

Leona Miyamura

A third-year at Suzaku High School and Miyamura's older sister. She likes Yamazaki, but after understanding Yamada's dilemma, she said she would help him out. What is her secret plan to "graduate seeing a smile on everyone's faces"?

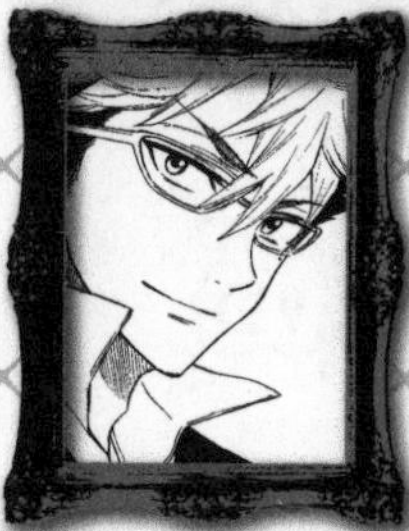

Ushio Igarashi

A second-year at Suzaku High School and Yamada's oldest and best friend. He looks cool on the outside but on the flipside is surprisingly poetic.

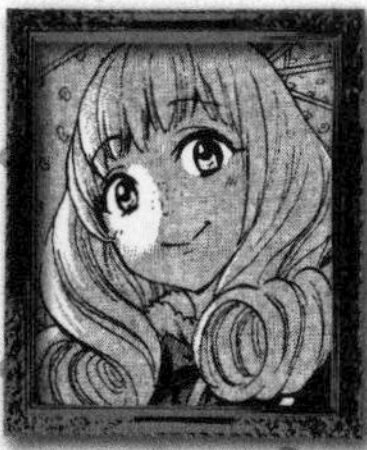

Rika Saionji

A third-year at Suzaku High School and a former "Seventh Witch." She also used to be Yamazaki's helper and plans to confess her feelings for him on graduation day!

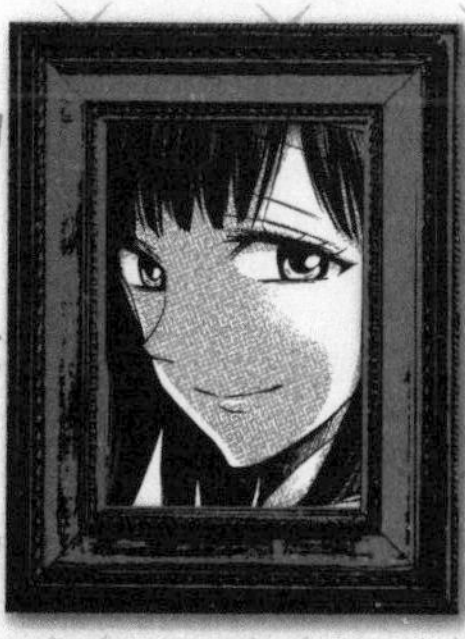

Mikoto Asuka

A third-year at Suzaku High School and former "Invisible Witch." A mysterious and beautiful woman who used to support Yamazaki as the vice president of the student council.

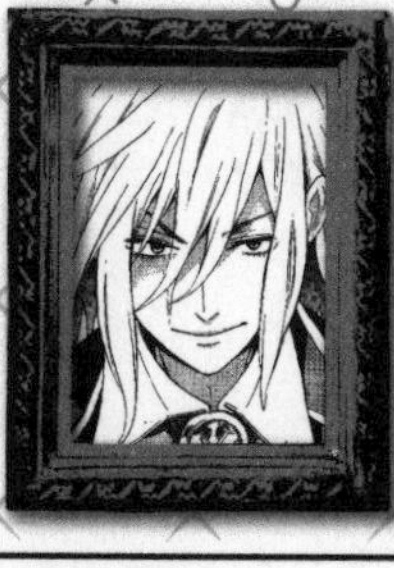

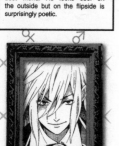

Rui Takuma

A second-year at Suzaku High School and a "Seventh Witch." He's a wily genius whose true intentions are inscrutable!

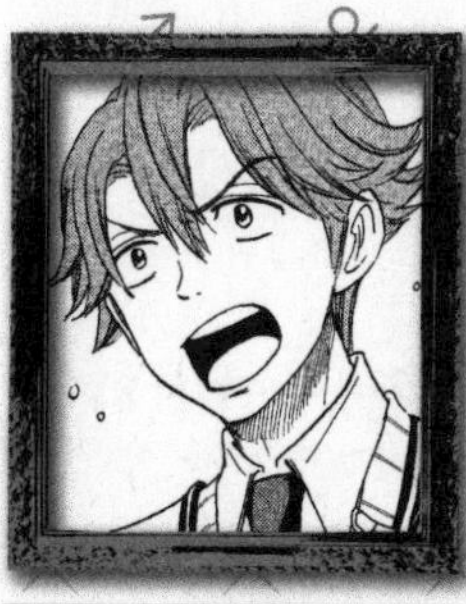

Shinichi Tamaki

A second-year at Suzaku High School and the new president of the Student Council. Trouble caused by the witches has been a nuisance for him and he's called upon Yamada for support.

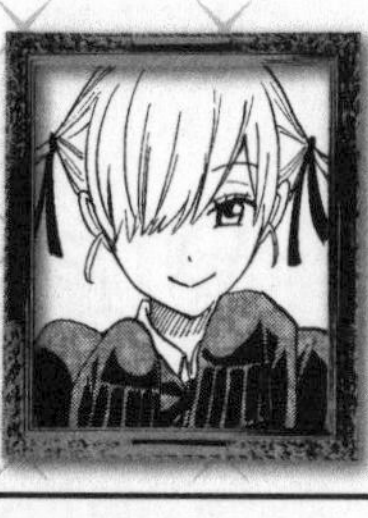

Noa Takigawa

A first-year at Suzaku High School and formerly a witch with the power to see into the past. She's a mischievous girl who has unrequited feelings for Yamada.

CONTENTS

CHAPTER 182: Well, it's true.

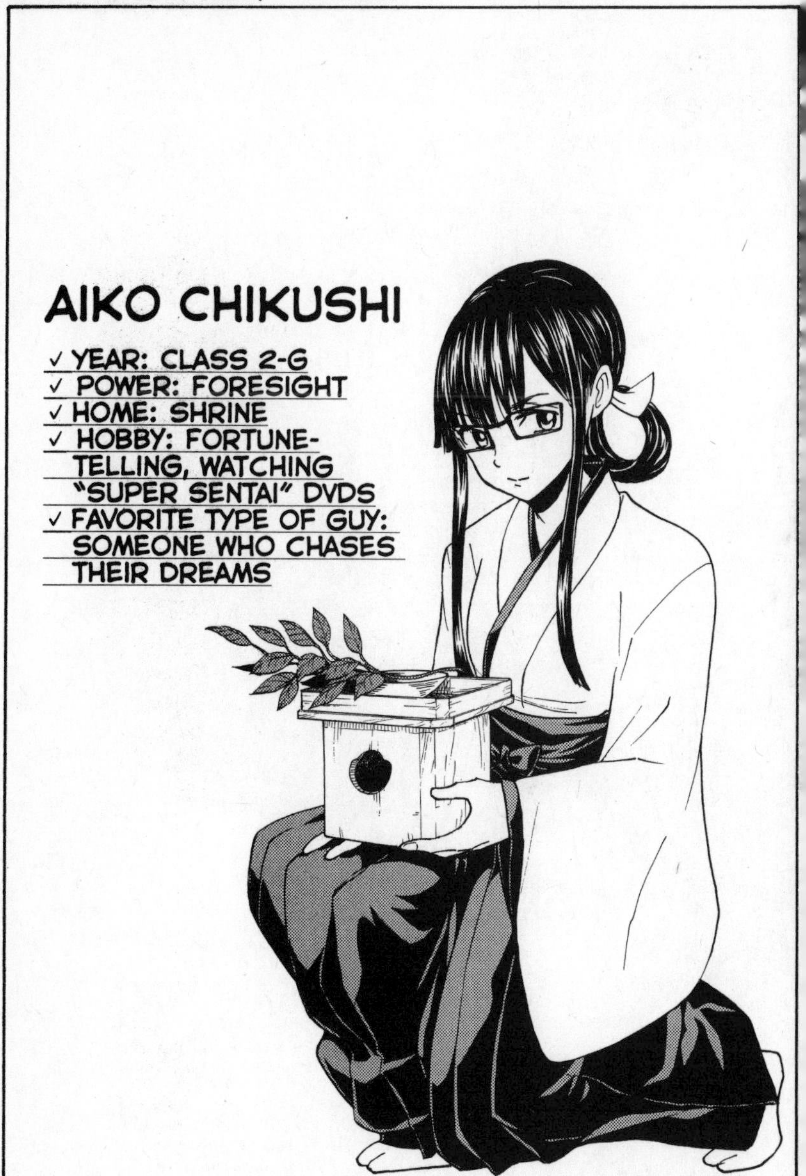
AIKO CHIKUSHI
✓ YEAR: CLASS 2-G
✓ POWER: FORESIGHT
✓ HOME: SHRINE
✓ HOBBY: FORTUNE-TELLING, WATCHING "SUPER SENTAI" DVDS
✓ FAVORITE TYPE OF GUY: SOMEONE WHO CHASES THEIR DREAMS

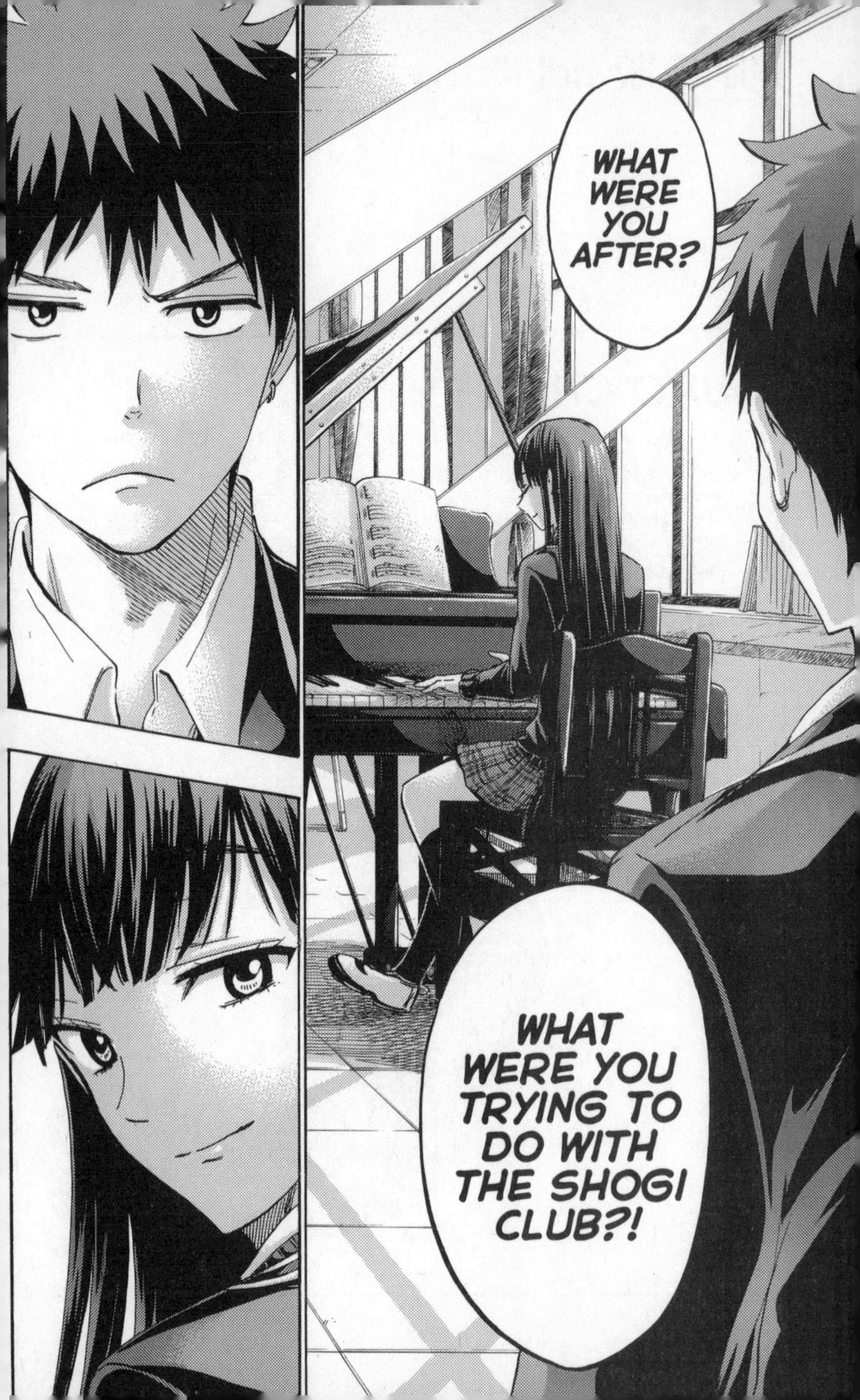
WHAT WERE YOU AFTER?
WHAT WERE YOU TRYING TO DO WITH THE SHOGI CLUB?!

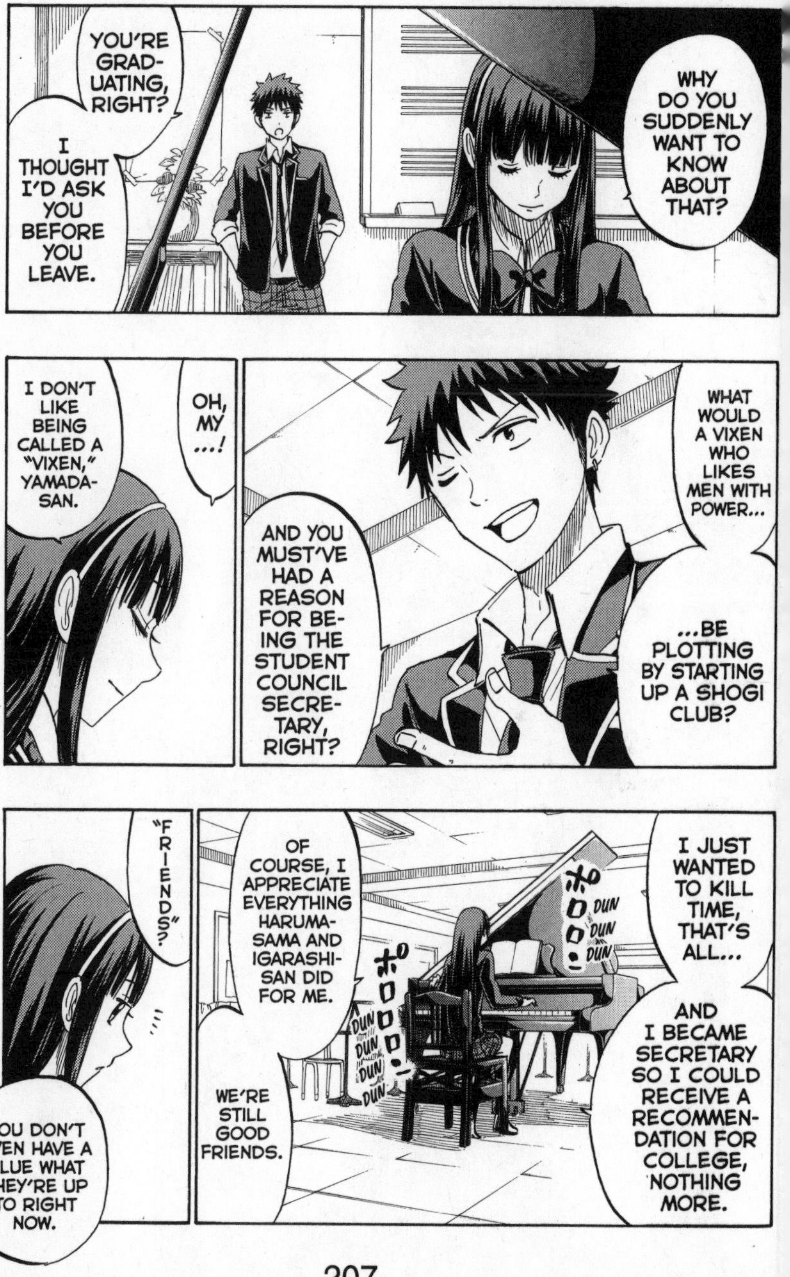
WHY DO YOU SUDDENLY WANT TO KNOW ABOUT THAT?
YOU'RE GRAD-UATING, RIGHT?
I THOUGHT I'D ASK YOU BEFORE YOU LEAVE.
WHAT WOULD A VIXEN WHO LIKES MEN WITH POWER...
...BE PLOTTING BY STARTING UP A SHOGI CLUB?
AND YOU MUST'VE HAD A REASON FOR BE-ING THE STUDENT COUNCIL SECRE-TARY, RIGHT?
OH, MY...!
I DON'T LIKE BEING CALLED A "VIXEN," YAMADA-SAN.
I JUST WANTED TO KILL TIME, THAT'S ALL...
AND I BECAME SECRETARY SO I COULD RECEIVE A RECOMMEN-DATION FOR COLLEGE, NOTHING MORE.
ポロロ・・
DUN DUN DUN
ポロロロロ・・
DUN DUN DUN DUN
OF COURSE, I APPRECIATE EVERYTHING HARUMA-SAMA AND IGARASHI-SAN DID FOR ME.
WE'RE STILL GOOD FRIENDS.
"FRIENDS"?
...!
YOU DON'T EVEN HAVE A CLUE WHAT THEY'RE UP TO RIGHT NOW.

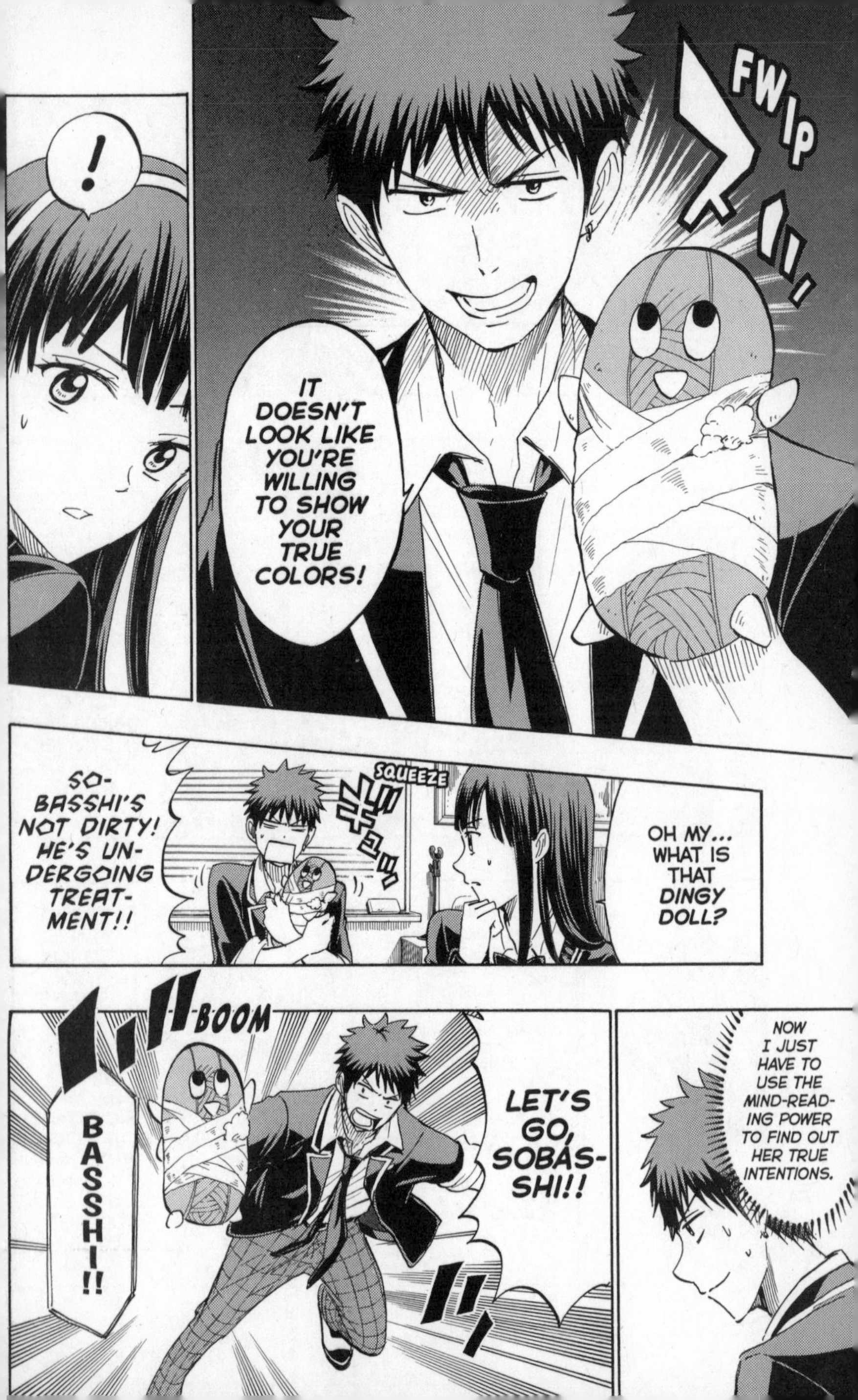
FWIP
IT DOESN'T LOOK LIKE YOU'RE WILLING TO SHOW YOUR TRUE COLORS!
!
OH MY... WHAT IS THAT DINGY DOLL?
SQUEEZE
SO-BASSHI'S NOT DIRTY! HE'S UN-DERGOING TREAT-MENT!!
NOW I JUST HAVE TO USE THE MIND-READ-ING POWER TO FIND OUT HER TRUE INTENTIONS.
BOOM
LET'S GO, SOBAS-SHI!!
BASSHI!!

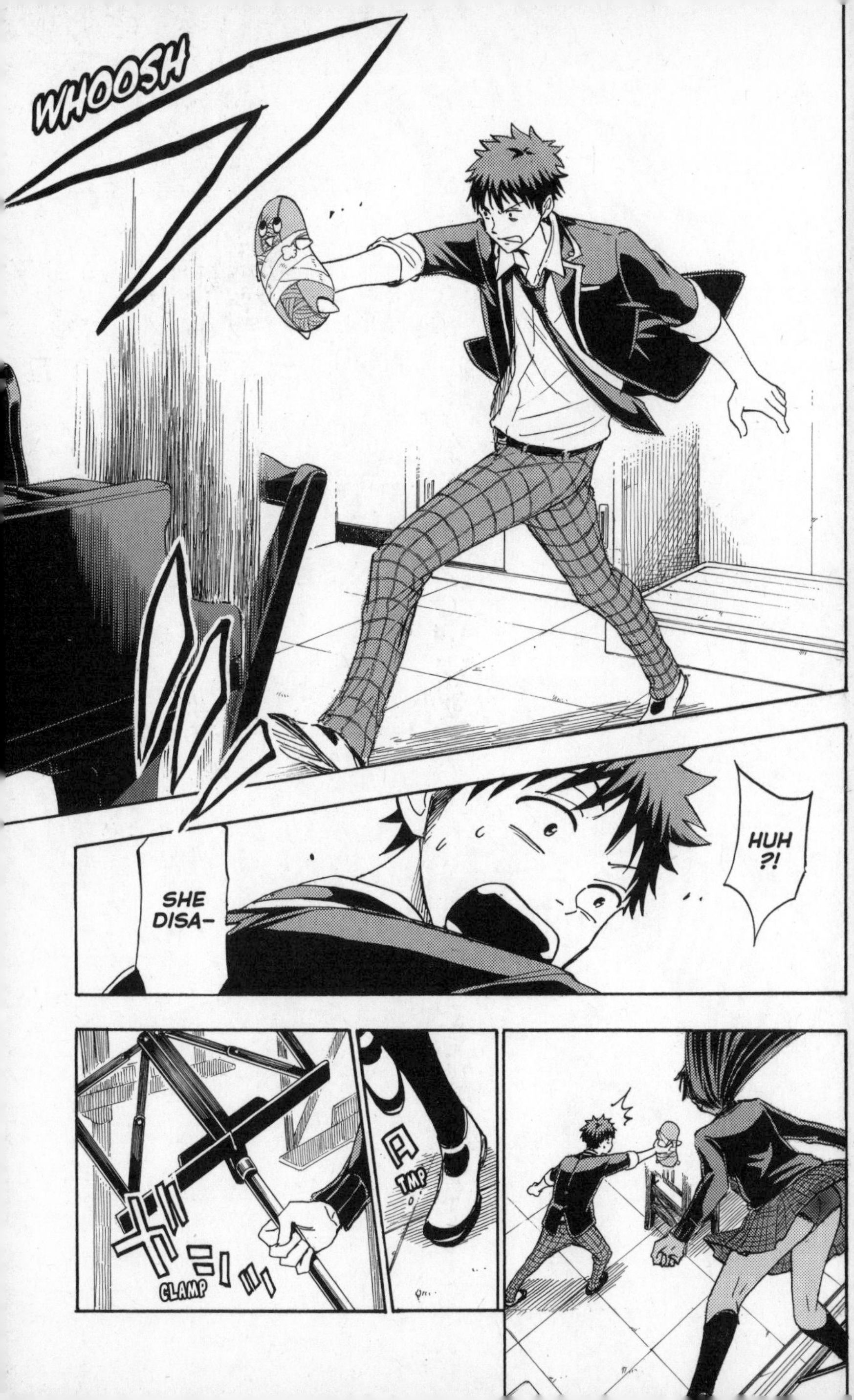
WHOOSH
HUH ?!
SHE DISA-
TMP
CLAMP

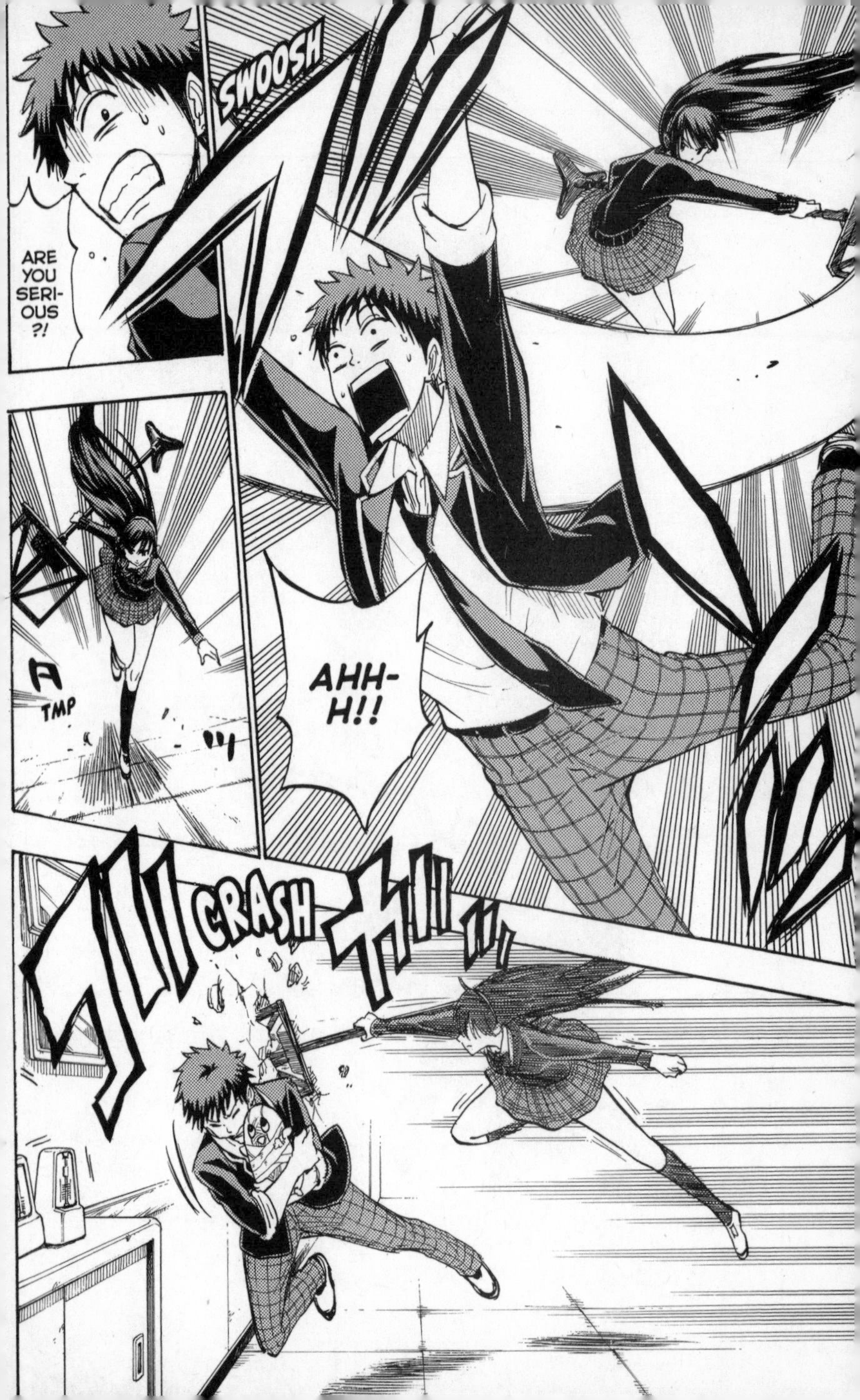
AHH-H!!
SWOOSH
ARE YOU SERI-OUS?!
TMP
CRASH

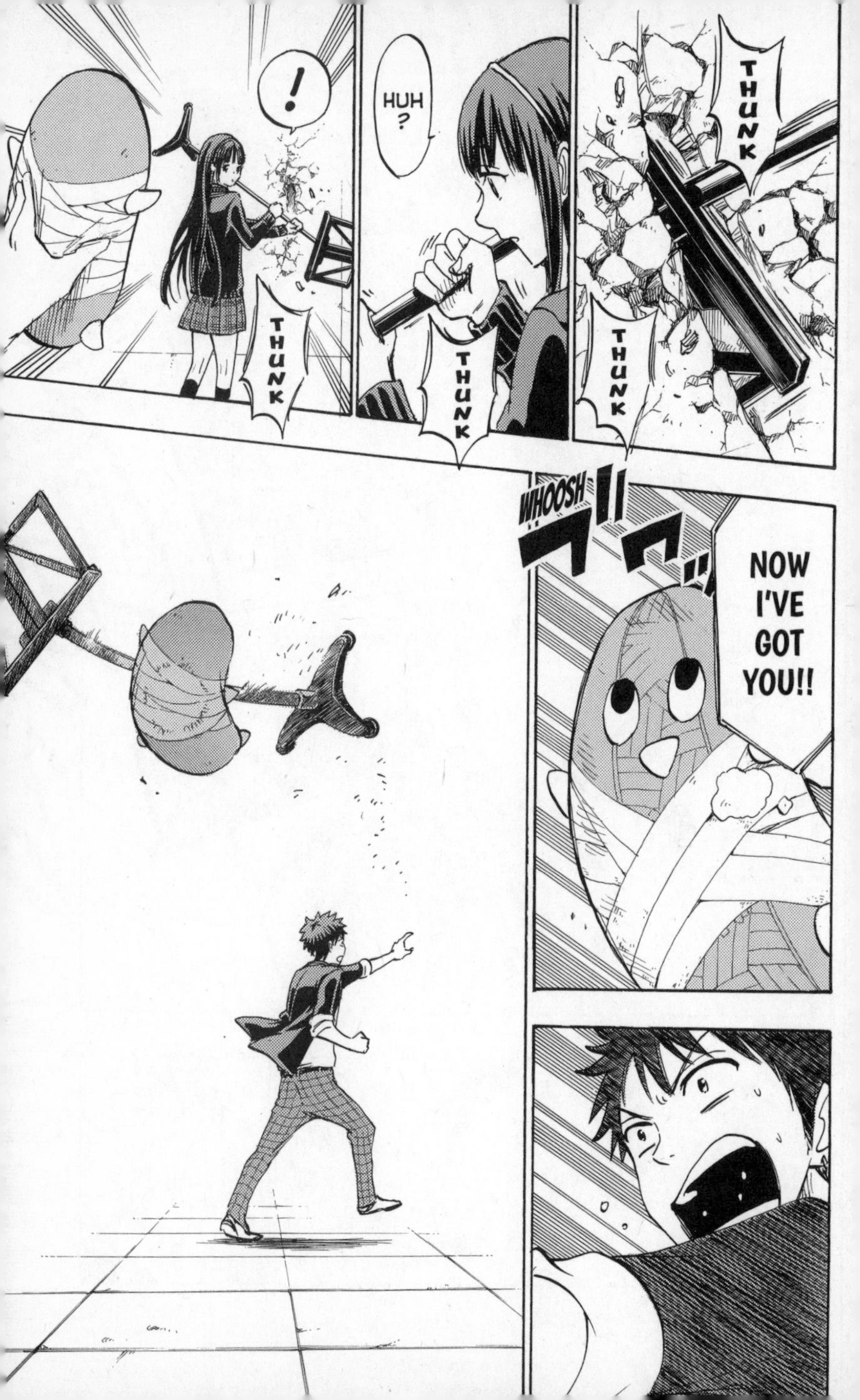
THUNK
THUNK
HUH?
THUNK
!
THUNK
WHOOSH
NOW I'VE GOT YOU!!

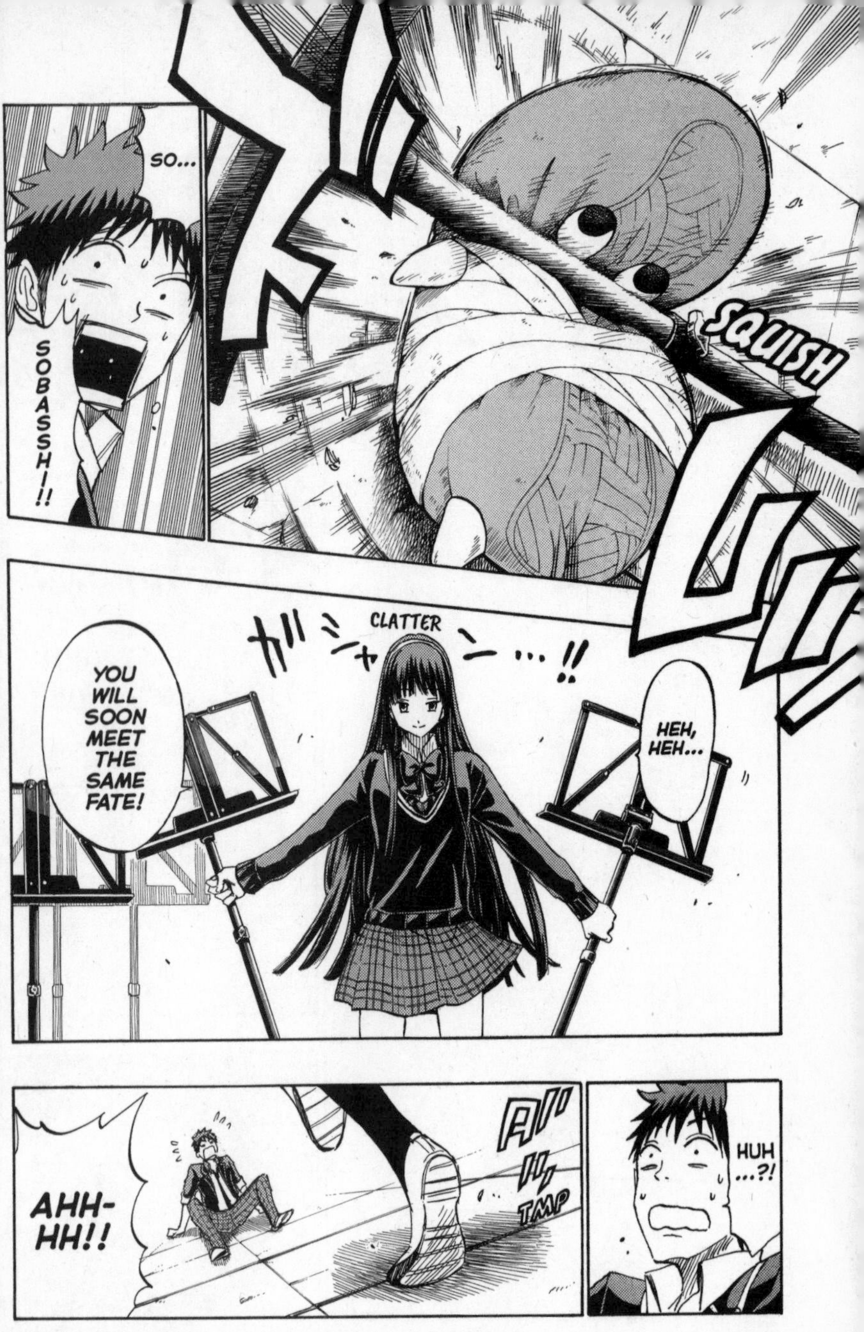
SQUISH
SO...
SOBASSHI!!
CLATTER
ガシャン…!!
HEH, HEH...
YOU WILL SOON MEET THE SAME FATE!
HUH ...?!
TMP
AHH-HH!!

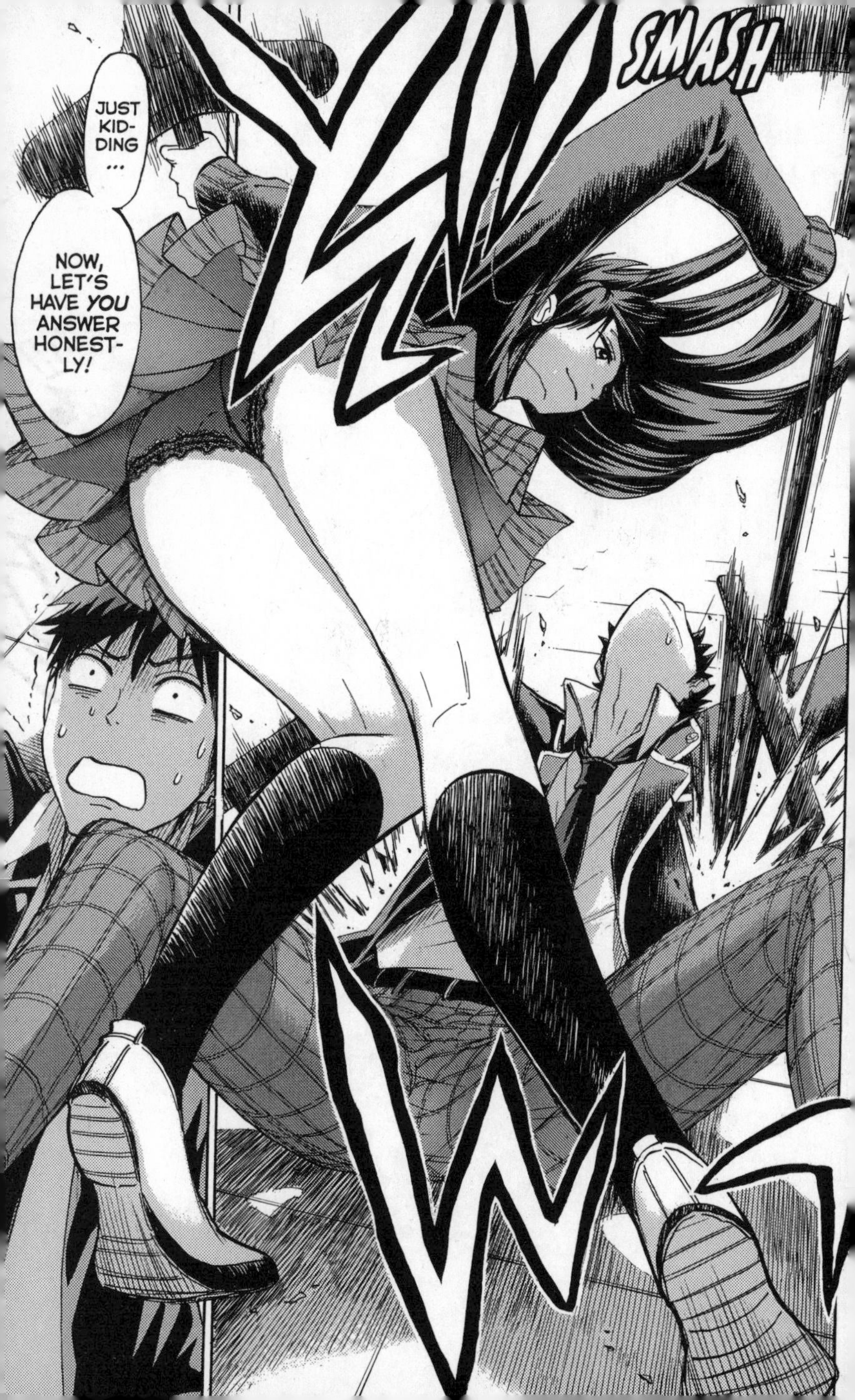
SMASH
JUST KID-DING ...
NOW, LET'S HAVE YOU ANSWER HONEST-LY!

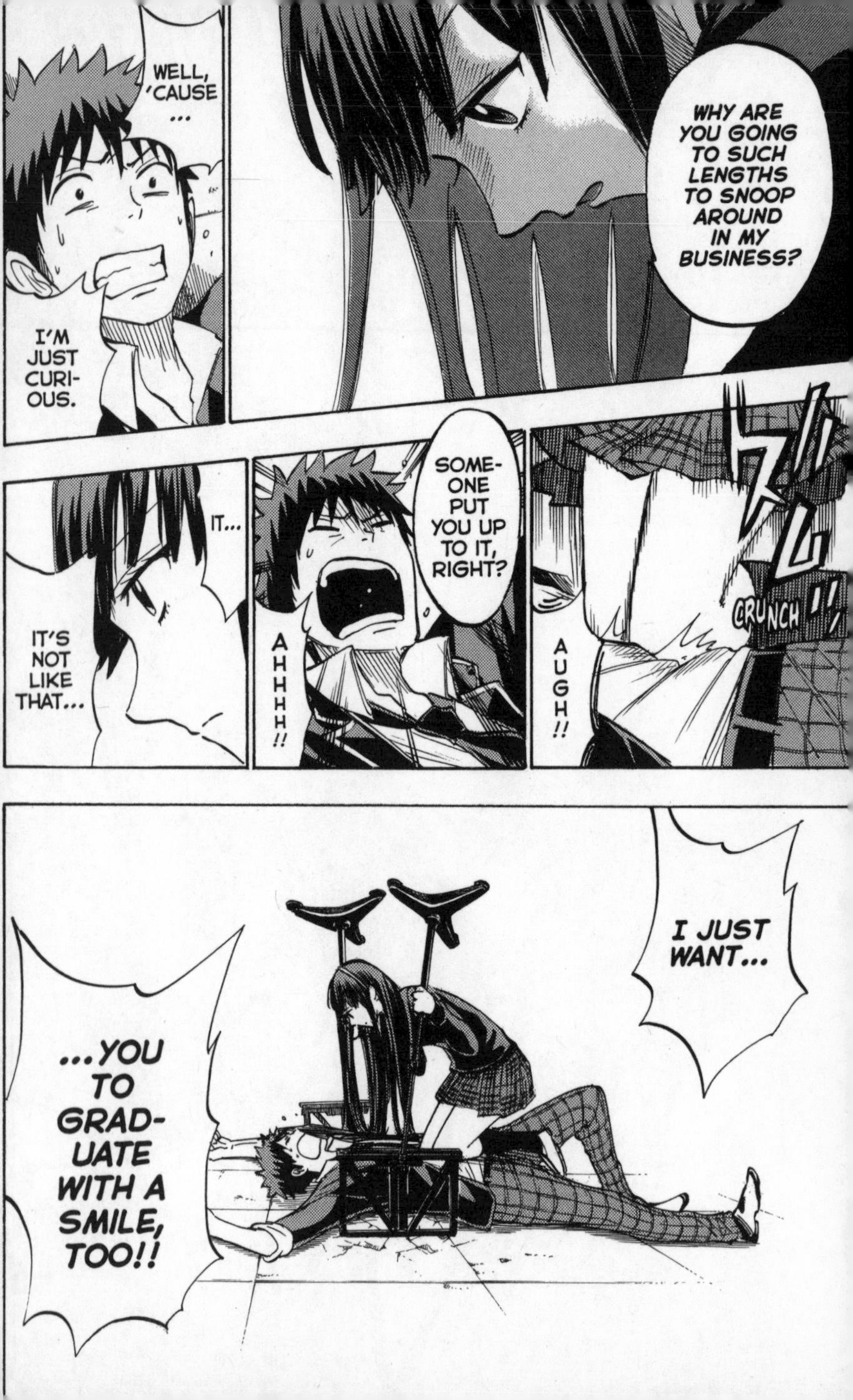
WHY ARE YOU GOING TO SUCH LENGTHS TO SNOOP AROUND IN MY BUSINESS?
WELL, 'CAUSE ...
I'M JUST CURI-OUS.
CRUNCH !!
AUGH!!
SOME-ONE PUT YOU UP TO IT, RIGHT?
AHHHH!!
IT...
IT'S NOT LIKE THAT...
I JUST WANT...
...YOU TO GRAD-UATE WITH A SMILE, TOO!!

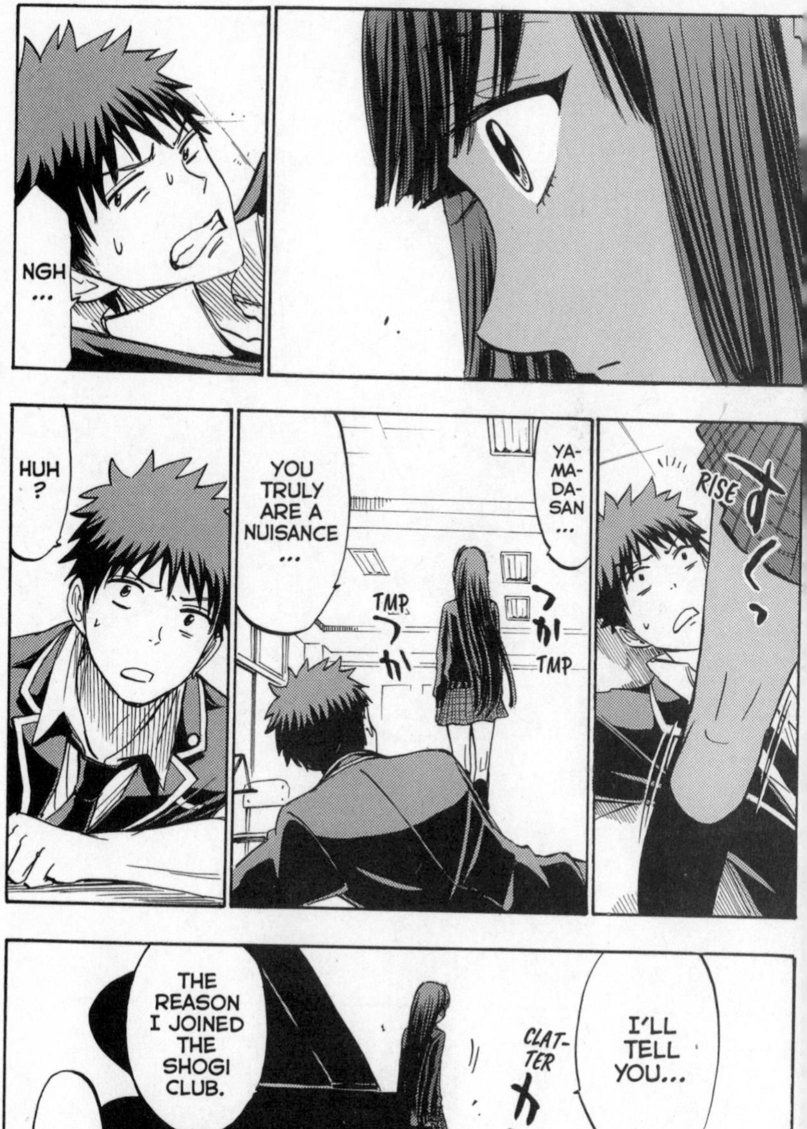
NGH ...
RISE
YA-MA-DA-SAN ...
TMP
TMP
YOU TRULY ARE A NUISANCE ...
HUH ?
I'LL TELL YOU...
CLAT-TER
THE REASON I JOINED THE SHOGI CLUB.
IT WAS...

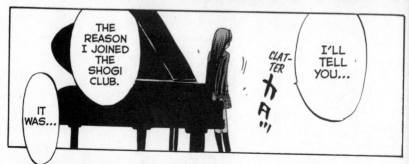

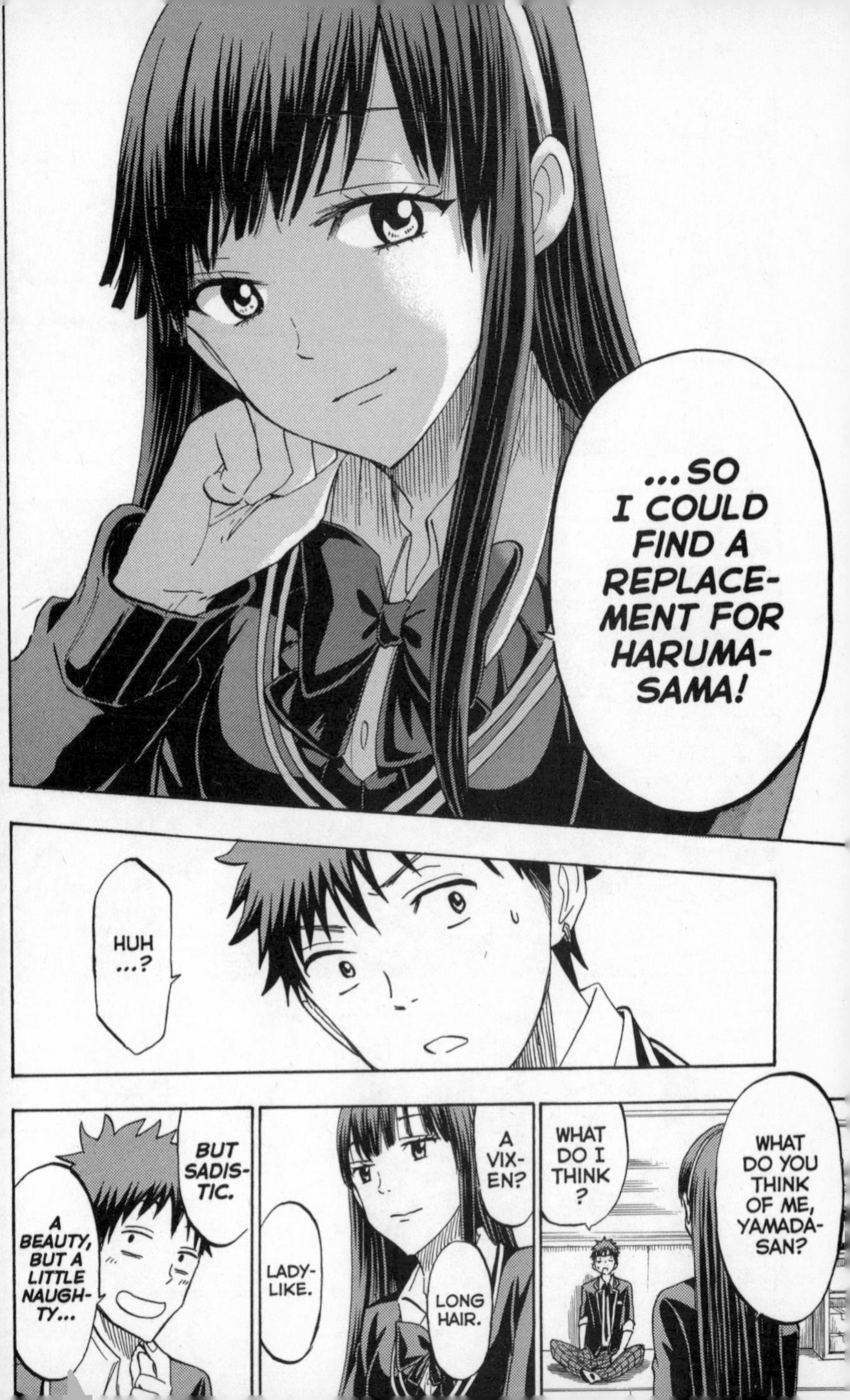
...SO I COULD FIND A REPLACEMENT FOR HARUMA-SAMA!
HUH ...?
WHAT DO YOU THINK OF ME, YAMADA-SAN?
WHAT DO I THINK?
A VIX-EN?
LADY-LIKE.
LONG HAIR.
BUT SADIS-TIC.
A BEAUTY, BUT A LITTLE NAUGH-TY...

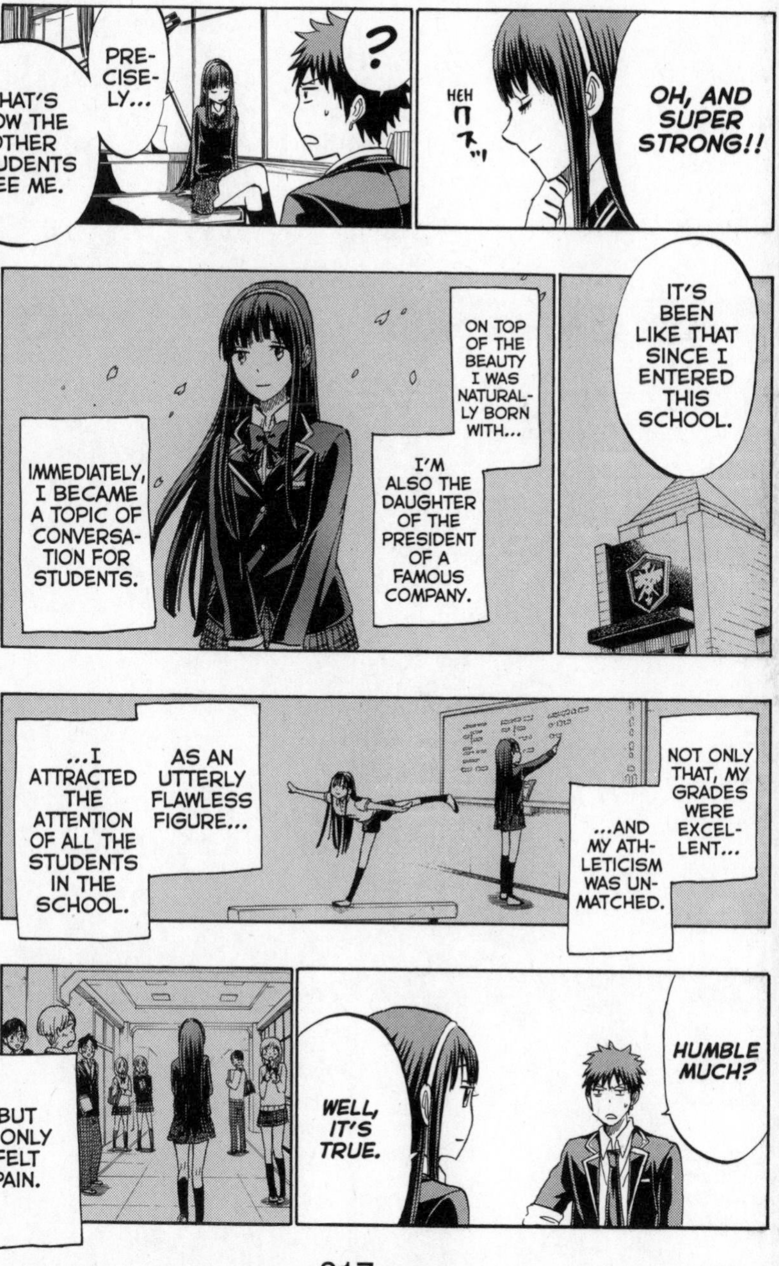
OH, AND SUPER STRONG!!
HEH
?
PRECISELY...
THAT'S HOW THE OTHER STUDENTS SEE ME.
IT'S BEEN LIKE THAT SINCE I ENTERED THIS SCHOOL.
ON TOP OF THE BEAUTY I WAS NATURALLY BORN WITH...
I'M ALSO THE DAUGHTER OF THE PRESIDENT OF A FAMOUS COMPANY.
IMMEDIATELY, I BECAME A TOPIC OF CONVERSATION FOR STUDENTS.
NOT ONLY THAT, MY GRADES WERE EXCELLENT...
...AND MY ATHLETICISM WAS UNMATCHED.
AS AN UTTERLY FLAWLESS FIGURE...
...I ATTRACTED THE ATTENTION OF ALL THE STUDENTS IN THE SCHOOL.
HUMBLE MUCH?
WELL, IT'S TRUE.
BUT I ONLY FELT PAIN.

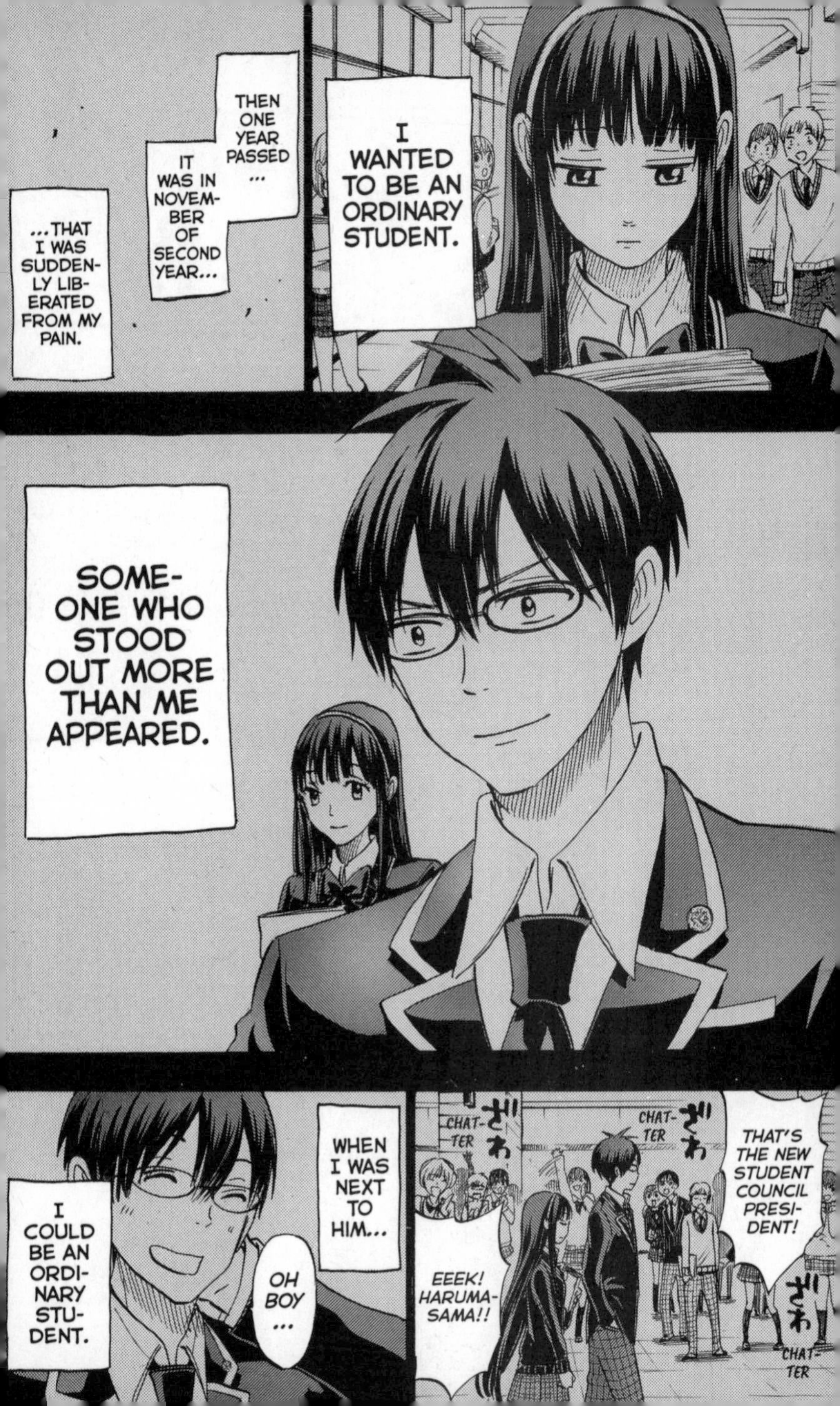
I WANTED TO BE AN ORDINARY STUDENT.
THEN ONE YEAR PASSED...
IT WAS IN NOVEMBER OF SECOND YEAR...
...THAT I WAS SUDDENLY LIBERATED FROM MY PAIN.
SOMEONE WHO STOOD OUT MORE THAN ME APPEARED.
ざわ CHATTER
THAT'S THE NEW STUDENT COUNCIL PRESIDENT!
ざわ CHATTER
EEEK! HARUMA-SAMA!!
ざわ CHATTER
WHEN I WAS NEXT TO HIM...
OH BOY...
I COULD BE AN ORDINARY STUDENT.

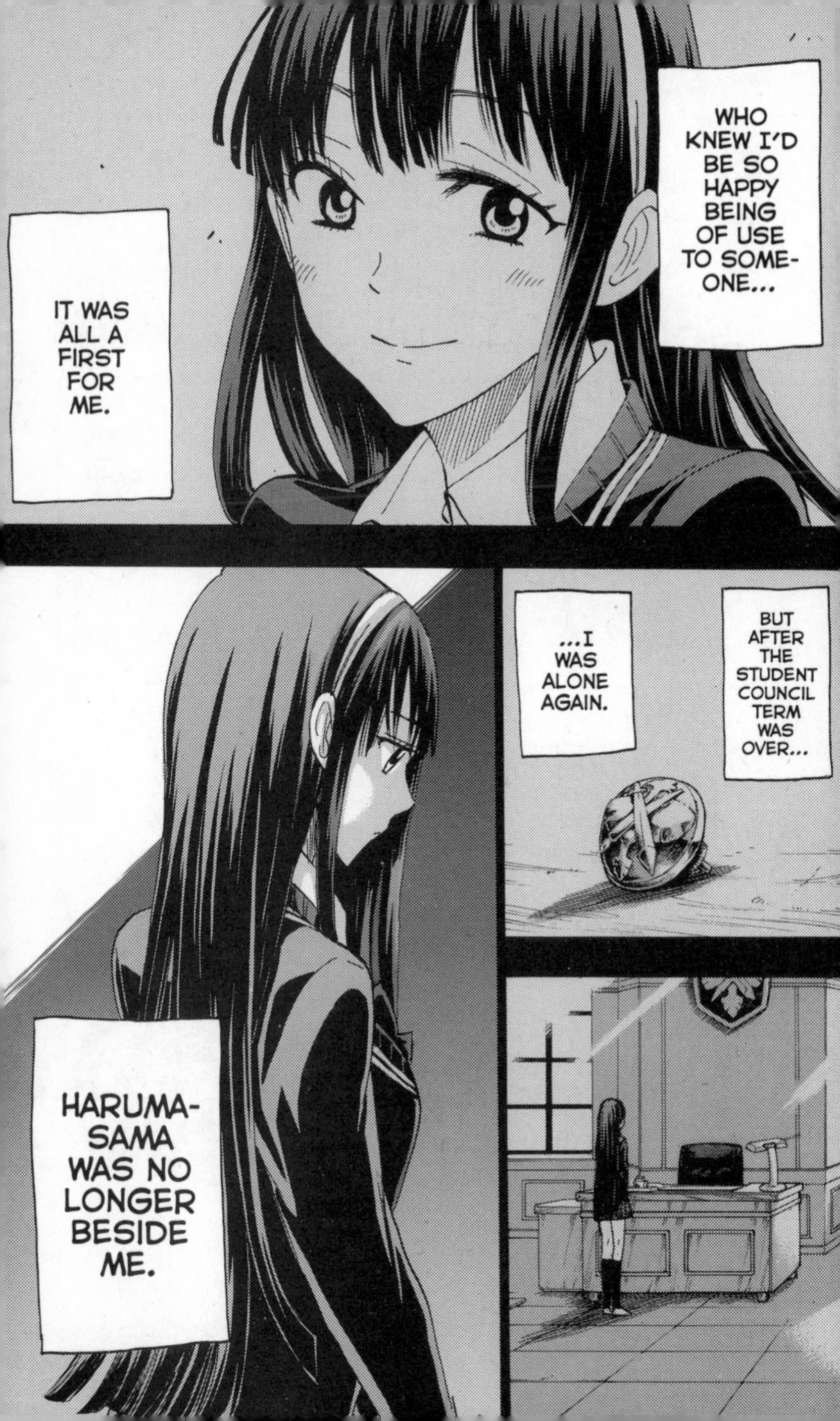
WHO KNEW I'D BE SO HAPPY BEING OF USE TO SOME-ONE...
IT WAS ALL A FIRST FOR ME.
BUT AFTER THE STUDENT COUNCIL TERM WAS OVER...
...I WAS ALONE AGAIN.
HARUMA-SAMA WAS NO LONGER BESIDE ME.

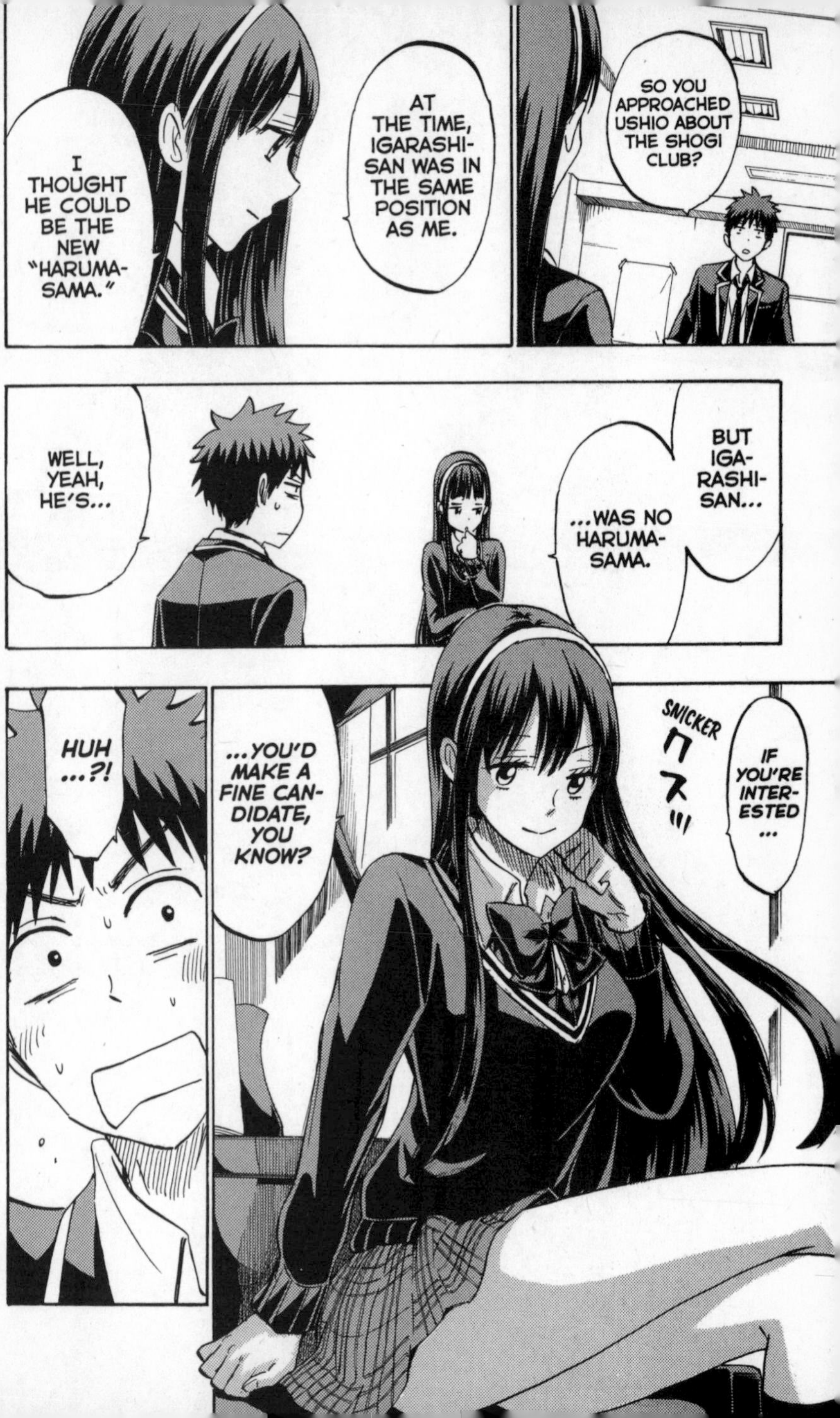

SO YOU APPROACHED USHIO ABOUT THE SHOGI CLUB?
AT THE TIME, IGARASHI-SAN WAS IN THE SAME POSITION AS ME.
I THOUGHT HE COULD BE THE NEW "HARUMA-SAMA."
BUT IGA-RASHI-SAN...
...WAS NO HARUMA-SAMA.
WELL, YEAH, HE'S...
SNICKER
クス
IF YOU'RE INTER-ESTED...
...YOU'D MAKE A FINE CAN-DIDATE, YOU KNOW?
HUH ...?!

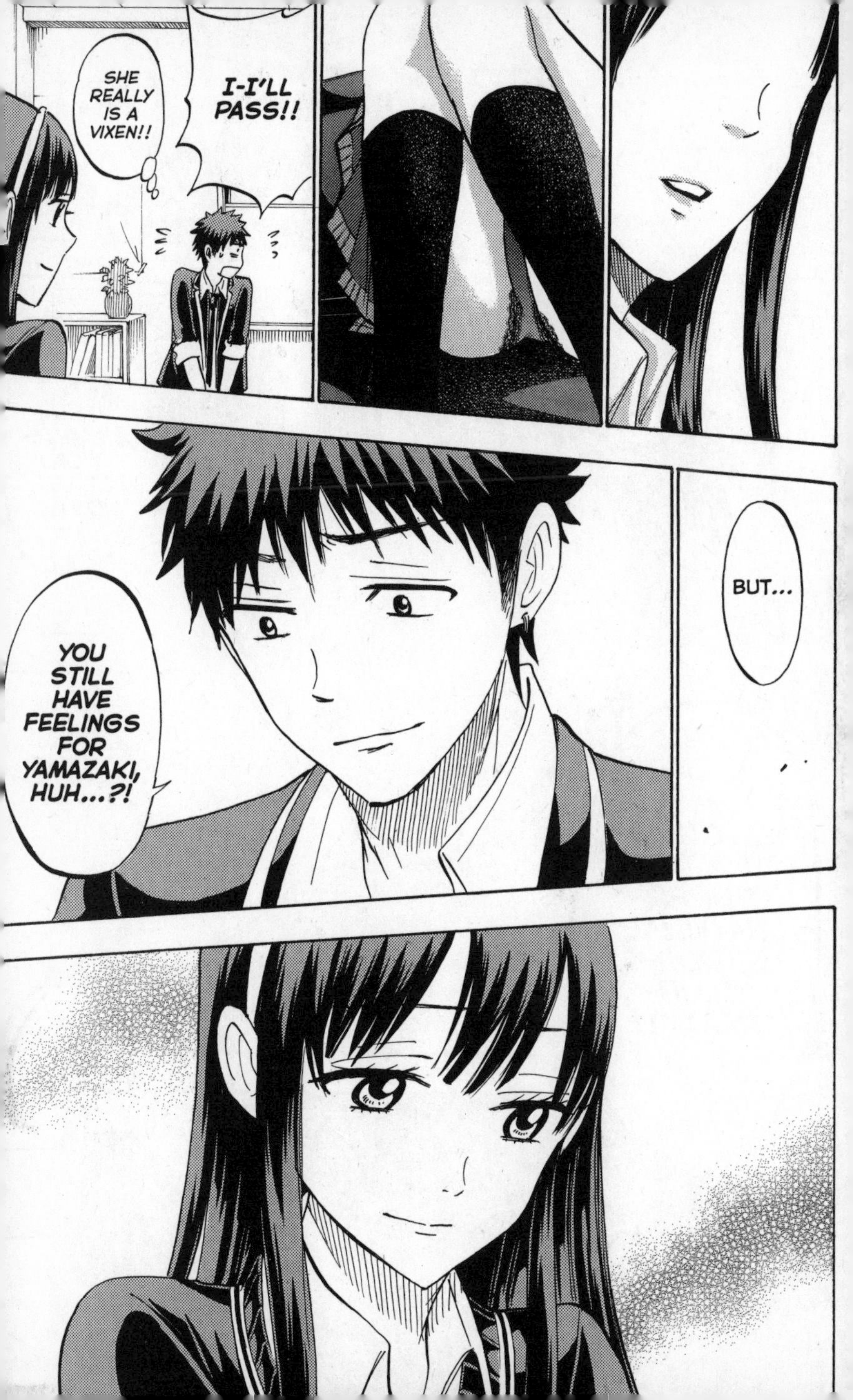
I-I'LL PASS!!
SHE REALLY IS A VIXEN!!
BUT...
YOU STILL HAVE FEELINGS FOR YAMAZAKI, HUH...?!

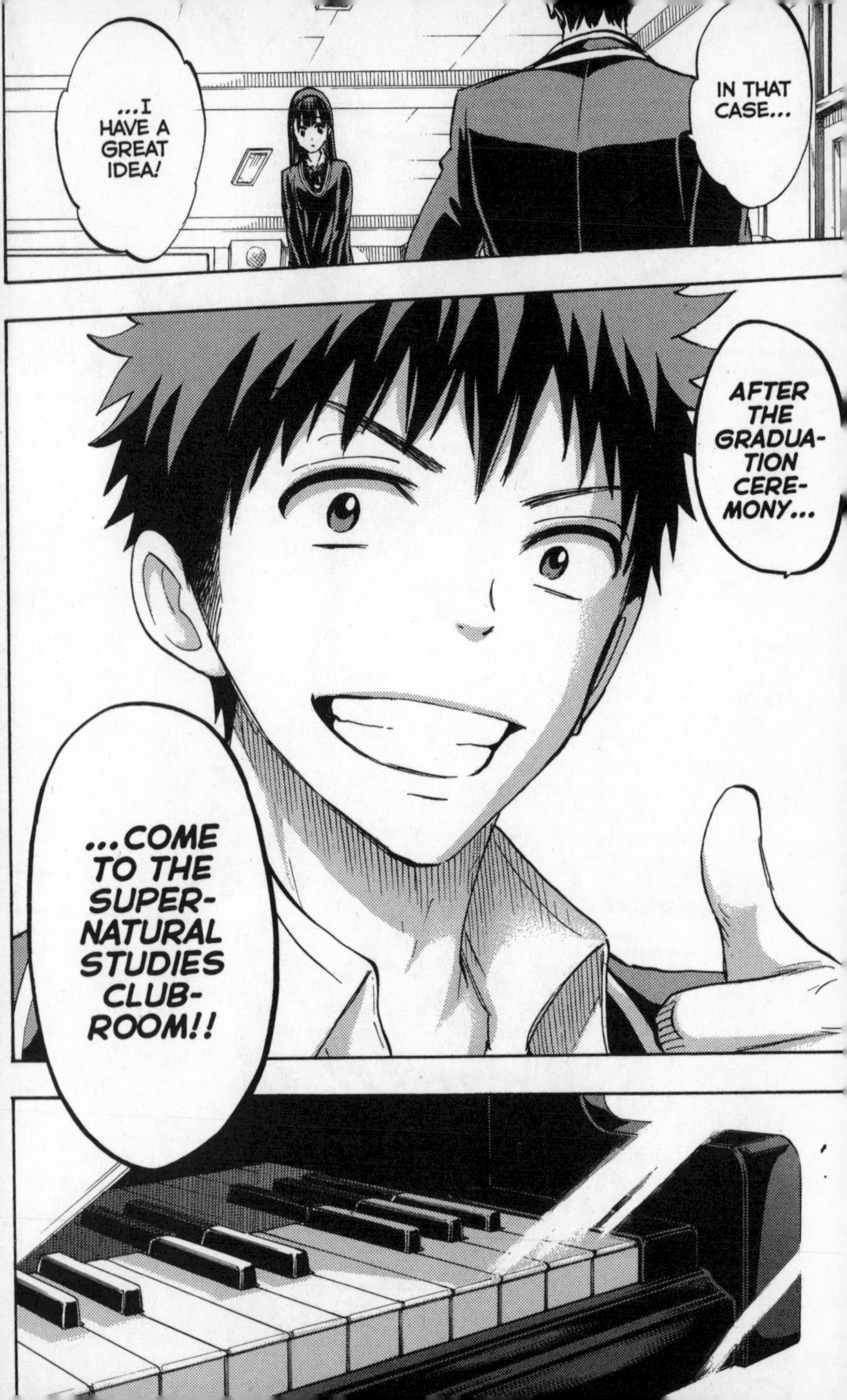
IN THAT CASE...
...I HAVE A GREAT IDEA!
AFTER THE GRADUATION CEREMONY...
...COME TO THE SUPERNATURAL STUDIES CLUBROOM!!

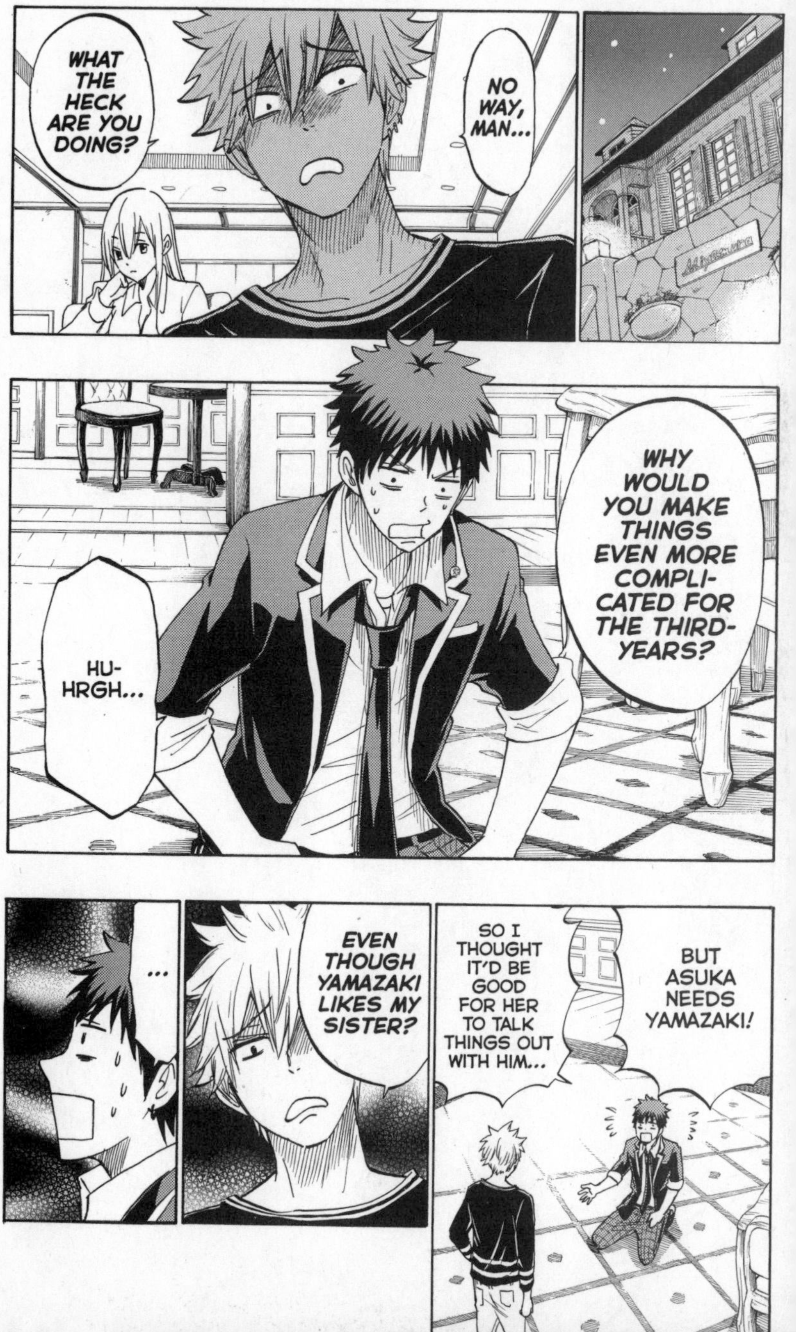
NO WAY, MAN...
WHAT THE HECK ARE YOU DOING?
WHY WOULD YOU MAKE THINGS EVEN MORE COMPLI-CATED FOR THE THIRD-YEARS?
HU-HRGH...
BUT ASUKA NEEDS YAMAZAKI!
SO I THOUGHT IT'D BE GOOD FOR HER TO TALK THINGS OUT WITH HIM...
EVEN THOUGH YAMAZAKI LIKES MY SISTER?
...

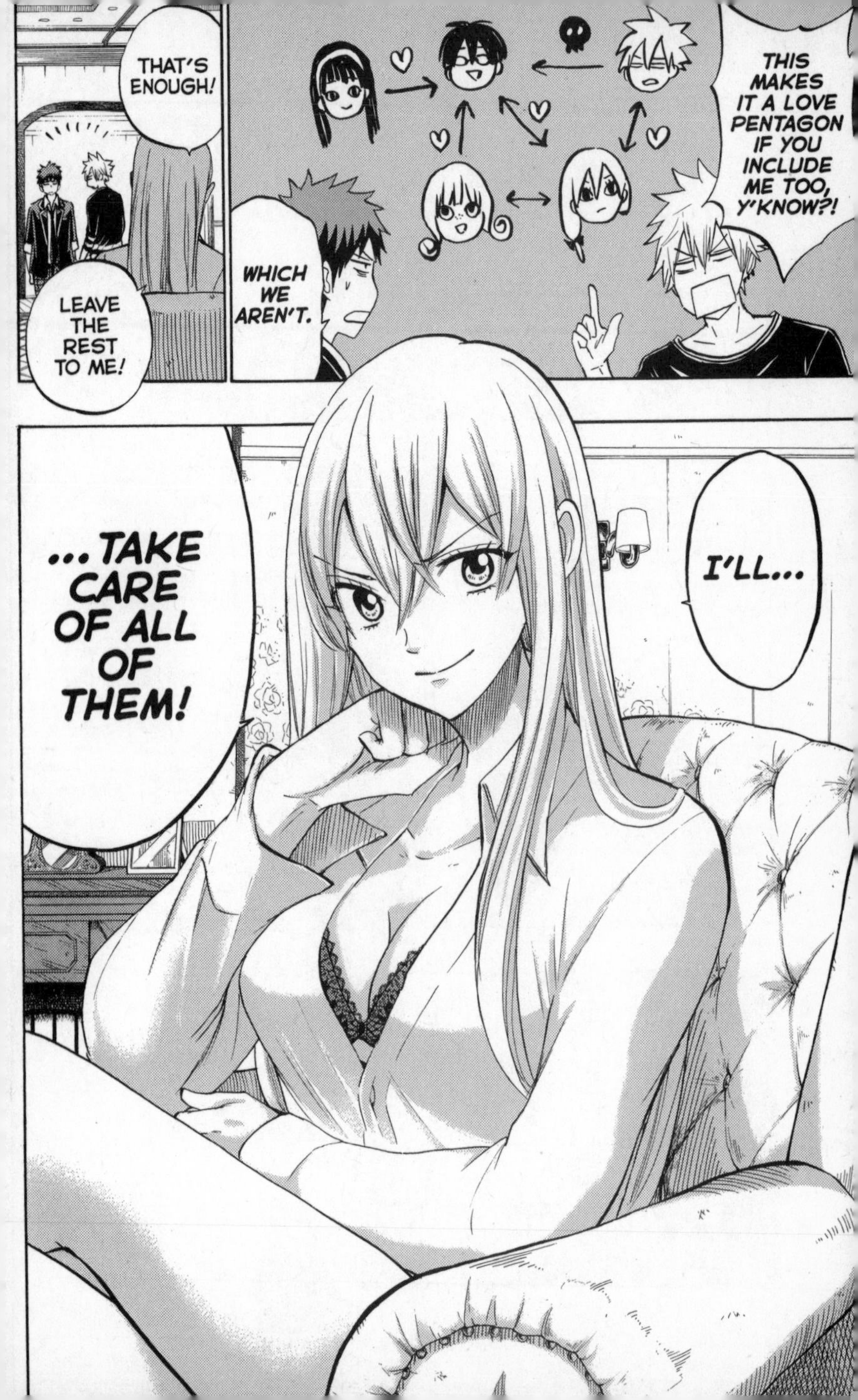
THIS MAKES IT A LOVE PENTAGON IF YOU INCLUDE ME TOO, Y'KNOW?!
WHICH WE AREN'T.
THAT'S ENOUGH!
LEAVE THE REST TO ME!
I'LL...
...TAKE CARE OF ALL OF THEM!

CHAPTER 183: Punch me, will you?

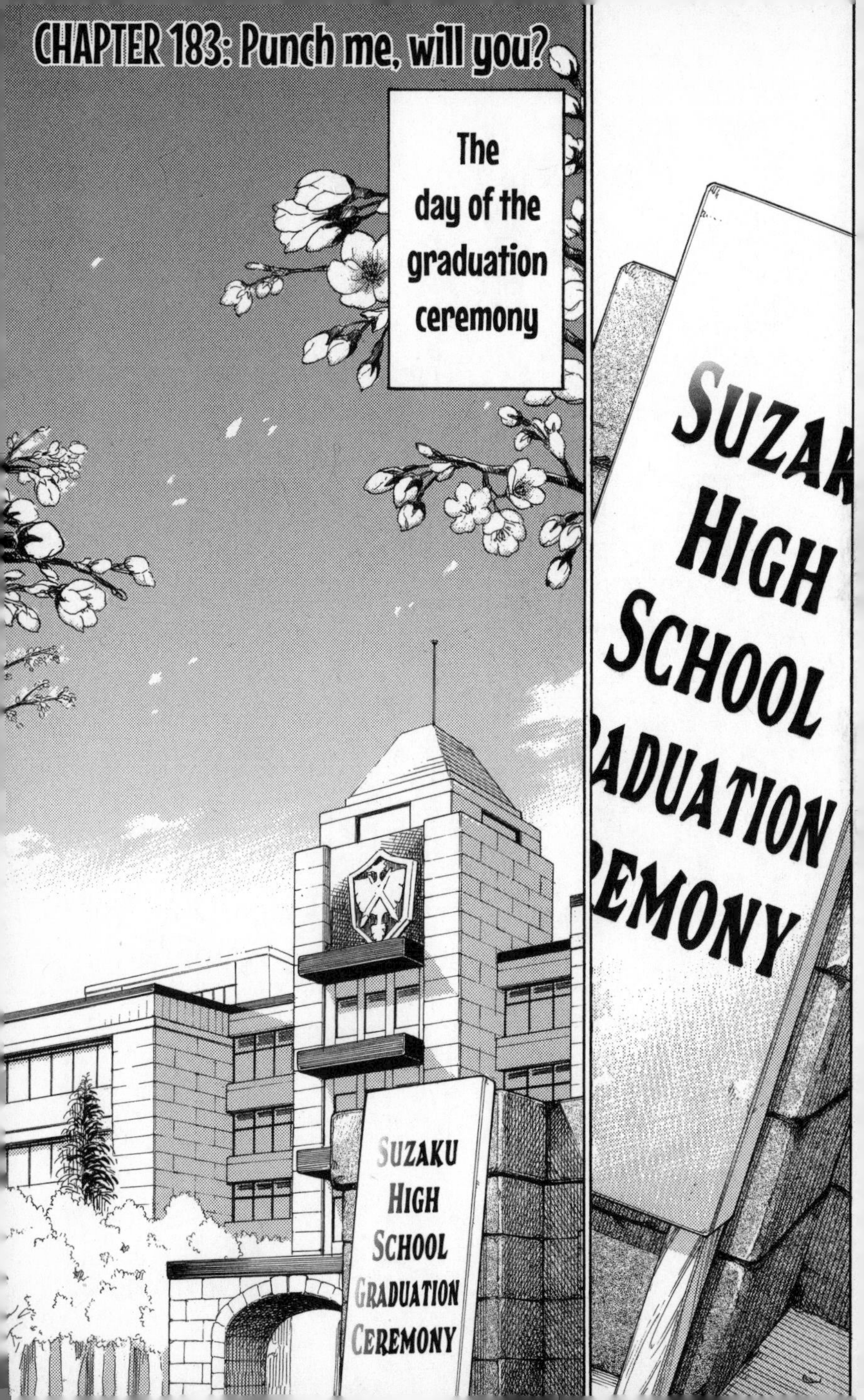
SUZAK
HIGH
SCHOOL
RADUATION
REMONY
The day of the graduation ceremony
SUZAKU HIGH SCHOOL GRADUATION CEREMONY

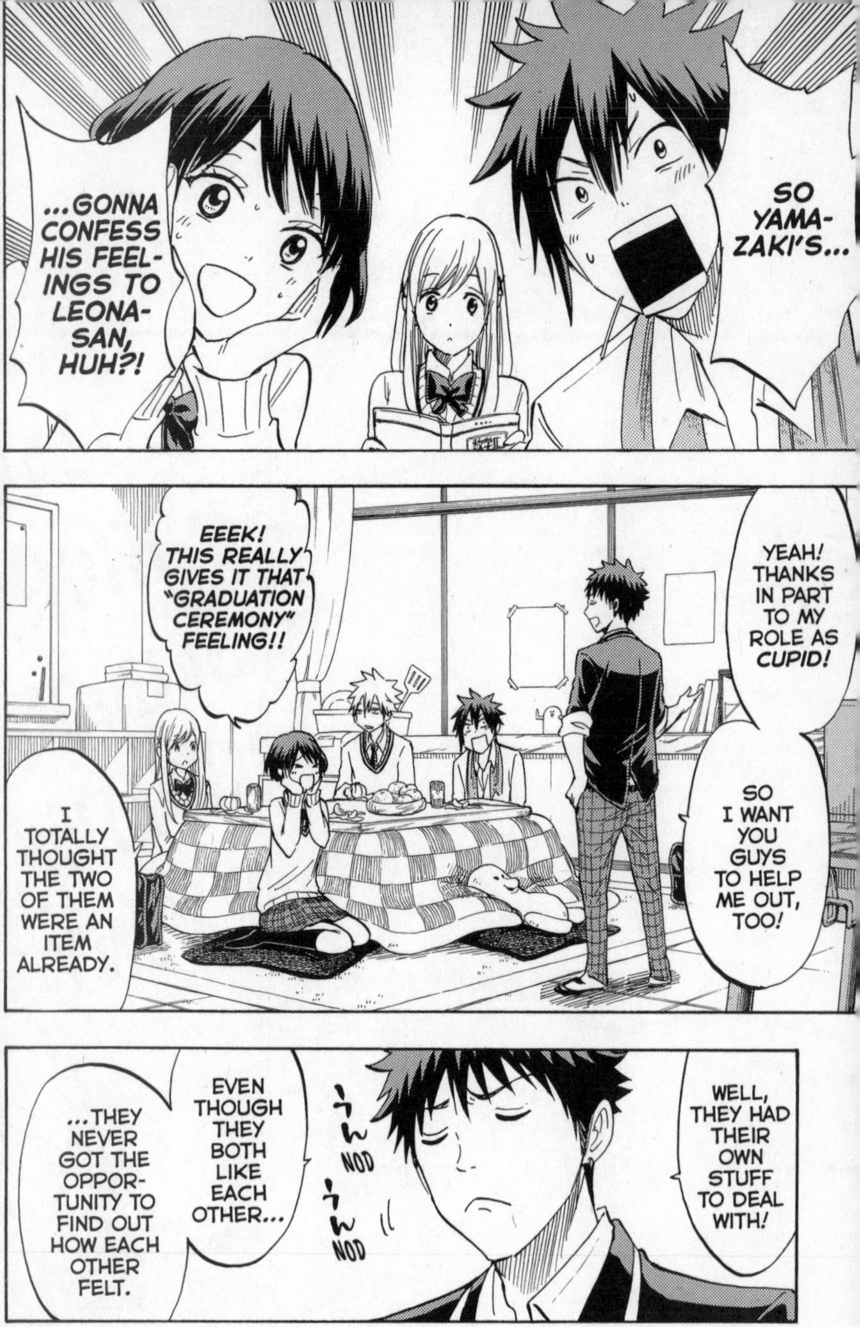
SO YAMAZAKI'S...
...GONNA CONFESS HIS FEELINGS TO LEONA-SAN, HUH?!
YEAH! THANKS IN PART TO MY ROLE AS CUPID!
SO I WANT YOU GUYS TO HELP ME OUT, TOO!
EEEK! THIS REALLY GIVES IT THAT "GRADUATION CEREMONY" FEELING!!
I TOTALLY THOUGHT THE TWO OF THEM WERE AN ITEM ALREADY.
WELL, THEY HAD THEIR OWN STUFF TO DEAL WITH!
うん NOD
うん NOD
EVEN THOUGH THEY BOTH LIKE EACH OTHER...
...THEY NEVER GOT THE OPPORTUNITY TO FIND OUT HOW EACH OTHER FELT.

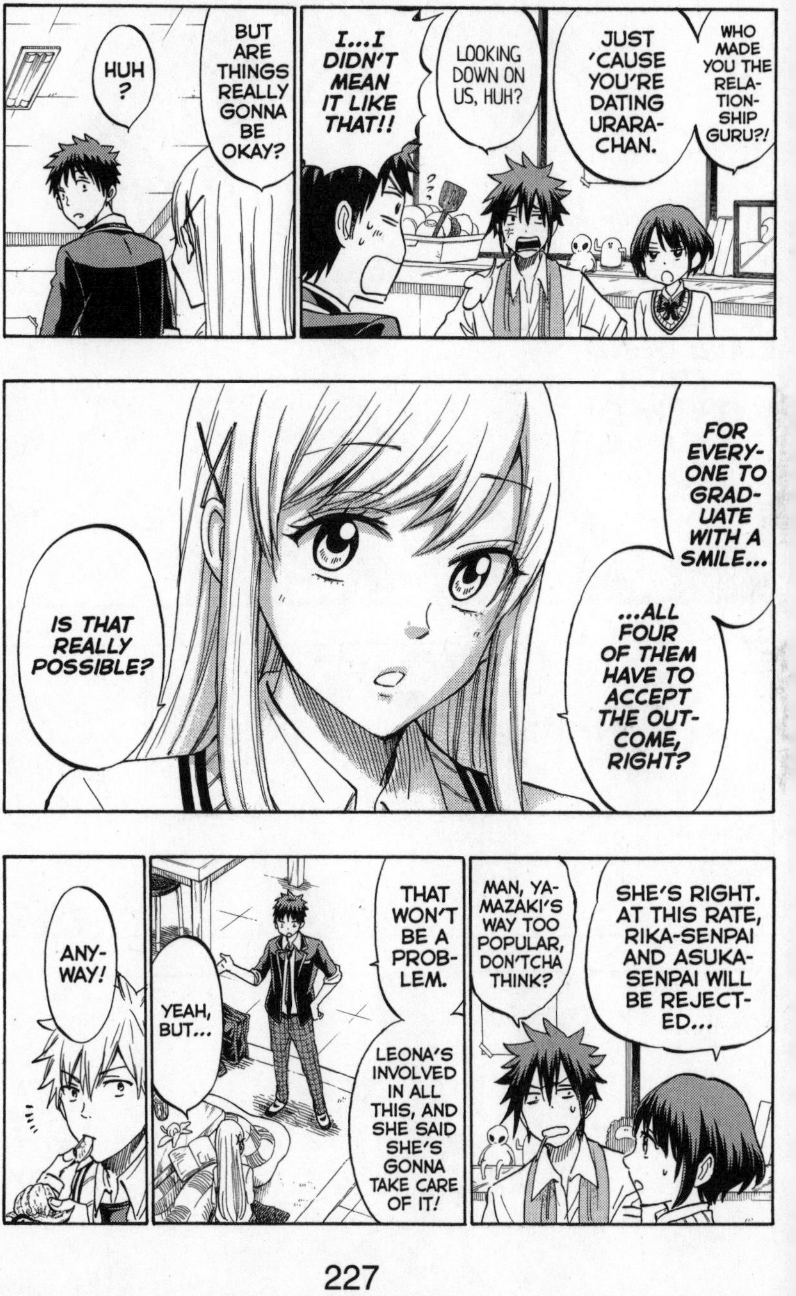
WHO MADE YOU THE RELATIONSHIP GURU?!
JUST 'CAUSE YOU'RE DATING URARA-CHAN.
LOOKING DOWN ON US, HUH?
I...I DIDN'T MEAN IT LIKE THAT!!
BUT ARE THINGS REALLY GONNA BE OKAY?
HUH?
FOR EVERYONE TO GRADUATE WITH A SMILE...
...ALL FOUR OF THEM HAVE TO ACCEPT THE OUTCOME, RIGHT?
IS THAT REALLY POSSIBLE?
SHE'S RIGHT. AT THIS RATE, RIKA-SENPAI AND ASUKA-SENPAI WILL BE REJECTED...
MAN, YAMAZAKI'S WAY TOO POPULAR, DON'TCHA THINK?
THAT WON'T BE A PROBLEM.
LEONA'S INVOLVED IN ALL THIS, AND SHE SAID SHE'S GONNA TAKE CARE OF IT!
YEAH, BUT...
ANYWAY!

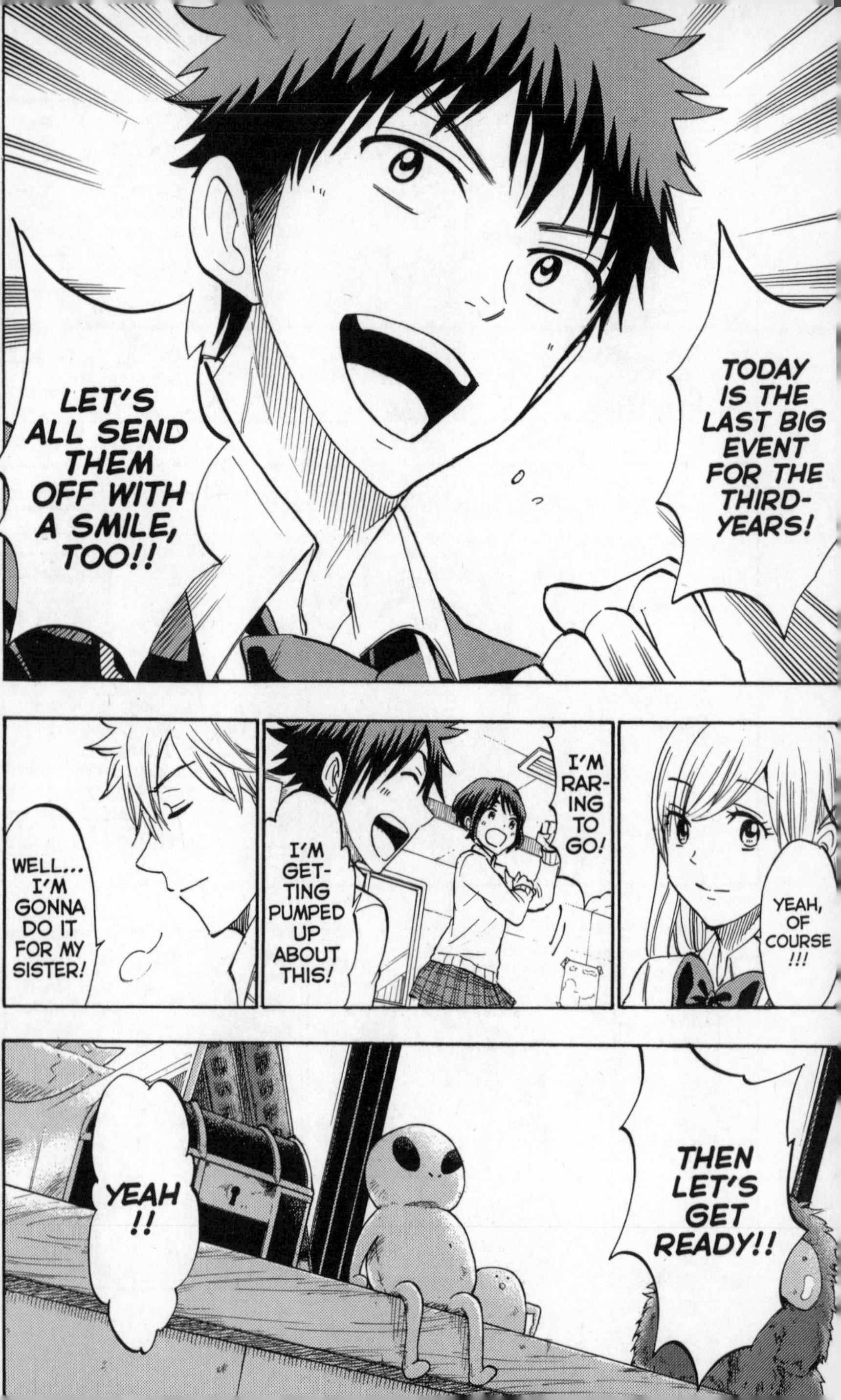
TODAY IS THE LAST BIG EVENT FOR THE THIRD-YEARS!
LET'S ALL SEND THEM OFF WITH A SMILE, TOO!!
YEAH, OF COURSE!!!
I'M RARING TO GO!
I'M GETTING PUMPED UP ABOUT THIS!
WELL... I'M GONNA DO IT FOR MY SISTER!
THEN LET'S GET READY!!
YEAH!!

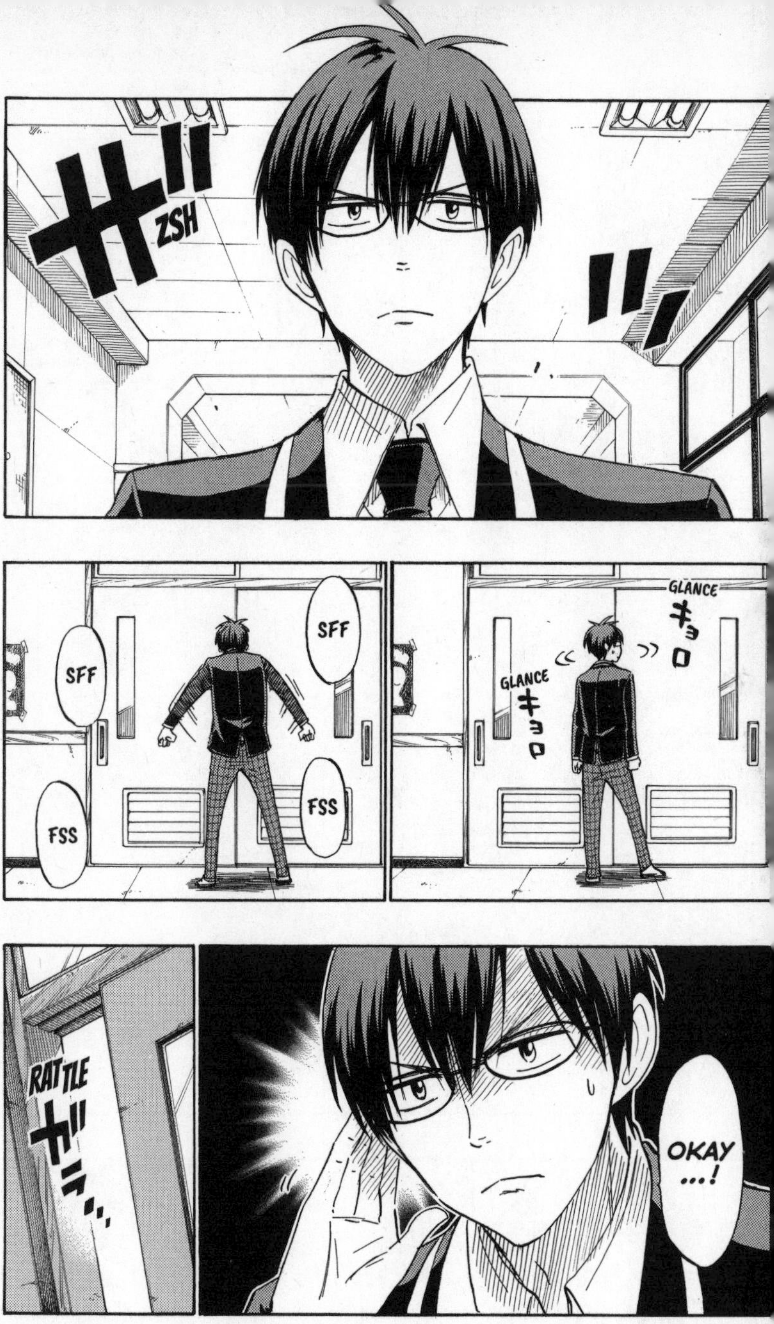
ZSH
GLANCE
キョロ
GLANCE
キョロ
SFF
SFF
FSS
FSS
OKAY ...!
RATTLE

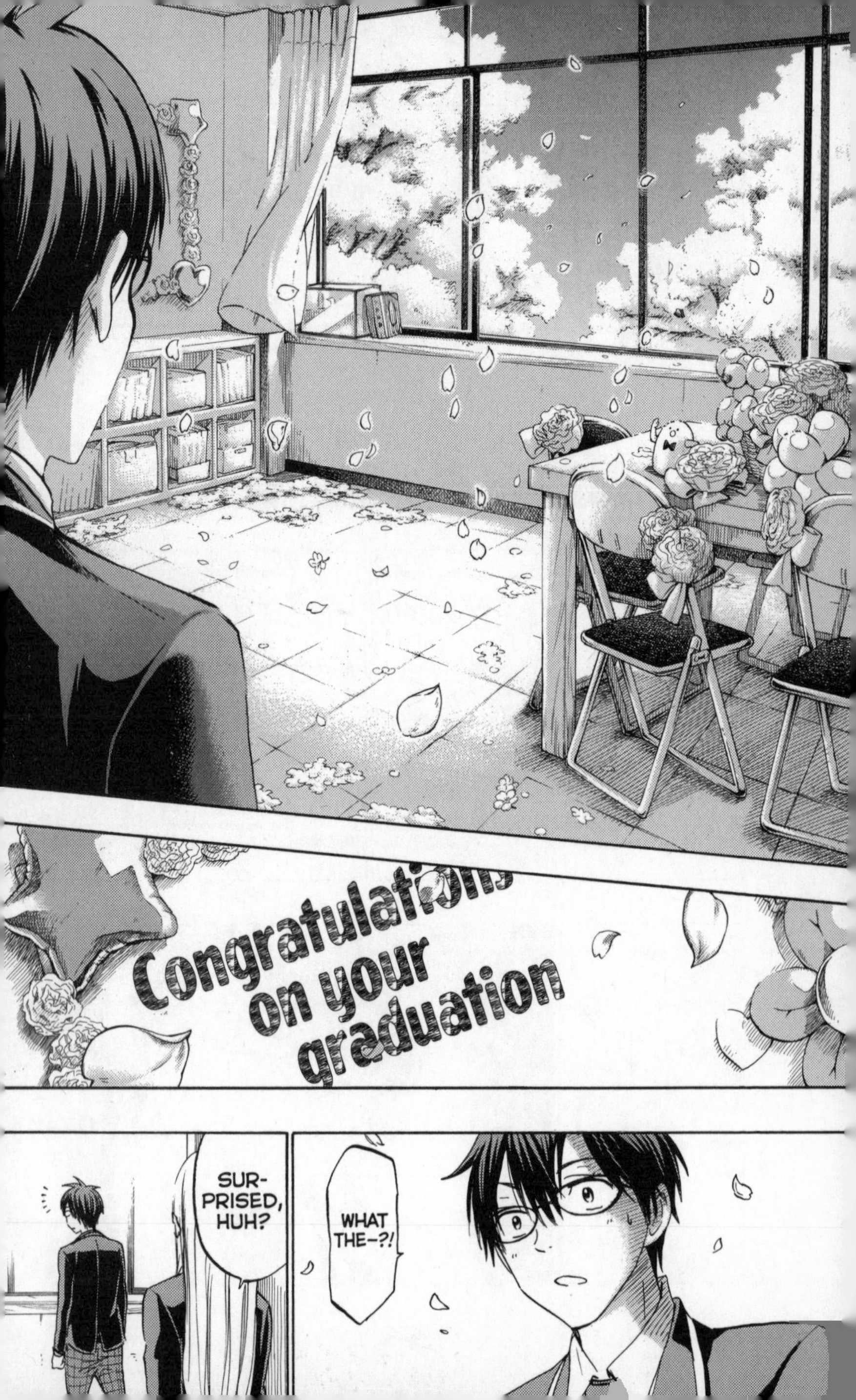
Congratulations on your graduation
WHAT THE-?!
SUR-PRISED, HUH?

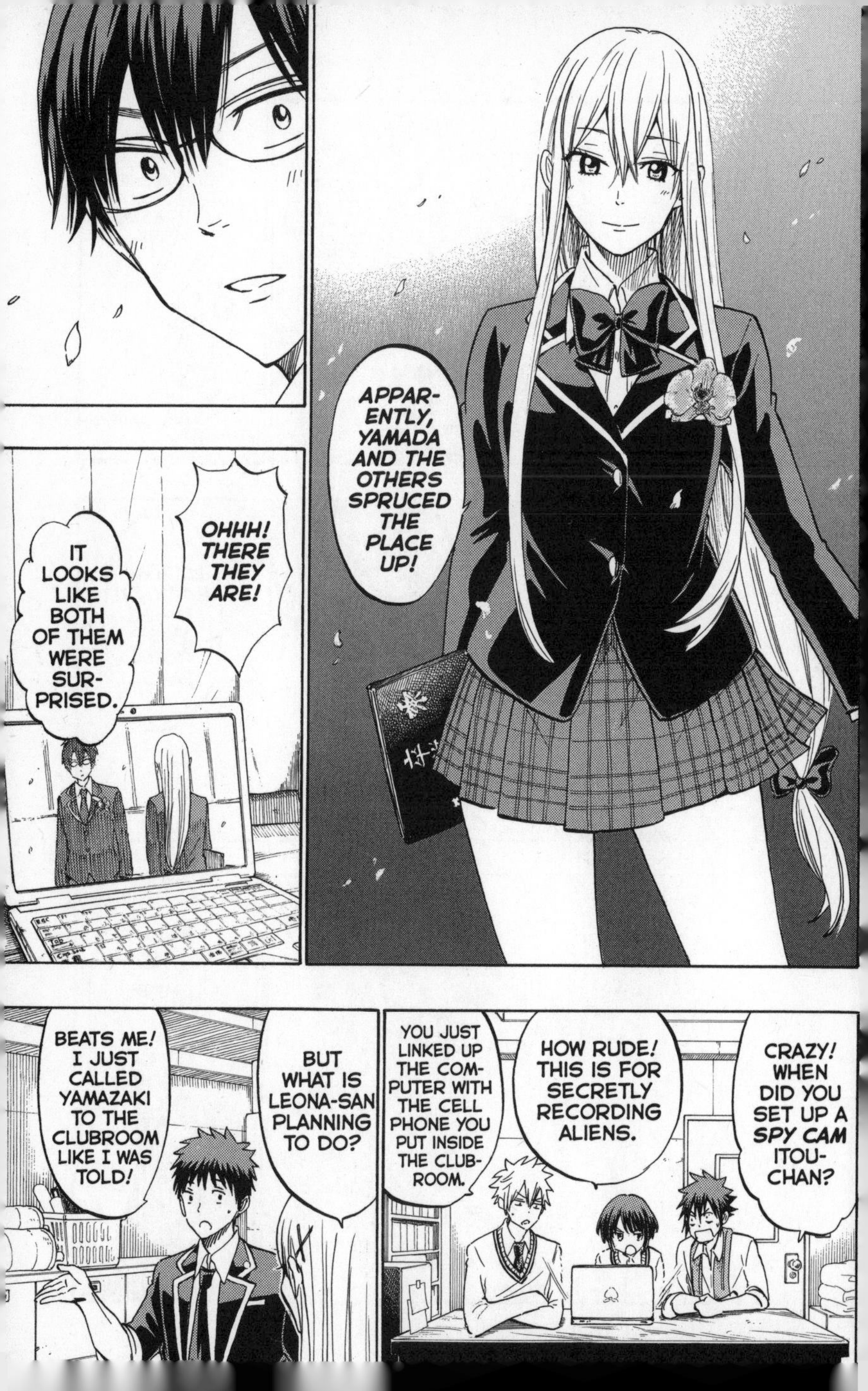
APPAR-ENTLY, YAMADA AND THE OTHERS SPRUCED THE PLACE UP!
OHHH! THERE THEY ARE!
IT LOOKS LIKE BOTH OF THEM WERE SUR-PRISED.
CRAZY! WHEN DID YOU SET UP A *SPY CAM* ITOU-CHAN?
HOW RUDE! THIS IS FOR SECRETLY RECORDING ALIENS.
YOU JUST LINKED UP THE COM-PUTER WITH THE CELL PHONE YOU PUT INSIDE THE CLUB-ROOM.
BUT WHAT IS LEONA-SAN PLANNING TO DO?
BEATS ME! I JUST CALLED YAMAZAKI TO THE CLUBROOM LIKE I WAS TOLD!

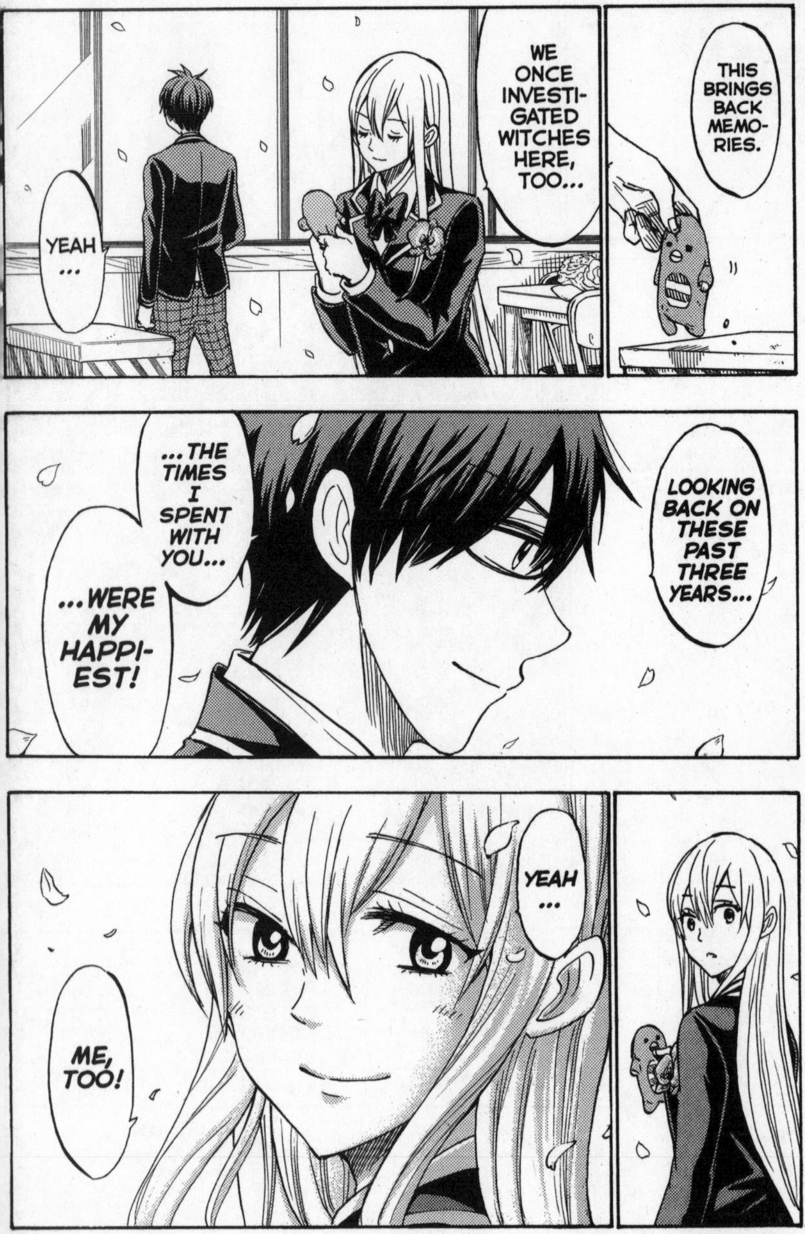
THIS BRINGS BACK MEMORIES.
WE ONCE INVESTIGATED WITCHES HERE, TOO...
YEAH...
LOOKING BACK ON THESE PAST THREE YEARS...
...THE TIMES I SPENT WITH YOU...
...WERE MY HAPPIEST!
YEAH...
ME, TOO!

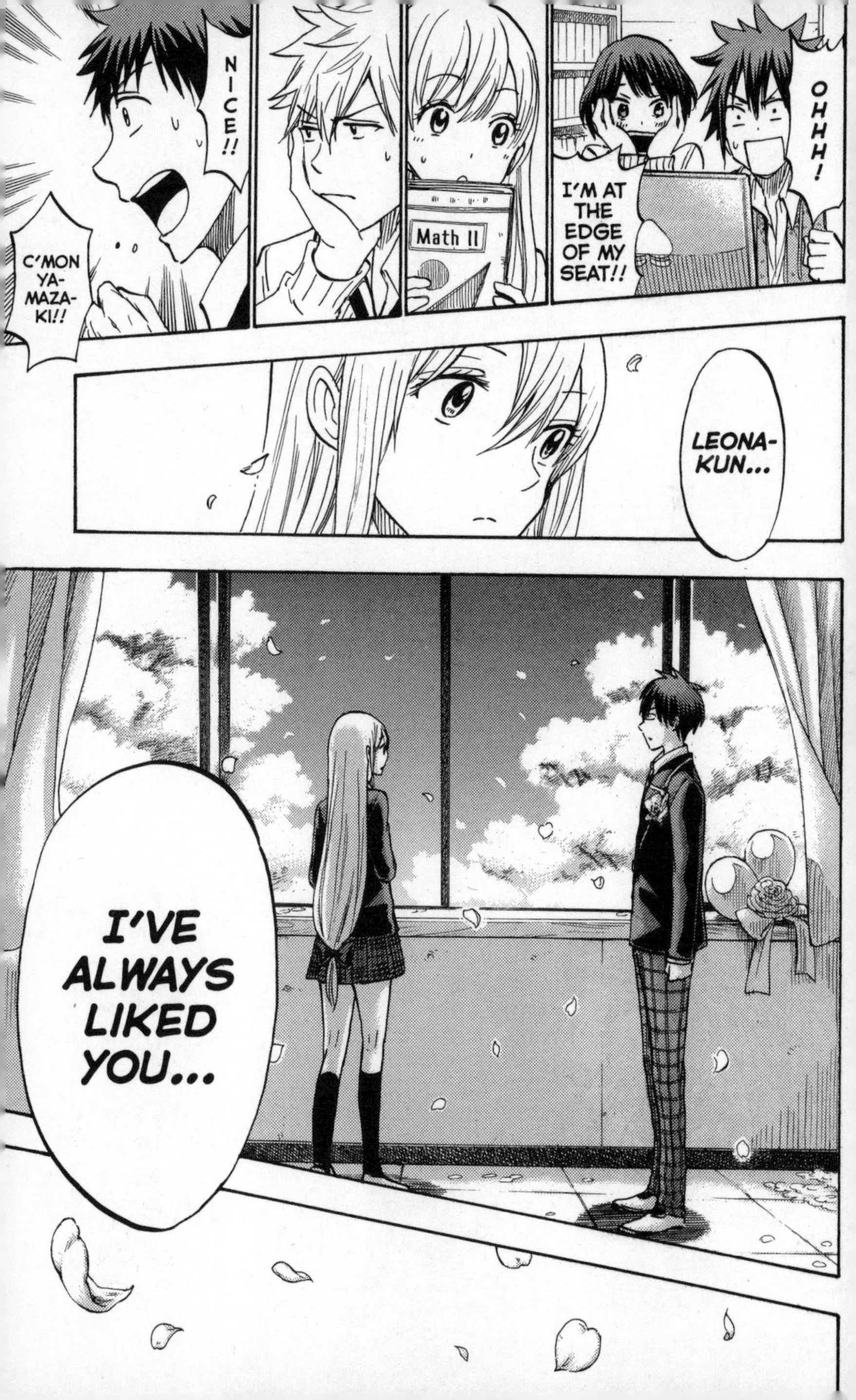
OHHHH!
I'M AT THE EDGE OF MY SEAT!!
Math II
NICE!!
C'MON YA-MAZA-KI!!
LEONA-KUN...
I'VE ALWAYS LIKED YOU...

PLEASE GO OUT WITH ME!!!

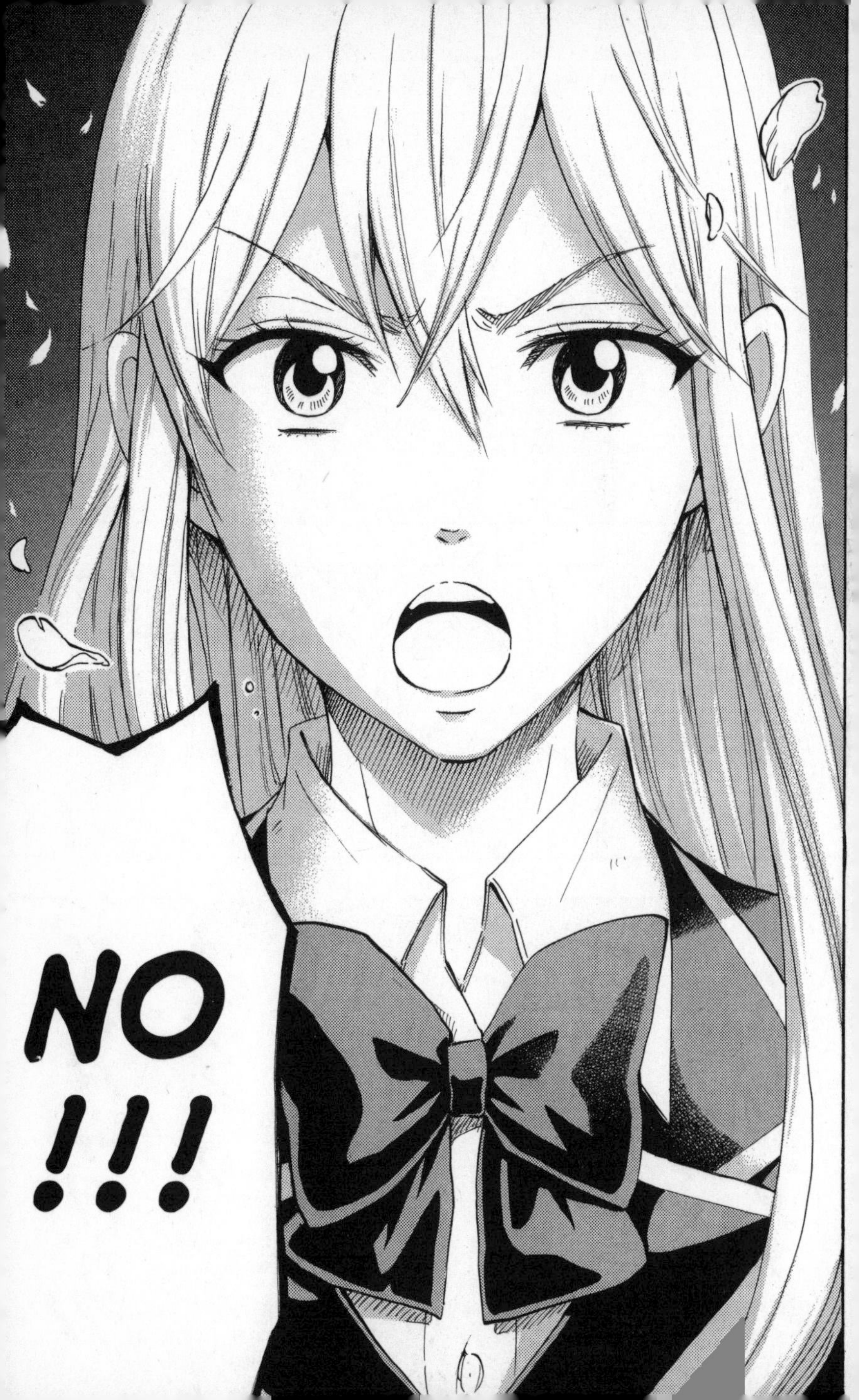
NO!!!

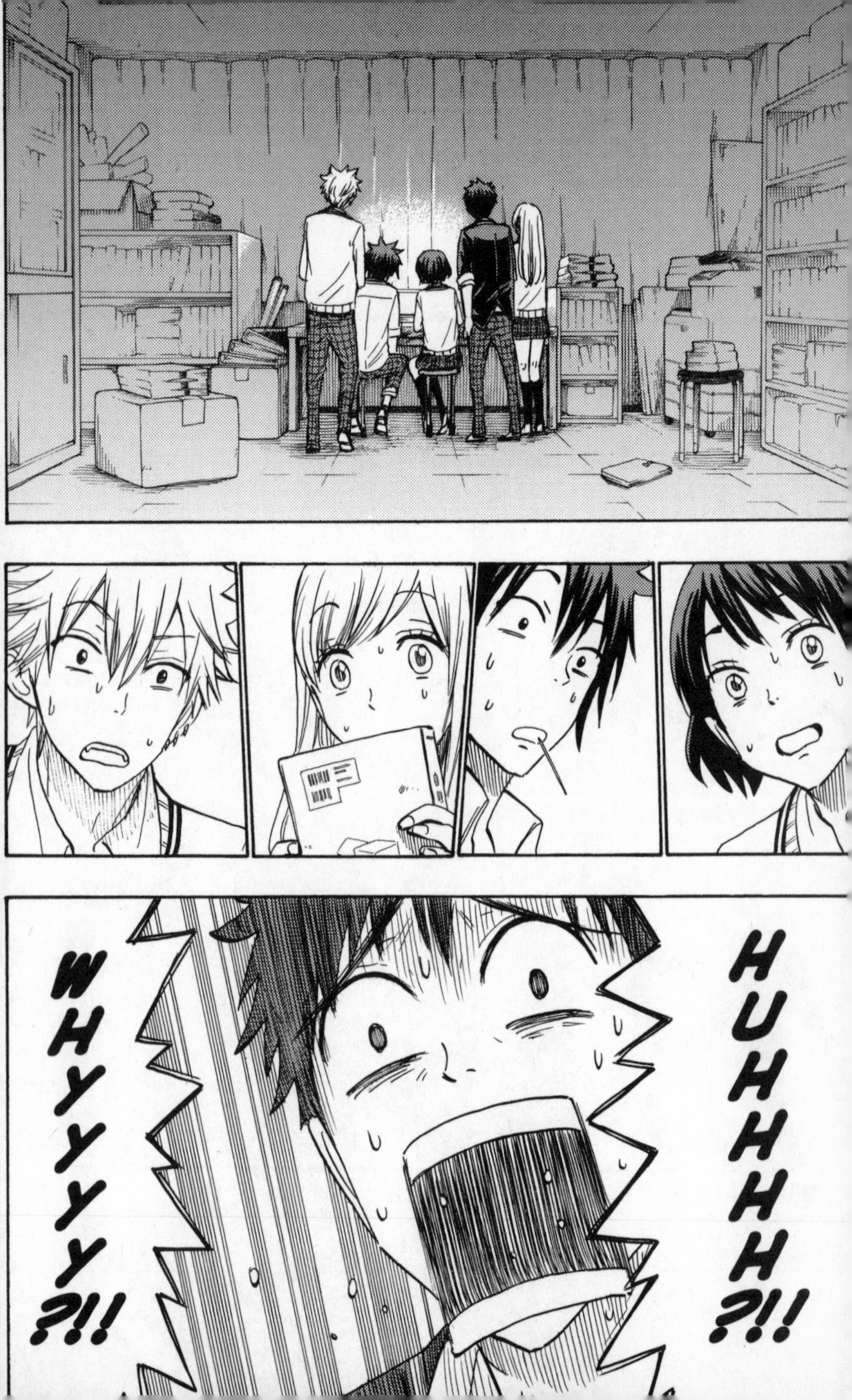
HUHHHH?!!
WHYYYY?!!

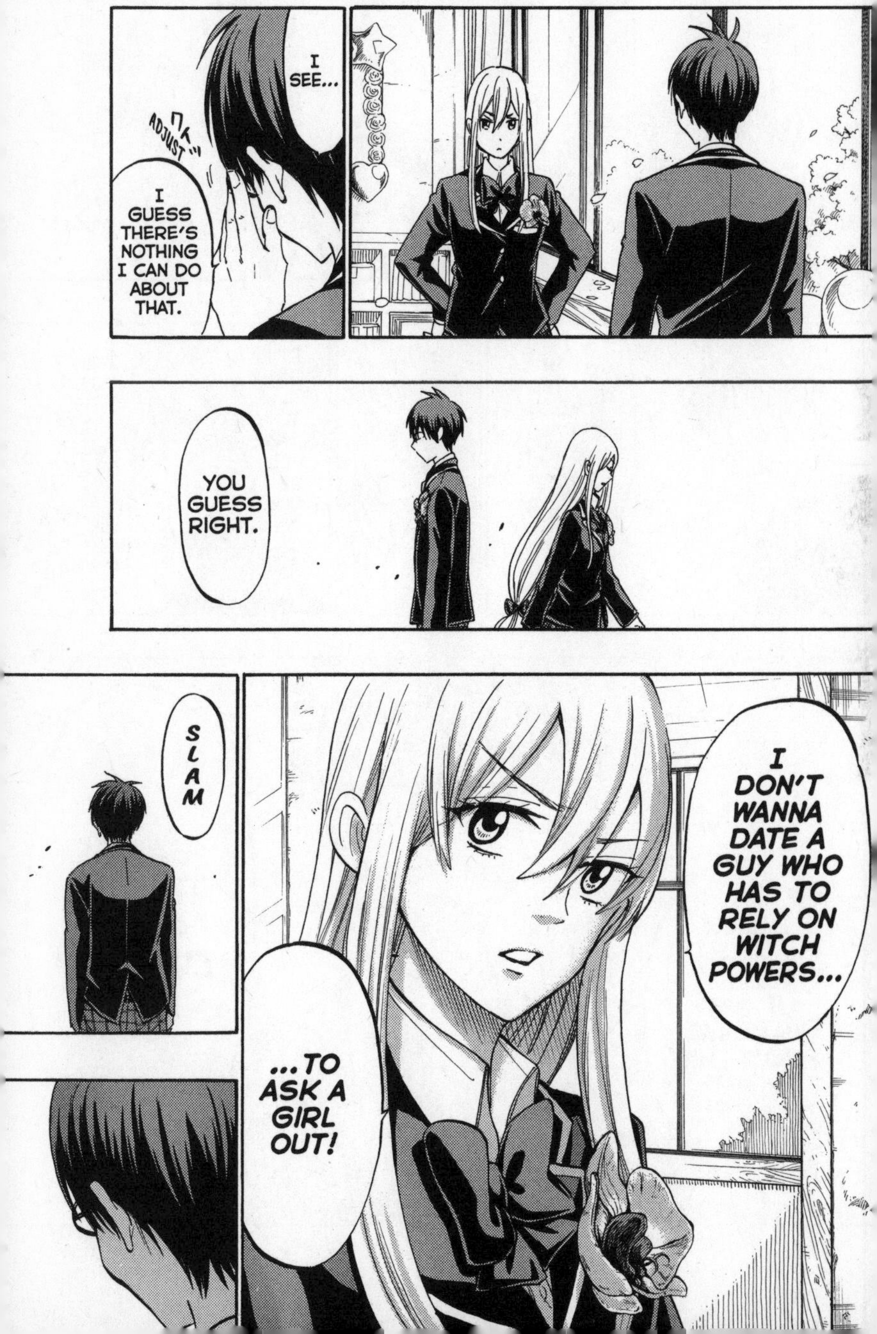
I SEE...
ADJUST
I GUESS THERE'S NOTHING I CAN DO ABOUT THAT.
YOU GUESS RIGHT.
I DON'T WANNA DATE A GUY WHO HAS TO RELY ON WITCH POWERS...
...TO ASK A GIRL OUT!
SLAM

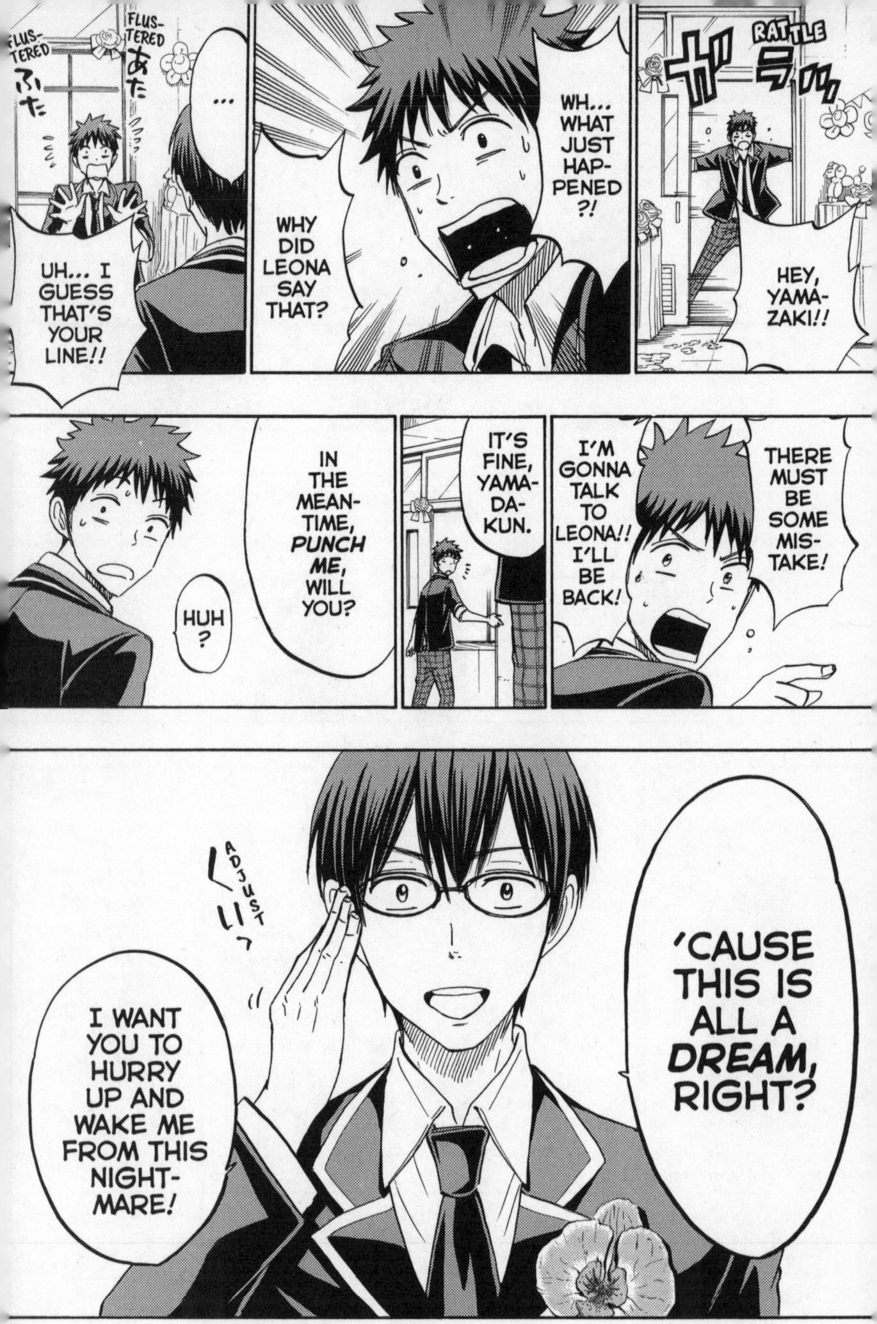
RATTLE
ガラッ
HEY, YAMAZAKI!!
WH... WHAT JUST HAPPENED?!
WHY DID LEONA SAY THAT?
FLUSTERED
あた
FLUSTERED
ふた
...
UH... I GUESS THAT'S YOUR LINE!!
THERE MUST BE SOME MISTAKE!
I'M GONNA TALK TO LEONA!! I'LL BE BACK!
IT'S FINE, YAMADA-KUN.
IN THE MEANTIME, *PUNCH ME*, WILL YOU?
HUH?
'CAUSE THIS IS ALL A *DREAM*, RIGHT?
ADJUST
くいっ
I WANT YOU TO HURRY UP AND WAKE ME FROM THIS NIGHTMARE!

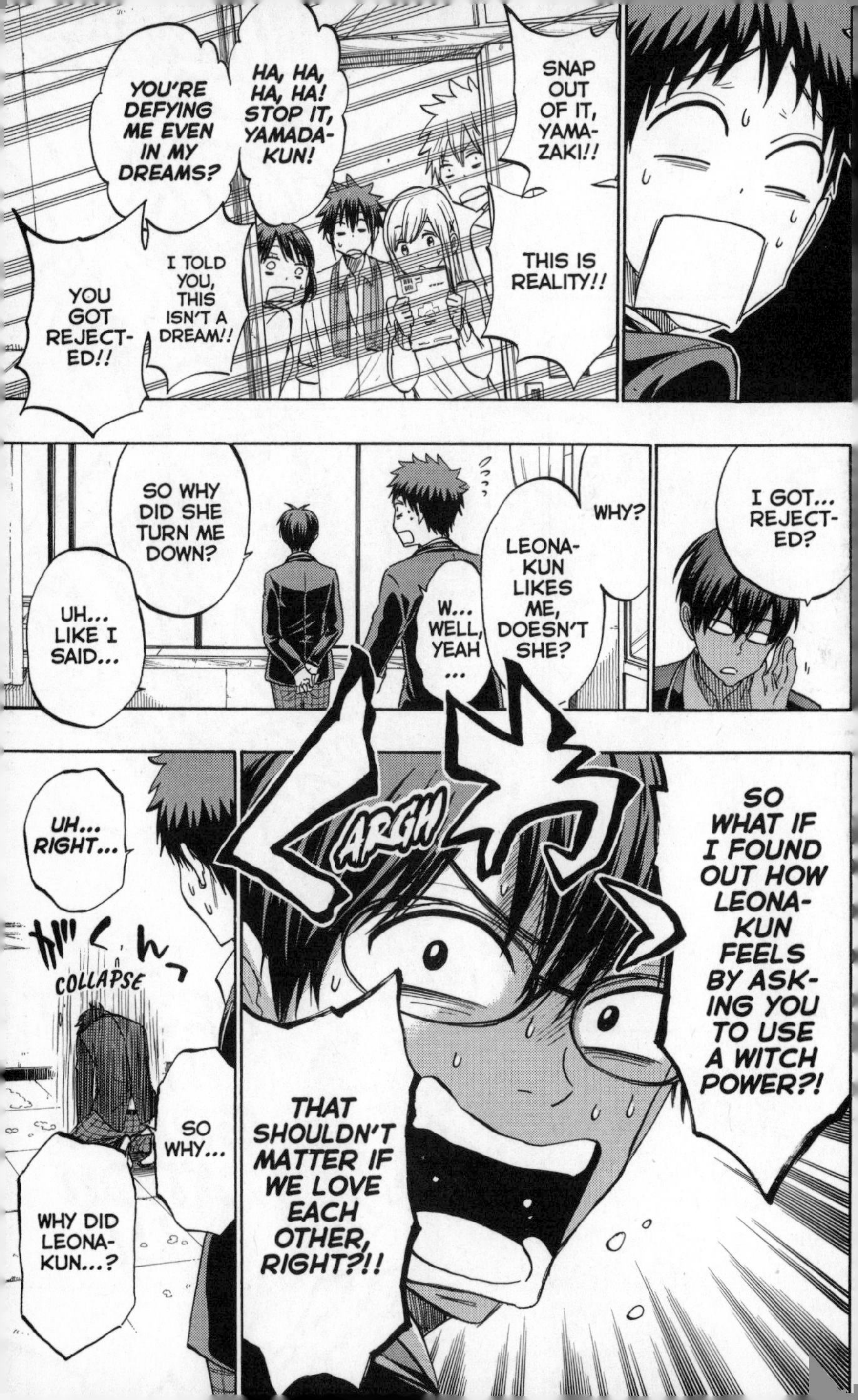
SNAP OUT OF IT, YAMAZAKI!!
THIS IS REALITY!!
HA, HA, HA, HA! STOP IT, YAMADA-KUN!
YOU'RE DEFYING ME EVEN IN MY DREAMS?
I TOLD YOU, THIS ISN'T A DREAM!!
YOU GOT REJECTED!!
I GOT... REJECTED?
WHY?
LEONA-KUN LIKES ME, DOESN'T SHE?
W... WELL, YEAH...
SO WHY DID SHE TURN ME DOWN?
UH... LIKE I SAID...
SO WHAT IF I FOUND OUT HOW LEONA-KUN FEELS BY ASKING YOU TO USE A WITCH POWER?!
ARGH
THAT SHOULDN'T MATTER IF WE LOVE EACH OTHER, RIGHT?!!
UH... RIGHT...
COLLAPSE
SO WHY...
WHY DID LEONA-KUN...?

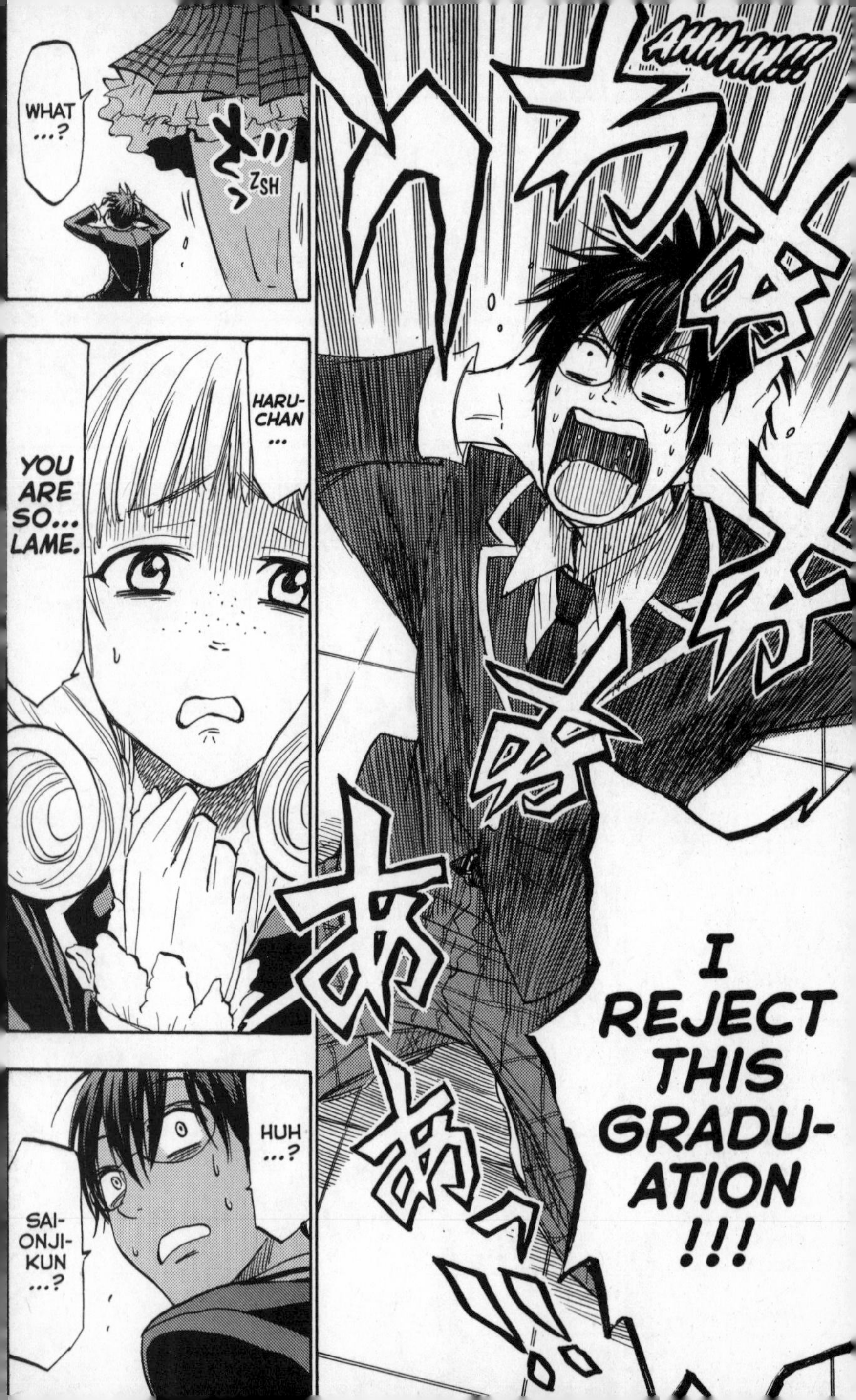
AHHHHH!!!
I REJECT THIS GRADUATION!!!
WHAT ...?
ZSH
HARU-CHAN ...
YOU ARE SO... LAME.
HUH ...?
SAI-ONJI-KUN ...?

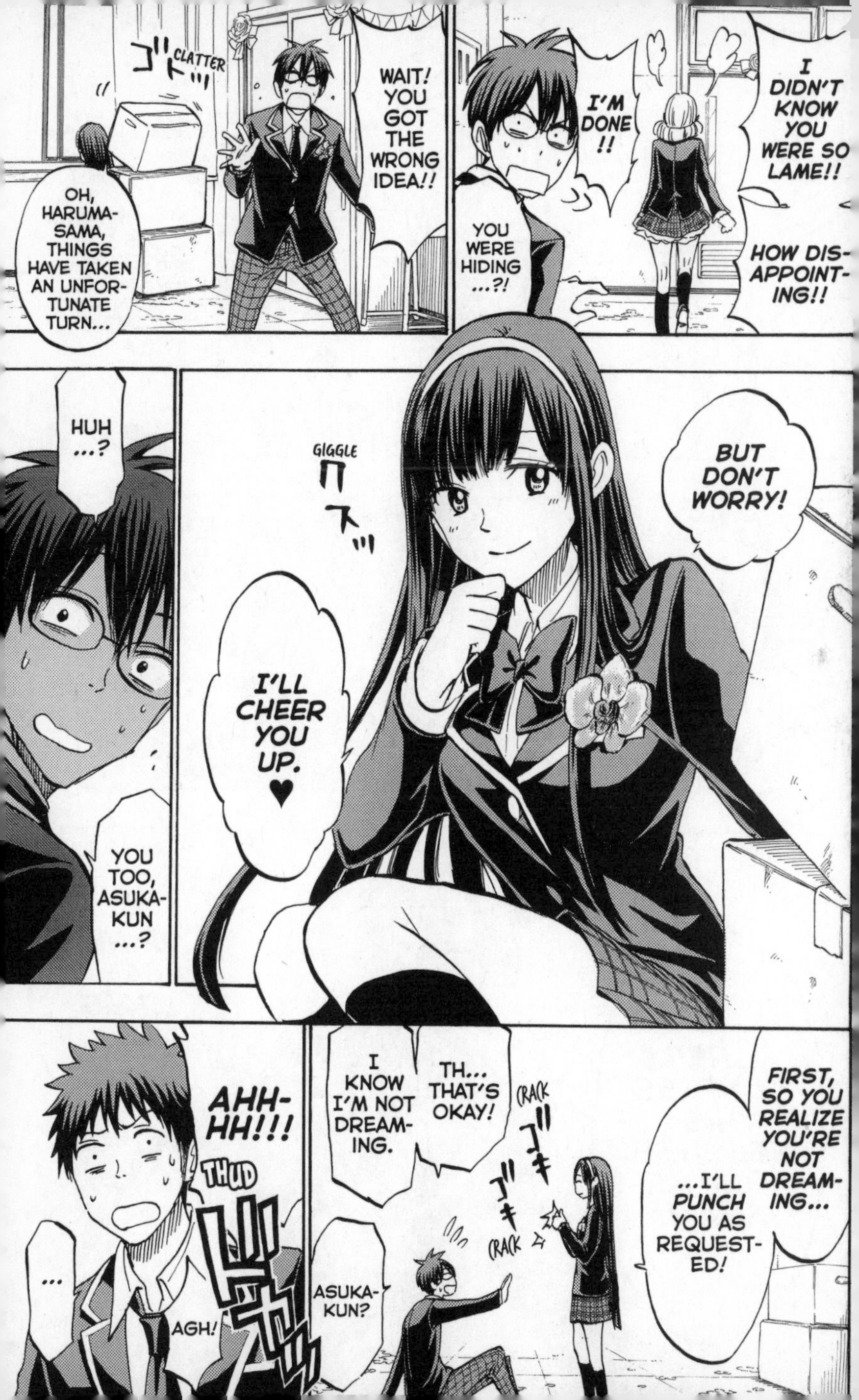
I DIDN'T KNOW YOU WERE SO LAME!!
HOW DISAPPOINTING!!
I'M DONE!!
YOU WERE HIDING...?!
CLATTER
WAIT! YOU GOT THE WRONG IDEA!!
OH, HARUMA-SAMA, THINGS HAVE TAKEN AN UNFORTUNATE TURN...
BUT DON'T WORRY!
GIGGLE
I'LL CHEER YOU UP. ♥
HUH...?
YOU TOO, ASUKA-KUN...?
FIRST, SO YOU REALIZE YOU'RE NOT DREAMING...
...I'LL PUNCH YOU AS REQUESTED!
CRACK
CRACK
TH... THAT'S OKAY!
I KNOW I'M NOT DREAMING.
ASUKA-KUN?
AHHHH!!!
THUD
...
AGH!

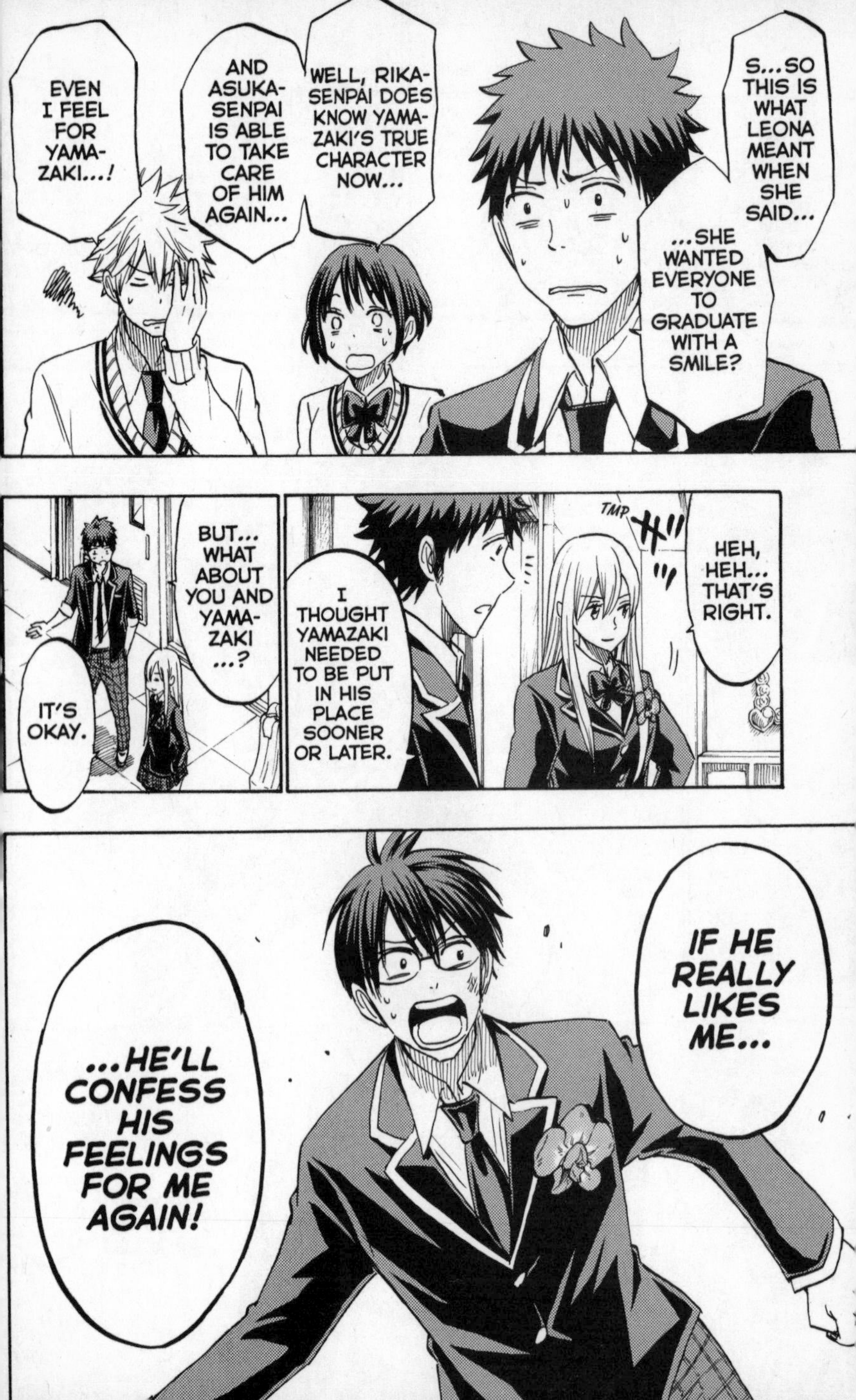
S...SO THIS IS WHAT LEONA MEANT WHEN SHE SAID...
...SHE WANTED EVERYONE TO GRADUATE WITH A SMILE?
WELL, RIKA-SENPAI DOES KNOW YAMAZAKI'S TRUE CHARACTER NOW...
AND ASUKA-SENPAI IS ABLE TO TAKE CARE OF HIM AGAIN...
EVEN I FEEL FOR YAMAZAKI...!
TMP
HEH, HEH... THAT'S RIGHT.
I THOUGHT YAMAZAKI NEEDED TO BE PUT IN HIS PLACE SOONER OR LATER.
BUT... WHAT ABOUT YOU AND YAMAZAKI...?
IT'S OKAY.
IF HE REALLY LIKES ME...
...HE'LL CONFESS HIS FEELINGS FOR ME AGAIN!

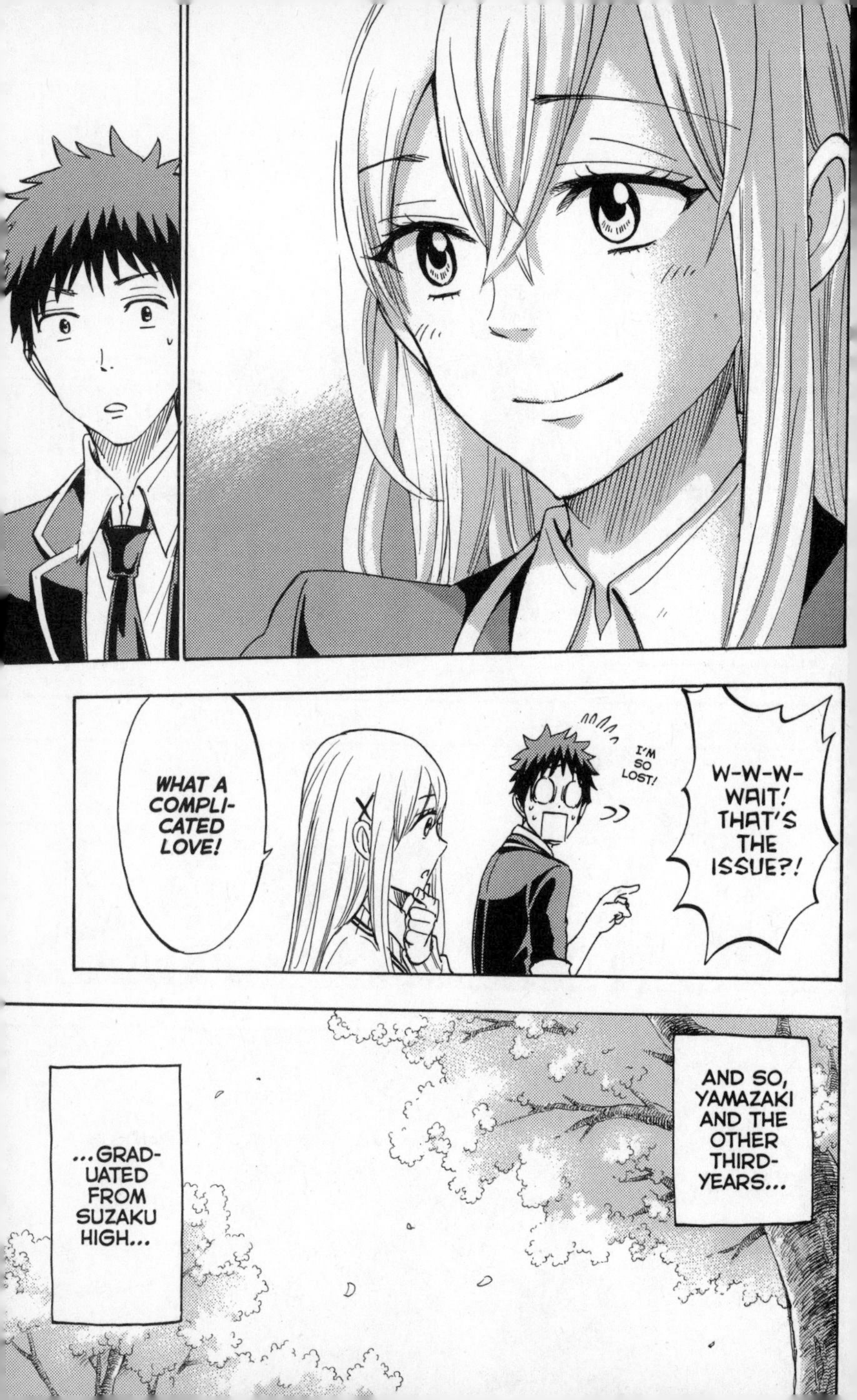
W-W-W-WAIT! THAT'S THE ISSUE?!
I'M SO LOST!
WHAT A COMPLICATED LOVE!
AND SO, YAMAZAKI AND THE OTHER THIRD-YEARS...
...GRADUATED FROM SUZAKU HIGH...

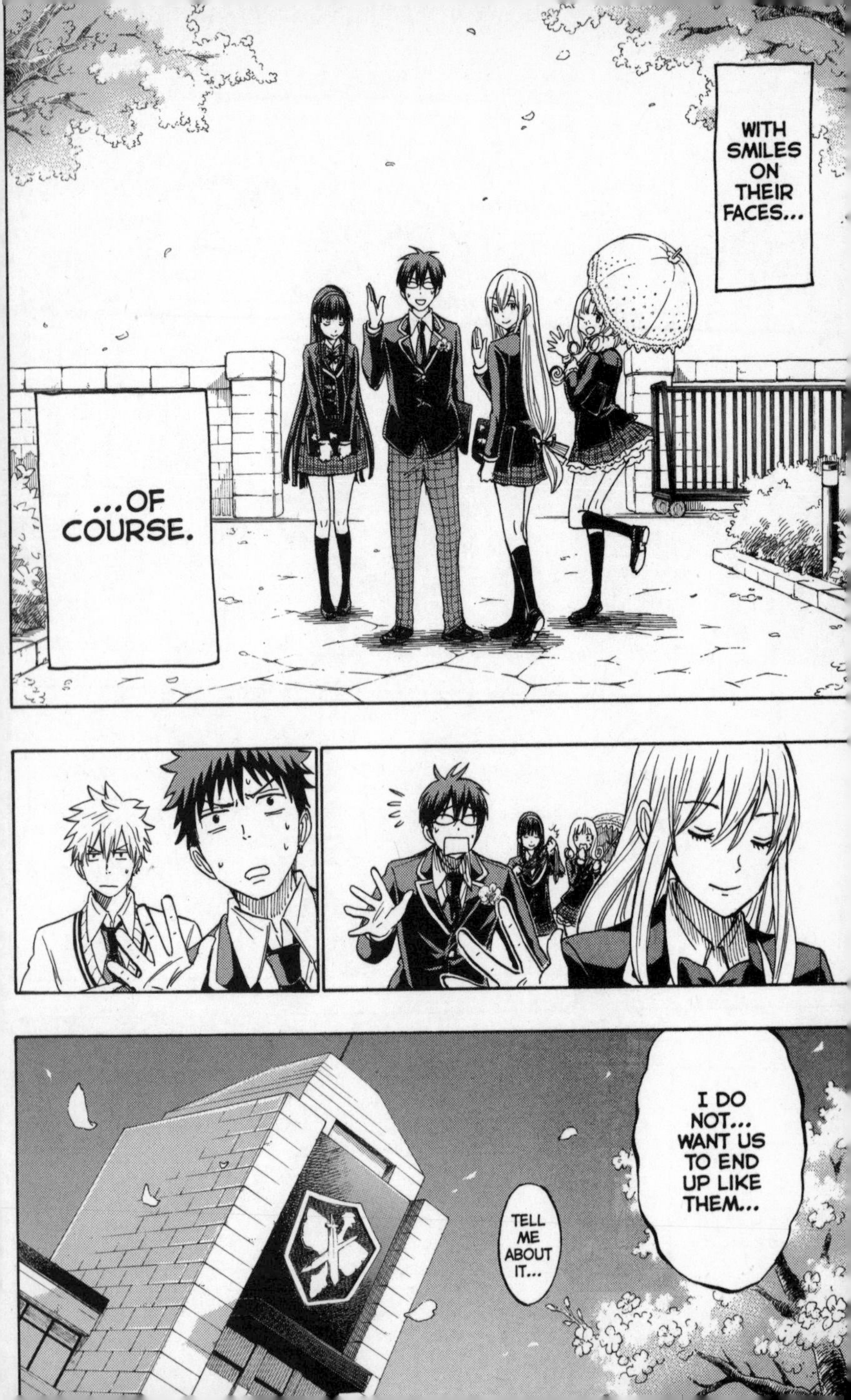
WITH SMILES ON THEIR FACES...
...OF COURSE.
I DO NOT... WANT US TO END UP LIKE THEM...
TELL ME ABOUT IT...

CHAPTER 184: Who wants mint chocolate chip?!

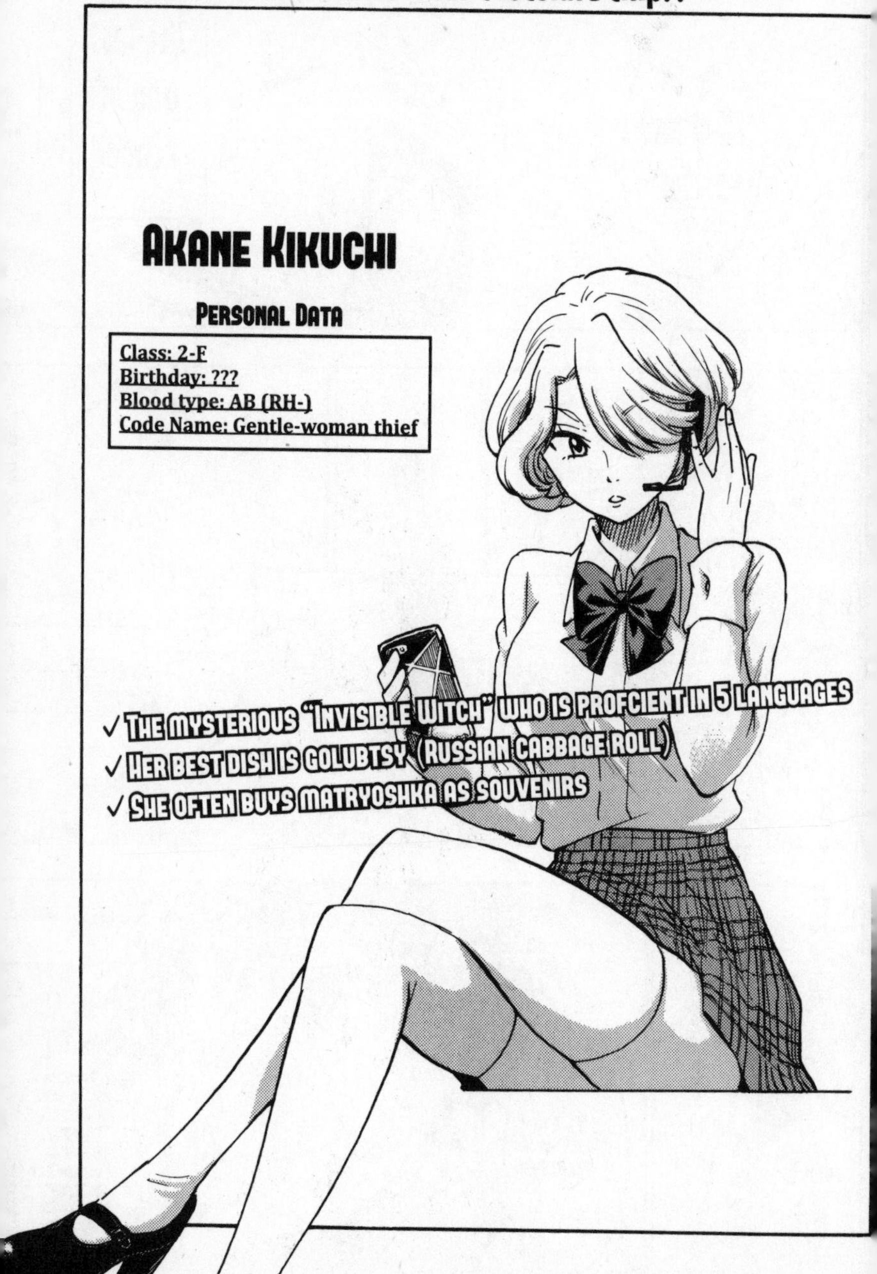
AKANE KIKUCHI
PERSONAL DATA
Class: 2-F
Birthday: ???
Blood type: AB (RH-)
Code Name: Gentle-woman thief
✓ THE MYSTERIOUS "INVISIBLE WITCH" WHO IS PROFCIENT IN 5 LANGUAGES
✓ HER BEST DISH IS GOLUBTSY (RUSSIAN CABBAGE ROLL)
✓ SHE OFTEN BUYS MATRYOSHKA AS SOUVENIRS

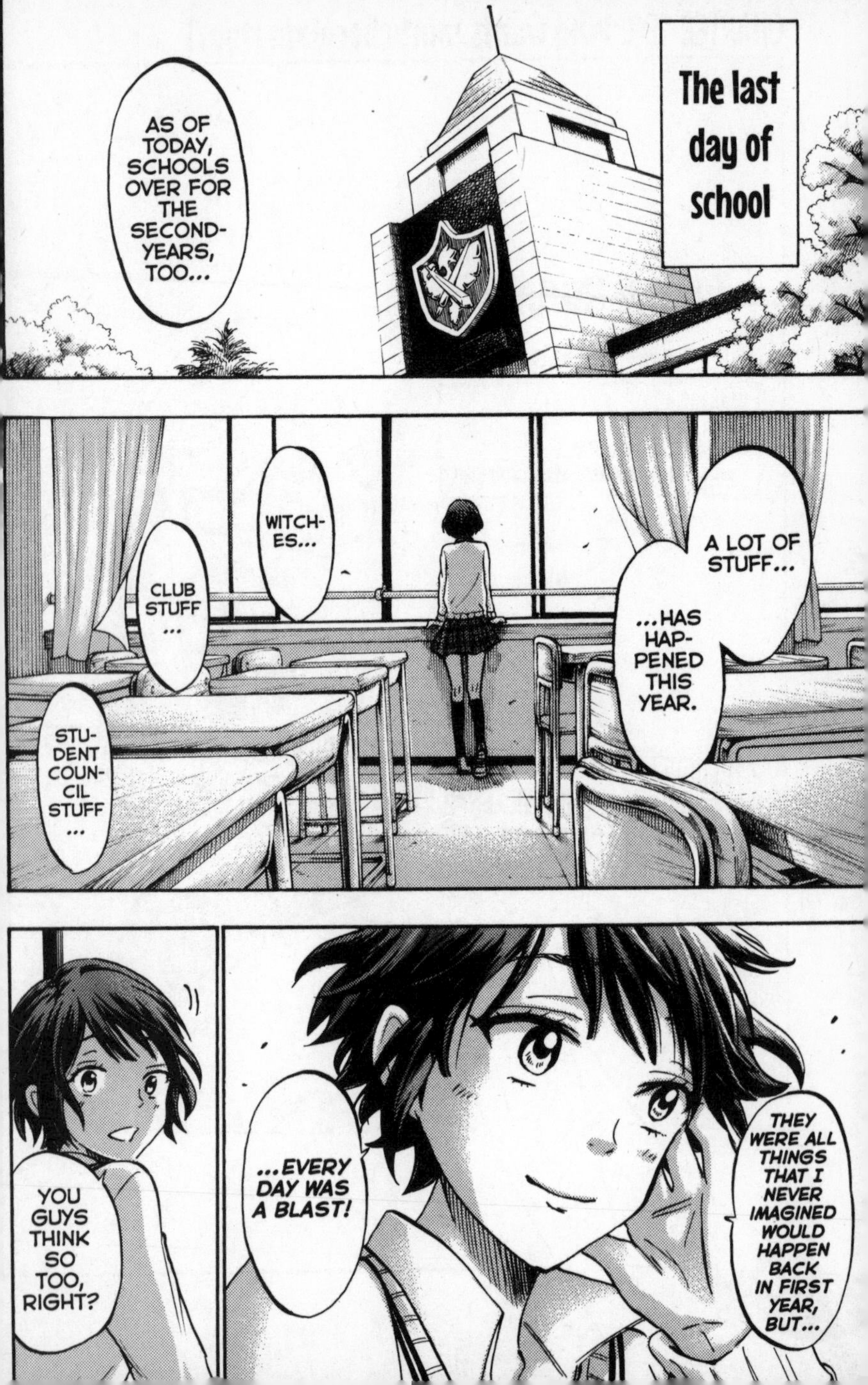
The last day of school
AS OF TODAY, SCHOOLS OVER FOR THE SECOND-YEARS, TOO...
A LOT OF STUFF...
...HAS HAPPENED THIS YEAR.
WITCHES...
CLUB STUFF...
STUDENT COUNCIL STUFF...
THEY WERE ALL THINGS THAT I NEVER IMAGINED WOULD HAPPEN BACK IN FIRST YEAR, BUT...
...EVERY DAY WAS A BLAST!
YOU GUYS THINK SO TOO, RIGHT?

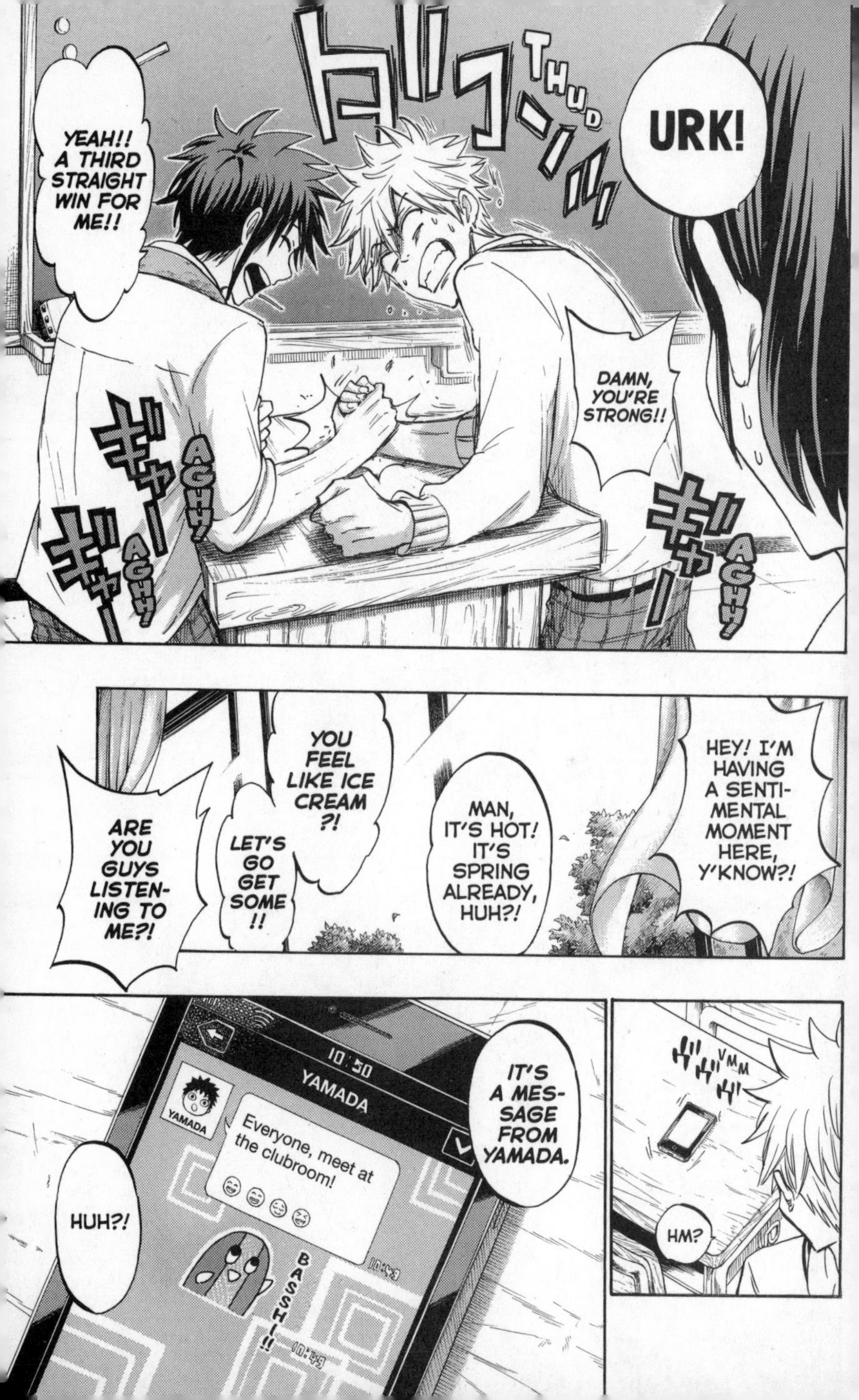
URK!
THUD
YEAH!! A THIRD STRAIGHT WIN FOR ME!!
DAMN, YOU'RE STRONG!!
AGHH
AGHH
AGHH
HEY! I'M HAVING A SENTI-MENTAL MOMENT HERE, Y'KNOW?!
MAN, IT'S HOT! IT'S SPRING ALREADY, HUH?!
YOU FEEL LIKE ICE CREAM?!
LET'S GO GET SOME!!
ARE YOU GUYS LISTEN-ING TO ME?!
VMM
HM?
IT'S A MES-SAGE FROM YAMADA.
10:50
YAMADA
YAMADA
Everyone, meet at the clubroom!
BASSH!!
10:49
HUH?!

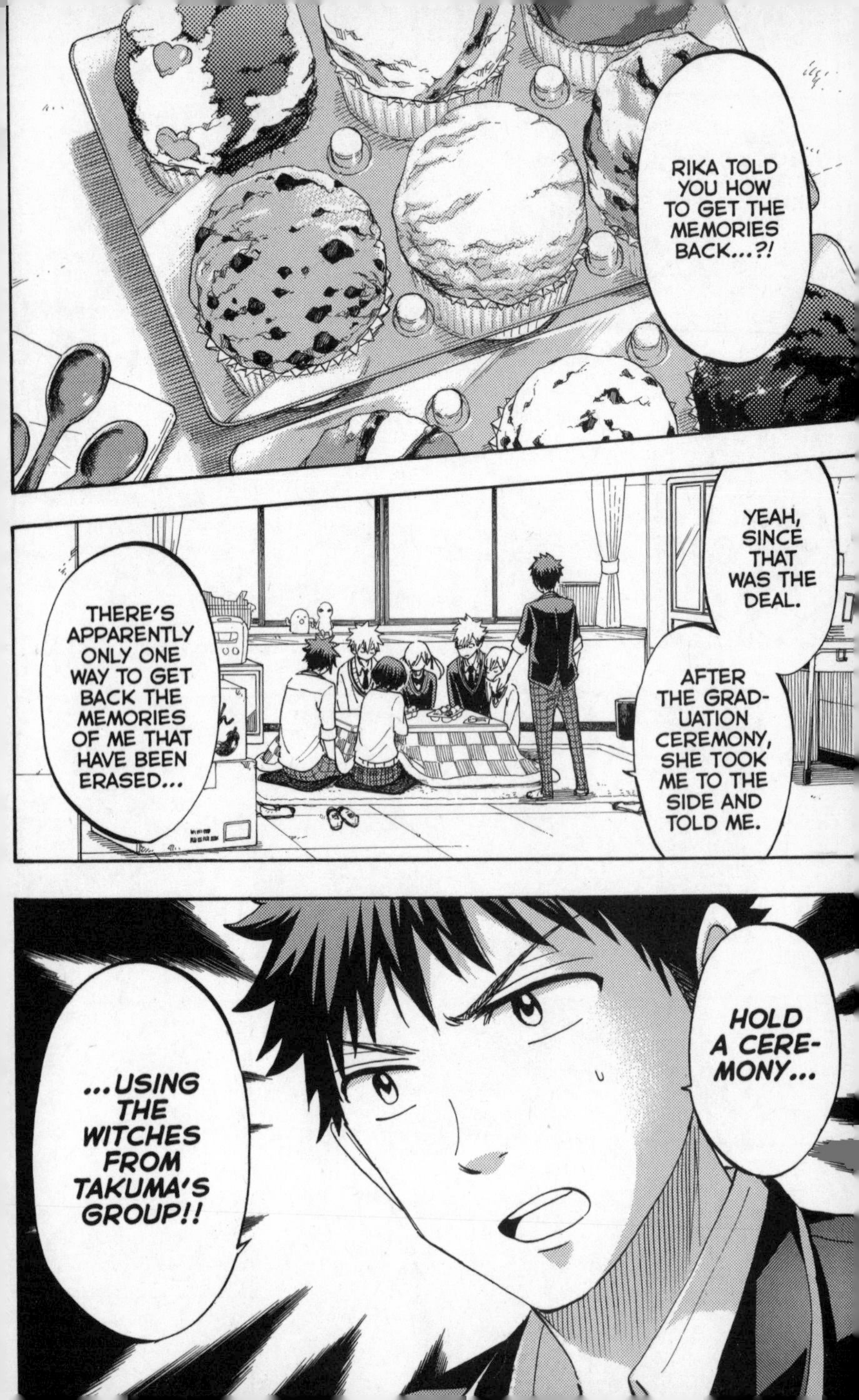
RIKA TOLD YOU HOW TO GET THE MEMORIES BACK...?!
YEAH, SINCE THAT WAS THE DEAL.
AFTER THE GRAD-UATION CEREMONY, SHE TOOK ME TO THE SIDE AND TOLD ME.
THERE'S APPARENTLY ONLY ONE WAY TO GET BACK THE MEMORIES OF ME THAT HAVE BEEN ERASED...
HOLD A CERE-MONY...
...USING THE WITCHES FROM TAKUMA'S GROUP!!

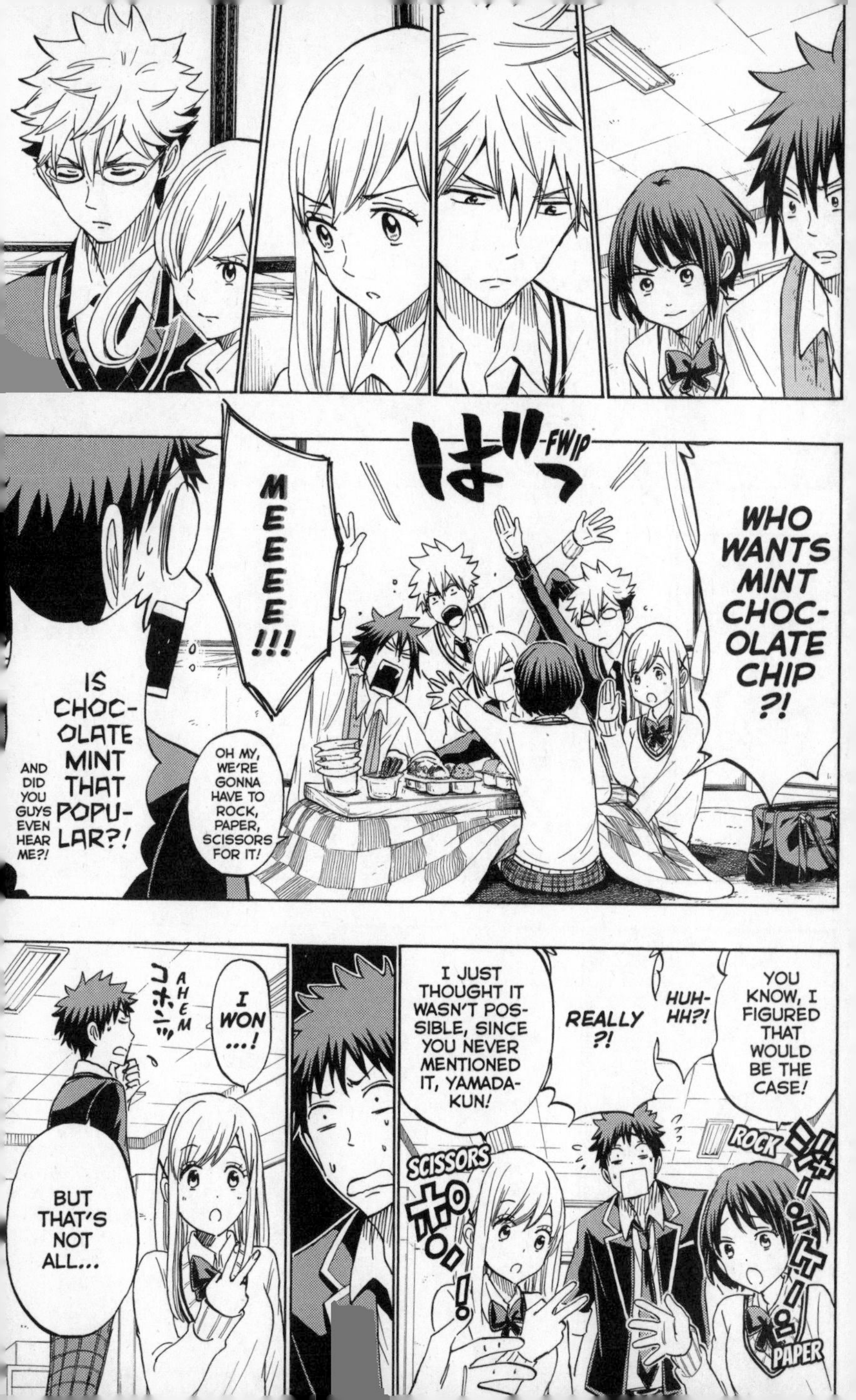
WHO WANTS MINT CHOCOLATE CHIP?!
ばっ -FWIP
MEEEEE!!!
OH MY, WE'RE GONNA HAVE TO ROCK, PAPER, SCISSORS FOR IT!
IS CHOCOLATE MINT THAT POPULAR?!
AND DID YOU GUYS EVEN HEAR ME?!
YOU KNOW, I FIGURED THAT WOULD BE THE CASE!
HUH-HH?!
REALLY?!
I JUST THOUGHT IT WASN'T POSSIBLE, SINCE YOU NEVER MENTIONED IT, YAMADA-KUN!
ROCK
PAPER
SCISSORS
I WON...!
AHEM
BUT THAT'S NOT ALL...

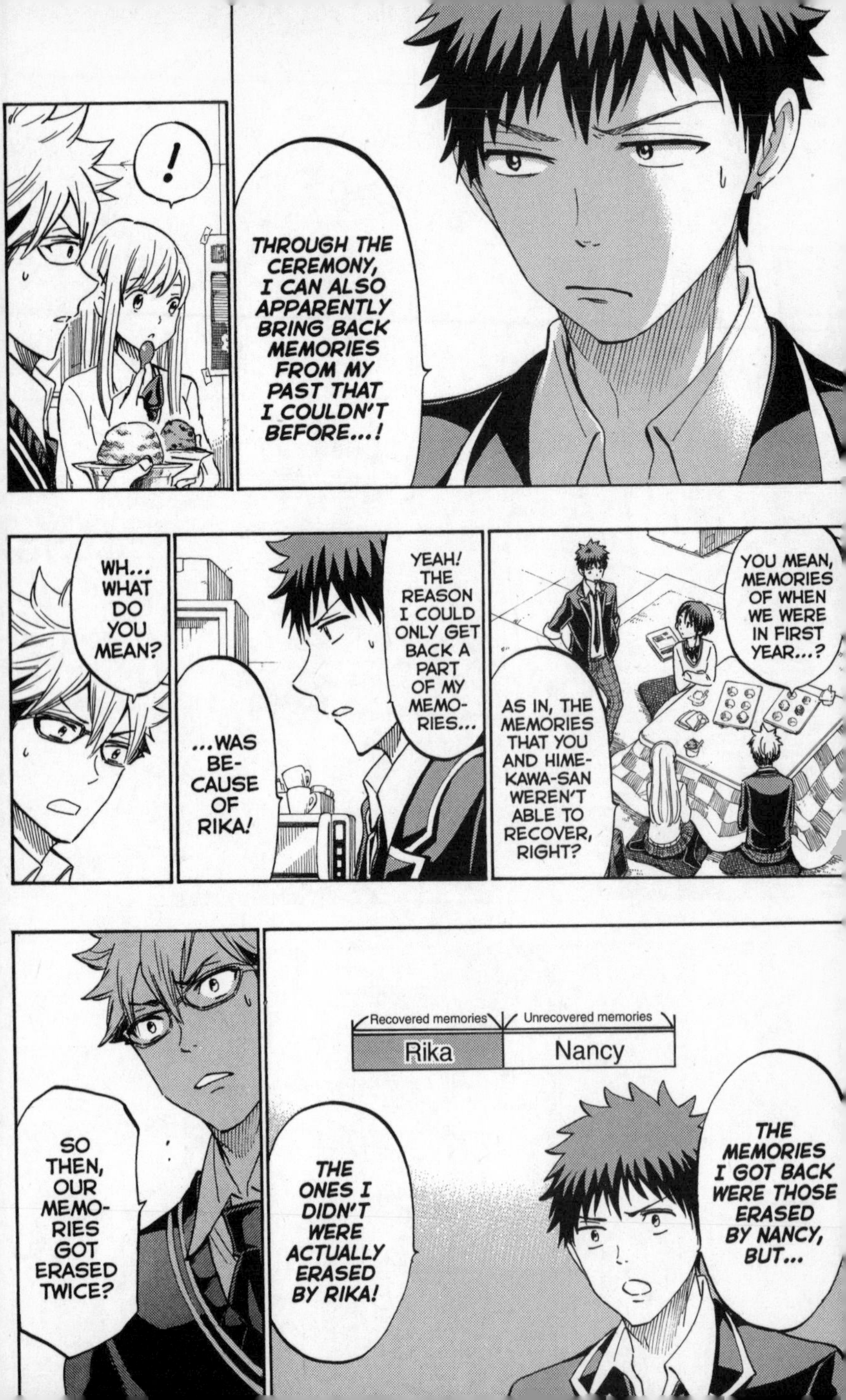
THROUGH THE CEREMONY, I CAN ALSO APPARENTLY BRING BACK MEMORIES FROM MY PAST THAT I COULDN'T BEFORE...!
!
YOU MEAN, MEMORIES OF WHEN WE WERE IN FIRST YEAR...?
AS IN, THE MEMORIES THAT YOU AND HIME-KAWA-SAN WEREN'T ABLE TO RECOVER, RIGHT?
YEAH! THE REASON I COULD ONLY GET BACK A PART OF MY MEMO-RIES...
...WAS BE-CAUSE OF RIKA!
WH... WHAT DO YOU MEAN?
Recovered memories
Unrecovered memories
Rika
Nancy
THE MEMORIES I GOT BACK WERE THOSE ERASED BY NANCY, BUT...
THE ONES I DIDN'T WERE ACTUALLY ERASED BY RIKA!
SO THEN, OUR MEMO-RIES GOT ERASED TWICE?

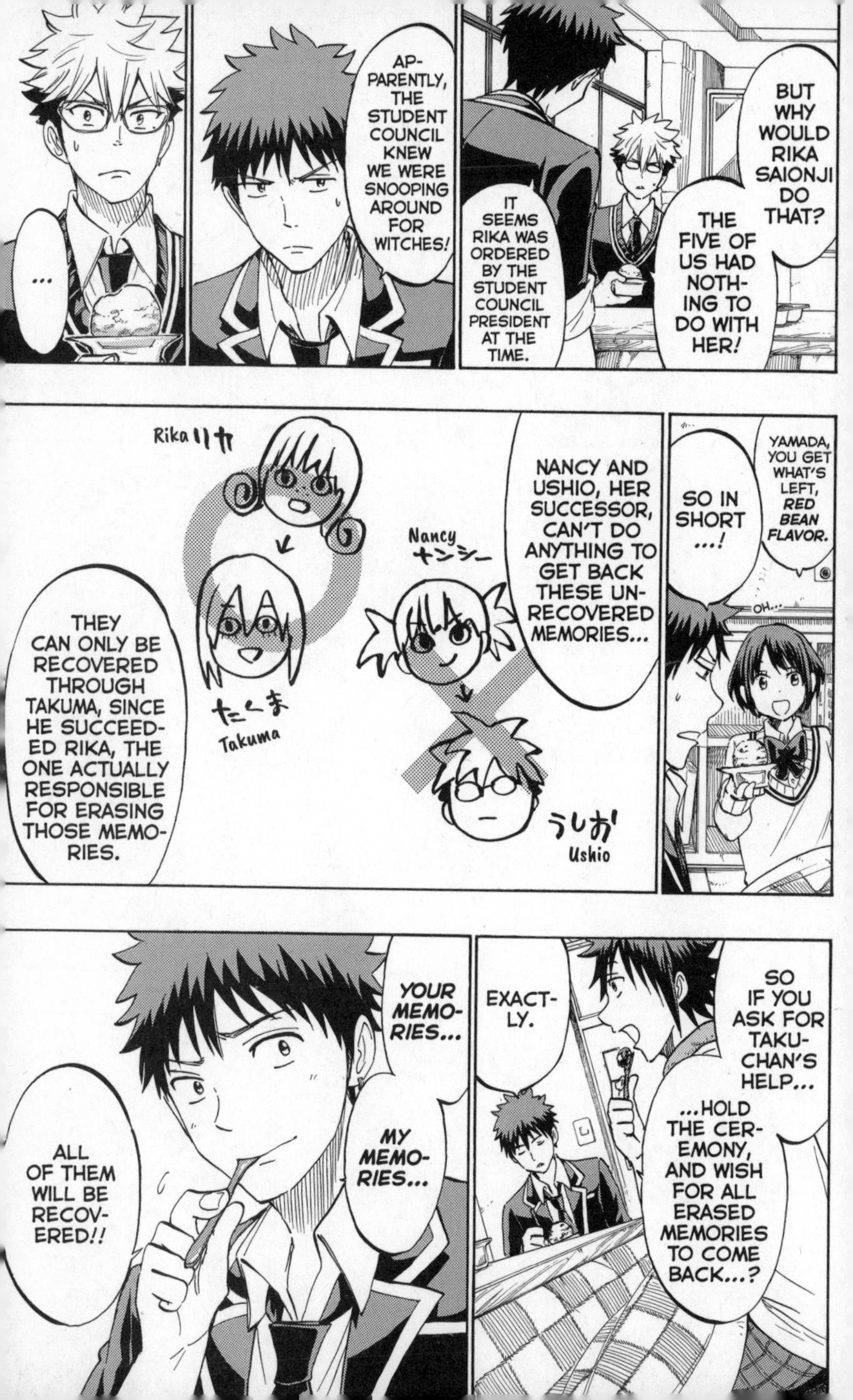
BUT WHY WOULD RIKA SAIONJI DO THAT?
THE FIVE OF US HAD NOTHING TO DO WITH HER!
IT SEEMS RIKA WAS ORDERED BY THE STUDENT COUNCIL PRESIDENT AT THE TIME.
APPARENTLY, THE STUDENT COUNCIL KNEW WE WERE SNOOPING AROUND FOR WITCHES!
...
YAMADA, YOU GET WHAT'S LEFT, RED BEAN FLAVOR.
OH...
SO IN SHORT...!
NANCY AND USHIO, HER SUCCESSOR, CAN'T DO ANYTHING TO GET BACK THESE UNRECOVERED MEMORIES...
Rika リカ
Nancy ナンシー
たくま Takuma
うしお Ushio
THEY CAN ONLY BE RECOVERED THROUGH TAKUMA, SINCE HE SUCCEEDED RIKA, THE ONE ACTUALLY RESPONSIBLE FOR ERASING THOSE MEMORIES.
SO IF YOU ASK FOR TAKU-CHAN'S HELP...
...HOLD THE CEREMONY, AND WISH FOR ALL ERASED MEMORIES TO COME BACK...?
EXACTLY.
YOUR MEMORIES...
MY MEMORIES...
ALL OF THEM WILL BE RECOVERED!!

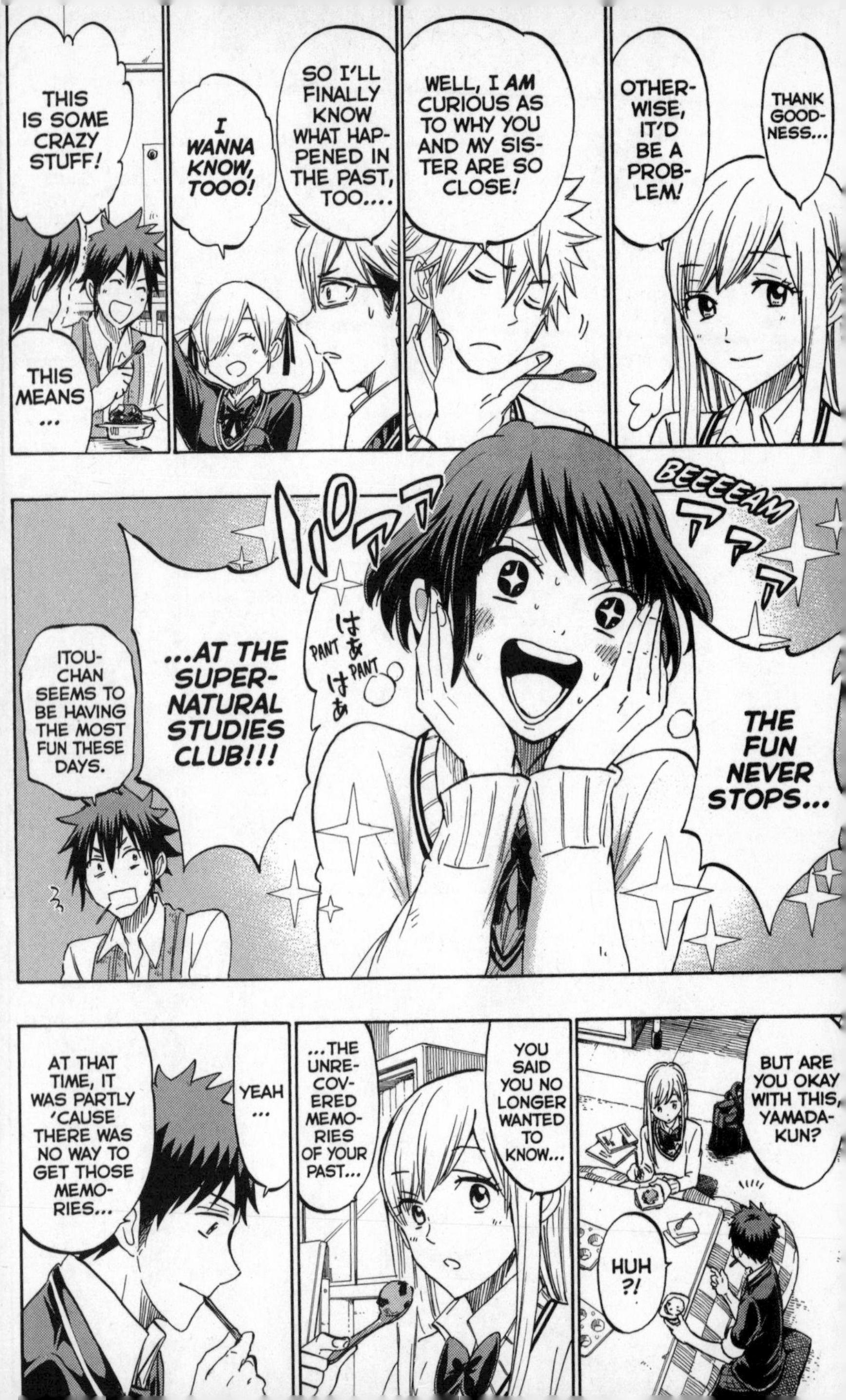
THANK GOODNESS...
OTHERWISE, IT'D BE A PROBLEM!
WELL, I *AM* CURIOUS AS TO WHY YOU AND MY SISTER ARE SO CLOSE!
SO I'LL FINALLY KNOW WHAT HAPPENED IN THE PAST, TOO....
I WANNA KNOW, TOOO!
THIS IS SOME CRAZY STUFF!
THIS MEANS ...
BEEEEAM
パァァァ
THE FUN NEVER STOPS...
...AT THE SUPERNATURAL STUDIES CLUB!!!
はあ PANT はあ PANT
ITOU-CHAN SEEMS TO BE HAVING THE MOST FUN THESE DAYS.
BUT ARE YOU OKAY WITH THIS, YAMADA-KUN?
HUH ?!
YOU SAID YOU NO LONGER WANTED TO KNOW...
...THE UNRECOVERED MEMORIES OF YOUR PAST...
YEAH ...
AT THAT TIME, IT WAS PARTLY 'CAUSE THERE WAS NO WAY TO GET THOSE MEMORIES...

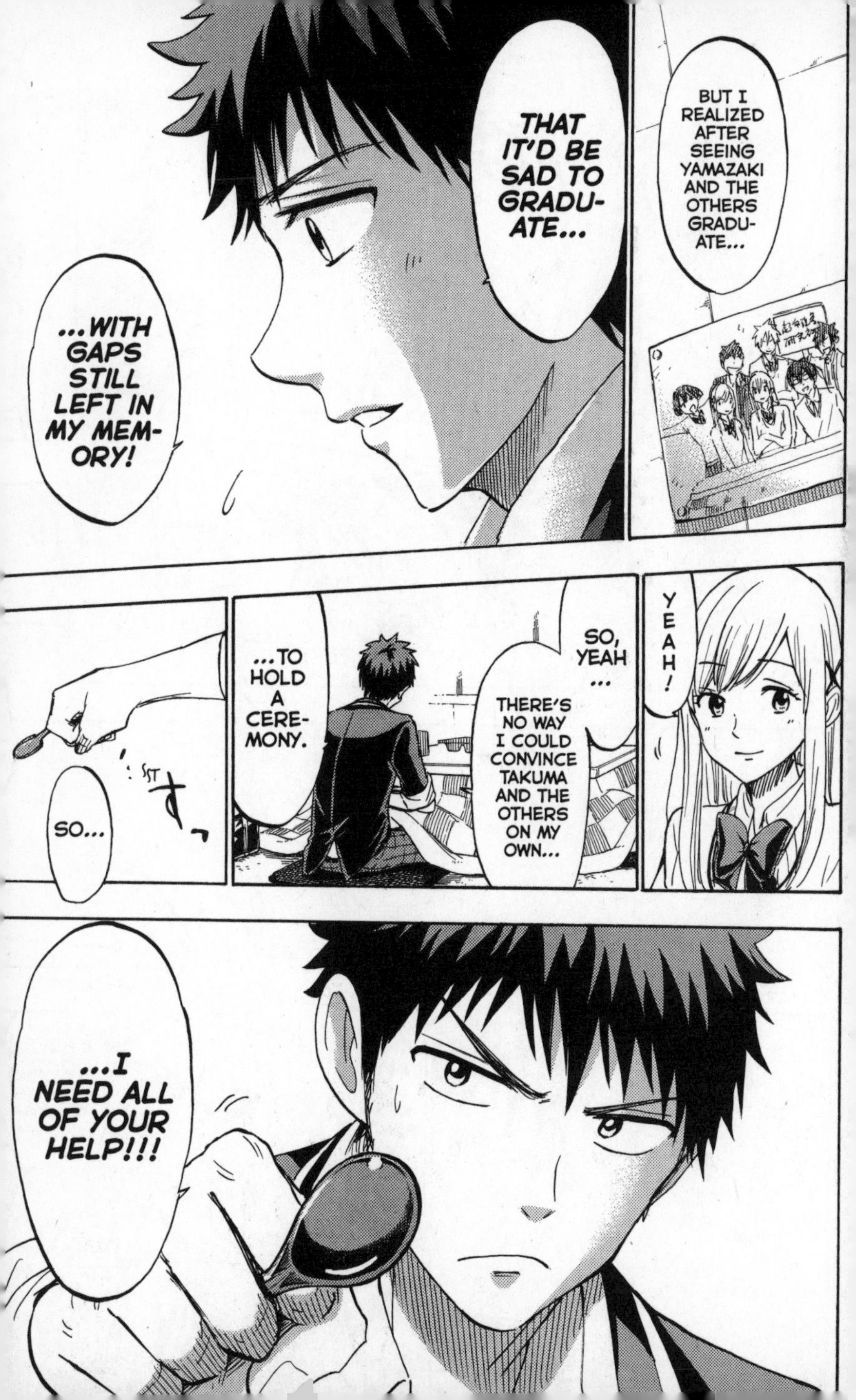
BUT I REALIZED AFTER SEEING YAMAZAKI AND THE OTHERS GRADUATE...
THAT IT'D BE SAD TO GRADUATE...
...WITH GAPS STILL LEFT IN MY MEMORY!
YEAH!
SO, YEAH...
THERE'S NO WAY I COULD CONVINCE TAKUMA AND THE OTHERS ON MY OWN...
...TO HOLD A CEREMONY.
SST
SO...
...I NEED ALL OF YOUR HELP!!!

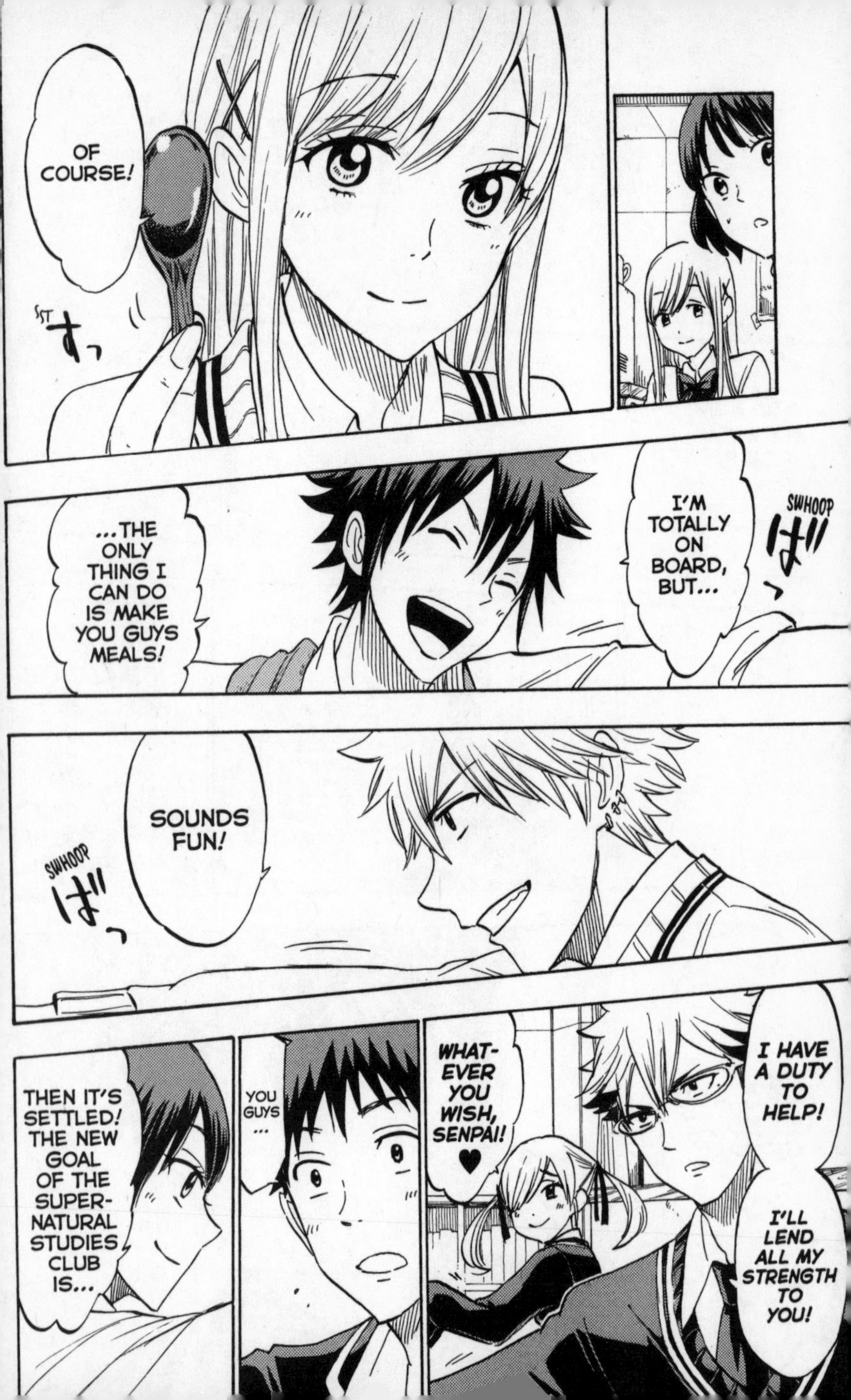
OF COURSE!
SST
すっ
SWHOOP
ばっ
I'M TOTALLY ON BOARD, BUT...
...THE ONLY THING I CAN DO IS MAKE YOU GUYS MEALS!
SOUNDS FUN!
SWHOOP
ばっ
I HAVE A DUTY TO HELP!
WHATEVER YOU WISH, SENPAI! ♥
I'LL LEND ALL MY STRENGTH TO YOU!
YOU GUYS...
THEN IT'S SETTLED! THE NEW GOAL OF THE SUPERNATURAL STUDIES CLUB IS...

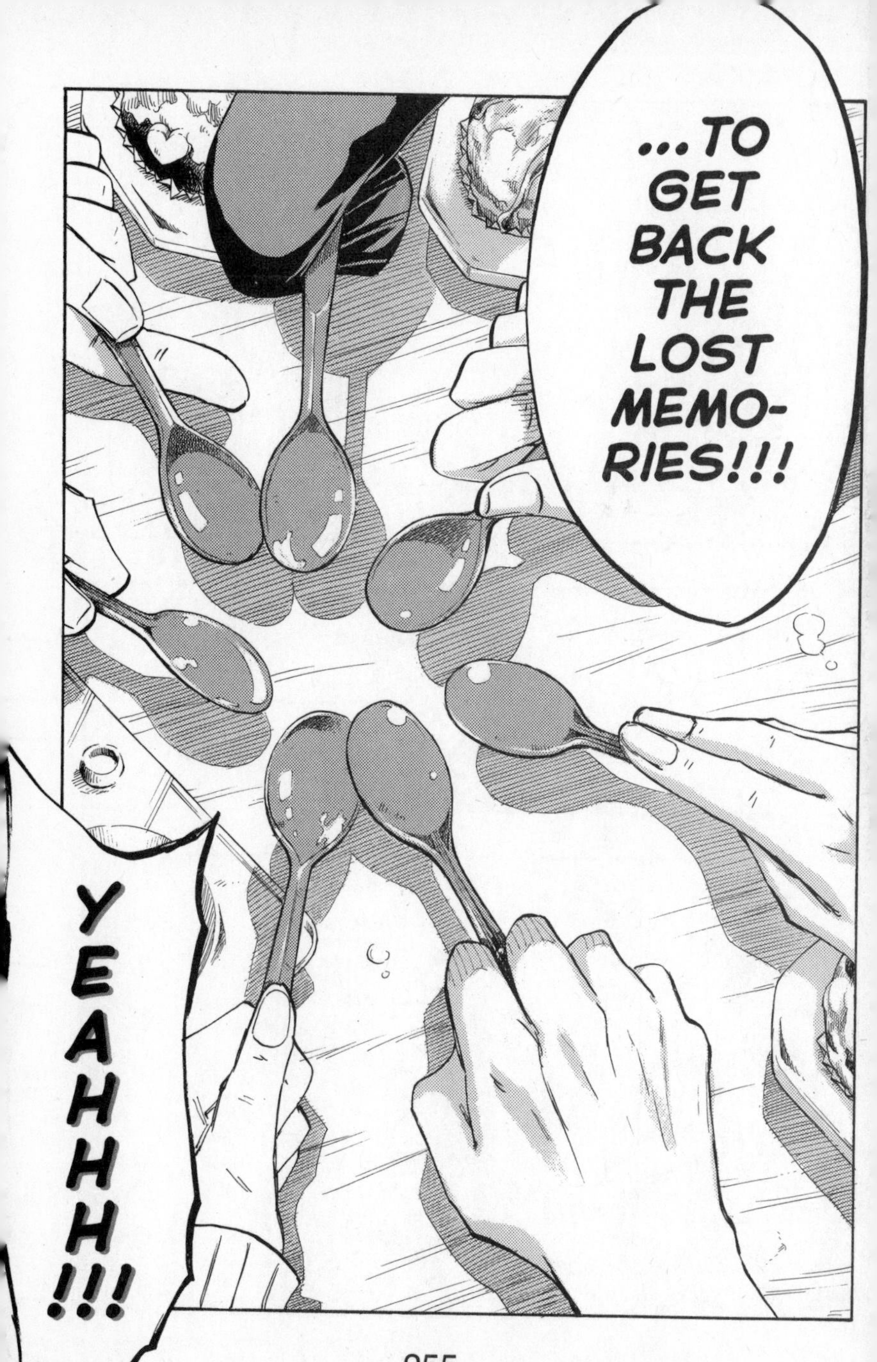
...TO GET BACK THE LOST MEMO-RIES!!!
YEAHHH!!!

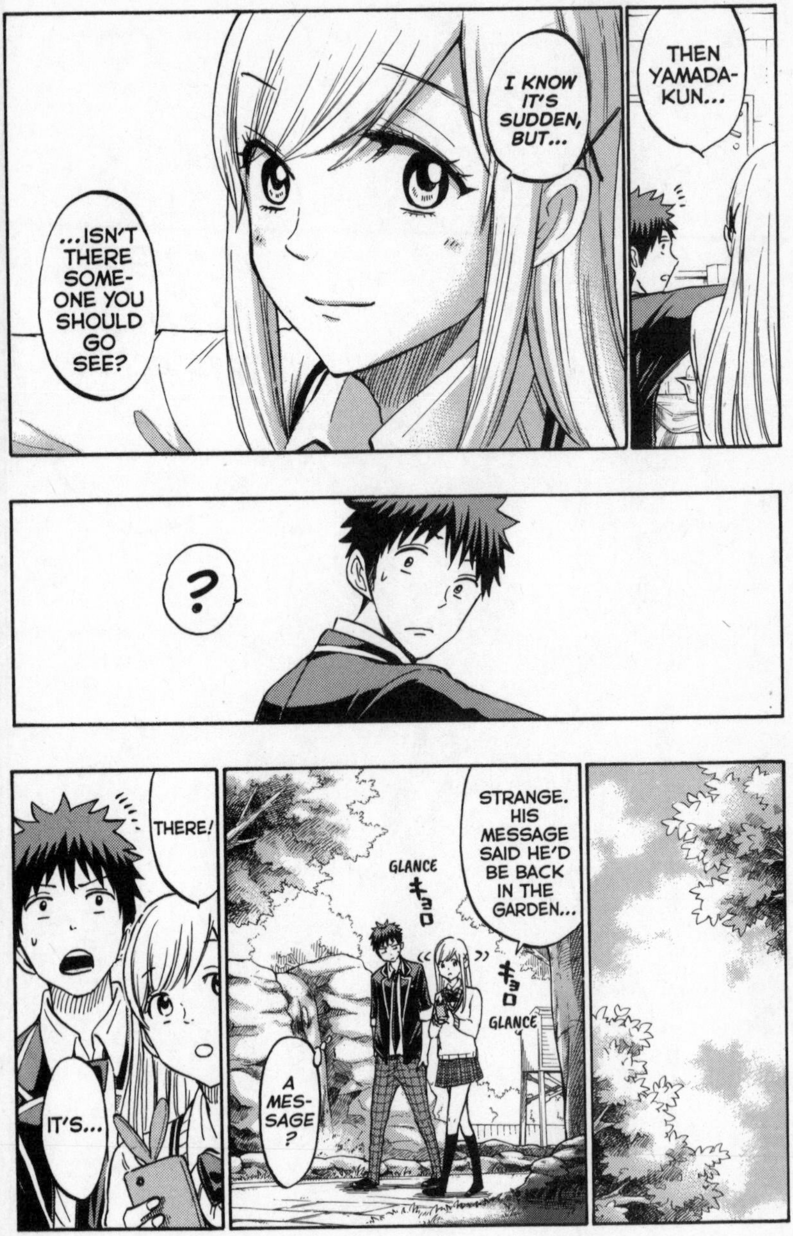
THEN YAMADA-KUN...
I KNOW IT'S SUDDEN, BUT...
...ISN'T THERE SOME-ONE YOU SHOULD GO SEE?
?
STRANGE. HIS MESSAGE SAID HE'D BE BACK IN THE GARDEN...
GLANCE キョロ
キョロ GLANCE
A MES-SAGE?
THERE!
IT'S...

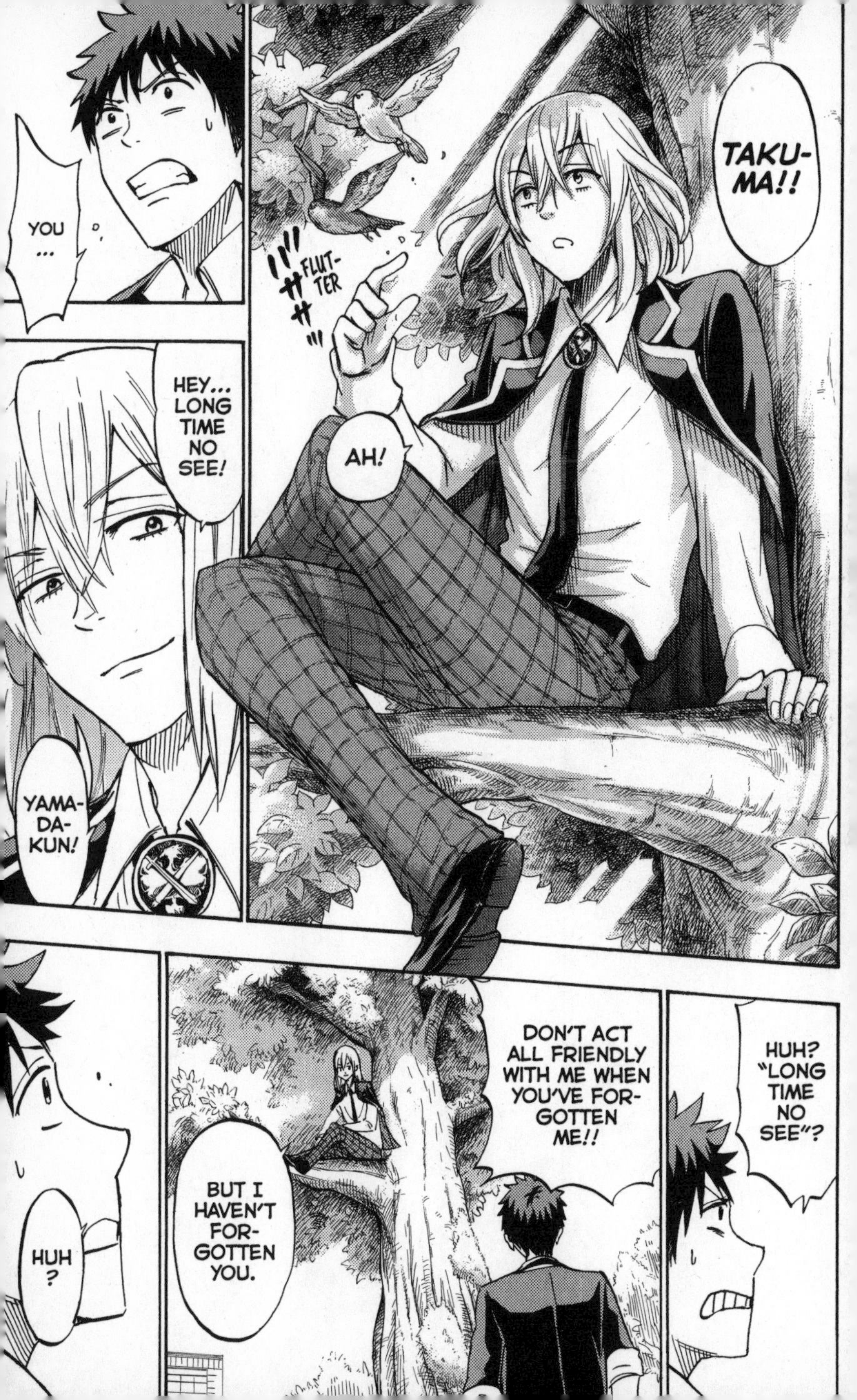
TAKU-MA!!
FLUT-TER
AH!
YOU...
HEY... LONG TIME NO SEE!
YAMA-DA-KUN!
HUH? "LONG TIME NO SEE"?
DON'T ACT ALL FRIENDLY WITH ME WHEN YOU'VE FOR-GOTTEN ME!!
BUT I HAVEN'T FOR-GOTTEN YOU.
HUH?

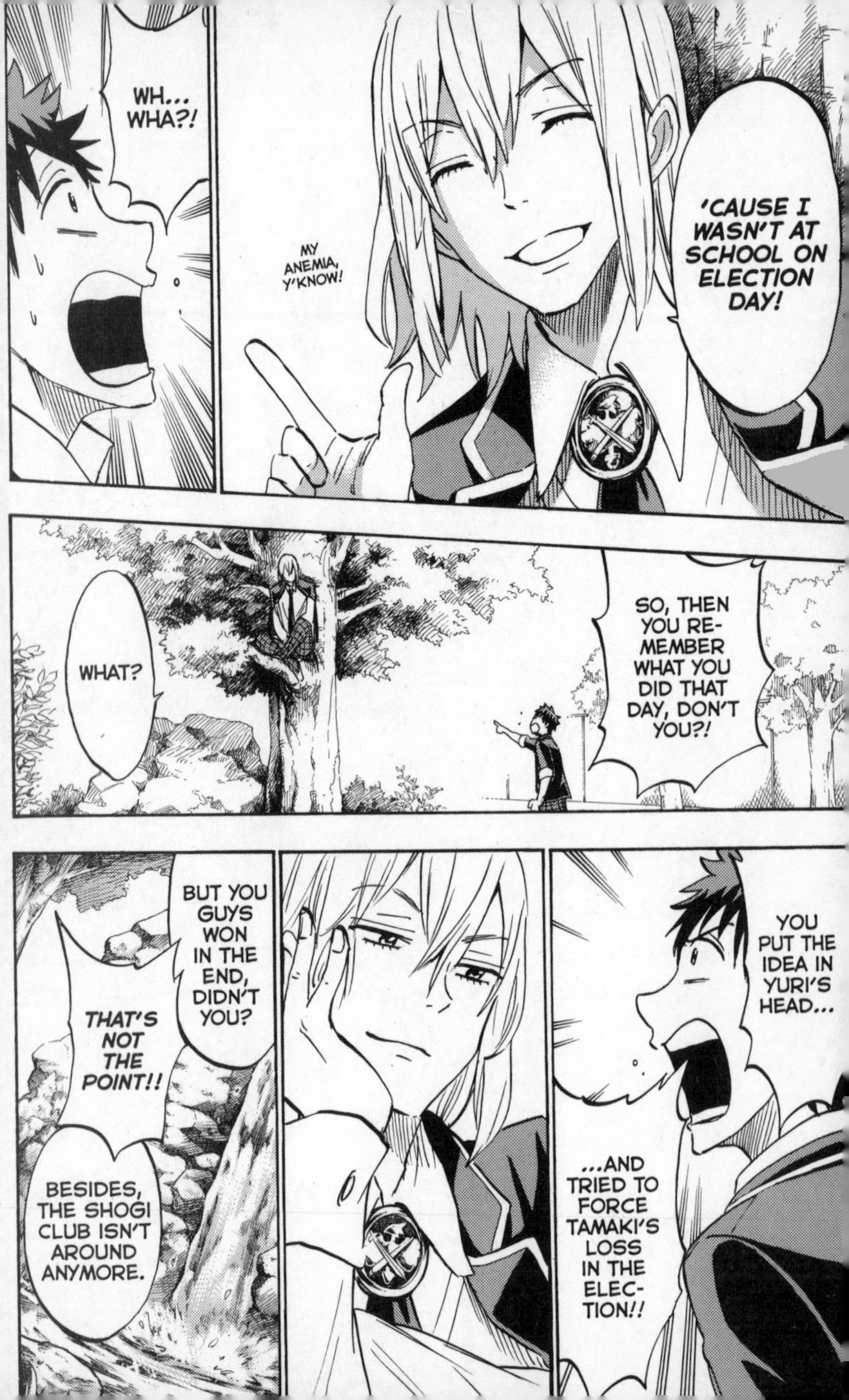
'CAUSE I WASN'T AT SCHOOL ON ELECTION DAY!
MY ANEMIA, Y'KNOW!
WH... WHA?!
SO, THEN YOU RE-MEMBER WHAT YOU DID THAT DAY, DON'T YOU?!
WHAT?
YOU PUT THE IDEA IN YURI'S HEAD...
...AND TRIED TO FORCE TAMAKI'S LOSS IN THE ELEC-TION!!
BUT YOU GUYS WON IN THE END, DIDN'T YOU?
THAT'S NOT THE POINT!!
BESIDES, THE SHOGI CLUB ISN'T AROUND ANYMORE.

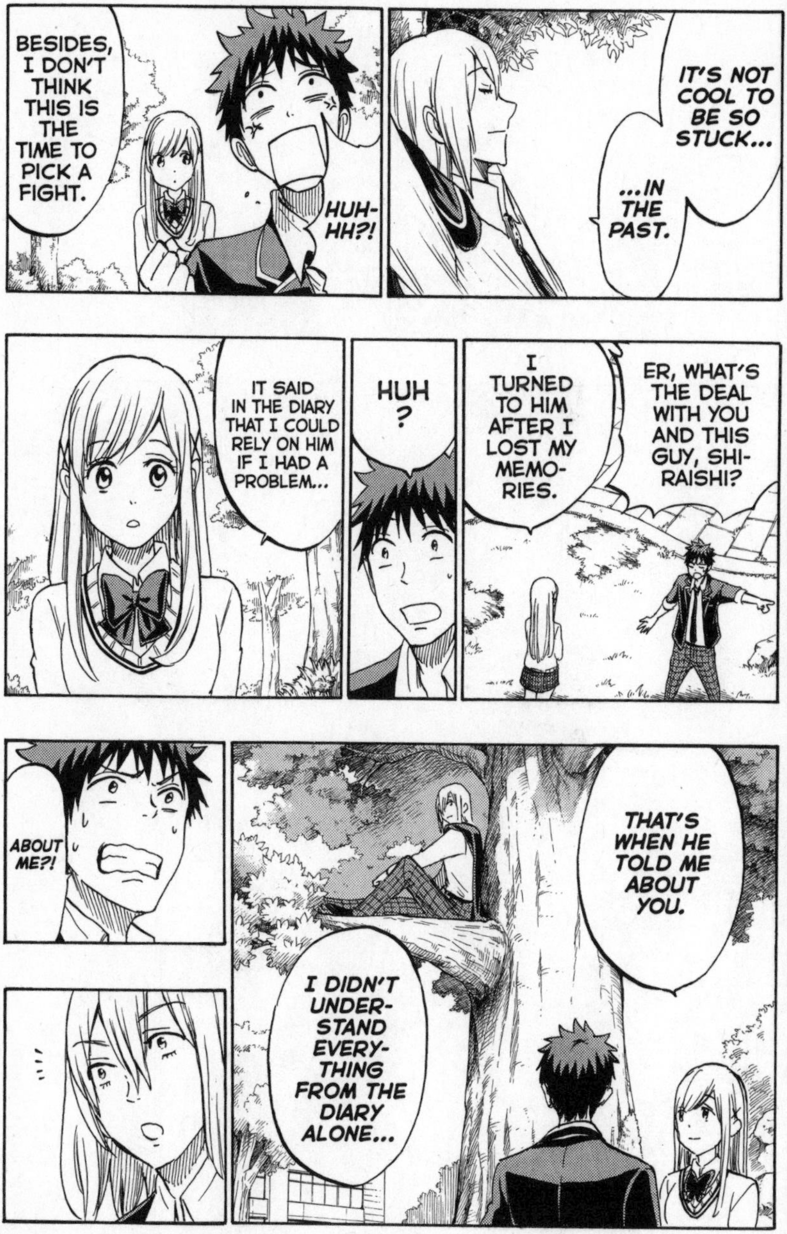
IT'S NOT COOL TO BE SO STUCK...
...IN THE PAST.
BESIDES, I DON'T THINK THIS IS THE TIME TO PICK A FIGHT.
HUH-HH?!
ER, WHAT'S THE DEAL WITH YOU AND THIS GUY, SHI-RAISHI?
I TURNED TO HIM AFTER I LOST MY MEMO-RIES.
HUH?
IT SAID IN THE DIARY THAT I COULD RELY ON HIM IF I HAD A PROBLEM...
THAT'S WHEN HE TOLD ME ABOUT YOU.
I DIDN'T UNDER-STAND EVERY-THING FROM THE DIARY ALONE...
ABOUT ME?!

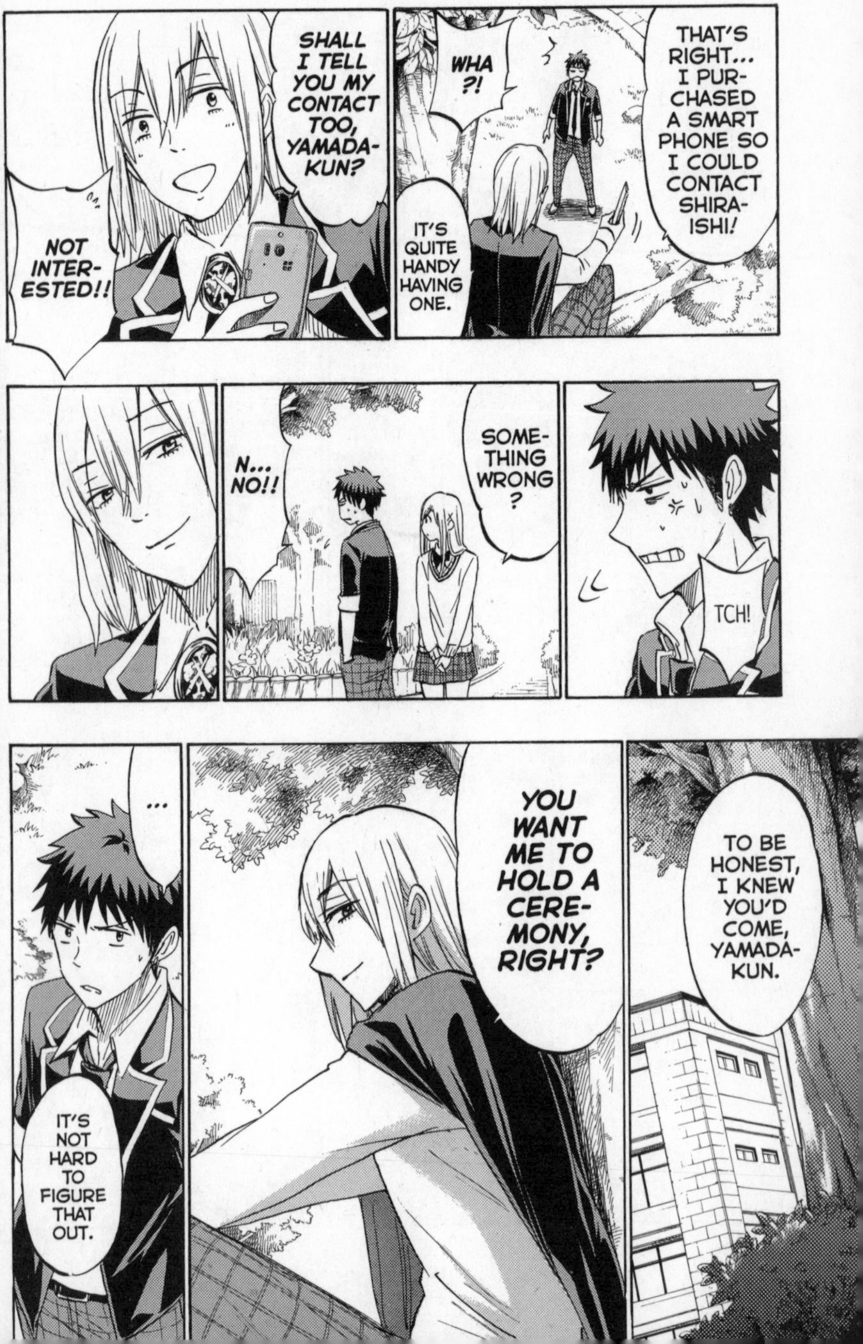
THAT'S RIGHT... I PURCHASED A SMART PHONE SO I COULD CONTACT SHIRAISHI!
WHA?!
IT'S QUITE HANDY HAVING ONE.
SHALL I TELL YOU MY CONTACT TOO, YAMADA-KUN?
NOT INTERESTED!!
TCH!
SOMETHING WRONG?
N... NO!!
TO BE HONEST, I KNEW YOU'D COME, YAMADA-KUN.
YOU WANT ME TO HOLD A CEREMONY, RIGHT?
...
IT'S NOT HARD TO FIGURE THAT OUT.

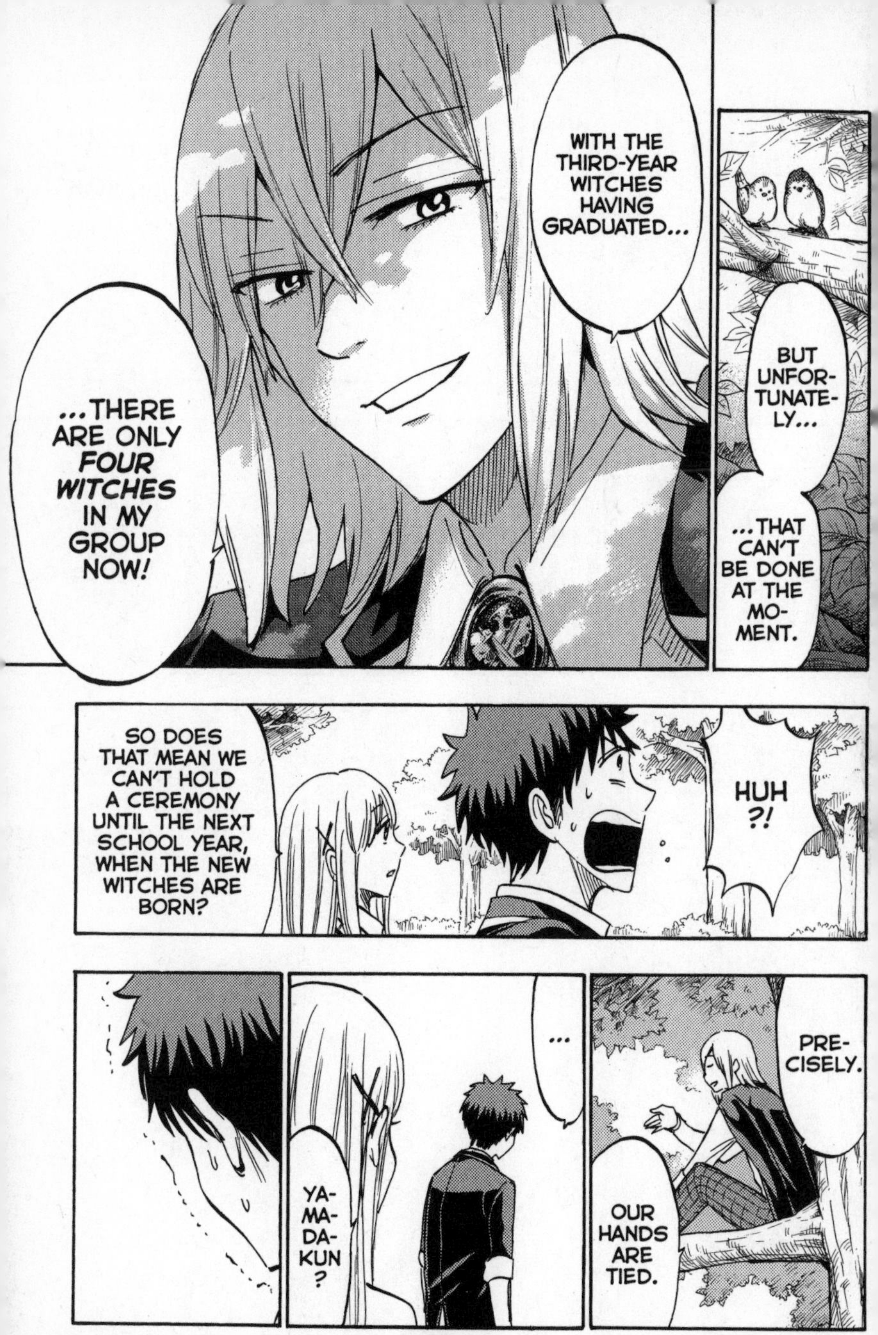
BUT UNFOR-TUNATE-LY...
...THAT CAN'T BE DONE AT THE MO-MENT.
WITH THE THIRD-YEAR WITCHES HAVING GRADUATED...
...THERE ARE ONLY *FOUR WITCHES* IN MY GROUP NOW!
HUH?!
SO DOES THAT MEAN WE CAN'T HOLD A CEREMONY UNTIL THE NEXT SCHOOL YEAR, WHEN THE NEW WITCHES ARE BORN?
PRE-CISELY.
OUR HANDS ARE TIED.
...
YA-MA-DA-KUN?

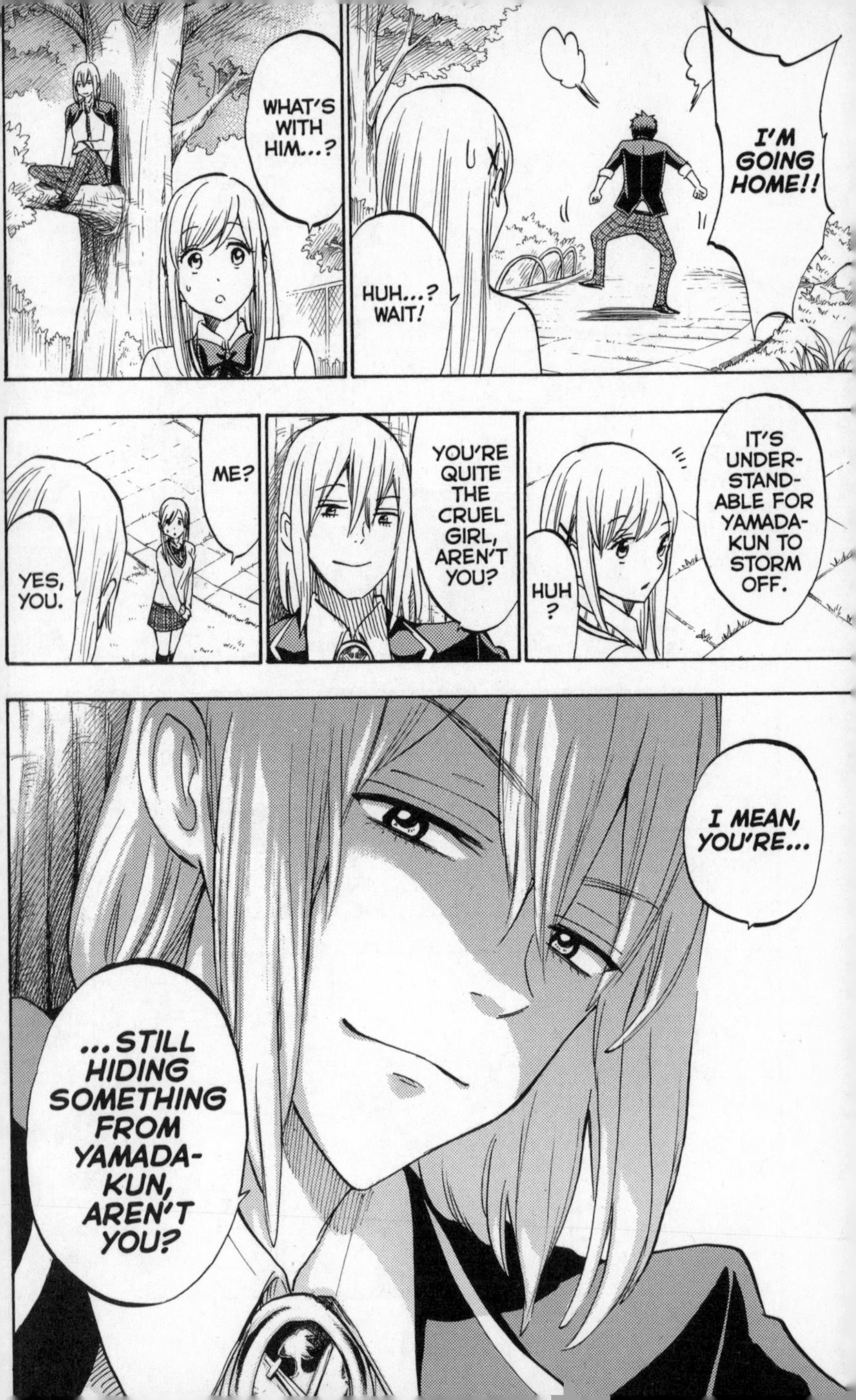
I'M GOING HOME!!
HUH...? WAIT!
WHAT'S WITH HIM...?
IT'S UNDERSTANDABLE FOR YAMADA-KUN TO STORM OFF.
HUH?
YOU'RE QUITE THE CRUEL GIRL, AREN'T YOU?
ME?
YES, YOU.
I MEAN, YOU'RE...
...STILL HIDING SOMETHING FROM YAMADA-KUN, AREN'T YOU?

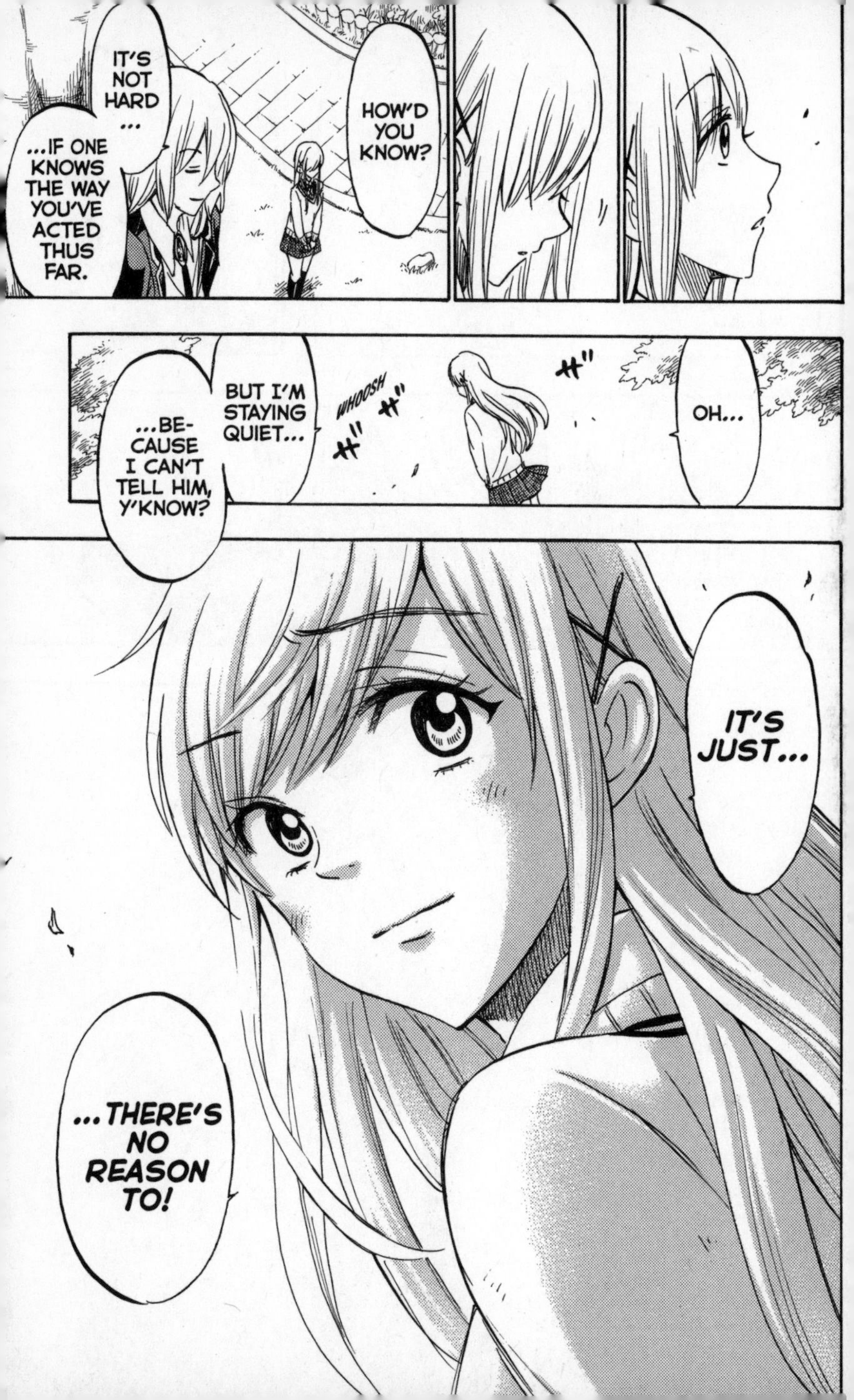
HOW'D YOU KNOW?
IT'S NOT HARD ...
...IF ONE KNOWS THE WAY YOU'VE ACTED THUS FAR.
OH...
WHOOSH
BUT I'M STAYING QUIET...
...BE-CAUSE I CAN'T TELL HIM, Y'KNOW?
IT'S JUST...
...THERE'S NO REASON TO!

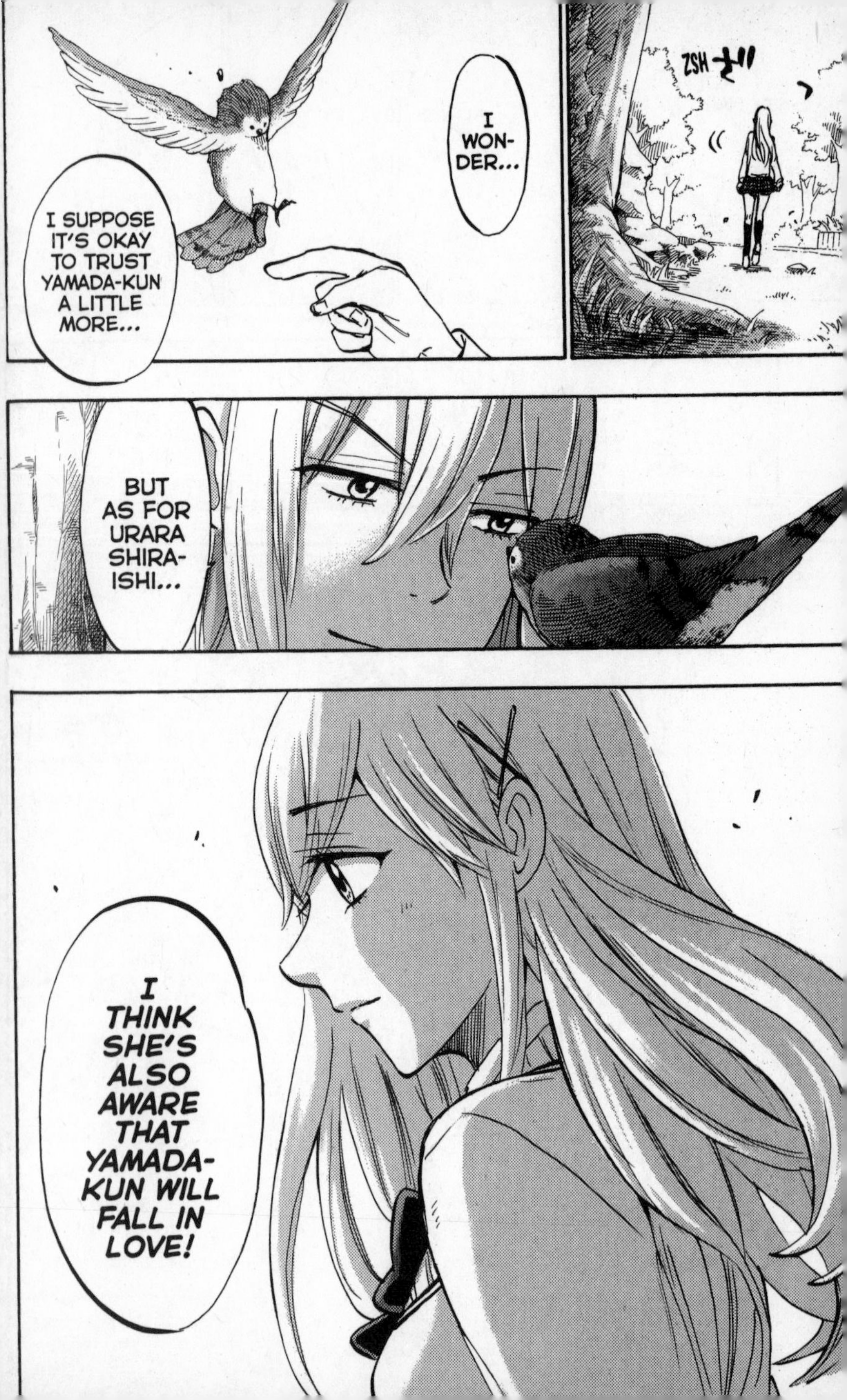
ZSH
I WONDER...
I SUPPOSE IT'S OKAY TO TRUST YAMADA-KUN A LITTLE MORE...
BUT AS FOR URARA SHIRAISHI...
I THINK SHE'S ALSO AWARE THAT YAMADA-KUN WILL FALL IN LOVE!

CHAPTER 185: What can't be learned at school.

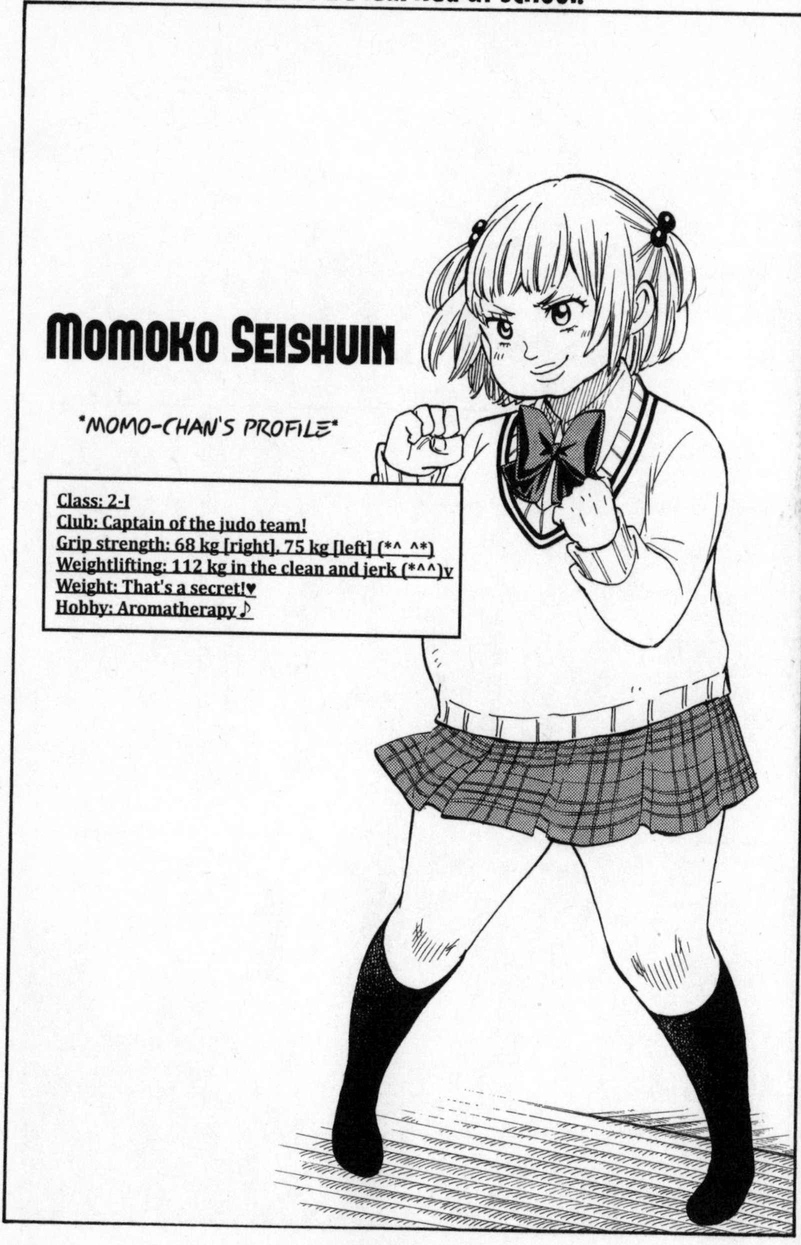
MOMOKO SEISHUIN
MOMO-CHAN'S PROFILE
Class: 2-I
Club: Captain of the judo team!
Grip strength: 68 kg [right], 75 kg [left] (*^_^*)
Weightlifting: 112 kg in the clean and jerk (*^^)v
Weight: That's a secret!♥
Hobby: Aromatherapy♪

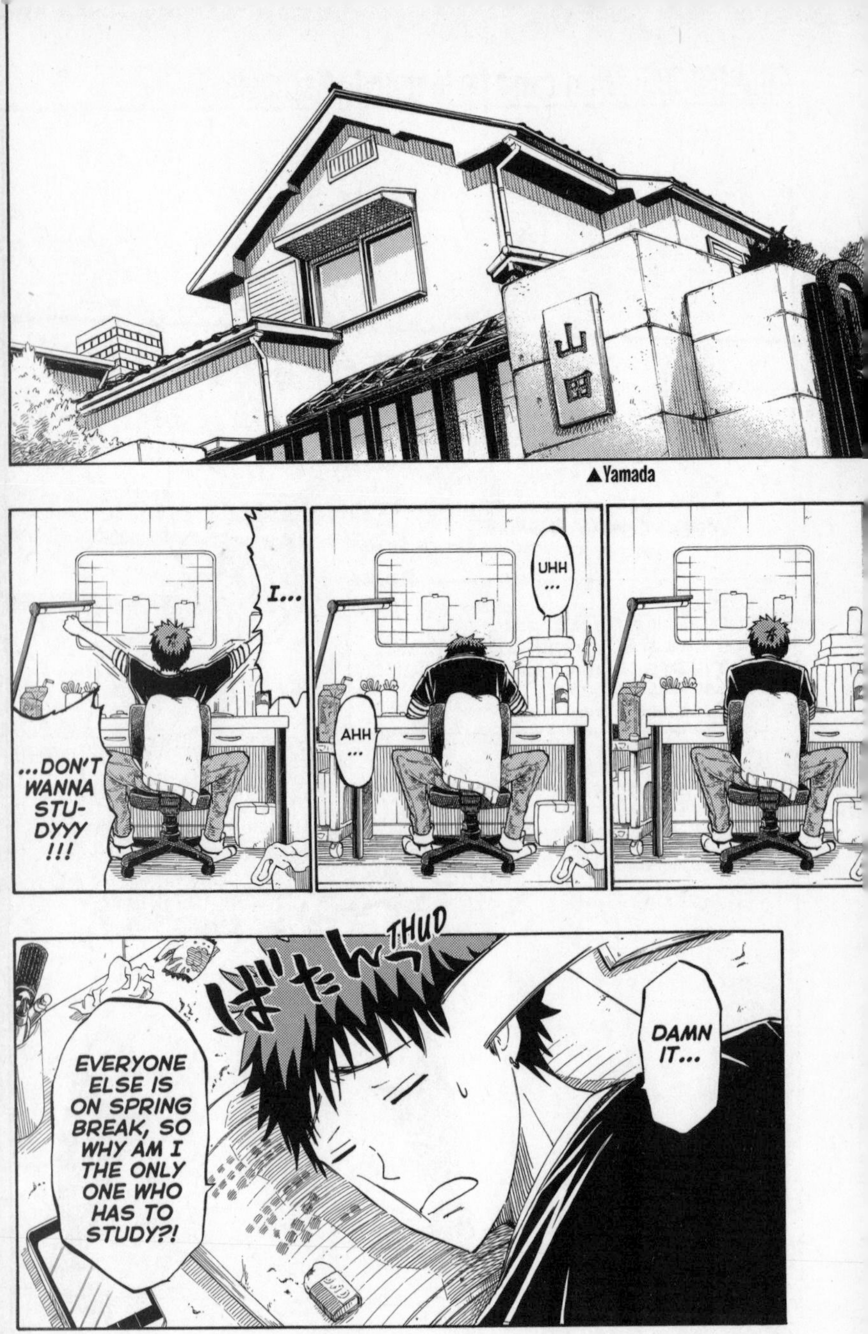
山田
▲Yamada
UHH ...
AHH ...
I...
...DON'T WANNA STU-DYYY !!!
ばたんっ THUD
DAMN IT...
EVERYONE ELSE IS ON SPRING BREAK, SO WHY AM I THE ONLY ONE WHO HAS TO STUDY?!

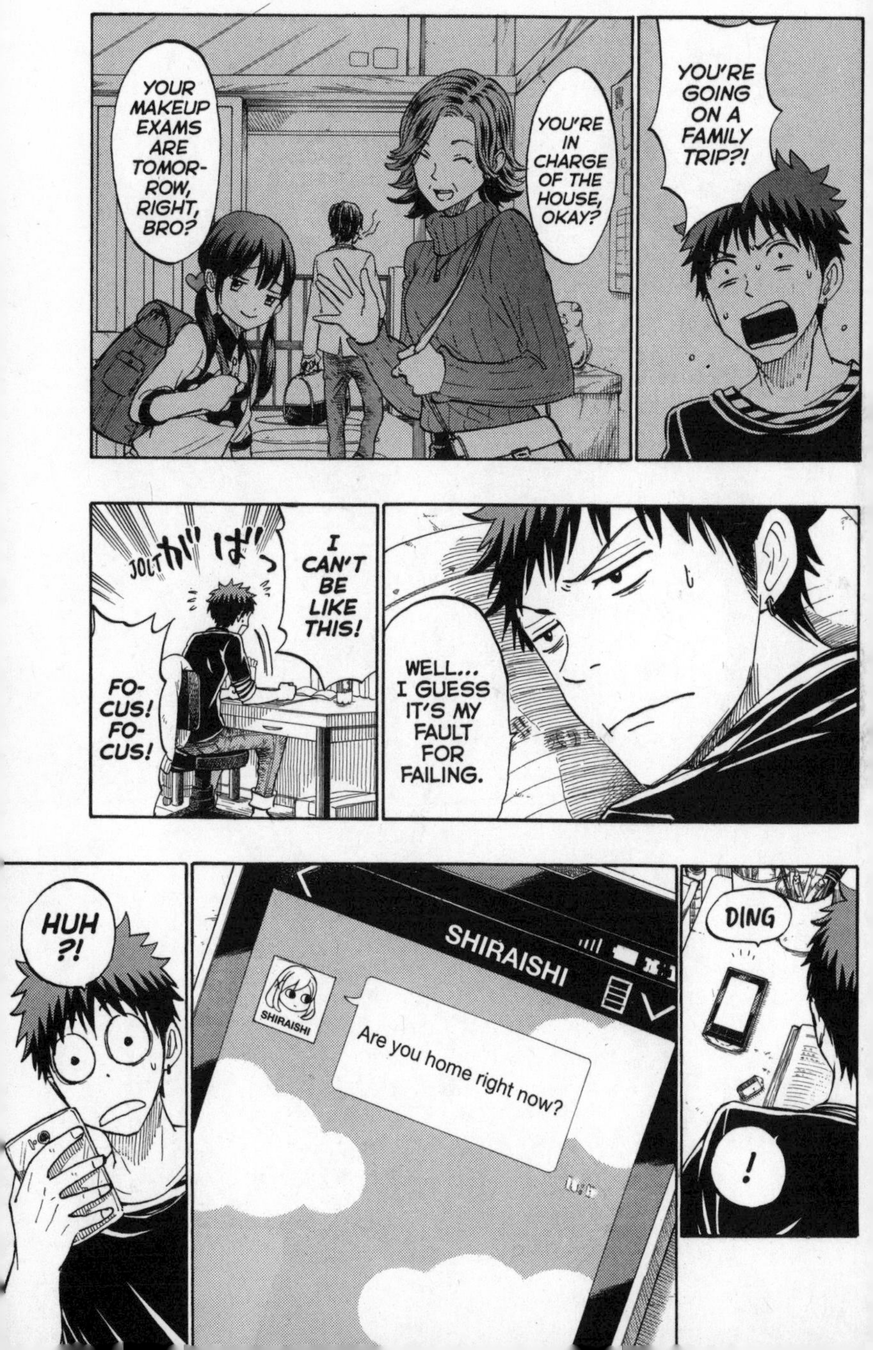
YOU'RE GOING ON A FAMILY TRIP?!
YOU'RE IN CHARGE OF THE HOUSE, OKAY?
YOUR MAKEUP EXAMS ARE TOMOR-ROW, RIGHT, BRO?
WELL... I GUESS IT'S MY FAULT FOR FAILING.
I CAN'T BE LIKE THIS!
JOLT がばっ
FO-CUS! FO-CUS!
DING
!
SHIRAISHI
SHIRAISHI
Are you home right now?
HUH ?!

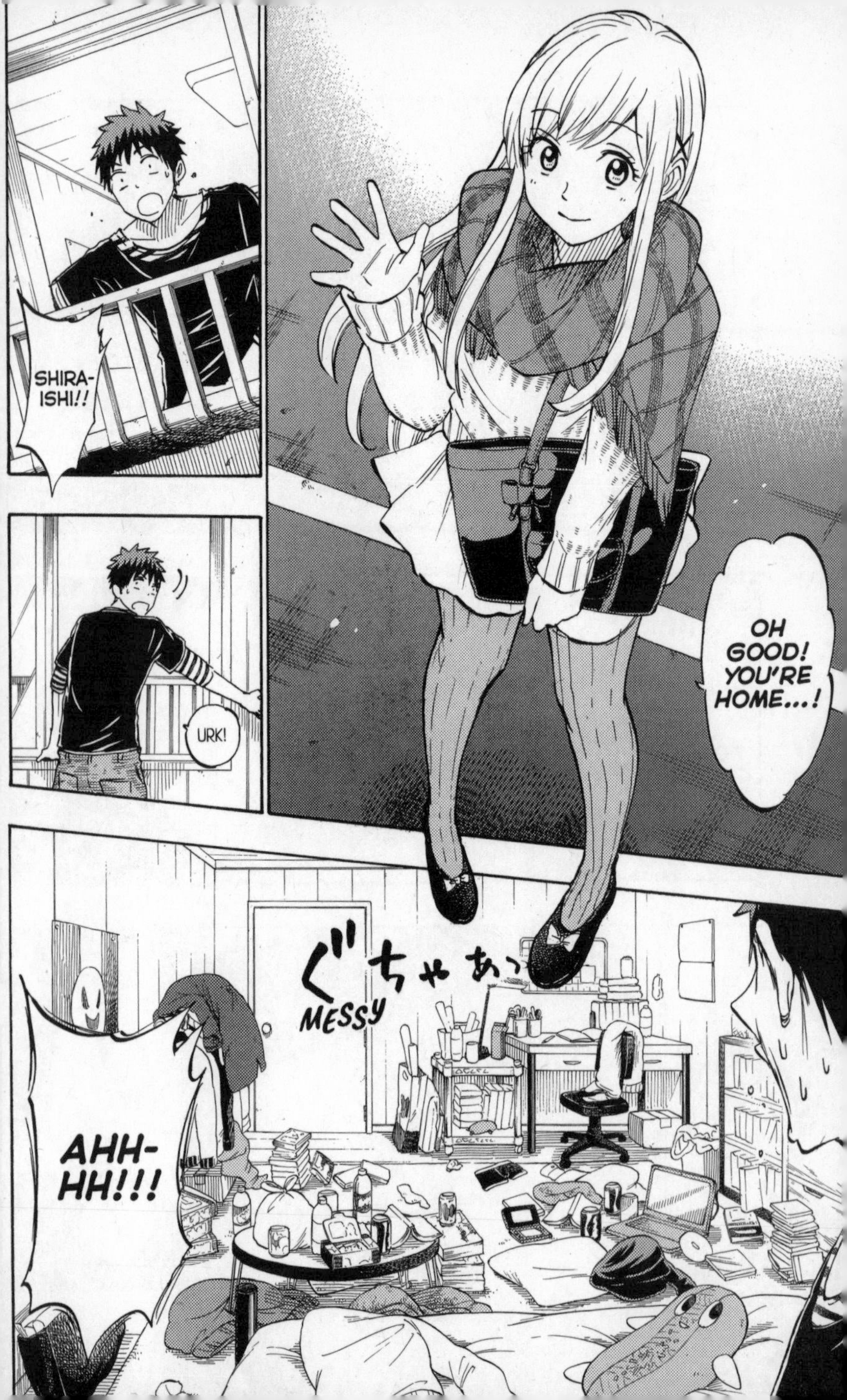
OH GOOD! YOU'RE HOME...!
SHIRA-ISHI!!
URK!
ぐちゃあっ
MESSY
AHH-HH!!!

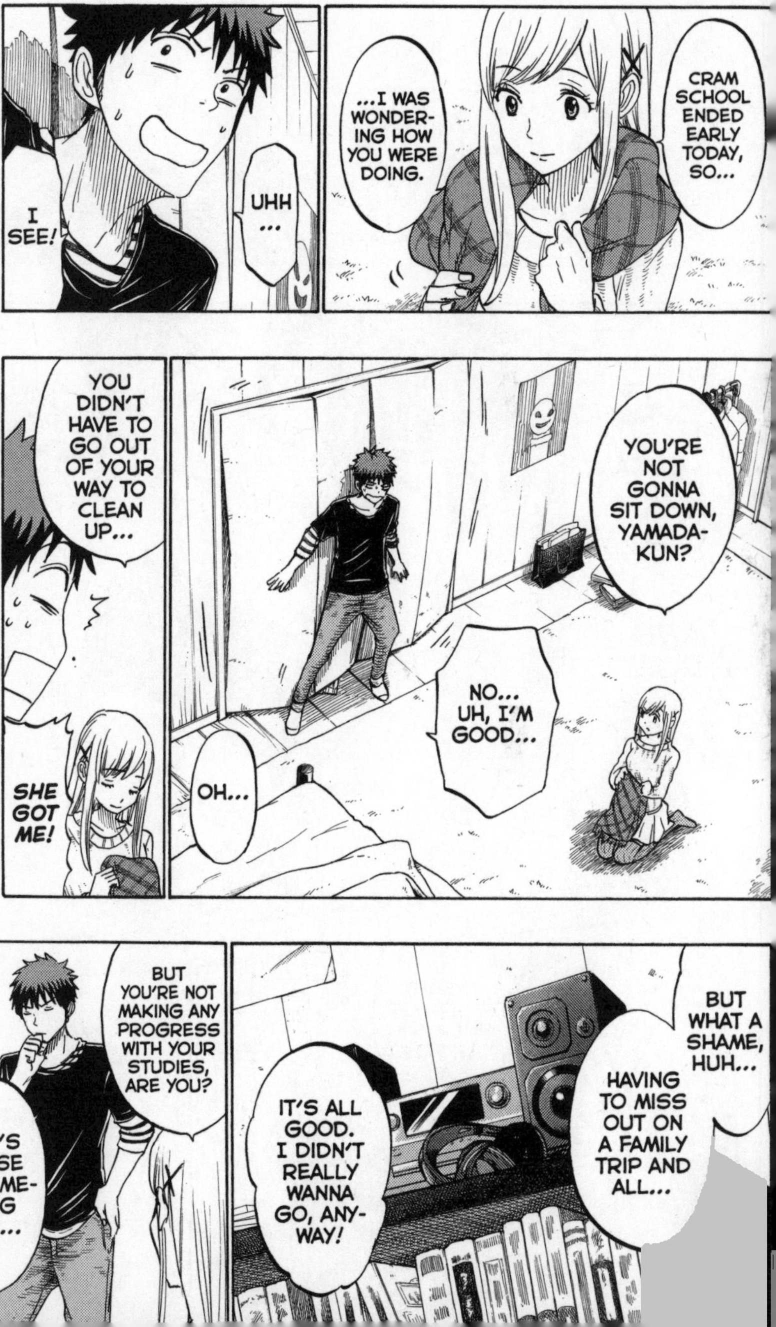
CRAM SCHOOL ENDED EARLY TODAY, SO...
...I WAS WONDERING HOW YOU WERE DOING.
UHH...
I SEE!
YOU'RE NOT GONNA SIT DOWN, YAMADA-KUN?
NO... UH, I'M GOOD...
OH...
YOU DIDN'T HAVE TO GO OUT OF YOUR WAY TO CLEAN UP...
SHE GOT ME!
BUT WHAT A SHAME, HUH...
HAVING TO MISS OUT ON A FAMILY TRIP AND ALL...
IT'S ALL GOOD. I DIDN'T REALLY WANNA GO, ANYWAY!
BUT YOU'RE NOT MAKING ANY PROGRESS WITH YOUR STUDIES, ARE YOU?
ゴホン
AHEM
THAT'S 'CAUSE OF SOMETHING ELSE...

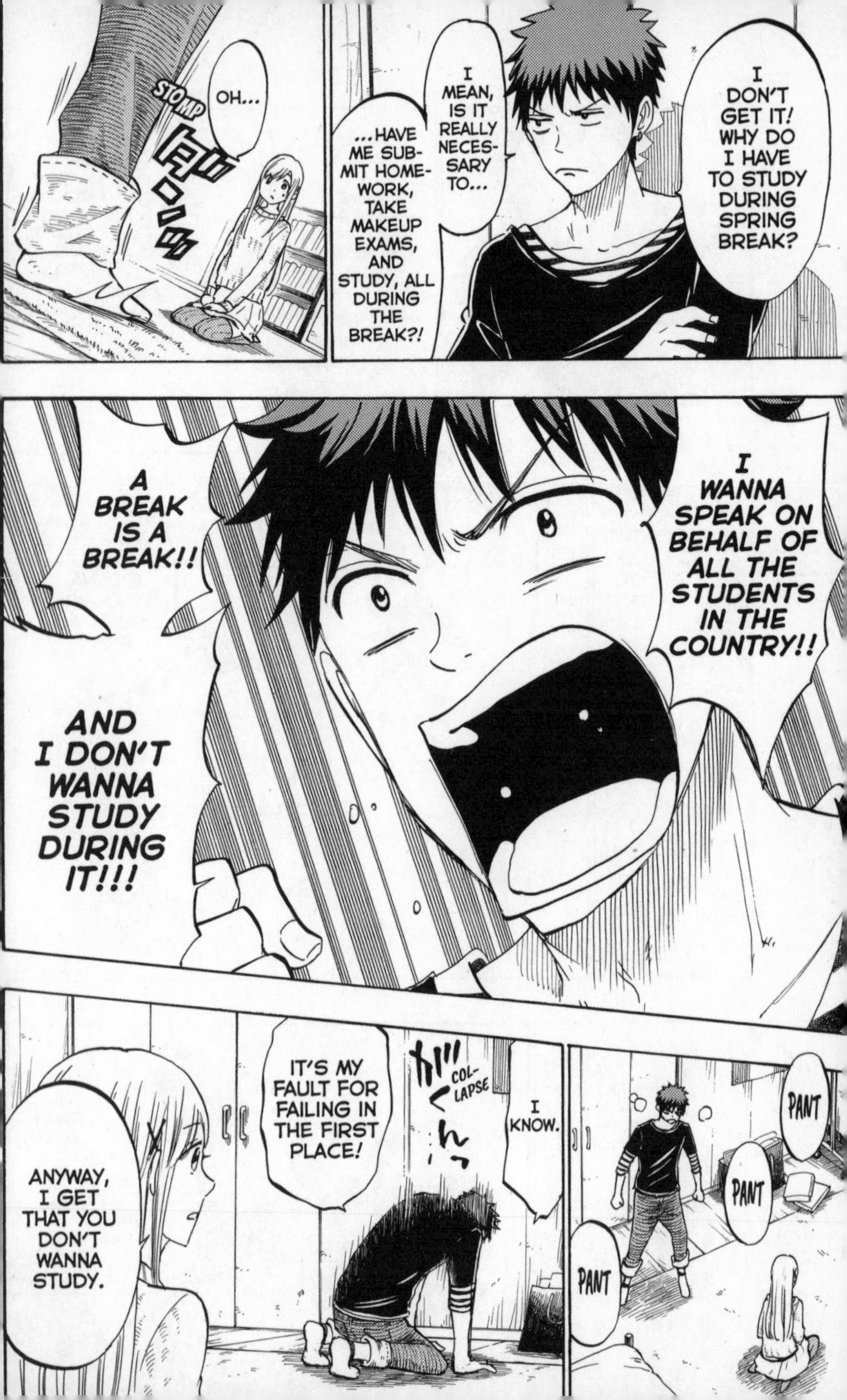
I DON'T GET IT! WHY DO I HAVE TO STUDY DURING SPRING BREAK?
I MEAN, IS IT REALLY NECESSARY TO...
...HAVE ME SUBMIT HOMEWORK, TAKE MAKEUP EXAMS, AND STUDY, ALL DURING THE BREAK?!
STOMP
OH...
I WANNA SPEAK ON BEHALF OF ALL THE STUDENTS IN THE COUNTRY!!
A BREAK IS A BREAK!!
AND I DON'T WANNA STUDY DURING IT!!!
PANT
PANT
PANT
I KNOW.
COLLAPSE
IT'S MY FAULT FOR FAILING IN THE FIRST PLACE!
ANYWAY, I GET THAT YOU DON'T WANNA STUDY.

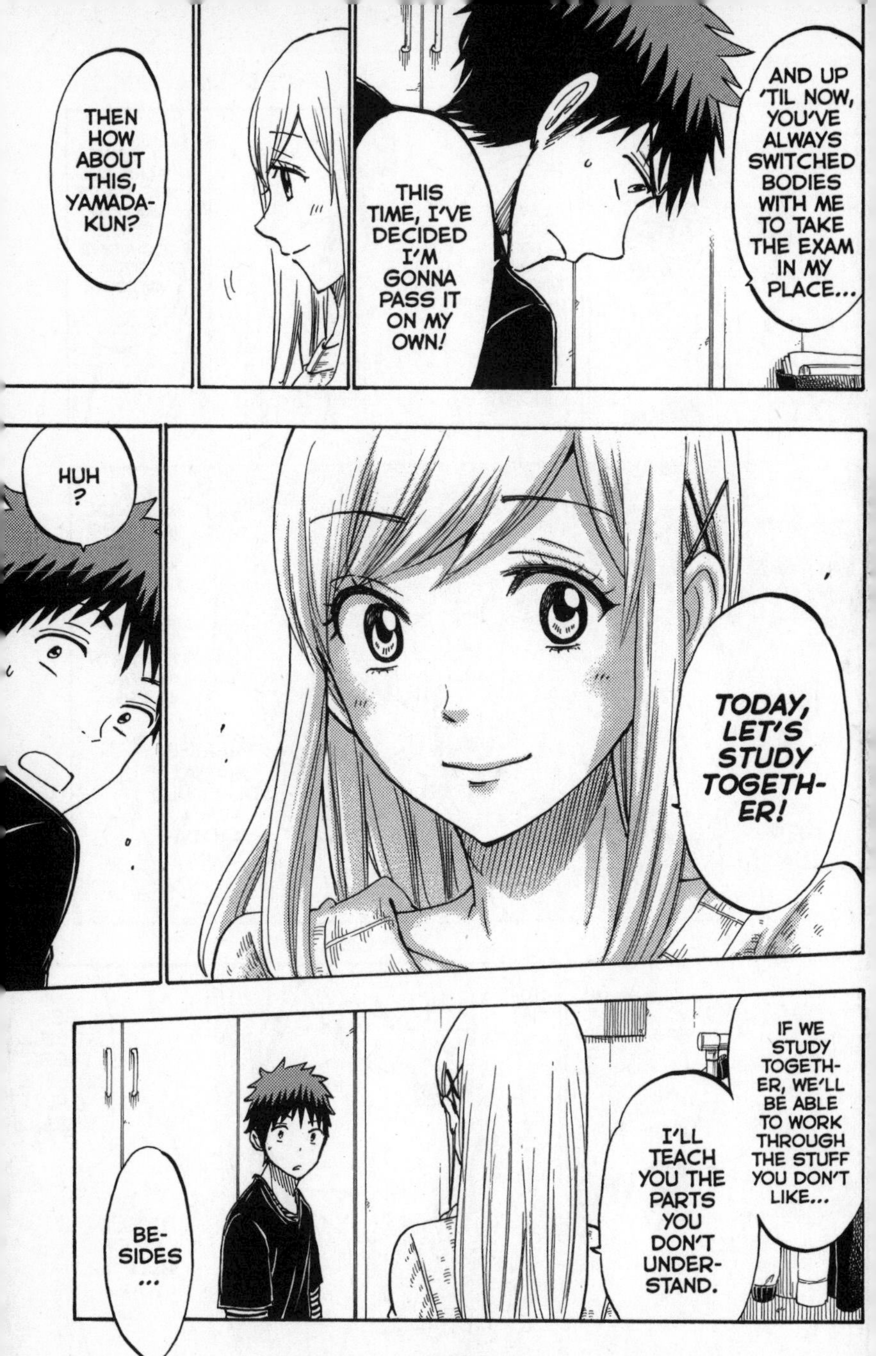
AND UP 'TIL NOW, YOU'VE ALWAYS SWITCHED BODIES WITH ME TO TAKE THE EXAM IN MY PLACE...
THIS TIME, I'VE DECIDED I'M GONNA PASS IT ON MY OWN!
THEN HOW ABOUT THIS, YAMADA-KUN?
TODAY, LET'S STUDY TOGETH-ER!
HUH?
IF WE STUDY TOGETH-ER, WE'LL BE ABLE TO WORK THROUGH THE STUFF YOU DON'T LIKE...
I'LL TEACH YOU THE PARTS YOU DON'T UNDER-STAND.
BE-SIDES...

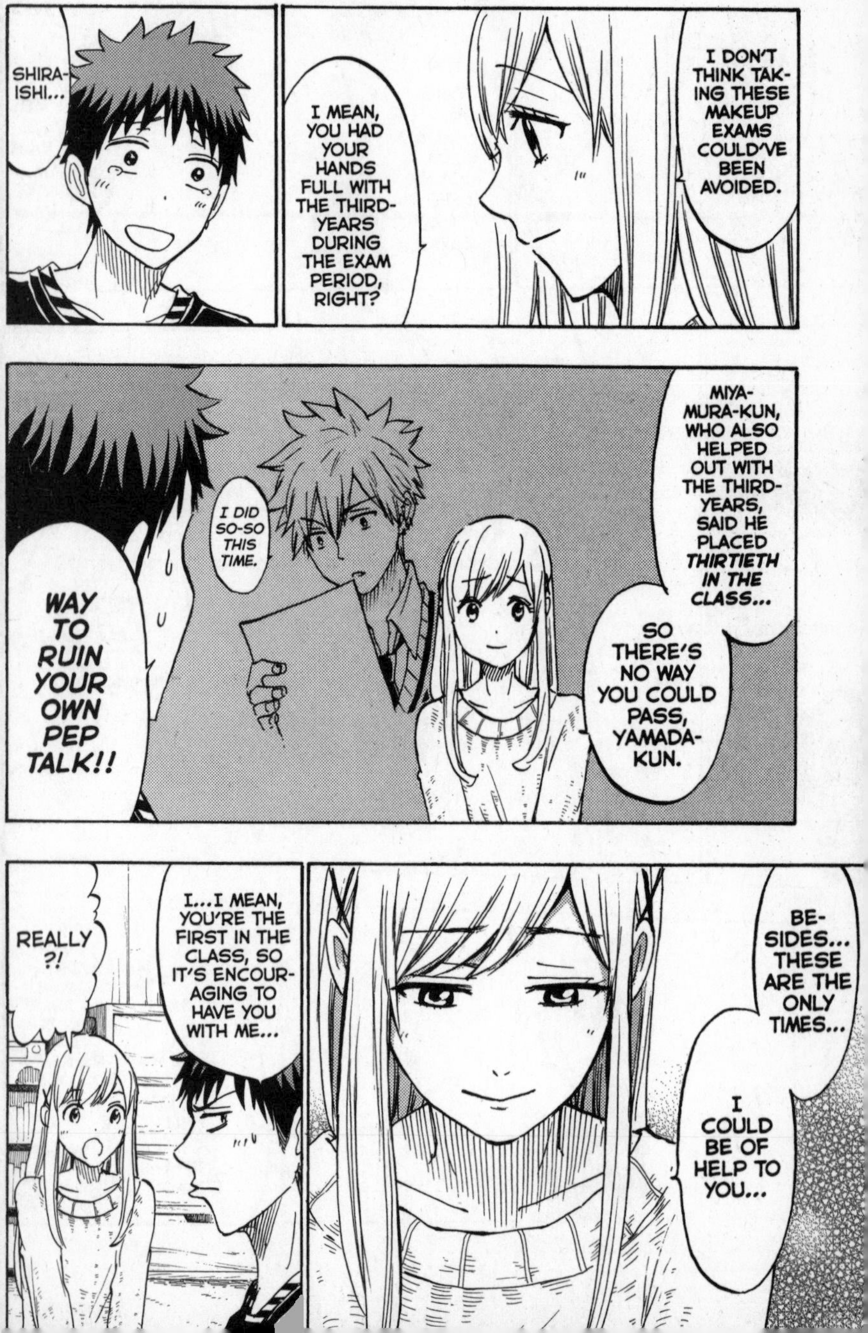
I DON'T THINK TAKING THESE MAKEUP EXAMS COULD'VE BEEN AVOIDED.
I MEAN, YOU HAD YOUR HANDS FULL WITH THE THIRD-YEARS DURING THE EXAM PERIOD, RIGHT?
SHIRAISHI...
MIYAMURA-KUN, WHO ALSO HELPED OUT WITH THE THIRD-YEARS, SAID HE PLACED *THIRTIETH IN THE CLASS*...
SO THERE'S NO WAY YOU COULD PASS, YAMADA-KUN.
I DID SO-SO THIS TIME.
WAY TO RUIN YOUR OWN PEP TALK!!
BESIDES... THESE ARE THE ONLY TIMES...
I COULD BE OF HELP TO YOU...
I...I MEAN, YOU'RE THE FIRST IN THE CLASS, SO IT'S ENCOURAGING TO HAVE YOU WITH ME...
REALLY?!

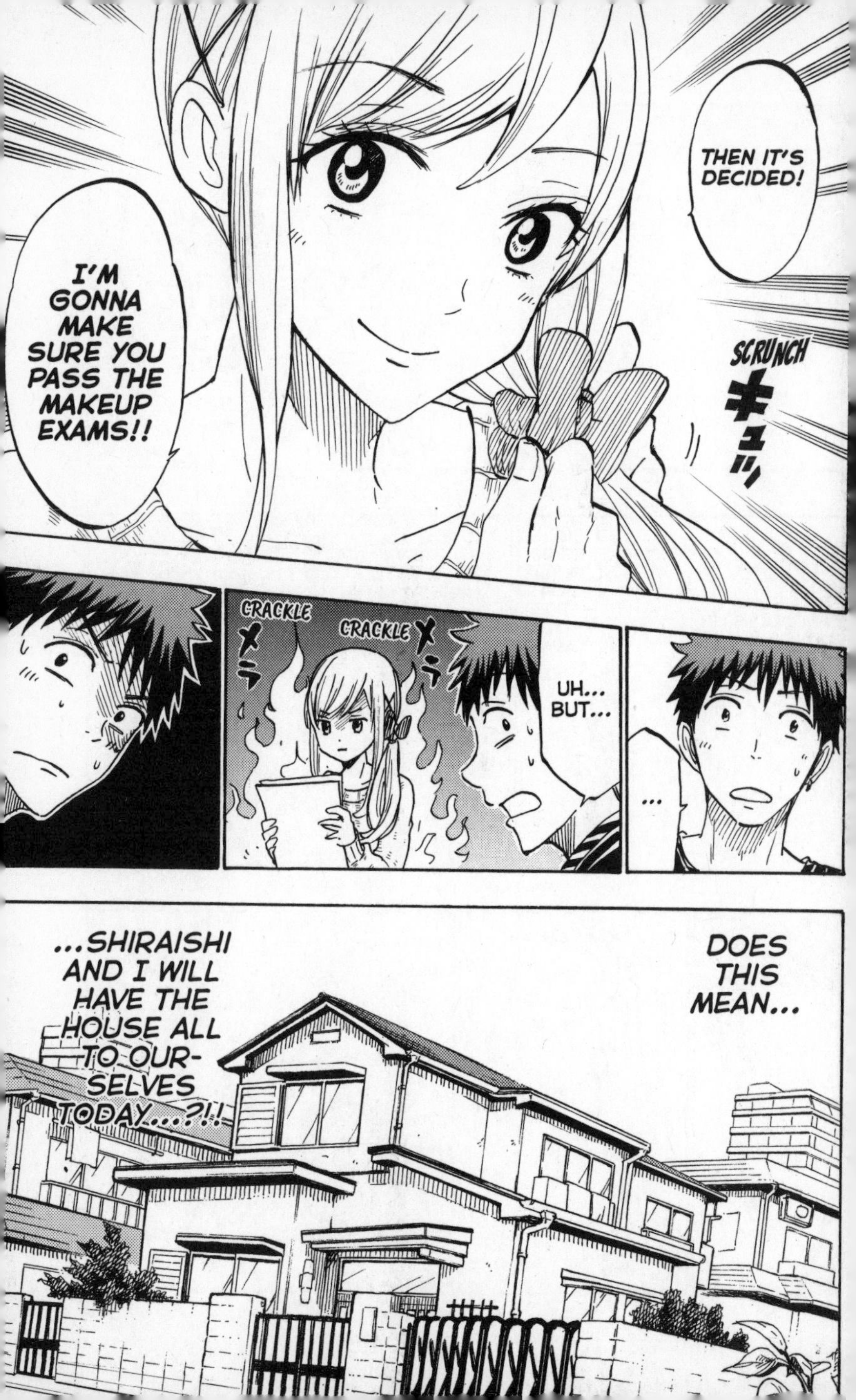
THEN IT'S DECIDED!
SCRUNCH
キュッ
I'M GONNA MAKE SURE YOU PASS THE MAKEUP EXAMS!!
...
UH... BUT...
CRACKLE
メラ
CRACKLE
メラ
DOES THIS MEAN...
...SHIRAISHI AND I WILL HAVE THE HOUSE ALL TO OUR-SELVES TODAY...?!!

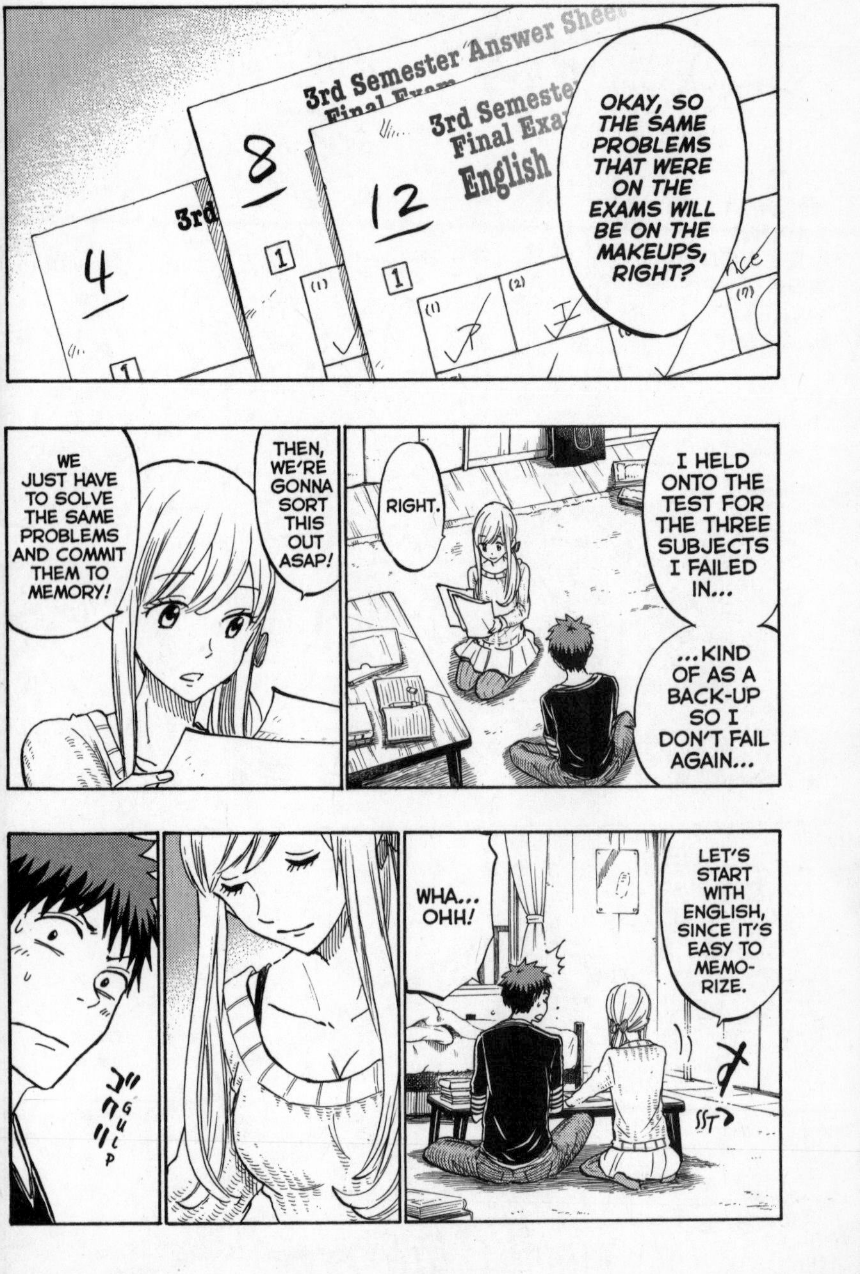
3rd Semester Final Exam
English
12
8
4
OKAY, SO THE SAME PROBLEMS THAT WERE ON THE EXAMS WILL BE ON THE MAKEUPS, RIGHT?
I HELD ONTO THE TEST FOR THE THREE SUBJECTS I FAILED IN...
...KIND OF AS A BACK-UP SO I DON'T FAIL AGAIN...
RIGHT.
THEN, WE'RE GONNA SORT THIS OUT ASAP!
WE JUST HAVE TO SOLVE THE SAME PROBLEMS AND COMMIT THEM TO MEMORY!
LET'S START WITH ENGLISH, SINCE IT'S EASY TO MEMO-RIZE.
WHA... OHH!
SST
GULP

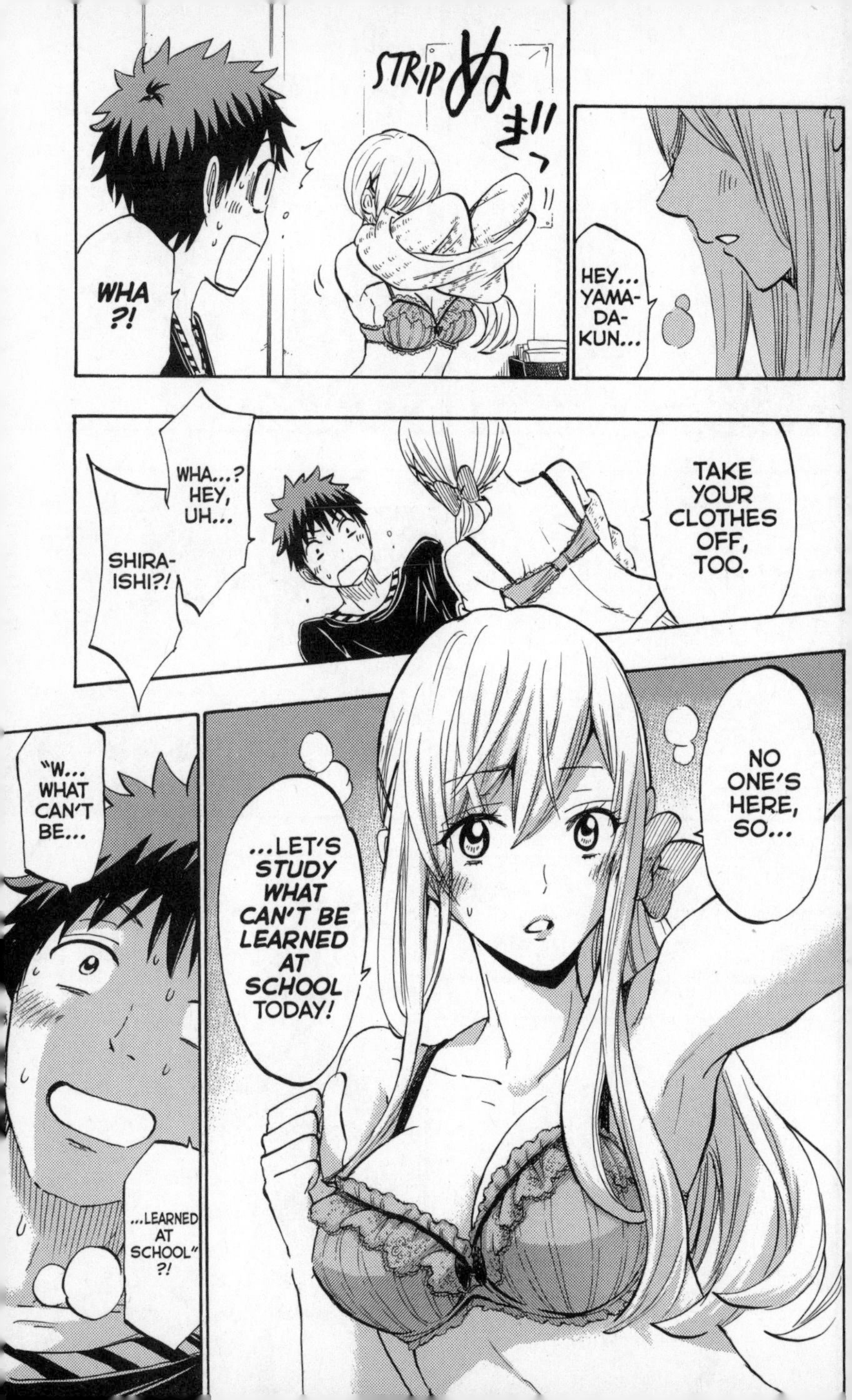
HEY... YAMA-DA-KUN...
STRIP ぬぎっ
WHA ?!
TAKE YOUR CLOTHES OFF, TOO.
WHA...? HEY, UH...
SHIRA-ISHI?!
NO ONE'S HERE, SO...
...LET'S STUDY WHAT CAN'T BE LEARNED AT SCHOOL TODAY!
"W... WHAT CAN'T BE...
...LEARNED AT SCHOOL" ?!

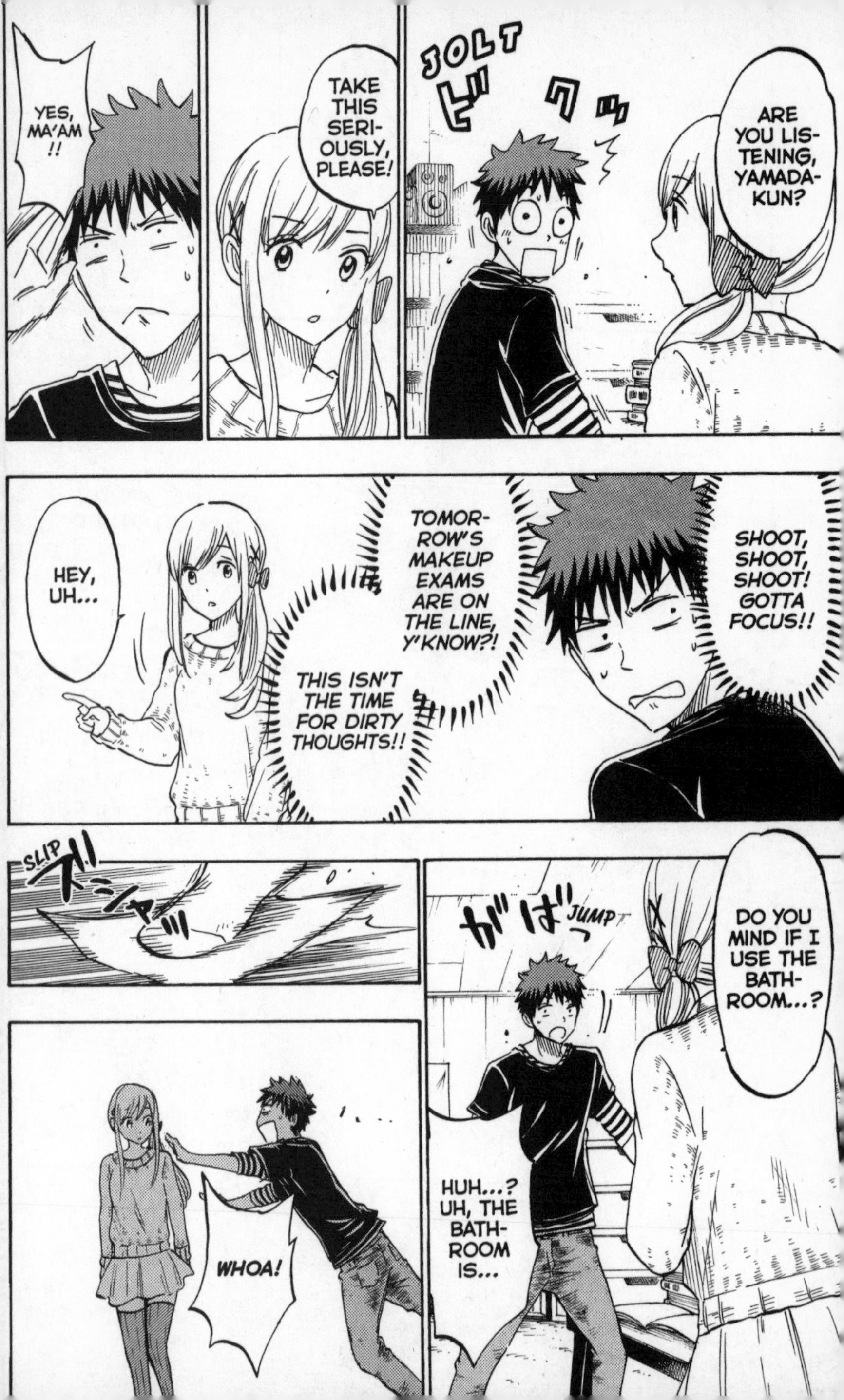
ARE YOU LISTENING, YAMADA-KUN?
JOLT
ビクッ
TAKE THIS SERIOUSLY, PLEASE!
YES, MA'AM!!
SHOOT, SHOOT, SHOOT! GOTTA FOCUS!!
TOMORROW'S MAKEUP EXAMS ARE ON THE LINE, Y'KNOW?!
THIS ISN'T THE TIME FOR DIRTY THOUGHTS!!
HEY, UH...
DO YOU MIND IF I USE THE BATHROOM...?
がばっ
JUMP
HUH...? UH, THE BATHROOM IS...
SLIP
ズシャッ
WHOA!

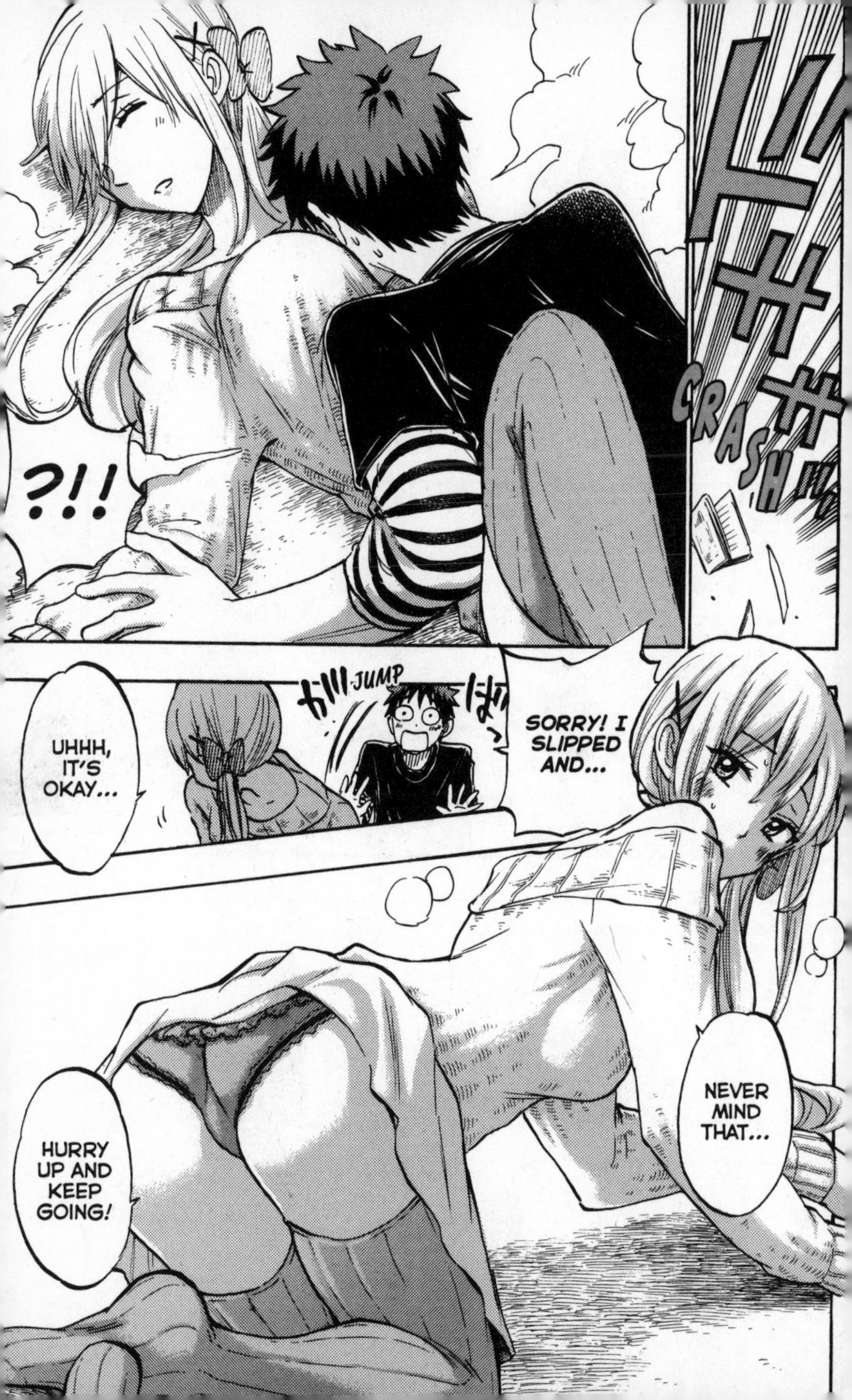
CRASH
?!!
SORRY! I SLIPPED AND...
JUMP
UHHH, IT'S OKAY...
NEVER MIND THAT...
HURRY UP AND KEEP GOING!

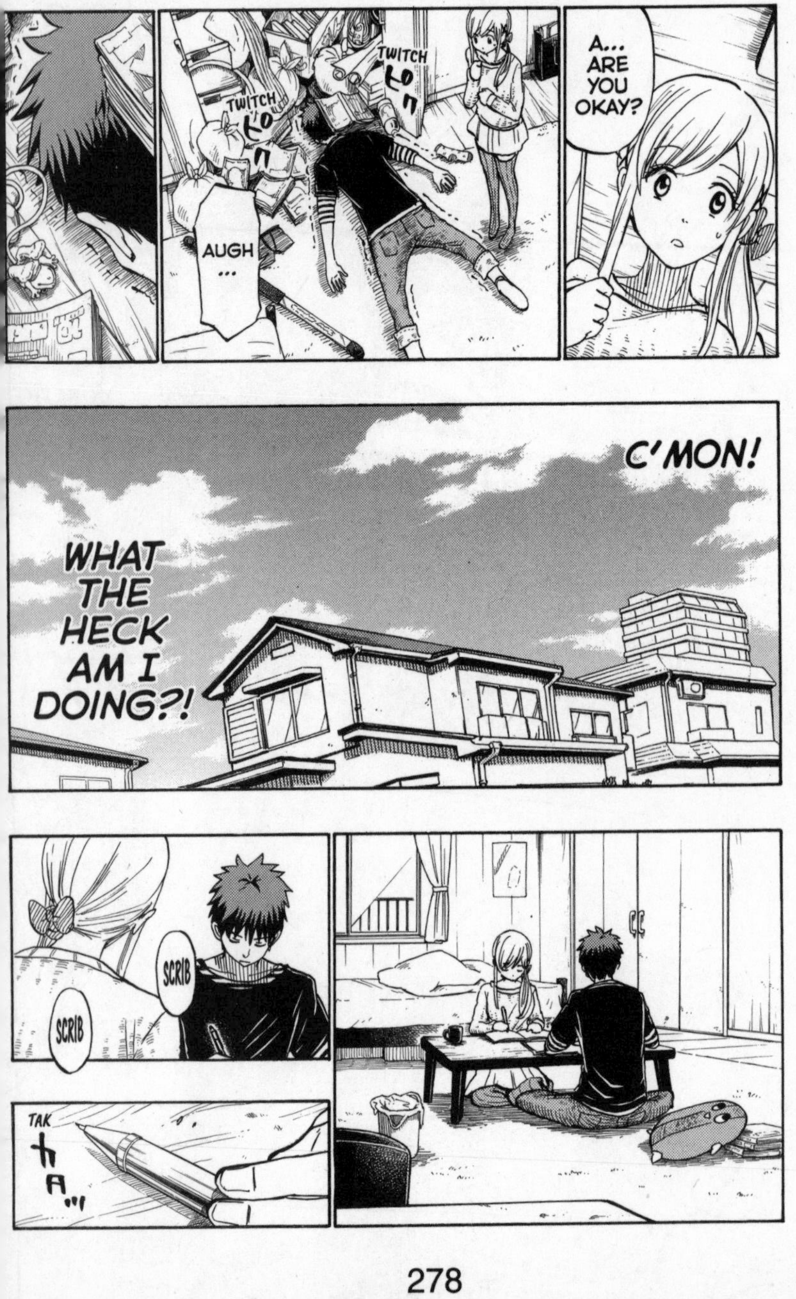
A... ARE YOU OKAY?
TWITCH
TWITCH
AUGH ...
C'MON!
WHAT THE HECK AM I DOING?!
SCRIB
SCRIB
TAK

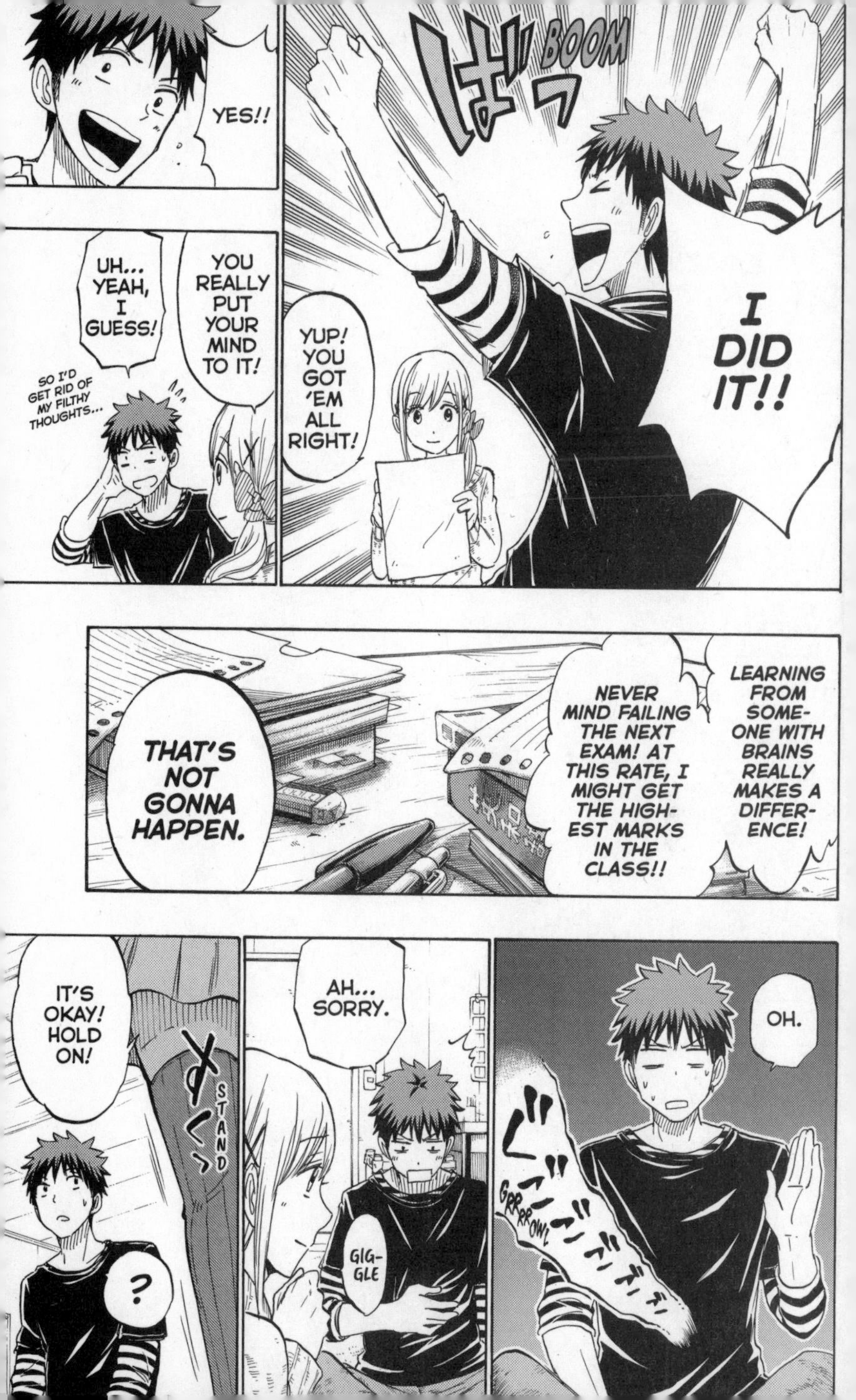
BOOM
I DID IT!!
YUP! YOU GOT 'EM ALL RIGHT!
YES!!
YOU REALLY PUT YOUR MIND TO IT!
UH... YEAH, I GUESS!
SO I'D GET RID OF MY FILTHY THOUGHTS...
LEARNING FROM SOME-ONE WITH BRAINS REALLY MAKES A DIFFER-ENCE!
NEVER MIND FAILING THE NEXT EXAM! AT THIS RATE, I MIGHT GET THE HIGH-EST MARKS IN THE CLASS!!
THAT'S NOT GONNA HAPPEN.
OH.
GRRRROWL
AH... SORRY.
GIG-GLE
IT'S OKAY! HOLD ON!
STAND
?

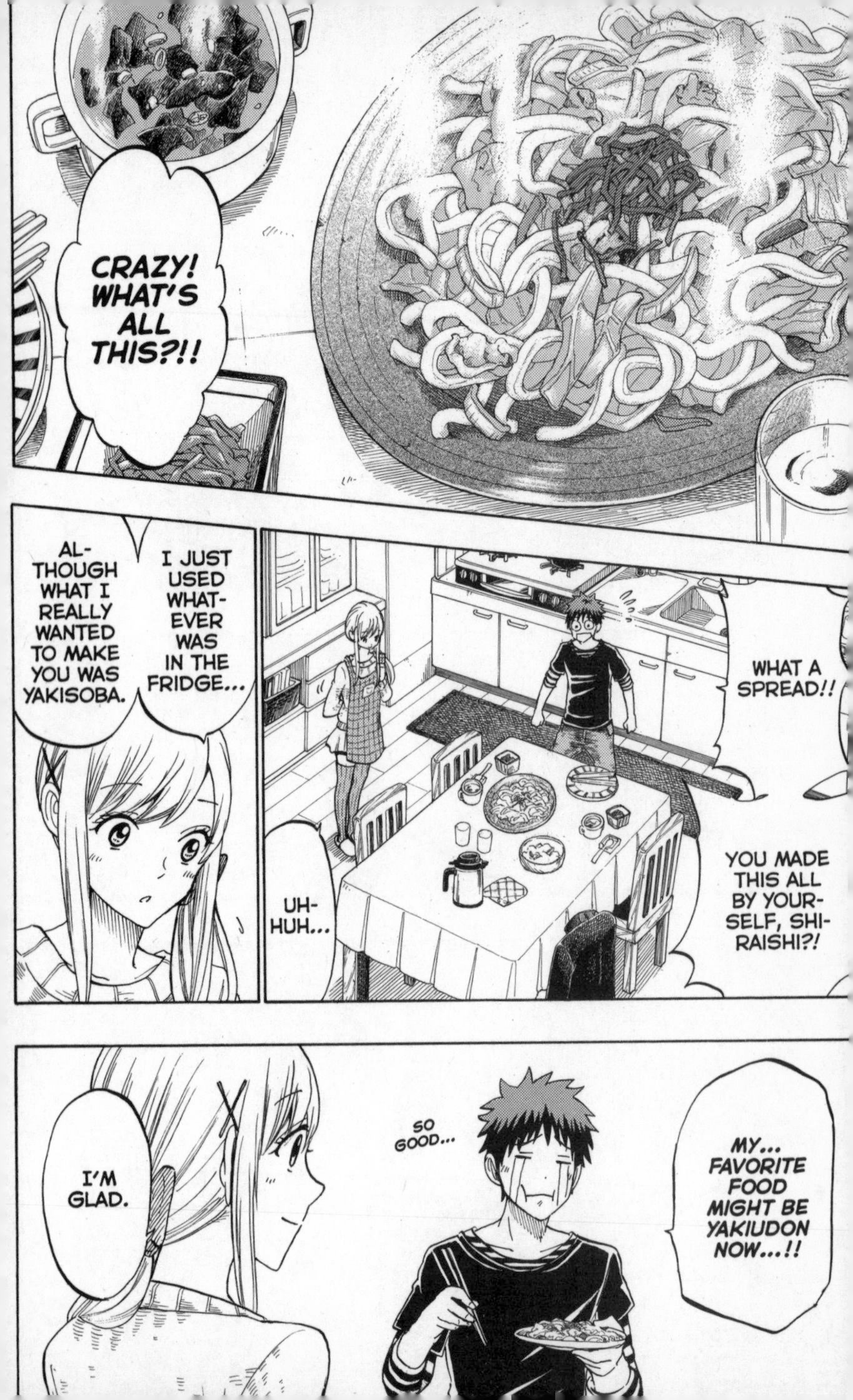
CRAZY! WHAT'S ALL THIS?!!
WHAT A SPREAD!!
YOU MADE THIS ALL BY YOURSELF, SHIRAISHI?!
UH-HUH...
I JUST USED WHATEVER WAS IN THE FRIDGE...
ALTHOUGH WHAT I REALLY WANTED TO MAKE YOU WAS YAKISOBA.
MY... FAVORITE FOOD MIGHT BE YAKIUDON NOW...!!
SO GOOD...
I'M GLAD.

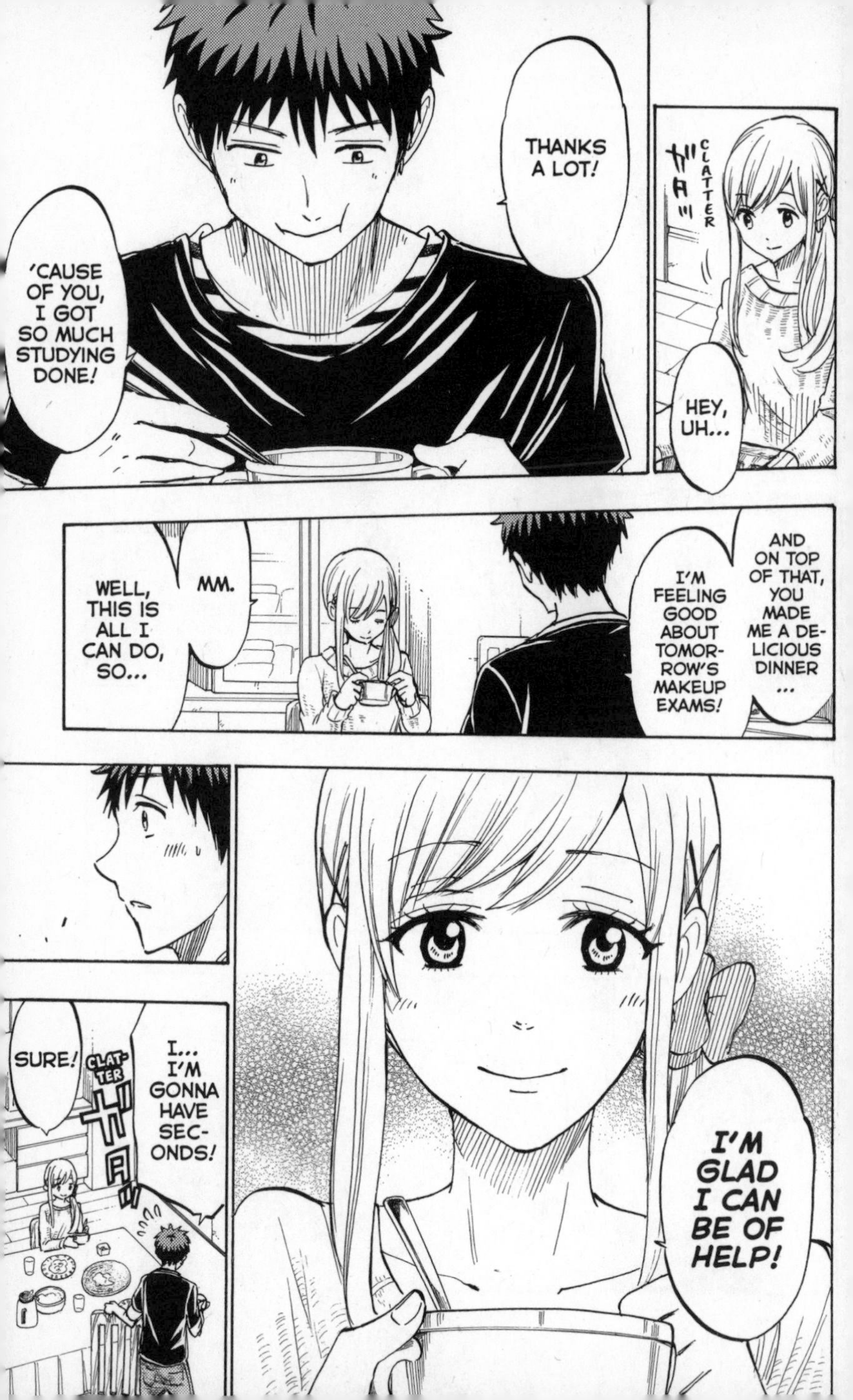
CLATTER
HEY, UH...
THANKS A LOT!
'CAUSE OF YOU, I GOT SO MUCH STUDYING DONE!
AND ON TOP OF THAT, YOU MADE ME A DE-LICIOUS DINNER ...
I'M FEELING GOOD ABOUT TOMOR-ROW'S MAKEUP EXAMS!
MM.
WELL, THIS IS ALL I CAN DO, SO...
I'M GLAD I CAN BE OF HELP!
I... I'M GONNA HAVE SEC-ONDS!
CLAT-TER
SURE!

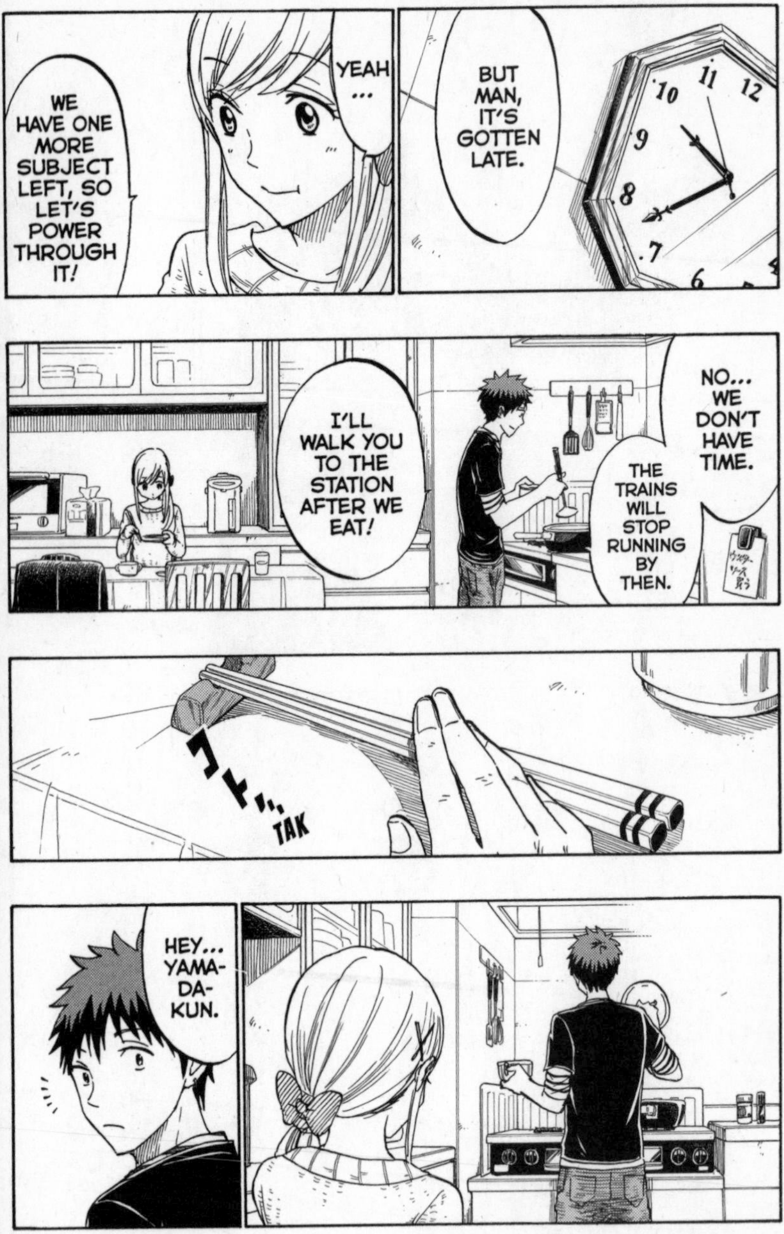
BUT MAN, IT'S GOTTEN LATE.
YEAH ...
WE HAVE ONE MORE SUBJECT LEFT, SO LET'S POWER THROUGH IT!
NO... WE DON'T HAVE TIME.
THE TRAINS WILL STOP RUNNING BY THEN.
I'LL WALK YOU TO THE STATION AFTER WE EAT!
TAK
HEY... YAMA-DA-KUN.

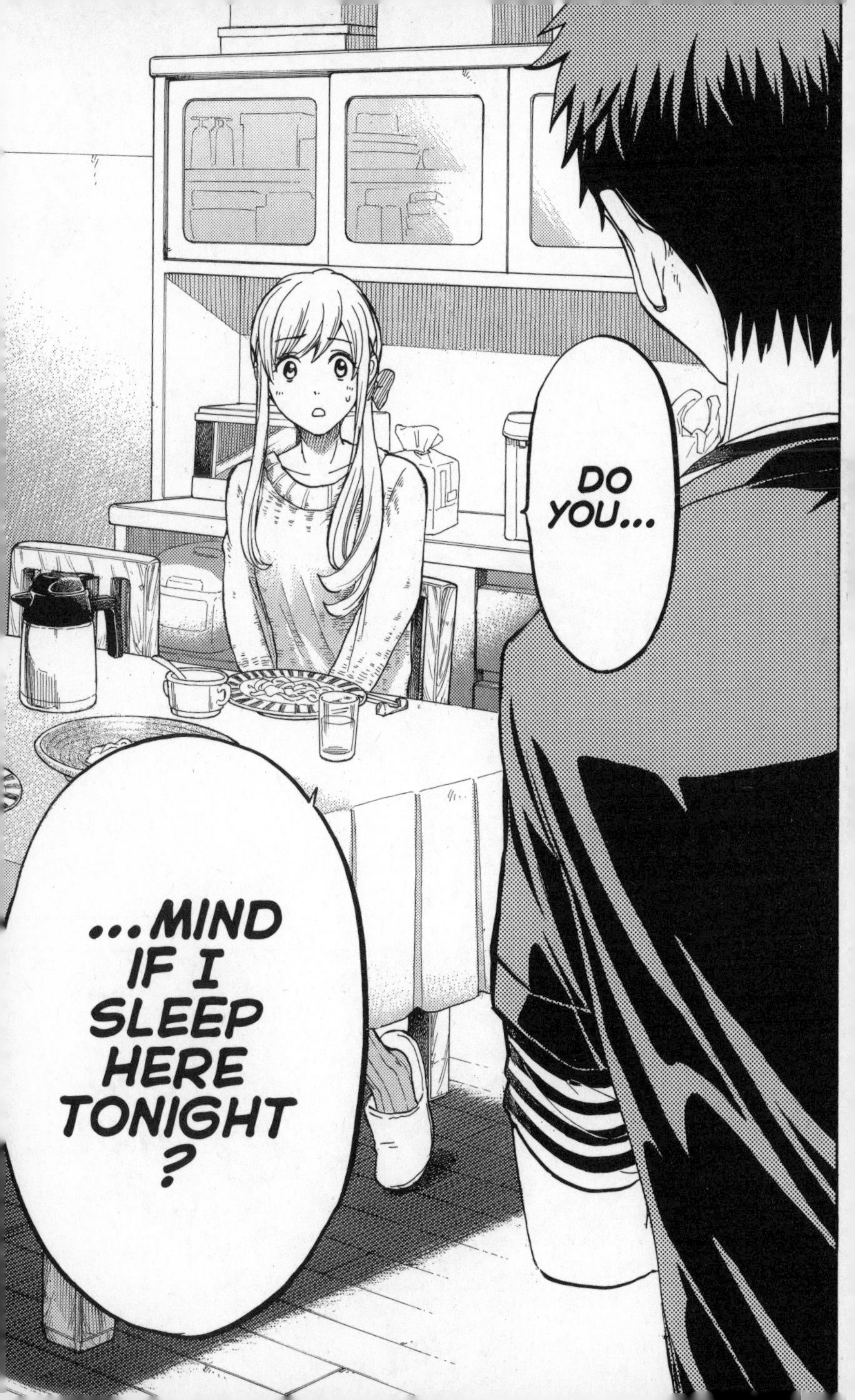
DO YOU...
...MIND IF I SLEEP HERE TONIGHT?

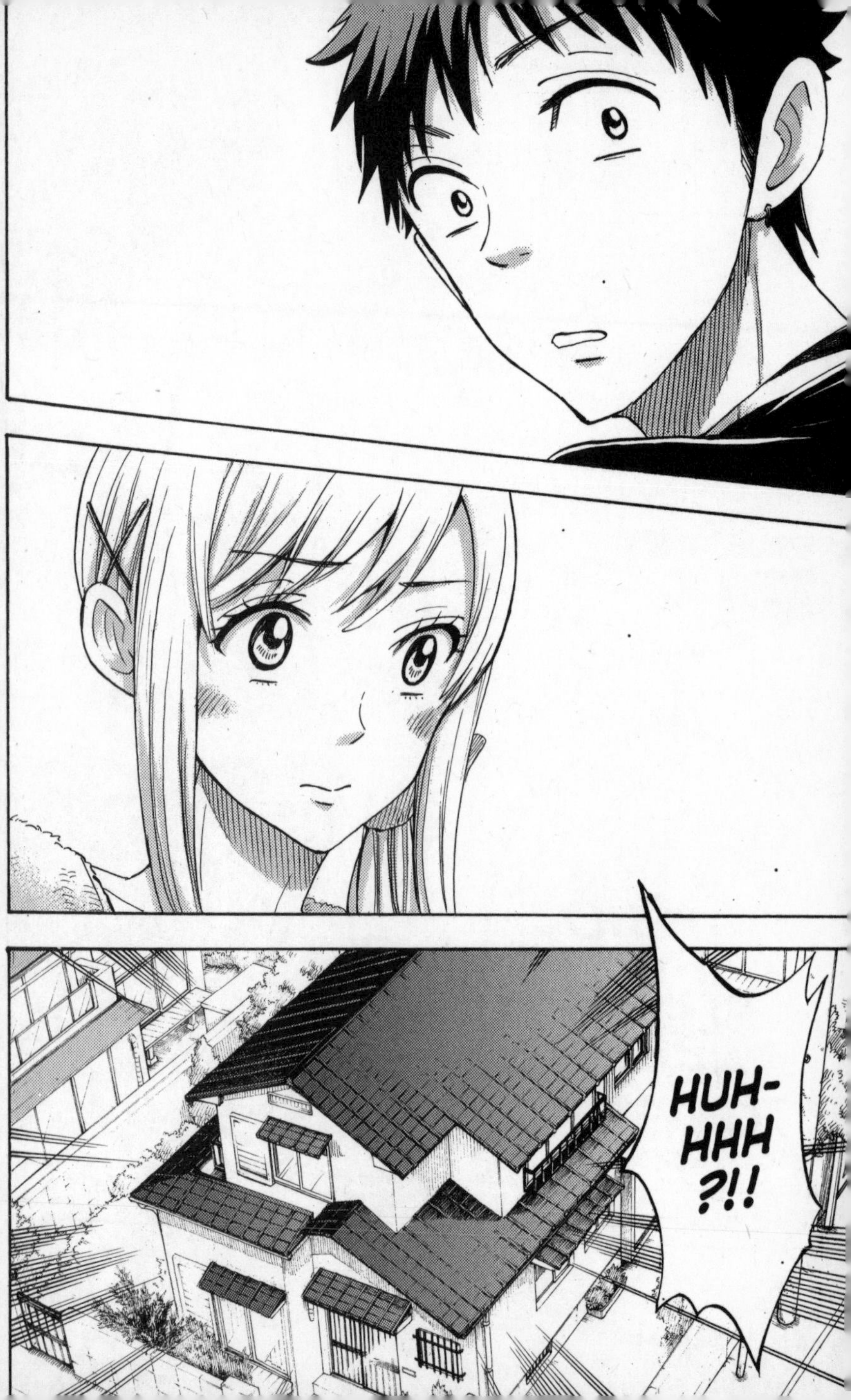
HUH-
HHH
?!!

CHAPTER 186: Are you gonna come in, too?

SORA HIMEKAWA

Q. What class are you in? A. Class 2-D

Q. What club are you in? A. The handicrafts club
✓ She can't sew properly, though!

Q. What's your power? A. Romance power
✓ After kissing someone, she can see a memory with the person they like!

Q. How do you feel about Yuri-kun? A. He's like a little brother.
✓ Yuri's gonna be so shocked if he hears that!

Q. Be honest, how far did you go with Yamada? A. ...
✓ **It's a secret! ♥**

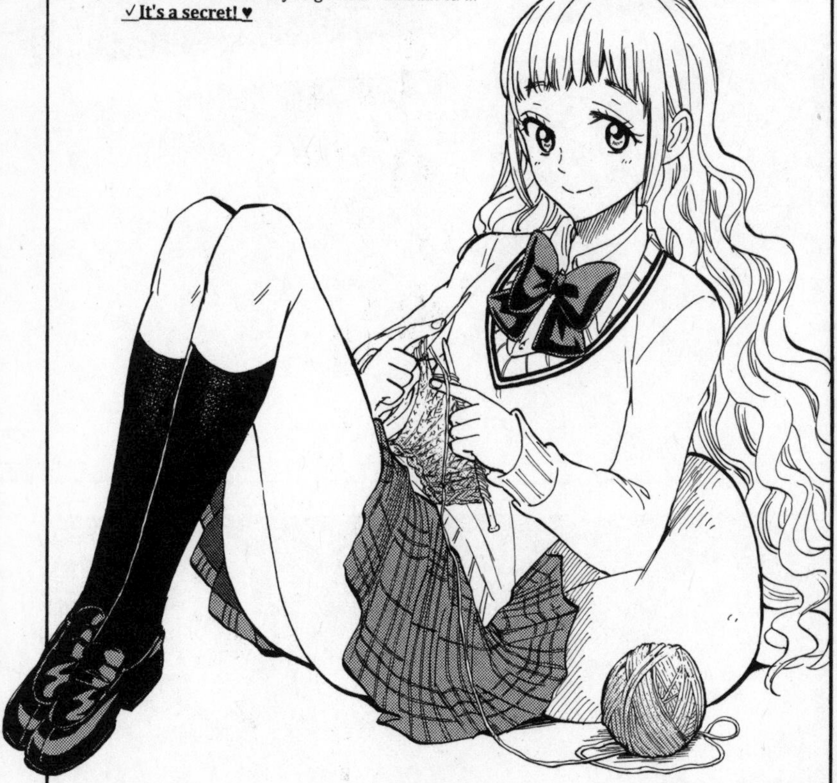

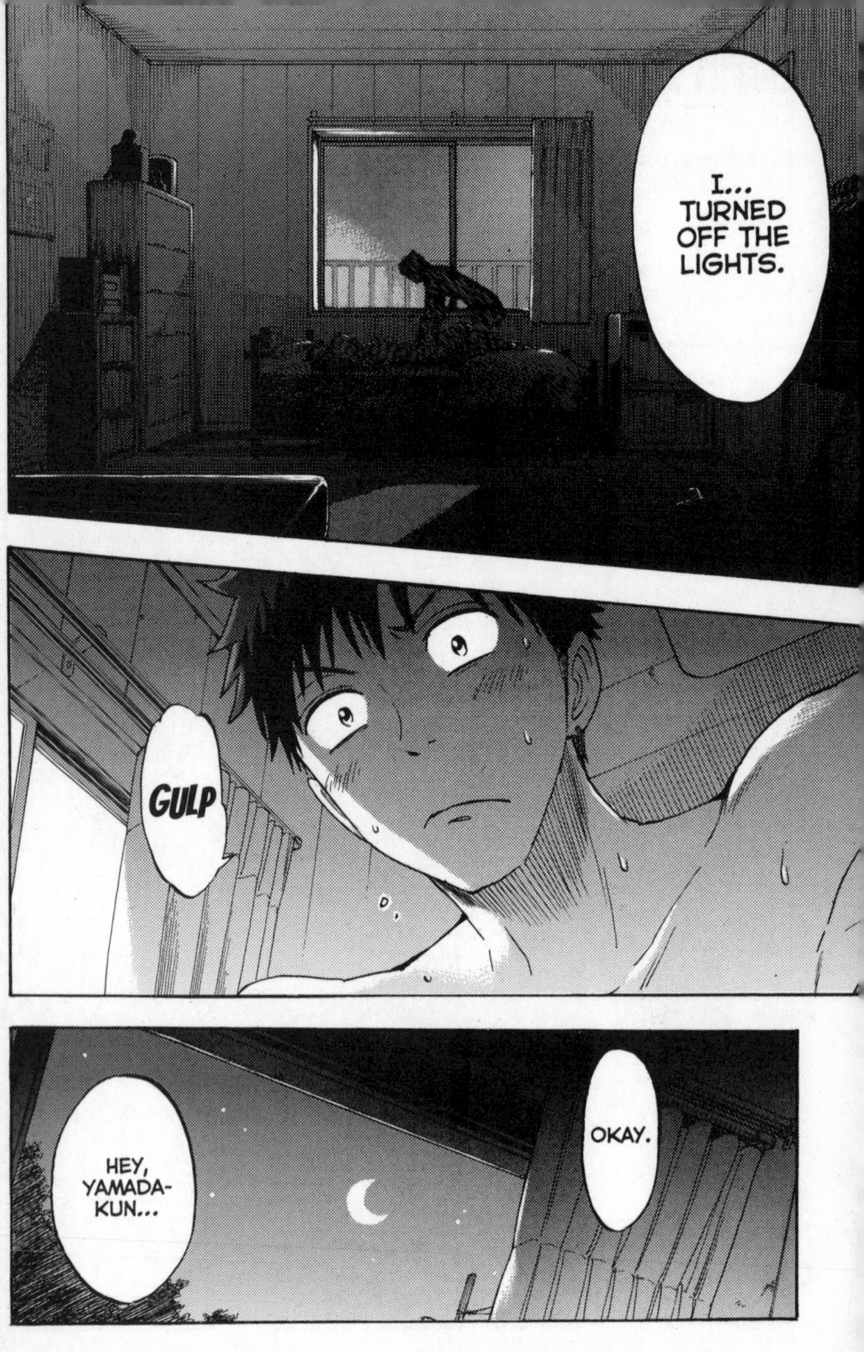
I... TURNED OFF THE LIGHTS.
GULP
OKAY.
HEY, YAMADA-KUN...

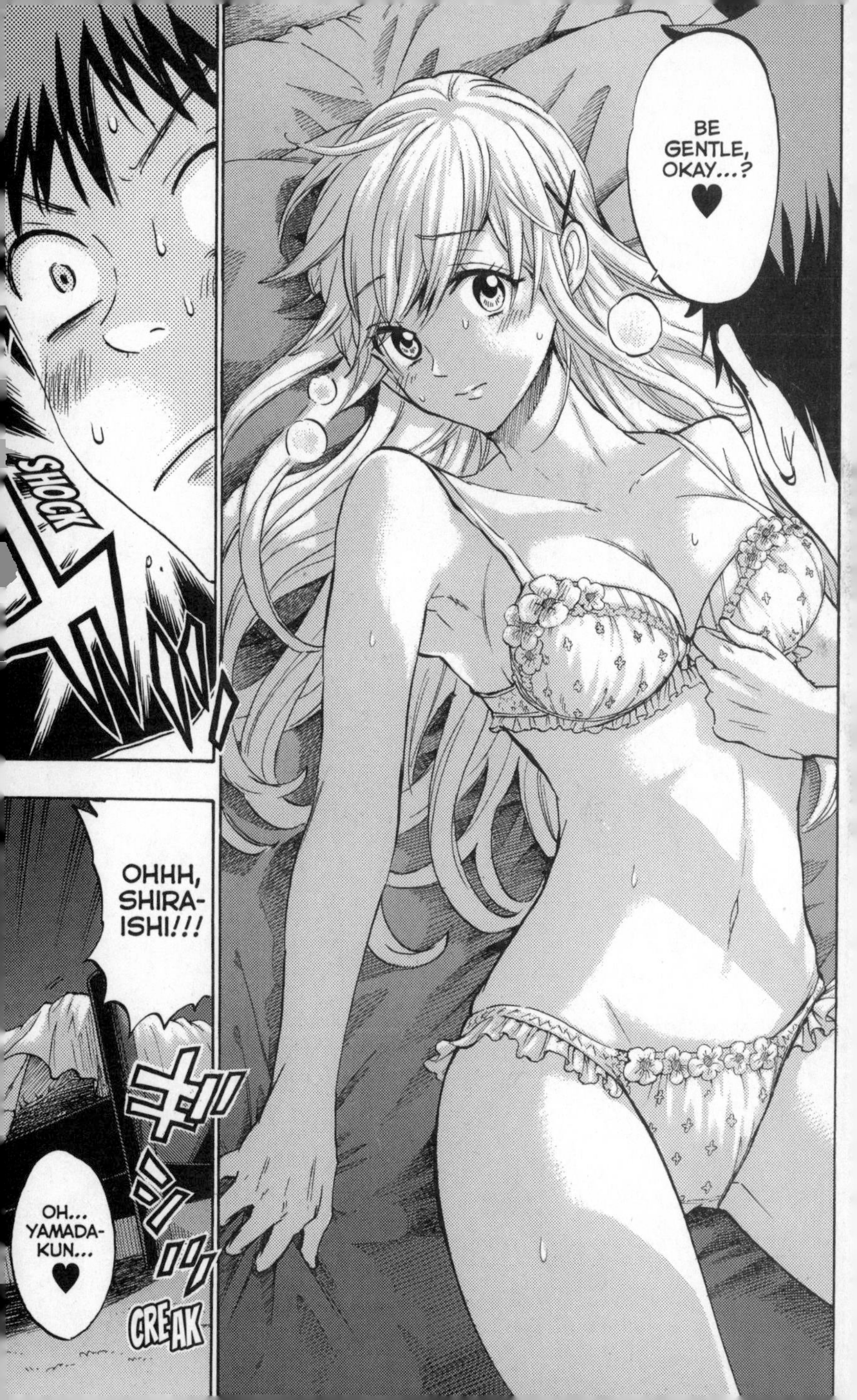
BE GENTLE, OKAY...? ♥
SHOCK
OHHH, SHIRA-ISHI!!!
OH... YAMADA-KUN... ♥
CREAK

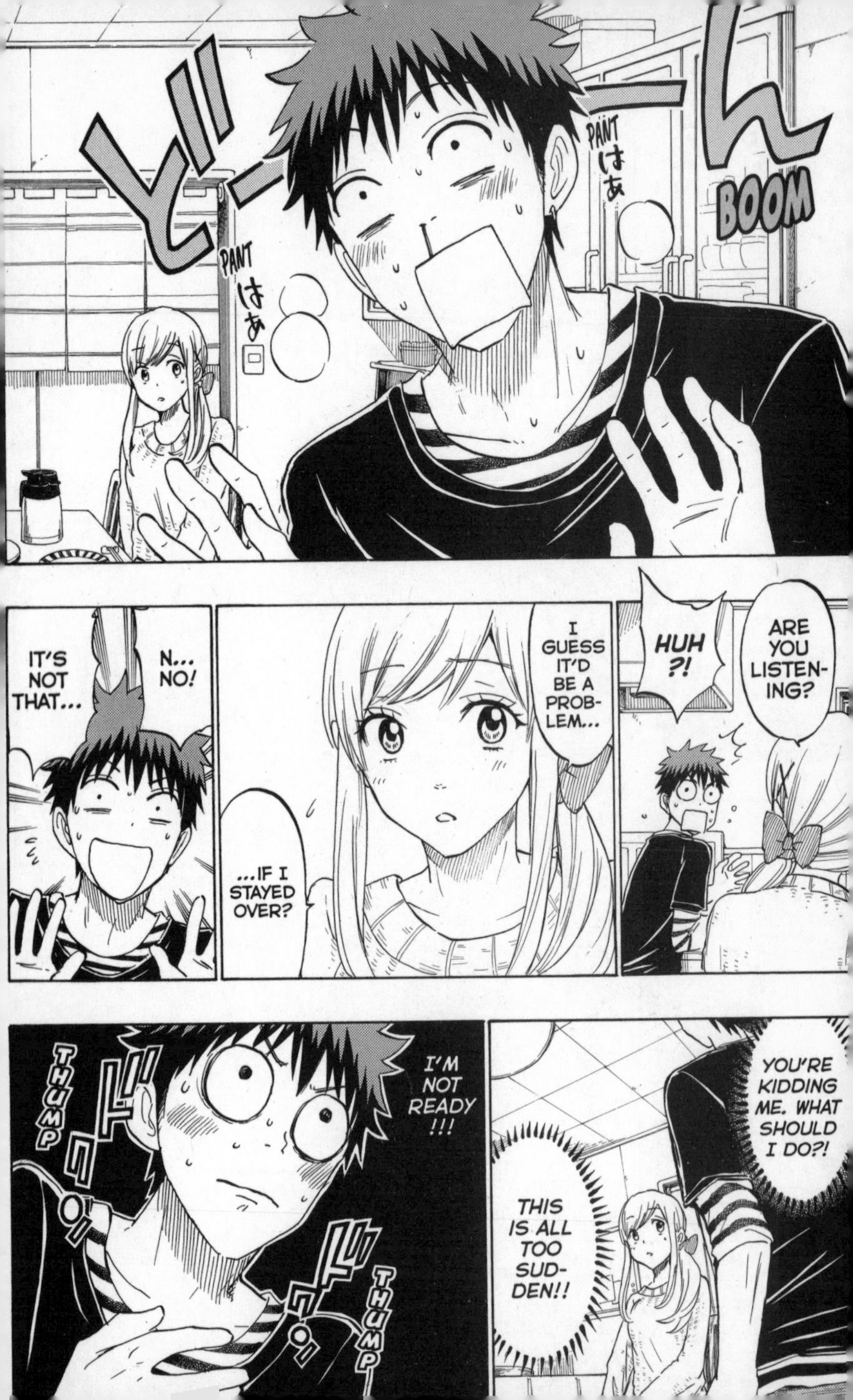
どーん
BOOM
PANT はあ
PANT はあ
ARE YOU LISTENING?
HUH?!
I GUESS IT'D BE A PROBLEM...
...IF I STAYED OVER?
N... NO!
IT'S NOT THAT...
YOU'RE KIDDING ME. WHAT SHOULD I DO?!
THIS IS ALL TOO SUDDEN!!
I'M NOT READY!!!
THUMP
THUMP

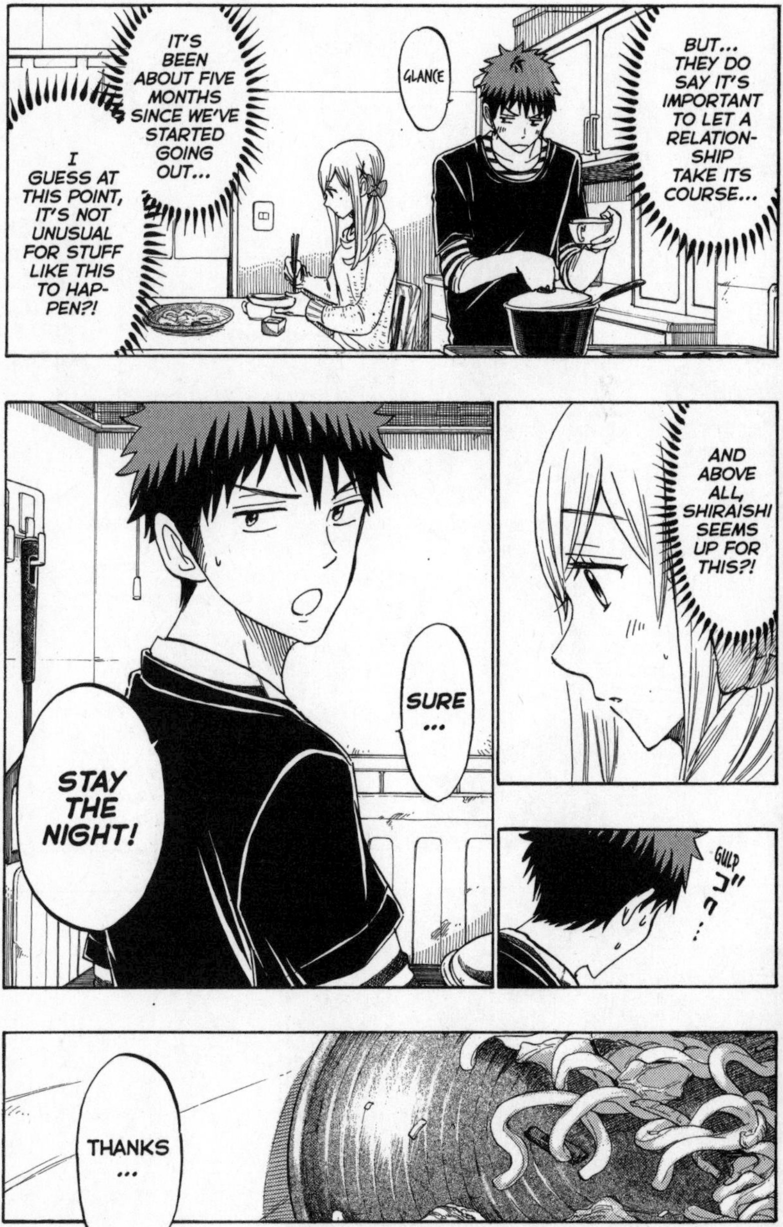
BUT... THEY DO SAY IT'S IMPORTANT TO LET A RELATIONSHIP TAKE ITS COURSE...
GLANCE
IT'S BEEN ABOUT FIVE MONTHS SINCE WE'VE STARTED GOING OUT...
I GUESS AT THIS POINT, IT'S NOT UNUSUAL FOR STUFF LIKE THIS TO HAPPEN?!
AND ABOVE ALL, SHIRAISHI SEEMS UP FOR THIS?!
GULP
SURE...
STAY THE NIGHT!
THANKS...

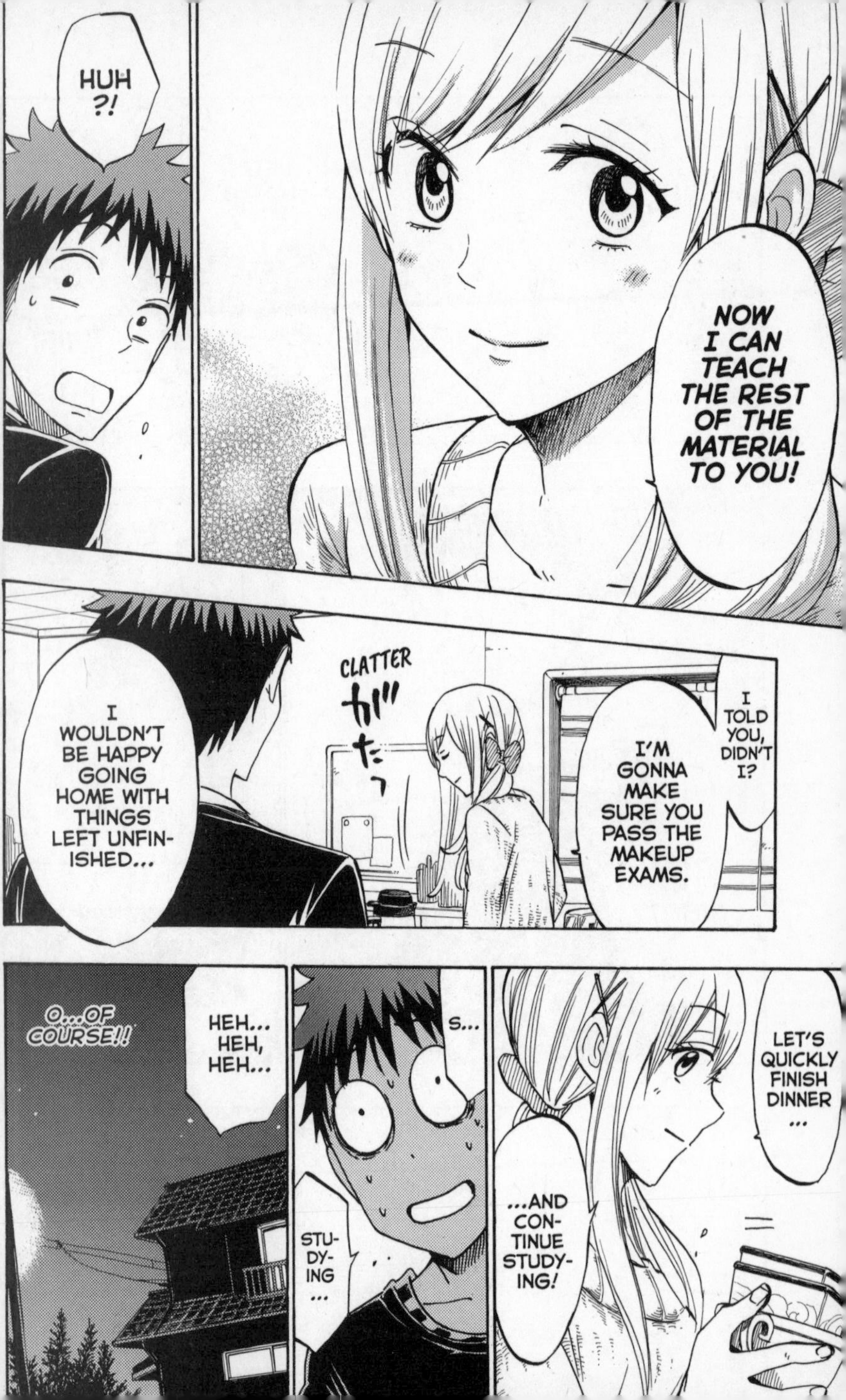
NOW I CAN TEACH THE REST OF THE MATERIAL TO YOU!
HUH ?!
I TOLD YOU, DIDN'T I?
I'M GONNA MAKE SURE YOU PASS THE MAKEUP EXAMS.
CLATTER
ガタッ
I WOULDN'T BE HAPPY GOING HOME WITH THINGS LEFT UNFIN-ISHED...
LET'S QUICKLY FINISH DINNER...
...AND CON-TINUE STUDY-ING!
S...
STU-DY-ING...
HEH... HEH, HEH...
O...OF COURSE!!

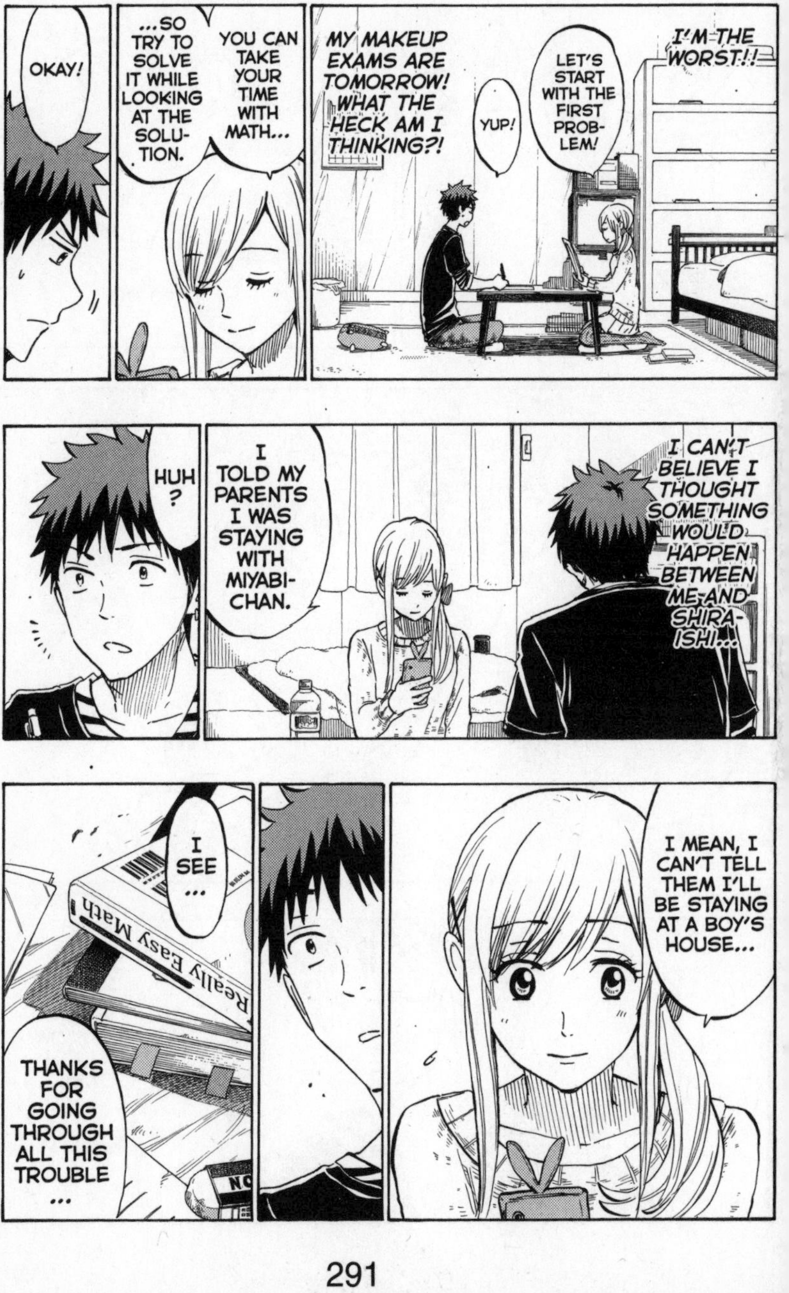
I'M THE WORST!!
LET'S START WITH THE FIRST PROBLEM!
YUP!
MY MAKEUP EXAMS ARE TOMORROW! WHAT THE HECK AM I THINKING?!
YOU CAN TAKE YOUR TIME WITH MATH...
...SO TRY TO SOLVE IT WHILE LOOKING AT THE SOLUTION.
OKAY!
I CAN'T BELIEVE I THOUGHT SOMETHING WOULD HAPPEN BETWEEN ME AND SHIRAISHI...
I TOLD MY PARENTS I WAS STAYING WITH MIYABI-CHAN.
HUH?
I MEAN, I CAN'T TELL THEM I'LL BE STAYING AT A BOY'S HOUSE...
I SEE...
Really Easy Math
THANKS FOR GOING THROUGH ALL THIS TROUBLE...

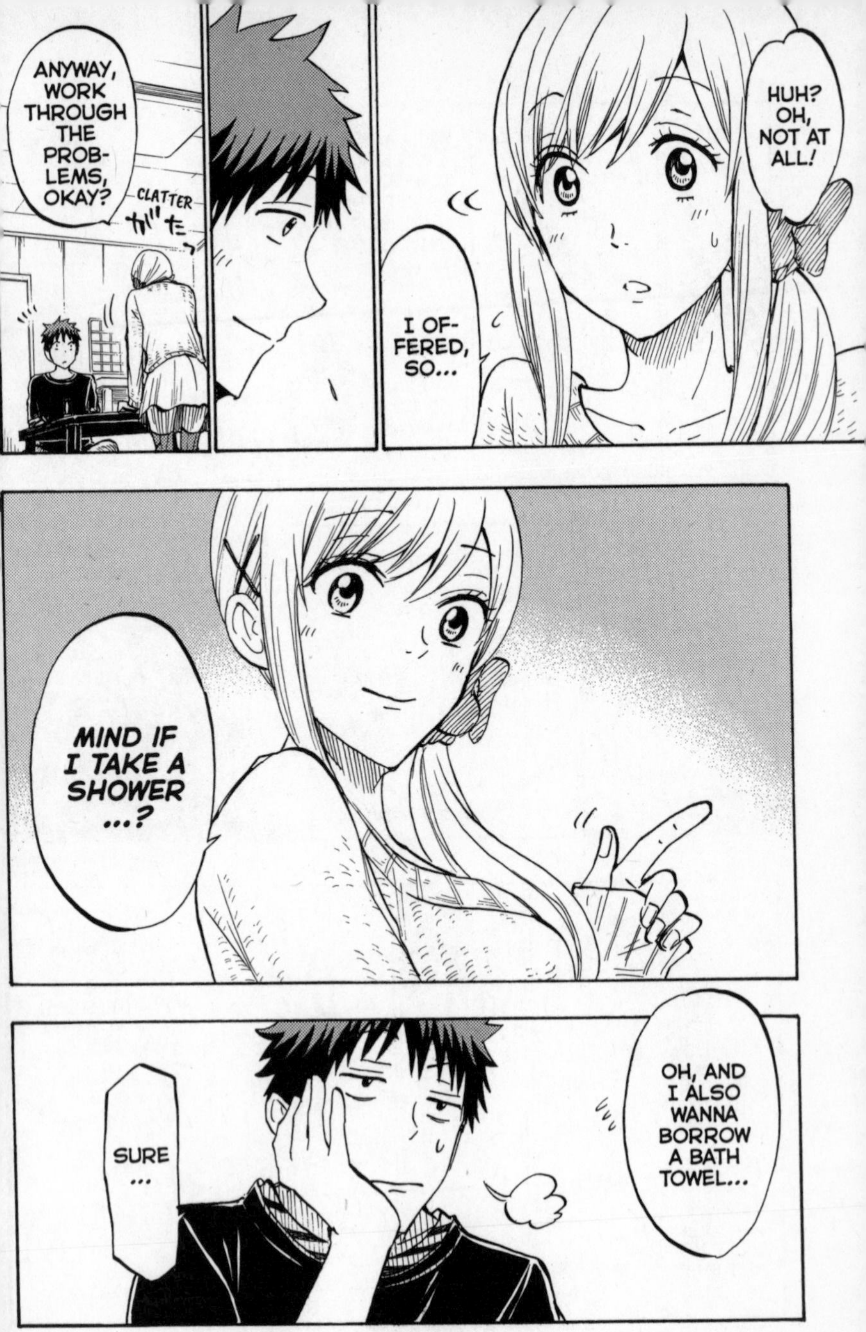
HUH? OH, NOT AT ALL!
I OFFERED, SO...
ANYWAY, WORK THROUGH THE PROBLEMS, OKAY?
CLATTER
ガたっ
MIND IF I TAKE A SHOWER ...?
OH, AND I ALSO WANNA BORROW A BATH TOWEL...
SURE ...

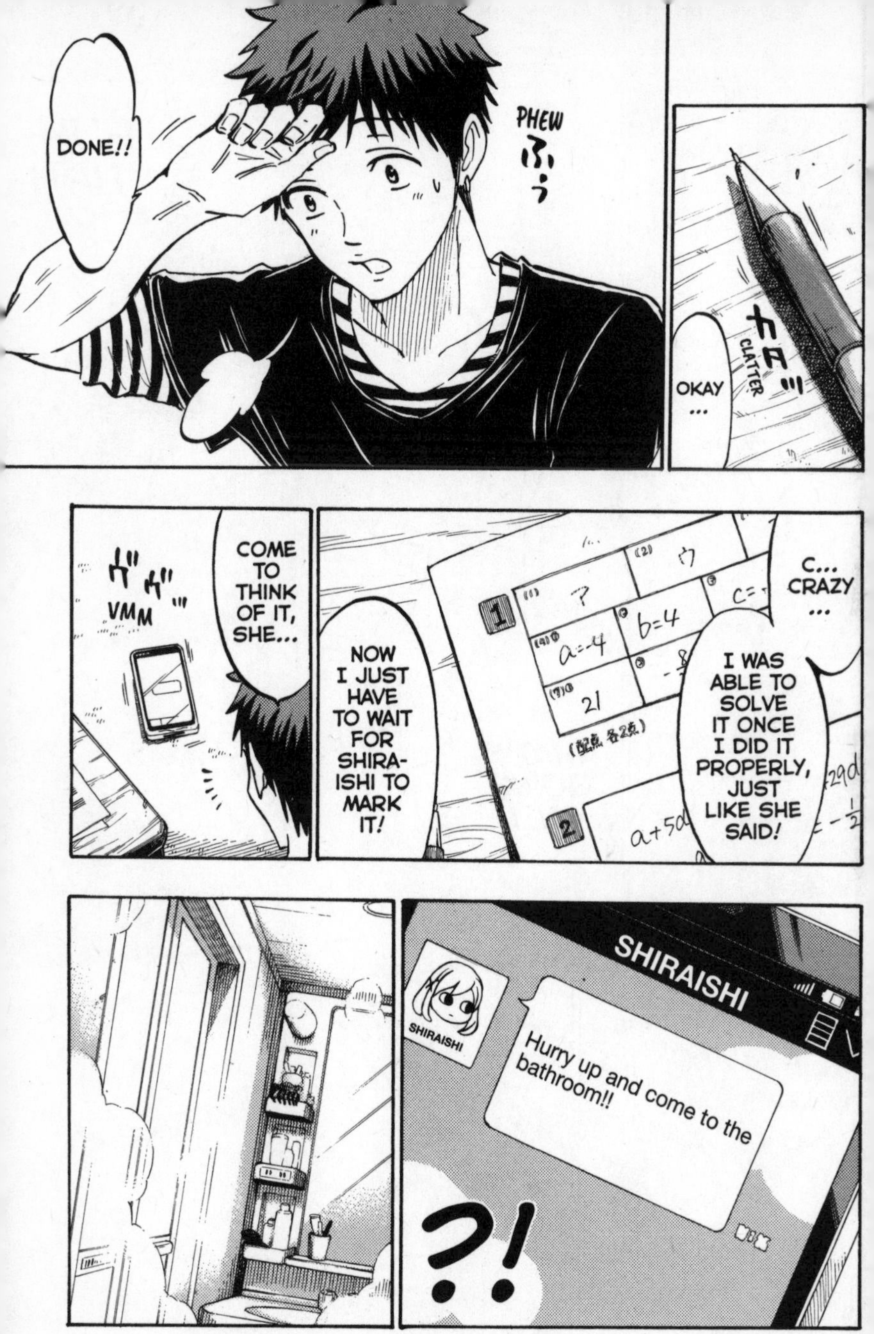
カタッ
CLATTER
OKAY...
DONE!!
PHEW
ふぅ
C... CRAZY...
I WAS ABLE TO SOLVE IT ONCE I DID IT PROPERLY, JUST LIKE SHE SAID!
NOW I JUST HAVE TO WAIT FOR SHIRAISHI TO MARK IT!
COME TO THINK OF IT, SHE...
VMM
SHIRAISHI
SHIRAISHI
Hurry up and come to the bathroom!!
?!

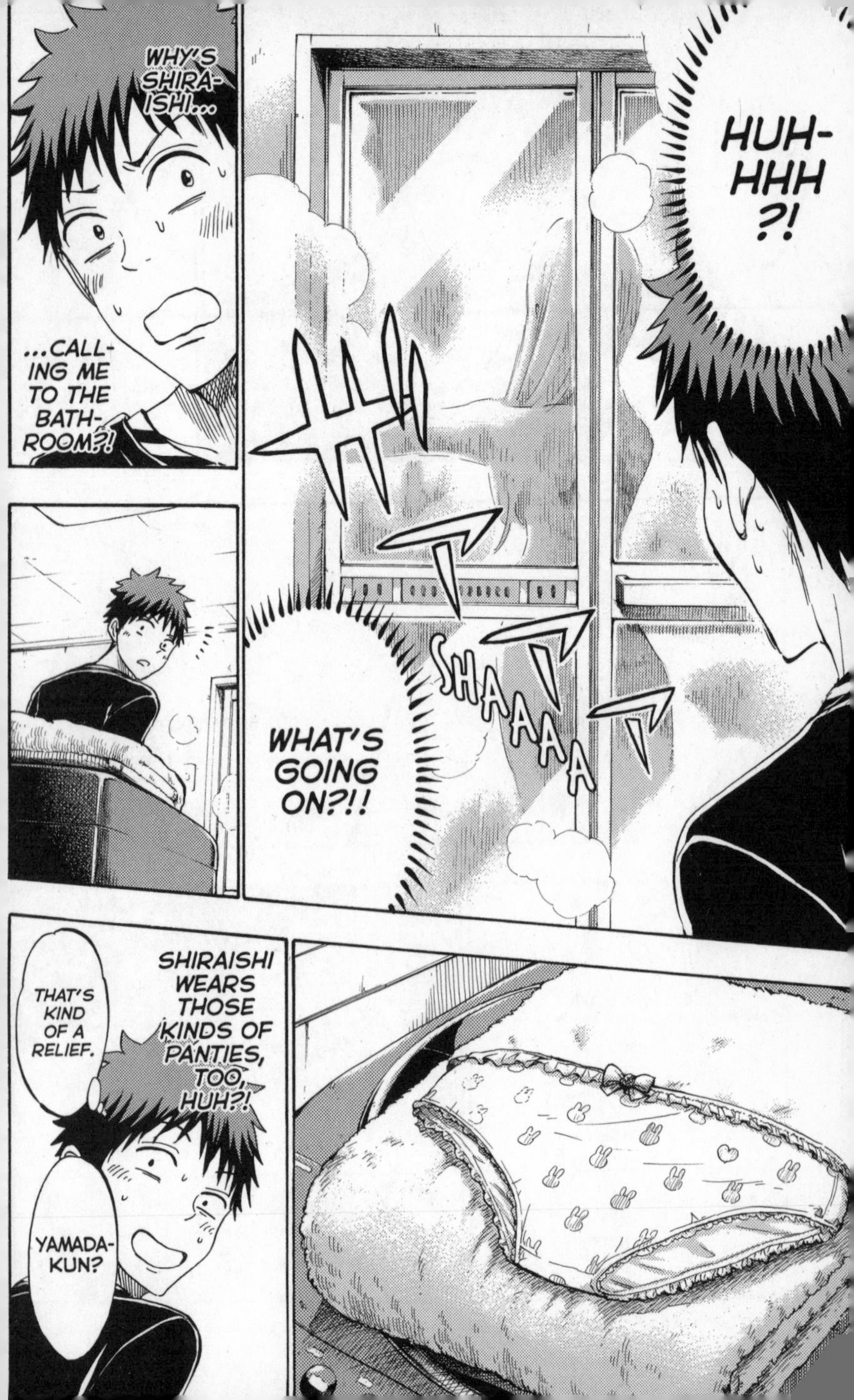
HUH-HHH?!
SHAAAAA
WHAT'S GOING ON?!!
WHY'S SHIRAISHI...
...CALLING ME TO THE BATHROOM?!
SHIRAISHI WEARS THOSE KINDS OF PANTIES, TOO, HUH?!
THAT'S KIND OF A RELIEF.
YAMADA-KUN?

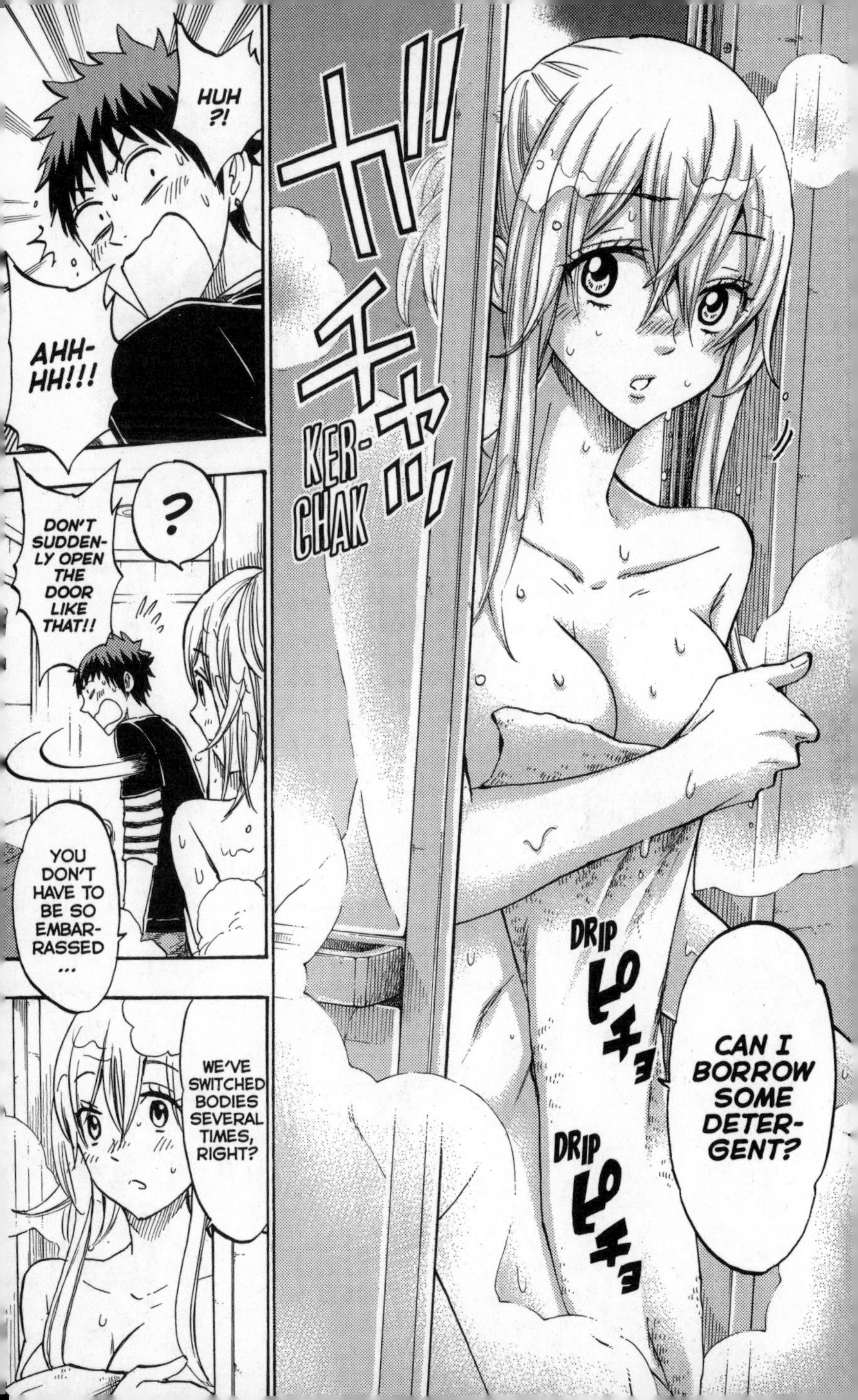

KER-CHAK
DRIP
DRIP
CAN I BORROW SOME DETER-GENT?
HUH?!
AHH-HH!!!
?
DON'T SUDDEN-LY OPEN THE DOOR LIKE THAT!!
YOU DON'T HAVE TO BE SO EMBAR-RASSED...
WE'VE SWITCHED BODIES SEVERAL TIMES, RIGHT?

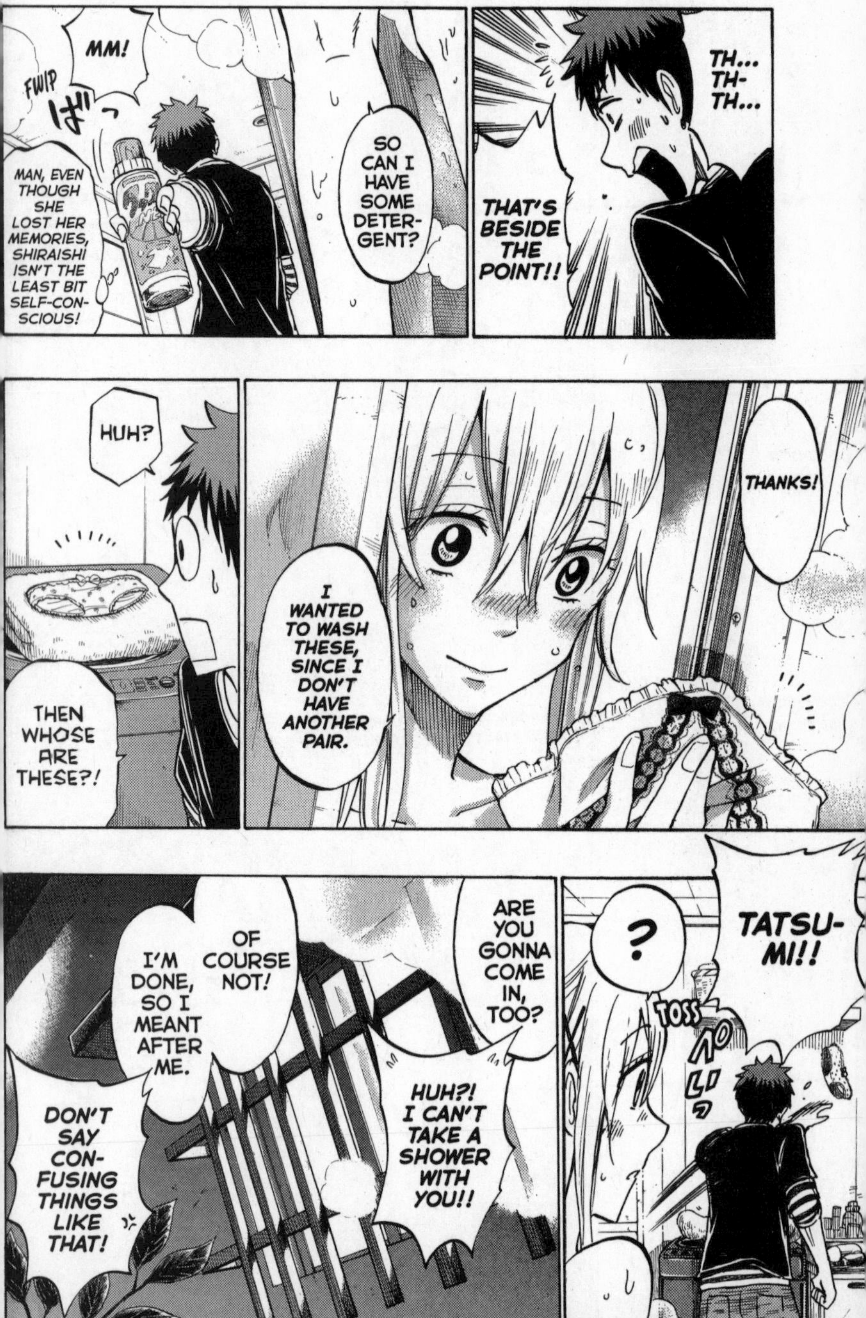
TH... TH- TH...
THAT'S BESIDE THE POINT!!
SO CAN I HAVE SOME DETERGENT?
MM!
FWIP
ばっ
MAN, EVEN THOUGH SHE LOST HER MEMORIES, SHIRAISHI ISN'T THE LEAST BIT SELF-CONSCIOUS!
THANKS!
I WANTED TO WASH THESE, SINCE I DON'T HAVE ANOTHER PAIR.
HUH?
THEN WHOSE ARE THESE?!
TATSUMI!!
?
TOSS
ARE YOU GONNA COME IN, TOO?
HUH?! I CAN'T TAKE A SHOWER WITH YOU!!
OF COURSE NOT!
I'M DONE, SO I MEANT AFTER ME.
DON'T SAY CONFUSING THINGS LIKE THAT!

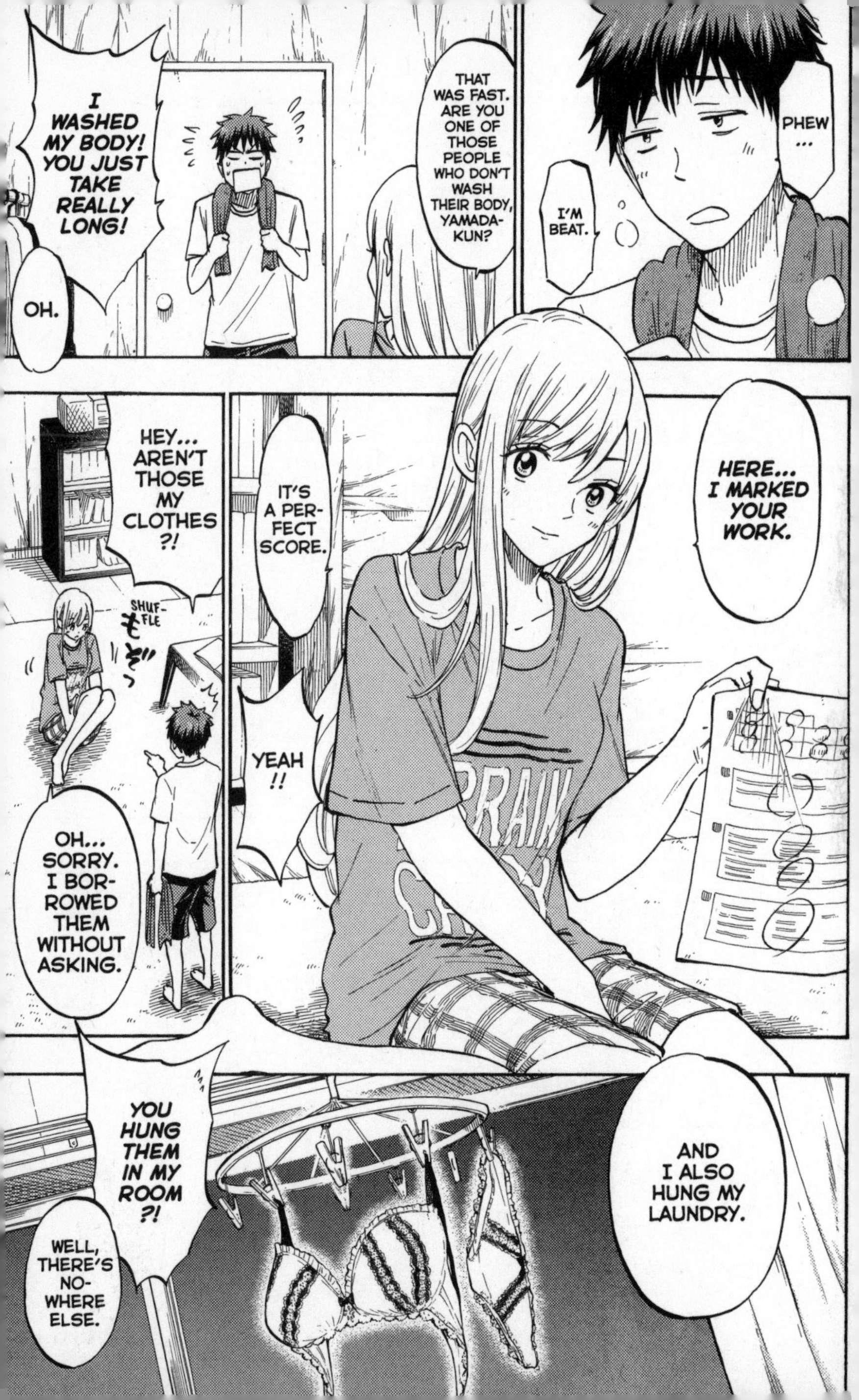
PHEW...
I'M BEAT.
THAT WAS FAST. ARE YOU ONE OF THOSE PEOPLE WHO DON'T WASH THEIR BODY, YAMADA-KUN?
I WASHED MY BODY! YOU JUST TAKE REALLY LONG!
OH.
HERE... I MARKED YOUR WORK.
IT'S A PERFECT SCORE.
YEAH!!
HEY... AREN'T THOSE MY CLOTHES?!
SHUFFLE
OH... SORRY. I BORROWED THEM WITHOUT ASKING.
AND I ALSO HUNG MY LAUNDRY.
YOU HUNG THEM IN MY ROOM?!
WELL, THERE'S NOWHERE ELSE.

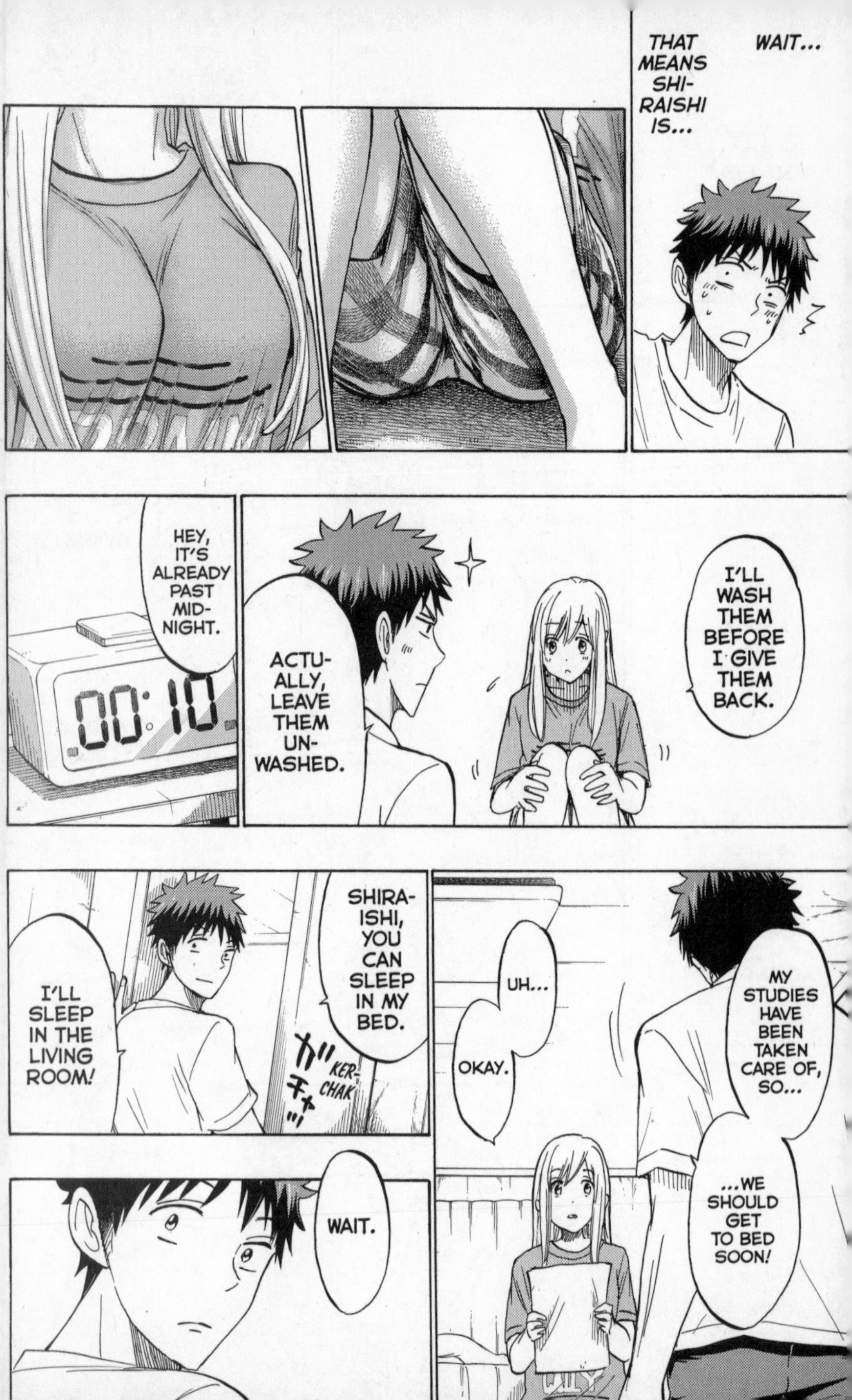
WAIT...
THAT MEANS SHIRAISHI IS...
I'LL WASH THEM BEFORE I GIVE THEM BACK.
ACTUALLY, LEAVE THEM UNWASHED.
HEY, IT'S ALREADY PAST MIDNIGHT.
00:10
MY STUDIES HAVE BEEN TAKEN CARE OF, SO...
...WE SHOULD GET TO BED SOON!
UH...
OKAY.
SHIRAISHI, YOU CAN SLEEP IN MY BED.
I'LL SLEEP IN THE LIVING ROOM!
ガチャッ
KERCHAK
WAIT.

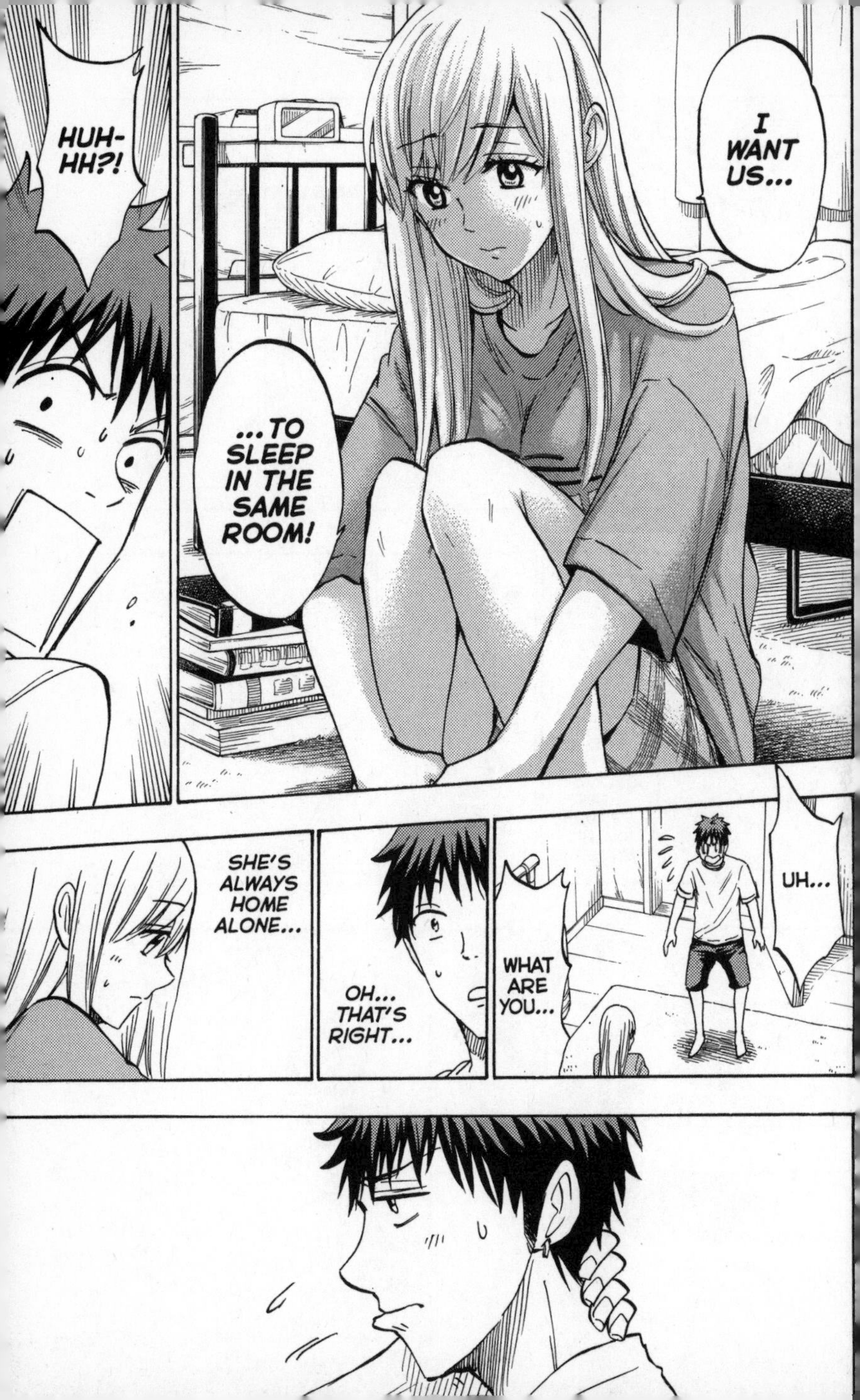
I WANT US...
...TO SLEEP IN THE SAME ROOM!
HUH-HH?!
UH...
WHAT ARE YOU...
OH... THAT'S RIGHT...
SHE'S ALWAYS HOME ALONE...

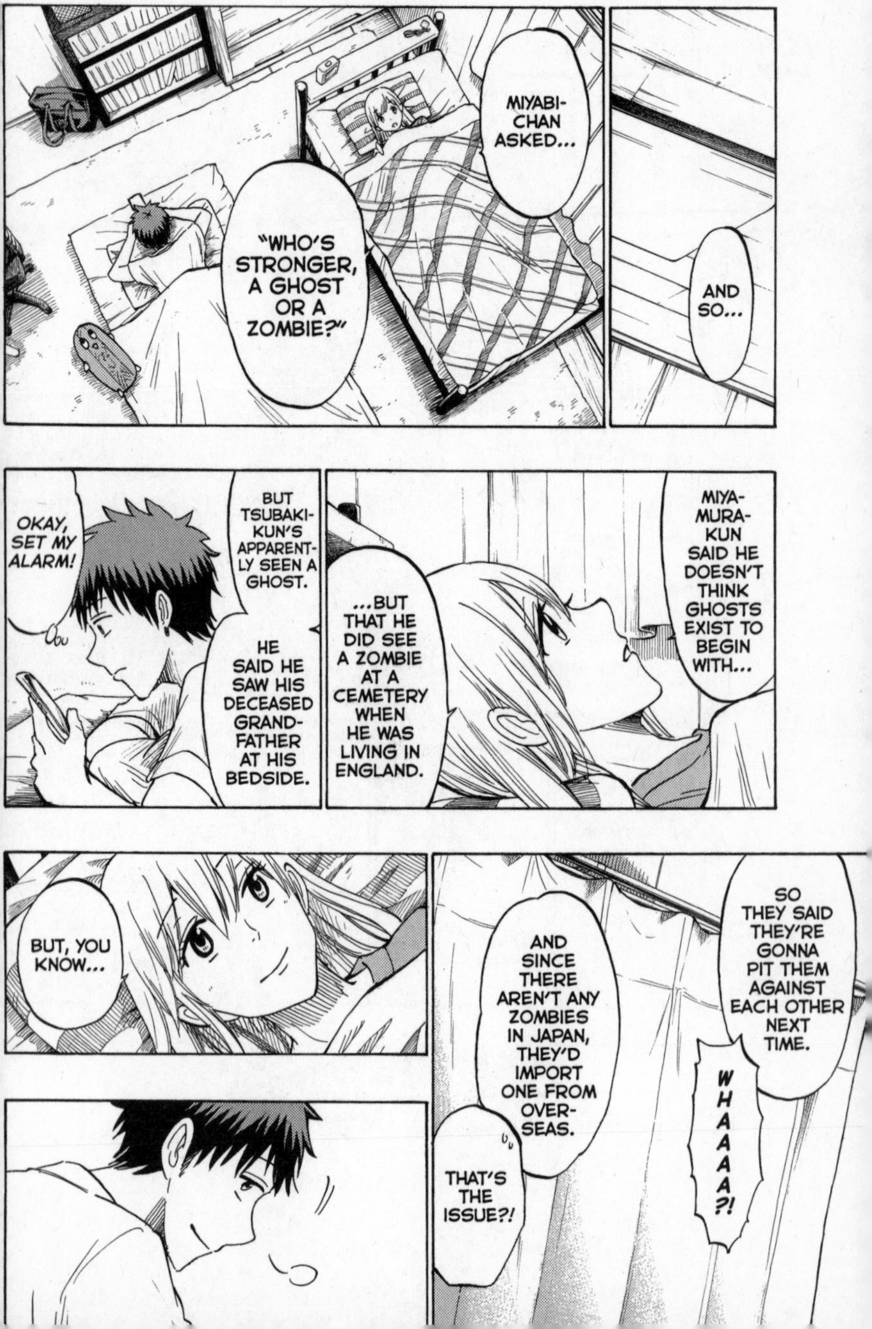
AND SO...
MIYABI-CHAN ASKED...
"WHO'S STRONGER, A GHOST OR A ZOMBIE?"
MIYAMURA-KUN SAID HE DOESN'T THINK GHOSTS EXIST TO BEGIN WITH...
...BUT THAT HE DID SEE A ZOMBIE AT A CEMETERY WHEN HE WAS LIVING IN ENGLAND.
BUT TSUBAKI-KUN'S APPARENTLY SEEN A GHOST.
HE SAID HE SAW HIS DECEASED GRANDFATHER AT HIS BEDSIDE.
OKAY, SET MY ALARM!
SO THEY SAID THEY'RE GONNA PIT THEM AGAINST EACH OTHER NEXT TIME.
WHAAAAA?!
AND SINCE THERE AREN'T ANY ZOMBIES IN JAPAN, THEY'D IMPORT ONE FROM OVERSEAS.
THAT'S THE ISSUE?!
BUT, YOU KNOW...

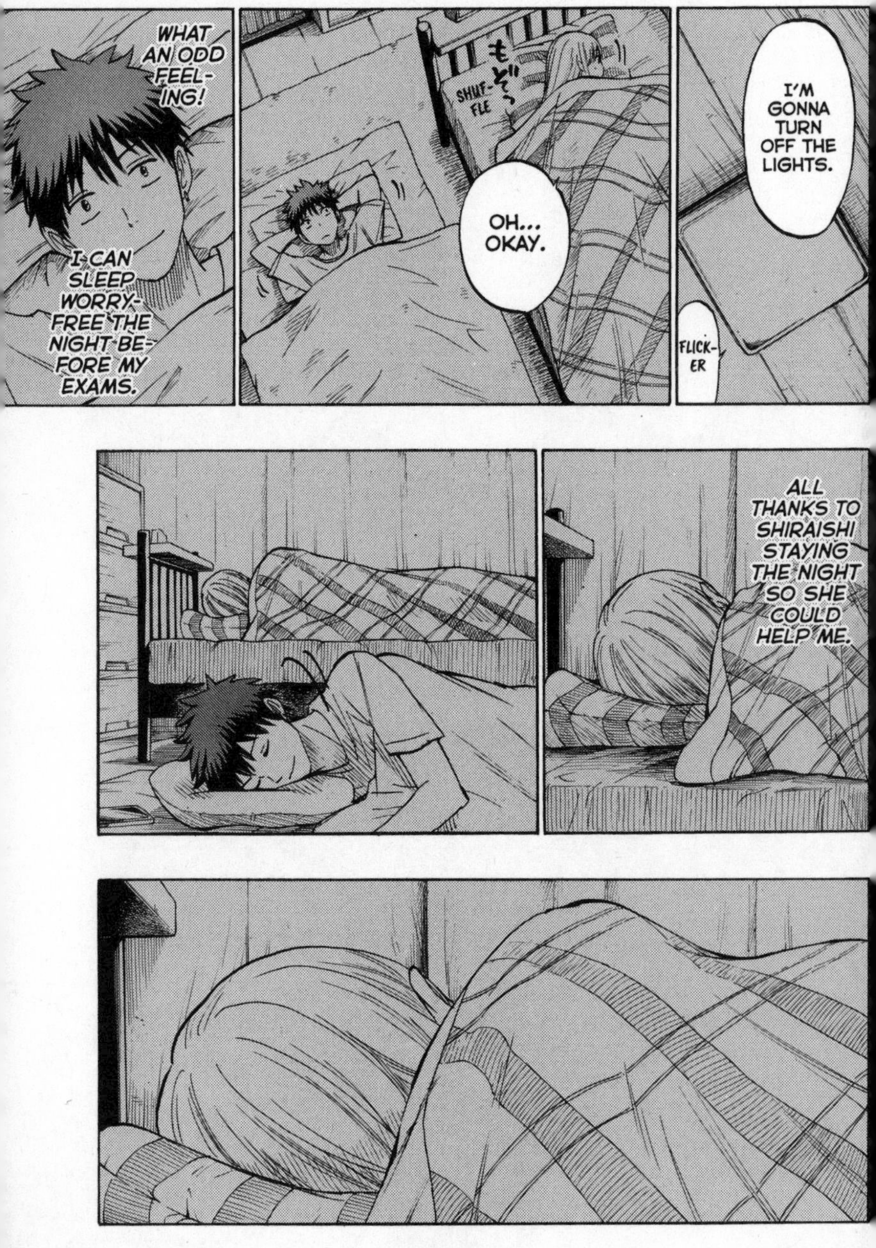
I'M GONNA TURN OFF THE LIGHTS.
FLICK-ER
もぞっ
SHUF-FLE
OH... OKAY.
WHAT AN ODD FEEL-ING!
I CAN SLEEP WORRY-FREE THE NIGHT BE-FORE MY EXAMS.
ALL THANKS TO SHIRAISHI STAYING THE NIGHT SO SHE COULD HELP ME.

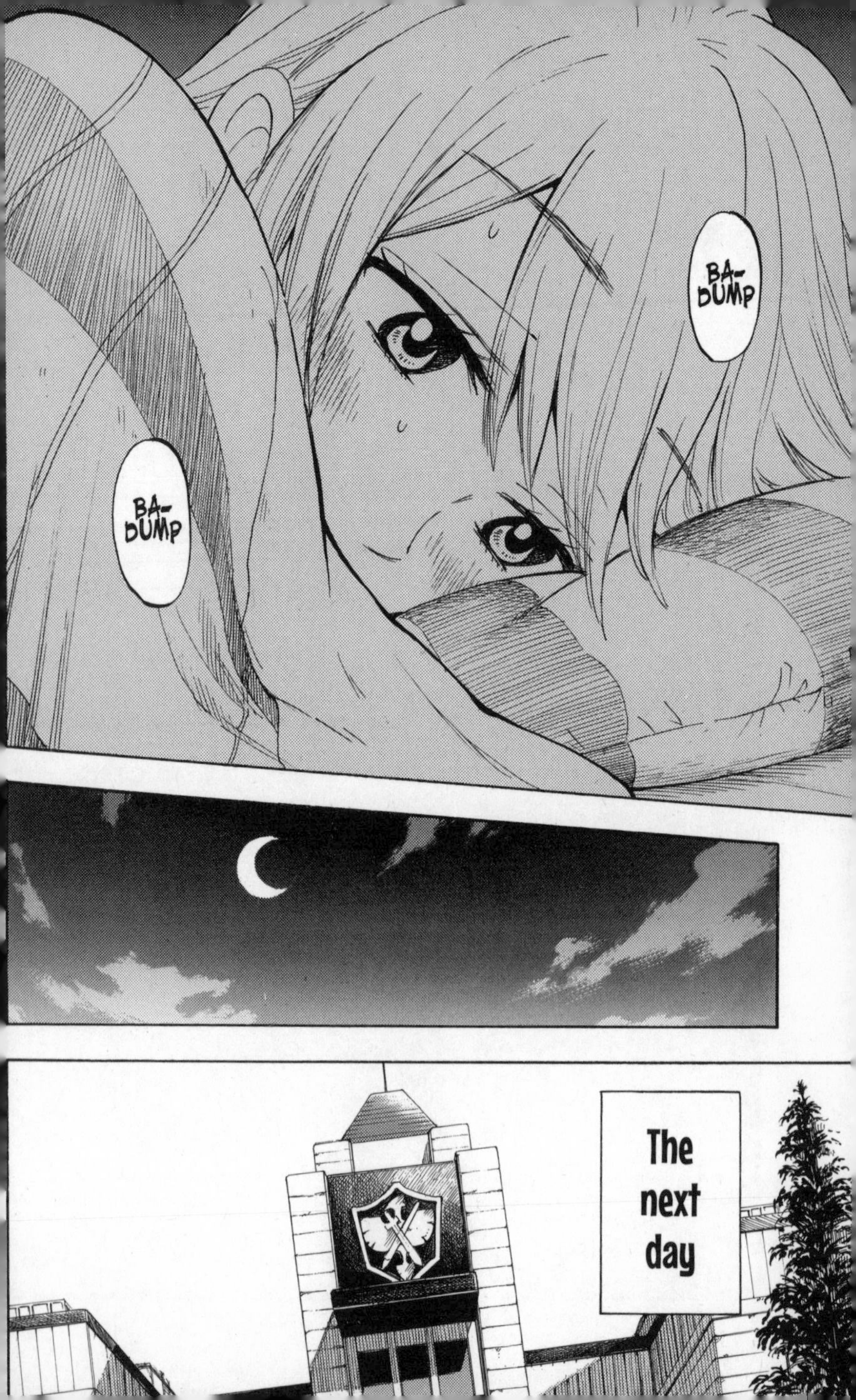
BA-DUMP
BA-DUMP
The next day

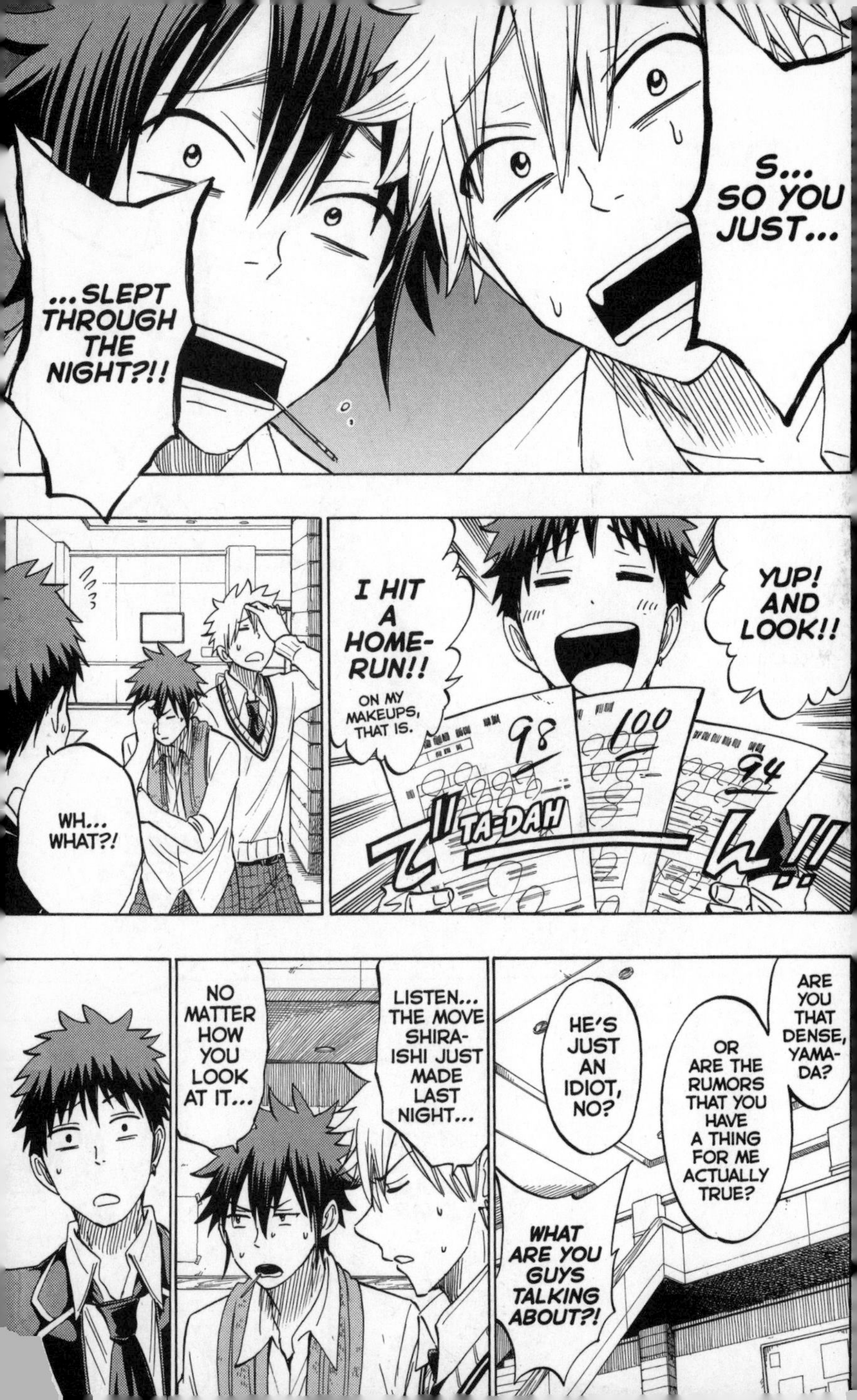
S... SO YOU JUST...
...SLEPT THROUGH THE NIGHT?!!
YUP! AND LOOK!!
I HIT A HOME-RUN!!
ON MY MAKEUPS, THAT IS.
100
98
94
TA-DAH
WH... WHAT?!
ARE YOU THAT DENSE, YAMADA?
OR ARE THE RUMORS THAT YOU HAVE A THING FOR ME ACTUALLY TRUE?
HE'S JUST AN IDIOT, NO?
WHAT ARE YOU GUYS TALKING ABOUT?!
LISTEN... THE MOVE SHIRAISHI JUST MADE LAST NIGHT...
NO MATTER HOW YOU LOOK AT IT...

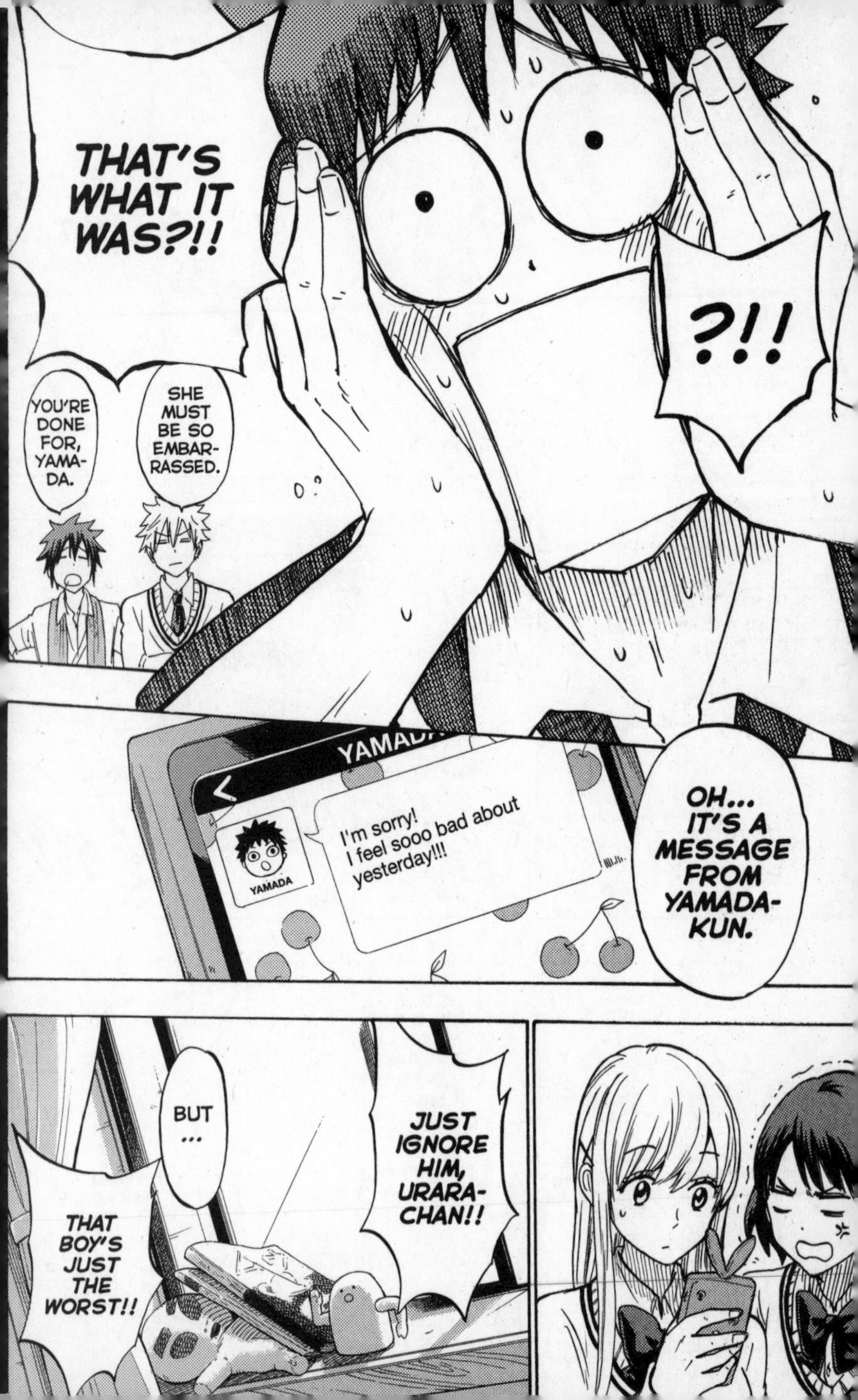
?!!
THAT'S WHAT IT WAS?!!
SHE MUST BE SO EMBARRASSED.
YOU'RE DONE FOR, YAMADA.
OH... IT'S A MESSAGE FROM YAMADA-KUN.
YAMADA
I'm sorry! I feel sooo bad about yesterday!!!
YAMADA
JUST IGNORE HIM, URARA-CHAN!!
BUT...
THAT BOY'S JUST THE WORST!!

CHAPTER 187: Come on over to the Poetry Club!

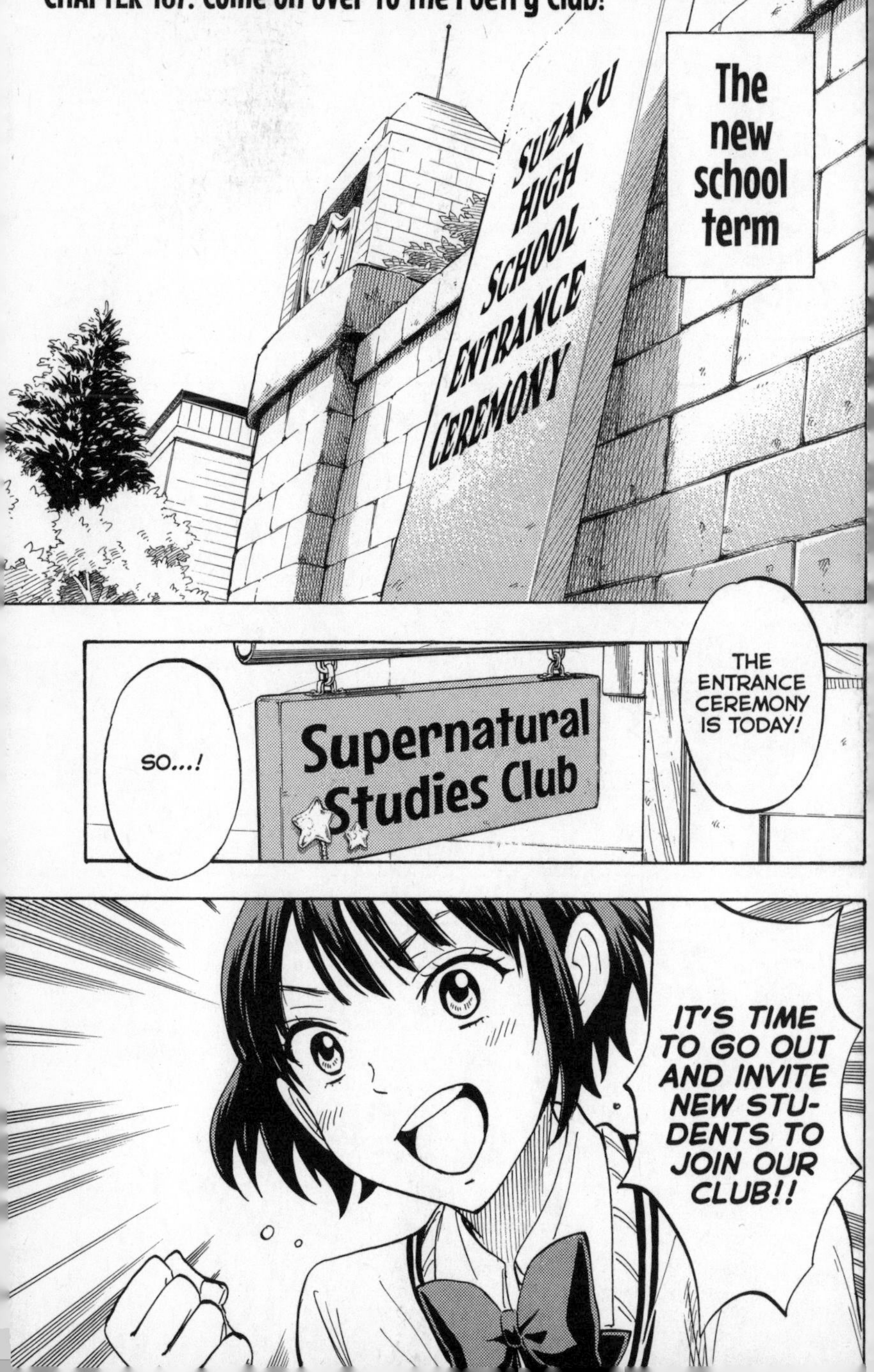
The new school term
SUZAKU HIGH SCHOOL ENTRANCE CEREMONY
THE ENTRANCE CEREMONY IS TODAY!
Supernatural Studies Club
SO...!
IT'S TIME TO GO OUT AND INVITE NEW STU-DENTS TO JOIN OUR CLUB!!

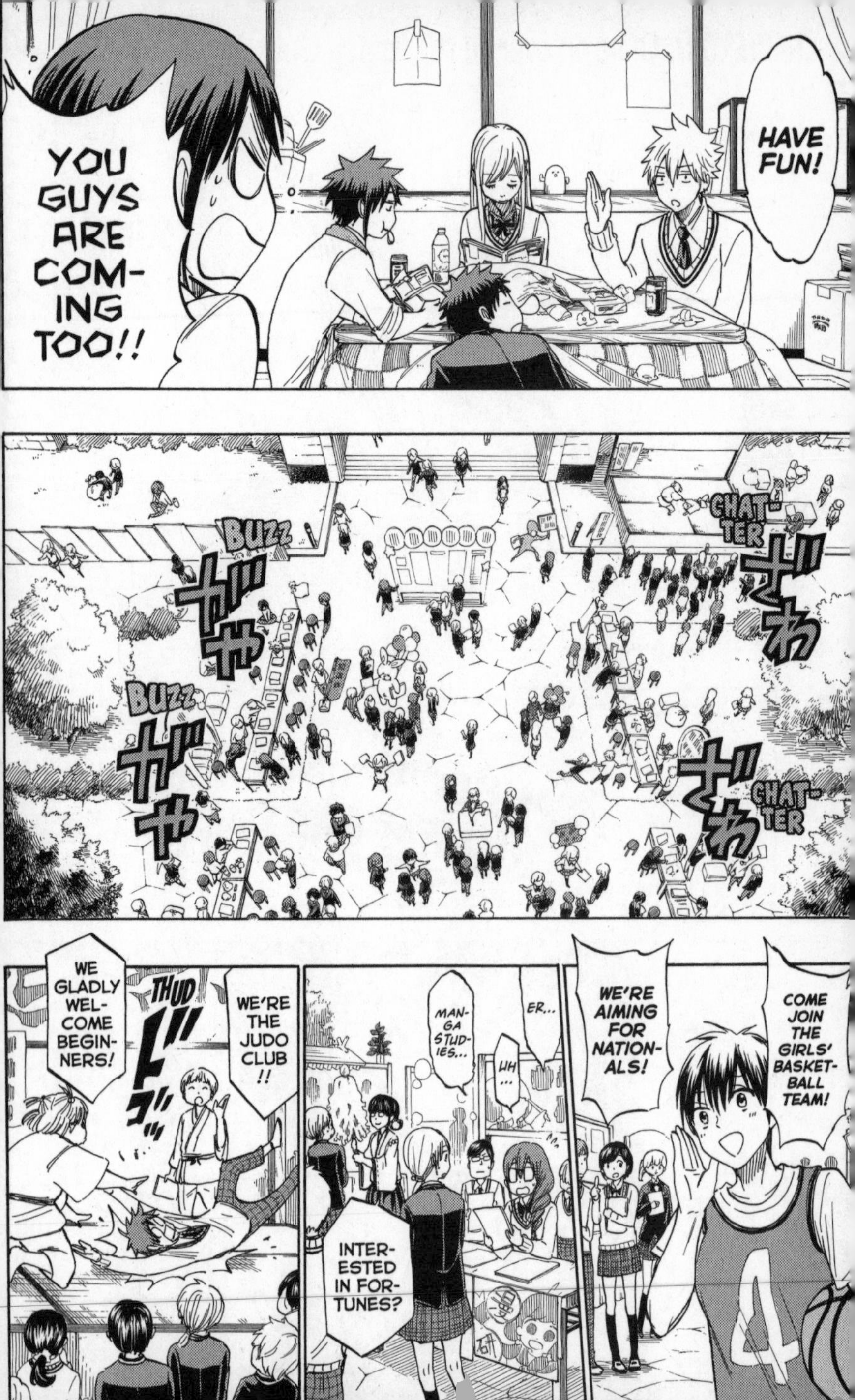
HAVE FUN!
YOU GUYS ARE COMING TOO!!
CHATTER
ざわ
BUZZ
ガヤ
BUZZ
ガヤ
ざわ
CHATTER
COME JOIN THE GIRLS' BASKETBALL TEAM!
WE'RE AIMING FOR NATIONALS!
ER...
UH...
MANGA STUDIES...
INTERESTED IN FORTUNES?
WE'RE THE JUDO CLUB!!
THUD
ドゴッ
WE GLADLY WELCOME BEGINNERS!

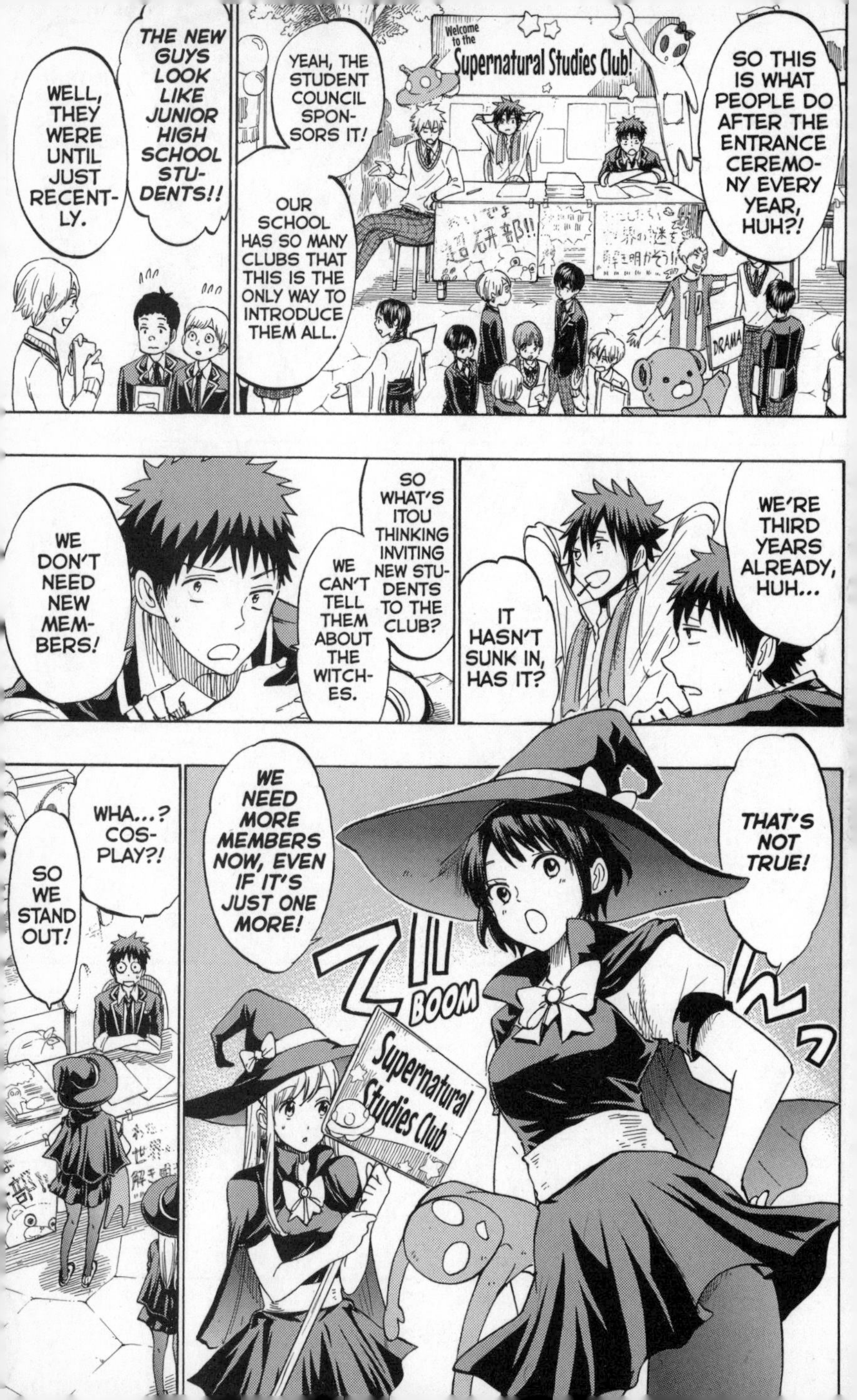

Welcome to the Supernatural Studies Club!
SO THIS IS WHAT PEOPLE DO AFTER THE ENTRANCE CEREMONY EVERY YEAR, HUH?!
YEAH, THE STUDENT COUNCIL SPONSORS IT!
OUR SCHOOL HAS SO MANY CLUBS THAT THIS IS THE ONLY WAY TO INTRODUCE THEM ALL.
DRAMA
THE NEW GUYS LOOK LIKE JUNIOR HIGH SCHOOL STUDENTS!!
WELL, THEY WERE UNTIL JUST RECENTLY.
WE'RE THIRD YEARS ALREADY, HUH...
IT HASN'T SUNK IN, HAS IT?
SO WHAT'S ITOU THINKING INVITING NEW STUDENTS TO THE CLUB?
WE CAN'T TELL THEM ABOUT THE WITCHES.
WE DON'T NEED NEW MEMBERS!
THAT'S NOT TRUE!
WE NEED MORE MEMBERS NOW, EVEN IF IT'S JUST ONE MORE!
BOOM
Supernatural Studies Club
WHA...? COSPLAY?!
SO WE STAND OUT!

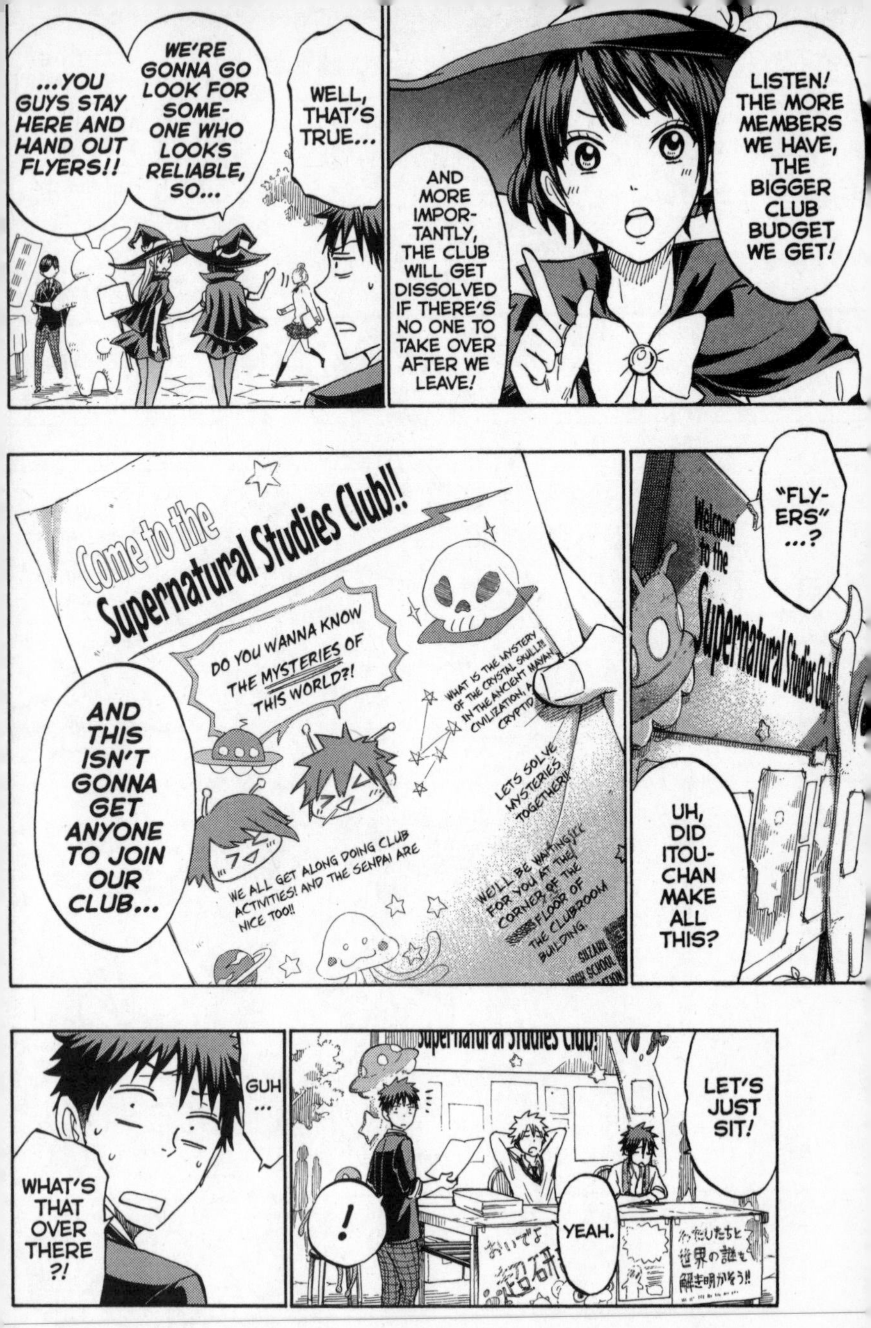
LISTEN! THE MORE MEMBERS WE HAVE, THE BIGGER CLUB BUDGET WE GET!
AND MORE IMPORTANTLY, THE CLUB WILL GET DISSOLVED IF THERE'S NO ONE TO TAKE OVER AFTER WE LEAVE!
WELL, THAT'S TRUE...
WE'RE GONNA GO LOOK FOR SOMEONE WHO LOOKS RELIABLE, SO...
...YOU GUYS STAY HERE AND HAND OUT FLYERS!!
"FLYERS"...?
Welcome to the Supernatural Studies Club!
UH, DID ITOU-CHAN MAKE ALL THIS?
Come to the Supernatural Studies Club!!
DO YOU WANNA KNOW THE MYSTERIES OF THIS WORLD?!
WHAT IS THE MYSTERY OF THE CRYSTAL SKULL!? IN THE ANCIENT MAYAN CIVILIZATION,
LETS SOLVE MYSTERIES TOGETHER!!
WE ALL GET ALONG DOING CLUB ACTIVITIES! AND THE SENPAI ARE NICE TOO!!
WE'LL BE WAITING FOR YOU AT THE CORNER OF THE FLOOR OF THE CLUBROOM BUILDING.
AND THIS ISN'T GONNA GET ANYONE TO JOIN OUR CLUB...
Supernatural Studies Club!
LET'S JUST SIT!
YEAH.
!
わたしたちと世界の謎を解き明かそう!!
おいでよ超研
GUH...
WHAT'S THAT OVER THERE?!

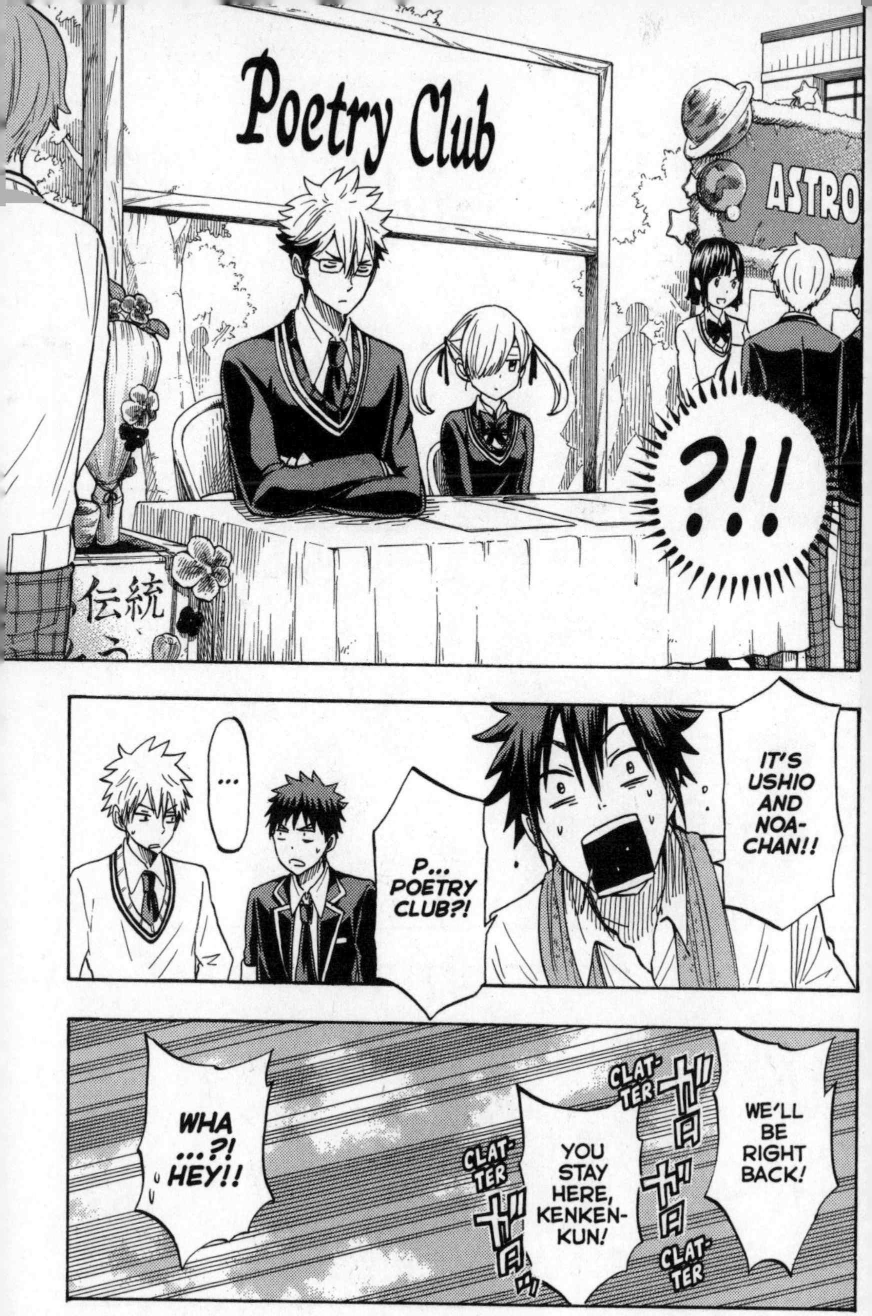
Poetry Club
ASTRO
伝統
?!!
IT'S USHIO AND NOA-CHAN!!
P... POETRY CLUB?!
...
WE'LL BE RIGHT BACK!
CLAT-TER
CLAT-TER
YOU STAY HERE, KENKEN-KUN!
CLAT-TER
WHA ...?! HEY!!

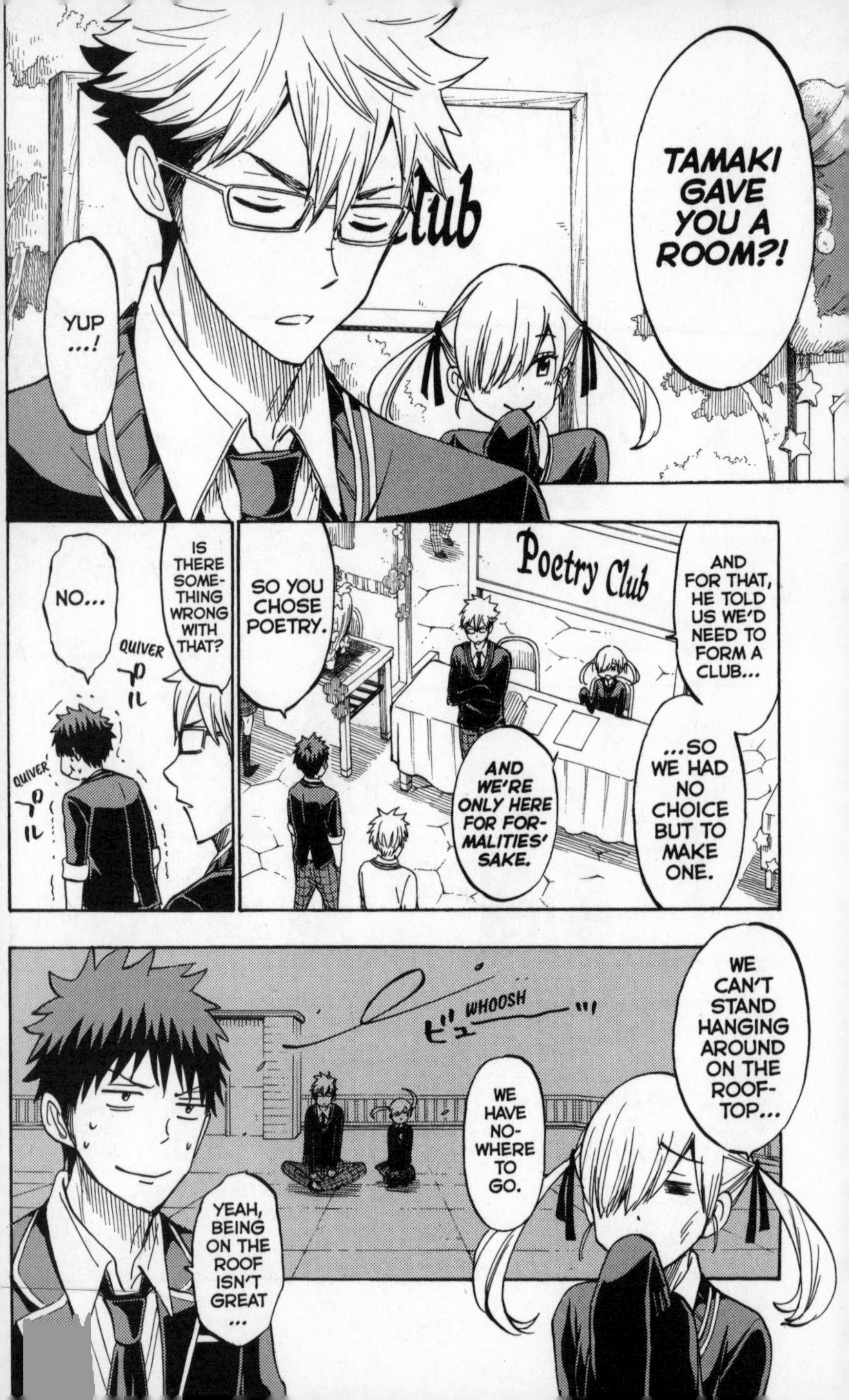
TAMAKI GAVE YOU A ROOM?!
YUP ...!
AND FOR THAT, HE TOLD US WE'D NEED TO FORM A CLUB...
...SO WE HAD NO CHOICE BUT TO MAKE ONE.
Poetry Club
AND WE'RE ONLY HERE FOR FORMALITIES' SAKE.
SO YOU CHOSE POETRY.
IS THERE SOMETHING WRONG WITH THAT?
NO...
QUIVER
プル
QUIVER
プル
WHOOSH
ビュ
WE CAN'T STAND HANGING AROUND ON THE ROOFTOP...
WE HAVE NOWHERE TO GO.
YEAH, BEING ON THE ROOF ISN'T GREAT ...

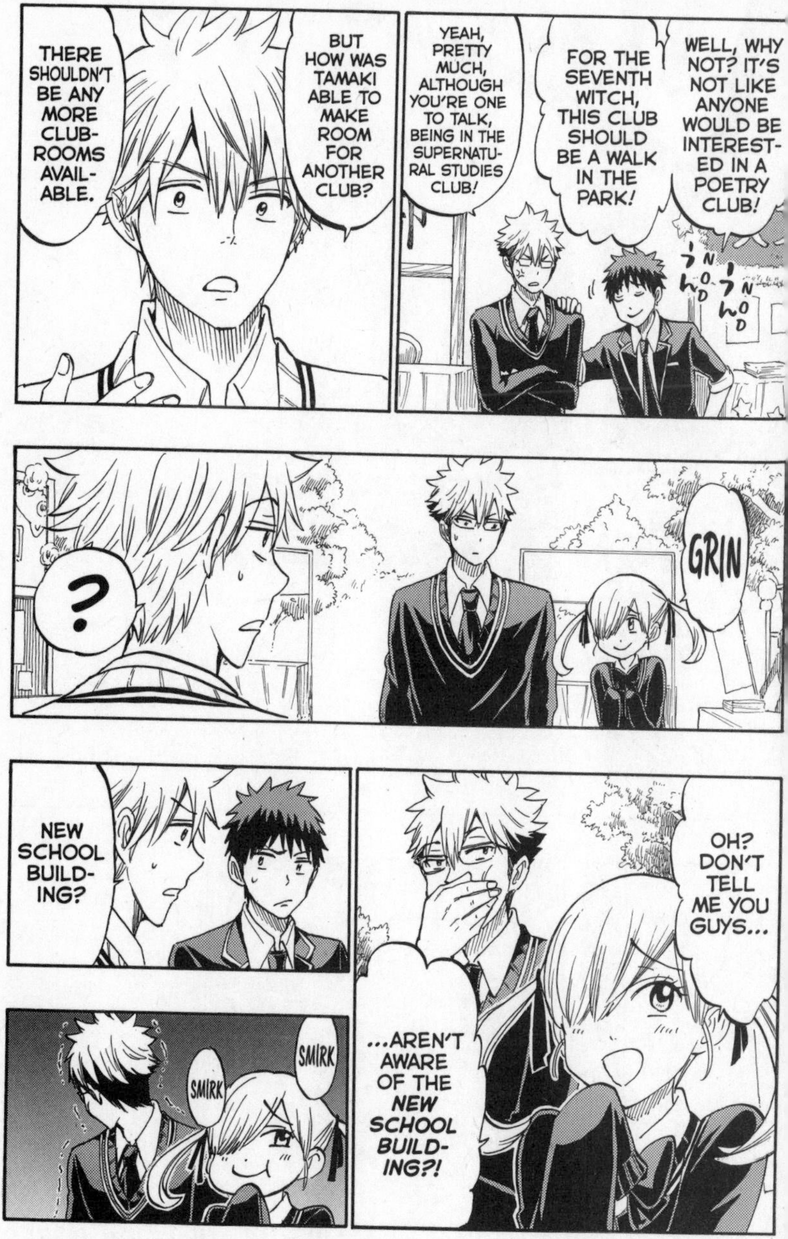
WELL, WHY NOT? IT'S NOT LIKE ANYONE WOULD BE INTEREST-ED IN A POETRY CLUB!
FOR THE SEVENTH WITCH, THIS CLUB SHOULD BE A WALK IN THE PARK!
NOD
NOD
YEAH, PRETTY MUCH, ALTHOUGH YOU'RE ONE TO TALK, BEING IN THE SUPERNATU-RAL STUDIES CLUB!
BUT HOW WAS TAMAKI ABLE TO MAKE ROOM FOR ANOTHER CLUB?
THERE SHOULDN'T BE ANY MORE CLUB-ROOMS AVAIL-ABLE.
GRIN
?
OH? DON'T TELL ME YOU GUYS...
...AREN'T AWARE OF THE *NEW SCHOOL BUILD-ING?!*
NEW SCHOOL BUILD-ING?
SMIRK
SMIRK

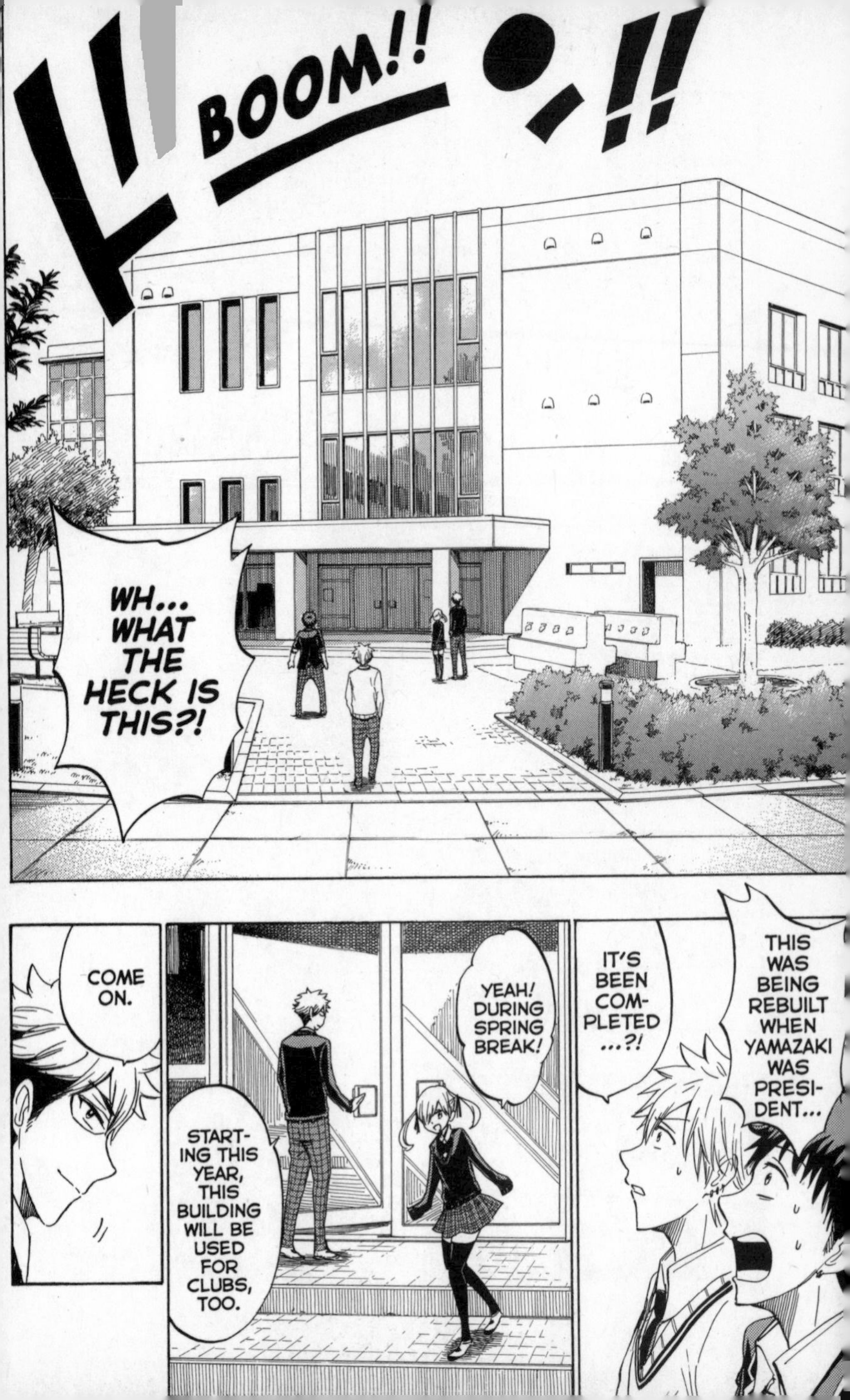
BOOM!!
WH... WHAT THE HECK IS THIS?!
THIS WAS BEING REBUILT WHEN YAMAZAKI WAS PRESIDENT...
IT'S BEEN COMPLETED...?!
YEAH! DURING SPRING BREAK!
STARTING THIS YEAR, THIS BUILDING WILL BE USED FOR CLUBS, TOO.
COME ON.

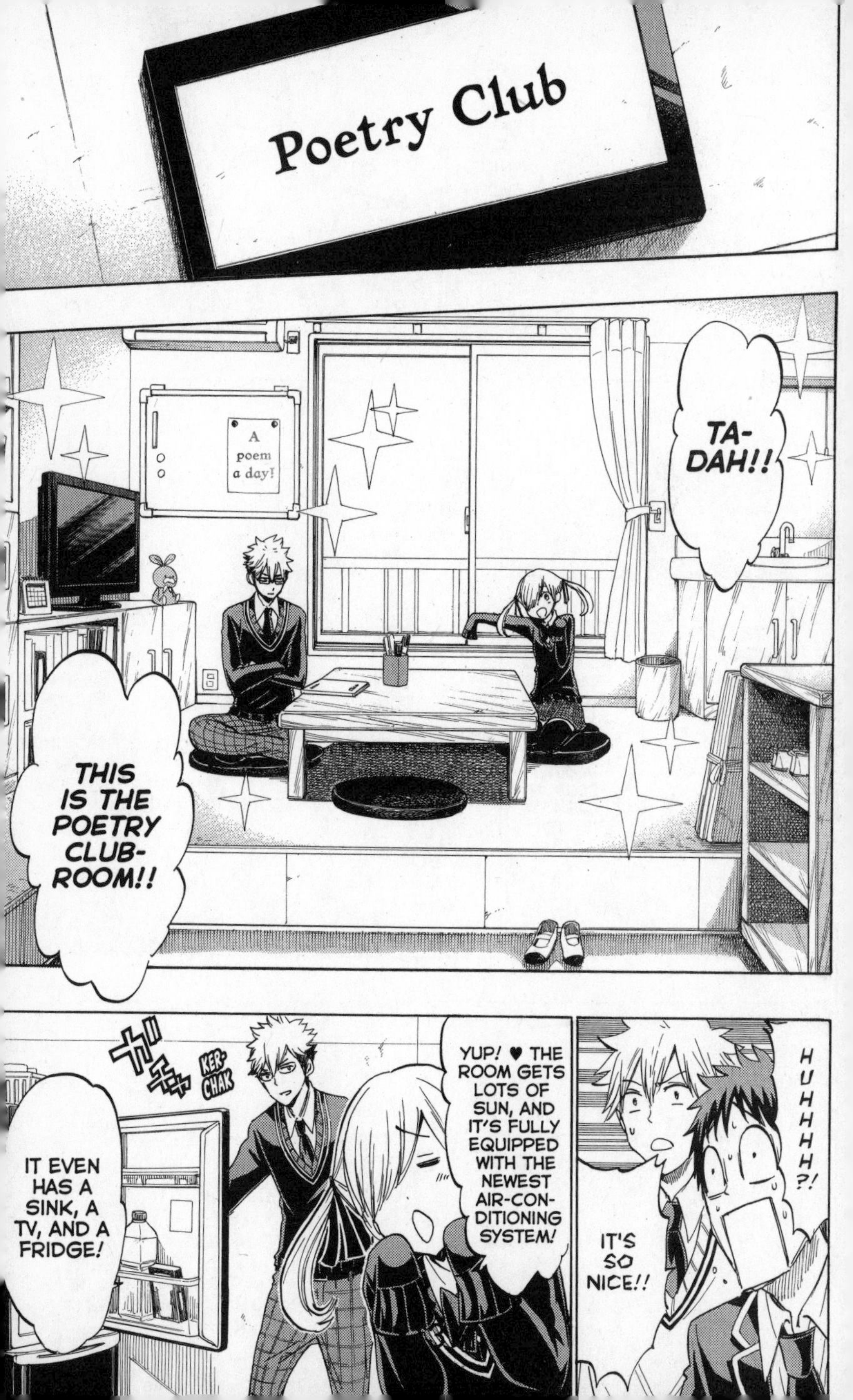
Poetry Club
TA-DAH!!
A poem a day!
THIS IS THE POETRY CLUB-ROOM!!
HUHHHHH?!
IT'S SO NICE!!
YUP! ♥ THE ROOM GETS LOTS OF SUN, AND IT'S FULLY EQUIPPED WITH THE NEWEST AIR-CONDITIONING SYSTEM!
KER-CHAK
IT EVEN HAS A SINK, A TV, AND A FRIDGE!

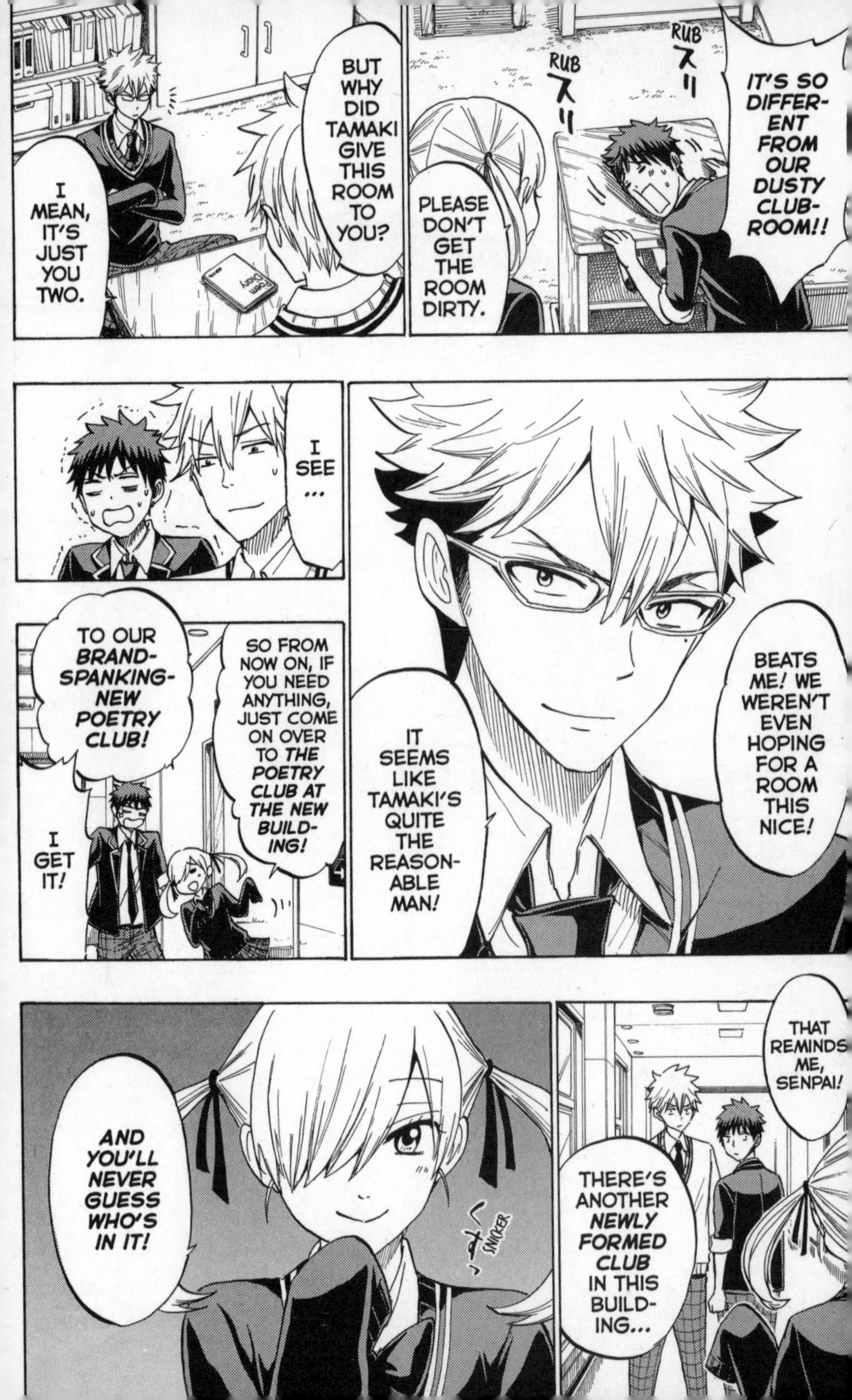
IT'S SO DIFFERENT FROM OUR DUSTY CLUBROOM!!
RUB スリ
RUB スリ
PLEASE DON'T GET THE ROOM DIRTY.
BUT WHY DID TAMAKI GIVE THIS ROOM TO YOU?
Poem Diary
I MEAN, IT'S JUST YOU TWO.
BEATS ME! WE WEREN'T EVEN HOPING FOR A ROOM THIS NICE!
IT SEEMS LIKE TAMAKI'S QUITE THE REASONABLE MAN!
I SEE...
SO FROM NOW ON, IF YOU NEED ANYTHING, JUST COME ON OVER TO THE POETRY CLUB AT THE NEW BUILDING!
TO OUR BRAND-SPANKING-NEW POETRY CLUB!
I GET IT!
THAT REMINDS ME, SENPAI!
THERE'S ANOTHER NEWLY FORMED CLUB IN THIS BUILDING...
くすっ SNICKER
AND YOU'LL NEVER GUESS WHO'S IN IT!

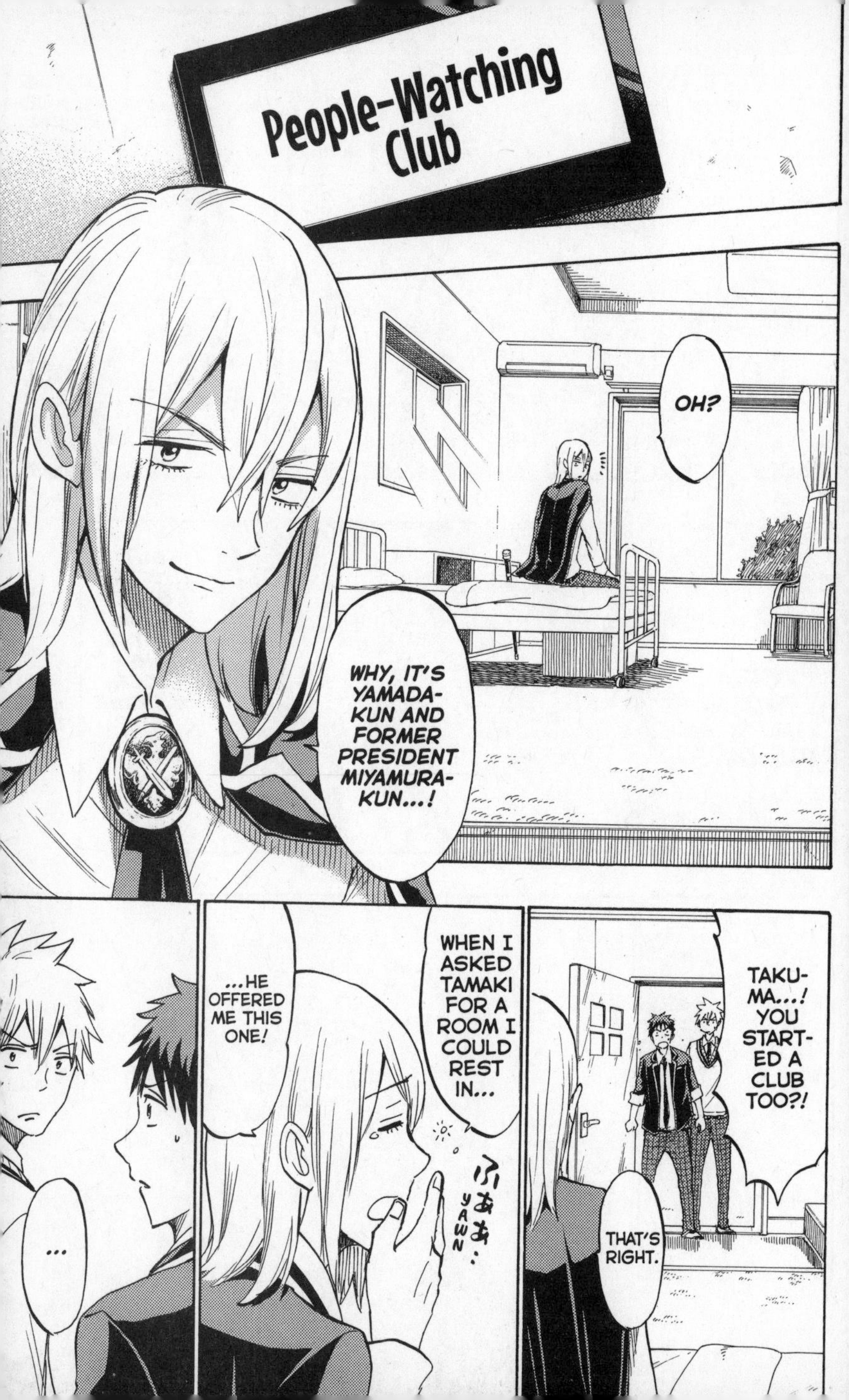
People-Watching Club
OH?
WHY, IT'S YAMADA-KUN AND FORMER PRESIDENT MIYAMURA-KUN...!
TAKU-MA...! YOU START-ED A CLUB TOO?!
THAT'S RIGHT.
WHEN I ASKED TAMAKI FOR A ROOM I COULD REST IN...
...HE OFFERED ME THIS ONE!
ふぁあ…
YAWN
...

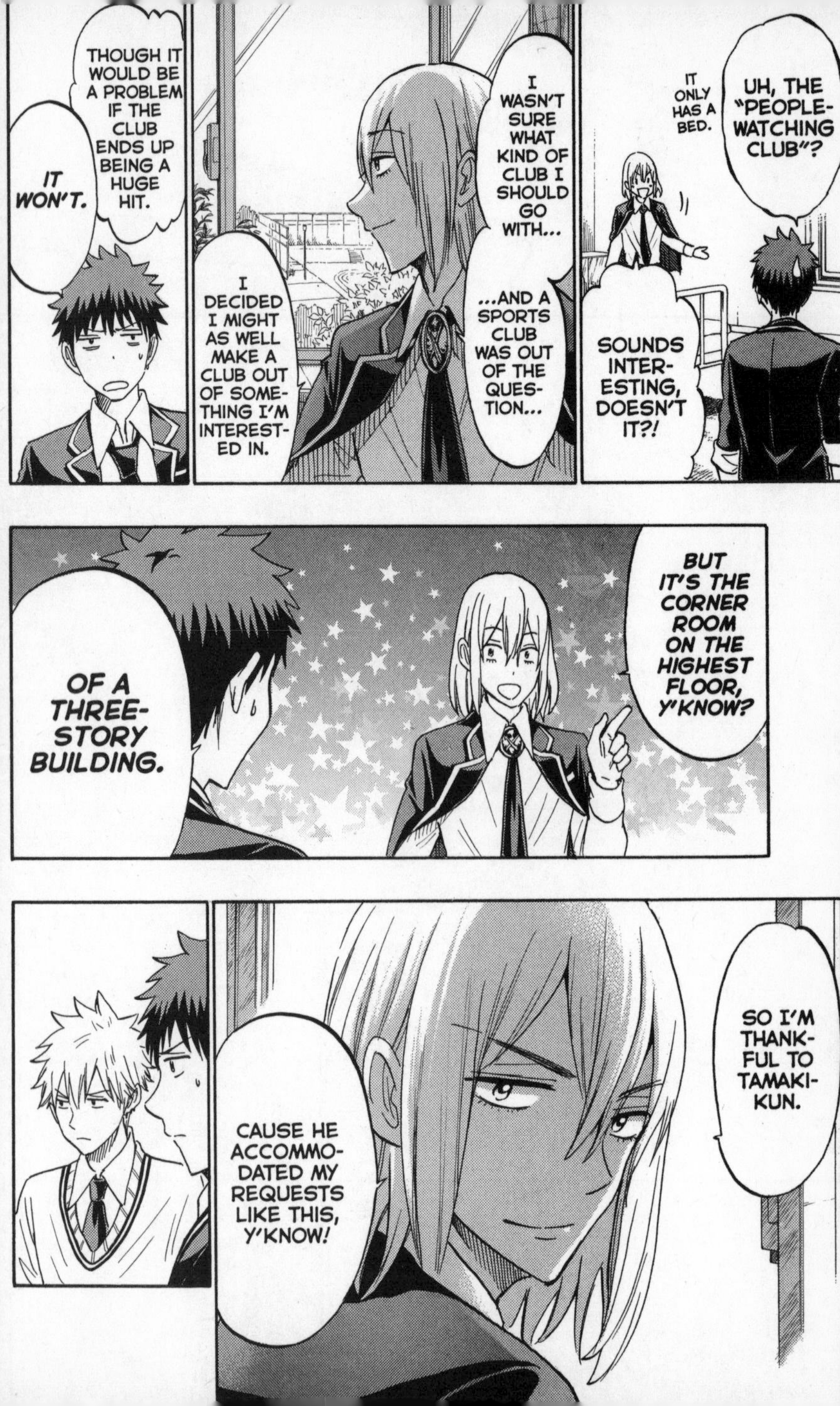
UH, THE "PEOPLE-WATCHING CLUB"?
IT ONLY HAS A BED.
SOUNDS INTERESTING, DOESN'T IT?!
I WASN'T SURE WHAT KIND OF CLUB I SHOULD GO WITH...
...AND A SPORTS CLUB WAS OUT OF THE QUESTION...
I DECIDED I MIGHT AS WELL MAKE A CLUB OUT OF SOMETHING I'M INTERESTED IN.
THOUGH IT WOULD BE A PROBLEM IF THE CLUB ENDS UP BEING A HUGE HIT.
IT WON'T.
BUT IT'S THE CORNER ROOM ON THE HIGHEST FLOOR, Y'KNOW?
OF A THREE-STORY BUILDING.
SO I'M THANKFUL TO TAMAKI-KUN.
CAUSE HE ACCOMMODATED MY REQUESTS LIKE THIS, Y'KNOW!

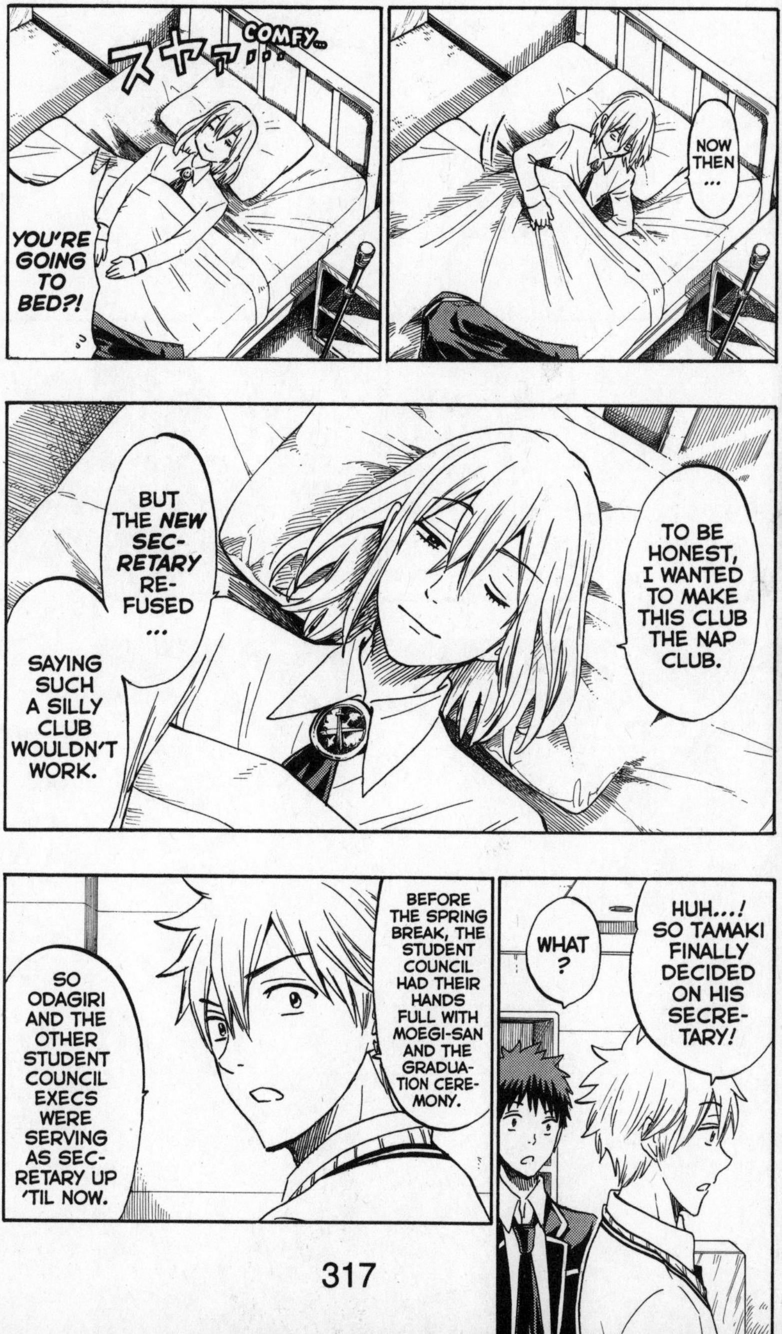
NOW THEN...
スヤァ...
COMFY...
YOU'RE GOING TO BED?!
TO BE HONEST, I WANTED TO MAKE THIS CLUB THE NAP CLUB.
BUT THE *NEW* SEC-RETARY RE-FUSED...
SAYING SUCH A SILLY CLUB WOULDN'T WORK.
HUH...! SO TAMAKI FINALLY DECIDED ON HIS SECRE-TARY!
WHAT?
BEFORE THE SPRING BREAK, THE STUDENT COUNCIL HAD THEIR HANDS FULL WITH MOEGI-SAN AND THE GRADUA-TION CERE-MONY.
SO ODAGIRI AND THE OTHER STUDENT COUNCIL EXECS WERE SERVING AS SEC-RETARY UP 'TIL NOW.

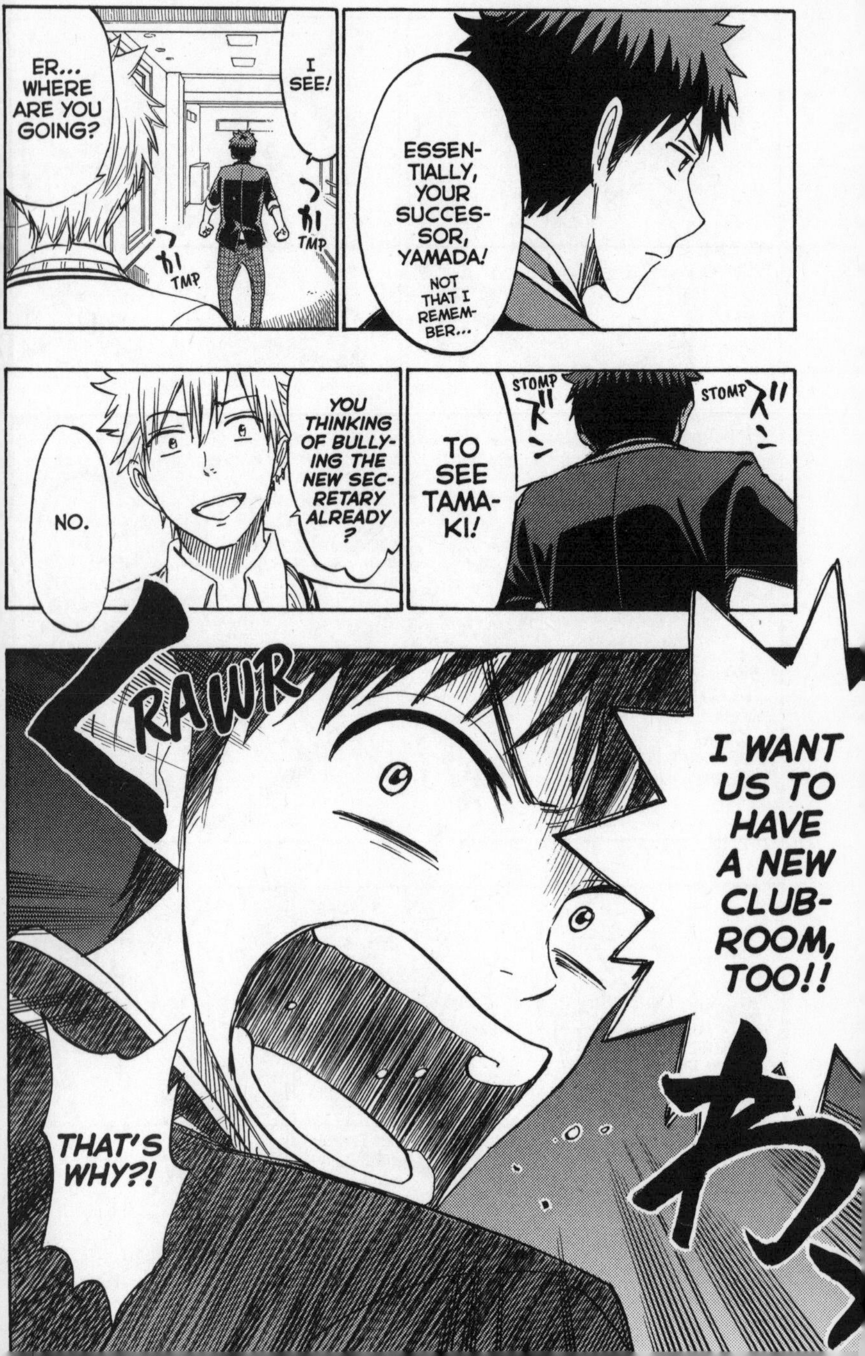
ESSEN-TIALLY, YOUR SUCCES-SOR, YAMADA!
NOT THAT I REMEM-BER...
I SEE!
ER... WHERE ARE YOU GOING?
TMP
TMP
STOMP
STOMP
TO SEE TAMA-KI!
YOU THINKING OF BULLY-ING THE NEW SEC-RETARY ALREADY?
NO.
I WANT US TO HAVE A NEW CLUB-ROOM, TOO!!
RAWR
THAT'S WHY?!

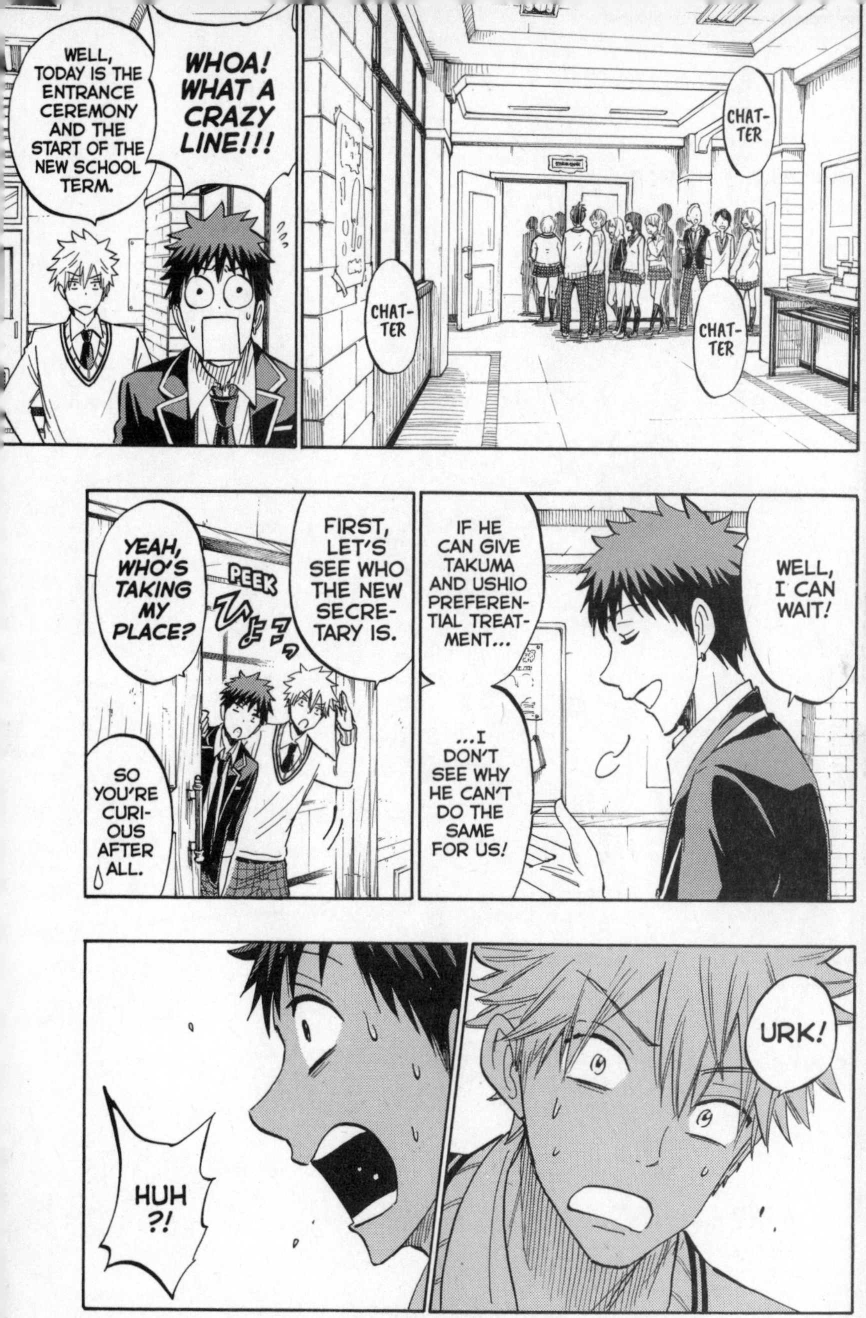
CHATTER
CHATTER
CHATTER
WHOA! WHAT A CRAZY LINE!!!
WELL, TODAY IS THE ENTRANCE CEREMONY AND THE START OF THE NEW SCHOOL TERM.
WELL, I CAN WAIT!
IF HE CAN GIVE TAKUMA AND USHIO PREFERENTIAL TREATMENT...
...I DON'T SEE WHY HE CAN'T DO THE SAME FOR US!
FIRST, LET'S SEE WHO THE NEW SECRETARY IS.
PEEK
YEAH, WHO'S TAKING MY PLACE?
SO YOU'RE CURIOUS AFTER ALL.
URK!
HUH?!

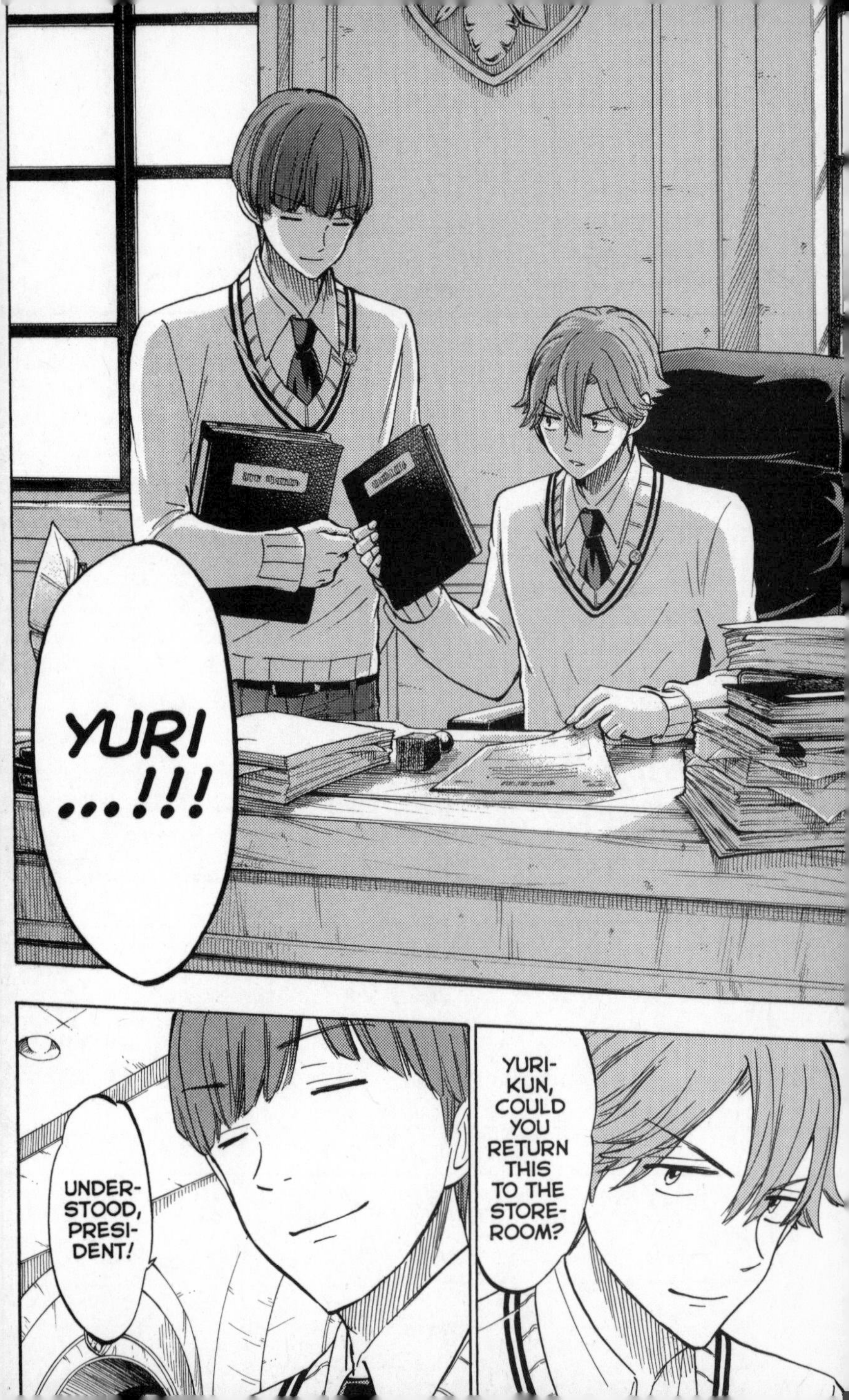
YURI ...!!!
YURI-KUN, COULD YOU RETURN THIS TO THE STORE-ROOM?
UNDER-STOOD, PRESI-DENT!

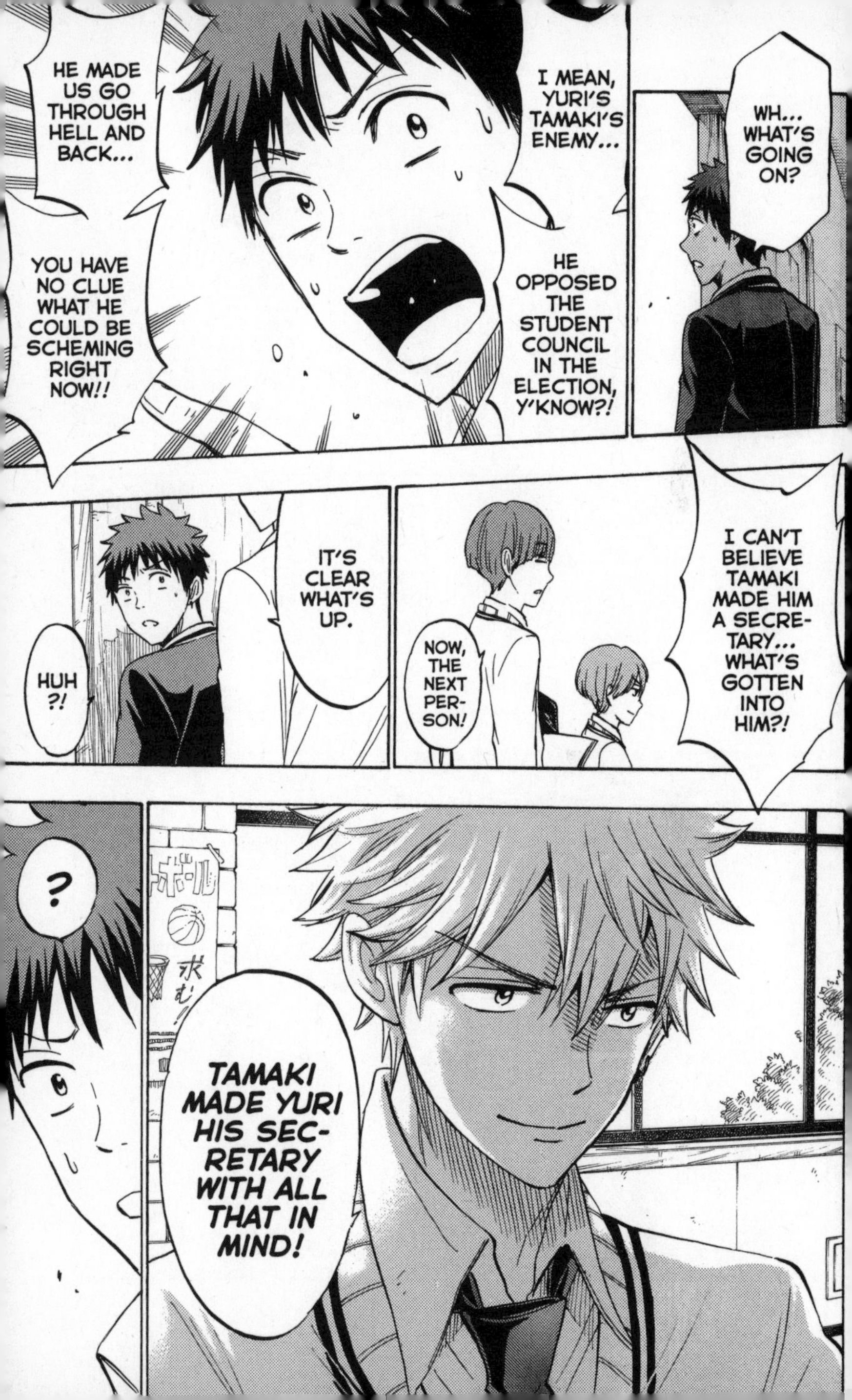
WH... WHAT'S GOING ON?
I MEAN, YURI'S TAMAKI'S ENEMY...
HE MADE US GO THROUGH HELL AND BACK...
HE OPPOSED THE STUDENT COUNCIL IN THE ELECTION, Y'KNOW?!
YOU HAVE NO CLUE WHAT HE COULD BE SCHEMING RIGHT NOW!!
I CAN'T BELIEVE TAMAKI MADE HIM A SECRETARY... WHAT'S GOTTEN INTO HIM?!
NOW, THE NEXT PERSON!
IT'S CLEAR WHAT'S UP.
HUH?!
TAMAKI MADE YURI HIS SECRETARY WITH ALL THAT IN MIND!
?

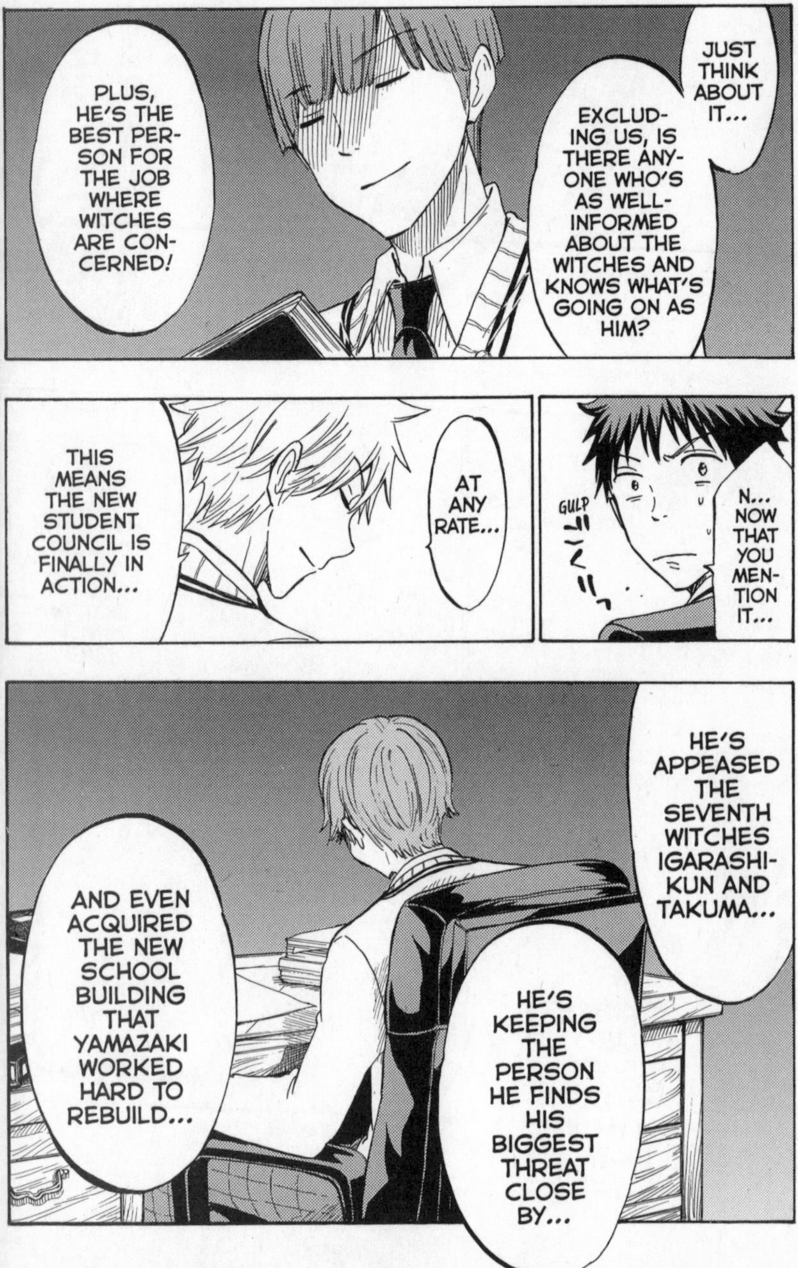
JUST THINK ABOUT IT...
EXCLUDING US, IS THERE ANYONE WHO'S AS WELL-INFORMED ABOUT THE WITCHES AND KNOWS WHAT'S GOING ON AS HIM?
PLUS, HE'S THE BEST PERSON FOR THE JOB WHERE WITCHES ARE CONCERNED!
N... NOW THAT YOU MENTION IT...
GULP
AT ANY RATE...
THIS MEANS THE NEW STUDENT COUNCIL IS FINALLY IN ACTION...
HE'S APPEASED THE SEVENTH WITCHES IGARASHI-KUN AND TAKUMA...
AND EVEN ACQUIRED THE NEW SCHOOL BUILDING THAT YAMAZAKI WORKED HARD TO REBUILD...
HE'S KEEPING THE PERSON HE FINDS HIS BIGGEST THREAT CLOSE BY...

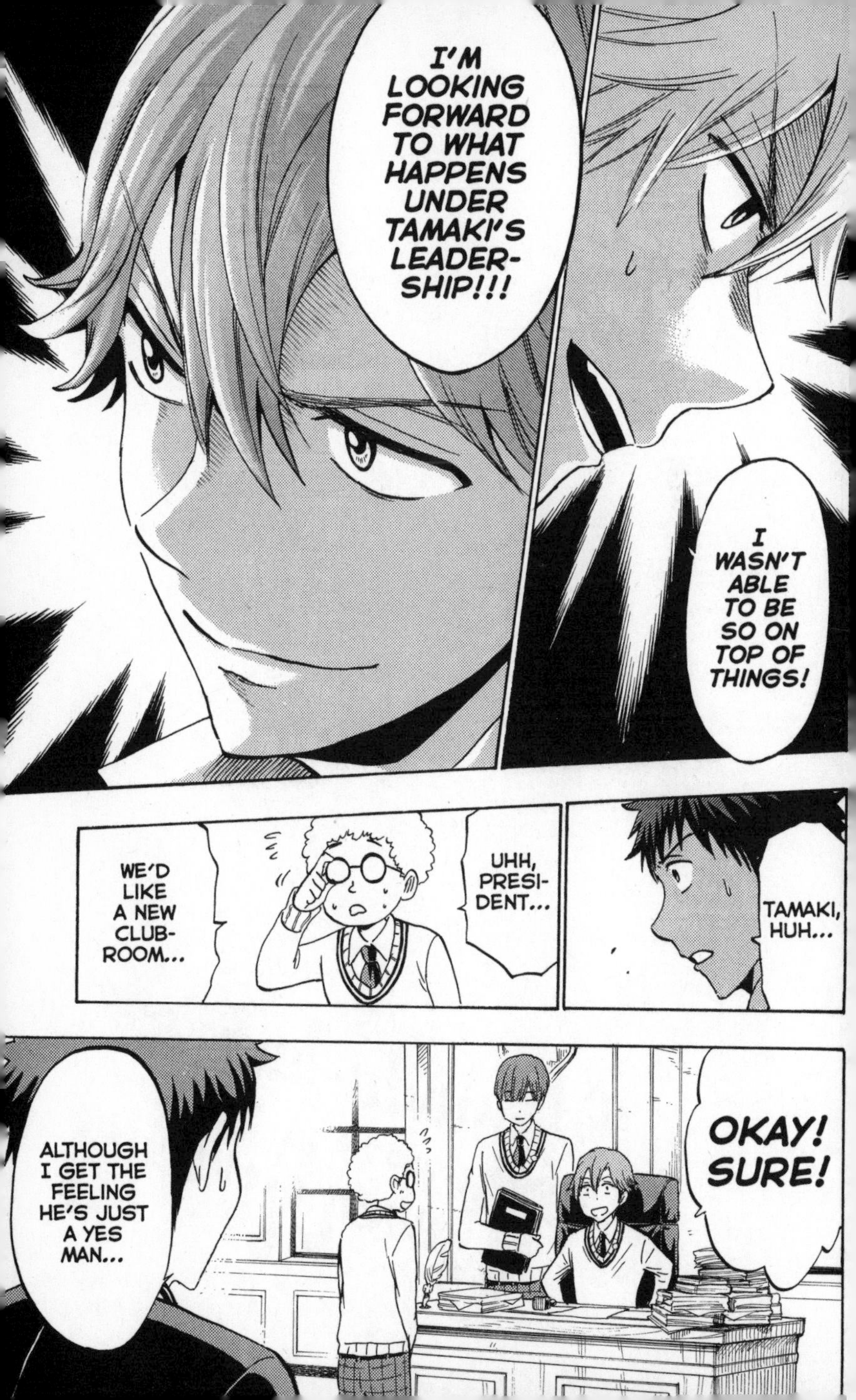
I WASN'T ABLE TO BE SO ON TOP OF THINGS!
I'M LOOKING FORWARD TO WHAT HAPPENS UNDER TAMAKI'S LEADER-SHIP!!!
TAMAKI, HUH...
UHH, PRESI-DENT...
WE'D LIKE A NEW CLUB-ROOM...
OKAY! SURE!
ALTHOUGH I GET THE FEELING HE'S JUST A YES MAN...

Yamada-kun and the Seven Witches

CHAPTER 188: Should I take off my pants, too?

NANCY

- ✓ Real name: Haruko Nijino
- ✓ Class: 2-C
- ✓ Club: Light Music Club (but she can't play an instrument)
- ✓ One thing about Yamada: I love you, you idiot!
- ✓ Nancy's most punk expression: Mt. Everest of garlic, extra-extra veggies, super-super spicy, plus oil!

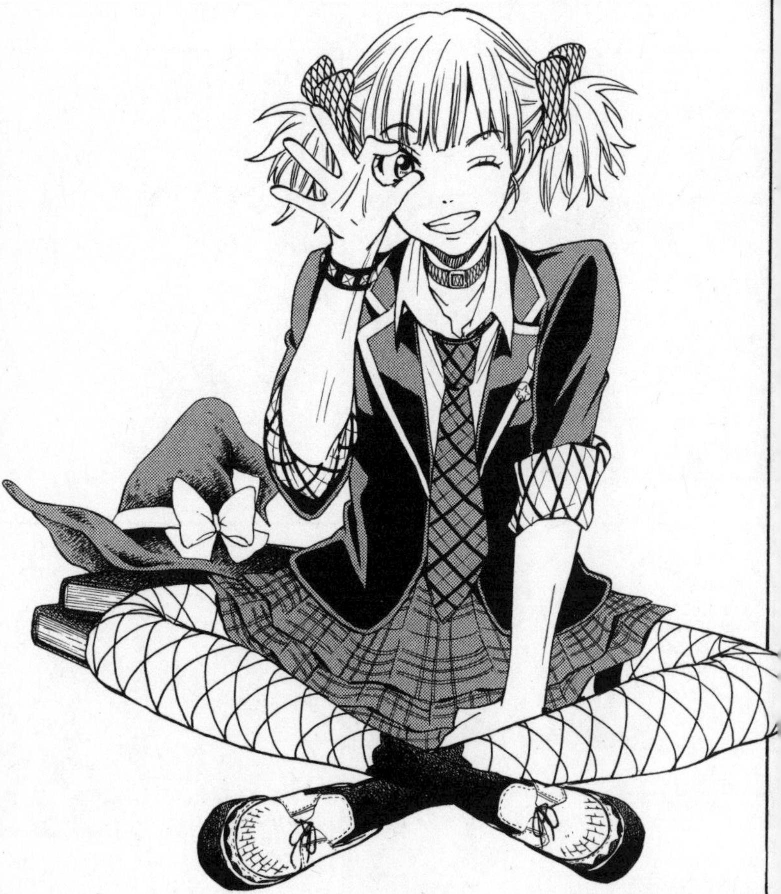

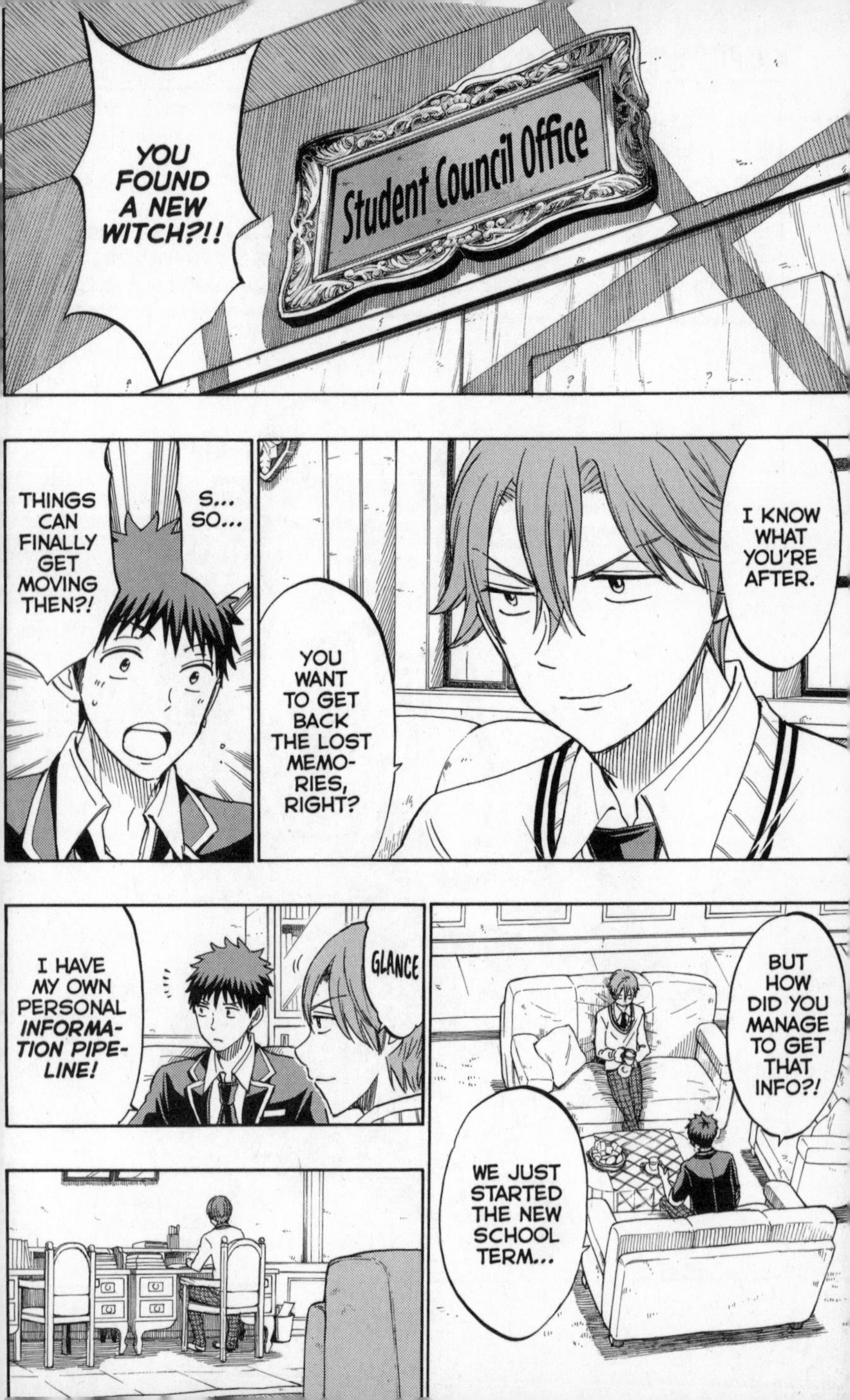
Student Council Office
YOU FOUND A NEW WITCH?!!
I KNOW WHAT YOU'RE AFTER.
YOU WANT TO GET BACK THE LOST MEMORIES, RIGHT?
S... SO...
THINGS CAN FINALLY GET MOVING THEN?!
BUT HOW DID YOU MANAGE TO GET THAT INFO?!
WE JUST STARTED THE NEW SCHOOL TERM...
GLANCE
I HAVE MY OWN PERSONAL INFORMATION PIPELINE!

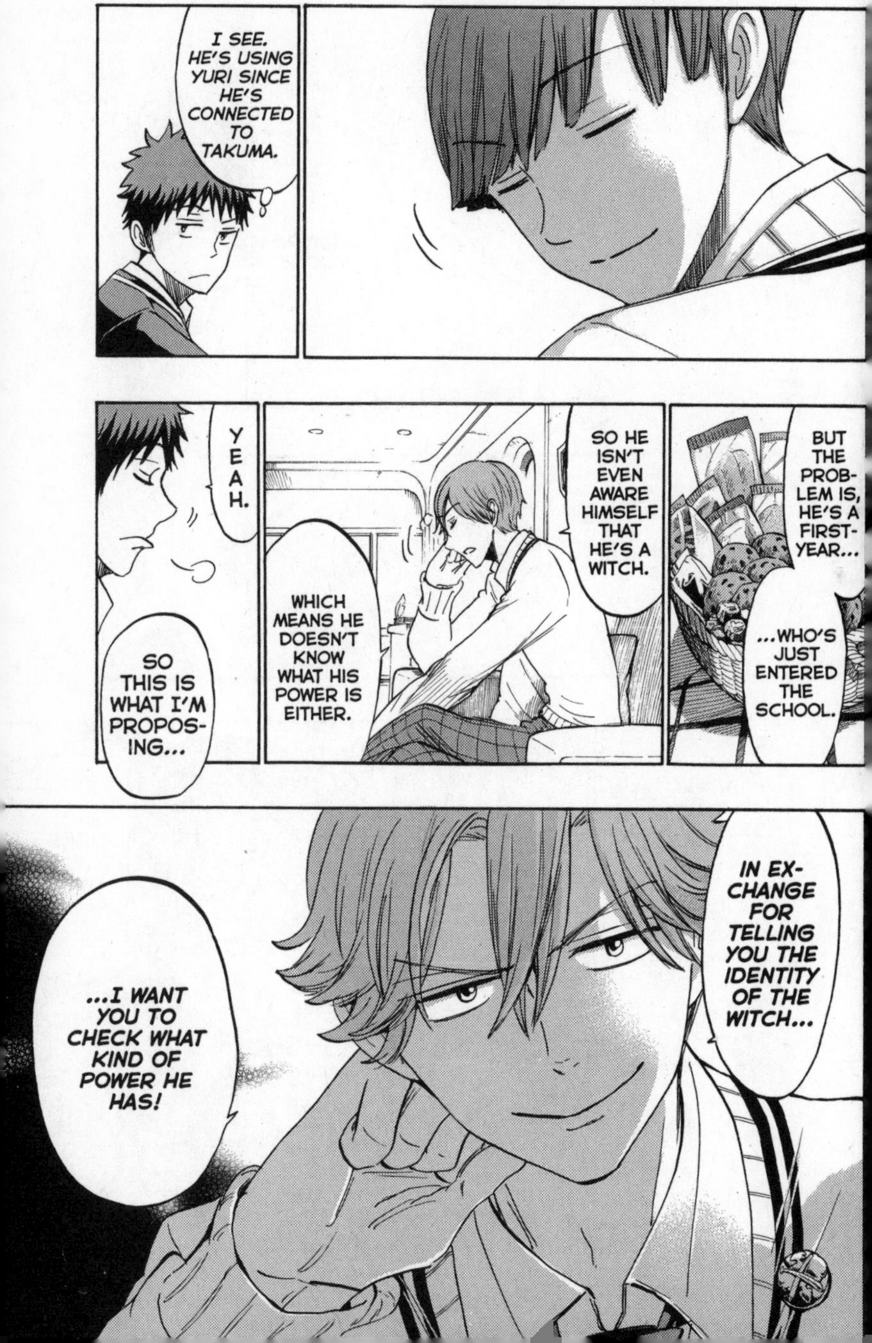
I SEE. HE'S USING YURI SINCE HE'S CONNECTED TO TAKUMA.
BUT THE PROBLEM IS, HE'S A FIRST-YEAR...
...WHO'S JUST ENTERED THE SCHOOL.
SO HE ISN'T EVEN AWARE HIMSELF THAT HE'S A WITCH.
WHICH MEANS HE DOESN'T KNOW WHAT HIS POWER IS EITHER.
YEAH.
SO THIS IS WHAT I'M PROPOSING...
IN EXCHANGE FOR TELLING YOU THE IDENTITY OF THE WITCH...
...I WANT YOU TO CHECK WHAT KIND OF POWER HE HAS!

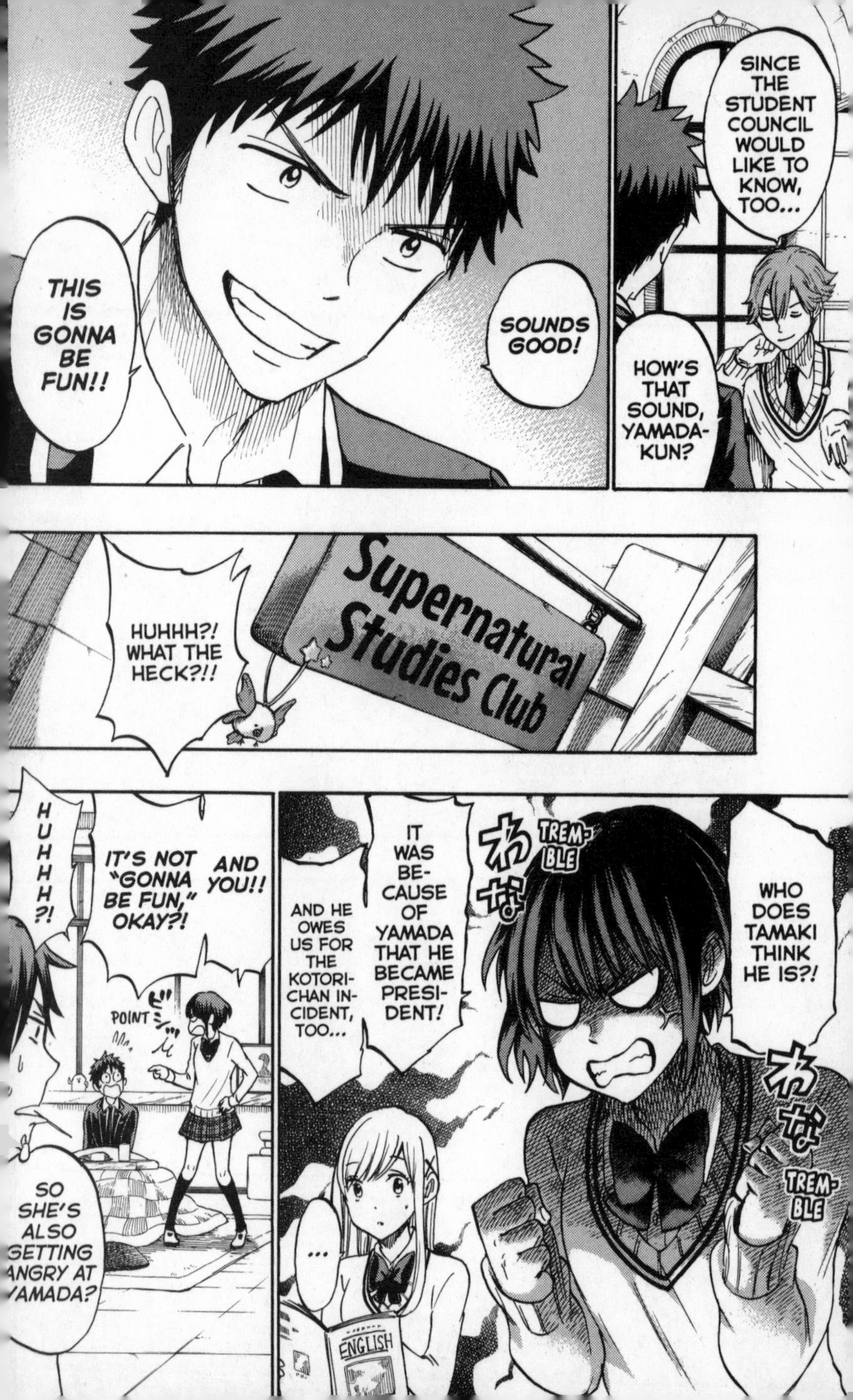
SINCE THE STUDENT COUNCIL WOULD LIKE TO KNOW, TOO...
HOW'S THAT SOUND, YAMADA-KUN?
SOUNDS GOOD!
THIS IS GONNA BE FUN!!
Supernatural Studies Club
HUHHH?! WHAT THE HECK?!!
WHO DOES TAMAKI THINK HE IS?!
わなわな
TREM-BLE
TREM-BLE
IT WAS BE-CAUSE OF YAMADA THAT HE BECAME PRESI-DENT!
AND HE OWES US FOR THE KOTORI-CHAN IN-CIDENT, TOO...
...
ENGLISH
AND YOU!!
IT'S NOT "GONNA BE FUN," OKAY?!
HUHHHH?!
POINT
SO SHE'S ALSO GETTING ANGRY AT YAMADA?

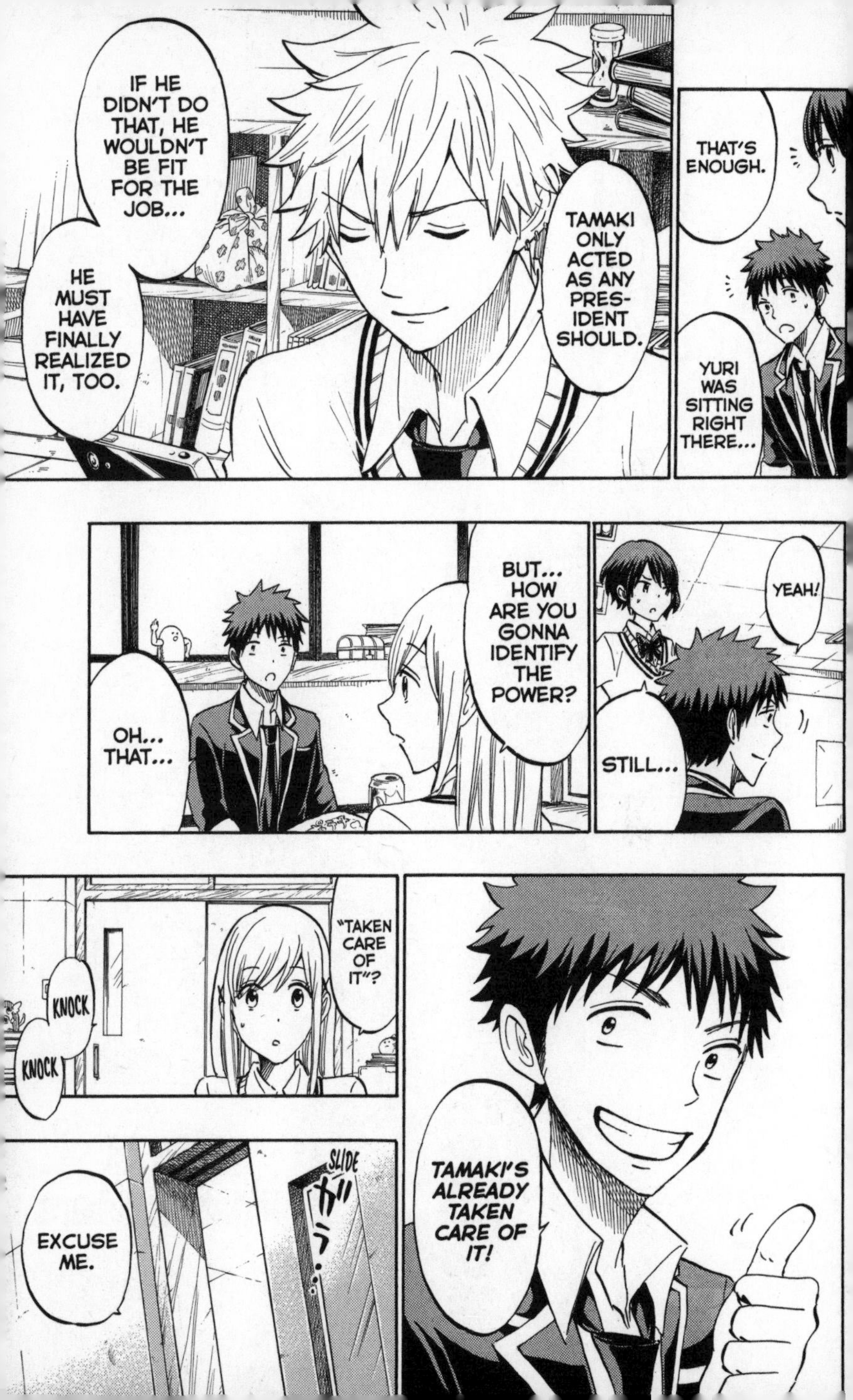
THAT'S ENOUGH.
YURI WAS SITTING RIGHT THERE...
TAMAKI ONLY ACTED AS ANY PRES-IDENT SHOULD.
IF HE DIDN'T DO THAT, HE WOULDN'T BE FIT FOR THE JOB...
HE MUST HAVE FINALLY REALIZED IT, TOO.
YEAH!
STILL...
BUT... HOW ARE YOU GONNA IDENTIFY THE POWER?
OH... THAT...
TAMAKI'S ALREADY TAKEN CARE OF IT!
"TAKEN CARE OF IT"?
KNOCK
KNOCK
SLIDE
EXCUSE ME.

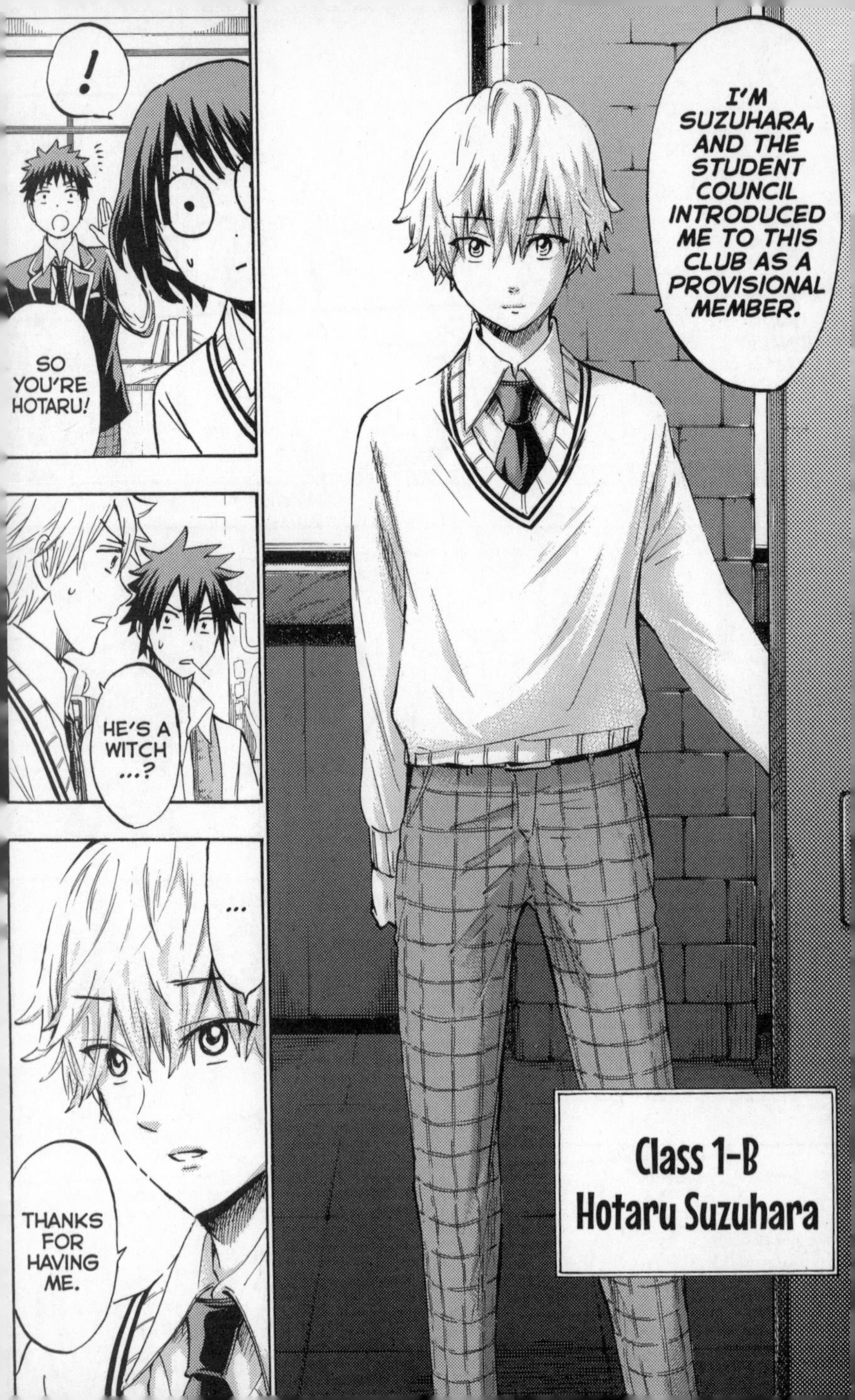
I'M SUZUHARA, AND THE STUDENT COUNCIL INTRODUCED ME TO THIS CLUB AS A PROVISIONAL MEMBER.
Class 1-B Hotaru Suzuhara
!
SO YOU'RE HOTARU!
HE'S A WITCH ...?
...
THANKS FOR HAVING ME.

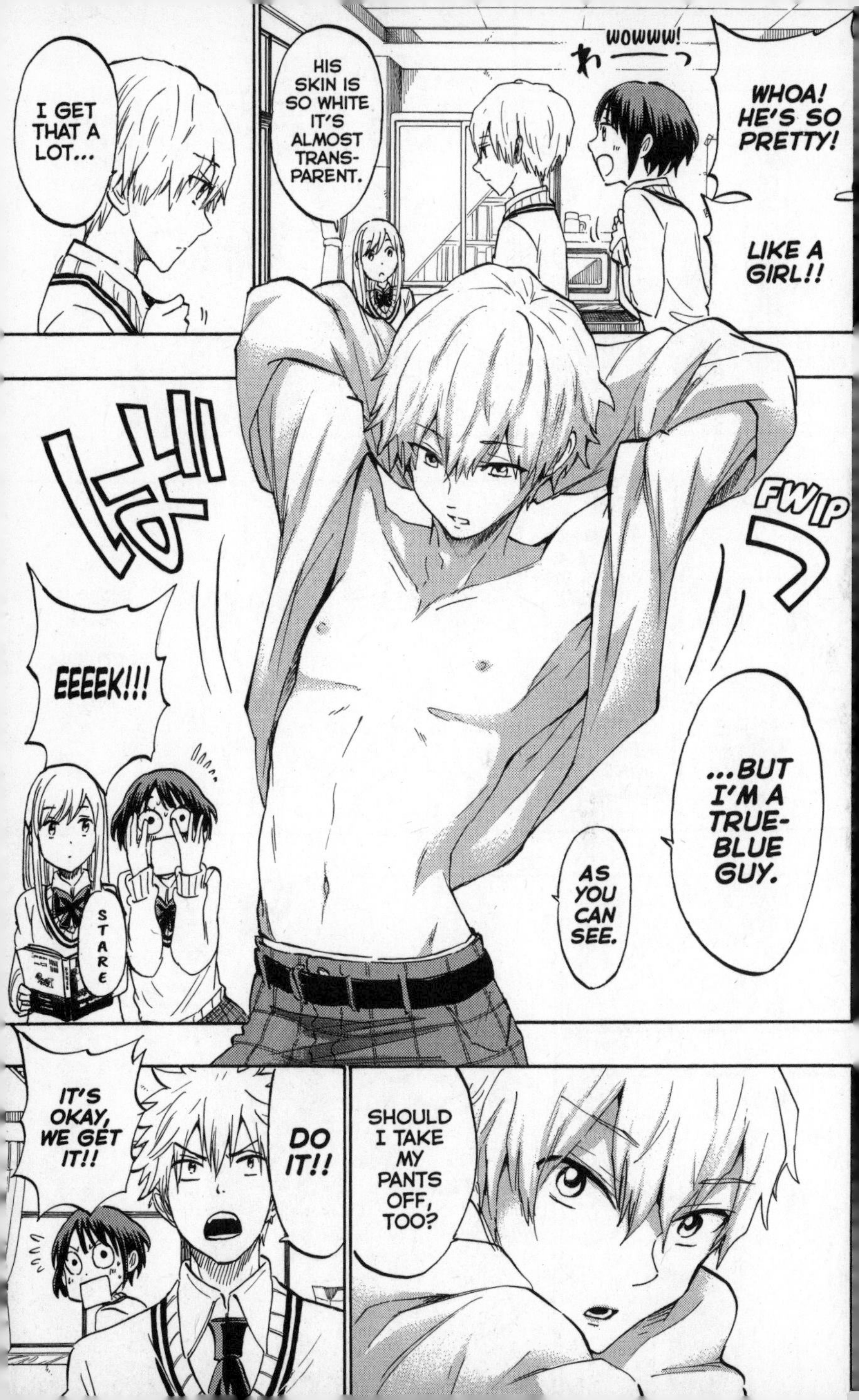
WOWWW!
WHOA! HE'S SO PRETTY!
LIKE A GIRL!!
HIS SKIN IS SO WHITE IT'S ALMOST TRANS-PARENT.
I GET THAT A LOT...
FWIP
...BUT I'M A TRUE-BLUE GUY.
AS YOU CAN SEE.
EEEEK!!!
STARE
SHOULD I TAKE MY PANTS OFF, TOO?
DO IT!!
IT'S OKAY, WE GET IT!!

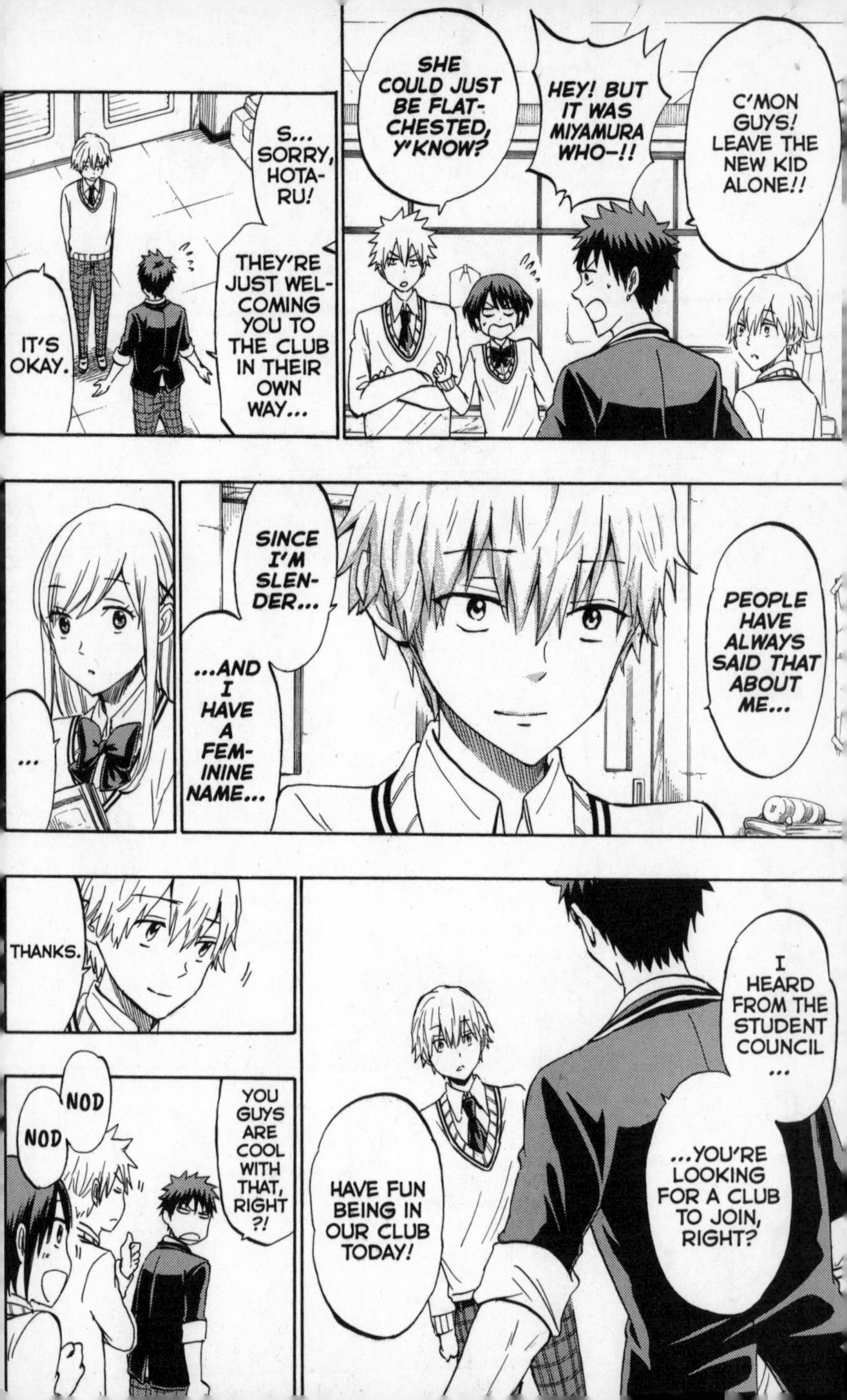
C'MON GUYS! LEAVE THE NEW KID ALONE!!
HEY! BUT IT WAS MIYAMURA WHO-!!
SHE COULD JUST BE FLAT-CHESTED, Y'KNOW?
S... SORRY, HOTARU!
THEY'RE JUST WEL-COMING YOU TO THE CLUB IN THEIR OWN WAY...
IT'S OKAY.
PEOPLE HAVE ALWAYS SAID THAT ABOUT ME...
SINCE I'M SLEN-DER...
...AND I HAVE A FEM-ININE NAME...
...
I HEARD FROM THE STUDENT COUNCIL ...
...YOU'RE LOOKING FOR A CLUB TO JOIN, RIGHT?
HAVE FUN BEING IN OUR CLUB TODAY!
THANKS.
YOU GUYS ARE COOL WITH THAT, RIGHT ?!
NOD
NOD

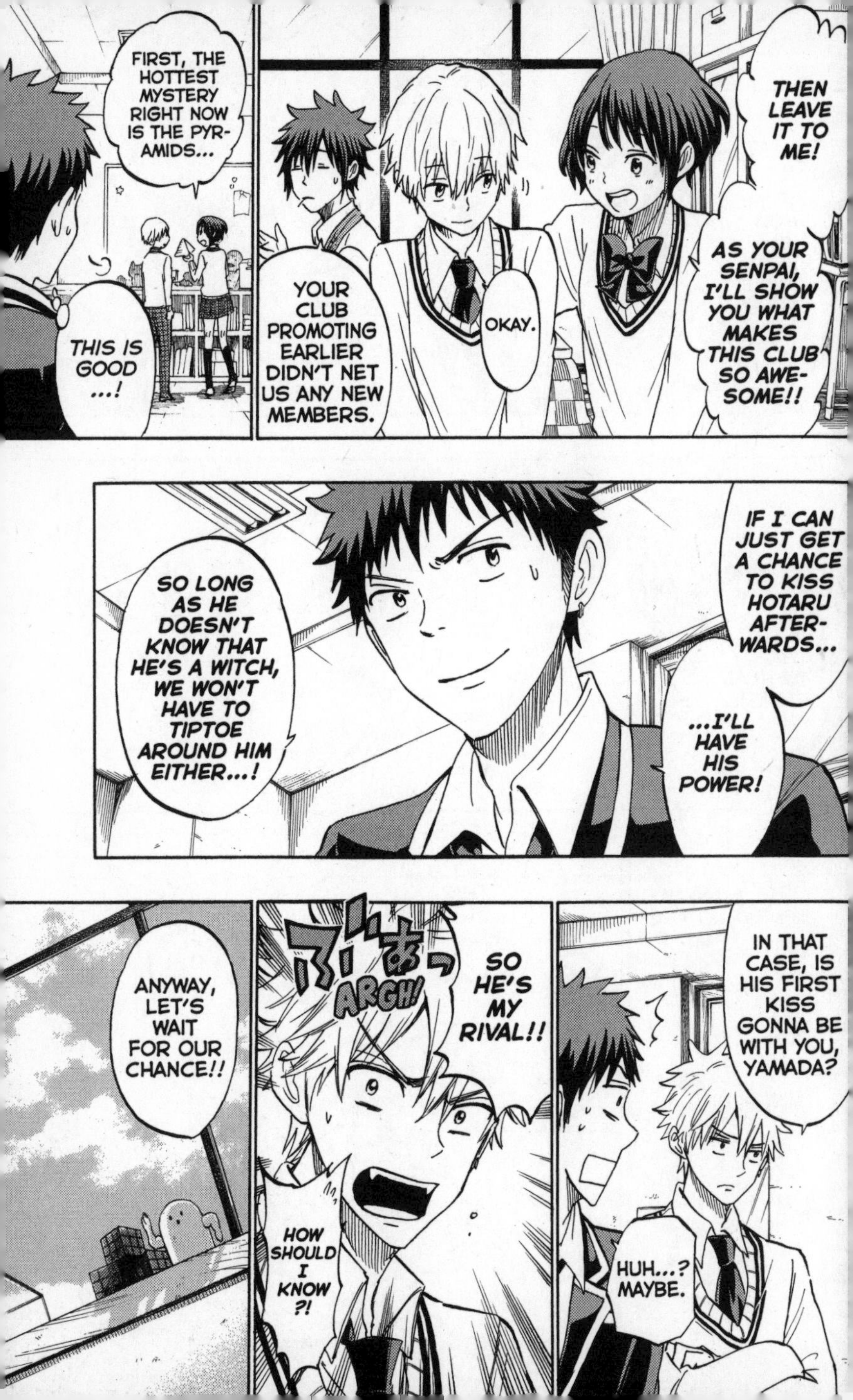
THEN LEAVE IT TO ME!
AS YOUR SENPAI, I'LL SHOW YOU WHAT MAKES THIS CLUB SO AWESOME!!
OKAY.
YOUR CLUB PROMOTING EARLIER DIDN'T NET US ANY NEW MEMBERS.
FIRST, THE HOTTEST MYSTERY RIGHT NOW IS THE PYRAMIDS...
THIS IS GOOD...!
IF I CAN JUST GET A CHANCE TO KISS HOTARU AFTERWARDS...
...I'LL HAVE HIS POWER!
SO LONG AS HE DOESN'T KNOW THAT HE'S A WITCH, WE WON'T HAVE TO TIPTOE AROUND HIM EITHER...!
IN THAT CASE, IS HIS FIRST KISS GONNA BE WITH YOU, YAMADA?
HUH...? MAYBE.
SO HE'S MY RIVAL!!
ぶあっ
ARGH!
HOW SHOULD I KNOW?!
ANYWAY, LET'S WAIT FOR OUR CHANCE!!

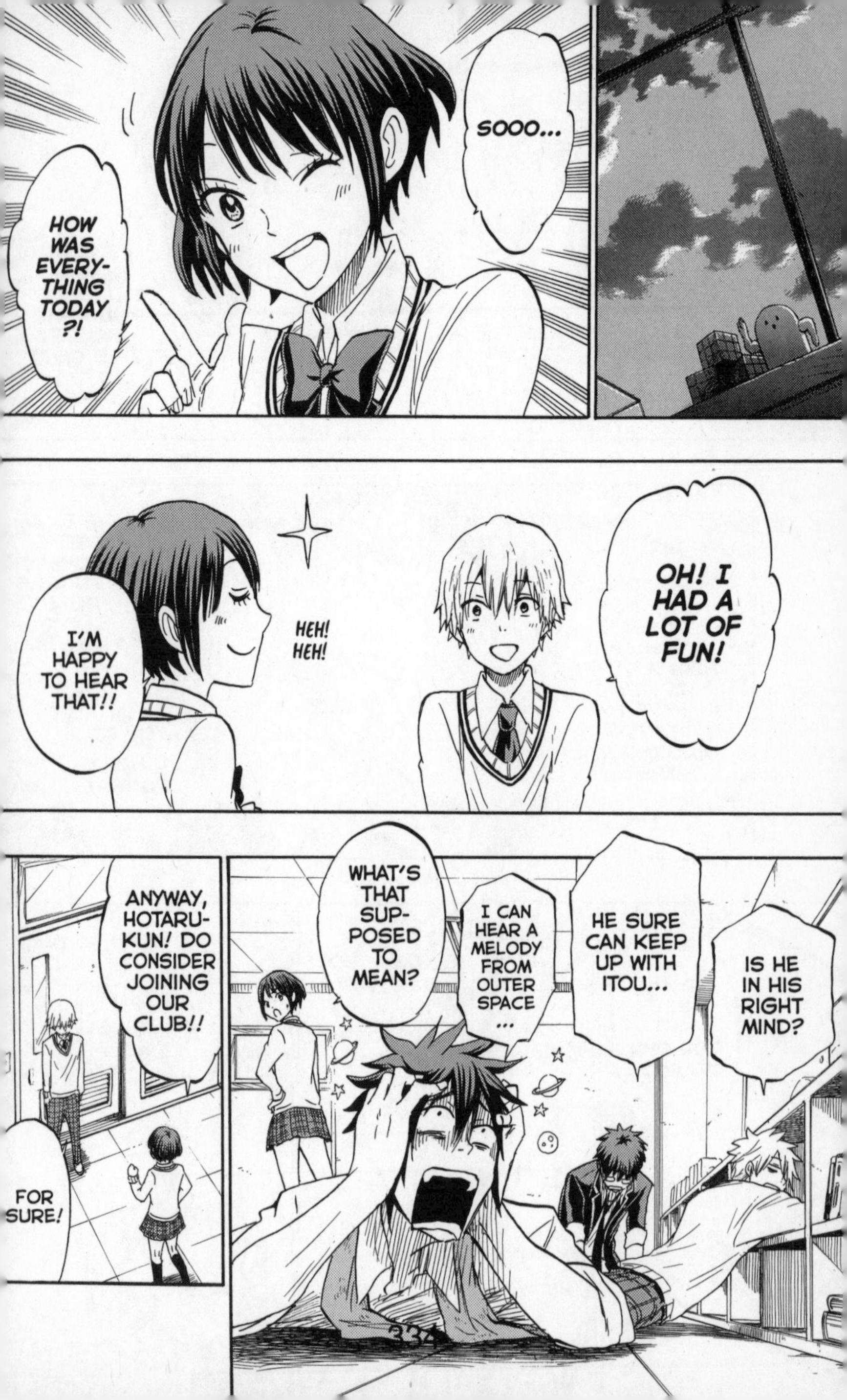
SOOO...
HOW WAS EVERYTHING TODAY?!
OH! I HAD A LOT OF FUN!
HEH! HEH!
I'M HAPPY TO HEAR THAT!!
IS HE IN HIS RIGHT MIND?
HE SURE CAN KEEP UP WITH ITOU...
I CAN HEAR A MELODY FROM OUTER SPACE...
WHAT'S THAT SUPPOSED TO MEAN?
ANYWAY, HOTARU-KUN! DO CONSIDER JOINING OUR CLUB!!
FOR SURE!

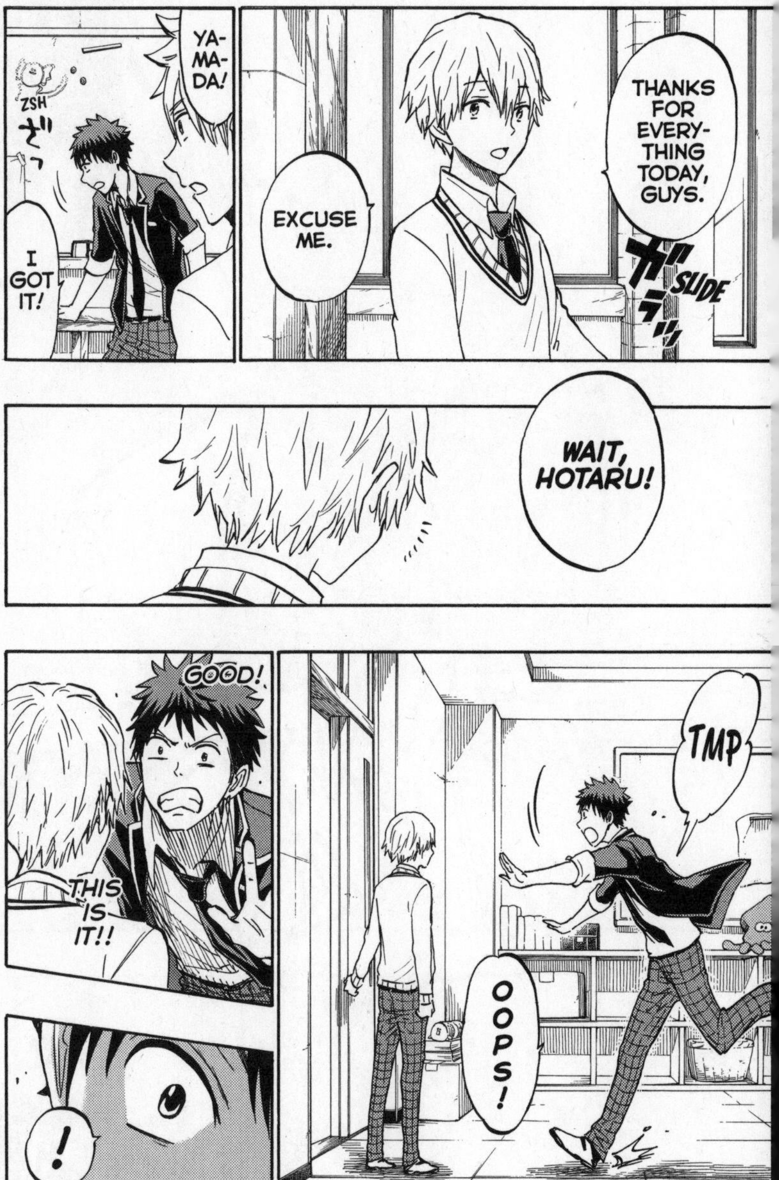
THANKS FOR EVERY-THING TODAY, GUYS.
ガラッ
SLIDE
EXCUSE ME.
YA-MA-DA!
ZSH
ざっ
I GOT IT!
WAIT, HOTARU!
TMP
OOPS!
GOOD!
THIS IS IT!!
!

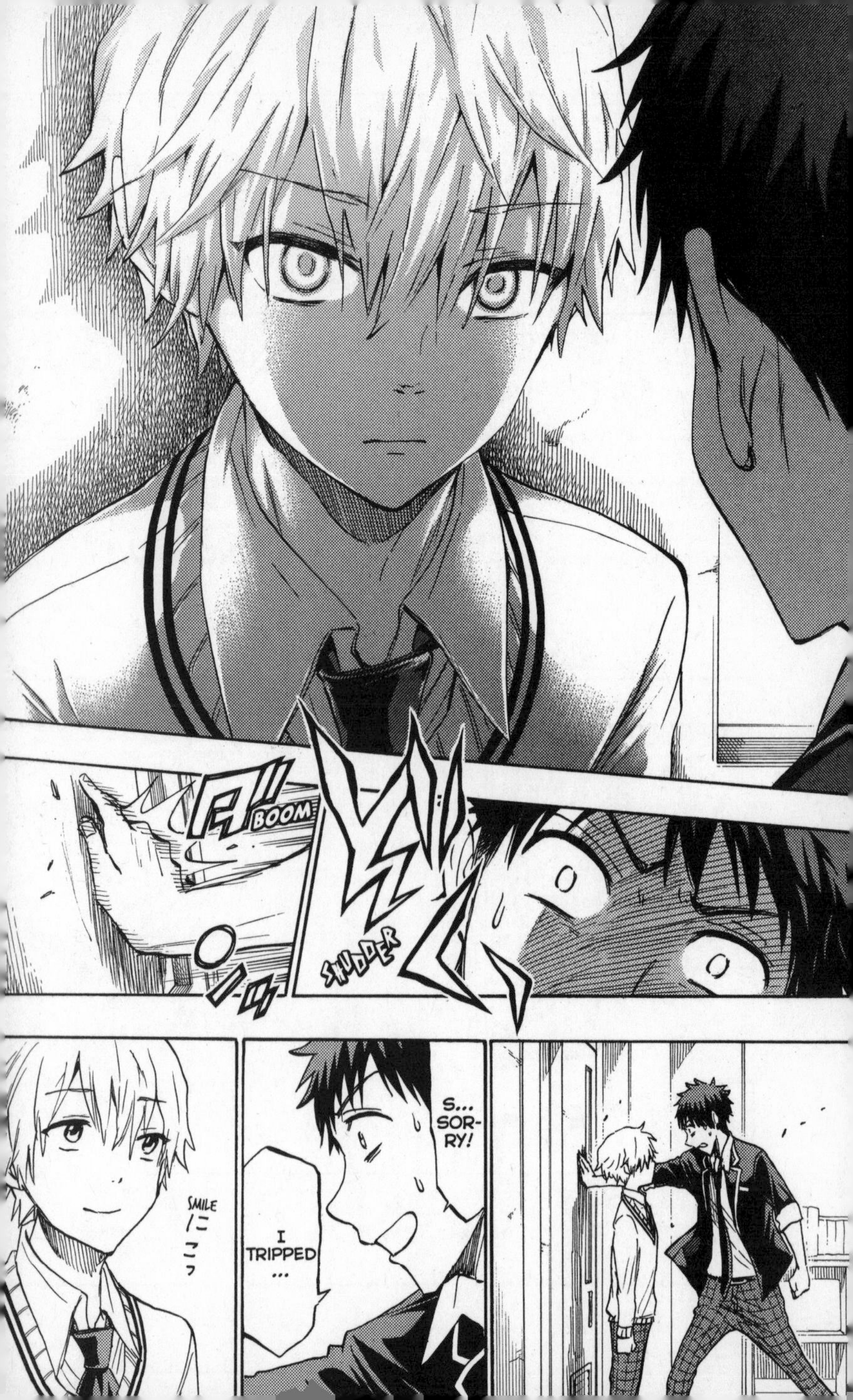
SHUDDER
BOOM
S... SORRY!
I TRIPPED...
SMILE
にこっ

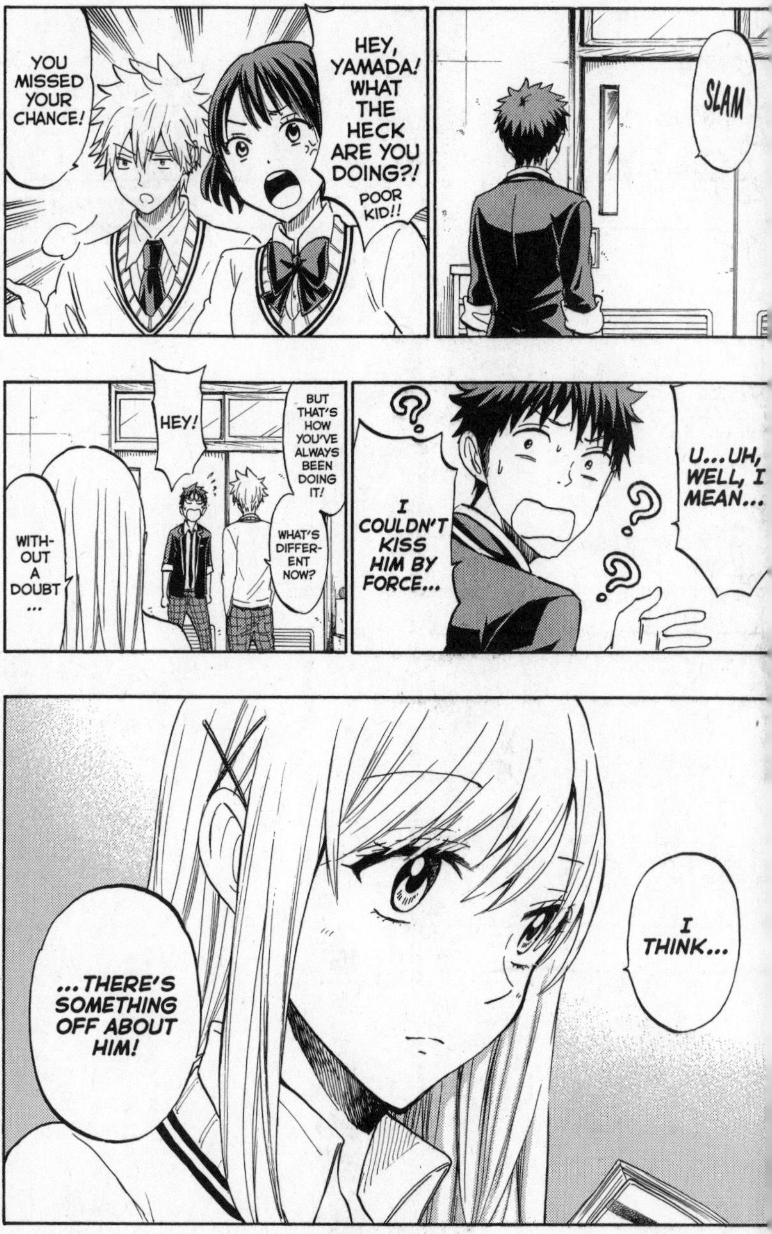
SLAM
HEY, YAMADA! WHAT THE HECK ARE YOU DOING?!
POOR KID!!
YOU MISSED YOUR CHANCE!
U...UH, WELL, I MEAN...
I COULDN'T KISS HIM BY FORCE...
BUT THAT'S HOW YOU'VE ALWAYS BEEN DOING IT!
HEY!
WHAT'S DIFFER-ENT NOW?
WITH-OUT A DOUBT ...
I THINK...
...THERE'S SOMETHING OFF ABOUT HIM!

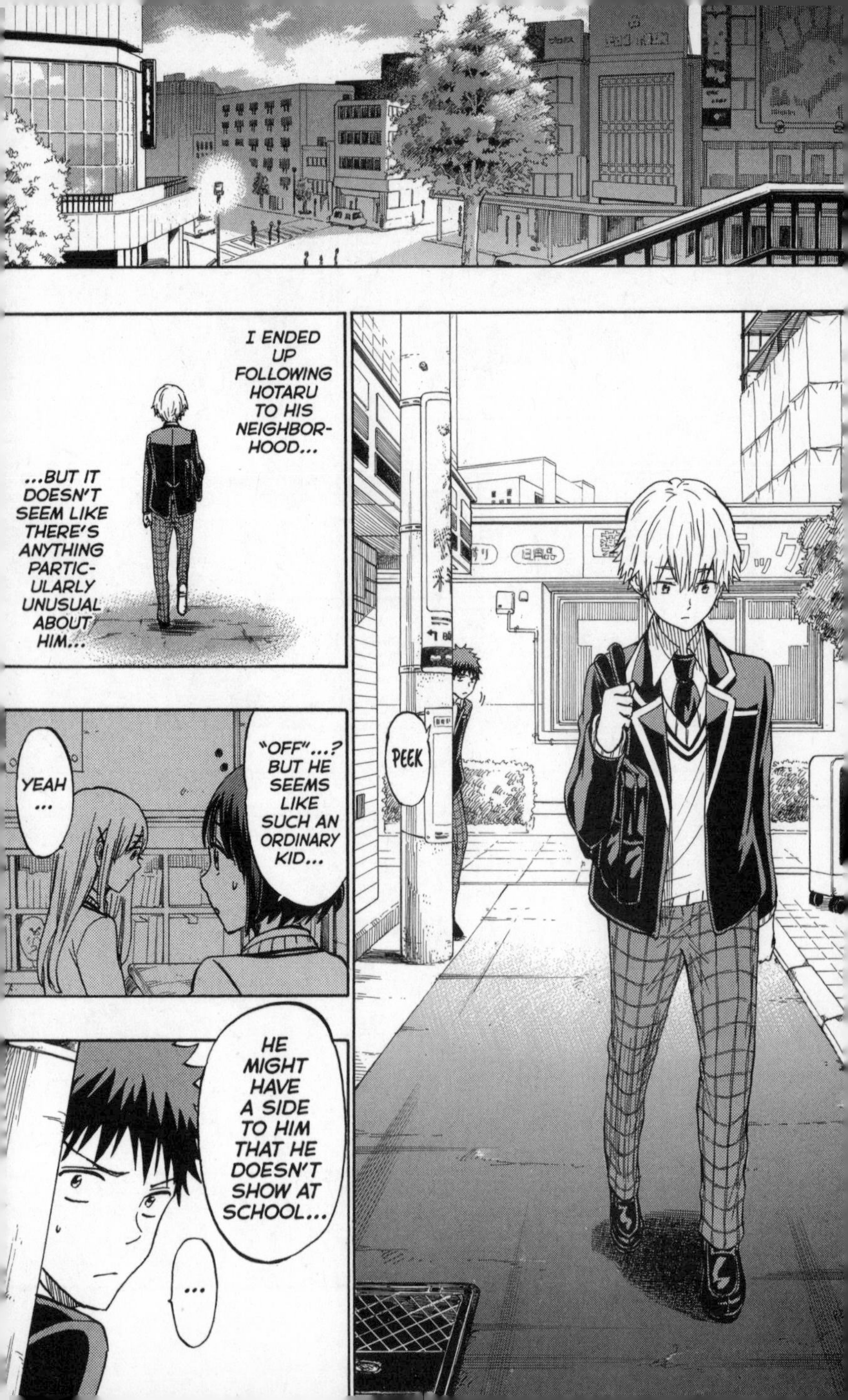
PEEK
I ENDED UP FOLLOWING HOTARU TO HIS NEIGHBOR-HOOD...
...BUT IT DOESN'T SEEM LIKE THERE'S ANYTHING PARTIC-ULARLY UNUSUAL ABOUT HIM...
"OFF"...? BUT HE SEEMS LIKE SUCH AN ORDINARY KID...
YEAH ...
HE MIGHT HAVE A SIDE TO HIM THAT HE DOESN'T SHOW AT SCHOOL...
...

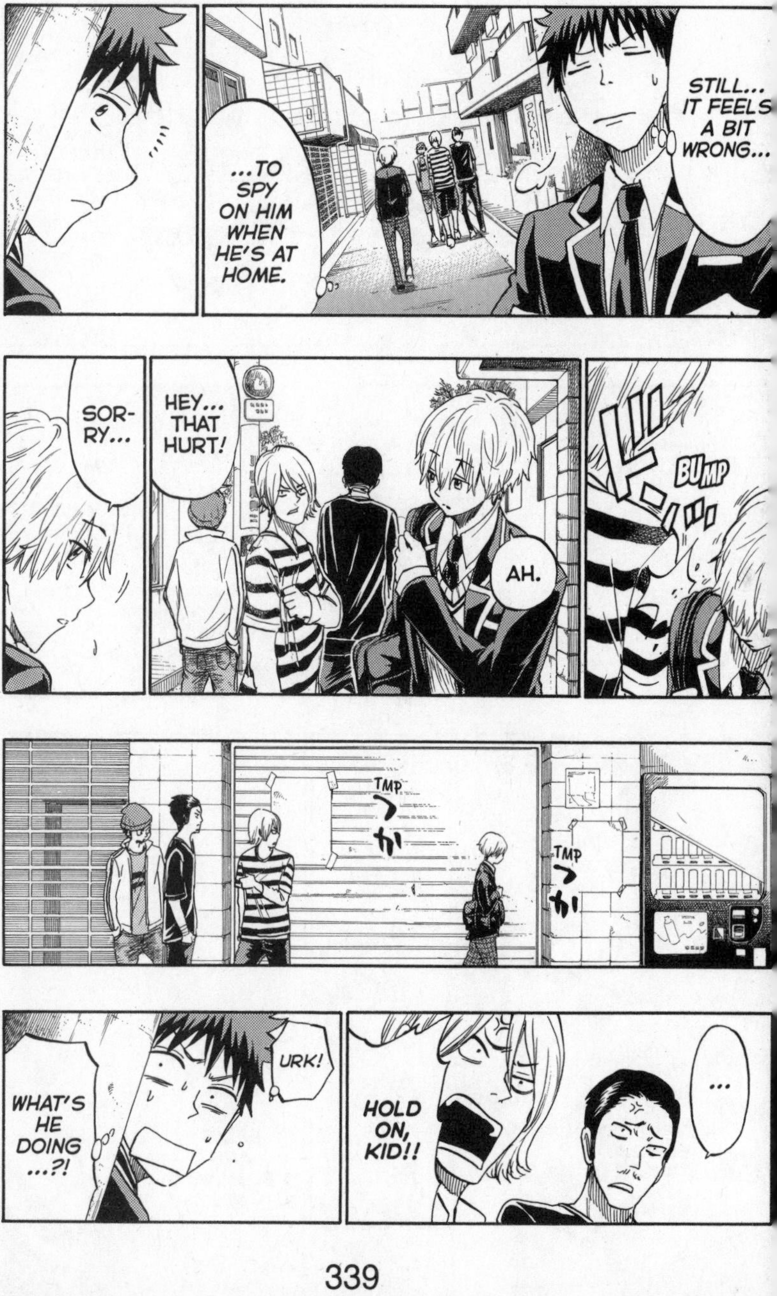
STILL... IT FEELS A BIT WRONG...
...TO SPY ON HIM WHEN HE'S AT HOME.
BUMP
AH.
HEY... THAT HURT!
SOR-RY...
TMP
TMP
...
HOLD ON, KID!!
URK!
WHAT'S HE DOING ...?!

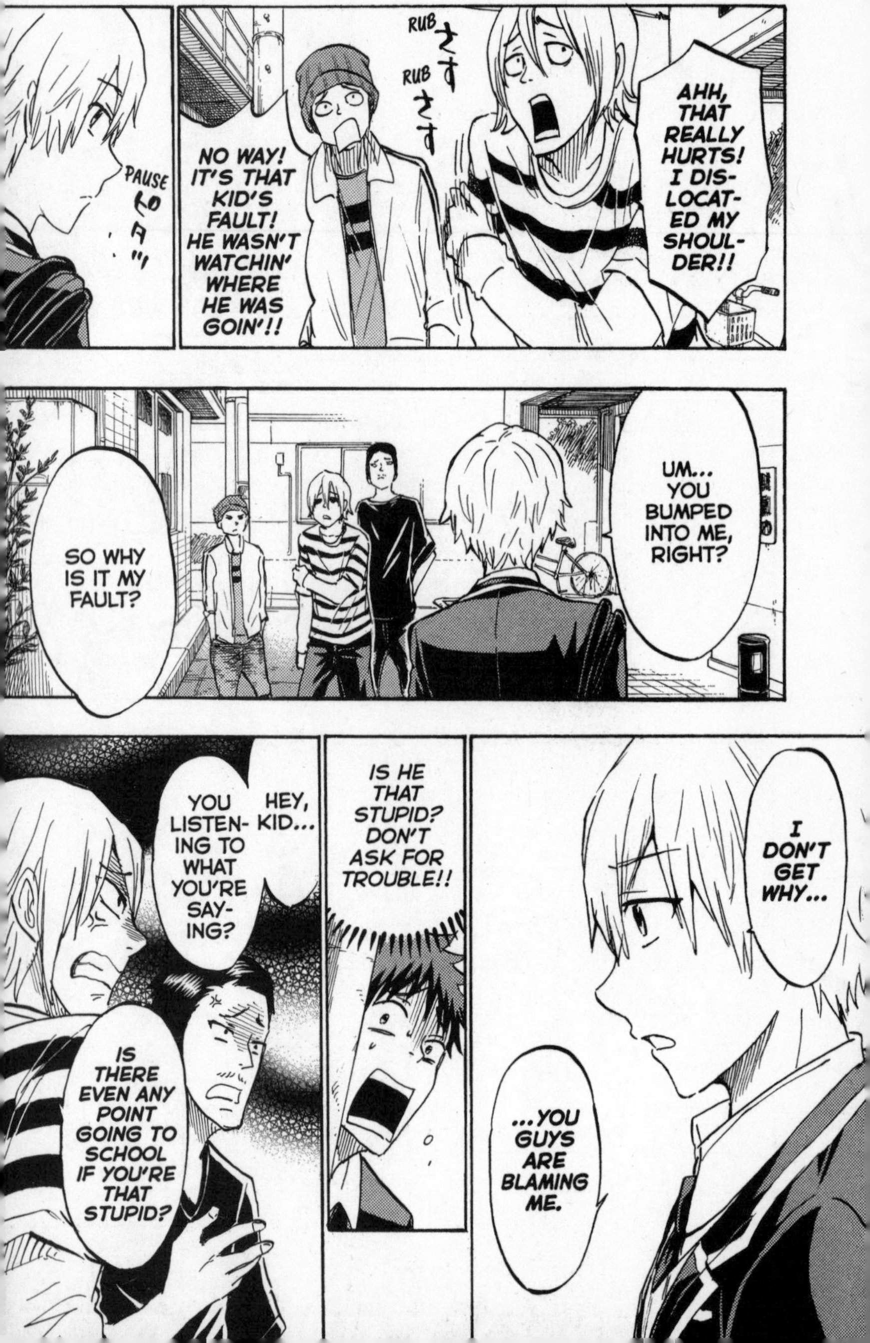
AHH, THAT REALLY HURTS! I DISLOCATED MY SHOULDER!!
RUB さす
RUB さす
NO WAY! IT'S THAT KID'S FAULT! HE WASN'T WATCHIN' WHERE HE WAS GOIN'!!
PAUSE
UM... YOU BUMPED INTO ME, RIGHT?
SO WHY IS IT MY FAULT?
I DON'T GET WHY...
...YOU GUYS ARE BLAMING ME.
IS HE THAT STUPID? DON'T ASK FOR TROUBLE!!
HEY, KID... YOU LISTENING TO WHAT YOU'RE SAYING?
IS THERE EVEN ANY POINT GOING TO SCHOOL IF YOU'RE THAT STUPID?

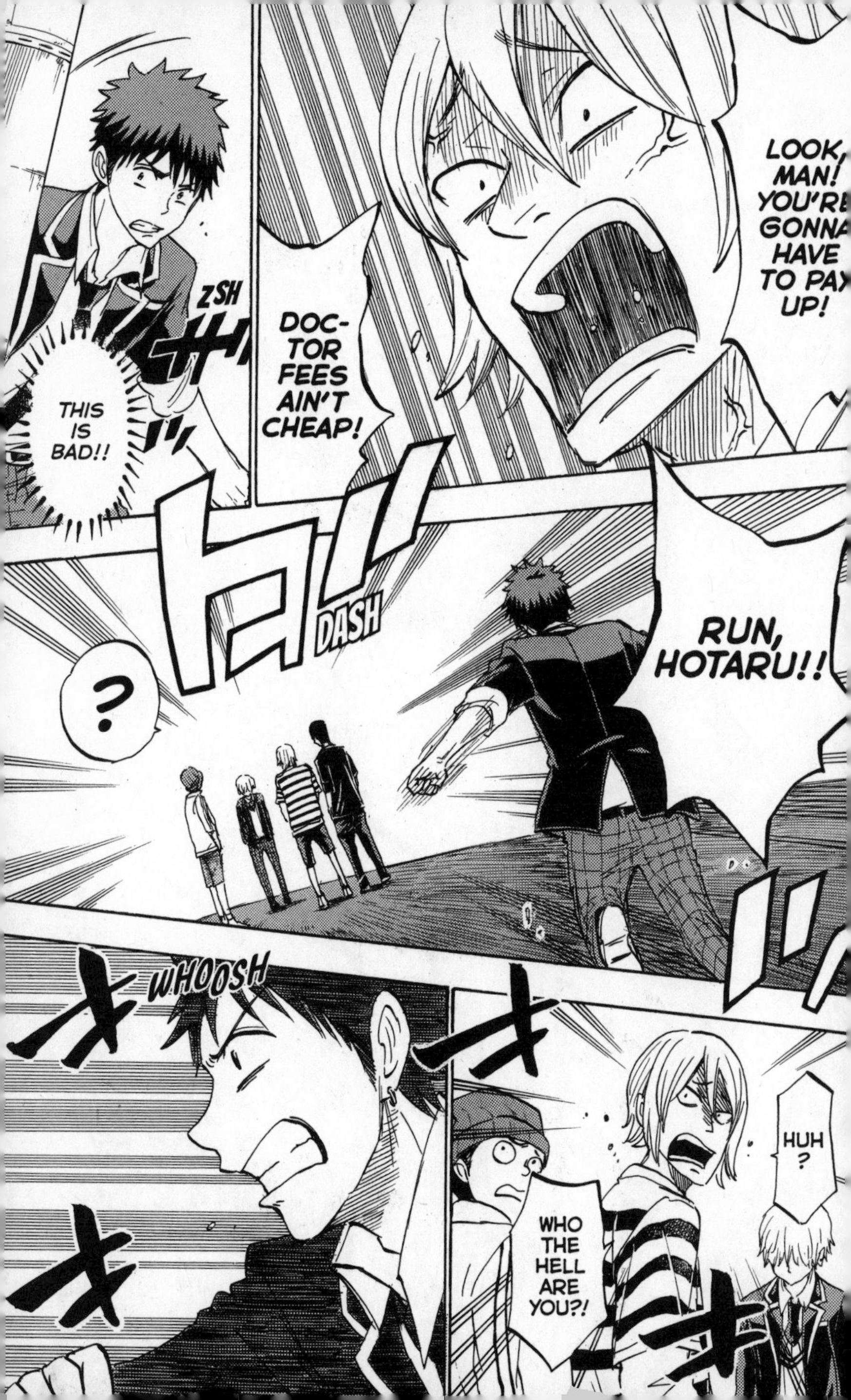
LOOK, MAN! YOU'RE GONNA HAVE TO PAY UP!
DOC-TOR FEES AIN'T CHEAP!
ZSH
THIS IS BAD!!
RUN, HOTARU!!
DASH
?
HUH?
WHO THE HELL ARE YOU?!
WHOOSH

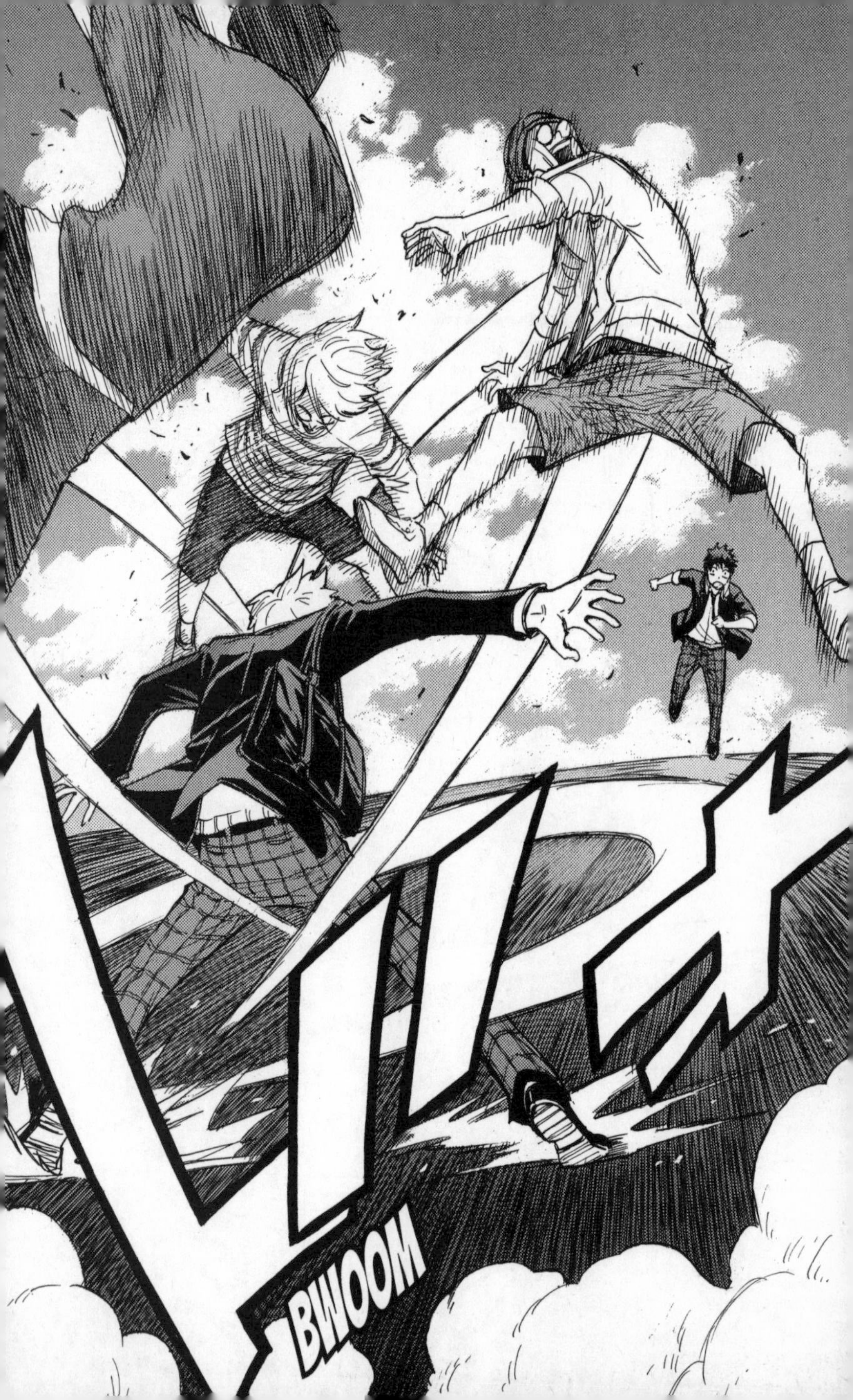
ドゴォ
BWOOM

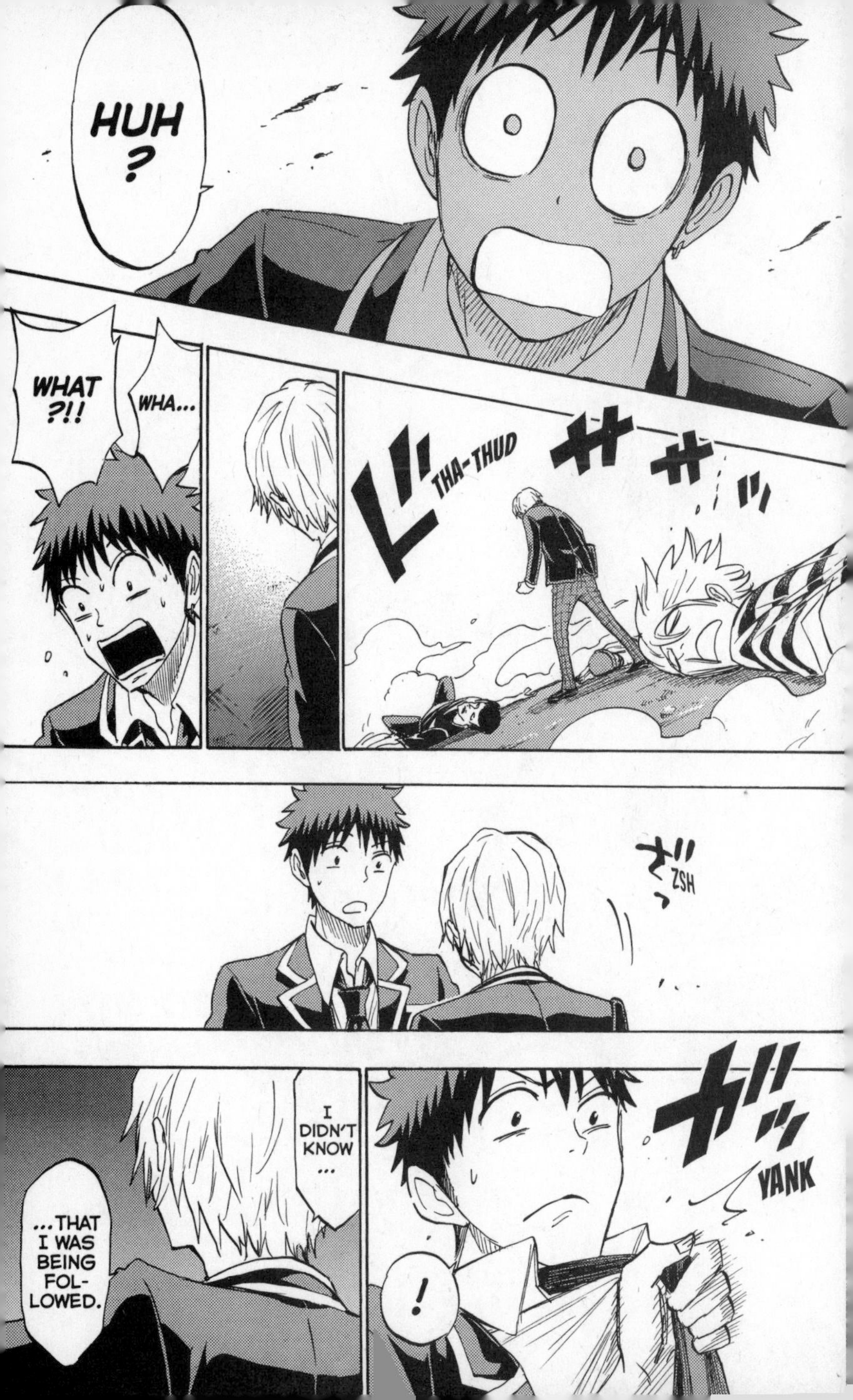
HUH ?
THA-THUD
WHA...
WHAT ?!!
ZSH
YANK
!
I DIDN'T KNOW ...
...THAT I WAS BEING FOL-LOWED.

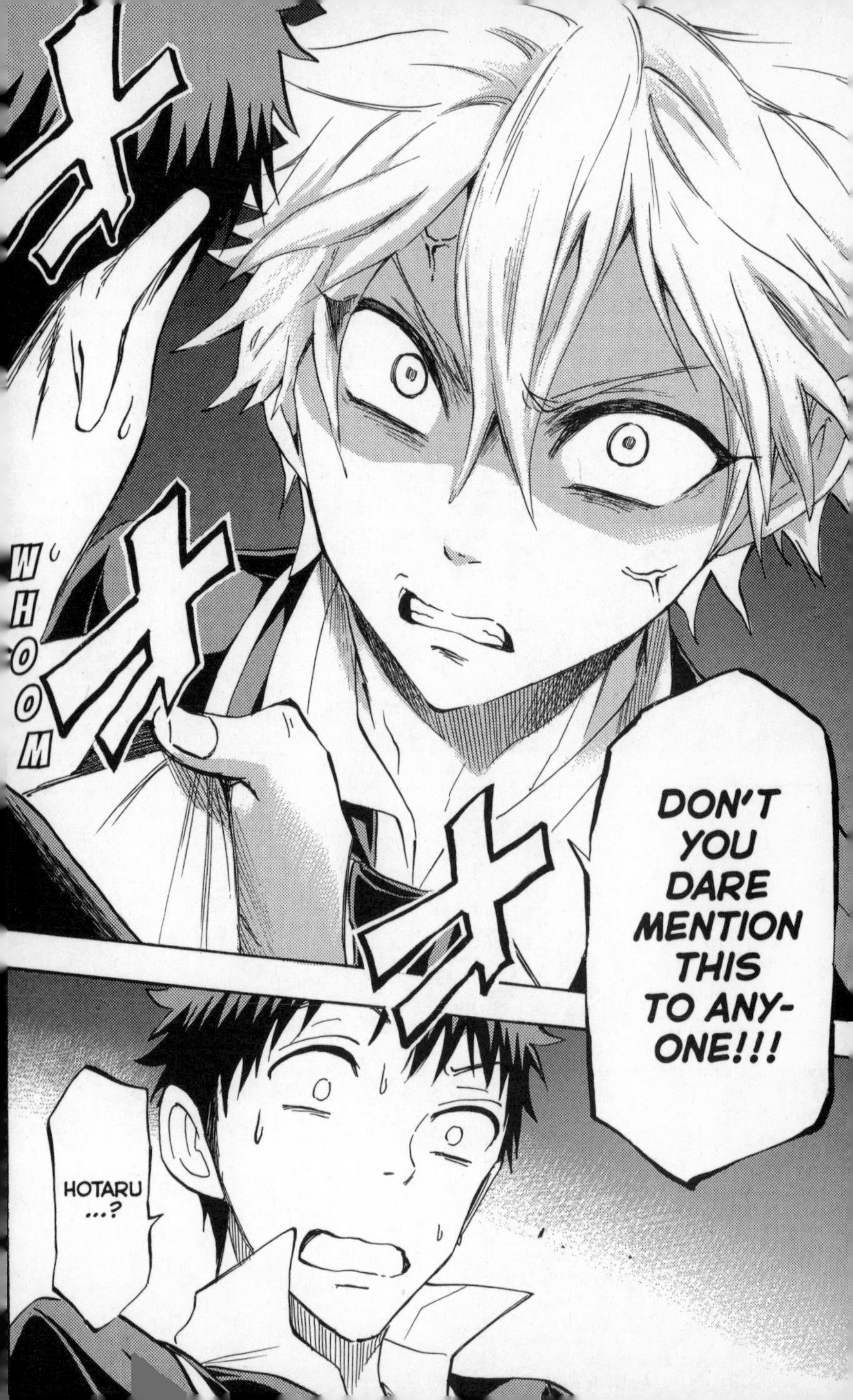
WHOOM
DON'T YOU DARE MENTION THIS TO ANY-ONE!!!
HOTARU ...?

CHAPTER 189: Perfect as my rival.

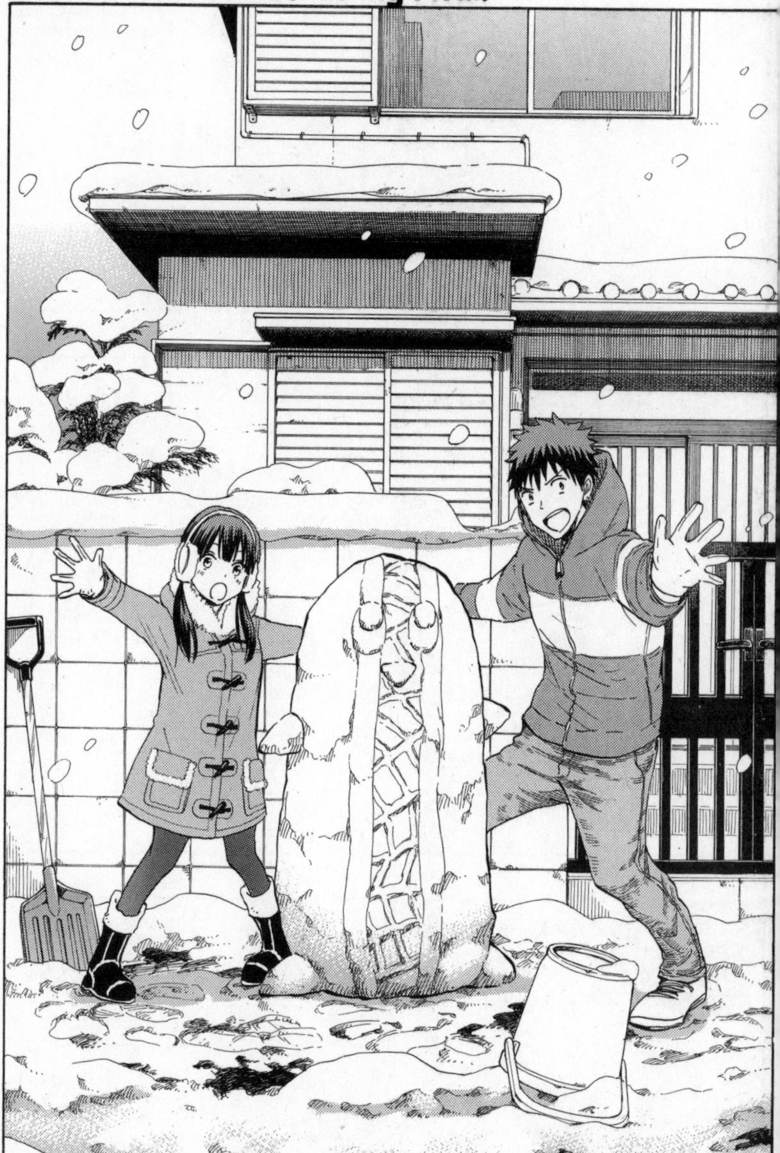

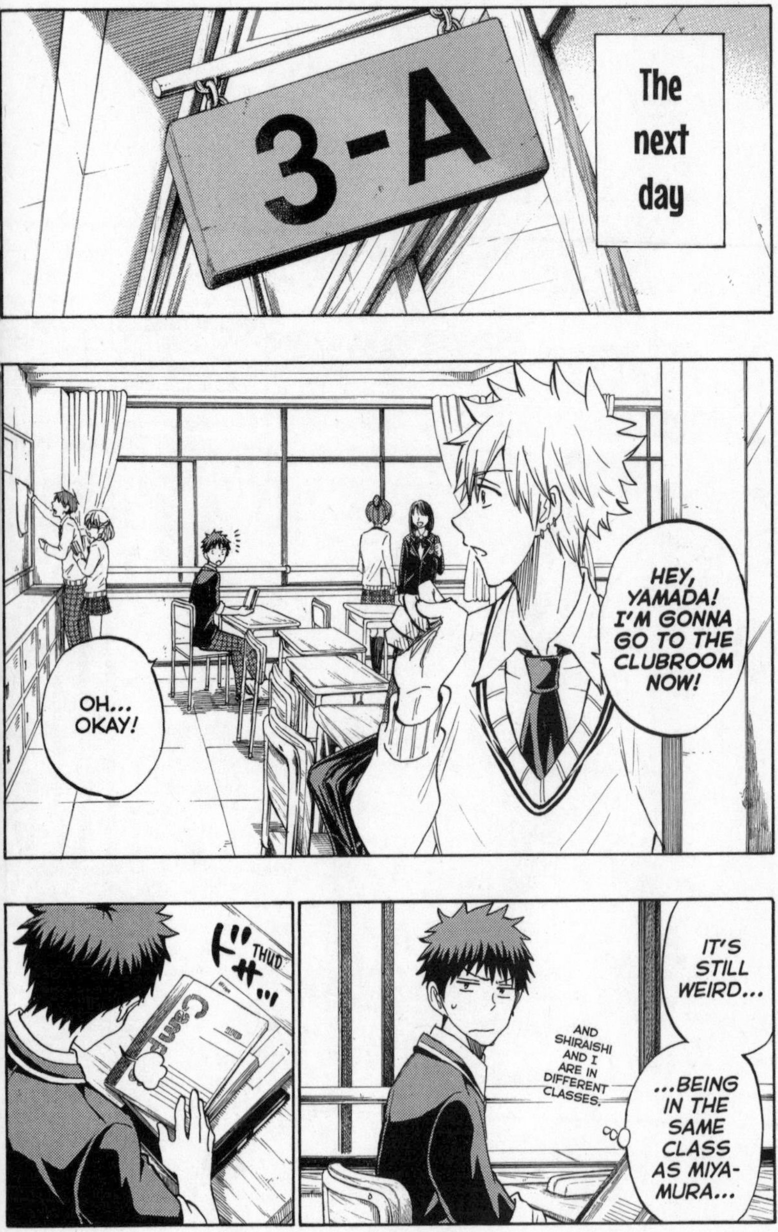
3-A
The next day
HEY, YAMADA! I'M GONNA GO TO THE CLUBROOM NOW!
OH... OKAY!
IT'S STILL WEIRD...
...BEING IN THE SAME CLASS AS MIYA-MURA...
AND SHIRAISHI AND I ARE IN DIFFERENT CLASSES.
ドサッ
THUD

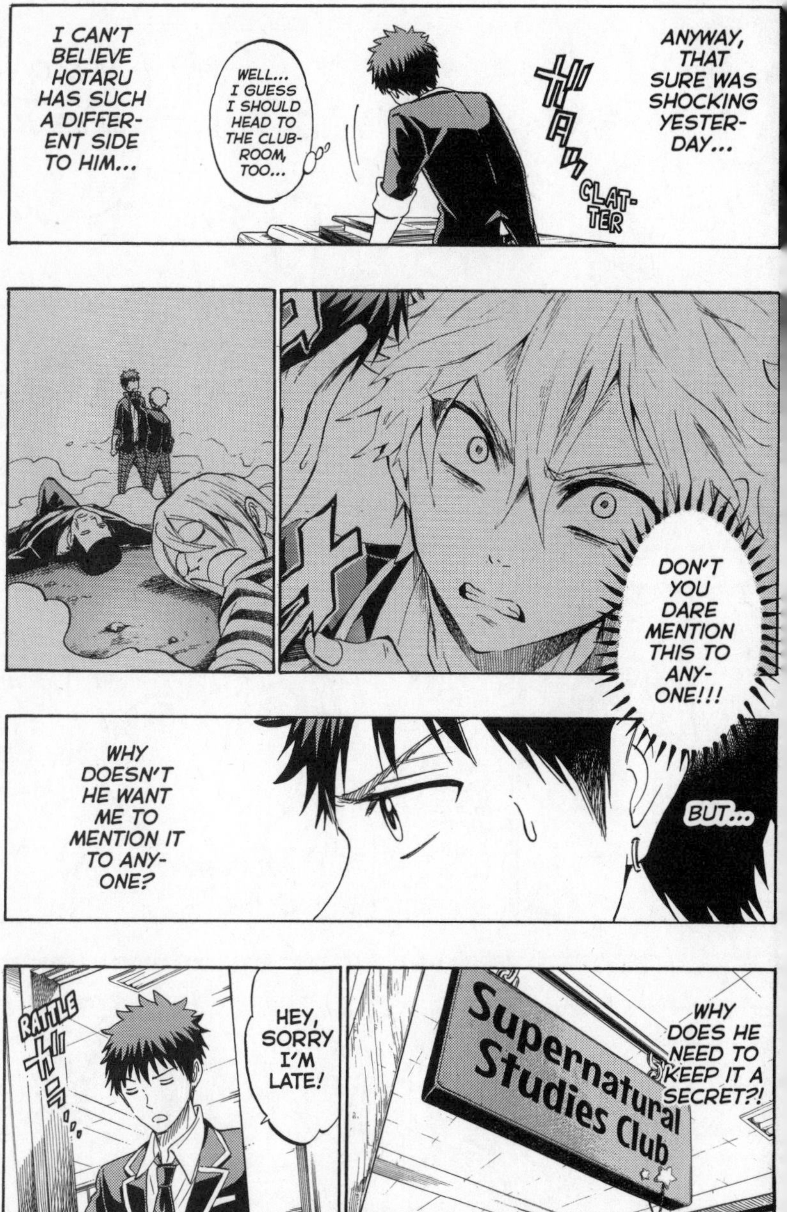
ANYWAY, THAT SURE WAS SHOCKING YESTERDAY...
CLATTER
WELL... I GUESS I SHOULD HEAD TO THE CLUBROOM, TOO...
I CAN'T BELIEVE HOTARU HAS SUCH A DIFFERENT SIDE TO HIM...
DON'T YOU DARE MENTION THIS TO ANYONE!!!
BUT...
WHY DOESN'T HE WANT ME TO MENTION IT TO ANYONE?
WHY DOES HE NEED TO KEEP IT A SECRET?!
Supernatural Studies Club
HEY, SORRY I'M LATE!
RATTLE

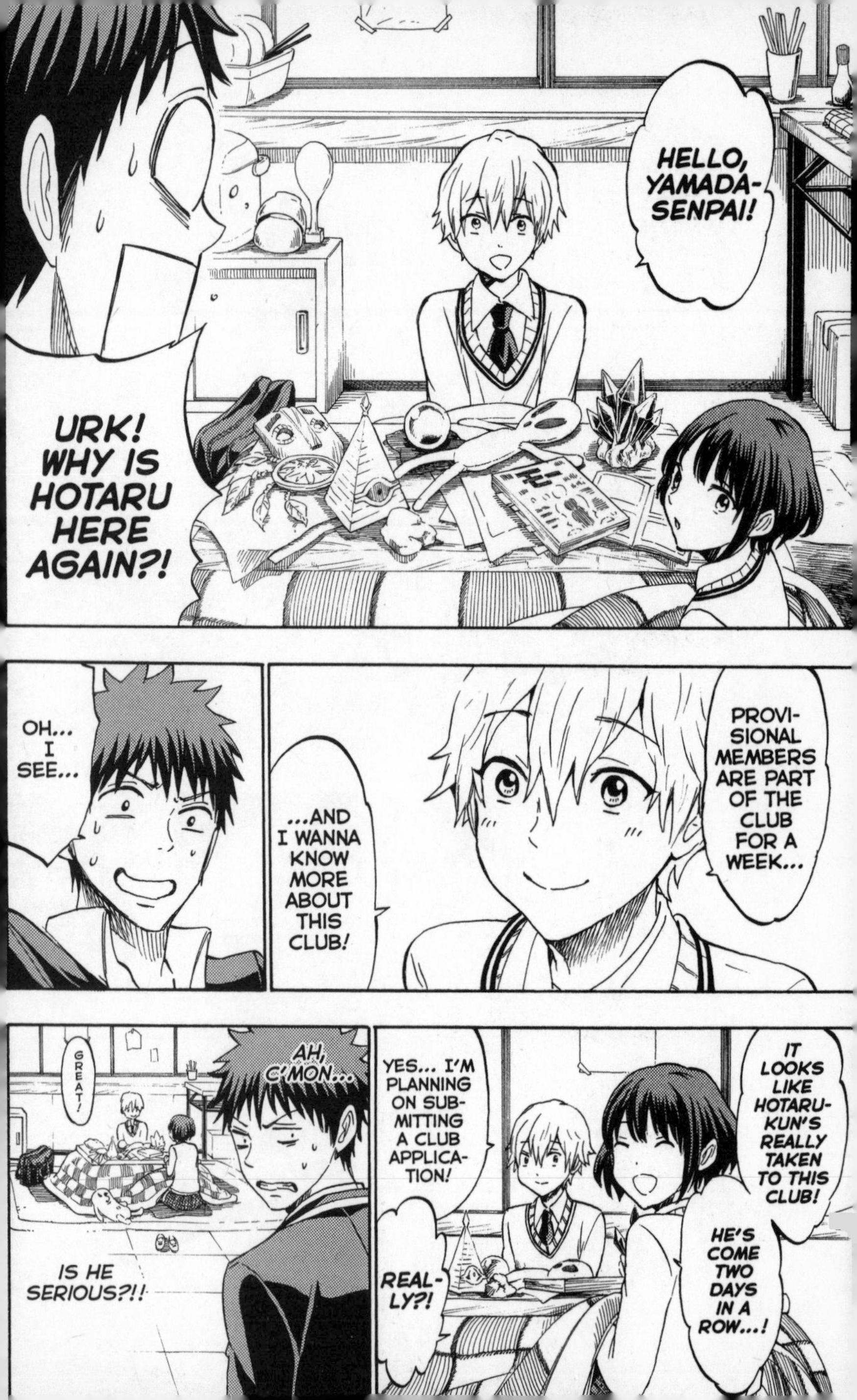

HELLO, YAMADA-SENPAI!
URK! WHY IS HOTARU HERE AGAIN?!
PROVISIONAL MEMBERS ARE PART OF THE CLUB FOR A WEEK...
...AND I WANNA KNOW MORE ABOUT THIS CLUB!
OH... I SEE...
IT LOOKS LIKE HOTARU-KUN'S REALLY TAKEN TO THIS CLUB!
HE'S COME TWO DAYS IN A ROW...!
YES... I'M PLANNING ON SUBMITTING A CLUB APPLICATION!
REALLY?!
AH, C'MON...
GREAT!
IS HE SERIOUS?!!

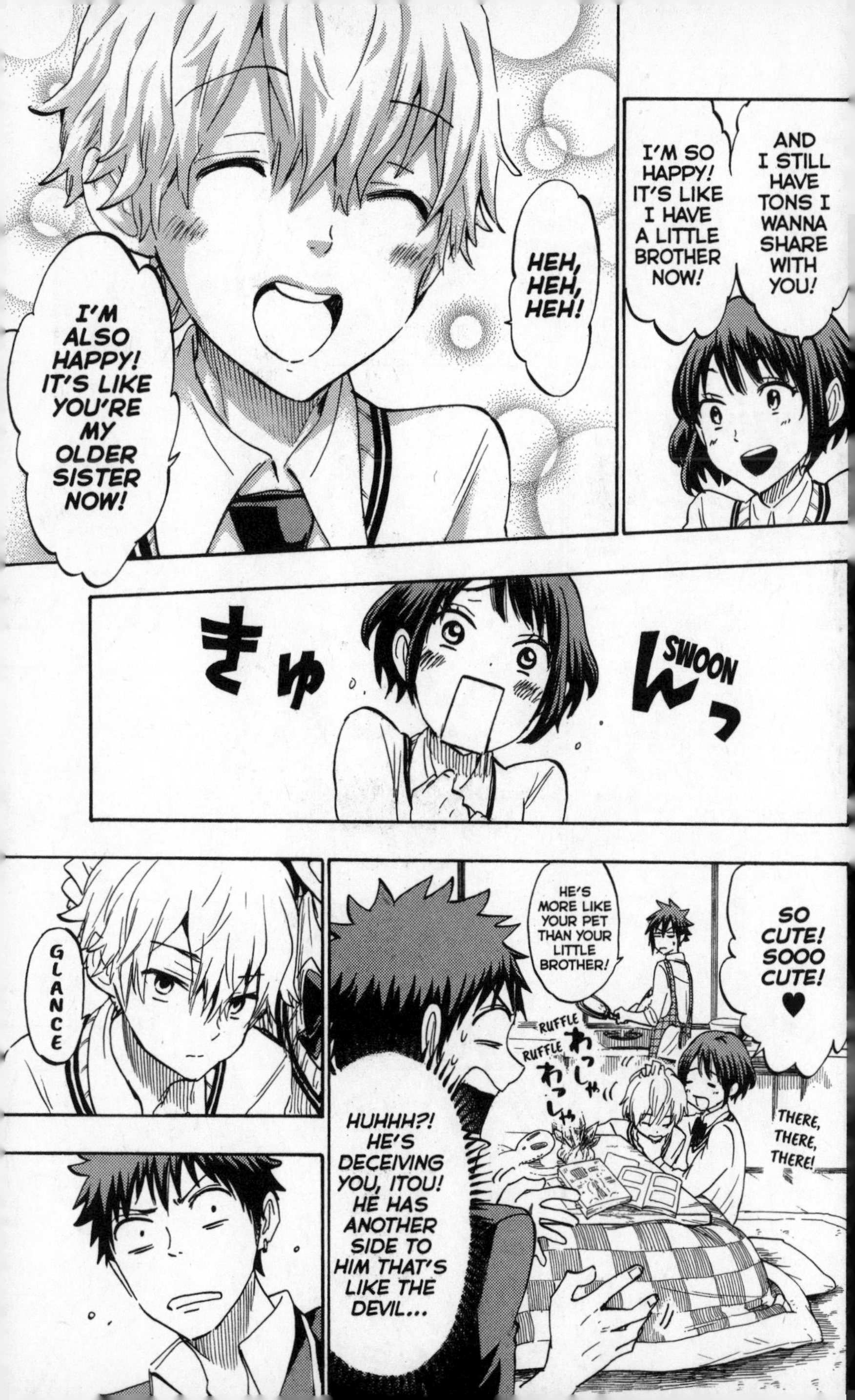
AND I STILL HAVE TONS I WANNA SHARE WITH YOU!
I'M SO HAPPY! IT'S LIKE I HAVE A LITTLE BROTHER NOW!
HEH, HEH, HEH!
I'M ALSO HAPPY! IT'S LIKE YOU'RE MY OLDER SISTER NOW!
きゅんっ
SWOON
SO CUTE! SOOO CUTE! ♥
HE'S MORE LIKE YOUR PET THAN YOUR LITTLE BROTHER!
THERE, THERE, THERE!
わっしゃ わっしゃ
RUFFLE RUFFLE
HUHHH?! HE'S DECEIVING YOU, ITOU! HE HAS ANOTHER SIDE TO HIM THAT'S LIKE THE DEVIL...
GLANCE

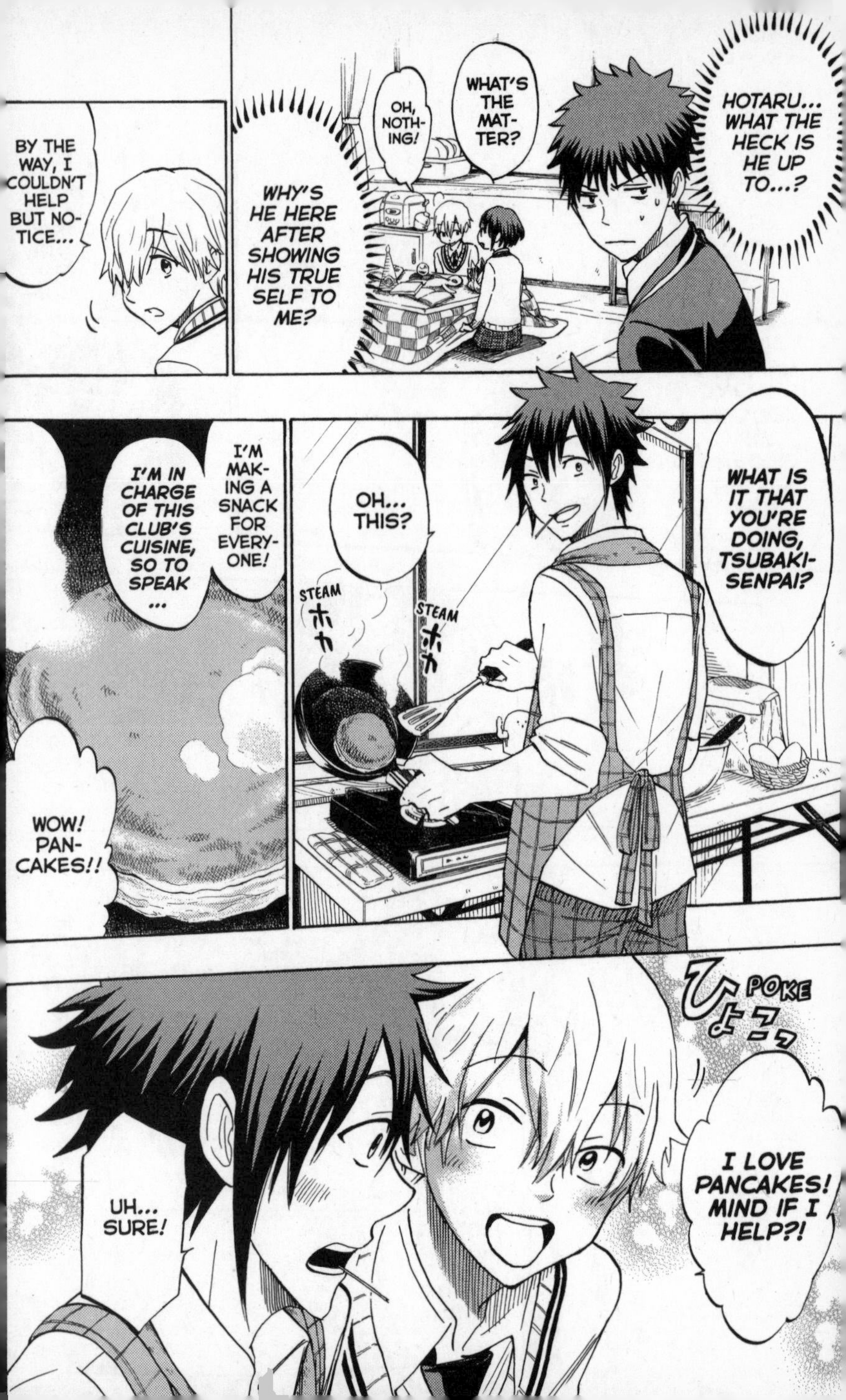
HOTARU... WHAT THE HECK IS HE UP TO...?
WHAT'S THE MATTER?
OH, NOTHING!
WHY'S HE HERE AFTER SHOWING HIS TRUE SELF TO ME?
BY THE WAY, I COULDN'T HELP BUT NOTICE...
WHAT IS IT THAT YOU'RE DOING, TSUBAKI-SENPAI?
OH... THIS?
STEAM
STEAM
I'M MAKING A SNACK FOR EVERYONE!
I'M IN CHARGE OF THIS CLUB'S CUISINE, SO TO SPEAK...
WOW! PANCAKES!!
POKE
I LOVE PANCAKES! MIND IF I HELP?!
UH... SURE!

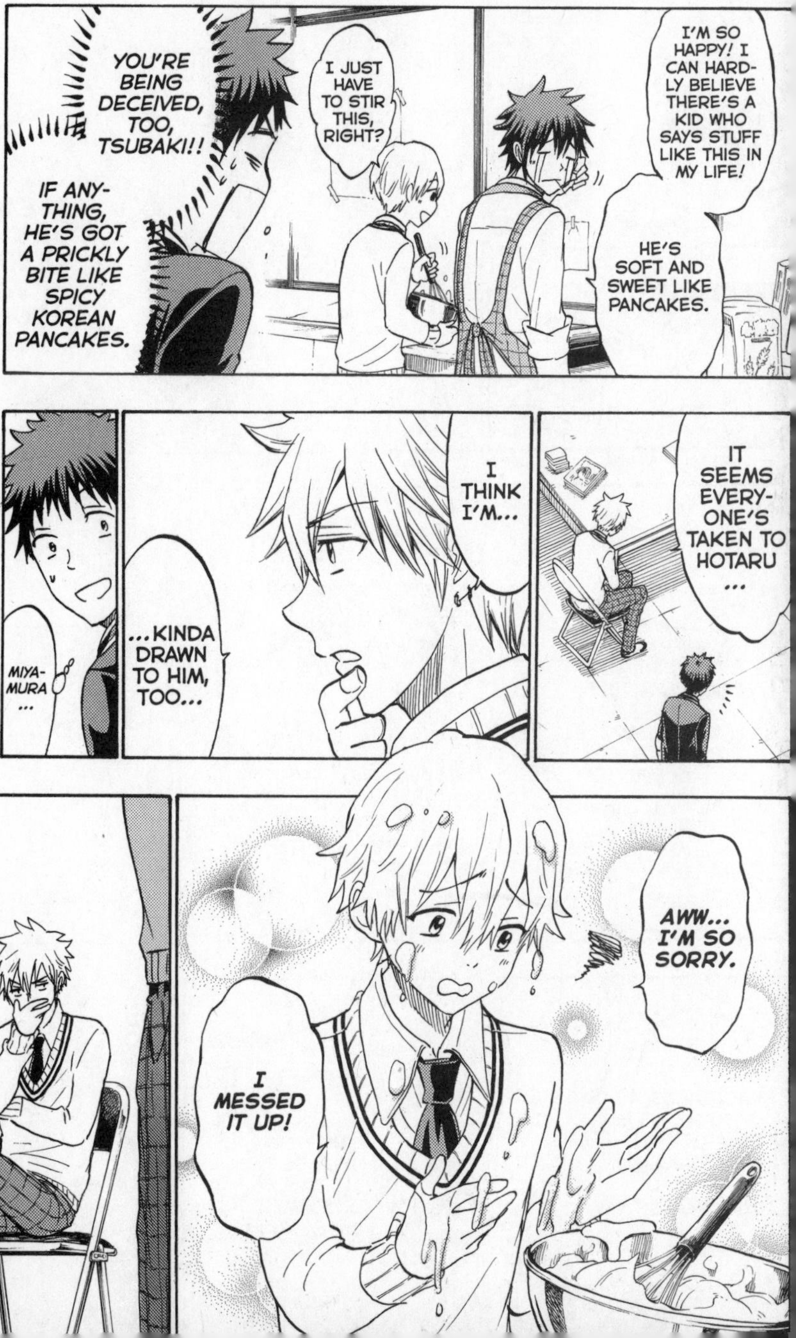
I'M SO HAPPY! I CAN HARDLY BELIEVE THERE'S A KID WHO SAYS STUFF LIKE THIS IN MY LIFE!
HE'S SOFT AND SWEET LIKE PANCAKES.
I JUST HAVE TO STIR THIS, RIGHT?
YOU'RE BEING DECEIVED, TOO, TSUBAKI!!
IF ANYTHING, HE'S GOT A PRICKLY BITE LIKE SPICY KOREAN PANCAKES.
IT SEEMS EVERYONE'S TAKEN TO HOTARU...
I THINK I'M...
...KINDA DRAWN TO HIM, TOO...
MIYAMURA...
AWW... I'M SO SORRY.
I MESSED IT UP!

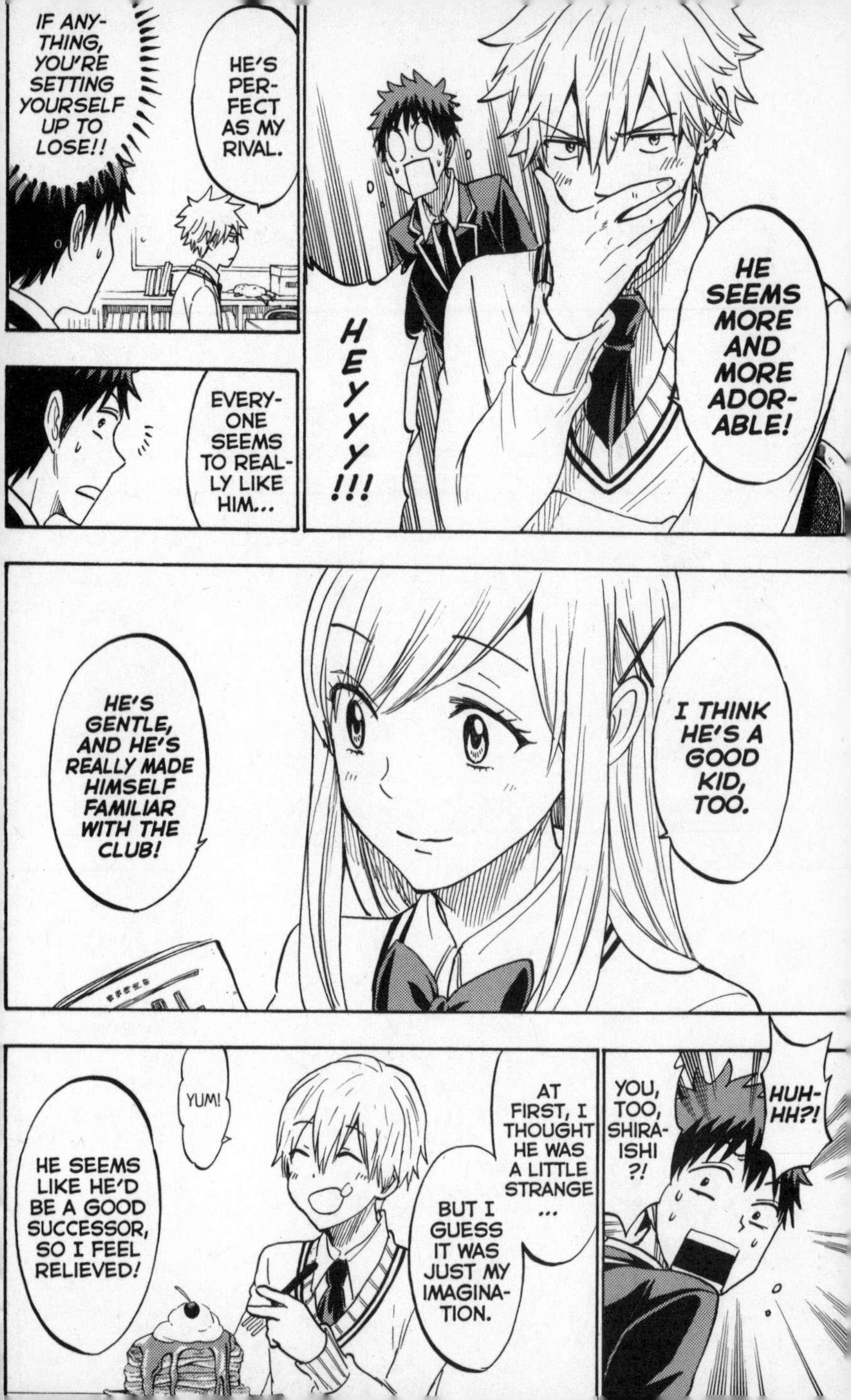
HE SEEMS MORE AND MORE ADORABLE!
HEYYY!!!
HE'S PERFECT AS MY RIVAL.
IF ANYTHING, YOU'RE SETTING YOURSELF UP TO LOSE!!
EVERYONE SEEMS TO REALLY LIKE HIM...
I THINK HE'S A GOOD KID, TOO.
HE'S GENTLE, AND HE'S REALLY MADE HIMSELF FAMILIAR WITH THE CLUB!
HUHHH?!
YOU, TOO, SHIRAISHI?!
AT FIRST, I THOUGHT HE WAS A LITTLE STRANGE...
BUT I GUESS IT WAS JUST MY IMAGINATION.
YUM!
HE SEEMS LIKE HE'D BE A GOOD SUCCESSOR, SO I FEEL RELIEVED!

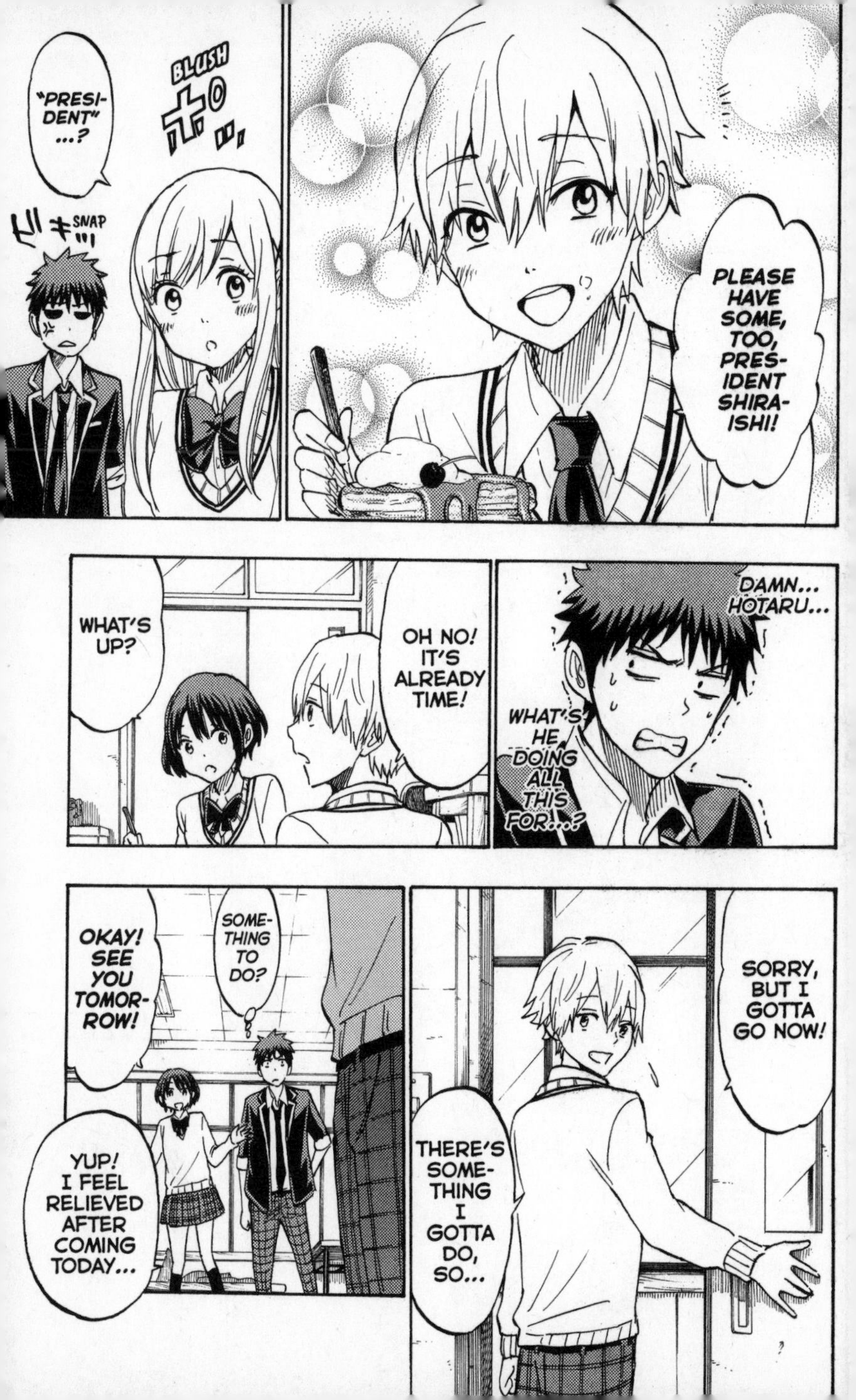
PLEASE HAVE SOME, TOO, PRESIDENT SHIRAISHI!
BLUSH
"PRESIDENT"...?
SNAP
DAMN... HOTARU...
WHAT'S HE DOING ALL THIS FOR...?
OH NO! IT'S ALREADY TIME!
WHAT'S UP?
SORRY, BUT I GOTTA GO NOW!
THERE'S SOMETHING I GOTTA DO, SO...
SOMETHING TO DO?
OKAY! SEE YOU TOMORROW!
YUP! I FEEL RELIEVED AFTER COMING TODAY...

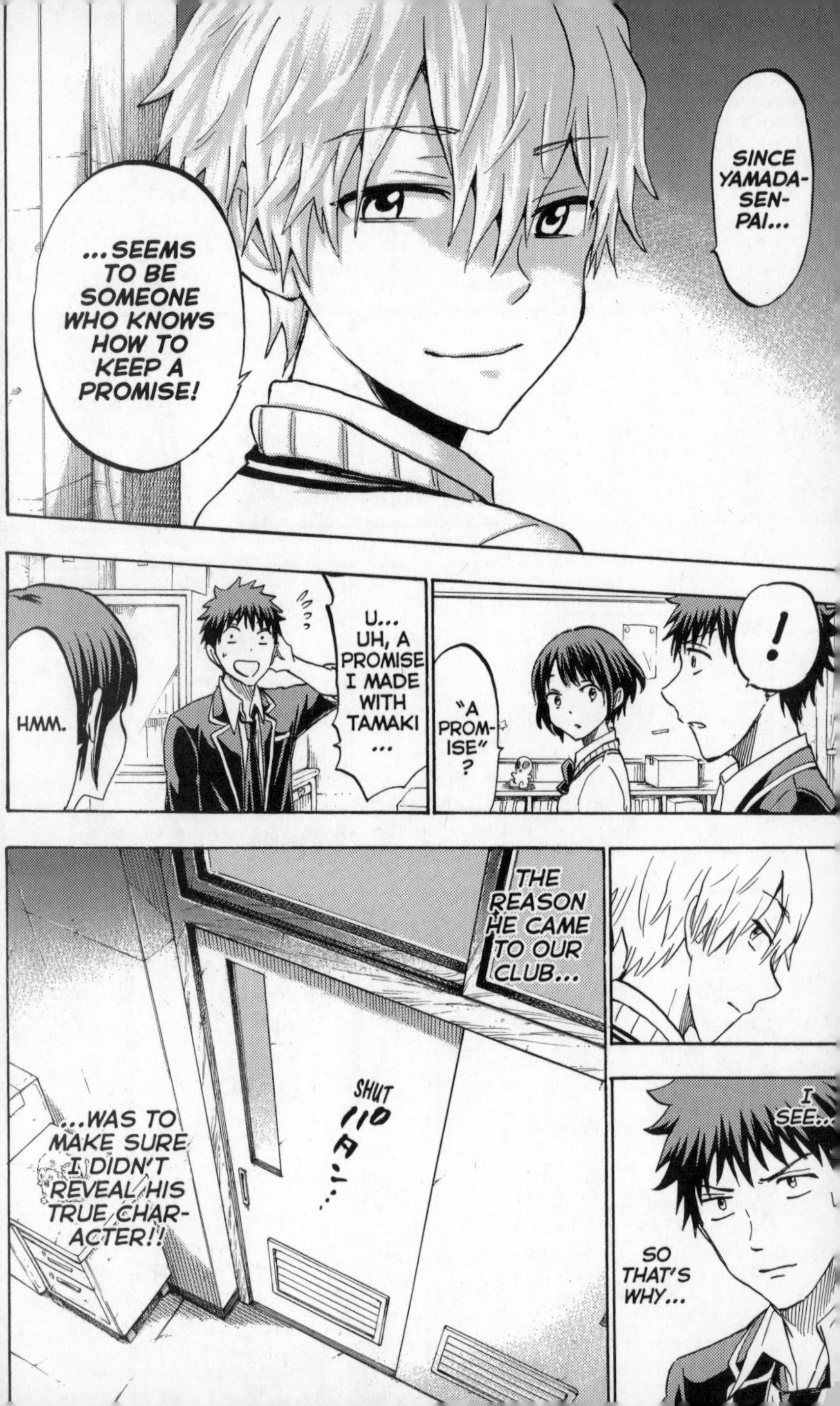
SINCE YAMADA-SEN-PAI...
...SEEMS TO BE SOMEONE WHO KNOWS HOW TO KEEP A PROMISE!
!
"A PROMISE"?
U... UH, A PROMISE I MADE WITH TAMAKI ...
HMM.
I SEE...
SO THAT'S WHY...
THE REASON HE CAME TO OUR CLUB...
SHUT
...WAS TO MAKE SURE I DIDN'T REVEAL HIS TRUE CHAR-ACTER!!

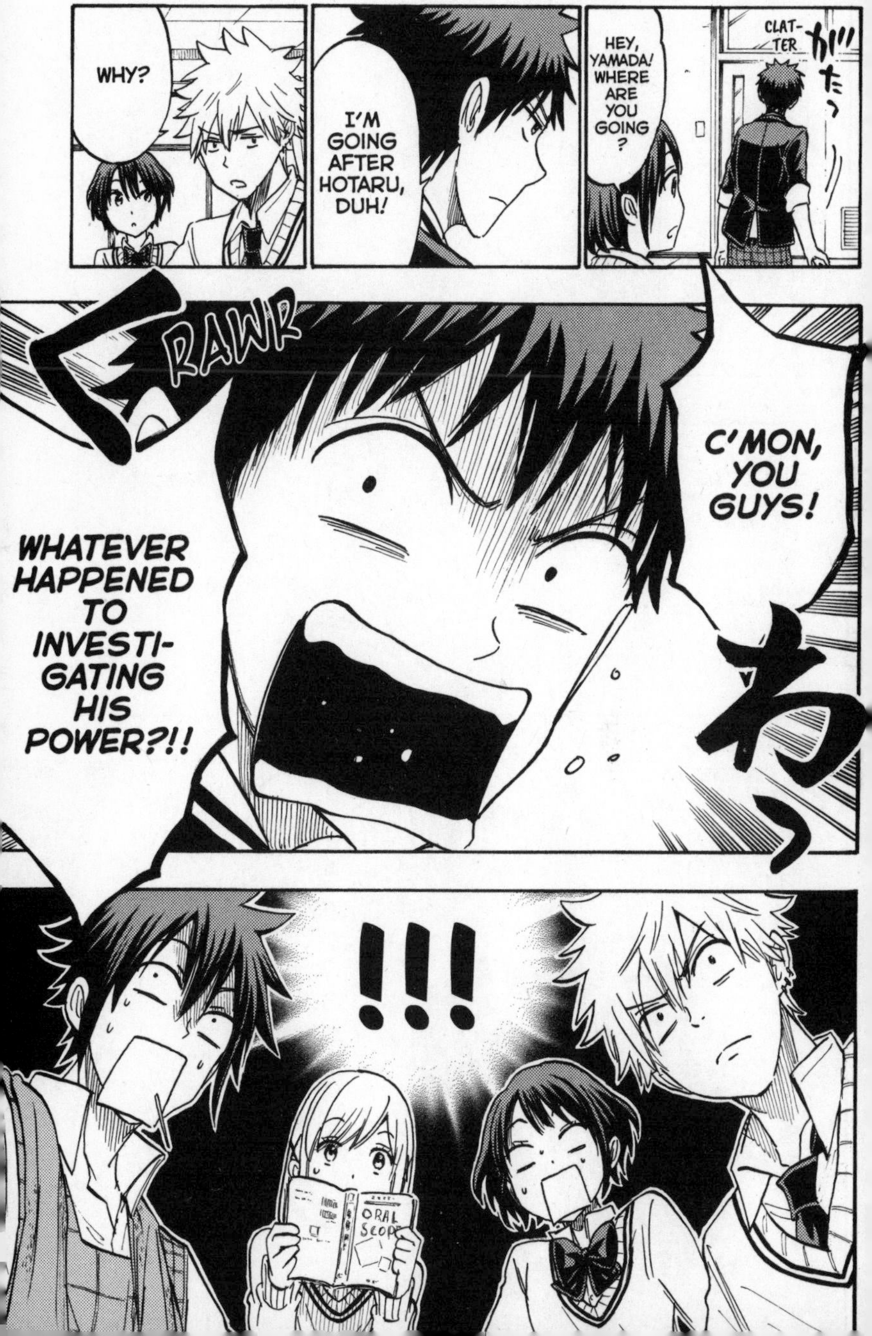
CLAT-TER
がたっ
HEY, YAMADA! WHERE ARE YOU GOING?
I'M GOING AFTER HOTARU, DUH!
WHY?
RAWR
C'MON, YOU GUYS!
WHATEVER HAPPENED TO INVESTI-GATING HIS POWER?!!
わっ
!!!

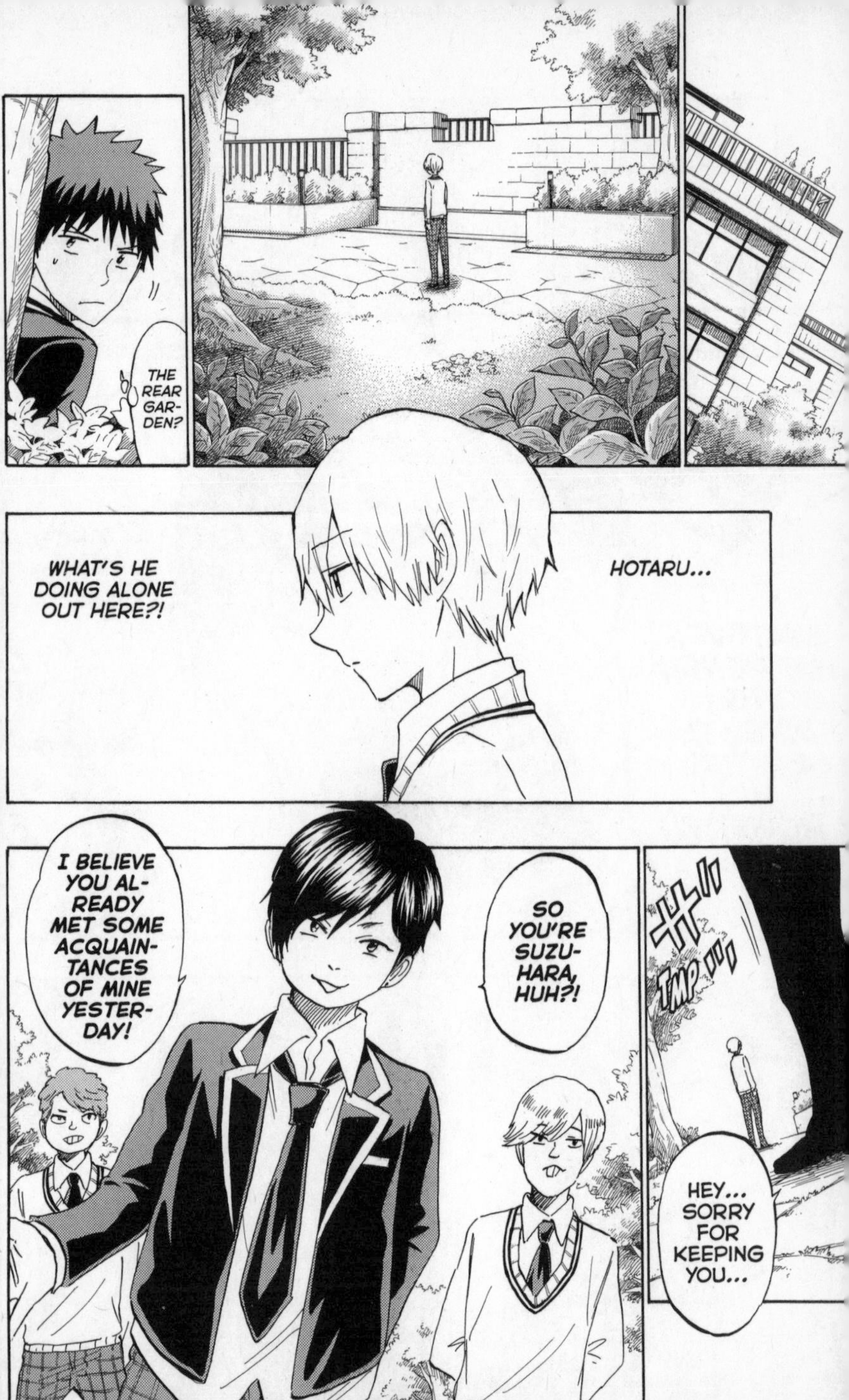
THE REAR GAR-DEN?
HOTARU...
WHAT'S HE DOING ALONE OUT HERE?!
TMP...
HEY... SORRY FOR KEEPING YOU...
SO YOU'RE SUZU-HARA, HUH?!
I BELIEVE YOU AL-READY MET SOME ACQUAIN-TANCES OF MINE YESTER-DAY!

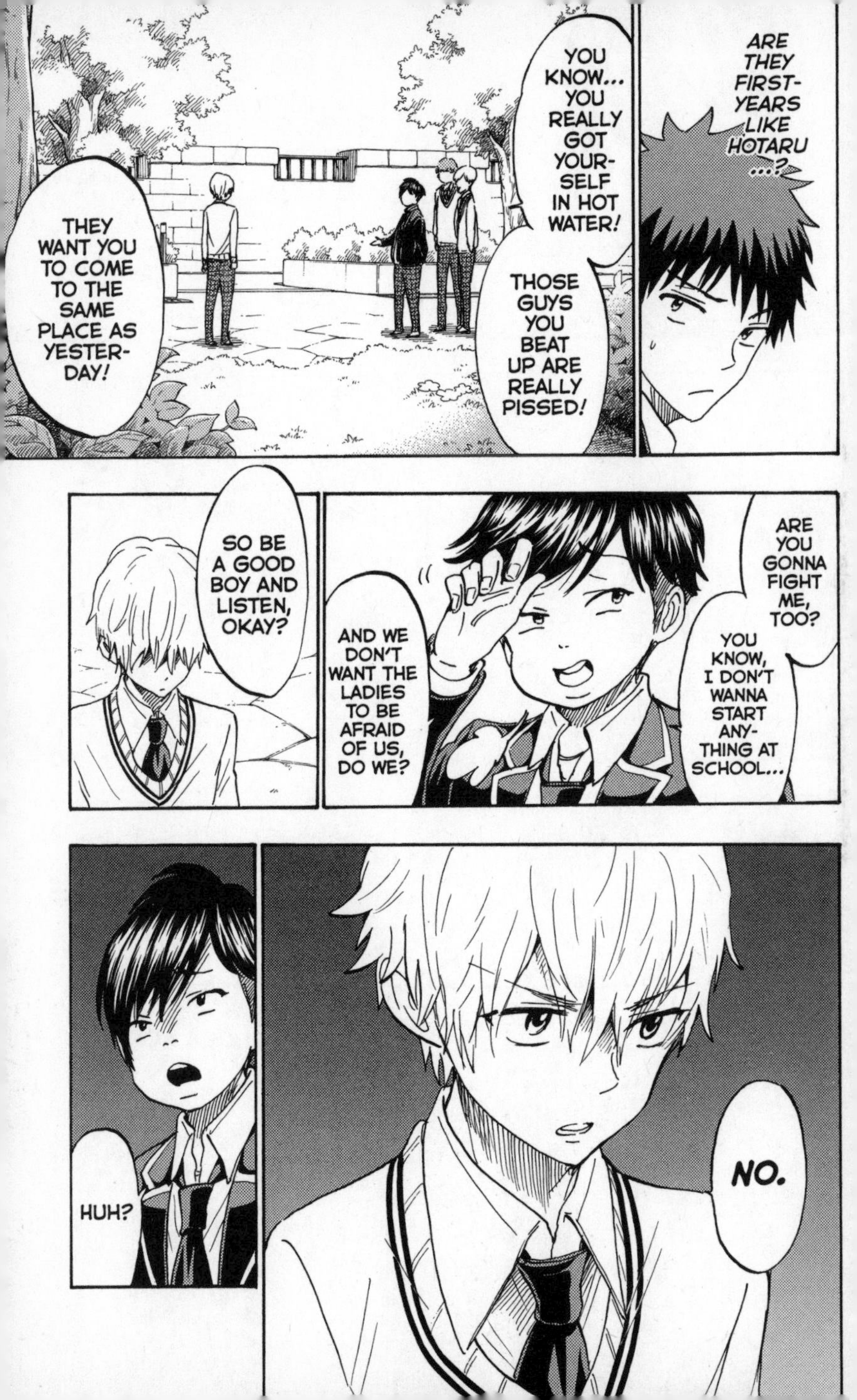
ARE THEY FIRST-YEARS LIKE HOTARU...?
YOU KNOW... YOU REALLY GOT YOURSELF IN HOT WATER!
THOSE GUYS YOU BEAT UP ARE REALLY PISSED!
THEY WANT YOU TO COME TO THE SAME PLACE AS YESTERDAY!
ARE YOU GONNA FIGHT ME, TOO?
YOU KNOW, I DON'T WANNA START ANYTHING AT SCHOOL...
AND WE DON'T WANT THE LADIES TO BE AFRAID OF US, DO WE?
SO BE A GOOD BOY AND LISTEN, OKAY?
NO.
HUH?

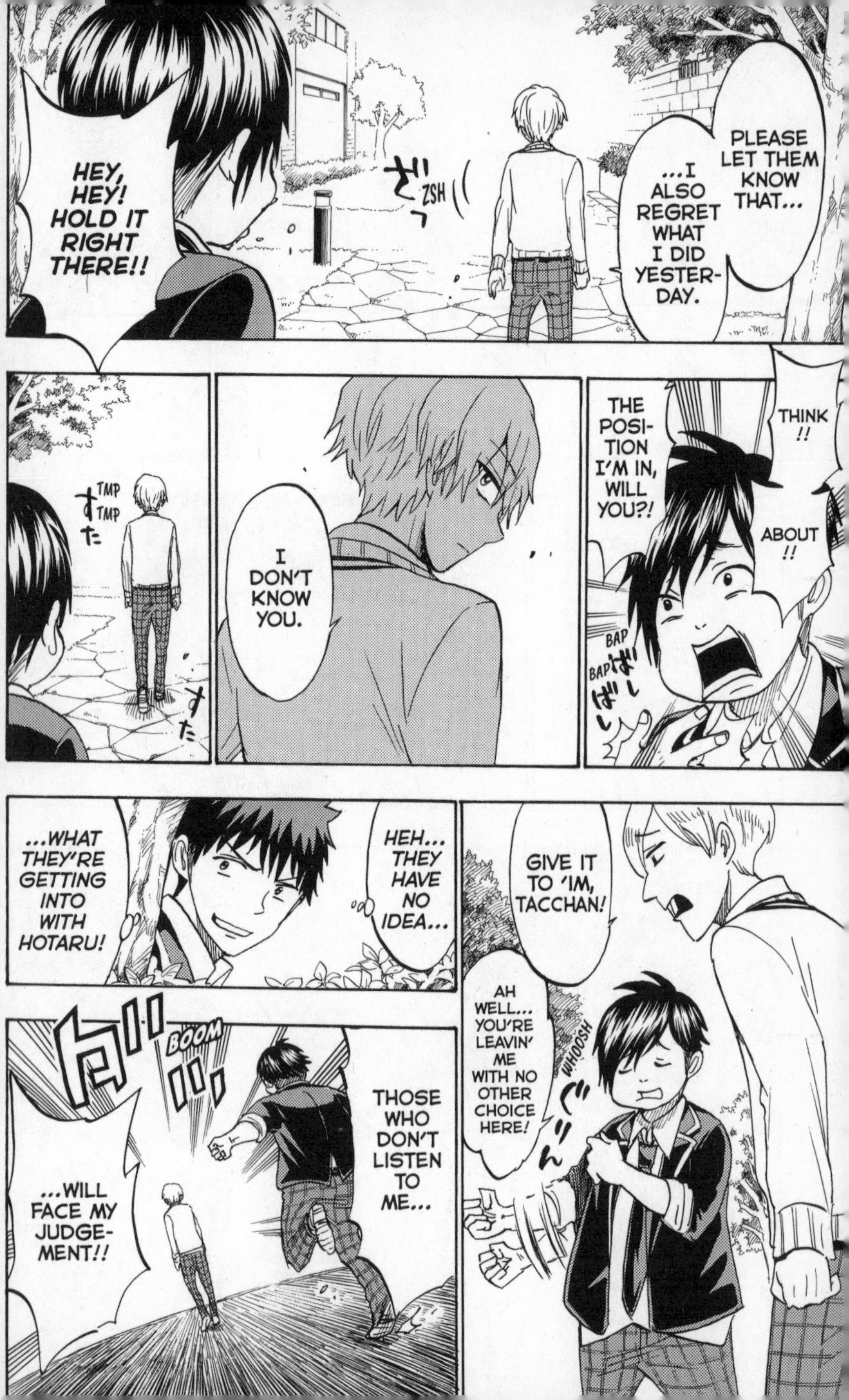
PLEASE LET THEM KNOW THAT...
...I ALSO REGRET WHAT I DID YESTERDAY.
ZSH
HEY, HEY! HOLD IT RIGHT THERE!!
THINK!!
ABOUT!!
THE POSITION I'M IN, WILL YOU?!
BAP
BAP
I DON'T KNOW YOU.
TMP
TMP
GIVE IT TO 'IM, TACCHAN!
AH WELL... YOU'RE LEAVIN' ME WITH NO OTHER CHOICE HERE!
WHOOSH
HEH... THEY HAVE NO IDEA...
...WHAT THEY'RE GETTING INTO WITH HOTARU!
THOSE WHO DON'T LISTEN TO ME...
BOOM
...WILL FACE MY JUDGEMENT!!

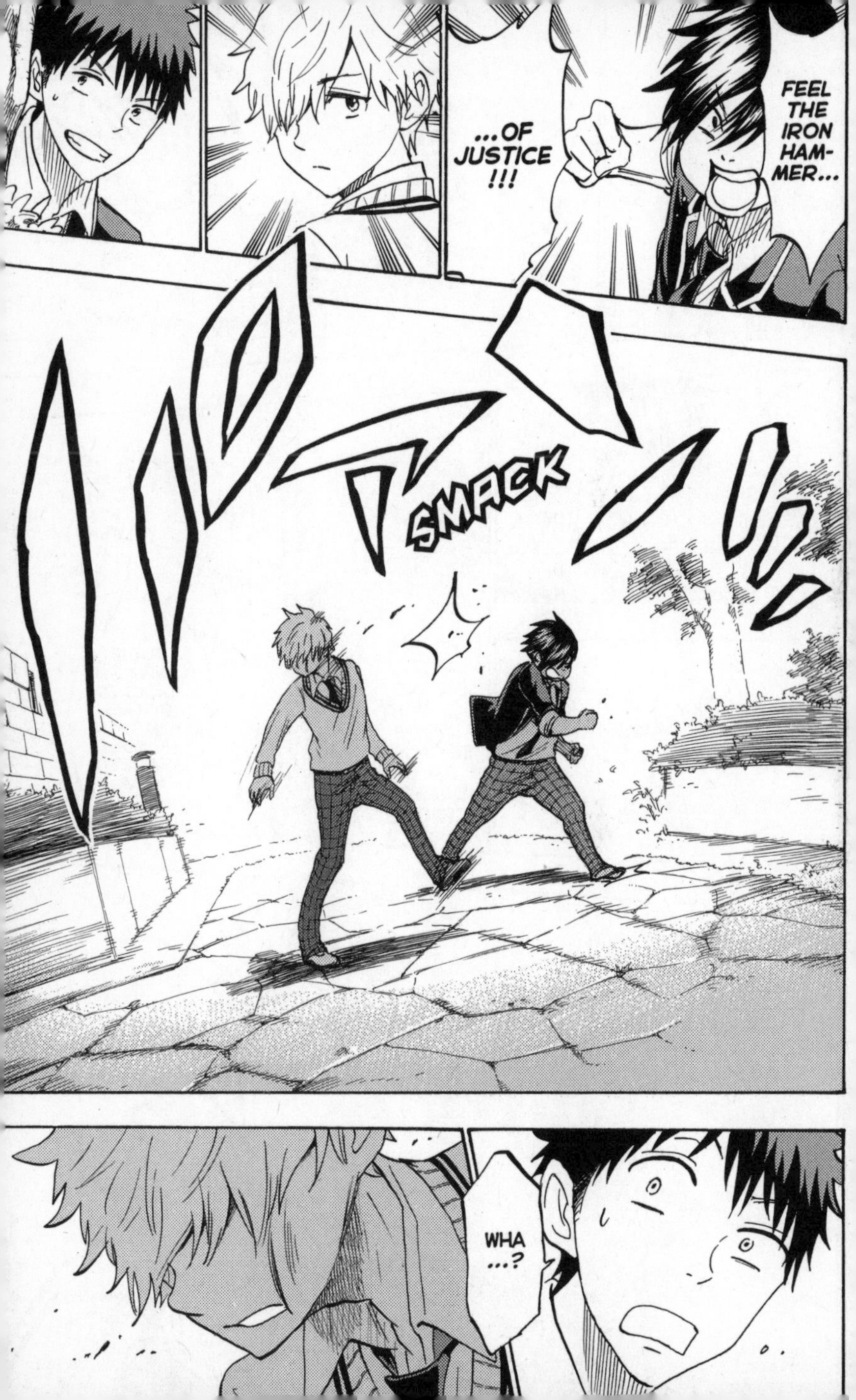
FEEL THE IRON HAMMER...
...OF JUSTICE!!!
SMACK
WHA...?

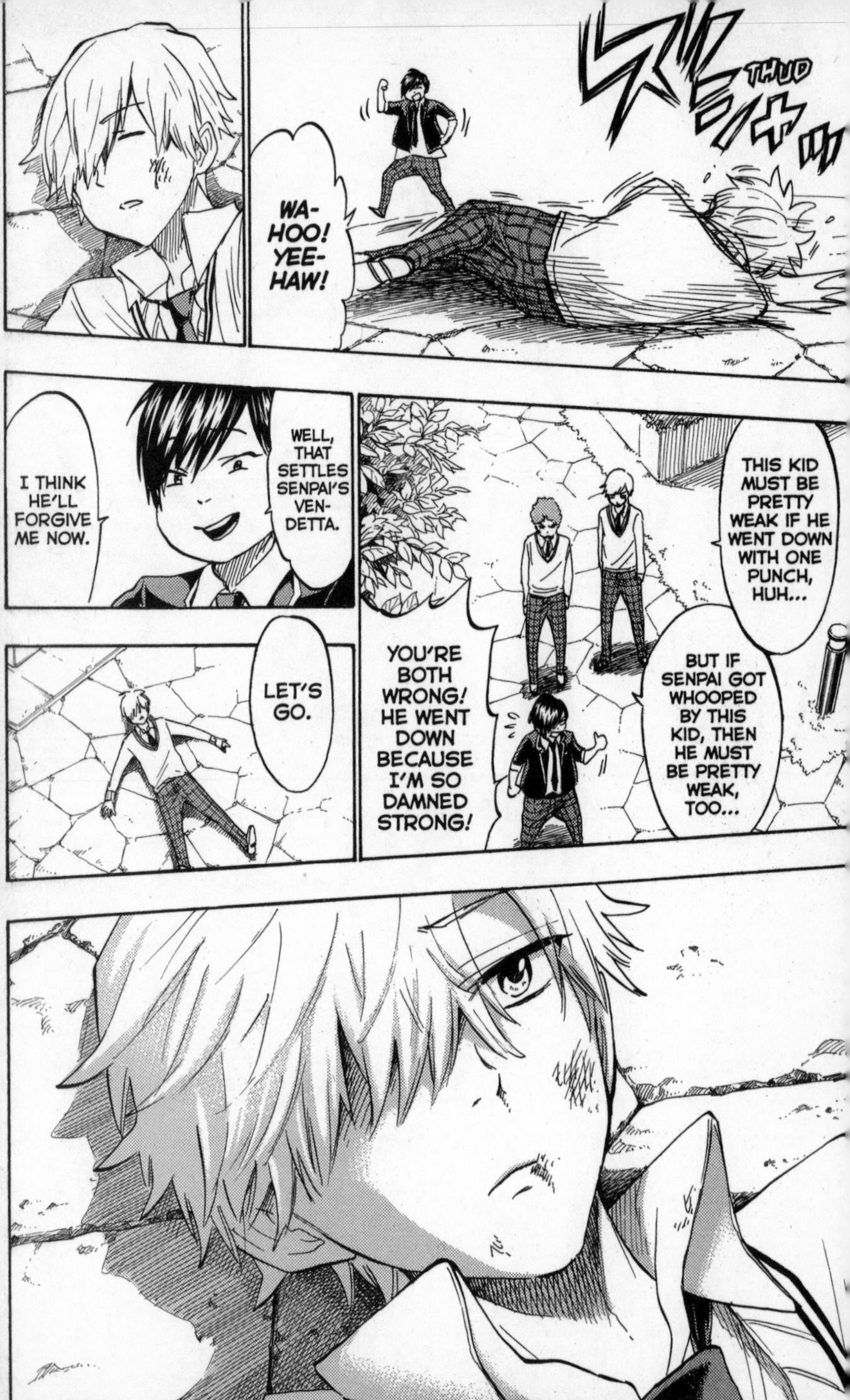
THUD
WA-HOO! YEE-HAW!
THIS KID MUST BE PRETTY WEAK IF HE WENT DOWN WITH ONE PUNCH, HUH...
BUT IF SENPAI GOT WHOOPED BY THIS KID, THEN HE MUST BE PRETTY WEAK, TOO...
YOU'RE BOTH WRONG! HE WENT DOWN BECAUSE I'M SO DAMNED STRONG!
WELL, THAT SETTLES SENPAI'S VEN-DETTA.
I THINK HE'LL FORGIVE ME NOW.
LET'S GO.

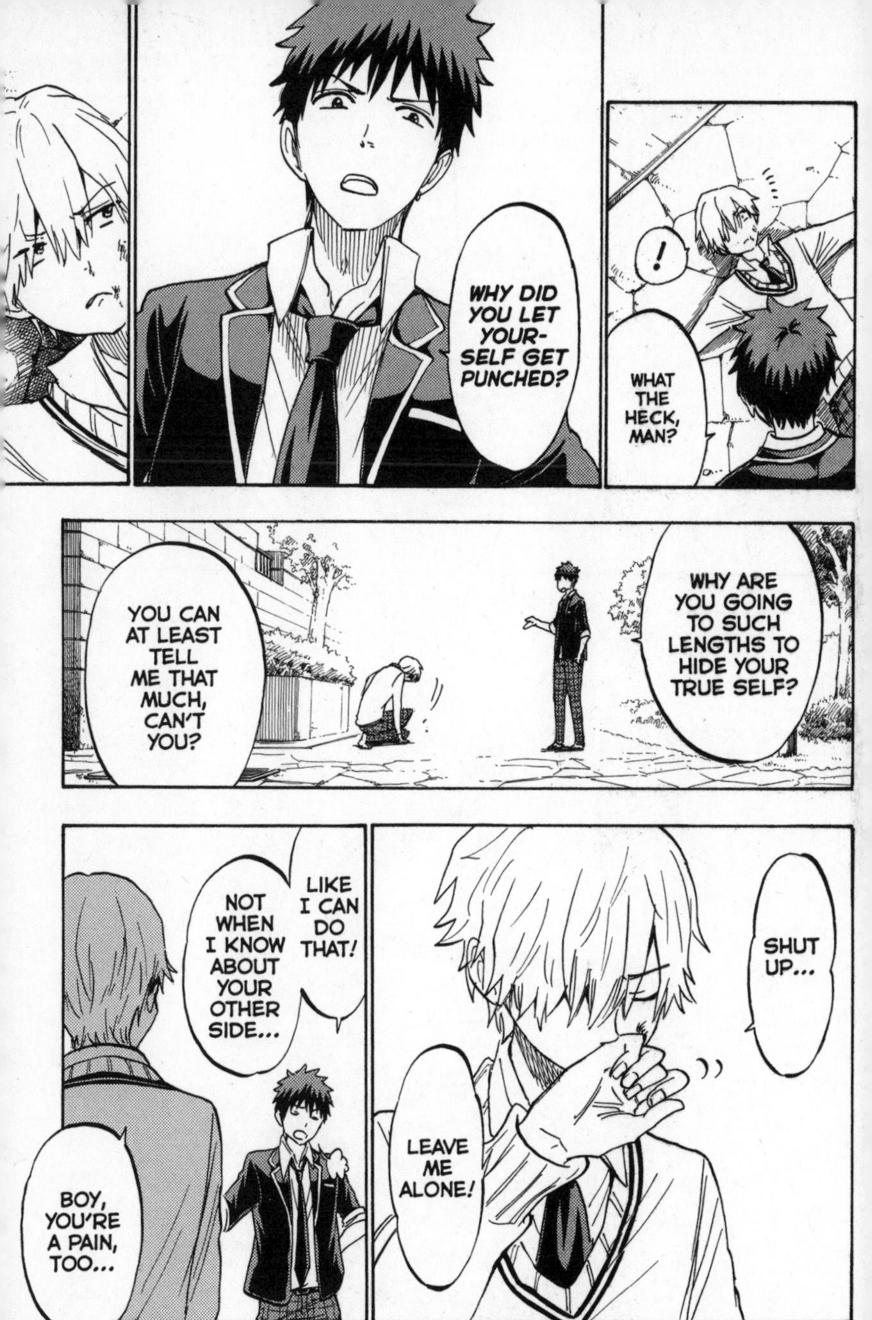
!
WHAT THE HECK, MAN?
WHY DID YOU LET YOUR-SELF GET PUNCHED?
WHY ARE YOU GOING TO SUCH LENGTHS TO HIDE YOUR TRUE SELF?
YOU CAN AT LEAST TELL ME THAT MUCH, CAN'T YOU?
SHUT UP...
LEAVE ME ALONE!
LIKE I CAN DO THAT!
NOT WHEN I KNOW ABOUT YOUR OTHER SIDE...
BOY, YOU'RE A PAIN, TOO...

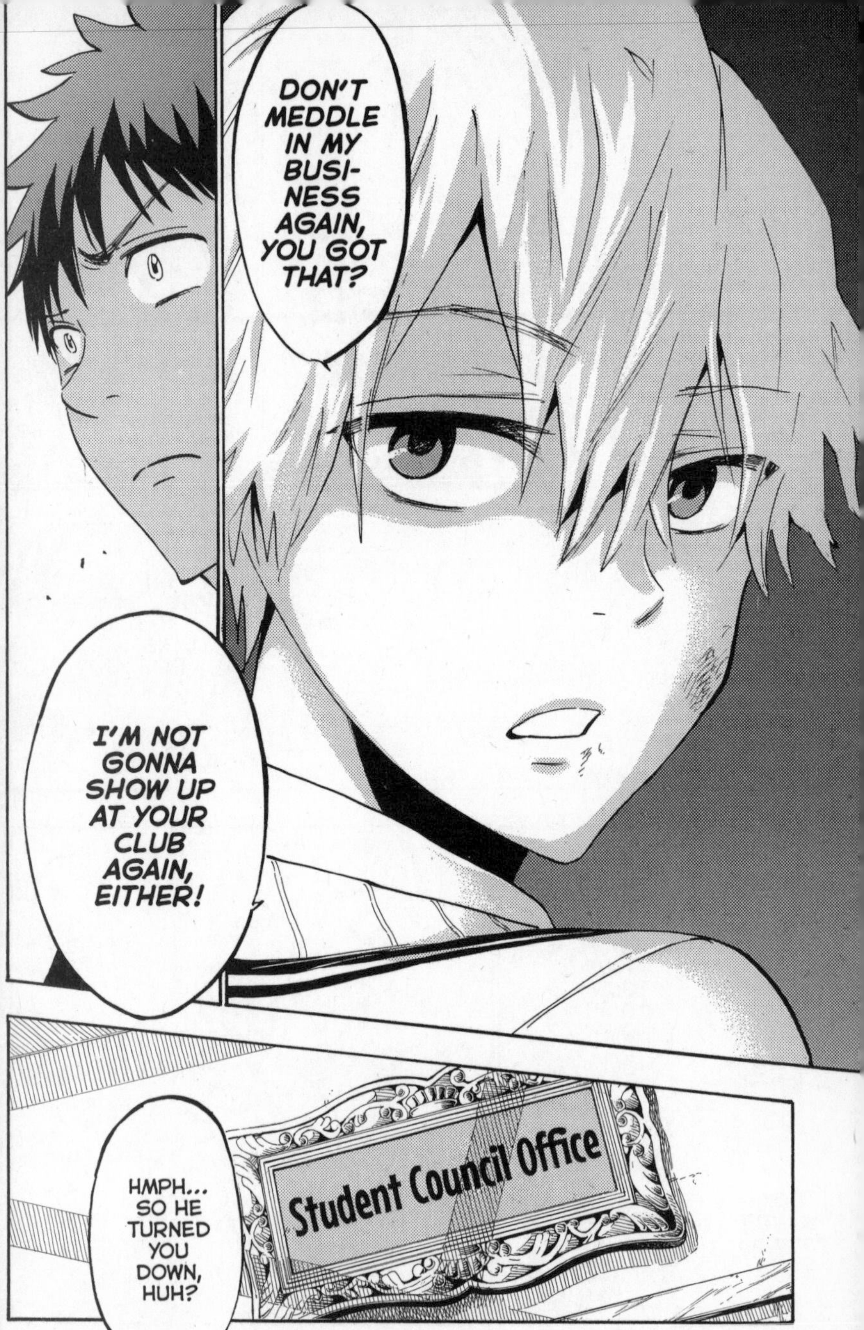
DON'T MEDDLE IN MY BUSI- NESS AGAIN, YOU GOT THAT?
I'M NOT GONNA SHOW UP AT YOUR CLUB AGAIN, EITHER!
Student Council Office
HMPH... SO HE TURNED YOU DOWN, HUH?

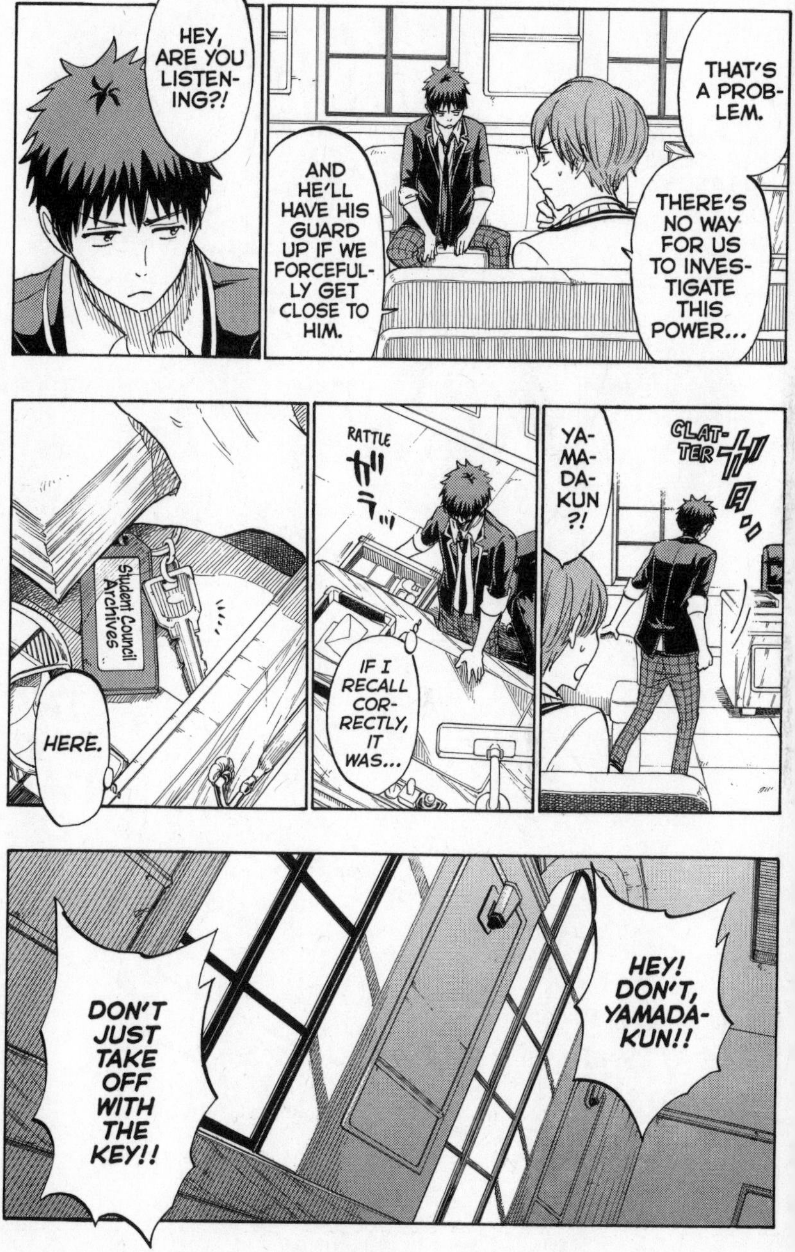
THAT'S A PROBLEM.
THERE'S NO WAY FOR US TO INVESTIGATE THIS POWER...
AND HE'LL HAVE HIS GUARD UP IF WE FORCEFULLY GET CLOSE TO HIM.
HEY, ARE YOU LISTENING?!
CLATTER
YAMADA-KUN?!
RATTLE
IF I RECALL CORRECTLY, IT WAS...
Student Council Archives
HERE.
HEY! DON'T, YAMADA-KUN!!
DON'T JUST TAKE OFF WITH THE KEY!!

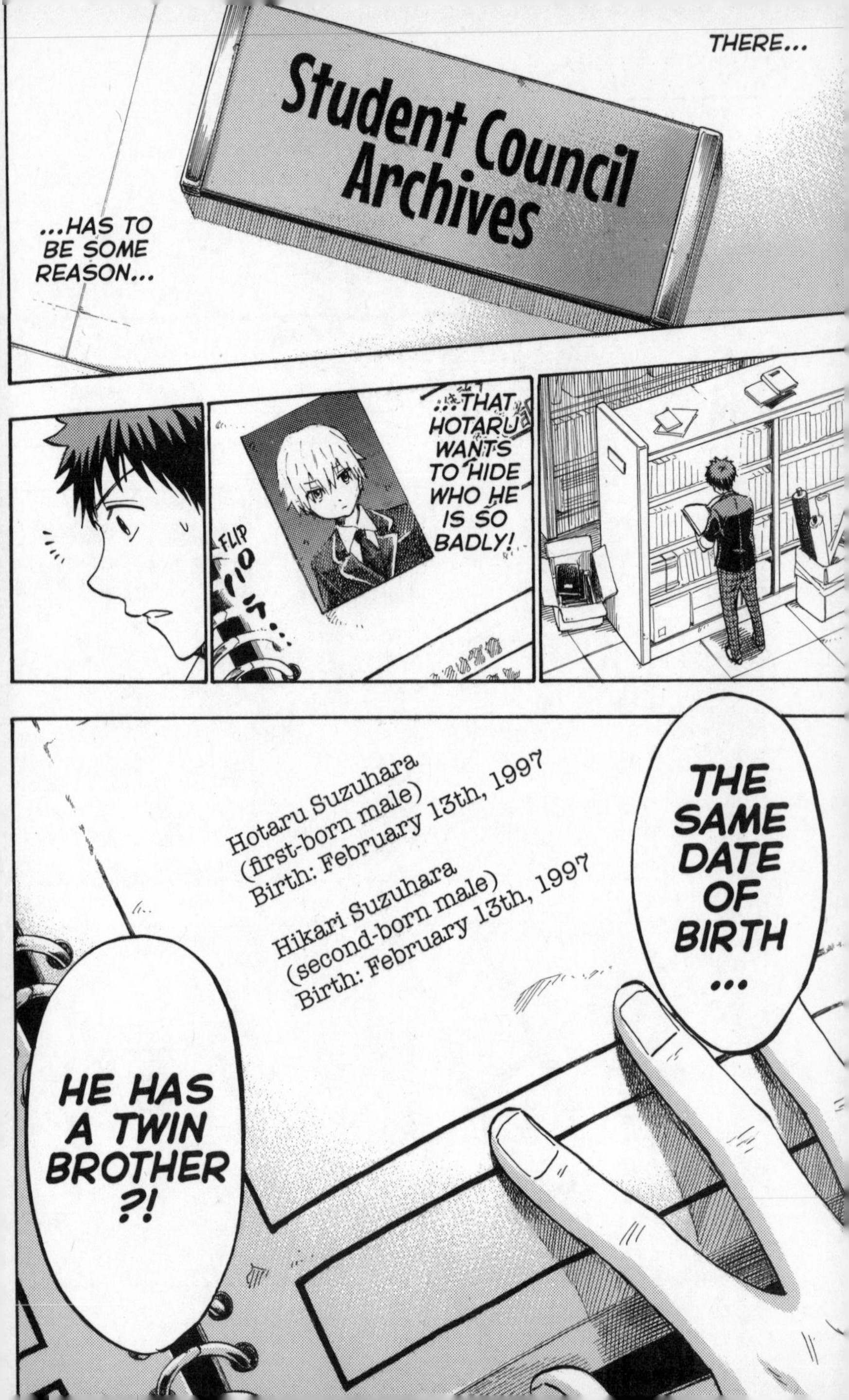
THERE...
Student Council Archives
...HAS TO BE SOME REASON...
...THAT HOTARU WANTS TO HIDE WHO HE IS SO BADLY!
FLIP
Hotaru Suzuhara (first-born male) Birth: February 13th, 1997
Hikari Suzuhara (second-born male) Birth: February 13th, 1997
THE SAME DATE OF BIRTH...
HE HAS A TWIN BROTHER?!

CHAPTER 190: You mean hosts?!

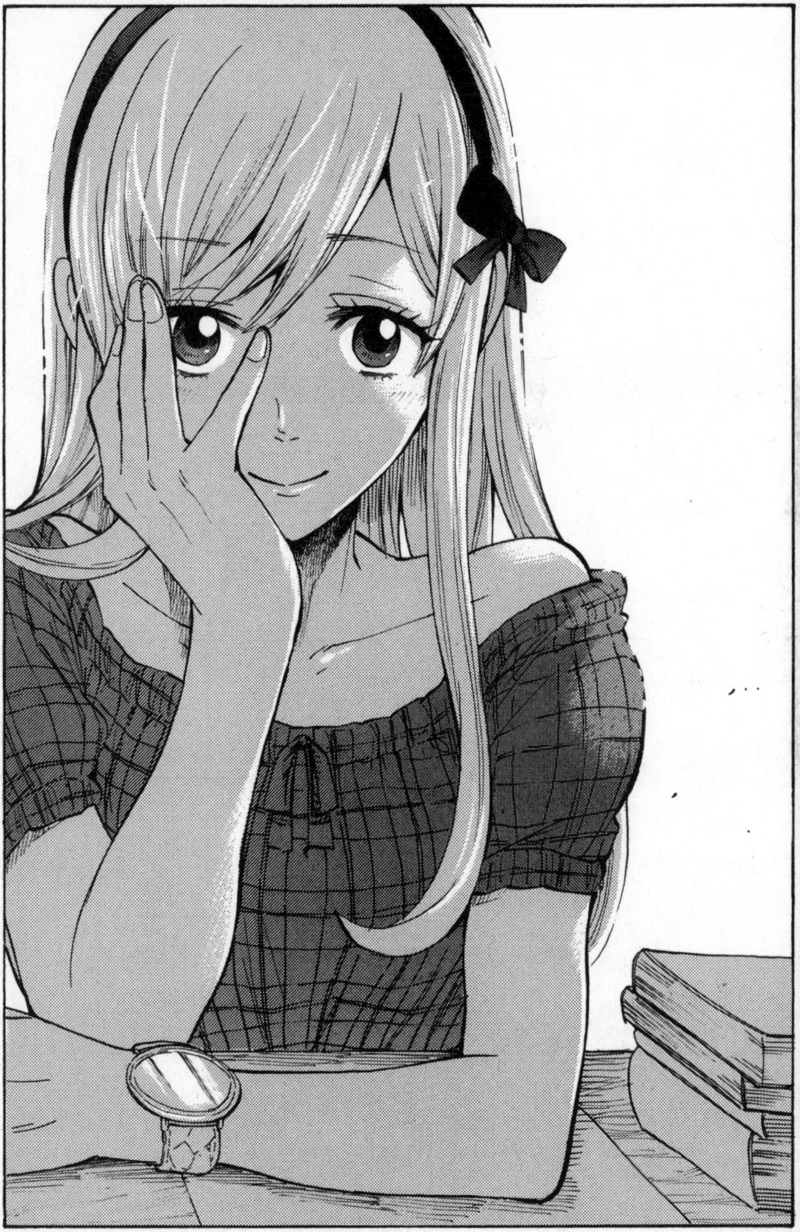

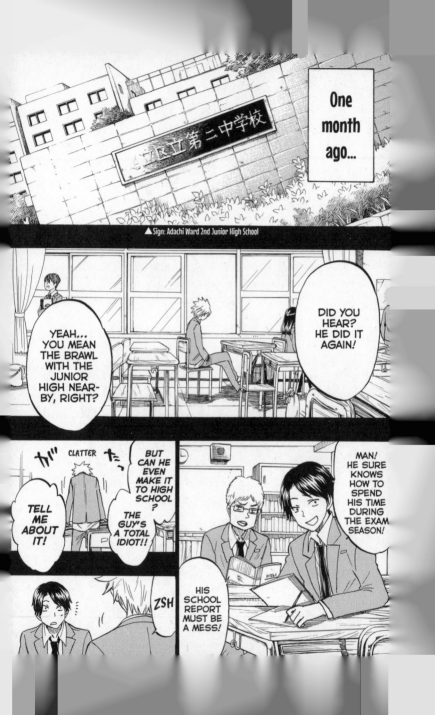

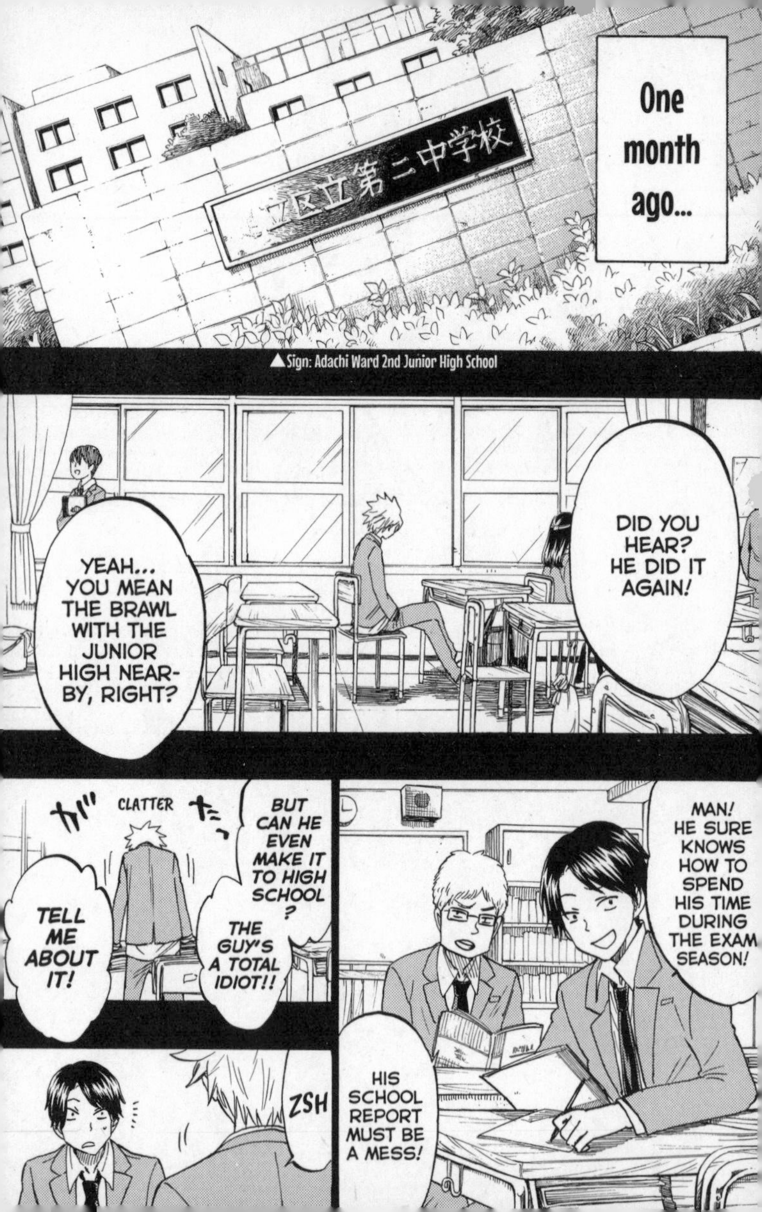
One month ago...
▲Sign: Adachi Ward 2nd Junior High School
DID YOU HEAR? HE DID IT AGAIN!
YEAH... YOU MEAN THE BRAWL WITH THE JUNIOR HIGH NEAR-BY, RIGHT?
MAN! HE SURE KNOWS HOW TO SPEND HIS TIME DURING THE EXAM SEASON!
HIS SCHOOL REPORT MUST BE A MESS!
BUT CAN HE EVEN MAKE IT TO HIGH SCHOOL?
THE GUY'S A TOTAL IDIOT!!
TELL ME ABOUT IT!
CLATTER
ZSH

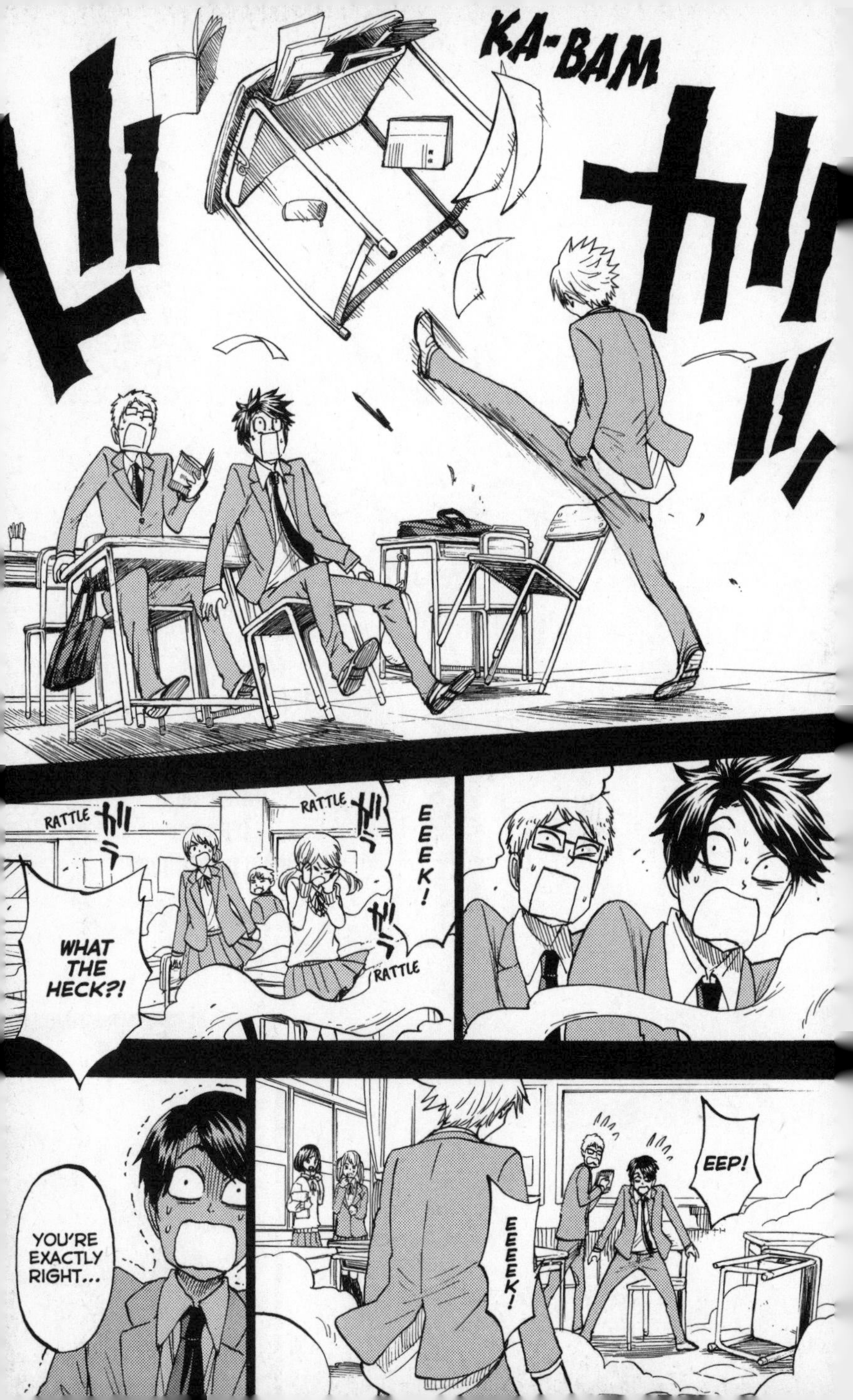
KA-BAM
RATTLE
EEEEK!
RATTLE
RATTLE
WHAT THE HECK?!
EEP!
EEEEK!
YOU'RE EXACTLY RIGHT...

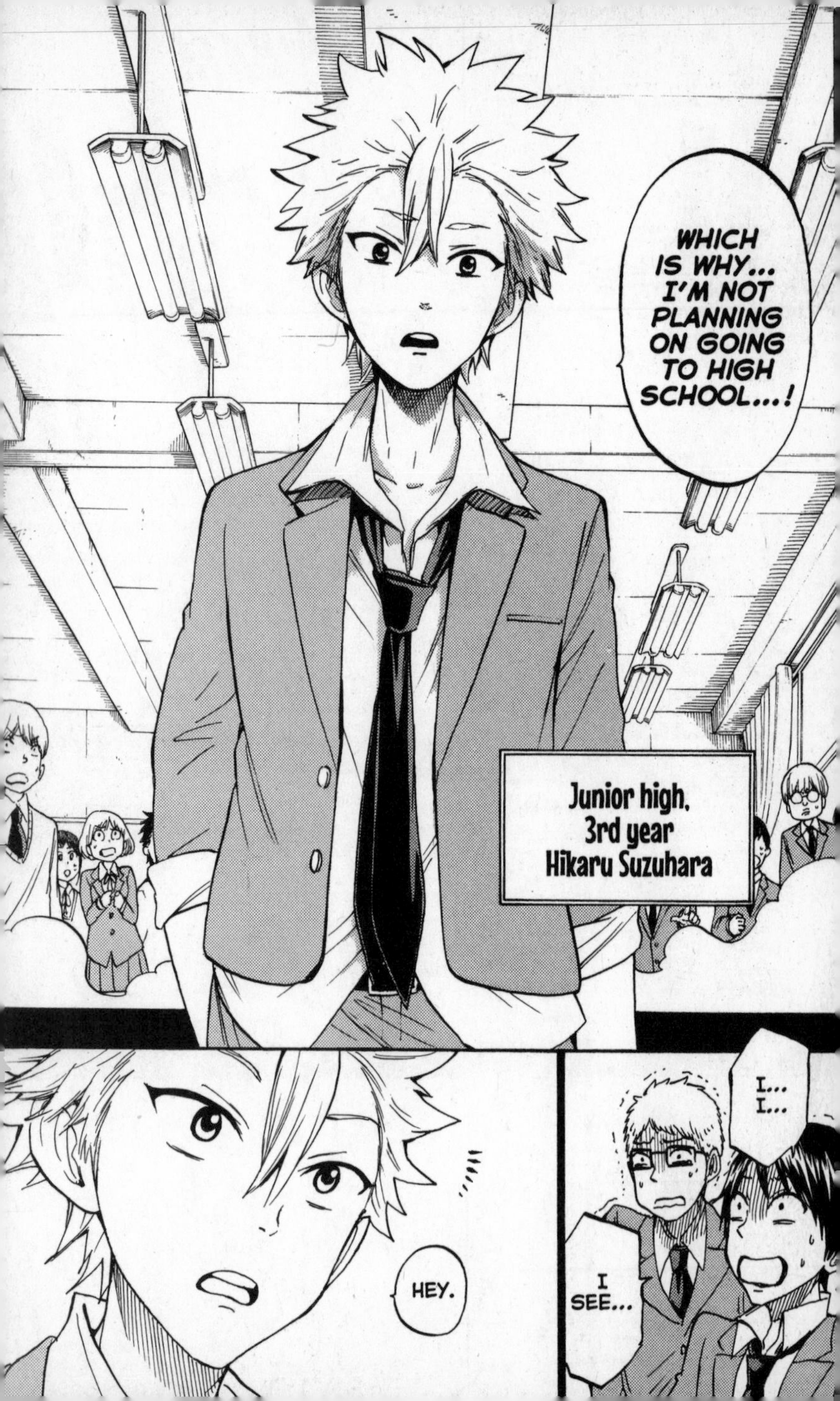
WHICH IS WHY... I'M NOT PLANNING ON GOING TO HIGH SCHOOL...!
Junior high, 3rd year Hikaru Suzuhara
I... I...
I SEE...
HEY.

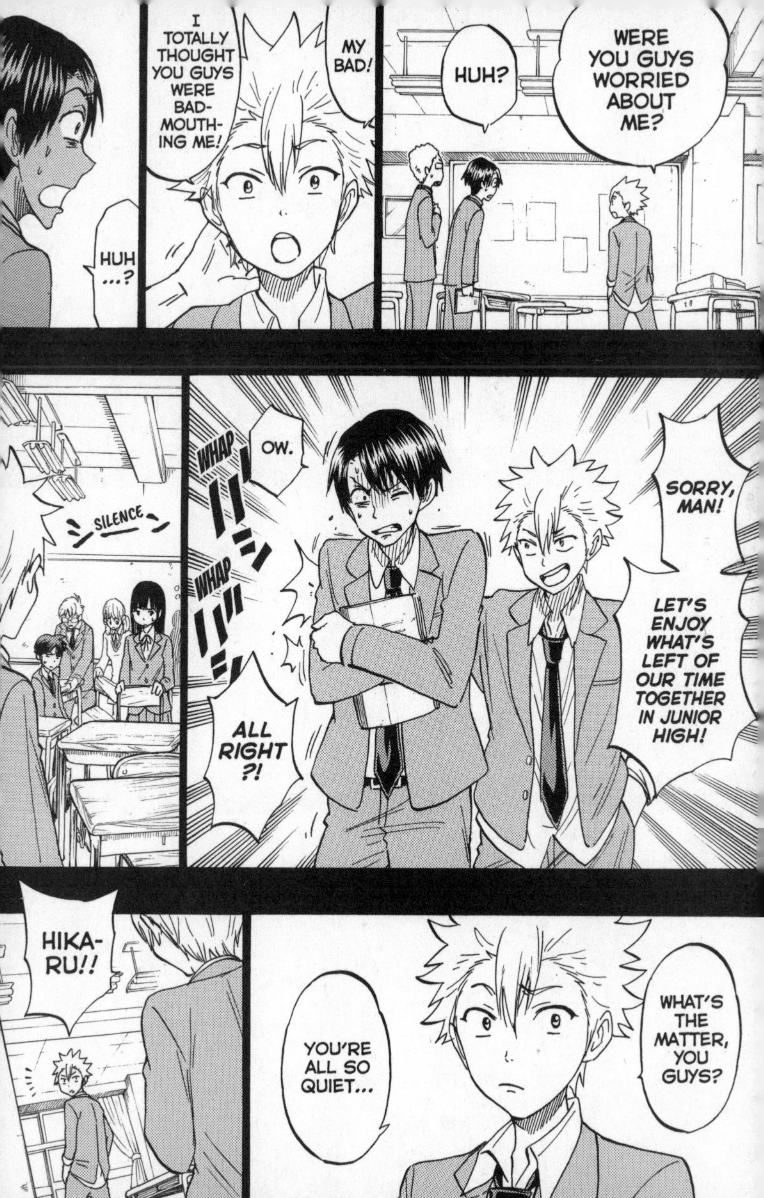
WERE YOU GUYS WORRIED ABOUT ME?
HUH?
MY BAD!
I TOTALLY THOUGHT YOU GUYS WERE BAD-MOUTHING ME!
HUH ...?
SORRY, MAN!
LET'S ENJOY WHAT'S LEFT OF OUR TIME TOGETHER IN JUNIOR HIGH!
OW.
WHAP
WHAP
ALL RIGHT ?!
SILENCE
WHAT'S THE MATTER, YOU GUYS?
YOU'RE ALL SO QUIET...
HIKA-RU!!

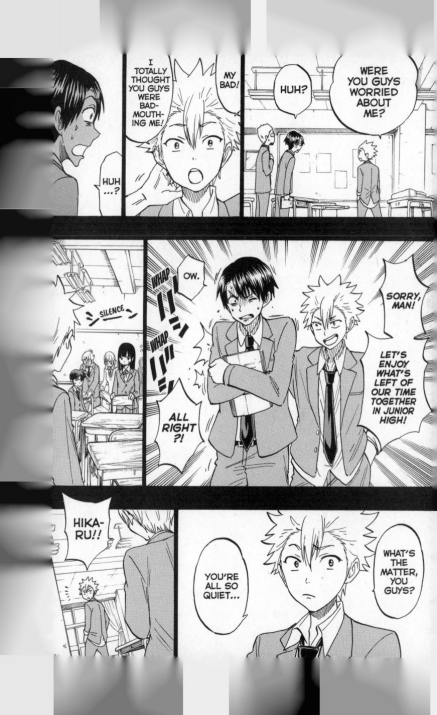

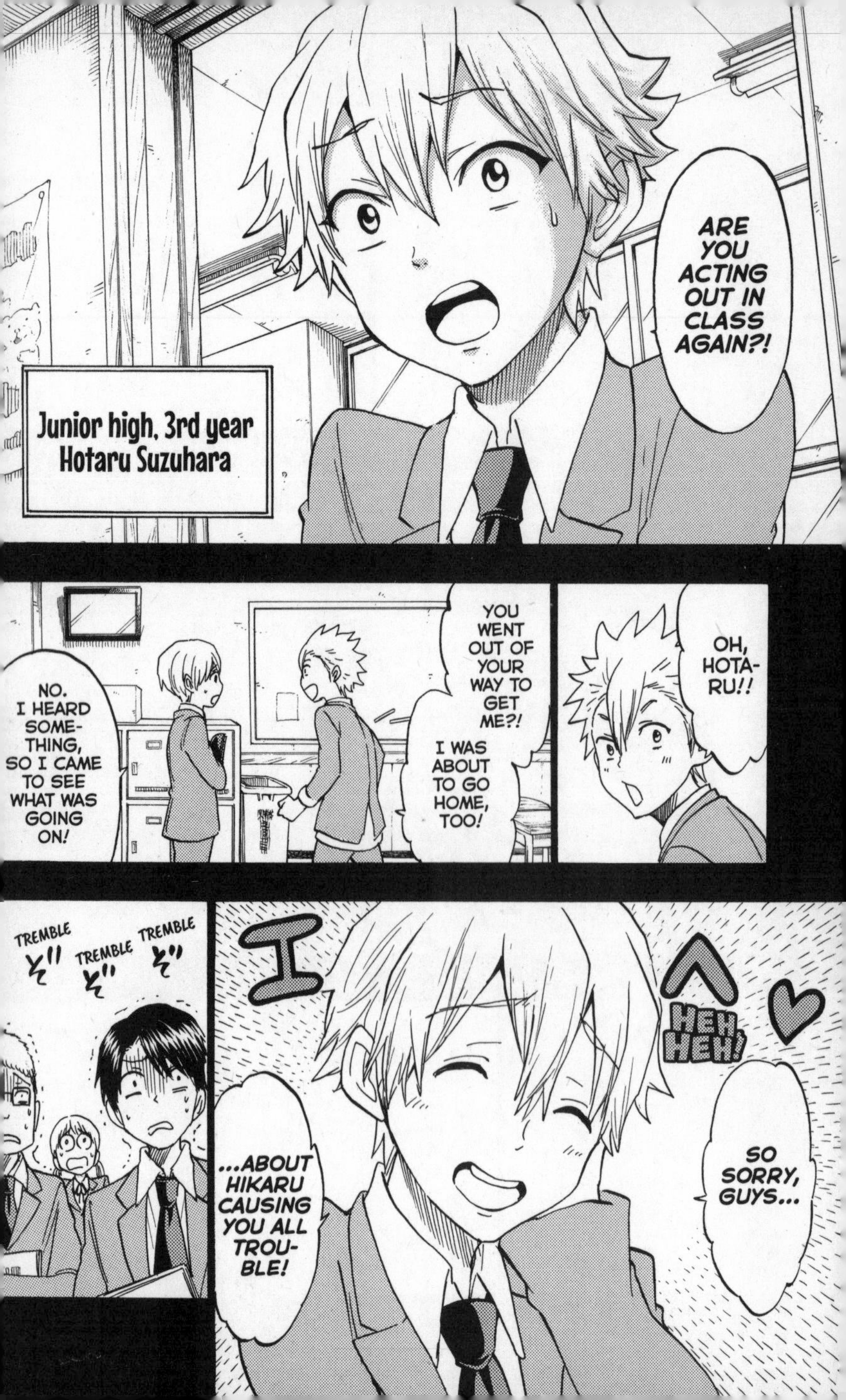
ARE YOU ACTING OUT IN CLASS AGAIN?!
Junior high, 3rd year Hotaru Suzuhara
OH, HOTA-RU!!
YOU WENT OUT OF YOUR WAY TO GET ME?!
I WAS ABOUT TO GO HOME, TOO!
NO. I HEARD SOME-THING, SO I CAME TO SEE WHAT WAS GOING ON!
HEH HEH!
SO SORRY, GUYS...
...ABOUT HIKARU CAUSING YOU ALL TROU-BLE!
TREMBLE
TREMBLE
TREMBLE

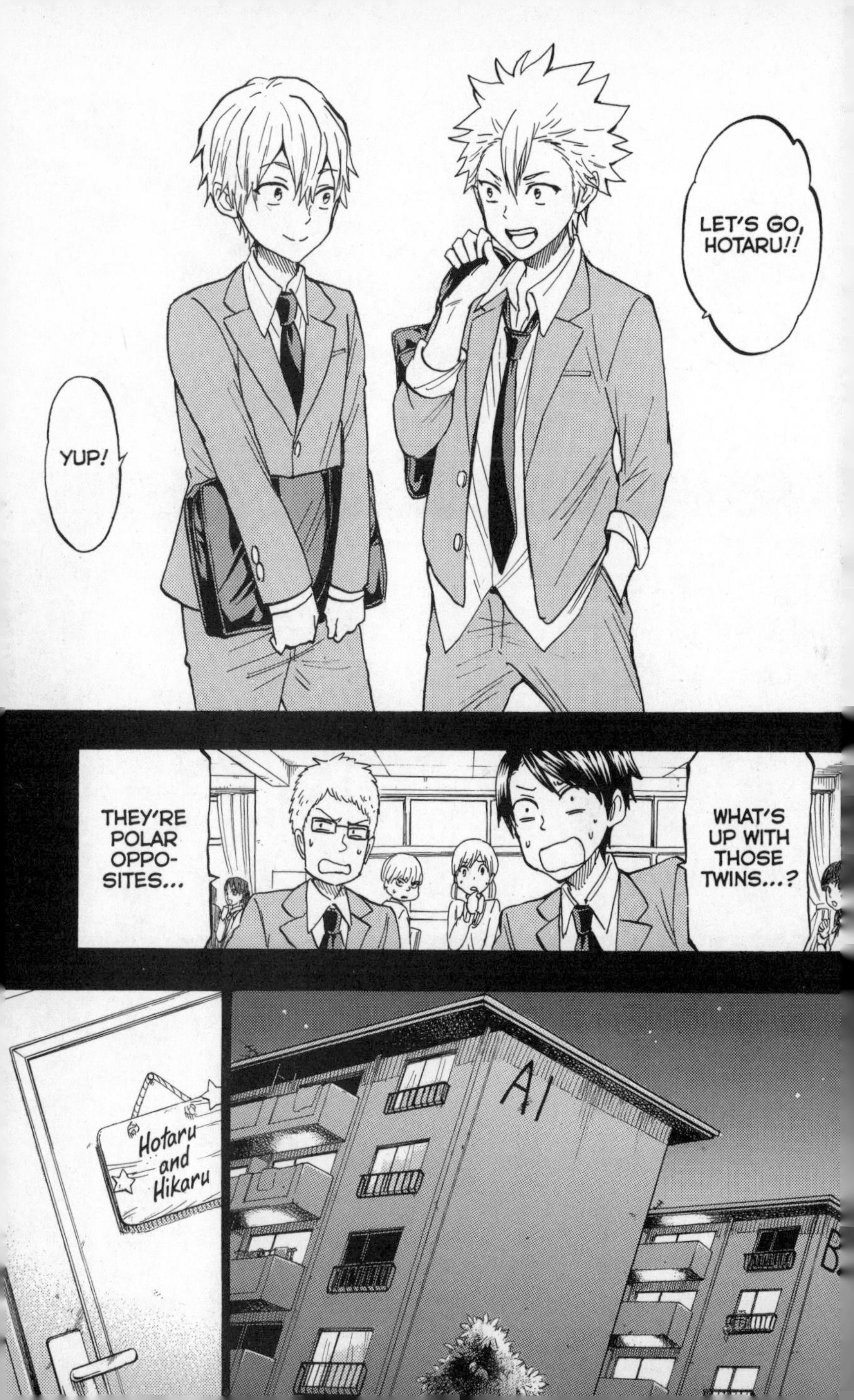
LET'S GO, HOTARU!!
YUP!
WHAT'S UP WITH THOSE TWINS...?
THEY'RE POLAR OPPO-SITES...
A1
Hotaru and Hikaru

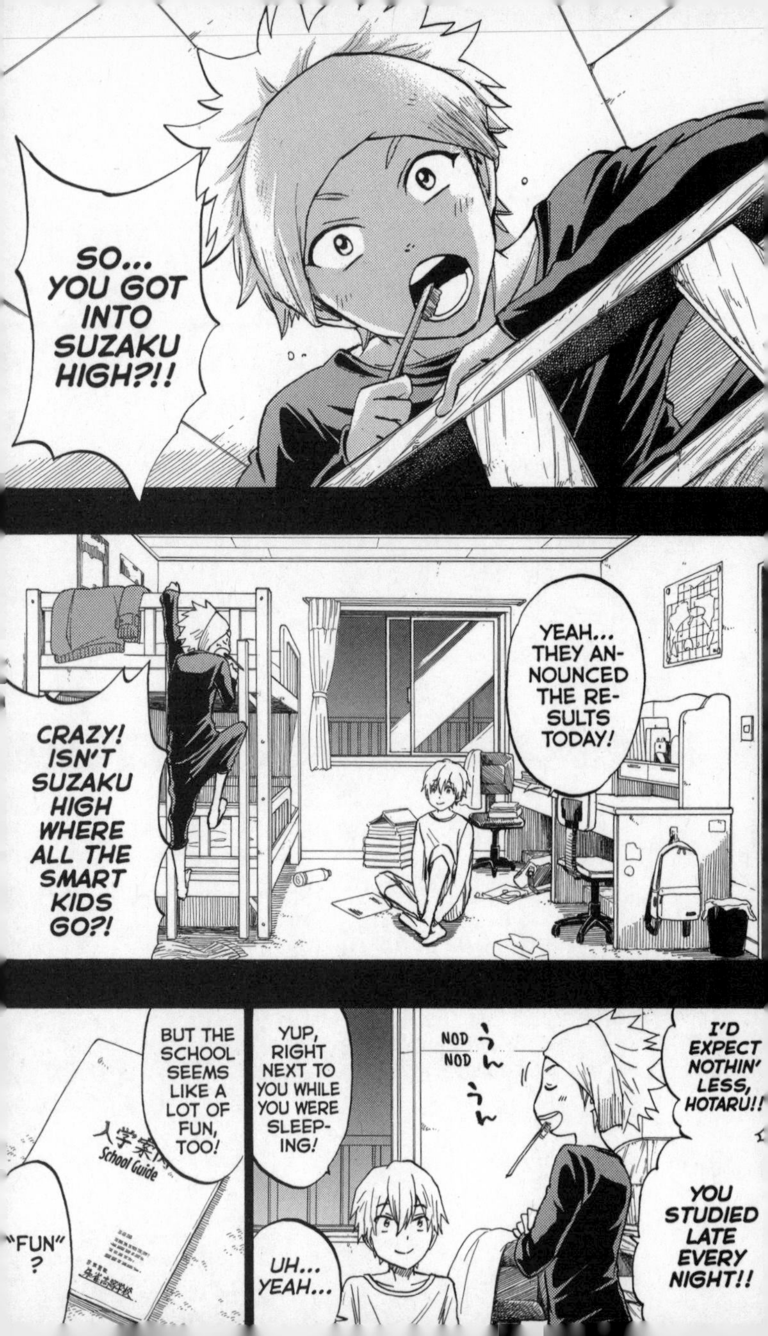
SO... YOU GOT INTO SUZAKU HIGH?!!
YEAH... THEY ANNOUNCED THE RESULTS TODAY!
CRAZY! ISN'T SUZAKU HIGH WHERE ALL THE SMART KIDS GO?!
I'D EXPECT NOTHIN' LESS, HOTARU!!
NOD NOD うん うん
YOU STUDIED LATE EVERY NIGHT!!
YUP, RIGHT NEXT TO YOU WHILE YOU WERE SLEEPING!
UH... YEAH...
BUT THE SCHOOL SEEMS LIKE A LOT OF FUN, TOO!
入学案内
School Guide
"FUN"?

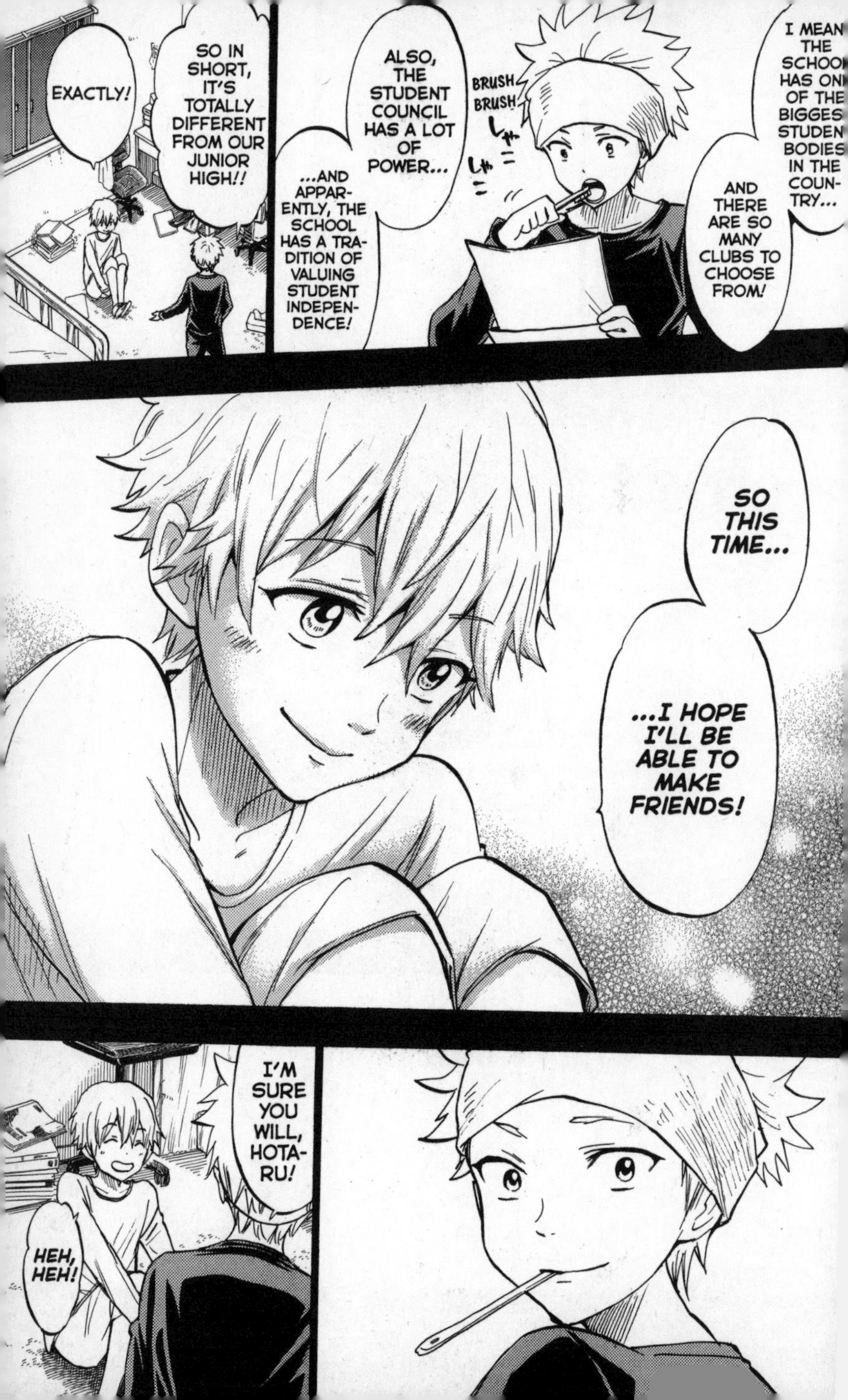
I MEAN THE SCHOOL HAS ONE OF THE BIGGEST STUDENT BODIES IN THE COUNTRY...
AND THERE ARE SO MANY CLUBS TO CHOOSE FROM!
BRUSH BRUSH
しゃ しゃ
ALSO, THE STUDENT COUNCIL HAS A LOT OF POWER...
...AND APPARENTLY, THE SCHOOL HAS A TRADITION OF VALUING STUDENT INDEPENDENCE!
SO IN SHORT, IT'S TOTALLY DIFFERENT FROM OUR JUNIOR HIGH!!
EXACTLY!
SO THIS TIME...
...I HOPE I'LL BE ABLE TO MAKE FRIENDS!
I'M SURE YOU WILL, HOTARU!
HEH, HEH!

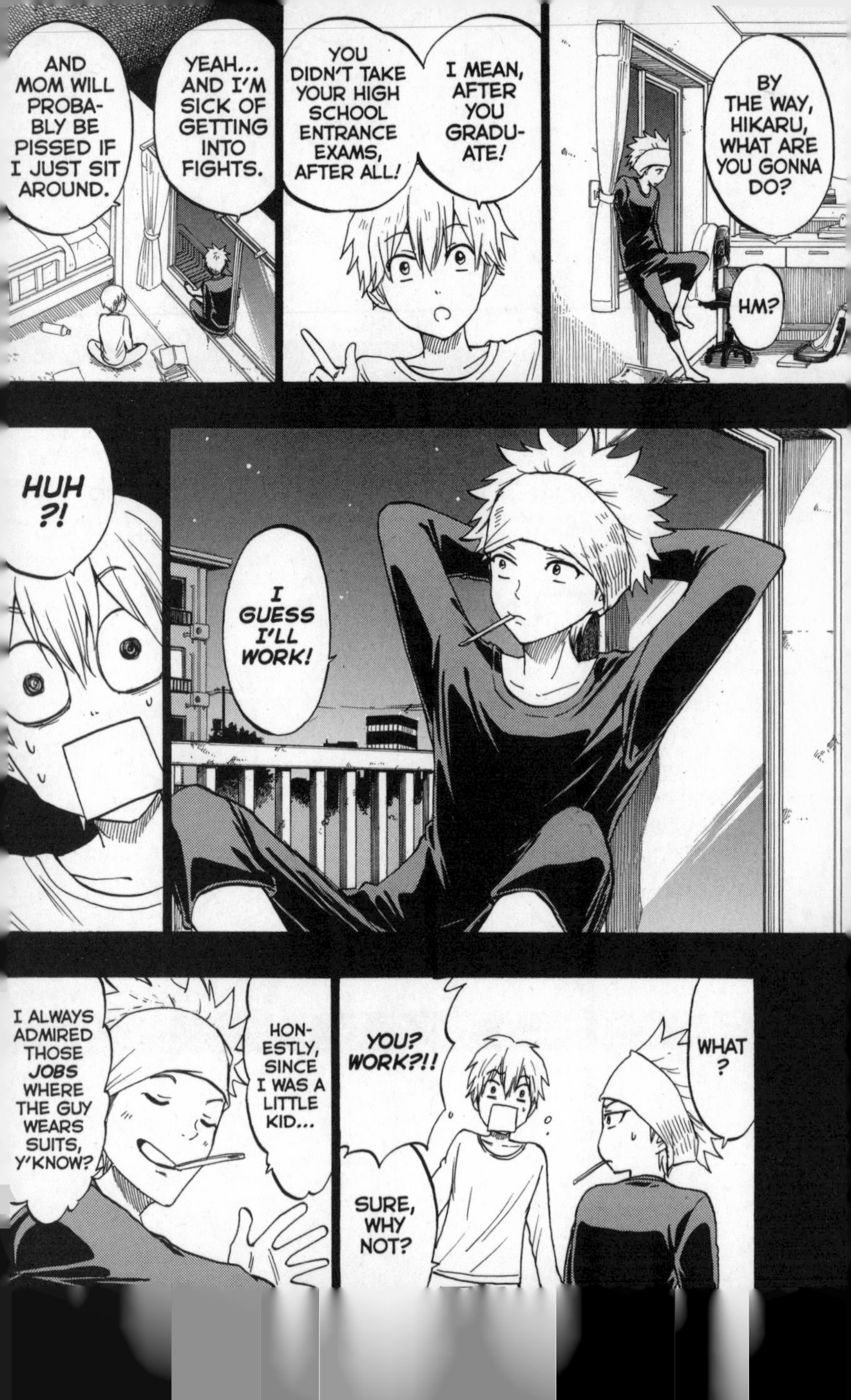
BY THE WAY, HIKARU, WHAT ARE YOU GONNA DO?
HM?
I MEAN, AFTER YOU GRADU-ATE!
YOU DIDN'T TAKE YOUR HIGH SCHOOL ENTRANCE EXAMS, AFTER ALL!
YEAH... AND I'M SICK OF GETTING INTO FIGHTS.
AND MOM WILL PROBA-BLY BE PISSED IF I JUST SIT AROUND.
I GUESS I'LL WORK!
HUH ?!
WHAT ?
YOU? WORK?!!
SURE, WHY NOT?
HON-ESTLY, SINCE I WAS A LITTLE KID...
I ALWAYS ADMIRED THOSE JOBS WHERE THE GUY WEARS SUITS, Y'KNOW?

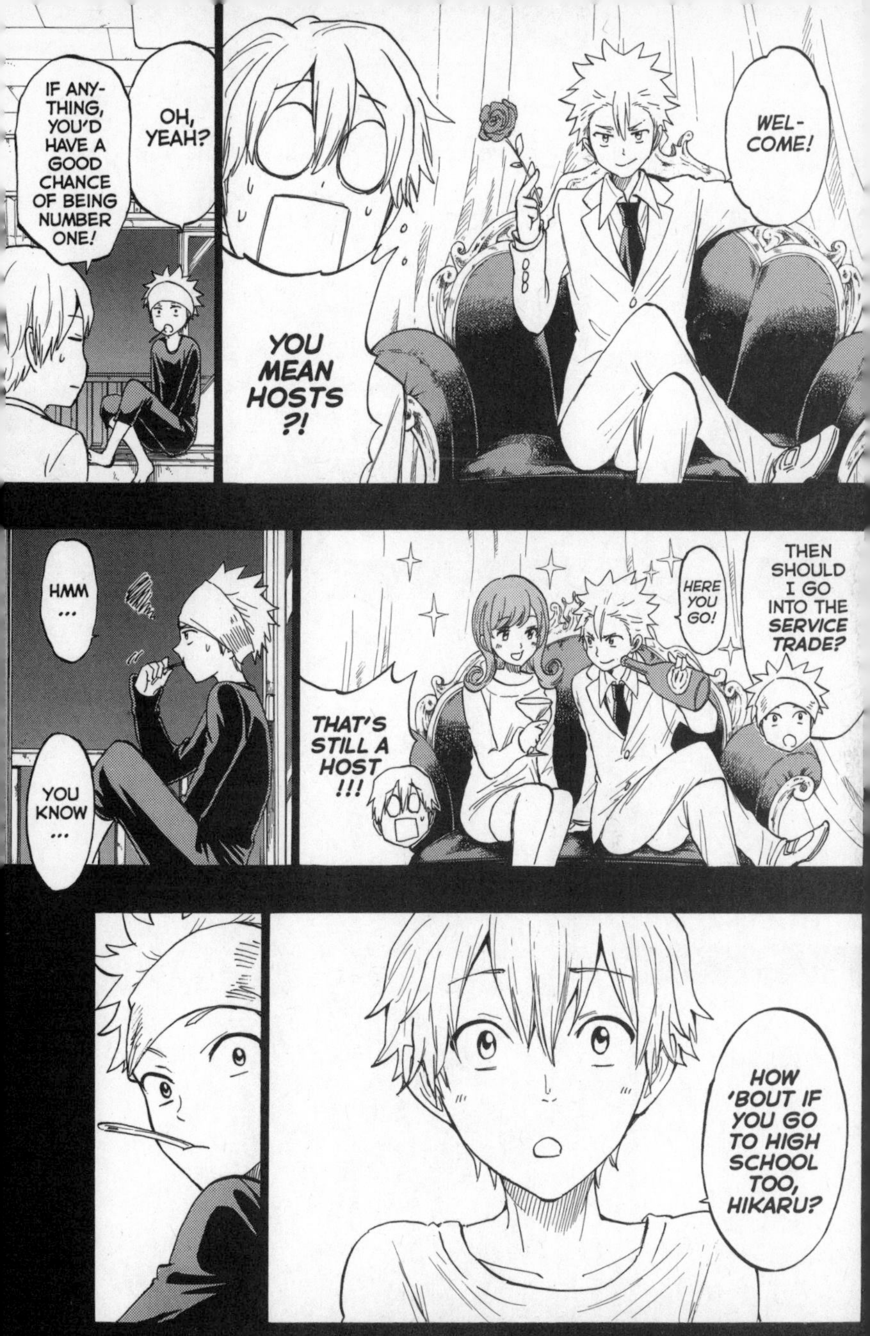
WEL-COME!
YOU MEAN HOSTS?!
OH, YEAH?
IF ANY-THING, YOU'D HAVE A GOOD CHANCE OF BEING NUMBER ONE!
THEN SHOULD I GO INTO THE SERVICE TRADE?
HERE YOU GO!
THAT'S STILL A HOST!!!
HMM...
YOU KNOW...
HOW 'BOUT IF YOU GO TO HIGH SCHOOL TOO, HIKARU?

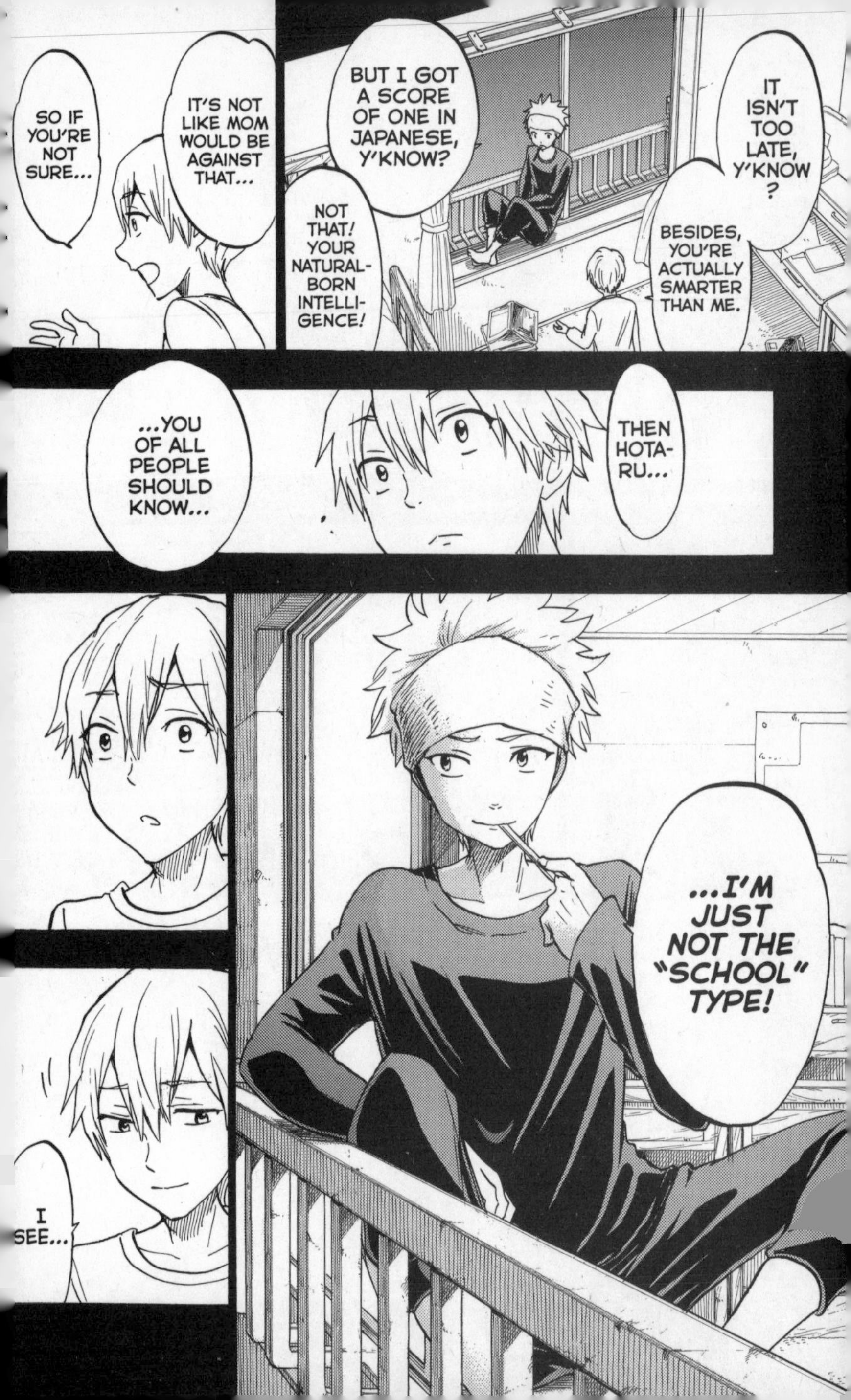
IT ISN'T TOO LATE, Y'KNOW?
BESIDES, YOU'RE ACTUALLY SMARTER THAN ME.
BUT I GOT A SCORE OF ONE IN JAPANESE, Y'KNOW?
NOT THAT! YOUR NATURAL-BORN INTELLIGENCE!
IT'S NOT LIKE MOM WOULD BE AGAINST THAT...
SO IF YOU'RE NOT SURE...
THEN HOTARU...
...YOU OF ALL PEOPLE SHOULD KNOW...
...I'M JUST NOT THE "SCHOOL" TYPE!
I SEE...

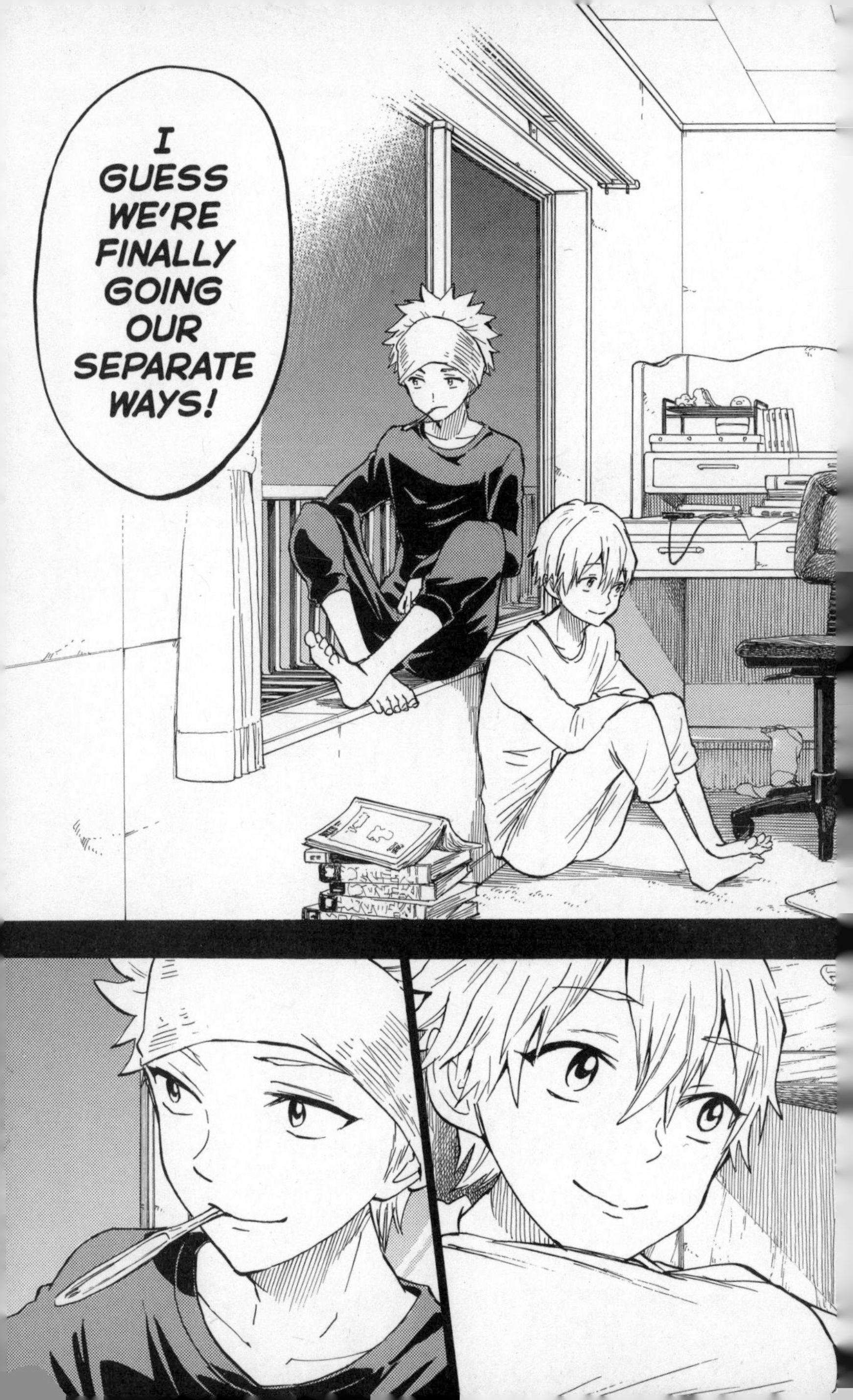
I GUESS WE'RE FINALLY GOING OUR SEPARATE WAYS!

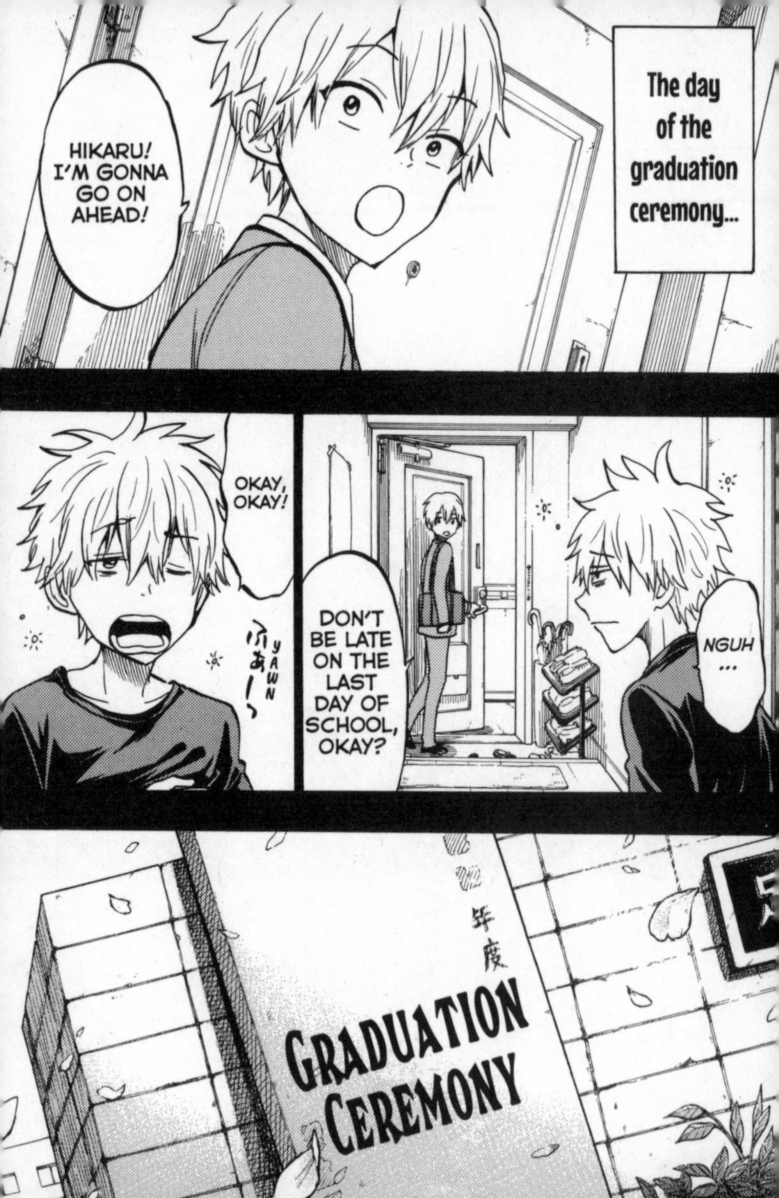

The day of the graduation ceremony...
HIKARU! I'M GONNA GO ON AHEAD!
NGUH ...
DON'T BE LATE ON THE LAST DAY OF SCHOOL, OKAY?
YAWN
OKAY, OKAY!
GRADUATION CEREMONY

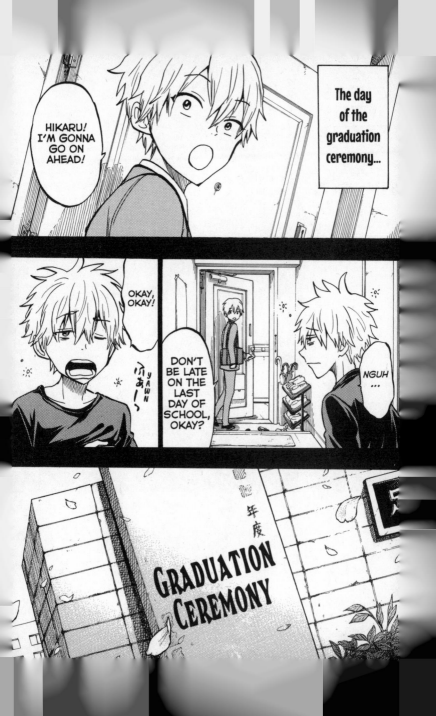

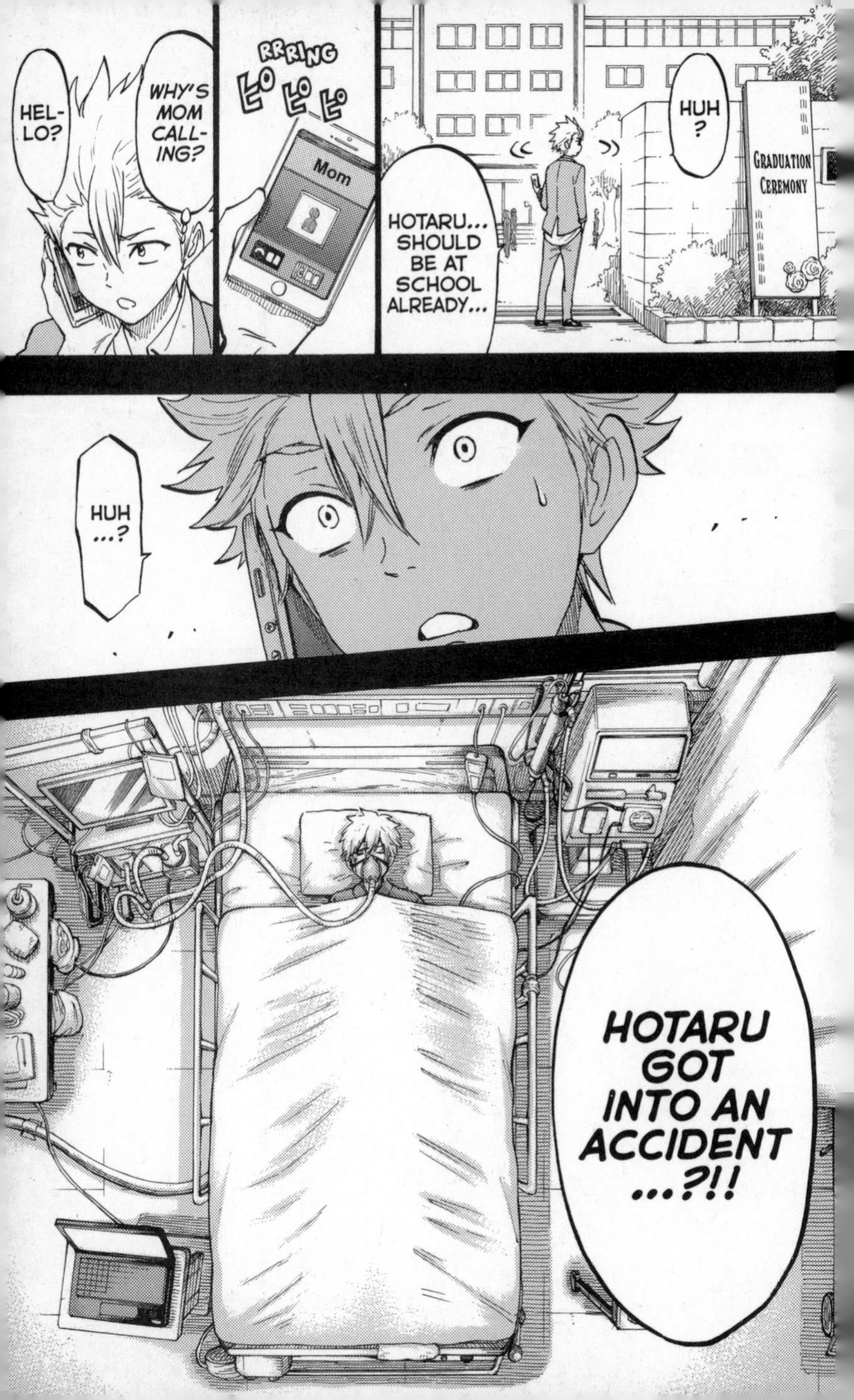
GRADUATION CEREMONY
HUH ?
HOTARU... SHOULD BE AT SCHOOL ALREADY...
RRRING
ピロピロピ
Mom
WHY'S MOM CALL-ING?
HEL-LO?
HUH ...?
HOTARU GOT INTO AN ACCIDENT ...?!!

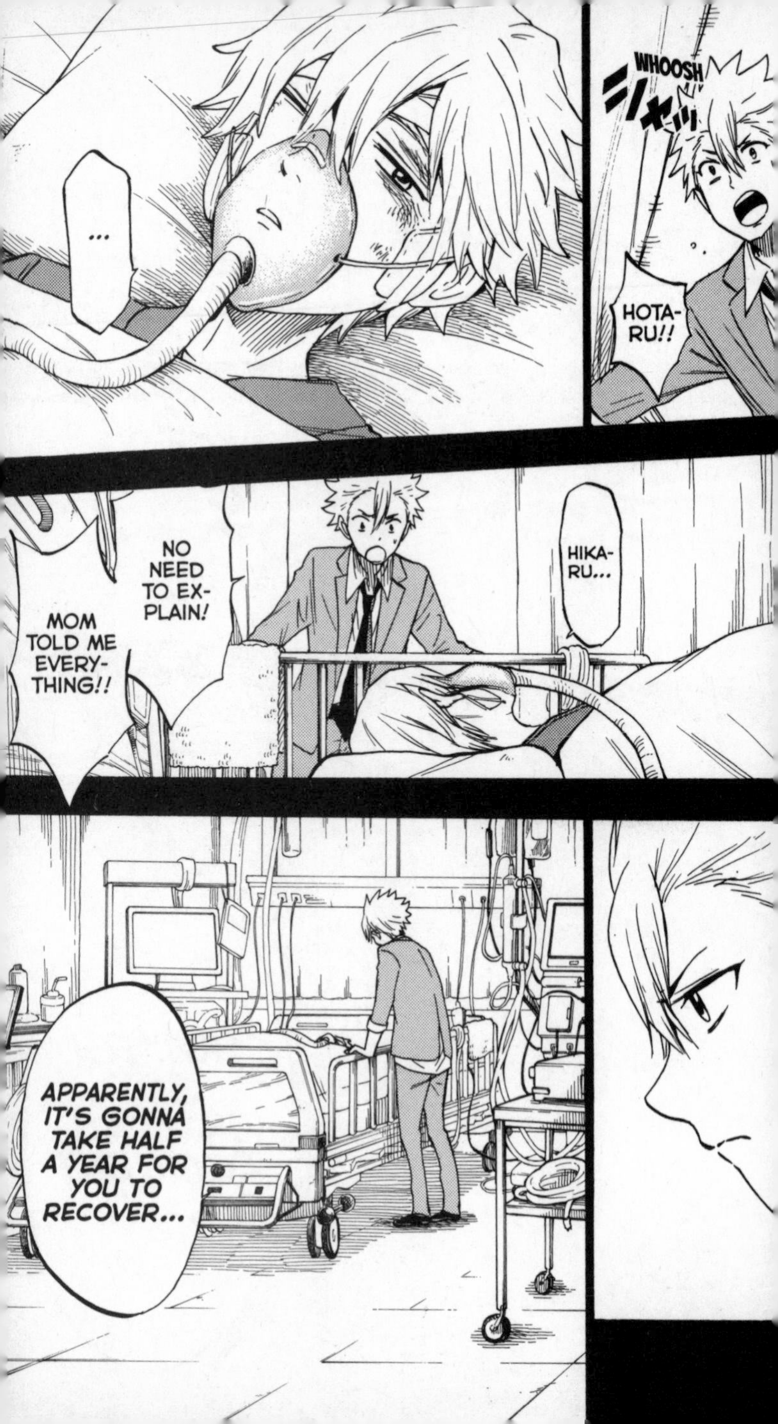
WHOOSH
HOTA-RU!!
...
HIKA-RU...
NO NEED TO EX-PLAIN!
MOM TOLD ME EVERY-THING!!
APPARENTLY, IT'S GONNA TAKE HALF A YEAR FOR YOU TO RECOVER...

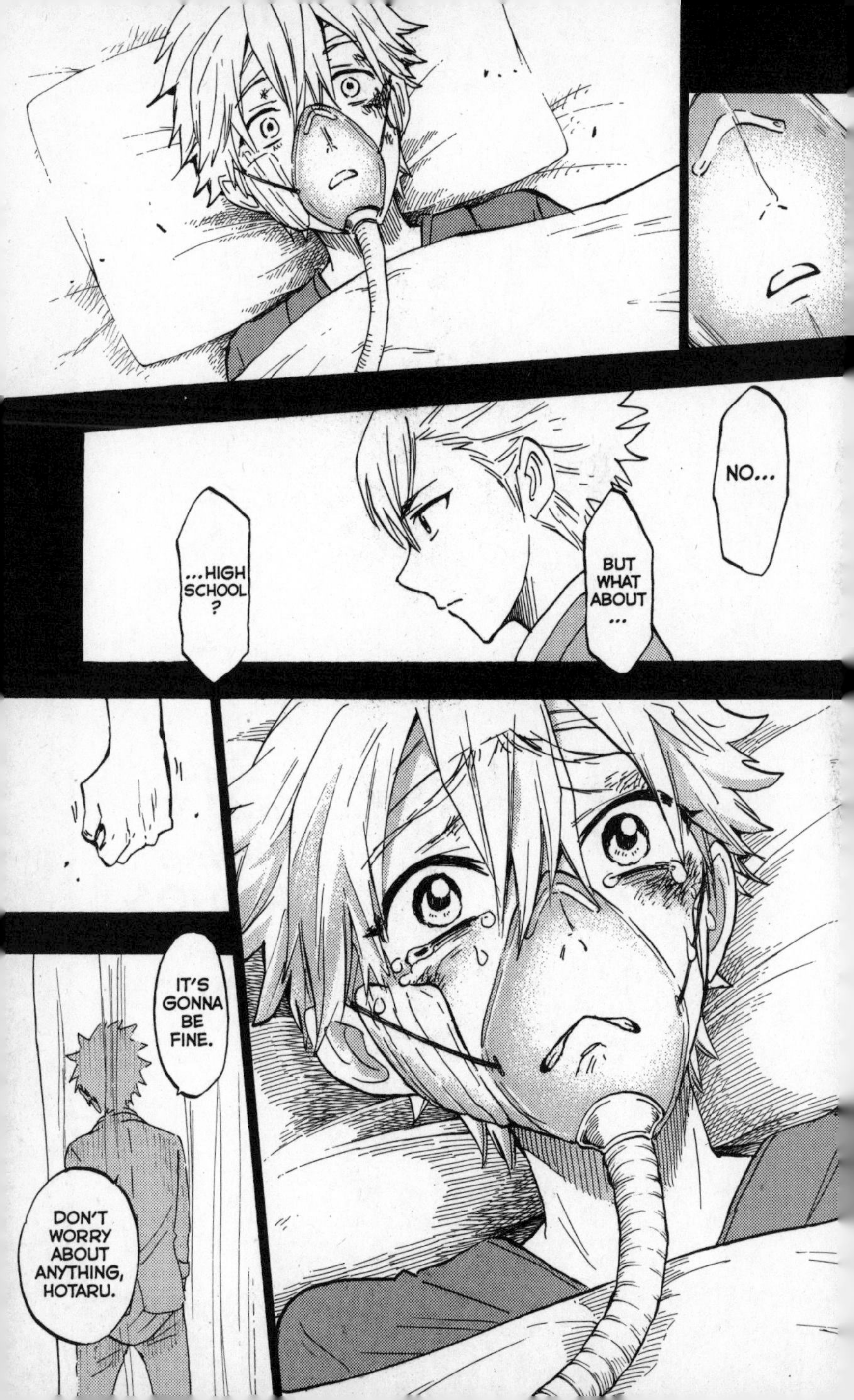
...
NO...
BUT WHAT ABOUT ...
...HIGH SCHOOL?
IT'S GONNA BE FINE.
DON'T WORRY ABOUT ANYTHING, HOTARU.

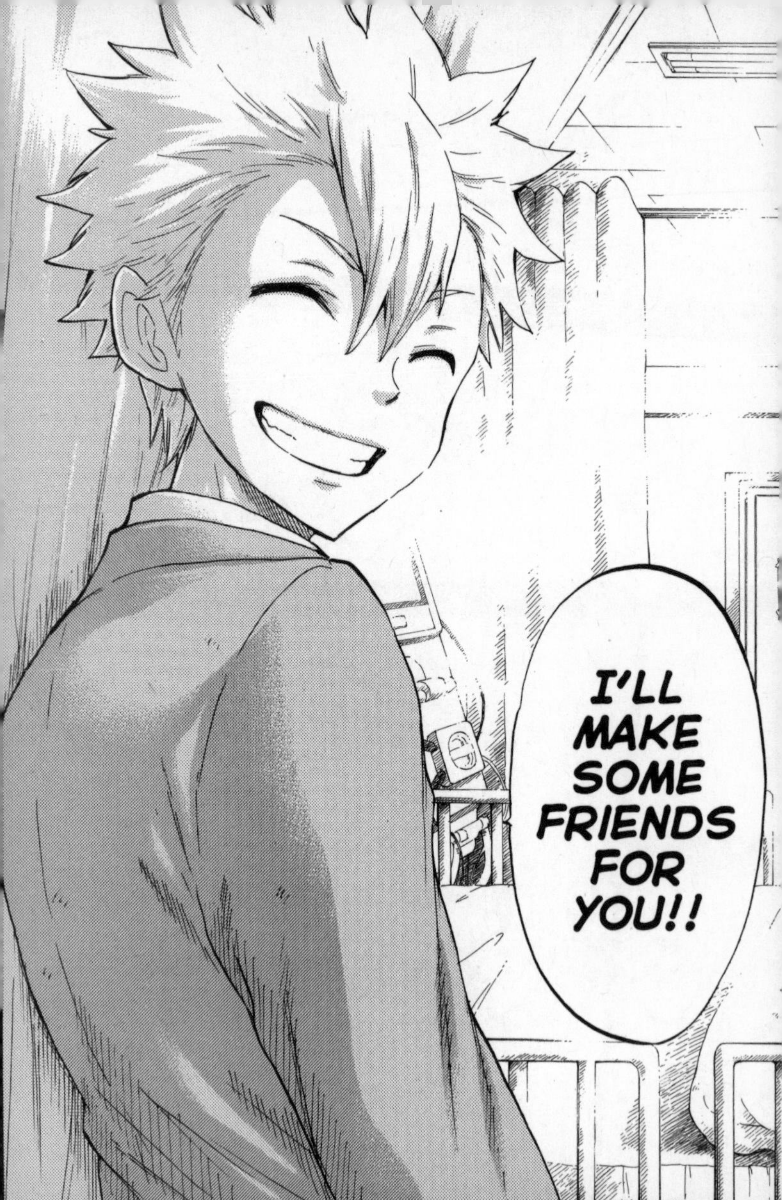
I'LL MAKE SOME FRIENDS FOR YOU!!

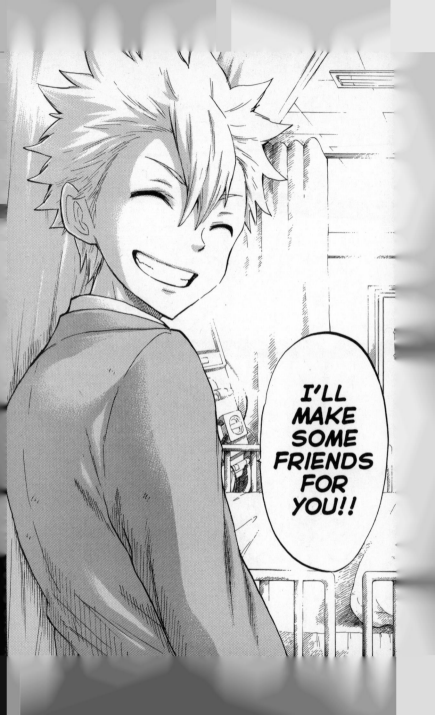

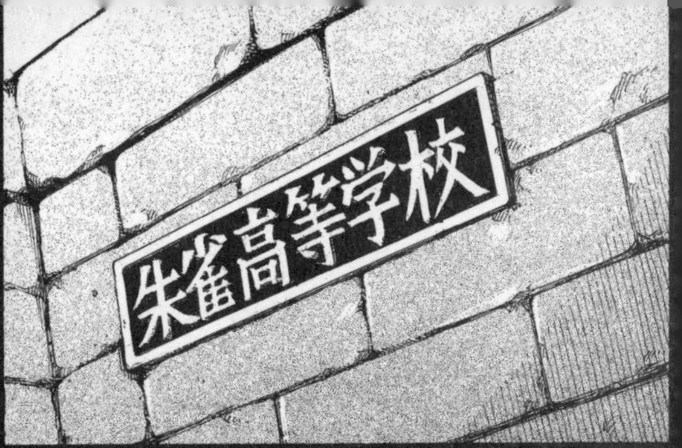
朱雀高等学校
▲ Sign: Suzaku High School

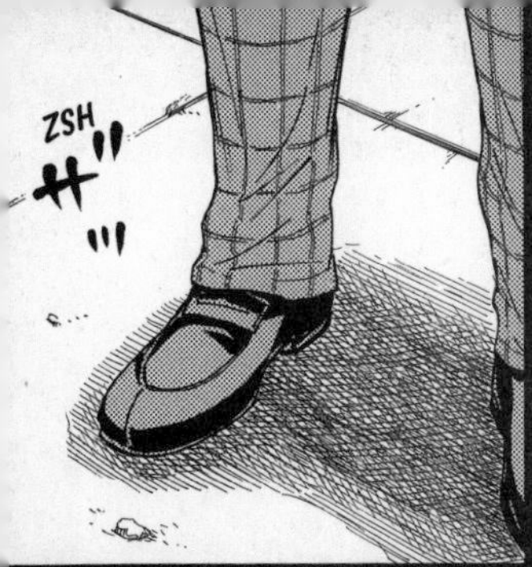
ZSH

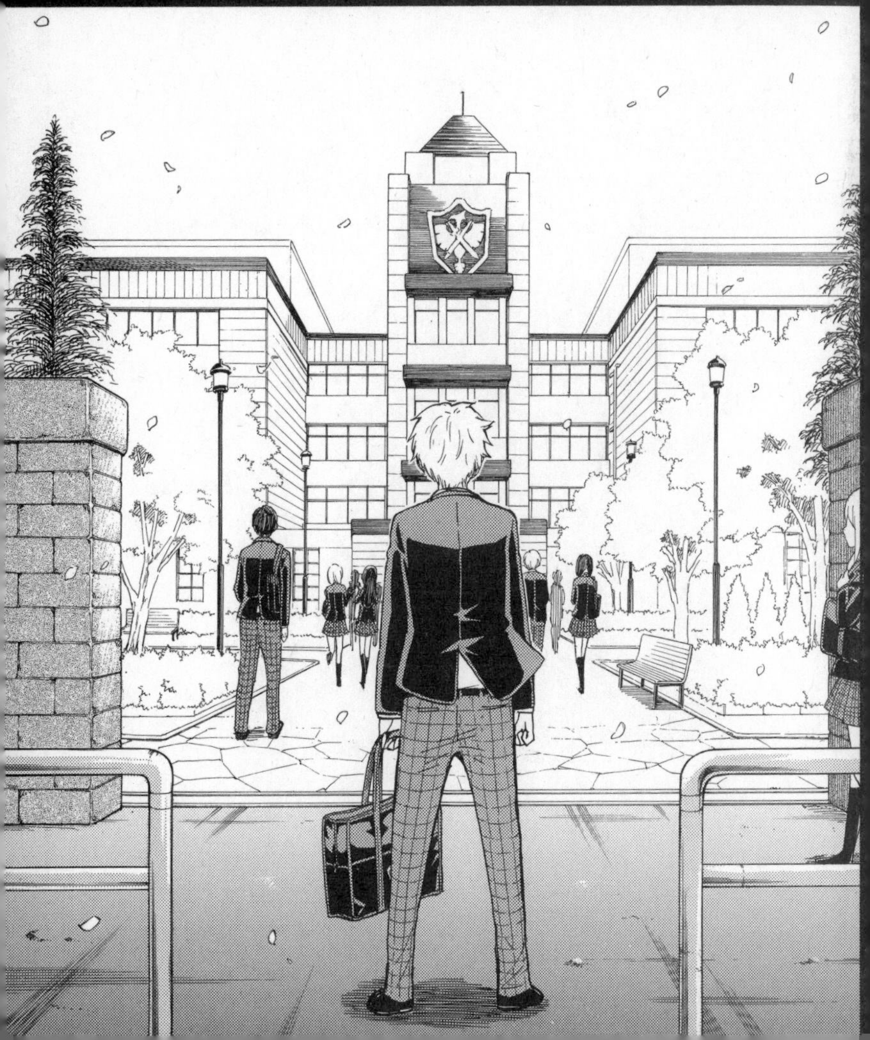

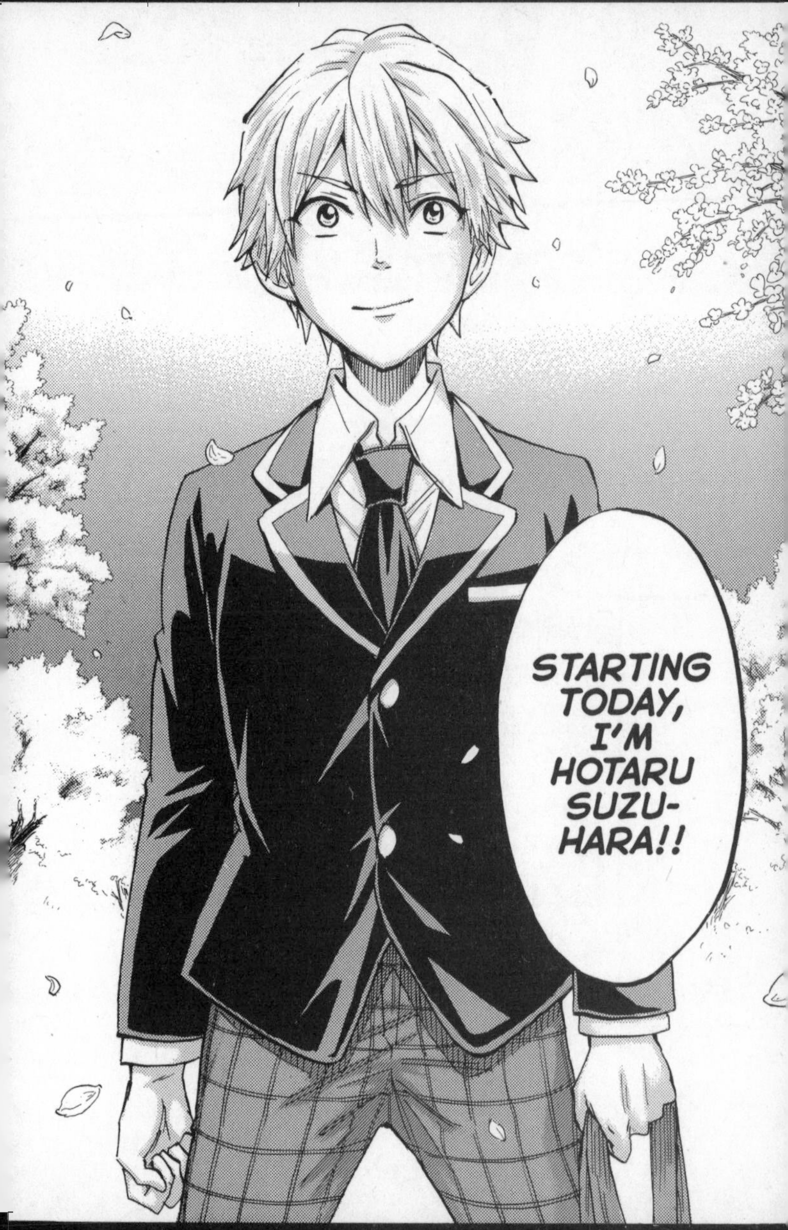
STARTING TODAY, I'M HOTARU SUZU-HARA!!

朱雀高等学校
裏ホームページ
SUZAKU HIGH SCHOOL UNDERGROUND WEBSITE

 Q&A Corner #15!!
Our guest today is Miyamura's older sister, Leona-san!

 I thank you for the invitation! I was looking forward to this day.
But first, I gotta strip down to my swimsuit!!!
BOOM

 Whaaaat?!!
Hold on, sis! We don't provide that kind of **service** on Q&A Corner!

 Hm? Really...?!

 It seems there's been a misunderstanding...

 I told you I had a bad feeling...!!

Q1. Why do you have so many scissors?

Tokyo, H.N. Yoshie-san

 Heh heh. The reason for that is...
So that I can scare Toranosuke!!!

 Eeeek!!

Just kidding!
Collecting scissors is a hobby of mine.

What the heck! You scared me.

You didn't think she was serious, did you?

I was a child when it became a hobby. When I first used scissors, I became fascinated by them. I would cut up everything in the house, which really pissed off my parents.

You got me, too... You took my favorite toy, and cut everything from the hair to the clothes...

Th...that happened, huh...

But I realized something after shredding everything up. It wasn't cutting things up that I liked; it was the scissors themselves. The shape, the structure, the power. I thought it was all wonderful!

So my dad, who travels for work, saw that in me, and bought me scissors from countries around the world. Of course, I collect them myself, too. Next time, I'll let you peruse my collection.

Having said that, you sure throw them at people a lot.

I...I'm looking forward to seeing the collection! (Honestly, I don't know...)

Q2. What are your feelings towards Miyamura-kun, Leona-san?

Kagoshima Prefecture, H.N. Ren Yuki-san

Since we were young, we've spent a lot of time together. He's been a **high-maintenance** little brother since way back. That still hasn't changed.

Huh? Who's really the high-maintenance one?

 You could say that the fact that you fight shows how close you are. I know what that's like... He went to school with you on your graduation day, right, Leona-san? (SMIRK)

 Y...you saw that?!

 The whole school saw you guys.
The Miyamura siblings stand out, y'know.

 Our housekeeper Hatsue-san suggested it since it was the last day we'd be going to the same school. Although Toranosuke was embarrassed...

 # I was not!!!

 You've been looking down and hiding your face this whole time. Why's that?!

Q3. The Special Miyamura Family Curry has appeared a few times, and it looks yummy! Is it different from regular curry?

Shizuoka Prefecture, H.N. Isosenbei-san

 Of course! That's because I prepare everything down to the seasoning. I bring out the flavor using ingredients you normally wouldn't expect.

 Oh, I totally get it! Like yogurt or chocolate, right?!

 Sis, that's all you have to say about your curry? Last time, you put in salted fish entrails and dumplings. And when it's really bad, you've put in eggs with the shell still intact, bat wings, tuna fish eyes...

It tastes good no matter what you put in! That's what makes it curry!

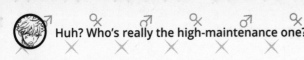

I never said it tasted good!

 Yet you still eat it... (That's a "sister complex" for ya...) Anyway, that's all the time we have for this Q&A Corner! Hope you enjoyed the Leona-san issue! Although it was Miyamura who enjoyed this issue the most.

 I'm very happy that I was able to make this my last school memory. Work together with Itou-san and keep doing your best, Toranosuke!

 The Q&A Corner isn't the place to get so serious, just so you know.

 Hey, but I'm serious! Also, I don't think you guys know, but Leona-san has been **in her swimsuit this entire time!!**

 I'm not one to shy away from giving a little extra!

 Sis... please!!

 Anyway, our next guest will be another graduating student, **Haruma Yamazaki**, the former Student Council President! Send us your questions!

Please send your correspondence here ↓

Yamada-kun and the Seven Witches: Underground Website
c/o Kodansha Comics
451 Park Ave. South, 7th Floor
New York, NY 10016

Don't' forget to include your handle name (pen name)!

 Well, Toranosuke, we don't always get the chance, so let's go home together today, too!

 Please, put on some clothes!

Suzaku Gallery

This is where we'll introduce illustrations that we've received from all of you!

Selected artists will receive **a signed shikishi from the series creator**! When you make a submission, please make sure to clearly write your address, name, and phone number! If you don't, we won't be able to send you a prize, even if you're selected! Looking forward to all your submissions!

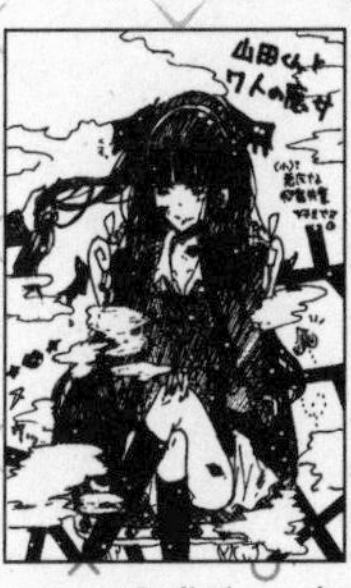
山田くんと7人の魔女

Gifu Pref., H.N. Yuyuna Nishikawa-san

Sadistic as she may be, Asuka-senpai really had a soft spot for me... Just kidding.

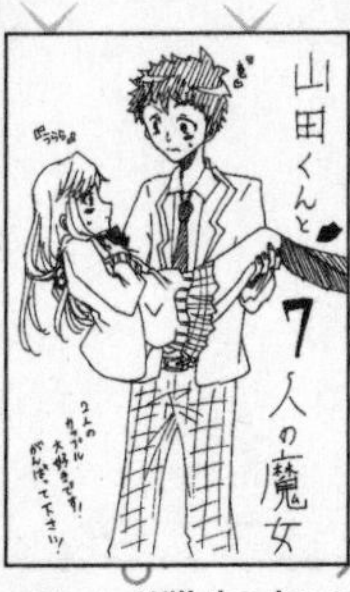
山田くんと7人の魔女

Aichi Pref., H.N. Kagamine-san

Will the day come where a prince appears and carries me like a princess?

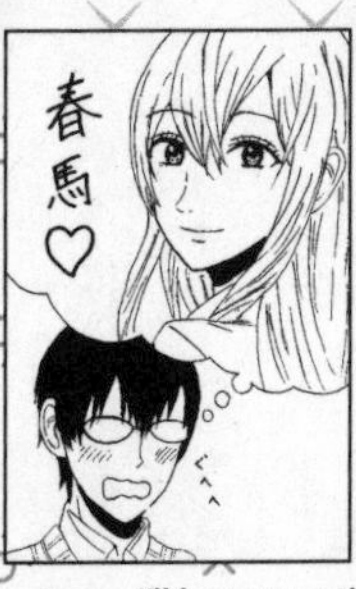
春馬♡

Tokyo, H.N. Yamada Itoku-san

I'll be supporting Yamazaki from now on. Just a little, though.

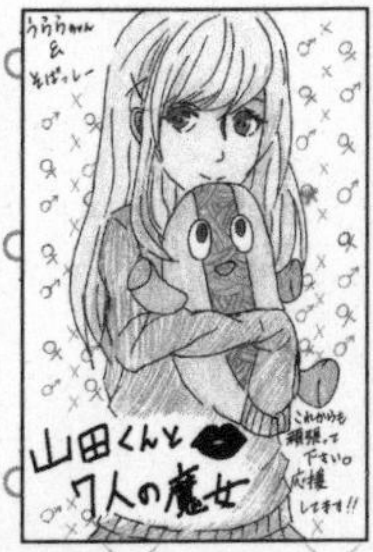
山田くんと7人の魔女

Aichi Pref., H.N. Toa-san

It's Urara-chan sweetly hugging Yamada's Sobasshi. It's super cute! ♥

Please send your art here ↓

Yamada-kun and the Seven Witches: Underground Website
c/o Kodansha Comics
451 Park Ave. South, 7th Floor
New York, NY 10016

※ Please clearly write your address, name, and phone number. If your address, name, and phone number aren't included with your submission, we won't be able to send you a prize.

※ And if necessary, don't forget to include your handle name (pen name)!

Please send your letters with the understanding that your zip code, address, name, and other personal information included in your correspondence may be given to the author of this work.

Bonus Gallery

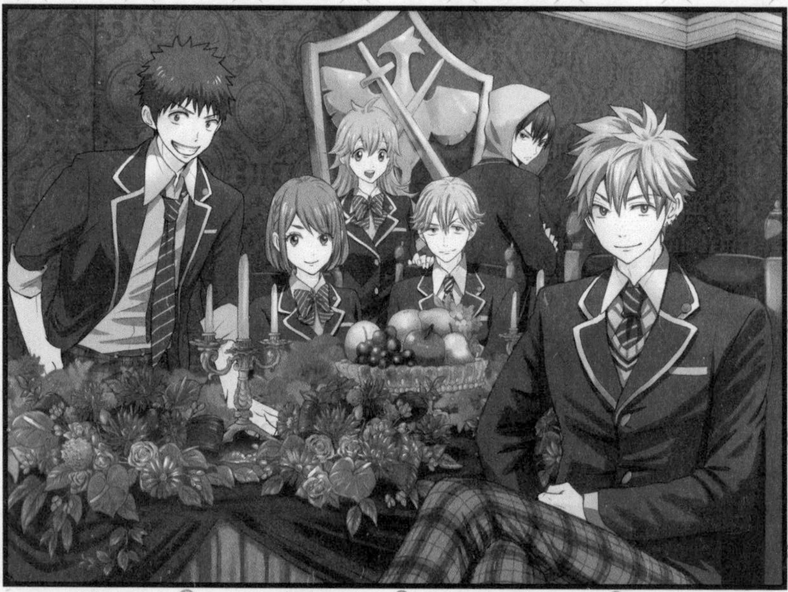

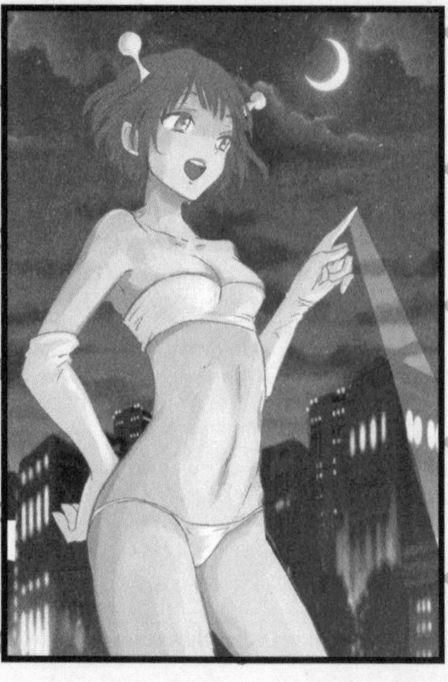

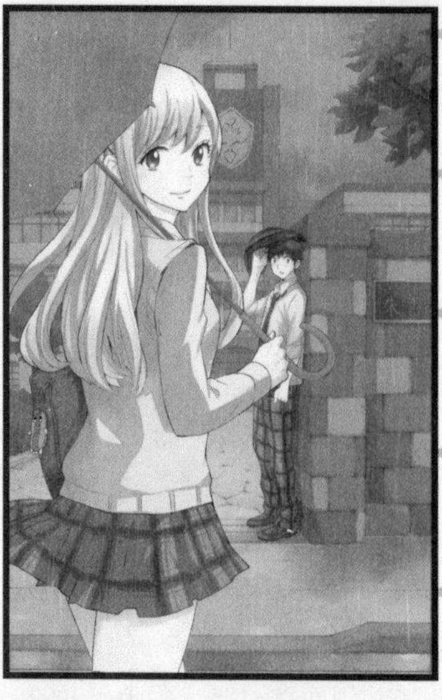

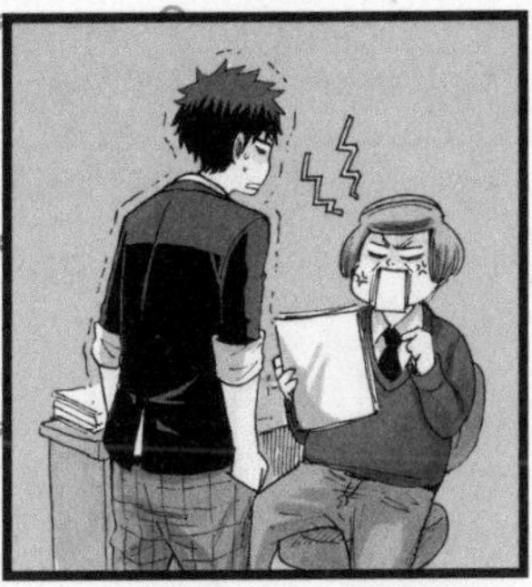

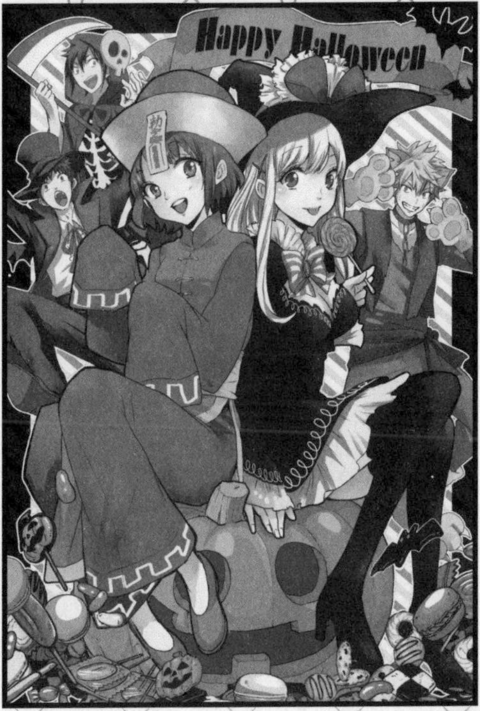
Happy Halloween

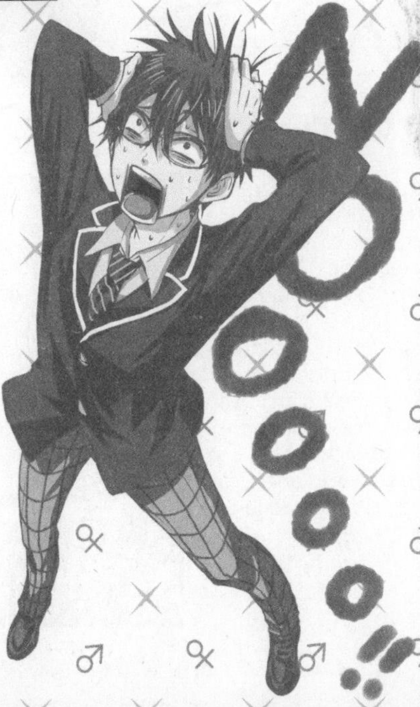
NOOOOO!!

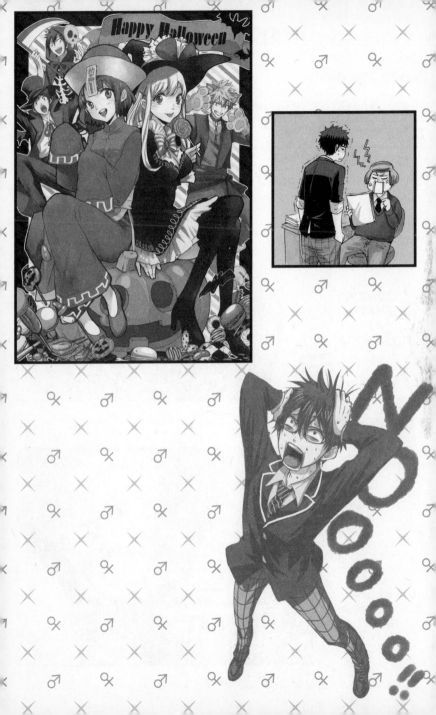

Translation Notes

Yakiudon, page 280

By now, you may be familiar with yakisoba (stir-fried buckwheat noodles) as Yamada-kun's favorite food, but another variation of stir-fried noodles uses udon, a thicker noodle made from wheat flour.

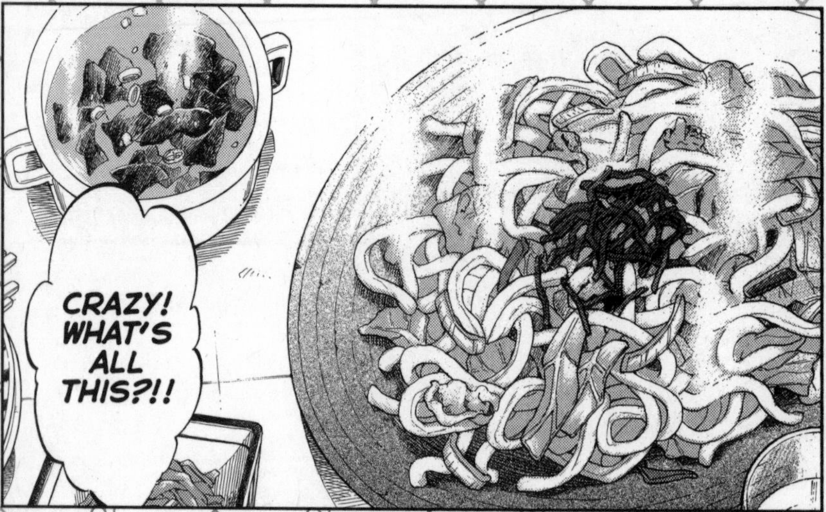
CRAZY! WHAT'S ALL THIS?!!

"I guess I'll work!", page 374

It might seem strange that Hikaru would choose to work after graduating from junior high school, but in Japan, the upper age limit for compulsory education is 15. This means that you are not required to go to high school and may work once you have graduated junior high.

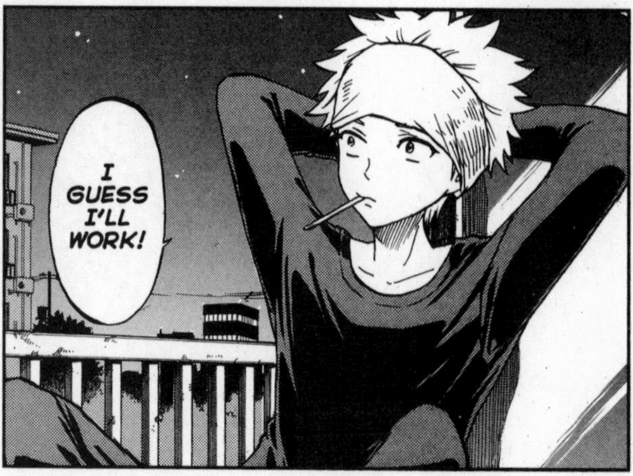
I GUESS I'LL WORK!

Hosts, page 375

In Japan, a "host" is a job where charismatic men entertain customers by talking and drinking with them in a bar or club-like setting. The typical image of a host is a flashy-looking, often handsome man with gelled hair.

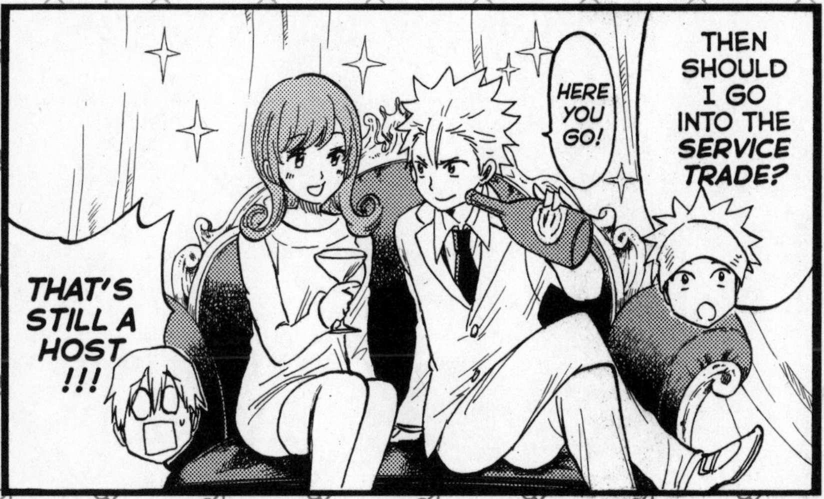
THEN SHOULD I GO INTO THE SERVICE TRADE?
HERE YOU GO!
THAT'S STILL A HOST!!!

"Carries me like a princess," page 389

The way that Yamada is holding Shiraishi in this illustration is commonly known as *himesama-dakko*, which directly translates to "princess hold" and is reminiscent of the way a prince would carry his princess after rescuing her from danger. The Western equivalent to this hold is the way that a newly married husband carries his wife over the threshold of their home.

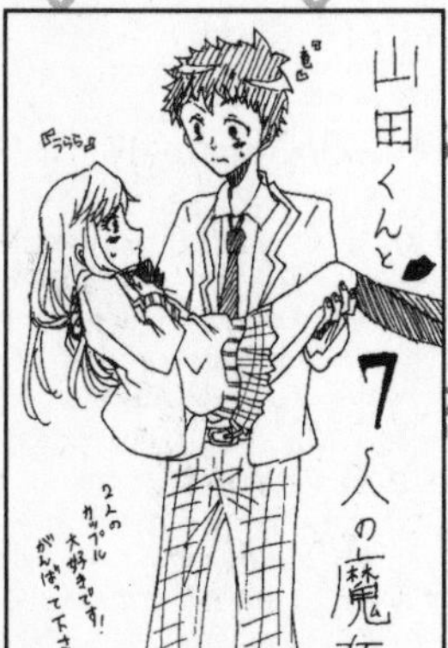
山田くんと7人の魔女
2人のカップル大好きです!
がんばって下さい!

◄ KAMOME ►
SHIRAHAMA

Witch Hat Atelier

A magical manga
adventure for
fans of Disney
and Studio
Ghibli!

Witch Hat Atelier © Kamome Shirahama/Kodansha Ltd.

The magical adventure that took Japan by storm is finally here, from acclaimed DC and Marvel cover artist Kamome Shirahama!

In a world where everyone takes wonders like magic spells and dragons for granted, Coco is a girl with a simple dream: She wants to be a witch. But everybody knows magicians are born, not made, and Coco was not born with a gift for magic. Resigned to her un-magical life, Coco is about to give up on her dream to become a witch…until the day she meets Qifrey, a mysterious, traveling magician. After secretly seeing Qifrey perform magic in a way she's never seen before, Coco soon learns what everybody "knows" might not be the truth, and discovers that her magical dream may not be as far away as it may seem…

KC
KODANSHA
COMICS

THE HIGH SCHOOL HAREM COMEDY WITH FIVE TIMES THE CUTE GIRLS!

"An entertaining romantic-comedy with a snarky edge to it." —Taykobon

Futaro Uesugi is a second-year in high school, scraping to get by and pay off his family's debt. The only thing he can do is study, so when Futaro receives a part-tim job offer to tutor the five daughters of a wealthy businessman, he can't pass it up. Little does he know, these five beautiful sisters are quintuplets, but th only thing they have ir common...is that they're all terrible at studying!

The Quintessential Quintuplets © Negi Haruba/Kodansha, Ltd.

THE QUINTESSENTIAL QUINTUPLETS

negi haruba

ANIME OUT NOW!

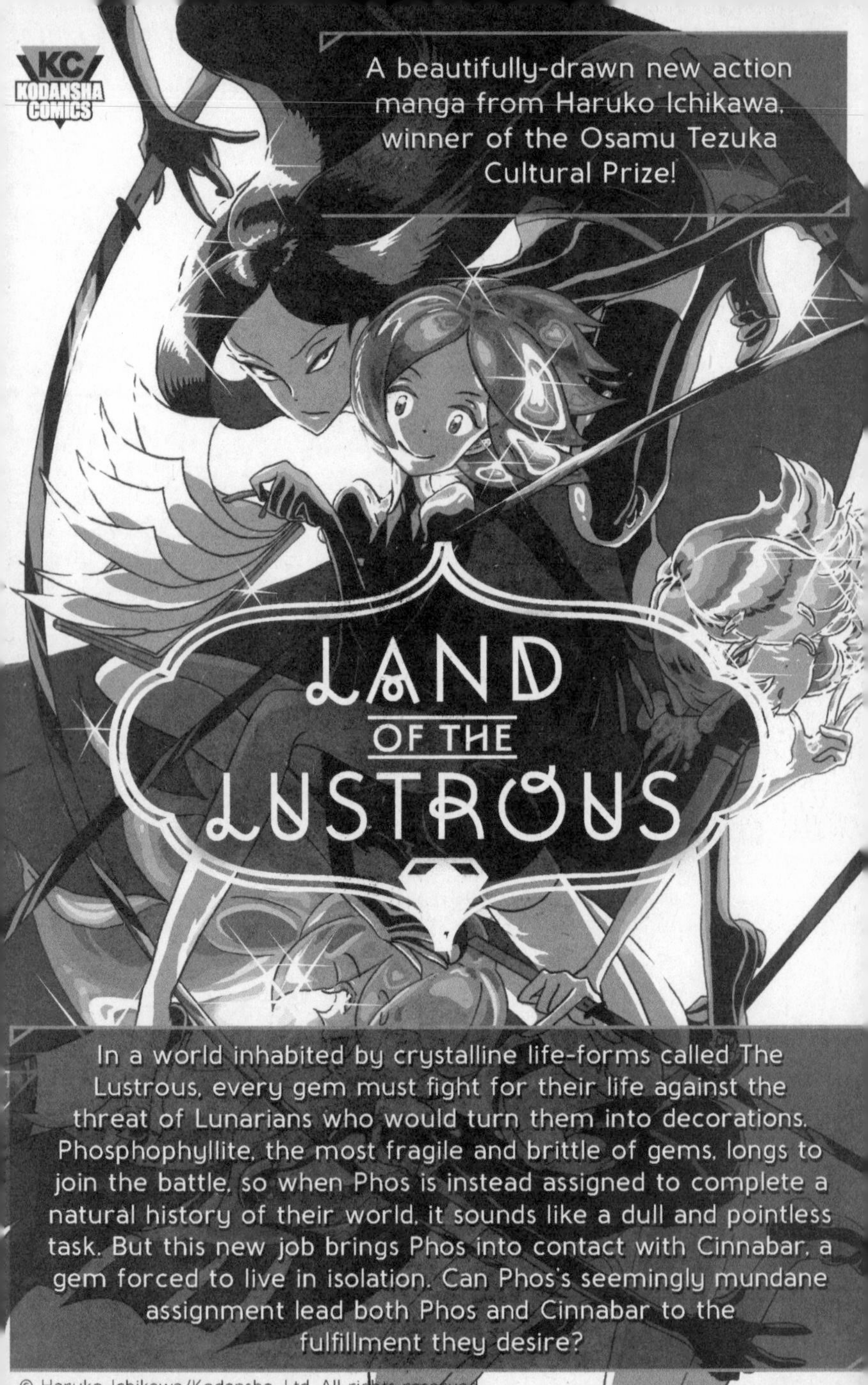
KC KODANSHA COMICS
A beautifully-drawn new action manga from Haruko Ichikawa, winner of the Osamu Tezuka Cultural Prize!
LAND OF THE LUSTROUS
In a world inhabited by crystalline life-forms called The Lustrous, every gem must fight for their life against the threat of Lunarians who would turn them into decorations. Phosphophyllite, the most fragile and brittle of gems, longs to join the battle, so when Phos is instead assigned to complete a natural history of their world, it sounds like a dull and pointless task. But this new job brings Phos into contact with Cinnabar, a gem forced to live in isolation. Can Phos's seemingly mundane assignment lead both Phos and Cinnabar to the fulfillment they desire?

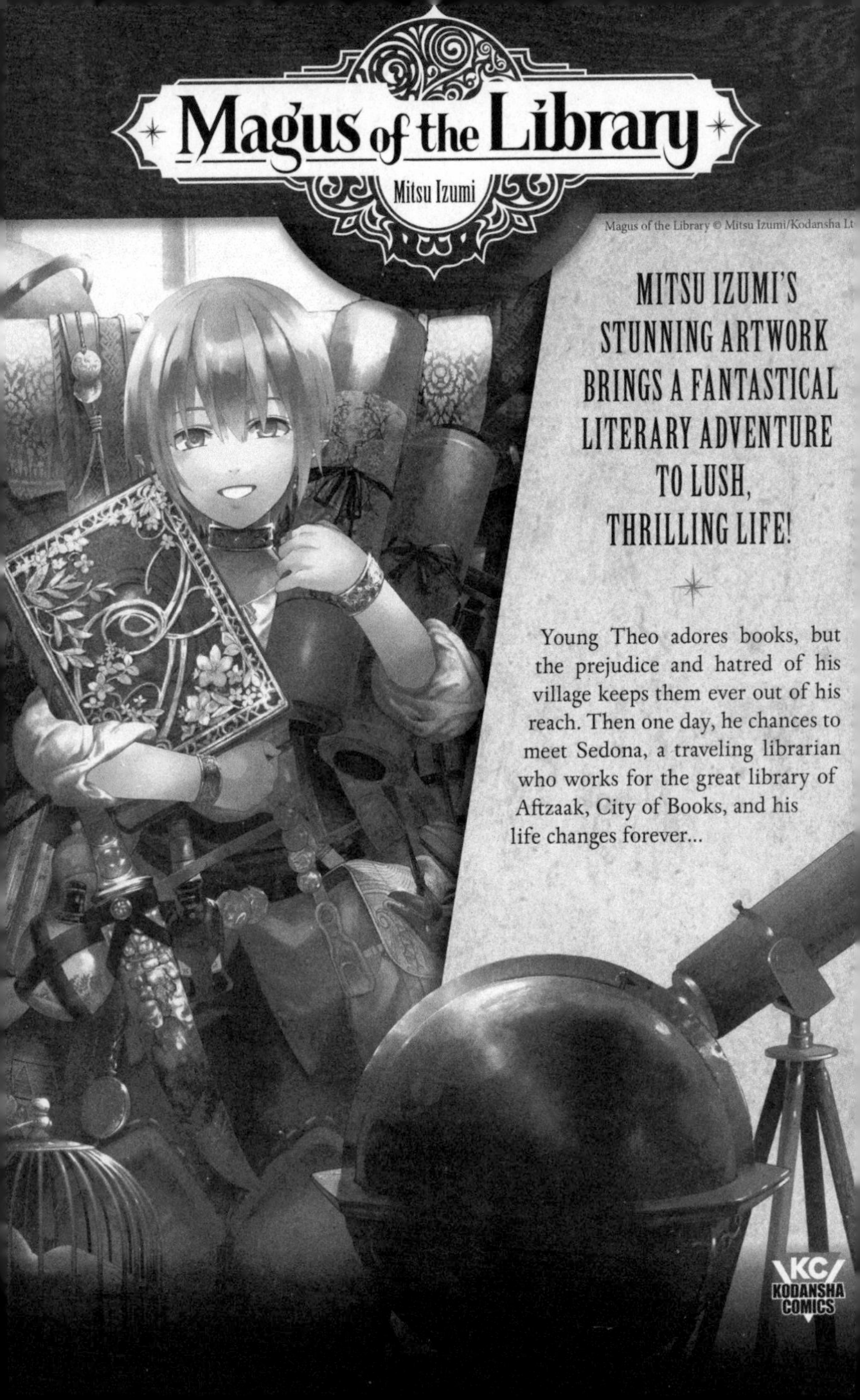
Magus of the Library
Mitsu Izumi
Magus of the Library © Mitsu Izumi/Kodansha Lt
MITSU IZUMI'S STUNNING ARTWORK BRINGS A FANTASTICAL LITERARY ADVENTURE TO LUSH, THRILLING LIFE!
Young Theo adores books, but the prejudice and hatred of his village keeps them ever out of his reach. Then one day, he chances to meet Sedona, a traveling librarian who works for the great library of Aftzaak, City of Books, and his life changes forever...
KC
KODANSHA COMICS

From the creator of *The Ancient Magus' Bride* comes a supernatural action manga in the vein of *Fullmetal Alchemist*!

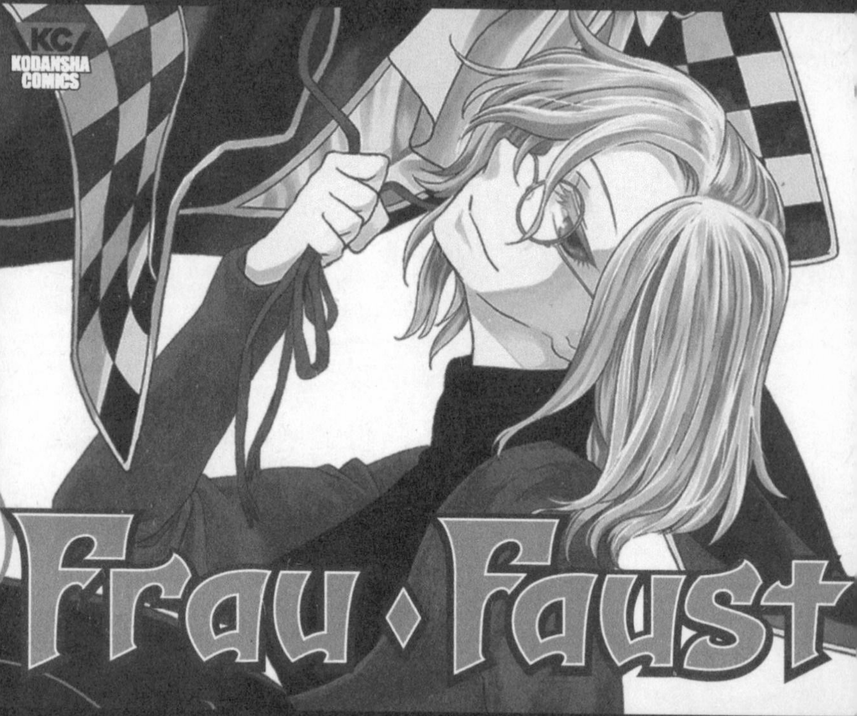
KC
KODANSHA COMICS
Frau · Faust

More than a century after an eccentric scholar made an infamous deal with a devil, the story of Faust has passed into legend. However, the true Faust is not the stuffy, professorial man known in fairy tales, but a charismatic, bespectacled woman named Johanna Faust, who happens to still be alive. Searching for pieces of her long-lost demon, Johanna passes through a provincial town, where she saves a young boy named Marion from a criminal's fate. In exchange, she asks a simple favor of Marion, but Marion soon finds himself intrigued by the peculiar Doctor Faust and joins her on her journey. Thus begins the strange and wonderful adventures of *Frau Faust*!

BATTLE ANGEL ALITA

After more than a decade out of print, the original cyberpunk action classic returns in glorious 400-page hardcover deluxe editions, featuring an all-new translation, color pages, and new cover designs!

KC
KODANSHA
COMICS

Far beneath the shimmering space-city of Zalem lie the trash-heaps of The Scrapyard... Here, cyber-doctor and bounty hunter Daisuke Ido finds the head and torso of an amnesiac cyborg girl. He names her Alita and vows to fill her life with beauty, but in a moment of desperation, a fragment of Alita's mysterious past awakens in her. She discovers that she possesses uncanny prowess in the legendary martial art known as panzerkunst. With her newfound skills, Alita decides to become a hunter-warrior - tracking down and taking out those who prey on the weak. But can she hold onto her humanity in the dark and gritty world of The Scrapyard?

Yamada-kun and the Seven Witches volume 21-22 is a work of fiction. Names, characters, places, and incidents are the products of the author's imagination or are used fictitiously. Any resemblance to actual events, locales, or persons, living or dead, is entirely coincidental.

A Kodansha Comics Trade Paperback Original.

Published in the United States by Kodansha Comics, an imprint of Kodansha USA Publishing, LLC, New York.

Publication rights for this English edition arranged through Kodansha Ltd., Tokyo.

First published in Japan in 2016 by Kodansha Ltd., Tokyo, as *Yamada-kun to Nananin no Majo* volumes 21 and 22.

ISBN 978-1-63236-900-0

Printed in the United States of America.

www.kodanshacomics.com

9 8 7 6 5 4 3 2 1

Translation: David Rhie
Lettering: Scott O. Brown
Editing: Ajani Oloye
Kodansha Comics edition cover design: Phil Balsman